Sixth Edition

Historical Introduction to Modern Psychology

GARDNER MURPHY

JOSEPH K. KOVACH

ROUTLEDGE & KEGAN PAUL
LONDON AND HENLEY

To M.K.M., L.B.M., and N.S.K.

First published 1928
by Routledge & Kegan Paul Ltd
39 Store Street
London WC1E 7DD and
Broadway House, Newtown Road
Henley-on-Thames
Oxon RG9 1EN
Second Edition 1929
Reprinted 1930
Third Edition 1932
Fourth Edition 1938
Reprinted 1948
Fifth Edition (revised and reset) 1949
Reprinted five times
Sixth Edition 1972
Reprinted 1979

Copyright 1949, © 1972 by Harcourt Brace Jovanovich, Inc.

Printed by Unwin Brothers Limited
The Gresham Press
Old Woking, Surrey

ISBN: 0-7100-7371-2

Sixth Edition

Historical Introduction to Modern Psychology

International Library of Psychology,
Philosophy and Scientific Method

Editor: C. K. OGDEN

PREFACE

Psychology has been rapidly changing in content and outlook since the last edition of this volume, in 1949. Despite the enormous changes in the field and, consequently, in the book, we hope we have remained true to the original intent: to share with students the excitement in the growth of a science, to mark and interpret the development of modern psychology.

This edition is the result of the full collaboration of its two authors, from the initial planning to the final draft. Joseph K. Kovach, the new coauthor, is a biopsychologist who has special interests in evolutionary thought, comparative and experimental psychology, and the rich Russian-language literature. But all the revisions represent our joint efforts.

Changes have been introduced wherever scholarship and research have suggested fruitful new interpretations and brought to light new information. The nature of our revisions varies from chapter to chapter, with the momentum gathering force as we approach our own sprawling times. The overall organization of the book has been retained, but we have consolidated, dispersed, or omitted certain sections and chapters for greater coherence and have introduced new chapters to bring our presentation up to date. For example, all of Part Four, Current Trends and Disciplines in Psychology, represents a new organization and wholly new material.

In Part One, The Antecedents of Modern Psychology, much has remained as it was in the previous edition, although new material has been introduced concerning the early origins of systematic psychologies.

In Part Two, The Rise of the Research Spirit, the two former chapters on physiology and neurology have been combined into a single chapter (Chapter 8), which includes some new material as well. In this part of the book, the major change is a fresh presentation of the theory of evolution (Chapter 9), especially timely, we believe, because of the increasing current interest in the subject and the new, strong ties between comparative and physiological psychology, genetics, and ethology. The sections on psychosomatic medicine (in Chapter 10), experimental psychology (in Chapter 11), and motor skills (in Chapter 12) have been rewritten. The chapters on Wundt and the spread of experimental psychology (Chapter 11) and on William James (Chapter 13) have been reorganized, and much of the material in them has been rewritten.

In Part Three, Gateway to the Present, the various schools and psychologies of the first half of the twentieth century are presented as immediate precursors of the current organization of the field. This part has been substantially expanded and extensively revised. Thus, Chapter 15 combines the former discussions of the Würzburg school and the acquisition of skills. The earlier chapter on modern conceptions of association has been deleted and its key ideas incorporated elsewhere. The chapter on behaviorism (Chapter 16) has been revised and updated. Gestalt and field theory are now combined in a single chapter (Chapter 17). The two chapters on Freud and the response to Freud (Chapters 18 and 19) bring the story up to date and include material on humanistic psychologies.

In the final and entirely new portion of the book (Part Four, Current Trends and Disciplines in Psychology), major areas of contemporary psychological thinking and research are examined. Separate chapters deal with learning theory; sensation, perception, and cognition; comparative and physiological psychology; Soviet psychology; developmental psychology; personality; and social psychology. Here, as elsewhere in the book, we have tried to integrate major lines of thought and research efforts and to bring the student to the very edge of the present frontier. In the final chapter, "History in the Making," we have presented a perspective on the relationships between psychology and other sciences and have tried to extend the student's vision beyond current frontiers.

The aim of the historical approach is to bring coherence and integration to a subject. We have attempted to display the whole fabric of the development of modern psychology as a science and to show how its many strands – the evolution of research and theory, important figures and schools, methods of thought and work, social and intellectual contexts – all contribute to the pattern. The dominant motifs – key figures, approaches, systems – get the major attention they deserve. We have tried to emphasize the main ideas of seminal minds and dominant personalities in the context of their own cultures, showing how they molded or broadened trends that were previously evident but less adequately focused.

A work of history must acknowledge its debts. In the comprehensive end-of-chapter References, we have provided the reader with bibliographical data on the hundreds of sources used. For the student who wishes to explore a given area further, we have also included, at the end of the book, a more general chapter-by-chapter annotated list of additional readings, emphasizing works currently available in paperbound editions. A good dictionary or the glossary of a good general introductory text is important for the student who is not yet familiar with basic technical terms.

The Menninger Foundation and The George Washington University have been strongly supportive of all our work over the years. Our undertaking was also aided by a Research Scientist Development Award from the National Institute of Mental Health (1–K2–MH–20, 140–01) to J.K.K., which is gratefully acknowledged.

We are most grateful for the secretarial help given by Winnie Anderson and Barbara Crites. In relation to the huge task of referencing, we are grateful for the assistance of Greg Wilson and the exceptional devotion and competence of Martha Carithers. We are also grateful for the helpful reading of portions of the manuscript by Riley Gardner, Herbert Spohn, and James Taylor of The Menninger Foundation; by Theodore M. Newcomb of the University of Michigan; and of the whole book by Wayne H. Holtzman of the Hogg Foundation and the University of Texas. Warm thanks are due Ernest R. Hilgard of Stanford University, under whose General Editorship the book has been published and who again provided substantial help with the entire manuscript.

GARDNER MURPHY
The George Washington University

JOSEPH K. KOVACH
The Menninger Foundation

CONTENTS

ix

Part IV: CURRENT TRENDS AND DISCIPLINES IN PSYCHOLOGY

Sixth Edition

Historical Introduction to Modern Psychology

Part One

THE
ANTECEDENTS
OF
MODERN
PSYCHOLOGY

1

The Intellectual Background

Their fine ways of explaining Nature mechanically charmed me.
LEIBNITZ

From color theories to defense mechanisms, from the functions of a white rat's vibrissae to the mystic's sense of unutterable revelation, from imaginary playmates to partial correlations—wherein lies that unity of subject matter which leads us to speak, compactly enough, of "contemporary psychology"? From behaviorism or Gestalt psychology to psychoanalysis or the objective measurement of character, the eye wanders over an interminable range of experiments, measurements, hypotheses, dogmas, disconnected facts, and systematic theories. In a sense it is true to say that through all this vast mélange the very birth cry of the infant science is still resounding. In another sense psychology is as old as civilization, and this seething multitude of investigations and opinions springs from a rich and variegated history. The complexity of contemporary psychology suggests that its understanding may well require the use of that *genetic* method which it has itself repeatedly demanded in recent years. Whatever difficulties there may be in finding unity in the various psychological disciplines, there is at least one unity to which we can cling for orientation and perspective, for appreciation and synthesis; and this is the tranquil unity of history.

The centuries since Descartes and Hobbes have woven together the psychology of antiquity and the physical science of the Renaissance, the nineteenth-century triumphs of biological science and the twentieth-century genius for measurement, while a multitude of social forces, as well as strokes of individual genius, have shown unities of method and conception underlying all the problems of psychology, and indeed of life itself. For experimental psychology sprang from the conception of a fundamental unity between psychology and physiology, and behaviorism from an attempt to make that unity more complete; psychoanalysis is an insistence on the fundamental

3

unity of normal and abnormal and of conscious and unconscious motives; Gestalt psychology strives to understand those Aristotelian "forms" which contribute the patterns of both the things of the physical world and the data of immediate experience.

Yet each of these movements toward unity is itself but a more comprehensive and systematic expression of movements that have been with us at least since the seventeenth century: behaviorism, for example, a refinement of Descartes's automatism and Hobbes's mechanism; the emphasis on the unconscious, a reminiscence of Leibnitz's idea of perceptions of which we are not aware; experimental psychology itself an application of that experimental and quantitative conception of nature which Galileo and Newton so brilliantly set forth. The venerable antiquity of psychology shows through the gloss of its newness and makes the finality of each new emphasis seem a little less absolute. Not, indeed, that there is great usefulness in asserting that each achievement of science gives but a new name to the discovery of some Hellenic thinker. But Western psychology has made its recent rapid advances only because of the richness of its own history and because of the centuries of general scientific progress which lie immediately behind us.

The Roots of Systematic Psychologies

Compared to the very large gaps between apes and even the most primitive men, the evolution of the human race, as shown by excavations, fossil bones, early tools, weapons, burial customs, traces of the perfection of skills, and the migrations of peoples, indicates the essential unity of human stocks. The modern human stock is uniform in its gross attributes. We shall deal later with the psychology of individuality; at this stage we wish only to indicate that there is reason to believe that there is such a thing as "human nature"—such a thing as a "characteristic" way of developing humanly from infancy to maturity. There is such a thing as the general growth of human intelligence and learning capacity and the growth of uniquely human temperamental, emotional, and instinctual attributes. There is, moreover, widespread evidence from contemporary preliterate societies —now quickly vanishing from the face of the earth—that they are fundamentally much alike and that the preliterate ancestors of our own modern stock were not very different from them or from us. We should think, therefore, that the attempts to describe systematically the story of psychology would give us rather similar pictures of psychologies over the face of the earth. Would not the Japanese, the Chinese, the people of Thailand, India, Egypt, and western Europe all present essentially similar histories in their attempts to understand their own psychology? Would not the essential unity of human nature imply that they all have passed through comparable stages of historical development and have developed comparable psychologies of their own growth?

Now, in fact, early men did *not* develop similar psychological systems. Psychology as an *organized discipline,* aimed at *understanding the experience and behavior of human beings,* is a very *late* development, taking shape after much social differentiation had already occurred. It therefore takes on very *different* forms in different cultural settings. Japanese civilization, for example, began to be systematically recorded in the sixth century of the Christian era. By that time assumptions about human nature had been influenced by native Japanese religious practices of Shinto, and later by Buddhist ideas brought from Korea and China. In that era Chinese psychology, depending rather largely upon the prophetic religious precepts of Confucius and Lao-tsu, had also grown into a distinctive form. The early philosophy of China had been profoundly integrated with and influenced by the Chinese political system.[1] The role and behavior of scholars in high governmental and bureaucratic positions was defined by hundreds of assumptions about what is "naturally good" and what is "naturally bad" and what can be remedied by the right kind of education—all very distinctive of the Chinese culture of the era. The ideas which had been developing in India, particularly ideas relating to the cultivation of the individual soul which could be absorbed into a cosmic soul, were very different from the prevailing Chinese and Japanese ideas; and even after these ideas were carried from India to China and Japan, they took on quite different forms, so that, for example, the psychological precepts of Zen Buddhism in Japan are very different from those of original Buddhism in India.

As we turn to our own immediate historical tradition and to the philosophy of the Greeks, from which Western psychology emerged, we may begin to realize that the first basic assumptions about human nature are by no means the same everywhere. Greek civilization fostered individualistic achievement and individualistic philosophy to a degree which would be hard to parallel in the Asian systems. Perhaps it was the tumultuous succession of military and political changes, the broken and discontinuous character of Greek life—in contrast to the rather static social order, lasting for centuries or millennia in most Asian civilizations—that stimulated a richer and more individualistic *variety* of psychologies in Greece and in the succeeding civilizations of the West.

However that may be, Greek ideas about human nature as expressed in the Homeric poems, in the work of early philosophers and tragedians, or in the *Lives* of Plutarch are very different from the ideas about human nature which appear in India, China, and Japan. Necessarily, then, the history of psychology begins to be colored by considerations of social change under different cultural settings. We need to recognize the special cultural bias with which we start our work; for we are dealing with a *Western* viewpoint regarding a *Western* development.

It is interesting to note the kinds of things that are noticed and the kinds

[1] See Needham (1947) for an excellent discussion of early Chinese science.

of things that are overlooked by Eastern and Western psychologies, by the questions that are posed and by the questions that are not. For example, the very rich psychology of India, despite the fact that Indian mathematics developed early and reached great heights, is almost wholly lacking in measurements or even in quantitative conceptions. Traditional Indian culture includes clear *ideas about education,* yet has no systematic *psychology of learning.* Western psychology, in contrast to Indian, has done almost nothing until very recently ·with the control of internal processes which predispose the individual to particular kinds of aesthetic and mystic experiences and the schooling in self-control which makes these experiences capable of being developed. Neither Western nor Indian psychology has paid much attention to the complex psychology of the impact of aesthetic objects upon the perceiver, as cultivated in China and Japan, while Western observers are almost totally innocent of any familiarity with the role which painting and spatial representation may play in giving one a sense of the relations of soul and body. Indeed, these questions are on the whole understood only by those who have posed them. Most of the questions of Western psychology are questions that are meaningful within Western history—its geographical, economic, military, and scientific backgrounds. Western psychology began with the special conditions of life in the Greek mainland, the islands of the Aegean, and the west coast of Asia Minor—the Greek world of 600 to 400 B.C.

The differences that existed, for example, between Greek and Roman ideas, or between Greek and Hebrew ideas, tend to be submerged as we try to present a generally representative history of Western psychology. Nevertheless we must try to recognize the various geographical, economic, political, military, and scientific events which made great impacts on the history of psychology. It is not enough to say that French psychology in the seventeenth century was very different from English psychology in the nineteenth; our task is to show *why* and *how* it was different. Why did the psychologists of each era choose the problems and come to the conclusions they did? We must also try to see why our own attempts to write a history of Western psychology involve profound bias because we are a part of it.

Is There a Universal Psychology?

But here the reader may well ask: "In all this sea of relativity are there no solid little islands of universal facts—facts both about universal human nature and about the development of thought about human nature?" Yes, indeed, there are such facts. If we look at Radin's work (1927) on primitive man we find profound and beautiful expressions of the brevity and sadness of human life; the glory of that kind of character which can exhibit both courage and self-control; the fact that youth is warm and old age cold; the intuitive perceptiveness of women; and the magnificence of loyalty to a friend and to a leader. There is the same wisdom here that we find in Aesop's

Fables and the Book of Proverbs. There have been many recent collections of folklore and wise sayings of many peoples, and it is an evening's delight to compare the proverbial wisdom of one human group with another. Often, however, the truths which emerge are vague: propositions like "water boils when you get it hot enough" have to be worked over before they can be called science. Or they give curiously opposed views of reality: compare "one man's meat is another man's poison" with "sauce for the goose is sauce for the gander." But these first primitive observations, even when thrown into systematic form, do not really make *psychology,* in the disciplined sense in which we find ancient men of India and of Greece trying to construct a psychology.

Psychology in this more disciplined sense is by no means found in all human cultures. In general, there is not much systematic psychology in pre-literate society. We may say, as a number of historians have said, that systematic philosophy has come into existence only a few times on the face of the earth. It is in the great river mouths and coastal harbors where trade flourishes that man could "keep the jungle down" and engage in local or international trade in such a way as to develop wealth and—for a few people—leisure. Leisure for speculation possibly arose under these conditions in India and in the Greek world of the eastern Mediterranean. The archeologists' diggings near Mohenjodaro in what is now West Pakistan are among the many archeological sources of information about a high civilization of 3000 B.C. and earlier, in which this kind of wealth and leisure existed. A dominant and exuberant invading host from the Persian uplands, speaking Indo-European languages, made its way into India, overran the sedentary people, borrowed much of their culture, and produced profound philosophical treatises, such as the *Upanishads.* These treatises teach the indivisible unity and permanence of the human soul and its identity with the cosmic spirit. Sometime later, the great *Gita* presented the problem of this eternal indivisible soul in the form of a poetic discourse between the Deity and a prince. By 500 B.C. another Indian psychological system came into existence: the teachings of Gautama, or Buddha, with their emphasis upon a "middle road" between self-indulgence and asceticism and a doctrine of mercy and compassion. Almost at the same moment, Confucius and Lao-tsu in China began to think psychologically. In almost exactly the same era, 600 to 500 B.C., after the biological and cultural fusion of invaders and invaded people in the eastern Mediterranean area, the beginnings of Greek systematic philosophy appeared, from which developed the psychological systems which are the beginnings of the psychology of the Western world.

Backgrounds in Greek Philosophy

The motions of the heavenly bodies are no more impressive than the rhythms of waking and sleeping, the rise and fall of emotion; the deviations from normality which invite the labors of the shaman stimulate also the speculations of the philosopher.

While primitive cultures differ as much in their psychology as they do in their basketry and pottery, or their kinship systems, they show a general preoccupation with one recurrent problem—the nature and attributes of the soul. The dramatic difference between a sleeping and a waking man invites the thought that something has gone out and then returned. The awakening man may recount a battle in which he took part while, manifestly, his body lay still upon the ground. In illness, especially in delirium or coma, something seems to disappear which may, upon recovery, reappear. The conception of a psychic entity—a detachable soul, we may say—makes sense to him. And such an opinion is greatly strengthened by the fact that those who dream and those who go into and out of coma or delirium or trance may encounter those who have died. Apparitions, hallucinatory forms, of the deceased are also familiar. Although lacking solidity, the apparition seems to perceive and to understand. The opening lines of Homer's *Iliad* refer to the souls which in combat have departed to Hades; and when Achilles is visited in the nether world, he is still, in a sense, the Achilles once known.

The conceptions summarized here are usually called "dualistic," for they make of soul and body two distinct things: two things capable, indeed, of continuous interaction but sharply and ultimately distinct as substances. There is a physical body and there is a ghost or detachable soul. Primitive psychology therefore usually has a place for the survival of the soul after bodily death, though the further abstraction of immortality—that is, permanent existence—is usually sketchy or completely absent. The applied psychology of primitive man includes devices for luring or coercing the soul to return to the body from which it has wandered and devices for strengthening the soul and enabling it to withstand life's difficulties.

All of these conceptions are perfectly evident in the religious systems of the Greeks in the first millennium before Christ: the Olympian religion, the mystery religions, and the speculative religious systems of the classical period. We shall, in commenting upon these three, emphasize both the thought and the language of Gilbert Murray (1925). When the curtain rises on the drama as revealed by the Homeric poems, a band of vigorous, magnificent "swashbuckling" warriors from the Danube basin is besieging a prosperous city on the east shore of the Aegean, and the gods and goddesses of their pantheon take a fully human role in the fracas. Within a few centuries, however, these long-haired buccaneers who produced such epic poetry have melted, both biologically and culturally, into the dark-skinned native population, a people of majestic architecture and sculpture and vast, dark, inexpressible thoughts, as betokened by the worship of nature in all its awesome aspects. The resulting cultural unity is neither naïve and childlike nor dark and mystical, but radiant, magnificent, subtle, inquisitive, and buoyant, turning ever to new problems with an audacity matched only by the capacity to give order and system to all that emerges.

The result is Greek philosophy, with its systems of interpretation of nature and, within these, its types of interpretation of the human body and soul. It is to be expected that the primitive "ghost soul," as Dessoir calls it, should appear in their speculations and that early Greek psychology should take the form of a relatively sophisticated study of the doings of souls and of the laws of their behavior. When therefore we find, along with those philosophers who reduce everything to water, or to fire, or to motion, or to numbers, those who reduce everything to mind, we may view it as an attempt to reconcile the traditional mind-body dualism with a monism which insists that mind is at the root of everything, all of nature making one harmonious whole. When, moreover, the Orphic mysteries provide expressly for the welfare of the soul, both within the body and after its departure, and when they encourage belief in the independent existence and collaboration of souls with one another after death, and when, finally, Plato tells us that souls perceive more clearly and reach to higher realities when freed of the body, we are encountering the refinement, rather than the abandonment, of the rudiments of primitive psychology.

We turn now specifically to the rise of types of psychology among the thinkers of Hellas. In particular, we shall look at five conceptions of the mind developed by Greek thinkers still to be found embedded in the tissue of our modern psychology: the conceptions associated with Pythagoras, Heraclitus, Democritus, Plato, and Aristotle.

Pythagoras was among the early Greek philosophers who thought that the universe could be explained in terms of a single central principle. Some had thought it was water; others fire; others looked for different origins. Pythagoras thought the first principle was *number*. As pioneers in geometry, he and his school found that the numerical relations of length, width, and height used in the construction of temples had a definite relation to the *beauty* of the structure. It was he who demonstrated that the square of the hypotenuse is equal to the sum of the squares of the other two sides. It was he who showed why, in tuning the lyre, the most beautiful chords are those in which simple mathematical relations are observed in the construction of the chords. The octave, for example, gives us one string twice as long as another; and other harmonious relations like the musical fifth and the musical fourth are based on simple whole number relations like four to three, or three to two. Pythagoras believed that the soul is at home with numbers, that the world of *science* and the world of *beauty* are ordered mathematically.

Different in temperament from Pythagoras but equal to him in philosophical power was Heraclitus, who taught that fire is the first principle, that "strife is the father of all things," and that a man cannot step twice into the same river.

Most explicitly representative of various "materialist" philosophies among the early Greeks was the extraordinary "atomism" of Democritus. He held that the world is made of tiny material particles. Living things, and the soul itself, are no exception. The principles of psychology, perception, memory, and thought are all expressions of the ways in which tiny bodily particles combine or interact with one another. Thought is thus a material process and life and thought come to an end with the death of the body. Democritus, though despised by Plato and Aristotle, strongly influenced such Greek thinkers of the later period as the celebrated Epicurus, organizer of a large school which in turn profoundly influenced the skeptical and materialistic outlook in later Greece and Rome.

Some modern philosophers believe that these early Greek thinkers exerted an immediate and marked influence upon Greek life itself, although their aristocratic and autocratic contemporaries belittled their literary output. We have only fragments of the work of Pythagoras, Heraclitus, and Democritus, while many of the works of Plato and Aristotle survived. At any rate, Plato and Aristotle are the two outstanding men of Greek philosophy; their work and ideas have been handed down to us in their original form, and our western European psychological history is profoundly indebted to the observations and speculations of these two great teachers.

Skepticism and Socrates's Answer

Wherever there is confident theoretical speculation about human nature, the destiny of human life, the ultimate nature of the universe and man's place in it, there is of course also skepticism, incredulity, and hostility. A single leader, however gifted, can never sway an entire population. In the period of ascendancy of the Athenian commercial and military power, about 440 to 400 B.C., as philosophically minded young men made their way to the Athenian marketplace, there were many winds of doctrine and many skeptical responses. On one side, there was a group of very astute and thoughtful men known as Sophists, who were sure that there is not much knowledge that transcends perception, not very much that we can hope to know about ultimate reality.

Then there was Socrates, an extraordinarily tough, vigorous, generous, humorous old soul, who appeared frequently in the marketplace. Having returned from soldiering to his philosophy, early plying a trade as a sculptor and making himself a controversial figure in Athens, this Socrates had something much more vivid and coherent to say than the Sophists expected. He was sure that there was much more in human knowledge than sheer perception; he was quite sure that man had genuine rational powers and that, moreover, these rational powers pointed not only to "correct" ways in business and in war, but to moral realities of individual life and socially right living which one could test for one's self. Thus in a period of conflict between the absolutists, who knew the final answers, and the Sophists, who doubted whether any answers could ever be found, Socrates with his conversational critical method would draw from his questioners the essentials of each broad philosophical issue; in these dialogues he led the young men of Athens to the view that there is a reality that can be grasped and that it can be ethically, socially, politically meaningful.

These dialogues of Socrates are recorded by his devoted pupil Plato. It is extraordinarily difficult to tell how much is Socrates and how much is Plato. Two other observers of Socrates's extraordinary dialogues with Athenian youth were Xenophon and Aristophanes. Xenophon, a general and "war correspondent" who went with the Greek mercenary armies to the wars of Cyrus the Younger, gives us a sharp, clear picture of Socrates as a fine, strong old man but gives us none of the subtleties, complications, and aesthetic charm that we find in the Socrates of Plato. The comic poet Aristophanes, in *The Clouds,* has Socrates, the visionary, literally walking on air. "I tread on air and take a good look at the sun," exclaims the Socrates of Aristophanes, who is Plato's Socrates being laughed at.

Plato and Aristotle

Socrates, as Plato reports him to us, defends the ancient belief that soul and body are fundamentally different things. While with primitive man and with the early Greeks, the *immaterial* soul had been confusedly regarded as possessing some qualities of a more or less *physical* nature—for example, it could be seen—the Platonic conception sharpens the distinction between soul and body, making them absolutely distinct kinds of things. The soul, moreover, being immaterial, may apprehend an ideal world, and it survives the death of the body. Among its manifest powers of transcending the concrete immediacy of physical objects is its capacity to deal with abstract relationships; the world of mathematics (as the Pythagoreans had earlier said) is a higher, more real world than the world of the senses; true philosophers must be mathematicians. As seen through Plato's eyes, the Socratic dialogues demonstrate the reality of the soul and the reality of knowledge about those things most precious and congenial to it: namely, the *universals* which transcend all concrete particulars—the beauty, the goodness, the mathematical relationships which represent the eternal and the ultimately real. The primitive man's ghost soul, winnowed and chastened in the fire of critical inquiry as to the nature of material and immaterial things, emerges as a real immaterial entity capable of knowing what is real.

We might expect, in this connection, a rich yield of psychological observation, based both upon introspection and upon studies of human behavior. This is not actually a task of primary interest to Plato. Since Plato's chief interest is in ultimates, we must not expect to find in him a rich yield of psychological detail. But such a yield was already coming from the medical men of the period. And an abundance of concrete psychological detail, in an ingenious new theoretical formulation, appears in the work of Plato's pupil Aristotle.

Aristotle was the sort of universal genius who makes three-paragraph summaries about him seem peculiarly lightheaded and perverse. His pertinence for the history of psychology lies in three contributions. First, in his orderly, architectural construction of a system of knowledge in which the study of the soul may be brought into relation, both empirically and rationally, with the study of living organisms. Second, in his definition of the nature of the soul and its activities in such fashion as to make the soul an expression of the living creature, and the living creature an expression of the soul, extirpating every rudiment of the dualism of soul and body which primitive man on the one hand, and his great master Plato on the other hand, had so carefully defined. Third, in his settling down to the workaday task of describing and interpreting human experience and behavior in concrete terms. The first and second contributions appear in the *De anima*.[2] The third task, appearing in the *Parva naturalia,* is expressed in vivid and readable accounts of youth and old age; of waking, sleeping, and dreaming; of the psychology of men and of women; of the processes of remembering and recognizing; and of that world of occult phenomena to which divination and prophetic dreams seemed to point; while in his volume on the orator (*De oratore*) he deals with the emotions the orator strives to sway, and in his *Ethics* and *Politics* he deals with problems of self-control and with interpersonal relations.

Aristotle was dissatisfied with the great gulf his master had placed between soul and body. Yet at the same time he could find little value in the mechanical theories of Democritus. He aimed to discover the intimate relation of mental and physical processes, yet to define the mental so as to show its differences from the physical. His solution lay in terms of a conception of *functions* carried out by the living organism. The raw stuff, or matter, of which a thing is made does not tell us what it is, nor what it does, but give it *form* and we can define it in terms of what it can do. Matter and form are always found together, but it is only through form that the potentialities inherent in matter can be actualized. The organs of the body would be mere matter were it not for the form which specifies how they must respond. Each of them can be said to have its own form, or, in a sense, its own soul. When the eye sees, we may say that seeing is its soul; the eye of a statue has no soul, for it does not see. The *potential* seeing which is an attribute of our eyes, even as we lie asleep, becomes *actual* when we open them and look at our environment. In the same way the potentiality of being seen is inherent in the objects around us; this potentiality is actualized when we see them. The living organism and the objects of its environment come together, are mutually responsive, actualized in reference one to the other.

We may properly use the term "soul" not only for the function of each organ, but for the living organism as a whole; the soul or mind is the *form* of the whole organism. The mind is not isolated from the thing known. In

[2] Some of Aristotle's books are best known to the English-speaking world under Latin titles.

knowing, "the mind is the object." This gives us a functional definition of mind or soul. *Mind is a process;* it is defined in terms of what it does. The environmental world can be fully defined only in terms of what we do as a response to it, just as we ourselves must be defined in terms of our interactions with it. Organism and environment are not independent but are two aspects of an interacting system of events.

Aristotle proceeds to a close study of the senses; of learning and memory; of emotion; of imagination and reasoning. Most influential of all his specific teachings is to the effect that we remember things by virtue of "contiguity, similarity, and contrast" (reference to contiguity and similarity had been made by Plato). We think of Paul because he was with Peter, or because he is like Peter, or because he contrasts with Peter. This doctrine of *association* later became the doctrine that all the operations of the mind depend upon associations laid down in experience.

During the great philosophical days of Socrates, Plato, and Aristotle, the Greek city-state, heart and core of Greek civilization, had undergone one mortal crisis after another. Sparta had overwhelmed Athens; Thebes had crushed Sparta. Thereupon Philip of Macedon and his son Alexander, whom Aristotle had tutored, had reduced the Greek world to vassalage, then spread through the world whatever was Greek in the civilization they knew. As the period of insecurity, or even despair, set in – a "failure of nerve," as Gilbert Murray calls it – those who had learned to philosophize went on philosophizing. Now, however, instead of the exultation of spirit which marked the absolutists, and the breezy casualness which marked the Sophists and the skeptics, there set in a long period of intellectual disillusionment, in which the primary aim was to find comfort through philosophy in a world whose reassuring marks of stability had disappeared.

Take, for example, the simple pleasure-pain philosophy which Socrates had espoused in the "Gorgias," in which we learn that the good man, though he be humiliated or tortured, has a kind of happiness which makes him, in a literal sense, more fortunate than the base man who is rewarded by mere wealth and status. In the period of disillusion and skepticism, this exuberant idealism seems a sort of forced heroics. The calm and honest Epicurus, looking sadly at the ruins of what was Greek civilization, prefers to say simply that men, born into a world of sorrow, will do well to find as much happiness as they can and to make happiness, while they can achieve it, their goal. The struggle of Aristotle to unify soul and body becomes, for others, a threat to the hope of immortality; they return to a body-mind dualism which will offer some hope that after passing through this vale of tears they may find eternal happiness. While at Alexandria, intellectual center of the world in the succeeding centuries, great strides were soon thereafter made in the physical and biological sciences, the Mediterranean world settled slowly into a period of rigidity and increasing hopelessness. This, of course, was not the viewpoint of the Roman gentleman of the first century

B.C., nor, indeed, of the emperors and their courts at any time; but from our vantage point, it is clear that the Roman Empire represented a slow but steady crushing of elemental emotional and aesthetic expression. The fire on the Greek hearth flickered more and more uncertainly, and after the defeat of the Maccabees, the Hebrew struggle for national freedom went the same way, while countless peoples about the Mediterranean, assimilating Roman civilization, learned also to acquiesce in the stolidity, the dead-level respectability, of Roman commerce and law. We should not expect "observations on man," psychologies worthy of the name, to appear.

It is thoroughly consonant with our expectations that the one kind of psychology which did take shape after the demise of the Greek creative spirit was that of the Church Fathers, based upon despair regarding this world, including despair regarding the goodness and the value of the living body, and appropriately saturated with two dominant motifs: first, Plato's mind-body dualism, and second, a moralistic prejudice against everything in human nature which seemed to bespeak a relation to the animal kingdom. Hence the intense preoccupation with problems of sin, guilt, restitution, and authority. Partly, of course, it was because Christianity spoke to men and women who had but little to live for: slaves, soldiers, fishermen, and the lowest level of artisans and farmers. The conception that the whole world was sick had, however, permeated every class. The need for the effacement of sin and for a sense of purification and reunion with the divine, known everywhere through the Mediterranean world through the flourishing mystery religions, was much more fully and adequately expressed in the Christian communion, through which oneness with the Son of God and the renewal of childlike intimacy with a loving Father was patently available to every earnest seeker, be he slave or emperor. The psychology of the Church Fathers, slowly taking shape in the writings of Paul, Origen, and Augustine, dominated philosophy until the full revival of Aristotelianism in the twelfth and thirteenth centuries. It was a psychology anchored in Platonic dualism, in the sense of guilt and the need of restitution, and in the conception of the will — both the will of God and the will of man — as cardinal instruments for weal or woe. The will, of course, transcended, as did everything else in the inner nature of the soul, those principles of explanation which held generally for natural objects.

The rediscovery of Aristotle in the twelfth and thirteenth centuries led to an interest in naturalism. The alert concern with physical and medical realities, so characteristic of the age, led to the revival of a scientific way of looking at nature. The human soul became articulated with other things encountered in everyday experience. Aristotle's psychology became the center of that vast new enterprise which sought to reconstruct the philosophy of the Church Fathers in a naturalistic direction. This is stating the issue, of course, not as a man of the thirteenth century would have stated it, but as it looks to us today.

The immediate practical test of the new Aristotelian philosophy, as shown definitely in the work of Thomas Aquinas, was its capacity to reconcile the humanity, urbanity, and naturalism of Aristotle with the body-mind dualism of Plato and the Church Fathers and to make a theologically acceptable treatise representing a union of ancient wisdom with those special doctrines upon which the salvation of the Christian soul depended. But once Aristotle had been rediscovered, and once he had been made the heart of scientific enterprise, the clock could not be set back; and from this time forward it is Aristotle very much more than Plato and the Church Fathers who shows the way to that modern psychology, that essentially Greek psychology, which took shape in the Renaissance period. For Greek psychology, especially the psychology of Aristotle, was brought into sharper focus and became central in the renewed efforts of men to understand man's own nature.

Backgrounds in the Renaissance

Our problem now is to take closer account of the intellectual temper of that new dawn of science and discovery which began with the end of feudalism and to study the manner in which this new intellectual temper made use of the great traditions. The manorial system, with its self-sufficient economic units, disintegrated as the military power of the knight in armor was successfully challenged and as traffic in commodities such as wool rapidly enlarged the area within which commerce was feasible. Travel by land and by sea became safer and more profitable. Moreover, the Crusaders of the twelfth and thirteenth centuries had discovered and carried back to Europe much of the civilization of the Near East, in which many elements of classical culture had been embedded. New phases of culture showed themselves; the new universities of the thirteenth century promoted the study of the classics, and a great artistic revival, the Proto-Renaissance, spread over southern Europe. The true Renaissance may be said to have begun as early as the fourteenth century and reached its greatest height in the sixteenth.

It gloried in explorations of all kinds, both physical and intellectual. But perhaps the realm of geographical discovery is as representative and enlightening as any. A beautiful epitome of the whole movement is found in the coinage of the Spanish Empire, changing as a result of the explorations of Columbus. In the days before the discovery of America, some of the coins of Spain bore the words *Ne Plus Ultra:* There Is Nothing Beyond. Spain and the Pillars of Hercules were the edge of the world. Then came Columbus and the age of the explorers. The inscription was changed. *Ne* was removed, and the motto read *Plus Ultra.* There *was* "more beyond."

For everywhere men sought for the new, both in the new appreciation of the culture of antiquity and in the search for new knowledge and new possessions, material and immaterial. Among the more obvious expressions of the movement was the search for new routes to the Far East and the beginning of the building of empires to include the "New World," the colonization of which was one of the great achievements of the sixteenth and seventeenth centuries. As the Holy Roman Empire slowly decayed, the new nation-states which came into being reached out for lands and wealth in the far corners of the world. During this period of discovery and expansion, the economic changes mentioned above went on at an accelerated pace, and Europe was caught in the vast upheaval of that Commercial Revolution which followed upon the collapse of the manorial system, the growth of towns, and the development of trade by land and sea, deriving from new routes to the East and from the general improvement in the means of communication. The political revolution in which Cromwell was the leader and Charles I was executed, and even more definitely the Revolution of 1688, in which the House of Orange was called to the throne, marked the emancipation of the commercial classes in Britain. This was the end of the traditional "divine right of kings" and the beginning of the self-assertion of a middle class, the great trading class which grew up as these economic changes occurred.

The spirit of unrest and of discovery became more and more conspicuous in the interests, spirit, and modes of thought of those who devoted themselves to art, to letters, to philosophy, and to practical affairs. In science a revival had begun as early as the twelfth century. The first great achievement was that of Copernicus (1543). His theory that the earth and the planets moved in circles about the sun (the revival of a theory dating from the third century B.C.) was the beginning of modern astronomy. In him and in his immediate successors can be seen the struggle and the ultimate union of the two great forces which generated modern science: the belief in a logically and aesthetically perfect "natural order" from which the laws of nature can be deduced and the determination to put every theory to an empirical test, a test permitting a decision through direct observation.

For after Copernicus came Tycho Brahe, who spent his life recording with scrupulous exactness such observations on the motions of the heavenly bodies as the best instruments of his time permitted. The Copernican system did not fit his observations, and he did not guess that the reason for the inconsistency lay in the fact that the orbit of the earth's motion about the sun is not a circle but an ellipse. Even Tycho, the observer, believed that heavenly bodies must of necessity move in perfect curves, and to him the perfect curve was the circle. Nevertheless, in the hands of Tycho and his immediate successors, science was beginning to take on a definitely empirical cast, the spirit of indifference to the perfection of theory, and eagerness for accurate data as the first step toward a sound hypothesis. In the work of Johannes Kepler there were elements of the work of these two predecessors. He succeeded in showing that Copernicus was essentially correct but that the figures accumulated by Tycho necessitated the assumption of elliptical rather than circular orbits. With Kepler the first great fusion of inductive with mathematical method came into being.

A somewhat similar step was being taken by Gilbert in England in the study of magnetism. For him, direct observation was the basic method; he varied the conditions of observation in a way genuinely deserving the modern term "experimental." The foundation was being laid for the development of experimental science; and in many branches of physical science such investigations were soon under way. This empirical work by Gilbert was admired by Galileo, an ardent believer in the Platonic (and the Pythagorean) doctrine that mathematics is the clue to nature's laws, who nevertheless had the most extraordinary genius for the invention of methods for empirical demonstration of such laws. At the end of the sixteenth century and in the opening decades of the seventeenth, Galileo extended the experimental method and went far beyond Gilbert both in the range and in the importance of his observations. Galileo and his followers concerned themselves primarily with the fundamental problems of mechanics and optics.

In all this group we can distinguish the leaders and the trumpeters, those collecting data and those blaring forth to the world what had been and what was to be done. Francis Bacon became the great herald of the new empirical spirit as it fought its way among the many forces of the Renaissance. He failed, unfortunately, to grasp the significance of many inductive studies going on about him, such as those of Gilbert; nevertheless, as a systematizer and an interpreter he contributed much to the rapid spread of enthusiasm for empirical methods.

The greatest combination of mathematical with empirical method in the seventeenth century was that effected by the genius of Sir Isaac Newton. Newton's work consisted both in the development of new mathematical methods and in the continuation of the work of Kepler in the elaborate logical use of experimental results. He utilized the empirical data of others as well as his own but contributed important original experiments, such as those with the prism demonstrating that white light may be split up so as to yield the spectral colors. Newton contributed much also to the philosophy of science, giving expression to a system of thought which could be used coherently in the advancement of knowledge. He sought to clarify those fundamental conceptions with which, as he conceived it, science must deal: space, time, mass, motion, force, and so on. Thus he well exemplified three different kinds of scientific work in the seventeenth century: the use of mathematical method; the impulse to vary conditions — that is, to experiment; and the study of the philosophical significance of the new acquisitions.

A few words about the organization of science. The only nation which had organized a definite means of scientific cooperation by the second half of the seventeenth century was France, and its work was confined chiefly to the city of Paris. The French Academy of Sciences began to receive royal support in 1671, which furthered the collaboration of investigators. The new impetus to scientific work given by the French Crown is in striking contrast to the situation in Britain. Newton at first worked alone. He helped to form a Royal Society, which was intended to give better means of cooperation, but he remained far greater than his own circle; and pitifully inadequate funds were granted by the Crown. The same condition existed in the German states. Germany, of course, was not a political unit, and naturally enough there was even less cooperation among its scattered men of science than in France and Great Britain, although the German university system was destined in the eighteenth century to serve as a center for the awakening interest in scientific effort. Galileo, in Italy, had worked alone, and under the suspicion of Church and State. The energies of Spain and Portugal were being expended in explorations and conquests in the New World. So if we are inclined to ask why a given "discovery" was announced when the facts were already known to contemporary investigators, the answer is that almost until the beginning of the nineteenth century scientific progress throughout western Europe was, with few exceptions, the fruit of the efforts of individuals, frequently working without knowledge of kindred efforts in their own and other lands, and destined to be forgotten until some scientist or scholar of a later day stumbled upon their work.

This holds strikingly true in the biological sciences. The revival of classical medicine, particularly in the Italian universities, was proceeding actively in the sixteenth century, and the desire to describe accurately, to understand in terms of observation rather than by speculative and deductive methods, was just as marked in biological science as in other fields, though generalizations were more difficult. The empirical movement was active generally and led in the seventeenth century to the spread of epoch-making clinical and post-mortem studies in anatomy. The reader will remember, for instance, Rembrandt's painting *The Anatomy Lesson,* a representation of the then novel and amazing art of dissecting the human body. The same clinical spirit was manifested in the study of mental diseases; Burton's *Anatomy of Melancholy* (1621) described familiar manic and depressed states. The swing from excitement and exultation to profound depression is described in convincing terms. The modern reader is carried from fresh firsthand empirical observations to the most curious patches of authoritarian lore coming down from the time of Galen, A.D. 200, and finds rational considerations of regimen and drugs mixed with purely fanciful and magical modes of treatment. Medicine was on its way from the authoritarian to the inductive and even the experimental methods of later centuries.

But the greatest discovery in the field of medicine and biology was William Harvey's. In 1628 he demonstrated how blood circulates. Harvey had studied water pumps and knew how they worked. Harvey wrote that the heart works like a "water pump," forcing the blue blood of the veins into the stream of the red blood of the arteries. Mechanism was taking possession of the bodily apparatus; in time philosophy of the soul would be involved too.

REFERENCES

Burton, R. *Anatomy of Melancholy*. Oxford: Cripps, 1621.
Murray, G. *Five Stages of Greek Religion.* Oxford: Clarendon Press, 1925.
Needham, J. *Science and Society in Ancient China*. London: Watts, 1947.
Radin, P. *Primitive Man as a Philosopher*. New York: Appleton, 1927.

NOTE: A list of further readings appears at the back of the book.

2

The
Seventeenth
Century

Heraclitus . . . says . . . that it is by something in motion that what is in motion is known; for he, like most philosophers, conceived all that exists to be in motion.

ARISTOTLE

The scientific movement of the seventeenth century was empirical; its appeal was primarily to observation rather than to authority. The systematic description of nature gradually led to systematic intervention in the ways of nature by the method of *experiment*. Nature's laws could thus be more precisely observed and understood and as mathematics developed could be made more clear, precise, and complete. These statements of nature's laws could then form *systems* of scientific ideas.

The new emphasis on objective observation and the attempt to establish laws capable of mathematical formulation had an immediate impact on psychology. Much of the psychology which resulted from this new spirit of inquiry was of course the restatement of the reinterpretation of the psychology — or the medicine — of antiquity, but the new mechanics and new mathematics were promptly put to work in redefining the ancient principles. Thus the knowledge of nerves and their functions of the Alexandrian school of medicine was combined with the new mechanics in the work of Descartes and his contemporaries in the seventeenth century.

Descartes

During the early decades of the seventeenth century, in the midst of his studies of theology and philosophy in various schools and in retreat in various parts of France and western Europe, René Descartes made himself expert in physiology and mathematics as well as in philosophy. It was he who conceived the systematic possibility of translating the equations of algebra into geometrical form (we still speak of "Cartesian coordinates"), showing the relationship of y to x, noting how the abstraction of an algebraic statement may give the beautiful form of a three-petal or four-petal rose when the lines are drawn out on a plane surface.

As a philosopher, he attempted to get at first principles: to discover the things that one may really know. Here, like Augustine before him, he came to the conclusion that his own doubts, his own uncertainty, gave him a fact from which he could start with certainty: namely, the fact of his own existence. He attempted then to show that reflection might give one knowledge of the nature of the soul—an "unextended" substance with its own kind of reality but not located in space—and its interaction with the body, which was definitely a physical substance located in space. He began to conceive of the body, with its sensory and motor nerves and its connections in the brain, as capable of functioning mechanically. The nerves could be conceived as tubes within which an obscure substance—the animal spirits—could travel, upon excitation, first through sensory nerves, then through centers, then through motor nerves so as to produce motor response.

But Descartes distinguished between animal and human behavior. He held that animals were simply machines: their bodies were controlled by physical laws. If this were true, then there must be specific mechanisms provided for these acts. Nervous and muscular reactions followed predictably from the stimulation of the sense organs; incoming and outgoing pathways provided fixed channels for the arousal of the animal's whole repertory of acts. Physiological psychologists have used the resulting conception of the *reflex* ever since to build an explanation of the more complicated life activities. Modern mechanistic psychology grew out of this seventeenth-century conception—greatly stimulated, of course, by progress in the science of mechanics in the hands of Sir Isaac Newton. Brett (1965) reminds us that in the gardens of the German nobility in those days manikins driven by water actually performed for amused visitors a wide variety of puppetlike movements, even uttering wordlike sounds, and he believes that this left its mark upon Descartes as he looked for a mechanical formulation of behavior.

While all of animal behavior could be thought of as mechanical, only the lower, more reflexive, type of human behavior could be so interpreted. Human acts involving understanding, thought, and rational decisions and action called for another explanation. What this explanation might be brought into sharp opposition the philosophical differences between "dualists," who accepted this distinction between bodily and mental realities, and "monists" like Spinoza (1677, Pt. 3, Chap. 2), who believed that soul and body are ultimately one—that is, merely *two aspects of one reality*.

Descartes himself recognized serious difficulties in his position. If mind and matter were totally different things, how could there be a working relation between the two? How could the body act upon the soul, and vice versa? This question caused much trouble; he had to look about for the point of interaction, the "seat of the soul." Some of the ancients had placed the soul in one place, some in another. But medical studies had begun to point to the importance of the brain. The trouble with the brain for Descartes's purposes was that it is "paired," right and left, and divided more finely into smaller structures which are arranged symmetrically on either side. But the pineal gland, the functions of which were unknown, is deeply embedded in the center of the brain. There is only one pineal gland; and it necessarily follows, thought Descartes, that it is the seat of the soul. This gland acted to transmit physical stimuli to the soul and to transmit impulses from the soul to the body. The soul's control of the body was through mechanical regulation of the connections between sensory and motor impulses in the nerves; the connection between the different sensory and motor impulses was controlled by the movements of the pineal gland. "This gland is variously affected by the soul . . . it impels the spirits which surround it toward the pores of the brain, which discharge them by means of the nerves upon the muscles" (1650, Pt. 1, Art. 34). This assumption reduced the problem of the action of the soul directly to control through the pineal gland, but no theory was vouchsafed as to the way in which an immaterial entity could exercise such mechanical effects. This dualism, or fundamental distinction between soul and body, so emphatically outlined by Descartes, has been the center of many psychological systems. But the acuteness of the difficulty was perhaps more apparent after Descartes's bold selection of the organ through which interaction was effected.

One other feature of Descartes's work, significant for later psychology, is the analysis of the emotions. The "passions" are treated almost like mechanical events; they are explained through motion in the brain, the blood, the "spirits," and the vital organs. Descartes's account of the "passions of the soul" reduces the complexity of emotional life to six elementary passions: wonder, love, hate, desire, joy, sadness. This process of dissecting human nature into elemental emotional experiences or impulses, which in their combination give all possible modes of emotion, is so fascinating that it has never ceased to occupy psychologists.[1] Yet the emotions listed by Descartes were described as though they were intellectual functions. Love, he believed, depends upon one's calculation of the pleasure an object may bring, and hate depends upon expected evil. The nonrational was translated into terms of the rational. The nineteenth-century "economic man," who avoided pain and sought pleasure, is another example of such rationalism.

The two great successors to Descartes in France in the hundred years which followed were Malebranche and La Mettrie. Malebranche (1674) so fully understood the *physiological definition of emotion* that he may be regarded as a forerunner of the James-Lange theory (see p. 199). La Mettrie (1748) held that if animals are automata then men are automata, that Des-

---

[1] Among the better-known attempts are those of Hobbes, Cabanis, Gall, Lotze, James, McDougall, and Watson.

cartes's interpretation of behavior in machine terms must be ruthlessly followed through to the end, granting man no immunities.

In the meantime, the extraordinary Baruch Spinoza, grinding away at lenses in the Netherlands, unknown to the world, was working out a philosophy of mind and body rich in ideas of a strangely modern cast—ideas far too modern to have any effect on his seventeenth-century contemporaries. Mind and body are aspects of one reality, so that physiology and psychology are utterly fused; memory is a sequence of mental events corresponding to a sequence of bodily events (arising from earlier impressions made on the body). The emotions and the motives of mankind are deeply irrational and often operate unconsciously so as to lead to self-deception. Spinoza's posthumously published *Ethics* (1677) was destined to sink deep into the minds of philosophers. But the intellectualistically minded men of his own era were not interested in the notion of unconscious motivation, and the unknown lens-grinder had no such easy access to an audience as had Descartes.

Leibnitz

In Germany in the meantime, soon after Descartes had worked out his application of physics and its methods to psychology, a somewhat similar approach was made by another mathematical genius, Gottfried Leibnitz (1695). He likewise sought an answer to the problem of the relation of mind to body. Leibnitz held, as did Spinoza, that it was impossible to accept the doctrine of an immaterial soul acting upon a material body. The relation of mind and body was actually stated by Leibnitz in terms nearly as dualistic as those of Descartes, but dispensing altogether with the troublesome concept of interaction. There is, Leibnitz taught, a body which follows its own laws: that is, the laws of mechanics. The acts of a human body are just as mechanical as are those of an animal. We must explain *all* acts of the human body in terms of known physical causes. Mental acts and sequences must on the other hand be explained in terms of mental principles. The soul carries on its acts without any direct reaction upon the body. Mental life displays an orderly sequence of events, while bodily life does the same; but these two never interact. His analogy was that of two clocks so constructed that they always perfectly agree, though neither acts upon the other (1696). Thus if we know what time it is by one clock, we know what time it is by the other. Mind and body *seem* to interact simply because of a "preestablished harmony" between them. We can understand mental changes only by understanding the preceding mental changes, and we can understand physical changes only by understanding the preceding physical changes; there is no causal connection between mental and physical. This doctrine made irrelevant the whole conception of interaction between mind and body and sought to do away with all those apparent contradictions involved in asking how a mental event occurs in consequence of a physical event. We have in Leibnitz's system a "parallelism" of mind and body to which many shades of contemporary parallelism bear close resemblance. Through Descartes's interactionism, Spinoza's monism, and Leibnitz's parallelism, the seventeenth century outlined three of the major body-mind theories which dominated eighteenth- and nineteenth-century thought.

Mental events were themselves classified and graded for Leibnitz according to their degree of clearness, ranging from the most definitely conscious to those which were most vague and obscure. This led to a distinction which remained prominent in German psychology and is now widely recognized: We may be totally unconscious of our obscure perceptions. Others are, at the same time, clearly grasped, or *apperceived*.[2] Perception is an internal condition "representing external things," and *apperception* is "*consciousness* or the reflective knowledge of this internal state" (1714).[3]

English Empiricism: Hobbes

But significant as were the psychological systems of these men, probably the most important stream of tradition for us to consider in order to understand the psychology of the eighteenth and early nineteenth centuries is the English "empiricism" of Thomas Hobbes and his successors. The starting point for Hobbes, even more obviously than for the other thinkers we have considered, was the social and intellectual environment in which he lived. He was, in particular, engaged in the study of the great political upheaval going on about him, that surging-forward of the commercial classes which weakened the grip of the nobility upon its exclusive power and prerogatives. Charles I was executed in 1649; and Hobbes published his *Leviathan* in 1651. It was the "heroic" age of Cavaliers and Roundheads, the lyrics of Lovelace, the leader sleeping in his armor, and the echo of wars across the Channel. But Hobbes bitterly hated both the commercial and the political revolution; he was a royalist, and his conception of life was aristocratic. The organization of society was for him based upon the authority of some individuals over others. The "natural" state of man (without organized society) would be "solitary, poor, nasty, brutish, and short" (Pt. 1, Chap. 13).

Nevertheless, he was an observer who, in spite of his prejudices, was singularly detached; and this in a hyperpolitical age in which every thinking Englishman was startled to witness the disruption of the time-honored order.[4] Though he was in a sense a part of this upheaval, he was still a spec-

[2] Aristotle had distinguished between "having" and "observing" an experience.

[3] Perception is a condition of a monad, a psychic individuality or soul. Monads are irreducible psychic entities.

[4] Milton, for example, attached greater importance to his political writings than to his poetry; it was his great regret that he was snatched away from politics by his blindness. The political intensity and bitterness of the age reverberates even in Gray's stately rhythms three generations later.

tator rather than a participant.[5] He observed in a spirit in which few before him had observed; even Machiavelli and Sir Thomas More, his great predecessors in political theory during the Renaissance, had had a case to prove and a practical goal to win. He sought to understand the revolution and the human nature which lies behind both war and peace. He was the first "social psychologist" among the moderns, and the principles which he laid down were epoch-making both for social and for individual psychology.

Hobbes drew the distinction between original nature and the products of experience (1651, Pt. 1, Chap. 6). Some human acts he attributed to innate constitution; but most specific activities he regarded as acquired. He started out to catalogue the inherited tendencies but quickly lost interest; hunger, thirst, and sex impulses were mentioned and passed over in a moment, being such obvious things that their psychology did not interest him. But in relation to social life, he gives a much fuller exposition of the principles of motivation. In this exposition, based largely on Aristotle's *Rhetoric*,[6] he described human motives not as purely impulsive forces, but as strivings based on expectation of pleasure and pain.[7] First and foremost came fear, fear conceived not as a blind impulse but as perception of pain inherent in an object, causing withdrawal from it. Fear is dependent upon calculation of evil results. The desire for honor is another dominant motive; it is based on the recognition of pleasure which must accrue from standing well with one's fellows.

Now these elements of human nature (hunger, thirst, sex impulses, fear, desire for honor, and, through all, the search for pleasure and the avoidance of pain) are the mainsprings of social conduct and the basis for social organization. Each individual in human society was conceived by Hobbes to have proclivities which he wished to satisfy and pains which he wished to avoid. Without society, each individual, alone, would directly seek pleasure and avoid pain. He would be obliged to engage in warfare with his neighbors in order to take from them the things he wished for himself and to ward off the attacks which they in turn made upon him. Man is competitive and if alone in his self-defense is necessarily miserable through the constant seizure of his possessions or the ceaseless task of self-defense. The only hope for men lies in the organization of commonwealths in which each man agrees to forego the pleasures of robbery in order to avoid attack from others.[8] In social groups each individual is prevented by the community from attacking his neighbor. A rational social organization thus prevents the selfishness of original nature from making for general chaos. Hobbes, like Machiavelli,

[5] He took refuge in France during some of the stormiest years.

[6] That is, the list of motives which the orator must sway.

[7] This simple hedonism was not particularly original. Many of the ancients assumed it; its elements were present also in More's *Utopia*. As was noted above, Descartes made a similar assumption.

[8] A similar conception of the commonwealth had been traced (by Glaucon) in Plato's *Republic*.

insisted that the mainsprings of human conduct were self-interested and that the most important was fear. Moralists had pointed out the essential baseness of humanity, and Augustine's and Calvin's emphasis on man's sinfulness was an expression rather than a cause of the age-long grudge which Western thought has cherished against man's moral nature. And this conception has been acceptable to penologists and to practical statesmen for centuries. Fear has been the central note of deterrent punishment, as of international politics and diplomacy.

Another mechanism of social control lay in the establishment of a nobility and of other special groups to whom honor was given in greater or lesser degree. Hobbes believed that gratification derived from high station, as well as from approval of one's acts, was a necessary part of the social order. But royalty is a very special form of noble rank, for the sovereign personalizes or represents society as a whole. The revolt against the sovereign is a contradiction in terms. The sovereign is the representative of all; by receiving supreme power he protects society against marauders. The king therefore rules not through an abstract "divine right," but by the collective values he holds within himself as representative of the commonwealth. Hobbes believed the overthrow of the sovereign to be vicious as well as ultimately futile. Subsequent events, especially the expulsion of the Stuarts, were not such as his scheme of society demanded, and the fact tended in some measure to discredit his theory of the state.

But there was here a system of ideas of immense importance, ideas rooted in the thought of antiquity and now revived in opposition to the doctrines of the Middle Ages. There was first the idea that human acts result from an objectively knowable human nature; that man is made in such a way that analysis may make possible prediction and control. Society can so organize itself as to control individuals and create for itself a complex but reasonably stable system of social relations. We shall see later how the "political economists," especially Bentham, continued another branch of Hobbes's thought, namely, "psychological hedonism," the doctrine that self-interest is the basis of conduct.

This description of social life, moreover, was supplemented by a systematic philosophical inquiry and by a keen analysis of the principles of general psychology. Philosophically, Hobbes was captivated by the desire to reduce everything to *motion*. He was delighted by Galileo's mechanical experiments and believed that through such methods the ultimate nature of "things natural" was to be discerned. This systematic (and dogmatic) emphasis on motion, even where motion could not be demonstrated, perhaps justifies the question whether Hobbes really was as purely "empirical" as is alleged. "He attempted a task which no other adherent of the new 'mechanical philosophy' conceived—nothing less than such a universal construction of human knowledge as would bring Society and Man . . . within the same principles of scientific explanation as were found applicable to the world of Nature"

(Robertson, 1910–11, p. 552). With the mechanical viewpoint, the notion of bodies as bits of matter moving in space and time, Hobbes built up the scheme of human nature as a purely mechanical thing, avoiding altogether the interactionism of Descartes. It is no exaggeration to say that Hobbes took the whole fabric of the seventeenth-century physical view of the world and fashioned from it a conception of human nature. Every thought, feeling, and purpose was simply internal *motion*.

It is sometimes held that his psychology is in large part Aristotelian; Aristotle gave him a "naturalism" which he could set in opposition to the "supernaturalism" of the Scholastics. Yet though Aristotle taught him a good deal, we find him making no use of the Aristotelian conception of form, preferring a mechanism like that of Democritus.

His psychology is in large part an empirical psychology. He uses the principle of motion chiefly in relation to motion as supposed to occur in the *brain,* an assumption which was supported by some evidence. And whatever may be thought of his metaphysics, his psychological observations have both a matter-of-fact empirical spirit and a richness of content very far indeed from the formalism which had characterized most psychological systems. Much of his psychological material evidently came from his own keen analysis. His work as a psychologist centers in close observation of his own mental processes, with the request that the reader "consider, if he also find not the same in himself" (1651, Introd.). He undertook, moreover, to show that the mind takes shape in consequence of natural forces operating upon the individual.

All experience, Hobbes held, was some special form of motion. He made, for example, no distinction between the *will* to do a thing and the doing it.[9] Appetites and fears were internal motions which led to action, and will was simply the last appetite or the last fear which in the course of deliberation precipitated overt movement (1650, Pt. 12, Chap. 2). Similarly, sensation was continuation of that motion which had impinged upon the sense organs, transmitting its motion through the nerves to the brain. Descartes had taught that in higher mental functions the soul, by means of the pineal gland, controlled the passage of an impulse from one nerve to another; but Hobbes did not require the intervention of the soul, for motion in the brain was sufficient.

The motion occurring within the brain substance constituted, moreover, the basis for all qualities of sensation. He proceeded, accordingly, to attack the popular conception that the qualities of experience are *inherent in* the objects we perceive.[10] "There is nothing *without us* (really) which we call

---

[9] A protest against a Scholastic teaching that the internal motion was merely metaphorical?

[10] Democritus had made a similar distinction. The astronomer Kepler had clearly distinguished half a century earlier between such objective reality as motion and such subjective phenomena as color. For the history of these concepts from Kepler to Berkeley, see Burtt (1925).

an *image* or colour . . . the said image or colour is but an *apparition* unto us of the *motion,* agitation, or alteration, which the *object* worketh in the *brain,* or spirits, or some internal substance of the head" (1650, Pt. 2, Chap. 4).[11] Moreover, after the external object has ceased to act upon the sense organ, the motion in the brain may continue. Such residual or "decaying" sensation constitutes the material of memory and imagination. As Aristotle had put it, imagination is "decaying sense."

There remains, however, the problem of the *order of events,* the "trains" of imagination and thought. This order of events depended upon the sequence of the original experiences caused by stimulation coming from the world about us. "Those motions that immediately succeed one another in the sense, continue also together after sense: insomuch as the former coming again to take place, and be predominant, the latter followeth" (1651, Pt. 1, Chap. 3). This doctrine is basic for all associationist teaching. *Associationism* is the doctrine that we connect things in memory, in thought, and in all mental life, simply because they were connected in our original experience with them; and since our first encounters with things are by means of our senses, the associationist maintains that all the complexity of mental life is reducible to sense impressions, the elementary components of consciousness, as connected in experience. The psychologists of ancient India, as well as of Greece, had speculated along these lines; what Hobbes is here doing is vigorously modernizing the doctrine, a task brilliantly pursued by Hartley in the following century.

But we cannot predict from a given thought which one of a variety of other thoughts may follow. A thought may have been followed, in different situations, by a variety of different thoughts. There may be many competitors, each one of which has a definite claim upon the next position in a mental series. A passage in *Human Nature* suggests that Hobbes believed that a knowledge of past experience is wholly sufficient to explain present associations: "The *cause* of the *coherence* or consequence of one conception to another, is their first *coherence* or consequence at that *time* when they are produced by sense: as for example, from St. Andrew the mind runneth to St. Peter, because their names are read together; from St. Peter to a *stone,* for the same cause" (1650, Pt. 4, Chap. 2). But in the *Leviathan* we read: "In the imagining of anything, there is no certainty what we shall imagine next; only this is certain, it shall be something that succeeded the same before, at one time or another" (1651, Pt. 1, Chap. 3). He failed to work out his position. Neither he nor his immediate successors realized the possibility of attaining a more adequate statement of the varieties of association. It was not, in fact, until the work of Thomas Brown, in the beginning of the nineteenth century, that this problem was fairly faced, reducing

---

[11] Hobbes constantly emphasizes the brain, as had some of the Greeks; but he is a good enough Aristotelian to emphasize the heart, and to give the latter a position of importance in mental life.

the problem of mental sequence to a large number of specific laws of association, taking into account the *competition* among experiences.

But Hobbes did take account of the vital distinction between such free or uncontrolled association on the one hand, and directed or purposive thinking on the other hand. "Mental discourse is of two sorts. The first is *unguided, without design* and inconstant. . . . The second is more constant; as being *regulated* by some desire, and design" (1651, Pt. 1, Chap. 3). He devoted much attention to the "regulated" type, taking account of the "desire" which guides the process, and of the tendency to seek causes for consequences and vice versa. He proceeds to give illustrations of the familiar (Platonic and Aristotelian) principles of association by contiguity and similarity.

Hobbes had, then, outlined an empirical psychology in which sensation was emphasized as the source of our ideas, and he had given a sketch of free and controlled association which served to explain the interconnections between the elements of experience.

Locke

The first great follower of Hobbes had an immense advantage over him as a molder of opinion. John Locke, the physician-philosopher, observed the continuing political turmoil and the success of the commercial and liberal elements against the landed aristocracies through the expulsion of the Stuarts in 1689. A liberal, he could genuinely communicate with the readers and thinkers of his era. To those who had struggled for freedom or uneasily pursued the liberal spirit sweeping over the Western world, he spoke of the fitness of man to live in a free society dominated by reason and forebearance. Indeed, a primary note in his great *Essay Concerning Human Understanding* (1690) is the rationality of man. Whereas Hobbes, the cynic, fought, argued, and mocked, Locke spoke in the idiom of his age. Men looked askance at the materialistic dogmas of "Hobbism," looked forward with Locke to a humane and enlightened social order. This conception was expressed in his discussions of politics and of education, as well as in his psychological studies which aimed to demonstrate the rationality of man and the relation of this rationality to the simpler associative laws of the mind.

Ideas, Locke noted, come from experience; [12] observation "supplies our understanding with all the materials of thinking." But ideas need not arise directly from sense impressions; they have two sources. They come either from sensation or from reflection, an "inner sense." Our minds are equipped not only with ideas directly derived from such sensory qualities as color,

---

[12] The mind before all experience is "white paper." The Latin *tabula rasa* (wax tablet, smooth and ready for writing) is a familiar epitome of Locke's conception of a mind upon which experience has as yet written nothing.

tone, and taste, but also with ideas derived from observing our own intellectual activity.

Locke agreed with Hobbes that "simple ideas of sensation" are the properties of experience and not of the objects outside us which excite these ideas in us. He proceeded, however, to distinguish between "primary" and "secondary" qualities. Primary qualities, such as size and motion, produce in us ideas resembling the physical stimuli which excite them. On the other hand, secondary qualities are those aspects of external objects which produce in us ideas unlike anything really existing in the external world; for example, such ideas as those of color and taste. He supposed that some aspects of experience are genuine duplicates of patterns existing in external bodies, while others bear, in fact, no such resemblance to external bodies.

Ideas, however, may be either simple or complex. The mind creates complex ideas by combining simple ideas. Many of our ideas designated by single words can in fact be analyzed in such a way as to show clearly that they are but combinations of simple sensory constituents. "Thus, if to substance be joined the simple idea of a certain dull, whitish colour, with certain degrees of weight, hardness, ductility, and fusibility, we have the idea of lead" (1690, Bk. 2, Chap. 12, Sec. 6). The principle was, as we shall see, far-leading. "Even the *most abstruse* ideas, how remote soever they may seem from sense, or from any operation of our own minds, are yet only such as the understanding frames to itself, by repeating and joining together ideas that it had either from objects of sense, or from its own operations about them" (1690, Bk. 2, Chap. 12, Sec. 8). While Locke's primary emphasis is upon the capacity of man to achieve understanding of the world and of himself, he agrees that the *sequences* of ideas which appear in the mind are often irrational, being due to the mere order in which earlier impressions were made, just as Hobbes had said. Such irrational, fortuitous mental connections exhibit the "association of ideas."

Three things were needed to make a systematic psychology out of these principles. One was to lay stress upon and give content to the notions of "repeating" and "joining," which constituted the basis for integration of simple into complex experiences. The second was to show how the entire mental life could be reduced to association. The third was to postulate a physical basis for mental interconnections. All three steps were soon to be taken.

Locke's greatest contribution to psychology thus lay in making explicit the possibilities of a theory of association which should start with the data of experience and work out the laws governing the interconnections and sequences among experiences. The germ of associationism had, of course, been apparent in the work of Hobbes, which in turn went back to Aristotle. But Locke's lucid exposition of the implications of empiricism, and of the possibility, through analysis, of clearly understanding the origin and organization of ideas, gave the empirical approach an appealing and challenging quality which greatly contributed to its strength and influence. Locke's confidence in human rationality was joined by a belief in the capacity of mankind for self-government and for liberal education, which contributed much to the political thought of the new era culminating in the American and French revolutions.

REFERENCES

Brett, G. S. *A History of Psychology*. Rev. ed. R. S. Peters, ed. Cambridge, Mass.: M.I.T. Press, 1965.

Burtt, E. A. *Metaphysical Foundations of Modern Physical Science*. New York: Harcourt Brace Jovanovich, 1925.

Descartes, R. *Les Passions de l'âme* [*The Passions of the Soul*]. Paris: Loyson, 1650.

Hobbes, T. *Human Nature*. London: Bowman, 1650.

———. *Leviathan*. London: Crooke, 1651. M. Oakeshatt, ed. New York: Collier, 1962.

La Mettrie, J.-O. de. *L'Homme machine* [*Man a Machine*]. Leyden: Luzac, 1748.

Leibnitz, G. W. *A New System of Nature*, 1695; *Second Explanation of the System of Communication Between Substances*, 1696; *The Principles of Nature and Grace, Based on Reason*, 1714. In *Opera omnia*. 6 vols. Louis Dutens, ed. Geneva, 1768; and *Leibnitz: Selections*. Philip P. Wiener, ed. New York: Scribner, 1963.

Locke, J. *Essay Concerning Human Understanding*. London: Basset, 1690.

Malebranche, N. de. *De la recherche de la vérité*. . . . 1674. 4th ed. Amsterdam: Desbordes, 1688.

Robertson, G. C. "Hobbes." In *Encyclopaedia Britannica*. 11th ed. Vol. 13. 1910–11.

Spinoza, B. *Ethica* [*Ethics*]. In *Opera posthuma*. N.p., 1677.

NOTE: A list of further readings appears at the back of the book.

3

The Eighteenth Century

> . . . it was the natural realism of English writing which seemed to the French a new revelation of the common thoughts and emotions of common people. With a burst of enthusiasm France embraced the idea that apart from monarchs and metaphysics there are ordinary mortals and a science of man.
>
> G. S. BRETT

The seventeenth century had paced, with seven-league boots, the road from medieval dogmatism to the agnostic mechanism of Hobbes and the empirical rationalism of Locke. In the bright light of the new physics —so fully empirical and so utterly rational—and with every breath of the new cultural atmosphere so stimulating to the intellectual adventurer, one may expect to find the psychology of the eighteenth century all the more eager to proceed by rigorous self-observation and relentless logic. These empirical yet rational trends are evident indeed in Berkeley, Hume, and Hartley, psychologists of the "century of rationalism."

Berkeley and Hume

Locke's distinction between primary and secondary qualities was rejected by his immediate follower, George Berkeley (1710), who showed with an indomitable logic that there are no qualities in experience except those qualities which Locke had already described as "secondary" or subjective; there are no "primary" qualities. We cannot assign to external objects a location, size, shape, mass, and movement; for we never know anything but our own experience. The whole objective world is a pure hypothesis supported by no evidence whatsoever. In analyzing our experience of a rose we encounter such qualities as redness, fragrance, softness of petals, sharpness of thorns: but these are plainly just sensations. And when we talk of external *objects* we do not know what they are; objects external to experience are nothing at all. He laid the cornerstone of that great edifice in modern philosophy, "subjective idealism," which portrays a world of experience qualities and denies, throughout, the existence of any other world. This was the logical end of the train of thought which began with Hobbes's denial that the qualities of things perceived are *in* the things themselves.

But Berkeley was eager to find some kind of unity in mental life, something that should hold these mental states together. There is no intrinsic reason why pain should follow the thrusting of the hand into fire, or why the odor of a rose should accompany the visual and tactual experience of the rose. Why do two persons see the same object or sequence of events? And what is it that holds together the collection of experiences which belong to a single mind? Experience, Berkeley concludes, is the property of the soul: the soul is the unobservable, but logically necessary, background of our experience. Furthermore, there must be an active cause for the succession of experiences, and this cause is to be found in God Himself.

This may seem to the modern reader to classify Berkeley (1709) as primarily a philosopher and a theologian; but in pursuing his problem he made an extremely important contribution to the theory of visual space perception, showing how the principle of association might be used to explain some of the most complicated facts of perception. Locke had recognized that in the compounding of ideas elements might be drawn from two or more sense modalities. Berkeley went further with this analysis of the origin of compound ideas. He asked how we perceive the relative distances of objects. The retina is spread out as a surface with an "up" and a "down," a "right" and a "left," but how can we, by means of this surface, perceive a third dimension? Berkeley answered in terms of tactual experiences. Through reaching and touching, the notion of distance is associated gradually with the elements given by the retina. Touch qualities are not directly perceived when we analyze our visual perception of three dimensions; but when visual impressions are combined with tactual memories derived from reaching for objects, we find a three-dimensional quality in our objects. The retina "gives" us three instead of two dimensions. Since Berkeley used the notion of compounding sensory qualities, he became one of the founders of association psychology.

Now appeared one who questioned the premises and conclusions, the beginning and end, of all these views which had been propounded with the confidence and perhaps the naïveté characteristic of the era. The central psychological contribution of David Hume (1739–40) was the analysis of the stream of thought into one endlessly changing kaleidoscopic series of experiences. For Berkeley a soul had been needed to bring all these experiences together, to make a coherent sequence. Hume declared that he had patiently examined his consciousness without succeeding in finding evidence for the soul. Even the thing that one calls the "self" turns out to be a group of sensations from the body. For the description of personality all that was necessary was a series of experiences. Empiricism had come to full term.

Hume took the position toward which Hobbes had groped, that psychology deals with experience as it comes to us and not with any logical postulate of the observer as a separate entity. Hobbes had not been able to see the real issue, because there had not been a Berkeley before him to make this sharp distinction between self and experience. Hume could do it because there *had* been a Berkeley. Hume, denying the validity of Berkeley's assumption of the soul, and of God as an active cause of experience, offered a psychology which was nothing but the study of a series of experiences combining and recombining, through the natural force of association. Here arose one of the great problems which association psychology had to face henceforward: What provided the basic unity of experience? This was long before the day of a detailed physiological psychology; the idea that there was an organism that holds things together could scarcely be worked out. Associationism had become, in the hands of Hume, a means of dissecting and describing experience, dispensing with any unifying agency, whether physical or mental.

Hartley and Associationism

By the middle of the eighteenth century associationism had thus begun to be the central point around which psychological problems revolved. But associationism as a psychological *system* is usually traced to David Hartley (1749).[1] He differed from his predecessors not so much in his enunciated principles as in the clearness with which he grasped the need of a thorough-going physiological basis for association. He undertook to define the physical facts upon which memory images and their sequences depend. Greatly interested in Newton's study of the movement of the pendulum, he held that if certain experiences follow in a given order it means that nerve fibers must be set in *vibration* in a given order. When a stimulus arouses a sense organ, and a moment later a second stimulus arouses a second sense organ, the vibrations in the brain caused by the first are followed by vibrations caused by the second. The parts of the brain are so connected that if now the first stimulus is again presented and arouses the first brain region, the arousal of the second region follows, with no need for the presentation of the second stimulus. A series of sensations A, B, C, D forms such a pattern in the brain that later the arousal of A will set going b, c, d—that is to say, *memory*

---

[1] The Preface to the work makes it clear that the core of his system of thought was suggested by a "Rev. Mr. Gay," whose views on association were stated nearly twenty years earlier. Hartley's own work was not widely noticed in England till the opening of the nineteenth century.

images of B, C, D. These images are produced by the vibration, on a *small* scale, of nervous tissue previously stimulated more actively.

He recognized the resemblance between motor habits—a series of acts in which, step by step, each act leads to the next—and mental activities like memory, in which a series of experiences follows in a certain order because of past experience in a certain order. There was, moreover, no distinction between sensation and image except insofar as differences in *intensity* of nerve function were concerned; the image had its seat in the *same region* which served as basis for the sensation.[2] Having found a way to explain the *succession* of ideas, it was easy for Hartley to use Locke's conception of *compound* ideas. A group of revived sensations might cohere so as to form a mental product. But this mental product was to be conceived as parallel to a physical product, a group of nerve excitations. Complex experiences were reduced to the elementary sensations which by association constituted them. In such complex experiences the component sensations may sometimes no longer be recognizable; in taking a new medicine, one may fail to recognize the components, though all of them have been experienced separately at an earlier time. He had, therefore, by physiological principles brought the whole realm of thought and of imagination into one explanatory system; clusters and sequences of sense impressions are the clue to mental life.

For Hartley, as for Locke, the child begins life without associations. But rejecting the notion of ideas derived from reflection, Hartley held that the child has simply the capacity for sensory experience. In the course of time, sensory experience, by making connections and establishing trains of association, building up complex objects of thought, becomes more and more intricate; and finally there arise systems of thought, such as philosophy, religion, and morals. Hartley had almost arrived at a complete psychical atomism, a reduction of mental life to atoms which in combination yield all observable events. He and his followers had as their goal such a thorough understanding of association as would enable them to take a number of psychical elements and show how their combination in various ways, acting according to a few simple laws, could produce every kind of psychological event. This fascinating game is one which had not yet been played with vigor and thoroughness.

The Scottish School

The tendency to simplify and mechanize mental processes led to a vigorous protest against Hobbes's mechanism, and, in particular, against Hume's whole skeptical approach, especially his indifference to the claims of the soul and its higher rational powers. The protest took shape in the Scottish universities, where Locke had made less headway than he had in England and where philosophers were alert to the claims of established

[2] A refinement of Hobbes's statement as to the relation of image to sensation.

religion — specifically the Church of Scotland as distinct from the Church of England and all other religious bodies. A wise philosopher reared in the stern Presbyterianism of the Scottish outlook must face the reality of man's rational and moral obligations to the Deity and to his fellow man. Religion and the state, closely allied, were threatened; popular education (through the parochial schools) was taken in real earnest, and public opinion could hardly brook an attack upon the core of its ethical and religious structure. Religious freedom was tolerated in some circles in England; respectability did not necessarily involve orthodoxy in religious thought. But Scottish Presbyterianism of the mid-eighteenth century helped create a new philosophy to combat skepticism.

The leader was Thomas Reid (1785; see 1853 ed.). He undertook to show that the skepticism of Hume was absurd, that we know perfectly well that we have minds, the capacity to perceive real things, to think, and to act rationally. Reid appealed to the practical reliability of our senses, pointing for example to Newton's studies in optics as showing the right way to approach the problem of our ability to make contact with the external world. Do we not, moreover, observe a profound difference between *reasoning* and mere *association?* Have we not intellectual powers upon which we can rely in solving problems, making it possible to understand the external world and to predict what will happen? The child is likewise endowed with the ability to know good and evil; and we are free to choose between right and wrong. In all this Reid sought not only to undermine the basis of association psychology, but to build a new system based upon confidence in our intellectual powers: a system based upon common observation as against the subtlety — the sophistry, he maintained — of the empiricists.

Reid's teaching was characteristic of the trend of the period. For such a revolution against prevalent philosophical thought would probably have taken in the thirteenth century, or in the sixteenth, the form of an appeal to authority. Demonstration of the soul would have been effected by means of deductive reasoning. But in the eighteenth century empiricism had taken such hold that rationalism was no longer trusted; even the enemies of the empirical movement resorted to experience rather than to deductive logic as their defense. Reid says in substance: "There are the facts on which *you* rely, but look at *my* facts; they are more conclusive than yours." One of the last bursts from the dying embers of medieval dogmatism had been Berkeley's supposed demonstration of the existence of the soul.

Because of its insistence upon the unity and coherence of mental life, and because it pictured the individual as an active entity, not as a mere field in which ideas assembled and reassembled, the greatest contributions of the Scottish school were necessarily general rather than specific. It contributed little to the solution of specific problems until the school became blended to some extent with the associationist movement. But Reid and his followers were influential, not only in Scotland but later in England, France, and the United States, because they appeared to save the individual and society from intellectual and moral chaos. In these countries, moreover, the new doctrines came to be known to the general reader as well as to philosophers; the Scottish school became almost popular.

Another tendency already at work grafted itself upon the Scottish school but also continued a separate existence in Germany: the "faculty psychology." This was never "founded," in the strict sense, at any one period; we find it implicit or explicit in the psychology of some of the ancients and some of the Scholastics. As the soul carried out the specific activities, for example, of remembering, reasoning, and volition, it made use successively of the different *faculties* of memory, reason, and will. But if one likes one may say, as is often done, that the first proponent of German faculty psychology was Christian von Wolff, whose *Rational Psychology* appeared in 1734. His central doctrine is simple and intelligible: there are definite and distinct faculties or capacities of the soul; the soul enters for the time being into each activity, just as the whole body may at different times take part in widely different acts. But the soul remains a unity, never a mere sum of constituent parts. German thought remained for more than a century steadfast to this general principle.[3] For this school of psychology a *faculty* was the *capacity* of the soul to carry out a certain activity. This gives us a double enumeration of all mental processes; there is not only the specific process of remembering, but the power of remembering. The distinction is convenient. But as a system, faculty psychology merely gives names to certain functions; it cannot analyze these functions. The Scottish school and the faculty psychology shared this approach. Beginning with the soul and the various ways in which it can act, the Scottish psychologists catalogued its capacities much as the Scholastics and the German faculty psychology had done.

As associationism matured into a self-confident system (see pp. 30, 35, 99, 358), it denied more and more vigorously the value of this approach. The child's mind, it asserted, was blank at birth and only by experience learned certain ways of functioning; it had no *innate capacities* to do things. The associationists, therefore, and the faculty psychologists stood at opposite poles; at poles which, however eroded in the currents of time, retain to this day their distinct identities and adherents in psychology.

French Psychology

French psychology before and during the French Revolution responded directly to the tendencies in British thought.

In the work of Condillac (1754) there arose a structure even more beautiful in its simplicity than the associationism of Hartley. Taking as his point

---

[3] Kant gave new life to the doctrine of the faculties at the same time that he elaborated his own theory of apperception.

of departure Locke's conception of sensation as the first source of ideas, Condillac went further and held that sensations alone are a sufficient clue to all mental life; no formulation of the principles of association, as entities, need be added to our primitive capacity for sensory experience. He asked his readers to imagine a *statue* and to imagine what would follow if it were given sensation, say the sense of smell, and nothing more. The sum total of all possible human mental processes would follow, with need to presuppose no laws of association whatever. Variations in the quality of sensation, for example, would necessarily produce those acts of judgment and comparison to which Locke referred. The fact of passing through experiences, one after another, is a sufficient clue to the way in which judgments and comparisons arise. Operations and functions are not added to the elements; the elements carry out their own functions. The mind is an assemblage of parts, and these parts in their relations explain mental functions of all describable varieties. A point implicit rather than explicit in Condillac's system is the assumption that pleasantness and unpleasantness are inherent in the nature of the sensory process itself; qualities of sense are by their very nature pleasant or unpleasant. He next assumes that pleasant experiences are inevitably (almost by definition) prolonged and repeated, while unpleasant experiences are as far as possible terminated. For Condillac's purposes we need consider only one of the senses; the other senses would contribute other *qualities,* but the laws formulated from observing them would be identical.

We may, to be sure, smile and remain unconvinced as we read how the experience of one sensation followed by another gives us, ipso facto, a comparison of the two, or how an inherently unpleasant sensation constitutes directly, and without further assumptions, the will to terminate the experience; but the logical construction comes to the modern reader as something exquisite in its simplicity and clarity.[4] It is the most nearly perfect modern example of *sensationism,* the effort to reduce mental life to sensory elements. The sensationist must indeed have a theory regarding the interaction and the succession of sense impressions, usually borrowing here from the associationist; and the associationist must agree with the sensationist's explanations of the sensory sources of the contents of the mind. In practice the two approaches are therefore very similar. But Condillac marks the most radical of modern efforts to find in sensation *all* the essential clues to psychology. This attempt to picture mental life as an aggregate of sensory bits became one of the dominant philosophies for the remaining years of the century, until the idealistic movement came into vigorous life again.

The success of Condillac's sensationism was due in part to the intellectual soil of the Enlightenment, to such influences as deism and the Encyclopedist

---

[4] A somewhat similar system, but with much more attention to physiology, was offered by Bonnet (1760). He described memory in terms of activities in nerve fibers (in language similar to Hartley's). He performed a rough experiment on the "span of attention." He suggested that each quality of sensation must depend upon the specific brain area excited.

movement. The middle of the eighteenth century had been a period of heroic intellectual achievements, concentrated above all in Paris. Here the influence of scientists and historians, especially of the antiecclesiastical group, had begun to simplify the picture of human life, as the English empiricists had done, by doing away with the supernatural and by making human experience the all-sufficient object of study. The great advances of physics, chemistry, and astronomy were making for the growth of the conception of natural law so important in the economic and political policies of French statesmen both before and during the Revolution. This scientific movement was destined to reach great heights in the work of two Frenchmen who are usually thought of as figures in the history of medicine: Cabanis and Bichat. Living at the time of the French Revolution, they were the most brilliant exponents of the movement which aimed to unite the science of the nonliving with the science of living things.

Cabanis first attracted attention as a student of a problem which arose from the facts of execution by guillotine (1799). He was interested in the philanthropic question whether the guillotine hurt its victims or acted so swiftly as to be painless. By questions of this kind he was prompted to a study of reflex action and to the formulation of a concept which has become an important principle in physiological psychology to this day. We can summarize his conception in the term "series of levels." The spinal-cord level was the simplest of a hierarchy; it carried out reflex acts in response to stimuli. At a higher level, semiconscious or semi-integrated activities were carried on; and at the highest level were such complicated functions as thought and volition.[5] Cabanis believed that unless the brain were involved there could be no mental processes, only mechanical responses. On this assumption he concluded that the guillotine was not painful; movements in the body after execution were reflexes of the lowest level.

Having postulated these levels, Cabanis went on to suggest an explanation of cerebral activities on the analogy of more elementary functions. He showed evidence that the same mechanical principles which govern reflex activity govern cerebral activity; he made use of data indicating the relation of brain disease to mental disease. He ventured upon a systematic physiological psychology, replacing many of Condillac's assumptions by the postulation of neural functions which served as the basis for an active adjustment to environment. He suggested a genetic approach, making much of the fact of increase in mental complexity arising from increase in the complexity of the nervous system. Finally, he conceived of a social psychology, based on laws of individual behavior and social stimulation, and was led to an empirical consideration of ethics. He was thus one of the first to realize that the biological observations of the eighteenth century had clear implica-

---

[5] This conception was elaborated by Jackson (Taylor, 1958) nearly a century later. Jackson supposed that the levels most recently achieved through evolution were most easily deranged, and he based a psychiatric classification upon this principle.

tions for social life. Starting from reflex action, he proceeded all the way to the most complicated problem with which psychologists have to deal — human conduct in its ethical aspects.

The writings of Cabanis were contemporaneous with the work of Bichat, whose medical researches led him also to the conception of a physiological psychology. From the time of Hippocrates, medicine had recognized the body as an assemblage of *organs;* in spite of the active prosecution of research with the aid of the microscope, the intimate knowledge of the composition of these organs had not been achieved. Bichat pushed analysis into the realm of the structure of the *tissues* and founded the science of histology. He showed that every part of the human body is composed of a few types of tissue, which combine in various ways to form the vital organs, muscles, glands, and so on. Here he came into contact with problems of neuropathology, and through these of psychopathology, viewing forms of mental disease in terms of the abnormality of anatomical and histological structure. Physiological psychology was taking shape. Descartes and Hobbes had outlined a physiological approach to psychology; Hartley had boldly attempted a physiology of association; but a thoroughgoing physiological psychology could arise only on the basis of a definite conception of the structures and the functions of the nervous system.

Another French scientist seems to sum up all these tendencies. Pinel was appointed in 1792 as director of the institution for the insane in Paris, the Bicêtre. Here he struck off the chains with which many of the insane were bound. He epitomized in this act a view which had been gaining ground steadily, the conviction that the insane are diseased: that instead of being simply queer or immoral, or in league with Satan, these individuals suffer from sick brains. Pinel epitomized on the one hand the great advances in neurology and pathology, holding that disorder in the brain meant disorder in the personality, and on the other hand the humanitarian movement, with its insistence on the mitigation of suffering. We break dramatically with the demonological conception of disease, which, although rejected by individuals in all ages, had held sway for centuries. Pinel was a practical psychiatrist of no mean ability. He won distinction in the classification of mental disorders, attempting wherever possible to correlate brain disorder with mental disease.

Humanitarianism, Hedonism, Utilitarianism

Pinel was representative of a wide and mounting tidal wave of humanitarianism. The nature of the trend appears in a new attitude toward the treatment of criminals. Among the factors responsible for earlier brutalities had been on the one hand the conception of original sin and on the other hand the emphasis on the principle of the freedom of the will, which made each individual personally responsible for his wickedness. These factors added to the severity of the treatment accorded to the criminal, treatment which of course had been brutal even under the "pax Romana." Torture was in use in France until the Revolution. Violent reaction now arose against such barbarism; human dignity demanded sympathy and the impulse to correct rather than simply to inflict pain upon wrongdoers. A still wider expression of the new mood was the effort to alleviate the sufferings of the poor and the publication of books proposing radical cures—anarchism, for example—for the inequities of human society.

Perhaps the whole movement of the Enlightenment, and in particular the humanitarian movement, had its ultimate origin, as some economists have suggested, in the discovery of the New World and in the Commercial Revolution, the bringing in of new goods and the raising of the general standard of living. With the breakup of the feudal system and the rapid rise of democracy, merchants began to compete with the nobility for economic and political power. In the Old World the guildsmen had raised themselves into a commercial class, and even those below them had risen to positions of genuine prosperity. And in the New World Europeans found a new opportunity to escape the oppression of a landed nobility; they might claim land for themselves and take part in the establishment of a democracy. Their constant emigration contributed to a rise in wages in western Europe; with the decrease of the number of available laborers, wages rose and the condition of the poor tended to improve.

Whether our emphasis on these factors be great or small, we find the humanitarian movement widespread by the middle of the eighteenth century. Pinel expressed it in the field of medicine. It was apparent in the work of Beccaria (1764), the founder of modern criminological theory. He protested against the brutality and the futility of the heavy sentences imposed for all sorts of petty crimes; capital punishment, for example, for petty larceny seemed to him barbarous and absurd. He carried into criminology that system of thought known as "psychological hedonism," which pictured each individual as motivated solely by desire for pleasure and aversion to pain. He outlined a theory of punishment which was designed to direct this human nature into conduct desired by the group. A man commits a crime only when he is impelled by a wish. A man steals bread because he is hungry; if he is terribly hungry, he steals more. If we institute a system of *graded* punishment, we may for each crime assign a punishment which will deter the individual from that act. This conception was an integral part of the humanitarian movement just considered. Had it not been for the violent repulsion against systems of torture and the use of capital punishment for dozens of crimes, such an application of hedonistic theory would not have been called for.

Closely bound up with the humanitarian movement and the eighteenth-century intellectualism were the writings of the political economists, especially the school of Adam Smith and the school of Jeremy Bentham. The

French economists known as the *physiocrats* had maintained that wealth came solely from land: primarily from agriculture, and to some extent from mining, forestry, and so on. All other forms of human activity were parasitic. Soon Adam Smith in England began to see the inadequacy of such a simple formula. His *Wealth of Nations* (1776) treated the principles involved in commerce: why it is that men trade with one another; what satisfactions they obtain from exchange of goods. He grasped the need of a psychological background for economic processes, just as in his work *The Theory of Moral Sentiments* (1759) he had already attempted a psychological explanation of fellow feeling and hence of morality. What had been a problem of mathematics with the French became a problem of psychology with the English; human motives were the key to social organization.

Smith's psychology differed much from Bentham's, and while Smith retained enormous influence as an economist, the psychology and the ethics of Bentham soon won equal influence. He championed the doctrine of "ethical hedonism," the doctrine that the only individual or social good is happiness. The phrases "the greatest good of the greatest number" and the "sum total of human happiness" are characteristic of the system. At the same time he insisted upon "psychological hedonism," the doctrine that all human acts are self-interested.[6] He was the first to formulate systematically this universal principle of psychological hedonism, which as we have seen many writers had assumed, but none had thoroughly worked out. He sought to explain all social behavior in terms of conscious search for pleasure and avoidance of pain. He and his followers sought to show a way to use this self-interest motive of each individual in the interests of society as a whole; in an ideal society, individual and social good would coincide. *Utilitarianism* was the resulting doctrine that the only defensible goal of society is to provide, through the control of behavior, for the greatest good of the greatest number. Just as Beccaria had explained that if the punishment is just great enough, the individual will refrain from stealing bread, so Bentham built up the doctrine that men will work just so much for their bread; that is, they will undergo labor and suffering only if their reward is sufficiently great. In his hands this became a method of explaining not only individual conduct, but the whole organization of society. The statesman's task is to guide the social order so that each individual's conception of his own greatest good will be one with that of society's greatest good.

Bentham's theory of motivation and his desire to use this motivation for the general welfare accorded with the humanitarian movement. But paradoxically, the resulting conception of the "economic man," who is motivated solely through pleasure and pain, became a great all-encompassing dogma of the industrialists, who found in it the inescapable law of all social behavior and hence the moral justification for every act of self-interest. The slogans

[6] Ethical hedonism does not necessarily involve psychological hedonism, nor vice versa, but Bentham embraced both.

of humanitarianism were often used in the rationalization of the hard prac-
ticalities of the Industrial Revolution, and even today the assumption of the
self-evident and obvious correctness of ethical and of psychological hedonism runs through the thinking of "practical men" in industrial society.

But there is one more link still to be fitted in. We have tried to make clear
that the dominant influence in English psychology during the eighteenth
century was associationism. What was the link between associationism and
these other developments? The link was that certain things in themselves
neutral become sources of pleasure and pain, and through association they
come to influence us as though they were the pleasure and pain themselves.
Specifically, a piece of paper that has no use and which is not feared is
neutral; but if the piece of paper has become associated with value, it becomes as *money* a direct object of satisfaction. Every symbol may be
pleasant or unpleasant, according to its associations. Associationism and
utilitarianism become intermingled.

A number of social and intellectual movements had now grown together.
They constituted almost a systematic view of life. The Commercial and
Industrial revolutions, the development of natural science, the rise of
political economy, associationism, humanitarianism, reform in the treatment
of criminals and the insane, deism and utilitarianism, as well as a number of
other movements, had led to a new and "naturalistic" conception of human
nature. Many historians of Western culture would make the economic factors, especially those arising from the Commercial Revolution, the origin
of most of the others; for our purposes it suffices to note the existence of all
these factors as they molded British psychology.

Though all these movements were international, their influence on Continental psychology was considerably less than on psychology in Britain.
Before the Revolution every one of these movements was clearly active in
France, but no psychological system took shape such as those constructed
by the associationists and the utilitarians. French psychology up to Cabanis
and Bichat had continued the Cartesian tradition and borrowed, through
Condillac and others, part of Locke's system.

German Psychology: Kant

German psychology was pursuing its independent career and had as yet
been but little affected by associationism and the kindred movements noted
above. It will be remembered that the "faculty psychology" of the seventeenth and eighteenth centuries had concerned itself with the various irreducible functions of the mind, maintaining that a unitary soul entered
fully at different times into each one of a number of distinct activities. This
conception is closely related to a view which has been widely advocated in
recent years, that each function is the function not of a part or an element of
the organism, but of the whole organism; every experience and every act

reflects the undivided individual. The main purpose of faculty psychology was to describe the primary powers exercised by the soul: memory, reason, will, and so on. This approach was congenial to the rationalistic tendency previously noted, because functions of intellectual and moral importance were accepted at their face value and freed from the humiliation of dissection into sensory bits in the manner favored by the associationists. Faculty psychology also emphasized religious values;[7] it became essentially and mainly "idealistic."[8]

Now in the course of time this faculty psychology, with its emphasis upon the "ultimate modes of psychical functioning," expressed itself most adequately in the writings of Immanuel Kant, one of the greatest figures in the history of thought. His celebrated doctrines received their initial impetus largely from Hume's skepticism. "It was Hume," said Kant, "who awoke me from my dogmatic slumbers." Thus awakened, Kant agreed that it was impossible by deductive methods to demonstrate the reality of the soul. But we are forced, said Kant, to a new and radical analysis of our rational powers in order to discover what the mind *can* actively achieve and what it can never hope to achieve. He proceeded to find in the complexity of mental processes a variety of ultimate cognitive functions which he believed to be not further analyzable. Psychologists are especially concerned with the sanction he gave to the notion of the three great subdivisions of mental activity: knowing, feeling, and willing. Analysis of the process of knowing is set forth in his epoch-making *Critique of Pure Reason* (1781); the processes of feeling and willing, though less exhaustively treated, are handled in the *Critique of Judgment* (1790), the *Critique of Practical Reason* (1788), and elsewhere.

Though his contribution to psychology was not comparable with his contribution to philosophy—and this just because he sought the ultimate, the transcendental, caring but little for the events of mental life as immediate data and entertaining no hope that they could become the subject matter of science—Kant's work nevertheless greatly influenced psychology. First, through his insistence on the unity of an act of perception. This attacked the very heart of associationism; many of the intellectual forces which in the nineteenth century contributed to the downfall of the associationist system are traceable to Kant's emphasis upon the unity of experience. When we cognize what we call objects, as in the case of touching a solid object with the fingers, we encounter certain mental states which are apparently com-

---

[7] Much of the psychological work of Britain in the seventeenth and eighteenth centuries was done quite outside of the religious atmosphere; and English empiricism, through Condillac, was amalgamated with French agnosticism. Germany was singularly free from these powerful agnostic trends. A strong empirical tendency flourished in Germany in the late eighteenth century, but it was unable to maintain itself.

[8] "Idealism" may be defined for our purposes as that type of philosophy which emphasizes the reality and the value of mental processes which appear to be remote from or independent of physical processes.

posed of sensory qualities; we seem to find the integration of bits of experience of which the associationists spoke. But we find these things coherent, meaningful; some operation has been performed by the mind in organizing these bits into a unitary experience.

Second, he emphasized the innate tendency to perceive in terms of space and time. A man looks and sees a tree in the world of outer space; he listens and hears a melody flowing forward in time. Locke had taught that the "primary" qualities (size, shape, motion, and so on) are independent of the observer. But all primary and secondary qualities become equally secondary to one who has assimilated Kant. Nevertheless quantitative observations are relatively free from inconsistencies in the hands of various observers. Though they fail to measure the "thing in itself," they give a systematic and orderly account of experience as qualitative observation cannot do. Kant sums up by saying that there is in any discipline as much of science as there is of mathematics. Since his time it has been the intellectual custom to believe that science deals with quantities, not with the inner quality or nature of the things measured; and that though science is a study of experience, it is subject to all the limitations of "knowledge."

Just as the ultimate nature of external things is unobservable, so the knower or inner self is unobservable; we know only phenomena, appearances. Yet the self is encountered in each act of will. The process of willing is independent of causality; the will is free. This is part of our moral nature. Kant therefore leads us back to that religious outlook which he had had to put aside in his study of the process of knowledge. He insists that the ultimate moral and religious reality lies not in the field of knowledge but in the process of the will. His adoption of a "faculty psychology" made feeling and willing each quite separable from knowledge.

The *transcendentalism* of Kant derives its name from the fact that its ultimate explanatory principles lie outside of the content of any particular experience. What is transcendental is *necessary* and *universally valid*. It was therefore in one important respect in violent conflict with empiricism; experience, taken without reference to its transcendental laws, was for Kant simply a meaningless chaos.

German Psychology: Romanticism

Kant's transcendentalism, springing from intellectualist soil, shortly underwent profound modification in the hands of men who had much less to offer in the analysis of cognitive functions, but who reproduced more adequately the new romanticism of their age. Two streams—transcendentalism and romanticism—come together in a strange kind of unity.

German romanticism was in part an expression of the delayed impact of the Renaissance, which was beginning to produce in Germany the intellectual and moral ferment it had produced much earlier in Italy, France, and

Britain. Germany had, on the whole, remained under Scholastic influences for a longer time than had Italy, France, or Britain. Experimental science, which had made rapid progress elsewhere, hardly brought an echo in Germany in these centuries, except among those educated in France. Germany was still locked in the mighty fortress of medieval culture. Now there came at last not only the influence of British empiricism through the work of Kant, but a series of profound changes in the life and the mood of the people, a rebellion against the didactic and the rationalistic.

One of the predisposing influences toward this *romantic movement* was an appreciative (or even mystical) attitude toward nature. The seventeenth and eighteenth centuries had expressed through landscape painting and poetry a new response to the beauty of nature; and nature, rather than human institutions, was being more and more eagerly studied as the clue to the wholesome and the morally sound. What had earlier happened in Italy, and then in France and England, now began with might in Germany: a turning away from the scholar's study into the bright day of the world outside. The love of nature and of the natural, which had reached passionate expression in Rousseau in the mid-eighteenth century, assumed in Germany toward the end of the century the form of youthful "storm and stress," which was none the less romantic when it took the majestic form of Goethe's *Faust*.

In consequence of the romantic movement there rapidly developed within transcendentalism a specific form of philosophy the whole purport of which was to show that nature is not merely a series of events but a system of interaction among spiritual entities; the events which science observes have spiritual meanings. From the contact of the post-Kantian transcendentalists, such as Fichte and Schelling, with the romantic movement there arose in the early nineteenth century a philosophy which was transcendentalist in its aim, romantic in its motivation: the "philosophy of nature." It was by no means indifferent to the progress of the sciences; its leader, Oken, stimulated research, and it concerned itself constantly with newly discovered facts, especially with facts from the biological sciences. Indeed, it was dealing with the same subject matter as science, but according to a law of its own. Ultimately it proved to be incompatible with the science it imitated. We shall see that this philosophy was one of the most potent factors in the early training of some of the greatest nineteenth-century physiologists. Its psychology was necessarily vitalistic rather than mechanistic, and its center of interest lay in the fact of the richness of experience rather than in detailed analysis.

Hegel

Comparable to Kant in power and in the impact of his thought on the nineteenth century was the philosopher Georg Hegel. Hegel conceived of all intellectual and cultural history as derived from an Absolute, making itself known through a great *thesis,* or affirmation, from which followed an *antithesis,* or apparent contradiction, and finally a *synthesis,* or high integration, in which the thesis and antithesis are reconciled.[9] This dynamic conception of history, offered also as a conception of specific histories like the history of philosophy and the history of science, became one of the dominant philosophical and scientific generalizations of the nineteenth century (Taylor, 1958). It was from Hegel that Karl Marx (turning Hegel's philosophy "upside down") derived the thought of materialism as first principle, consciousness as antithesis or contrasting principle, and the whole integrity of life as the higher-level integration — the "dialectical materialism" of Soviet philosophy and Soviet science.

Let us review briefly these various schools with which we have been dealing so far and see their interrelations at the beginning of the nineteenth century. The Scottish school emphasized primarily cognitive processes which were thought to be self-evident: we can by direct observation discover that we have ways of obtaining valid knowledge. In Britain the work of the empirical school went on, under Locke's followers on the one hand and Bentham's and the utilitarians' on the other. The French psychology was to some extent modeled upon the English, especially upon the sensationalist principles formulated by Locke. But the tradition of Descartes, especially as it related to the theory of reflex action and to a conception of bodily mechanics, had in the persons of Cabanis and Bichat led to the vision of a physiological psychology much in advance of that of Hartley. In Germany the rationalistic tendency prevailed, bearing fruit in the transcendentalism of Kant, which insisted on realities beyond experience; and on the other hand, the romantic movement appealed directly to the spiritual meaning of nature. Hegel's dialectic conception of the dynamics of history was one of the early developmental conceptions. It sought to demonstrate a wide generalization as to the laws of philosophical, scientific, and, indeed, all development.

REFERENCES

Beccaria, C. B. *Trattato dei delitti e delle pene.* Leghorn, 1764.
Berkeley, G. *An Essay Towards a New Theory of Vision.* Dublin: Pepyat, 1709.
———. *A Treatise Concerning the Principles of Human Knowledge.* Dublin: Pepyat, 1710.
Bonnet, C. *Essai analytique sur les facultés de l'âme.* Copenhagen: Philibert, 1760.
Cabanis, P. *Rapports du physique et du moral de l'homme.* Paris: Sorbonne, 1799.
Condillac, É. *Traité des sensations.* 2 vols. Paris: Londres, 1754.

[9] Hegel went further than this. He attempted to show that all human history is more than a succession of events; there is a spiritual thread, a series of embodiments of the "Idea."

Hartley, D. *Observations on Man. His Frame, His Duty and His Expectations.* London: Johnson, 1749.

Hume, D. *A Treatise of Human Nature.* London: Noon, 1739–40.

Kant, I. *Kritik der reinen Vernunft [Critique of Pure Reason].* Riga: Hartknoch, 1781.

———. *Kritik der praktischen Vernunft [Critique of Practical Reason].* Leipzig: Reclam, 1788.

———. *Kritik der Urteilskraft [Critique of Judgment].* Leipzig: Reclam, 1790.

Reid, T. *Essays on the Intellectual Powers of Man.* 1785. 4th ed. Cambridge: Bartlett, 1853.

Smith, A. *The Theory of Moral Sentiments.* London: Millar, 1759.

———. *An Inquiry into the Nature and Causes of the Wealth of Nations.* 2 vols. London: Strahan and Cadell, 1776.

Taylor, J., ed. *Selected Writings of John Hughlings Jackson.* New York: Basic Books, 1958.

Wolff, C. von. *Psychologia Rationalis [Rational Psychology].* Frankfurt: Officina Libraria Regeriana, 1734.

NOTE: A list of further readings appears at the back of the book.

4

The Early Nineteenth Century

All our thoughts [the Stoics believe] are formed either by indirect perception, or by similarity, or analogy, or transposition, or combination, or opposition.

DIOGENES LAERTIUS

We must next take account of the influence of British associationism upon German thought. Transcendentalism had been gaining in momentum in Germany but yielded to associationism in the doctrines laid down by Herbart (1816), whose significance is equally great for the history of psychology and of education.

Herbart

J. F. Herbart, a vigorous and respected philosopher, with a strong bent for mathematics and a deep concern for an educational process built upon the laws of psychology, appeared on the scene in the heyday of Kant's philosophy. Essentially conservative in his emphasis upon the unity and activity of the soul, he was nevertheless radical in his attention to the process of learning and to the dynamics of the actual steps by which human knowledge and skills are acquired. Herbart's obligations to the English and German traditions are equally obvious. From the Hobbes-Locke-Hartley tradition he accepted the sensory elements which make up the observable conscious mind as it is seen at work in our perceiving and thinking. Whereas, however, the Greek sensationists and the English associationists had thought that sensations were passively impressed upon the mind, the German thinkers, from Leibnitz forward, had emphasized *activity*. In Herbart each sensory particle is active, is dynamic. In its inherent push, it tends to coalesce with other sensory particles or to resist such coalescence. Among the massive sensory impressions, some compete successfully with

49

others; indeed, they press down, so to speak, upon them, drive them out of consciousness. The mental particles which make up the conscious mind at any one time constitute a seething system of component parts interacting and, from time to time, dislodging or rejecting some of their members.

Mental functions were regarded by Herbart as expressions of psychical forces and were treated from a dynamic — and from a mathematical — point of view. Had he been more of a mathematician and less of a metaphysician, he could perhaps have constructed his beautiful associationism without reference to *forces,* the notion of which had come down from the physicists of the seventeenth century and especially from Newton (Burtt, 1925). But Herbart not only constructed a mathematical system to explain how bits of experience became associated; he not only showed the formulae by which we can create a calculus of the mind; he also defined the principles according to which something, as yet unknown, actively puts these parts together. He closely interwove these distinct conceptions, a mathematical system and the doctrine of an activating principle. The bits of experience coming through the senses combine with each other through the operation of certain measurable forces in the mind, as in the physical world.

Elementary bits of experience may combine harmoniously into wholes; the resulting composite ideas are closely similar to those described by Locke and Hartley. But there are also, Herbart taught, ways in which ideas may come into relation with each other through *conflict* or *struggle.* That is to say, ideas which are incapable of combining compete with one another — compete for a place in consciousness. A systematic theory of the conscious and the unconscious thus becomes necessary. Following out the dynamic implications of the system, a system in which ideas were active forces, Herbart had to show not only exactly what happens when ideas combine, but also exactly what happens when they exclude one another from consciousness. His mathematical formulae are designed to treat of the ascent of ideas into fuller consciousness and their descent from it into the unconscious. The conception of the unconscious was indeed a logically necessary result of such an analysis. Our ideas wax and wane in degree of consciousness as we observe them, and when they sink and are lost to view, we have no choice but to say that they have entered the realm of unconscious ideas. In discussing the "opposition" which leads some ideas to be ejected from consciousness by the superior force of other ideas, he simply needed a place for those which had lost the battle, yet were destined to return.[1]

For when an idea is ejected from consciousness, it is not *lost;* it may reappear later. How does it come back? Either by the weakening of the idea which repressed it, or by its combination with an ally, a cooperating idea

---

[1] Recent authors, including the psychoanalysts, point out that objects of thought do not conflict with each other because they are in logical opposition, but because they lead to divergent lines of conduct. Ideas are in conflict if they lead us to do opposite things.

which may, through joining forces with it, enable it to regain supremacy in consciousness. There is thus a tendency toward the recurrence of ideas which have once been banished. No purpose was served for Herbart by trying to describe the *nature* of unconscious ideas; he insisted simply that when ideas leave consciousness they have a tendency to return. This is a clear recognition of the fact that psychology must deal not only with what is present in consciousness, but with psychological factors beyond the reach of introspection; it involves, moreover, a theory so free from ambiguities that it can be applied to the phenomena of memory and to every phase of mental conflict. As the ideas in the field of consciousness pass from it they cross a *threshold;* the same threshold is crossed in the reverse direction when the idea reappears. It was over fifty years before a more adequate description of the unconscious in terms of empirical findings was attempted.[2]

This conception of the comparability and the interdependence of conscious process with other somehow similar processes occurring outside of consciousness has been a storm center in psychology for a century. Some regard it as an unfortunate and superfluous assumption, one that is unnecessary for empirical psychology, one which clutters up psychology with confusion and contradictions. Others regard consciousness as only one of many expressions of psychological reality; indeed, many psychologists think that the recognition of a psychological realm far greater than the conscious realm is the great emancipating principle of all modern psychology.

Herbart had no interest in neurological formulae such as those of Hartley. He wanted a purely psychological statement without assumptions regarding echoes and re-echoes of the nerve substance. He achieved this by applying his mathematics directly to the mental processes themselves, using force and time as two of the variables which preside over the uprisings and downsittings of all the different bits of sensory experience in their different combinations. If we experience a series of events in a given order, the dynamic relations established between them provide the basis for subsequent experience. In place of Hartley's statement of associative sequence through patterns once established in the brain, we have in Herbart a series following in order because certain dynamic relations inherent in the ideas themselves have been set up. This conception received an impressive vindication in the experiments of Ebbinghaus upon memory half a century later.

Many of our sensory experiences are not attributable solely to a new stimulus, but to a stimulus augmenting an unconscious deposit of experience. This is equivalent in some cases to the statement that although we had not noticed a stimulus before we now have the background to notice it as soon as it is presented. We may take as an example the case of a professional tea-taster seeking and finding a particular flavor or quality. Most of us might

[2] By Janet, James, Freud, and F. W. H. Myers. The theoretical studies by Schopenhauer and Von Hartmann seem to have been less important forerunners than the clinical work of Charcot.

seek in vain for a certain quality which is present, but the tea-taster has so frequently given attention to such qualities that now, when the stimulus is presented, he is able to detect it because of his accumulated past experience; it rises into his consciousness. This brings us to Herbart's most celebrated conception, the *apperceptive mass*. This comprises all those past experiences which we use when we perceive something new. In the illustration used, the perception of a certain quality in the tea is dependent upon the fact that there is a myriad of past tea flavors in the man's accumulated experience; the elements of flavor immediately find a place and are assimilated in consciousness.

Herbart applied his theory significantly to the process of learning. The child is learning, for example, the meaning of numbers. If he has observed his fingers often enough and has learned a group of words which apply to one, two, and three fingers, and so on, with other objects, and if we now attempt to teach him the general idea that one plus two equals three, he can assimilate this idea because he has observed it in specific cases. He can understand a map of Europe if he knows how land, water, and mountains are represented on the map of a region he already knows. His teacher builds in his mind a certain structure and now gives him a map of Europe. Immediately all these new sensory stimuli combine with the ideas which lie already assimilated in his mind. This background of ideas constitutes the "apperceptive mass," and instead of merely gazing at the map, he apperceives it. The term "apperception" has for Herbart much the same meaning that it had for Leibnitz, with whom it began; it borrows also from Kant. The process of apperception is a combination of a number of sensory bits into a unity. But instead of emphasizing an innate unifying power, as did Kant, Herbart presupposed that a background of experience already well organized in the mind makes possible the assimilation of a new idea which could never otherwise be learned.[3] This seemingly obvious common-sense doctrine has enjoyed the most extraordinary influence in education.

A revolution in educational theory and practice was already taking place in the closing years of the eighteenth and the opening years of the nineteenth centuries. It came mainly in the form of a protest against the mechanical implanting of information. It emphasized the new idea of developing the child's inherent capacities. Rousseau, in his time, had done much to disseminate this doctrine in speaking of the natural as opposed to the artificial. The aim of education would be to bring out the natural responses of the child. But no one knew just what was "natural." It remained for Pestalozzi and Froebel to clarify the idea. Pestalozzi believed one must start by developing the child's ability to observe. He did not confine this doctrine to the classroom but applied it to work on the farm, in the garden, and in the

[3] Herbart did indeed regard the soul as necessary to the coherent function and organization of mind. But from our contemporary viewpoint this seems little more than lip service to it, since the apperceptive mass sets the limits on what the soul can do and appears to be the central agency in the process of learning and knowing.

home. The implanting of information in the child's mind was reduced to a very subordinate position. Froebel carried the idea further, emphasizing the use of vivid stimuli, such as brightly colored toys, as means of attracting and holding attention and exercising the child's capacities for dealing with things; he made much of the educational value of play and founded the *kindergarten* as a means of making use of the "natural" in the child's development.

Herbart realized the importance of this emphasis upon observation. He saw that there were all kinds of ways of reacting to the same stimuli, depending upon the child's background. Education could make use of this principle throughout the whole course of life, starting with physical stimuli and gradually reaching more and more complicated forms of experience. Systematic use was thus made of the doctrine of apperception. Just as counting the fingers may lead to a general knowledge of numbers, so each contact with the world gives a background for the handling of more and more complex situations. But each idea must be offered to the child's observation only when the child, through previous observations, is ready to assimilate the new. This led to the idea of a curriculum so devised that the child passes systematically from familiar to closely related unfamiliar subject matter.

These ideas were epoch-making. Educational method became an empirical study. Herbart established an experimental school; he conducted classes for teacher training and compared different methods of presenting school material. The mathematical aspirations of Herbart's work were themselves ill-suited to the "apperception mass" of his immediate contemporaries. Yet his mathematical conception of a systematic psychology was consonant with the experimental approach which took shape a little later in the hands of Weber and Fechner; specifically, his conception of the *threshold* was highly relevant to the experimental program which Weber, Fechner, and their followers launched. The basic conception of conflict-within-the-mind — the conflict which Herbart described as continuously going on between the components of consciousness at any given time — was surely "dynamic" enough, rich enough in conceptions of "struggle" and "intrapsychic turmoil" to fit easily into the general dynamic emphasis of this romantic period and of the evolutionary period which followed. It may be difficult to prove that Freud's ideas of the unconscious and of the continuous conflict between psychic tendencies were inspired by Herbart. The relation was probably less direct and Freud's observations more dependent upon his own observations in psychiatric practice.

Herbart's permanent place in psychology rests on his thoroughgoing effort at mathematical analysis of psychological functions as later appreciated by Weber and Fechner, and later still by Ebbinghaus (see pp. 82, 181–82); his conception of attention and integration as formulated in the conception of the apperception mass; and his determined effort to make the process of learning an empirical and quantitative field of study.

Herbart's Contemporaries

German psychological literature in the age of Herbart was of considerable quantity. One group of writers reached out toward a unified science of man. They tried to relate the accounts of primitive cultures to those more complex; the raw material of travelers' records and memoirs was woven into a system of conceptions about man in his "natural state"[4] and as a social being. There appears to have been an increase in the practice of traveling for its own sake. The improvement of roads in France and later in England was important in knitting together more closely the nations of western Europe,[5] while longer journeys ceased to be ventures of discovery and became almost a part of a liberal education. The traveling naturalist and philosopher, Von Humboldt, striving to unify the intellectual life of western Europe, was typical. Mark Twain (*Innocents Abroad* and *A Tramp Abroad*) spoke to a public that thrived on travel and stories of travel.[6] The growing knowledge of many civilizations, primitive and advanced, gave an inductive basis for the work of these students of man. But they needed a theory as to how the mind works; they had to build some kind of bridge between the mind of the individual and the life of the group. The first vague intimation of "folk psychology" is found in this period.

One of the most influential psychologists of this era, J. F. Fries (1820–21), placed Kant's approach upon a biological, empirical foundation. He agreed with Kant about the futility of hoping to know anything ultimate about reality. But the process of cognition, instead of being attributed to a soul which lies beyond experience, was for Fries a function of the constitution of the organism. Man is forced by his biological make-up to see things in a certain way. Instead of introducing a transcendental principle, we should attribute human perception and reasoning to laws inherent in organic make-up. The Kantian categories, instead of being transcendental, are empirical. Such men as Fries helped pave the way for skepticisms and relativities — the fear of absolutes, so characteristic of modern science.

Phrenology

At the same time that these rather academic modes of thinking were going on, an extremely widespread movement was taking place which enormously exceeded in popular influence any of the writings just discussed. With the possible exception of Rousseau, none of the psychologists that we have

---

[4] The reader will recall that Hobbes and Rousseau, among many, had pictured a nonsocial human existence.

[5] Laurence Sterne, *A Sentimental Journey:* "they order . . . this matter better in France." Oliver Goldsmith's *The Traveller* is an equally celebrated expression of the tendency noted.

[6] Van Wyck Brooks in *The Dream of Arcadia* gives a vivid picture of American travelers in Italy in the nineteenth century.

considered had enjoyed what we might call a genuinely popular standing. But with the founding of phrenology by Gall (1809) in Germany early in the century, a tendency began which was destined to attract wide attention.

Gall's first thesis was that the mind exhibits numerous identifiable functions; his second, that each of these functions is located in a specific region of the brain. The last vestige of doubt that the brain was the seat of mental life had disappeared as a result of clinical investigations. Nor was the subdivision of the brain into regions possessing independent functions original in itself. But it was one thing to suggest that memory lies in the forebrain, another to itemize the way in which supposedly fundamental traits of man, such as imitativeness, destructiveness, the poetic gift, find their appropriate seats in minute corners of the brain. Gall's list included over thirty such localized traits. Thus while associationism broke up the mind into sensory particles, phrenology broke it up into functions.

Gall held that the degree to which any trait was developed depended on the hereditary development of the appropriate brain area. Such development of the brain tended to exert local pressure on the skull and to press it outward in the form of a "bump." The final assumption was that feeling the skull with the fingers can detect those regions in which there is rich endowment and thus make possible an analysis of the individual's chief traits.

This was a fascinating game. Gall's hypotheses, with the exception of the one relating to the pressing out of the skull, seemed plausible enough at the time; but instead of seeking full clinical evidence, men went on the road to lecture and to give character demonstrations on the basis of bumps. The practice came rapidly into vogue in France, Britain, and America. In a series of lectures on "Domestic Duties" for young housewives, popular in the thirties, the well-informed young woman is warned against the hasty acceptance of the generally discussed tenets of phrenology. The continuance in popular speech today of such phrases as "the bump of locality" does not imply that those who use it are believers in phrenology; but it does show the continuance of the doctrines of faculty psychology through phrenology. The phrenological scheme reinforced faculty psychology by keeping alive the notion of independent mental functions.

Along with a theory of localization in the brain, Gall was utilizing the conception, developed by Cabanis, that the organism is equipped by nature with basic reaction tendencies in the nervous system which enable it to adjust itself. Many of the instincts, he thought, have their accompanying emotional quality.[7] This was fifty years before the publication of Darwin's *Origin of Species* (1859) and the resulting emphasis in psychology upon instincts. Thus in relation to the idea of specialized brain areas, and in relation to the necessity for dynamic units in the study of behavior, Gall was a person of no mean significance. Nevertheless, he fared but ill in academic circles.

[7] Compare McDougall's analysis of instinct (1908).

His unverifiable assumptions and the popular degradation of his system led to the general neglect of his work among psychologists and physiologists. The later studies of localization of function within the brain made practically no use at all of the early efforts of Gall, except, of course, the general notion that brain structures are associated with localizable brain functions.

The French Revolt Against Mechanism

As we turn to the development of psychology in France, we encounter two traditions: the tradition of Descartes and the associationist's tradition. The sturdiest figure at the turn of the century had been Cabanis, a physiologist whose emphasis upon reflex action and whose whole dynamic approach made him a worthy disciple of Descartes.

But a revolt was brewing; mechanism did not suit the intellectual climate of the Napoleonic era; an idealistic movement was rapidly coming into its own. The spirit of this revolt was largely empirical. Thomas Reid, in founding the Scottish school, had tried as we have seen to base his idealism not on dogma but on confidence in the trustworthiness of the senses. Even those who attacked the empirical findings of mechanism used empiricism as a method. The same thing is true, to some extent, of the new French idealism, in which Maine de Biran was the dominant figure.

Biran began with an attempt at empiricism: the analysis of the genesis of habit, will, and self-consciousness in the child. His chief concern was the development of the self, of an individuality which is capable of integrated activity. He represented, moreover, a reaction against the mechanistic method, believing that the self is an experiencing *agent* and something more than a series of experiences; it is a unified spiritual principle. Now the self is not at first aware of its own existence; it is not directly experienced. But, by the process of adjustment to the environment, it becomes conscious of the distinction between the self and the not-self. There are two steps in this process. Such activities as crying and movement of the limbs are first called out mechanically. They take place by virtue of those principles which Cabanis had emphasized. But when the same stimulus is repeated later, there is in the field of experience a division into two parts, the object or thing upon which we react, and the self that reacts. In other words, the exercise of will is the first and dominant principle which causes the development of self-consciousness. It is because of our reactions, especially when resistance is offered to them, that we become aware of ourselves as individuals. As activity becomes more complex, self-consciousness develops greater richness.

This is a genuinely dynamic psychology. But its importance lay in giving a new turn to French thought, rather than in providing a specific set of ideas for the use of later generations. The details of Biran's system had little influence even in France a generation after his death. Yet he remained a sort of guardian spirit constantly present with French psychology, not indeed as a stimulus to the use of the genetic method, but as an embodiment of voluntarism, emphasizing the central place of the will.

Joining in the antimechanist protest came another movement: a French version of the Scottish philosophy. For the writings of Royer-Collard, who became professor at the Sorbonne in 1811, were simply continuations of the work of Reid. But in giving psychology a "spiritual" interpretation,[8] the school of Royer-Collard made use of the doctrines of Biran; specifically, they emphasized the fact of activity, which the associationists had almost without exception disregarded. His voluntarism had opened the way for a psychology which could meet their requirements. The will remained dominant in French psychology for the next forty or fifty years (idealism almost necessarily clings to the will as an independent function). But no clear facts about the will were available. With Biran as their presiding genius and Royer-Collard as their recognized head, French psychologists now settled down into an unimaginative and unproductive eclecticism. In the second quarter of the century the greatest figure was Cousin, whose contribution lay more in wide scholarship than in original observation. Eclecticism was so general that during the entire half-century which followed Biran French psychology may be characterized as the influenced rather than the influencing psychology of western Europe. But, as we shall see, France later did far more than its share in the development of psychiatry and in the task of bringing psychiatry and psychology together.

The Fusion of Scottish and English Psychology: Brown

Thomas Brown (1820) was a representative of three schools of thought: Scottish, English, and French. He was Scottish in his background, his education, and his academic position, ideally fitted for his post as Professor of Moral Philosophy at Edinburgh. He never abandoned that claim to prestige which the Scottish school had maintained through its emphasis upon the dignity of man. And he derived from the Scottish school one cardinal doctrine, the conception of a unitary substance or principle: in other words, the soul, whose affections and functions are the phenomena of psychology. The mind was not a mosaic of pieces, but a unity of substance with varying manifestations.

Yet he borrowed copiously from the associationists and had constant recourse to their methods of observation. Beginning with the work of Brown, the Scottish school came definitely under the influence of the English tradition. The chief importance of Brown's system of psychology lay in his wise and mature development of associationist theory. Using the term "suggestion" rather than "association," he sought an empirical treatment of the problem of mental connections.

[8] The term "*spiritualisme*," which is still in general use in French psychology, corresponds, roughly, to our "idealism."

He accepted Hartley's reduction of mental connections to one basic principle, which he called "coexistence." But this basic principle manifested itself in three forms, dependent on *resemblance, contrast,* and *nearness in time and space.* But now we come to this vital problem: When one thing is somehow connected with *two* or more other things, what is it that determines each particular course of association? When, for example, *tiger* resembles both *leopard* and *lion,* why does *tiger* in some cases make us think of *leopard* and in other cases of *lion?* Hobbes, in the middle of the seventeenth century, had vaguely seen the problem but had given no satisfactory solution. Hartley had concerned himself with the analysis of complex life situations but had never undertaken to show how his laws worked in the determination of particular sequences to the exclusion of others; why, for example, the same experience will prompt in the same man different ideas on different occasions. Brown, grasping the significance of the problem, undertook an analysis of the many factors determining the course of association, the celebrated "secondary laws of association." These have a peculiarly modern ring. It was not until the last decades of the century that German and American experimentalists discovered the necessity of taking such an analysis into account.[9]

The first four of Brown's secondary laws have perhaps the most vital significance, but all are important as modifications of the associationist tendency to oversimplify. Brown's laws are thus summarized by Warren (1921, p. 73).

1. The relative *duration* of the original sensations: "The longer we dwell on objects, the more fully do we rely on our future remembrance of them."

2. Their relative *liveliness:* "The parts of a train appear to be more closely and firmly associated as the original feelings have been more lively."

3. Relative *frequency:* "The parts of any train are more readily suggested in proportion as they have been more frequently renewed."

4. Relative *recency:* "Events which happened a few hours before are remembered when there is a total forgetfulness of what happened a few days before."

5. Their coexistence in the past with *fewer alternative associates:* "The song which we have never heard but from one person can scarcely be heard again by us without recalling that person to our memory."

6. *Constitutional differences* between individuals modify the primary laws. They give "greater proportional vigor to one set of tendencies of suggestion than to another."

7. Variations in the *same individual,* "according to the varying emotion of the hour."

8. "Temporary *diversities of state,*" as in intoxication, delirium, or ill-health.

9. Prior *habits of life* and thought—the influence of ingrown tendencies upon any given situation, however new or irrelevant the experience may be.

[9] Notably Külpe (1893) and Calkins (1896).

The general laws of "suggestion" were now seen to operate in terms, for example, of the relative *recency, frequency,* and *liveliness* of particular experiences. The emphasis on emotional and constitutional factors was also significant and quite in contrast with the associationists' usual neglect of individual differences. It was a contribution of great moment to see the need of working out such specific laws and to think in terms of the individual as a whole in the determination of each specific sequence of thought.

Brown championed Locke's position as to the presence of certain capacities of a reflective nature as well as those of a merely sensory nature. Locke had taught that in addition to ideas derived directly from the senses, we have ideas derived from reflection upon the data given by the senses. Brown, unwilling to use the nervous system as an explanatory principle, could not regard images or ideas as mere reverberations of sensations, reducing them to faint copies of their sensory originals. The memory elements were not for him identical with the sensory elements; they were independent entities. But if two objects are observed at the same time, and if we immediately become aware of the relation between the two, this is not a sensory function; it is a function of the mind, as a mind. To perceive that one man is taller than another, or one light brighter than another, is to grasp directly a relation present in experience. This was another blow at associationism. Mental life was not a mere concatenation of sense data, but was characterized by capacities to grasp relations. This was "relative suggestion," as opposed to the "simple suggestion" by which one idea follows another by virtue of sensory experience. "Relative suggestion" was not treated as a part of perception, but was emphasized only as it appeared in such processes as comparison and judgment. These relational elements have been successively forgotten and rediscovered. Bain, for example, recognized them; German psychologists rediscovered them in various guises late in the century. They have again come into their own in connection with the Gestalt school in recent years.

In addition to these obvious influences of the Scottish and the English schools, we have to take into account the fact that Brown had immersed himself in the writings of those French philosophers who were gently but effectively reinstating idealism in opposition to the mechanistic trend of the late eighteenth century. It was noted above that the reduction of the mind by Condillac and Cabanis to simple, mechanically conceived components was in harmony with a widespread revolt against religious and spiritual interpretations. Similarly, the return of the pendulum to idealism after the French Revolution gave strength to the hands of those who sought to overthrow the mechanistic schools. The followers of Condillac were amending his system by attributing some degree of *activity* to the individual. Among their greatest names were Laromiguière and De Tracy; the former, greatly influenced by Biran's activism, influenced in turn the work of Brown. Cabanis, though himself a mechanist, had helped to point out the significance of activity in personality. An idealistic and religious turn of mind found therefore close at hand the materials for the construction of a new system. This group of "ideologists" took hold upon that polite part of society which was interested in philosophy. They would not call ideas by unpleasant names, such as "mere sensation." But they were not so direct and flamboyant as Reid; their protest was orderly and courteous. Their central principle was that mind is not a passive instrument for receiving impressions. In specific revolt against Condillac, they held that mind is essentially a thing which reacts, which has spontaneous activities of its own. But theirs was scarcely a constructive movement. It was an attempt to restore the broken handle rather than to mold a new vessel.

This philosophy had all the elements necessary to make it become popular in Scotland. It was not only in harmony with the spiritual views of the Scottish school; it had, in fact, much that had been absorbed indirectly or borrowed directly from Scotland. Its specific alterations of associationist doctrine were useful and welcome to the Scottish school. Brown mastered both Scottish and French systems; his introduction of the French viewpoint and the French critique was, in fact, an enriching influence in his own system and responsible in part for his popularity. It was through French conceptions rather than Scottish ones that he saw how he could safely use the methods of the associationists while still rejecting their viewpoint. Regarding the soul as a living and acting entity, he could without compromise accept most of the empirical analysis of Hartley and his followers.

The French influence was especially clear in Brown's emphasis on the "muscular sensations," the sensations which give awareness of the position of the limbs and of opposition which they may meet in contact with outside objects. Some attention had been given to the muscle sense by physiologists; its introduction into psychology was, however, chiefly the work of Brown. The muscle sense, said Brown, gives us our notion of resistance. This was an elaboration of the ideologists' position; it was similar also to the point which Biran was making, the idea that the self is, in fact, engendered by the resistance offered to the blind movements of early infancy. But Brown's treatment of the concept differs materially from Biran's. Instead of Biran's almost mystical treatment of the will, leading to self-consciousness in the child, Brown's was chiefly a simple statement of the part played by muscular sensation in giving us awareness of the solidity of material things.

Brown's chief significance lay perhaps in the fact that he served to make the Scottish school more empirical. He made the school so closely acquainted with genuinely analytical methods that it could never quite go back to the firmly implanted dogmatism of its founder. In becoming amalgamated with empiricism and associationism, it lost its identity. But in Brown's hands associationism had for the first time undertaken a specific narrative of why we think and act in the particular ways forced upon us by particular occasions, while the interaction of "ideas" was replaced by acting individuals. Psychic atomism remained, to be sure, for a while; as we shall see, it was incorporated in the thoroughgoing associationism of James Mill, with whom it reached its logical perfection and systematization. But Brown's work was the beginning of the end both of associationism and of the Scottish school. He had given new life to the bold endeavors of those who wished to analyze and systematize the furious complexity of experience. He had put an end forever to the naïve formalism and pompous barrenness of Reid's approach. At the same time his conception of personality as a unity did much to give associationism that maturity and caution through which it attained its greatest achievements in the work of Spencer and Bain.

REFERENCES

Brown, T. *Lectures on the Philosophy of the Human Mind*. Edinburgh: Tait, Longman, 1820.

Burtt, E. A. *Metaphysical Foundations of Modern Physical Science*. New York: Harcourt Brace Jovanovich, 1925.

Calkins, M. W. "Association." *Psychological Review*, 3 (1896), 32–49.

Darwin, C. *The Origin of Species*. London: Murray, 1859.

Fries, J. F. *Handbuch der Psychischen Anthropologie*. Jena: Croker, 1820–21.

Gall, F. J. *Recherches sur le système nerveux en général, et sur celui du cerveaux en particular*. Paris: Schoell, 1809.

Herbart, J. F. *Lehrbuch zur Psychologie* [*A Textbook in Psychology*]. Königsberg: Unzer, 1816.

Külpe, O. *Grundriss der Psychologie* [*Outlines of Psychology*]. Leipzig: Engelman, 1893.

McDougall, W. *An Introduction to Social Psychology*. London: Methuen, 1908.

Warren, H. C. *A History of the Association Psychology from Hartley to Lewes*. Baltimore: Johns Hopkins University Press, 1921.

NOTE: A list of further readings appears at the back of the book.

Part Two

THE RISE
OF THE
RESEARCH
SPIRIT

5

Some Intellectual Antecedents of Experimental Psychology

. . . the whole conception of the Natural Universe has been changed by the recognition that man, subject to the same physical laws and processes as the world around him, cannot be considered separately from the world, and that scientific methods of observation, induction, deduction and experiment are applicable, not only to the original subject-matter of pure science, but to nearly all the many and varied fields of human thought and activity.

SIR WILLIAM DAMPIER

The origins of experimental psychology are to be sought in the intellectual development of western Europe in the late eighteenth and early nineteenth centuries; and most of all in the progress of experimental science in France and Germany. We must turn first to the progress of the exact sciences, particularly mathematics, chemistry, and physics; next, to that of the biological sciences, especially physiology. For experimental psychology grew out of the soil of an experimental physiology which was dependent upon all of these for its existence.[1]

Experimental methods had yielded many and cumulative results in the natural sciences since the days of Galileo. The Newtonian mathematics had been eagerly adopted and developed in France and became a central feature of French science. Whereas the experimental approach was more characteristic of English science, the most characteristic feature of science in France was the development of mathematical methods. By the middle of the eighteenth century French mathematicians had won world preeminence.

[1] For a fuller treatment of the history of science in the eighteenth and early nineteenth centuries see Merz (1896–1914).

French Science

As early as the middle of the seventeenth century the French Academy of Sciences had found favor with Louis XIV; and from that time onward it served as a central repository of scientific methods and results, as well as a center for the mutual stimulation and encouragement of scientific men—a center not merely for France, but for the world. This was utterly unlike anything to be found in Britain or Germany. It is true that Newton took a leading part in the formation of the Royal Society in England, but it was never favored by much support. A great British astronomer of the period was forced to give part of his time to tutoring in order to get the wherewithal for his researches. The French, on the other hand, offered much encouragement to astronomical work. This matter of patronage was a prominent factor in the rapid rise of the exact sciences in France. There sprang up departmental centers for scientific study and research all over France, so that French science attained some degree of integration. Local groups had opportunities to exchange ideas with one another, and many individuals went to Paris for study. Journals were founded which served to give quick dissemination to new ideas. Such close affiliation for scientific work was not dreamed of in England, nor in Germany.[2] But the departmental centers and the journals were dependent on an all-important element, without which French intellectual leadership would have been impossible: namely, national solidarity and a unity both political and cultural.

Whichever of these advantages we see fit to emphasize, the preeminence of the French in the exact sciences was apparent. The French had borrowed to such an extent the mechanical view of the universe, founded upon Newton's work, that we begin to find literary expression of it in the mid-eighteenth century: for example, in Voltaire. This gave to the reading public the unified view of the mechanical universe which had been developed by Kepler, Galileo, and Newton. Voltaire was almost a popularizer of Newton; he conveyed to the reading public that conception of the world which mathematics and physics had outlined.

This popularization was, of course, limited; it spread rapidly among the elite, but it was scarcely designed for the laborer and the peasant. But the French Revolution, with its mass appeal and its attempts at democracy, brought about an immediate change. Educators sought to dispense with traditional subjects and to put the whole system of public instruction upon the foundation of natural science. Condorcet made the point that the mathematical sciences were of immediate importance to all citizens; they strengthened the powers of observation and the capacity for clear thinking. Moreover,

[2] The German states which were parts of the empire were held together in the loosest fashion; while Prussia, though powerful, had a negligible influence as yet in the intellectual integration of the German-speaking states.

they were of practical value; as France soon found itself engaged in war with most of the powers of Europe, the scientific application of mathematics for artillery, of chemistry for explosives, and of biology in the training of military surgeons was important.

The Revolution interfered at first with research work, and the great Lavoisier was among those to lose their lives; but it is surprising to note how much scientific investigation, even in fields not immediately practical, was carried on in France during this period of relative isolation. Some individuals suffered, but most of the scientific work in progress was publicly recognized. Napoleon acknowledged the importance of science and mathematics, for this added to his own personal prestige as well as to the value of his engineering and artillery officers.

Some of the specific contributions of French science may serve to show its spirit. By means of differential and integral calculus it had been possible to work out the laws of the movements of heavenly bodies more adequately than seventeenth-century mathematicians had dared to dream. A little more than a century after Newton's *Principia* (1687), Laplace (1796) published his great books on celestial mechanics. He also undertook to describe the evolution of the solar system from nebular substances — the view known as the "nebular hypothesis." His "theory of probability" was of great importance. Tables of births, marriages, and deaths had long been in use, but Laplace supplied the theory necessary for a mathematical understanding of the means of prediction from such tables. Although his interest lay chiefly in pure rather than in applied mathematics, it was natural that he should become statistician to Napoleon. The relatively simple conception of *quantities*, offered by Newton, was also subjected by French mathematicians to a critical analysis.

It was chiefly through the work of Lavoisier just before the Revolution that an experimental quantitative chemistry came into being. In discovering, moreover, the nature of respiration (the union of carbon with oxygen), he brought chemistry into close relation with the life sciences. The scope of chemical experimentation is indicated by the founding of journals for the publication of research. This advance of chemistry in France was slow in reaching other nations, as the military situation tended to isolate France in respect to science and its applications. Furthermore, the tradition of the isolation of individual investigators from one another still held sway in Great Britain, in sharp contrast to the cooperation and centralization which characterized French research.

German Science

On the other hand, it happened through a fortunate concatenation of circumstances that early in the nineteenth century Germany began to occupy itself with chemistry and physics. Chemistry in the German universities had been dependent on French sources.[3] Practically all textbooks in the exact sciences in use in German (as in British) universities were in French, or were translations from the French. But within the university system of Germany there began to arise shortly after the close of the Napoleonic era a group of men (some of them trained in France) who were prepared to introduce French ideas. The first decade of their work was essentially a continuation of the French tradition, but German chemistry soon acquired a distinct individuality.

Liebig founded in 1826 a university laboratory for the systematic study of chemistry. He became, indeed, the founder of a new division of chemistry; he devised suitable methods for the chemical study of some of the functions of living creatures, and for these the term "organic chemistry" came into use.[4] Borrowing freely from contemporary French work, he probably did more than any other man to give German chemistry its enviable position in the three generations which followed. Wöhler, his pupil, succeeded as early as 1828 in actually creating synthetically an organic compound, urea, and thus in throwing a bridge across the gulf which separated the inorganic from the organic.

At the same time other investigations which served to establish connections between the physical and the biological sciences were going on in many other countries. In 1791, Galvani discovered the electrical current generated by stimulation of the frog's sciatic nerve. This was thought by many to have tremendous philosophical significance. Some hastened to conclude that the intimate nature of life processes had been found and that these processes were fundamentally different from the mechanical processes supposed to dominate the nonliving. On the other hand, mechanists derived an equal consolation from it; it proved for them that physical principles were sufficient for the explanation of life. Many men, of many philosophical expressions, were dreaming of bringing together on a scientific level both those disciplines which we call physical and those which we call biological. The dream had been dreamed by many before; but these strange electrical phenomena which were actually under investigation gave new ground for the hope of unifying the physical with the biological sciences.

Other contributions bringing the life sciences into closer touch with the physical sciences came from a series of discoveries in acoustics and optics. Chladni's work in acoustics was followed by Young's celebrated studies (1807) in the wave theory of light and in the theory of retinal function.[5] Optical phenomena necessitated physiological and psychological assumptions. Young formulated a three-color theory, later supported by Helmholtz, according to which the retina is equipped with three kinds of color receptors,

[3] The dissemination of French science into Germany had, of course, been possible to some extent even during the Revolution and the Napoleonic era.
[4] The term gradually acquired its present meaning: the study of the compounds of carbon.
[5] The wave theory of light goes back to the pioneer work of Huygens, a Dutch contemporary of Newton.

whose cooperative function gives the entire range of colors experienced. The Bohemian physiologist Purkinje made important observations on the brightness of color in relation to the intensity of light. From such developments followed that experimental physiology of audition and vision which was later on to play so great a role in the establishment of an experimental psychology.

The Biological Sciences

In turning to the development of the biological sciences, attention must first be given to the classifications of species. Ray's seventeenth-century classification of species was extended by Linnaeus (1735). Not only did Linnaeus know and classify thousands of plants and animals, but, more significantly, he devised a *system* of classification, grouping individuals into species, and species into genera, both indicated by Latin, hence international, names. The conception of a "species" has undergone notable changes; but the Linnean system has been of inestimable value.

The work of classification was carried forward and greatly enriched by Cuvier (1769–1832). "To name well," he remarked, "you must know well." His many contributions extend through the Revolutionary and Napoleonic eras. They give him rank with the histologist Bichat and the physiologist Cabanis as a representative of French biology. His contribution consists first of all in carrying out Linnaeus's idea of systematically grouping organisms and noting the elements of similarity and difference observed in members of various species and genera. He sought to make possible a classification which would not only give names to organisms, but would show their true resemblances and differences by noting which similarities were significant and fundamental and which were superficial or without significance. In spite of the lead taken by Lamarck, Erasmus Darwin, and others, Cuvier definitely opposed the evolutionary theory, which would have been most useful as a genetic method of classification. But he was an anatomist of such insight that he was able to lay down fundamental principles of wide general validity; he is generally recognized as the father of modern comparative anatomy. It is interesting to note that Cuvier relied chiefly not on the structure of bones, muscles, or sense organs, but on the central nervous system, as the most reliable single criterion in classification.

It was Cuvier's task to make a systematic survey of all the scientific work done each year; these surveys were in the form of reports to Napoleon. Together with *Eloges* delivered upon the deaths of great scientists, they mark a further advance in the establishment of central storehouses of scientific information. The group of physiologists and anatomists to which Cuvier belonged gave France—in fact, we may say specifically the city of Paris—almost as definite a position of leadership in biological science as it enjoyed in physical science.

But in the early nineteenth century a new place in the study of the biological sciences, as well as in the study of physical sciences, was won by Germany. To understand how this came about, we must turn our attention to the German university system, in which a series of important developments had been taking place during the eighteenth century.

The typical German university during the Middle Ages included three faculties: a faculty of theology, a faculty of law, and a faculty of medicine. These three faculties were virtually professional schools. No general or liberal-arts course was provided. If a student went to the university, he usually prepared himself for one of these three professions. There was a general neglect of scientific courses, except as they forced themselves into the medical curriculum. In 1734 a faculty of philosophy was founded at Göttingen, the aim of which was to give instruction not for the specific purpose of training for a professional career, but for the purpose of providing what we should now call a "liberal education." This involved the establishment of chairs for some subjects which had traditionally been a part of the three older faculties and some chairs for subjects newly introduced. The faculty of philosophy included such subjects as mathematics and physics; history; history of literature; Oriental languages; as well as two chairs for various subdivisions of philosophy, and a professorship of philosophy "without special definition." Carlyle's Teufelsdröckh, professor of "things in general," would have been an ideal holder of such a chair without portfolio. This new faculty was rapidly copied all through the German-speaking world.

During the eighteenth century, science became an important part of the German university curriculum; but "science" — "*Wissenschaft*" — took on a distinctive meaning. In France, "*science*" had come to mean mathematics and "exact science." German scholars attacked the problem of phonetics and of language; they developed philological technique. They began to apply critical methods to the study of literature, developing in time, for example, the technique of Biblical criticism and working out general principles by which it was possible to ascertain the date and the authorship of ancient manuscripts. They improved the methods of history and archeology. They devoted themselves to the problem of evaluating historical source material. Baumgarten's attempt to found a science of aesthetics, Kant's critical approach to the process of cognition, and Hegel's revision of logic under the term "dialectic" are parts of an extensive movement already well under way; they were works of *Wissenschaft* just as truly as were experiments in physics.[6]

We may say, to put it negatively, that the reason why the French and the British had given biology and the cultural sciences a secondary place was their preference for quantitative analysis. They could approach physics and chemistry with mathematical methods; they could not understand that the

[6] But "cultural sciences" (*Geisteswissenschaften*) are of course to be distinguished from the "natural sciences" (*Naturwissenschaften*).

biological and cultural sciences could be experimentally or mathematically approached. While the British and the French thought the physical sciences alone capable of being genuinely scientific, the Germans thought every field of knowledge could be equally scientific. Even the analysis of the knowing process itself, as Kant undertook to show, could become a systematic discipline. The German university teacher and student had but little of the departmental turn of thought which inevitably influenced the French teacher and student. The German faculty of philosophy served as a means of attaining a broad view of civilization as a whole. The German university was an engine with which to create a unified knowledge of the world.

Together with this ideal of the unity of all human knowledge there was also the feeling that the phenomena of life, as represented by the biological sciences, were to be viewed not merely in the perspective of chemistry and physics, but in their relation to all these other disciplines. No single approach could suffice in the study of so complex a thing as life; there must be some kind of unity or connection, at least in treatment if not in subject matter. There had been in both Britain and France a considerable skepticism about the possibility of building up a scientific technique for the study of living things. But in the German university the phenomena of life were subjected to the same critical treatment and seen in the same perspective as was required in any other specialty. The study of life must be undertaken from a unified philosophical world-view.

It is natural to ask how there could be uniformity of treatment in view of the fact that there were over twenty universities in Germany, politically separated, and with each man teaching from his own point of view. Such a possibility resulted from the exchange of professors between universities and the students' habit of moving about from one institution to another, customs vitally important in the unification of German thought. It never occurred to the German student that there ought to be any local continuity in his course toward a degree. This exposure to many influences augmented the tendency to seek for a unified view of the world and the desire to see life as a whole.

One who did much to point out the unity between the sciences was Haller, the physiologist of Göttingen, who flourished in the middle of the eighteenth century. Profoundly influenced by his teacher, the Dutch physiologist Boerhaave, he sought to treat human and animal life, chemistry and physics, as a unity. He gave to German students the conception that the empirical approach—in particular, the experimental method—which the British and French were using in the physical sciences, could be applied to life processes; the notion of physiology as an experimental science was established. The importance of this conception can be realized only when we consider the extraordinary degree to which biological science had been occupied with the astrological and the occult. Even the great teacher Paracelsus, who did so much to establish a chemical view of life processes, had made extensive use of astrological principles; even the intrinsically helpful notion of humors in the blood was confused with much that was incapable of any sort of verification. Haller has been called the father of modern physiology.[7] He published a textbook which remained the standard text on physiology for the world for three quarters of a century: until Johannes Müller (1833–40).

But we have to consider another factor which this statement disregards. We may recall the extraordinary development of the interest which Germany of the "romantic" period showed in living things as something distinct from the world of matter and motion. The German temperament of the time reached out toward the comprehension of life. Eighteenth-century France and Britain witnessed striking romantic movements. Yet the tendency to speak of the "romantic movement" as essentially German is perhaps evidence for the view suggested. But we are dealing with a question of degree. There is, of course, no need to designate this as a permanent national trait; the same general tendency was apparent in Italy during the Renaissance. One might be tempted, and not entirely without justice, to say that this is the arrival of the Renaissance in Germany. One might be tempted to say that Germany, isolated from the rest of western Europe through a series of wars and through such influences as the surviving feudalism of the Holy Roman Empire, had its awakening in the eighteenth century, so that problems of the nature of life won a prominent place outside of as well as within the university system. All this development of the biological sciences in Germany might be regarded as part of a general cultural movement. It would be out of perspective to say that the German university was the sole explanation for the rise of biology.

A familiar illustration of the German spirit of the time is the personality and career of Goethe, who was so great as a poet that few people thought of him as a scientist. But he was, in fact, responsible for two important biological contributions. He was one of the first of the moderns to put forward a theory of organic evolution; and he elaborated a significant theory of color vision (1810). In opposition to Young's three-color theory, he undertook to show that one cannot account for the facts of color blindness, color contrast, and negative afterimages without postulating at least four primary colors. Goethe made also a number of contributions to botany which would have sufficed to render him illustrious were they not overshadowed by his position in literature and philosophy. It was not only in the universities that the growing study of life processes was manifest.

On the other hand, the main current of this development undoubtedly did flow in the universities. It reached its greatest height after the Napoleonic period in the brilliant physiological researches of Weber and Müller and their pupils. (To these men we shall later devote special attention; for the

---

[7] Harvey had of course shown the way, and many clinicians had contributed important empirical studies of physiological functions, side by side with the rapid progress of anatomy.

present it is important only to show their relation to the general movement indicated.) We saw above how Liebig and Wöhler worked together to found the science of organic chemistry and how a link had been forged between the inorganic chemistry of Lavoisier and the study of life. While this was going on, botanists and zoologists sought with the aid of the microscope to discover a connection between physical principles and the principles of form which underlie the structure of living things. They were trying to do in the field of morphology what Liebig had done in the field of chemistry. A great step had already been taken in France in the closing years of the eighteenth century when Bichat demonstrated the relation between organs and the fundamental structures (the tissues) which compose them. In Germany a new step was now taken by Schleiden, who demonstrated in 1838 that all plant tissues were made up of cells, each cell being in some respects an independent unit. Two years later Schwann succeeded in showing that the same principles held for animal tissues. The study of life processes was enormously furthered by these two noteworthy discoveries; the knowledge of the cellular constitution of living matter greatly facilitated the analysis and classification of microscopic structures. The discovery of such structural units was of far-reaching consequence not only for anatomy but for physiology. Germany held, by the middle of the century, a position of leadership in biological science, which, as we have seen, was due very largely to a certain background of intellectual history that differentiated its specific problems from those of France and Britain.

While all this went on in Germany, there were many brilliant biological researches under way in England, in the hands of individuals who enjoyed no such cooperation and no such profound intellectual stimulus as were vouchsafed to the German scientist. The most notable of these, as far as scientific psychology was concerned, was Sir Charles Bell's discovery of the principle of differentiation of sensory and motor nerves. Galen, to be sure, had known of sensory and motor nerve functions. But it was supposed that nerves possessed in general *both* sensory and motor functions, and it remained for Bell to show that some structures are sensory, others motor—that immediately before entering the spinal cord the sensory fibers group themselves into the dorsal, and the motor fibers into the ventral, root of each nerve. His *Idea of a New Anatomy of the Brain* (1811) was followed by a number of papers read before the Royal Society.[8] He laid the foundation for a detailed study of nervous physiology in terms of the incoming and outgoing pathways. He suggested also that the division of labor might be still more detailed; that in spite of morphologic similarity the *variety* of mental functions might be based on a variety of specialized tasks carried out by many functionally distinct nervous elements. In essence, the idea is really a very old one, and the eighteenth century had revived it. Bonnet had grasped

[8] See Carmichael (1926).

it quite clearly: ". . . there are in each sense certain fibers which are appropriate to each kind of sensation. . . . There are consequently still among the fibers of vision certain differences corresponding to those which exist among the rays" (1769). The lack of scientific intercommunication across national boundaries in this period is well shown in the fact that many years passed before Johannes Müller undertook the elaboration of these two doctrines of Bell, experimentally verifying the former and stating the latter in the famous formula of "specific energies." Though Magendie, in France, did experimental work on the problem in the twenties, Bell's epoch-making discovery regarding sensory and motor roots seems not to have been fully appreciated until Müller's time.

Throughout this era of intellectual ferment, the vigorous and imaginative work in science and philosophy was a response to the rapid scientific advances and changes in the conditions of human life. Even so, there was as yet no concept of "psychology" as we would use the term. There was a philosophy of life in its biological aspects, as seen by medical men, by naturalists, and by students of health and disease. There was a vigorous philosophy of social change, arising from the moral problems posed by the coexistence of vast wealth with enormous poverty. There were challenges to authoritarian and orthodox beliefs. The lands to be "won" in the New World encouraged individualism, democracy, and independence of thought.

These many ways of facing the new picture of life, however, did not add up to a "psychology." They did add up to a concept of the mind on one hand and of the social order on the other. Here and there, a creative thinker was able to bind some strands of thought together: Cabanis in France, Kant in Germany, James Mill and John Stuart Mill in Britain. But it took more than isolated thinkers to see a new territory. It took the labor of many men to create anything like a unified view of the human predicament, or psychology, which could be soundly rooted both in the individual life experience and in the collective experience within the social order. Indeed, one of the major attempts of nineteenth- and early twentieth-century science was to foster conditions under which this broader view developed — psychology as a biological and social science.

REFERENCES

Bell, C. *Idea of a New Anatomy of the Brain.* London: Strahan and Preston, 1811.
Bonnet, C. *Analyse abrégée de l'essai analytique.* Paris: Sorbonne, 1769.
Carmichael, L. "Sir Charles Bell: A Contribution to the History of Physiological Psychology." *Psychological Review,* 33 (1926), 188–217.
Cuvier, G. *Le Règne animale.* 20 vols. Paris: Fortin, Masson, 1769–1832.
Goethe, J. W. von. *Zur Farbenlehre.* 2 vols. Tübingen: Cotta, 1810.
Laplace, P. S. *L'Exposition du système du monde.* Paris: Courcier, 1796.

Linnaeus, C. *Systema naturae*. Lugduni Batavorum, apud Theodore Haak, 1735.

Merz, J. T. *History of European Thought in the Nineteenth Century*. 4 vols. Edinburgh: Blackwood, 1896–1914. New York: Dover, 1965.

Müller, J. *Handbuch der Physiologie des Menschen*. 3 vols. Coblenz: Hölscher, 1833–40.

Newton, I. *Philosophicae naturalis principia mathematica*. London: Streater, 1687.

Young, T. *A Course of Lectures on Natural Philosophy and the Mechanical Arts*. 2 vols. London: Johnson, 1807.

NOTE: A list of further readings appears at the back of the book.

6

The Beginnings of Psychological Experimentation

> *The art of measurement would do away with the effect of appearance.*
> *... They err not only from defect of knowledge in general, but of that*
> *particular knowledge which is called measuring.*
>
> PLATO

The rise of the biological sciences in Germany led quickly to a brilliant personification of the movement in E. H. Weber. He was one of three brothers illustrious in the natural sciences. Whereas the others devoted themselves to physical science, his own work was centered in the physiology of the sense organs. Research in Germany upon the sense organs and their functions, as well as in France and England, had been confined almost entirely to the higher senses, seeing and hearing. Weber's work consisted largely in opening up new experimental fields, notably research upon the cutaneous and muscular sensations, and in perceiving psychological implications in his results.

Weber

Weber began shortly before 1820 to teach anatomy and physiology at the University of Leipzig, where he remained throughout his career. His life there was characterized by the constant publication of new work and the stimulation of a large number of students—medical students for the most part, for medicine was supreme among the biological sciences, and physiology as an independent science did not yet exist. Though he was more or less under the influence of the "philosophy of nature," with its belief in spirit expressing itself through physical symbols, this did not mar the solidity of his experimental and theoretical work as a physiologist.

A few examples may be given of his widely varied studies in sensory physiology. His experiments on the temperature sense led him to formulate a theory to the effect that the experience of warmth and cold is not dependent directly on the temperature of the stimulating object, but on the *increase* and *decrease* of the temperature of the skin. If the hand is placed in warm water, the rising temperature of the skin leads to the experience of warmth. The skin temperature may rise or fall without occasioning the experience of warmth or cold if the change is very gradual. This theory accounts well for the adaptation or habituation which makes warmth or cold less noticeable after the skin has been exposed to it for some time. One of his minor experiments tried to determine whether liquids or gases are the true stimuli for the sense of smell. He put a 10 per cent solution of Eau de Cologne into his nose and tilted his head so as to bring the liquid into contact with the nasal mucous membrane. Finding that no sensation of smell was received, he concluded that liquids are not direct olfactory stimuli. An instance of his work on audition was the discovery that if he held a ticking watch at each ear he was less proficient in judging whether the ticks were simultaneous than if the two watches were held at the same ear. As an example of his experiments in vision, he undertook to determine the smallest arc that would permit discrimination of two lines. When the lines are exceedingly close together we get the impression of one line, while if they are not so close we see two distinct lines; he measured the arc necessary for such distinction.

To several of Weber's experiments much more attention must be given. One of these had to do with the distance that must separate two stimuli applied to the skin, in order to bring about the perception of doubleness (1842–53, Vol. 3, pp. 481–588). This was, of course, the same experiment within the field of *cutaneous* sensation which we noted above in the field of vision. Precautions being taken to exclude the use of vision, the subject's skin was stimulated, sometimes with one compass point, sometimes with two, the distances between the two points being constantly varied. As the distance increased with two-point stimulation, the subject passed from the impression of one clear-cut stimulus to an impression of blurring, or uncertainty as to whether there was one or two, and thence on to a state where he was quite definitely aware that there were two points of stimulation. There was, in other words, a threshold (*limen*) to be crossed before the impression of doubleness could be evoked. He established a "two-point threshold." The concept of the *threshold*, so widely used in the measurement of stimuli and the relations between them, was first systematically used by Weber. Now Weber found that the two-point threshold, the distance necessary to make possible the discrimination of doubleness, varied in different parts of the body — in fact, varied enormously. It was smallest on the tips of the fingers and the tip of the tongue. It was somewhat greater on the lips, greater still on palm and wrist, and increased toward the shoulder. Further, the threshold for a given region varied from one individual to another.

In explanation, Weber put forward the hypothesis that the "sensation circles" (areas within which doubleness is not perceived) must contain a number of nerve fibers and that unstimulated fibers must lie between the two stimulated if doubleness is to be perceived. Difficulty was encountered because subjects showed marked effects of training; the circles became smaller with practice. Other difficulties have arisen, and the theory has lost ground: the work of Blix (1884) showed that there are many "touch spots" in each sensation circle. Even so, Weber's experimental method remains of much greater permanent significance than his explanation of his results.

Even more important, perhaps in Weber's own mind the most important of his contributions, was his examination of the muscle sense (1834). It was while exploring the muscle sense that he made the discovery with which he is chiefly identified. Physiologists had come to recognize that sensory impulses arise not only from the outside but from the interior of the limbs. Thomas Brown (1820) had emphasized the important part which the muscular sensations play in detecting resistance offered to our movements. Weber undertook to find to what extent muscular sensations function in the discrimination of weights of different magnitude. If the subject lifted weights with his hand in such a way as to experience not only tactual sensations, but also muscular sensations from the hands and arms, he discriminated very much more accurately than when weights were laid upon the resting hand. Weber made use of four subjects whose results were quite consistent in showing the great superiority of those judgments in which the muscle sense was used. He worked with two sets of weights, the standard weight being 32 ounces in the one set and 4 ounces (32 drachmae) in the other. He later undertook another series of experiments with a standard weight of 7½ ounces. In the latter experiment the conditions were systematically varied; the weights were, for example, applied both simultaneously and successively. In all these experiments, the fact emerged that discrimination depended not upon the absolute magnitude of the difference between two weights, but upon the ratio of this magnitude to the magnitude of the standard. Under the most favorable circumstances, the difference between the weights was correctly perceived when they bore roughly the ratio 29:30. Using touch alone, the necessary difference was roughly one-fourth of the standard weight, but again it proved to be not an absolute quantity, but a fraction depending on the relative magnitude of the stimuli.

From these facts of muscular and cutaneous sensation Weber reached the conclusion that the ability to discriminate between two stimuli depends not on the absolute magnitude of the difference, but upon a relative difference which can be stated in terms of their ratio to one another. The "just noticeable difference" could be stated as a fraction which, while varying with the sense tested, was constant within a given sense modality. This led him to inquire whether there was not evidence from other sense modalities to support the general principle that discrimination depends not on the absolute difference of stimulus magnitudes but on their relation to one another. Accordingly, he undertook experiments in vision which bore on the same problem. He presented pairs of straight lines, requesting the subject to state which of the lines was longer. The results of this experiment confirmed the principle of "relativity" which he had already found. Here the fraction was even smaller than in the case of the muscle-sense experiments; visual discrimination between two lines was possible if one was from one-hundredth to one-fiftieth longer than the other; that is, 1 or 2 per cent. (This holds for simultaneous presentation. With successive presentation a 5 per cent difference was needed.) The fraction for a given subject at a given time was roughly constant and independent of the length of the "standard" line. This led Weber to offer the generalization that we can lay down for *each* of the senses a *constant fraction* for "just noticeable differences."

The generalization was overbold. These experiments with visual stimuli involved to some extent sensations from the external eye muscles and did not directly settle the question of the discrimination of visual intensities. Having become enamored of his principle, he thought he found it exemplified also in another field. Just before the period of these experiments Delezenne (1827), who was working in the field of acoustics, had unearthed some facts that seemed to Weber to support a similar generalization. Weber seized upon this observation as another instance of his law. From the results of all the experiments noted, Weber believed that his general principle was founded on facts from skin, muscle, eye, and ear. But though the data at hand warranted no such sweeping generalization, the effort to find by experiment a truly psychological law relating to the experiences derived from different sense-modalities marked a turning point in the history of science.

It would be hard to overemphasize Weber's importance in the genesis of an experimental psychology. His interest in physiological experimentation served to turn the attention of physiologists to the legitimacy and the importance of approaching in the laboratory certain genuinely psychological problems which had throughout history been neglected. Not only did he set problems which occupied men of the ability of Helmholtz, Fechner, and Lotze, but he himself attacked a great many of these problems and pointed the way to their systematic study. His conception of "just noticeable differences" and his broad assumption that our responses to the world are subject to measurement have leavened the study of everything in psychology from the simplest feelings to the most complex social attitudes.

An illustration will show the extent to which he could transform the problems of the physicist and the physiologist. An experiment had been carried out in France by Bouguer a generation before Weber's time, in which the sensitiveness of the eye to light was measured by varying the relative positions of candles and pinholes through which light reached a screen beyond. In order to make a faint shadow distinguishable from a shadowed area adjacent to it, it was found that the illumination of the two must differ by

one sixty-fourth. The problem led to no principle of any particular consequence. Yet it was in embryo the problem of "just noticeable differences."
It was just such a problem as in the hands of a Weber might have become a
cornerstone of epoch-making research.

It is no accident that work like Weber's came when and where it did.
German intellectual history for a century had paved the way; the influence
of Haller still lived, enriched by the brilliant French discoveries of the late
eighteenth century, which had been adopted with new energy by the
German universities in the early years of the nineteenth century. Important
as it may be to plant wisely the seed of an experimental project, the soil is no
less important. When Hamilton, a few years later, undertook to study
experimentally some problems in attention, nothing of significance resulted
in British psychology; associationism and the Scottish school were alike
uninterested. The crucial point was that in Germany experimental physiology was solidly established with quantitative methods and with a wide
outlook. The measurement of the cutaneous two-point threshold, the study
of visual acuity, and the study of "just noticeable differences" in the field
of the muscle sense were throughout envisaged in quantitative terms; and
problems were so stated that they quickly became experimental in the more
restricted modern sense, several different factors being varied in order to
isolate the significance of each. Weber ventured, moreover, to bring together
an array of results under a common law, a universal principle. Important as
this law was to become as a hypothesis for voluminous research, Weber's
greatest significance lies rather in his conception of an experimental approach to psychological questions and in the stimulation of research through
which ultimately a vast variety of problems other than his have been in-
cisively studied.

Fechner and Psychophysics

Nothing could be more misleading than to study Gustav Fechner as a
follower of Weber, as if he were simply an echo or a reflected light from the
great physiologist. A moment's glance at Fechner's early life shows how
soon his characteristic genius displayed itself.

He started his career as a student of medicine, and of physics and chemistry, at Leipzig, where he began to give instruction a few years later. He
interested himself especially in contemporary discoveries in mechanics
and electricity. His earliest writings, consisting of scientific treatises and
translations from French experimental contributions, show how, as a young
man, he mastered the physical sciences of his day. But he began before long
a series of brief articles of purely literary design. Among these, one of the
purest gems is *Das Büchlein vom Leben nach dem Tode* (The Little Book
of Life After Death, 1866). In this he strove to show how we are, as it were,
all parts of one another, living in each other so fully that as long as human

life continues no individual can die. He was studying the philosophy of Fichte and Schelling also and beginning to give literary expression to the feelings it kindled within him. And he was deeply stirred by the "philosophy of nature," which was dominated by the desire to find a spiritual meaning in all the events of the natural order.

The source of this many-sided distribution of interests was the problem: "How can quantitative science teach us to study the human spirit in its relation to the universe? How can those exact methods which have been applied so successfully in the natural sciences be turned to advantage in the study of the inner world? How can we ever see the soul under conditions of direct and reportable observation?" As we are told by J. T. Merz:

> He became acquainted with the philosophy of Schelling, Oken, and Steffens, which dazzled him, touched the poetical and mystical side of his nature, and, though he hardly understood it, had a lasting influence on him. The simultaneous occupation with the best scientific literature of the day (he translated French textbooks such as those of Biot and Thénard, and verified Ohm's law experimentally), however, forced upon him the sceptical reflection whether, "of all the beautiful orderly connection of optical phenomena, so clearly expounded by Biot, anything could have been found out by Oken-Schelling's method?" This mixture or alternation of exact science and speculation, of faithfulness and loyalty to facts as well as to theory, runs through all Fechner's life, work, and writings (1896–1914, Vol. 2, p. 508 n).

It is easy to see why Fechner was both a follower of the "philosophy of nature" and one of its most ardent opponents. He did not come to this attitude hastily; he felt about for a way. He knew vaguely what it was that he sought, but there was no movement which undertook the thing he wanted, no school with which he could affiliate. Reaching in one direction and another, he was bewildered by the complexity of the spiritual heritage and the futility of stating and cataloguing it in the terms of those sciences in which he was at home. He began then, in a series of satirical writings under the name of Dr. Mises, to assert a negative expression of what he felt; he began to satirize mechanistic science. The attempt to bring the biological sciences into terms similar to those of mathematics and physics seemed to him to involve the repudiation of biology and psychology, because this attempt seemed to repudiate life and mind at the outset. The attempt to transfer the methods of physics and chemistry into biology and psychology meant for him a retreat from the self-evident world of life of which we are a part; it meant also the denial of the living reality of the whole universe, every fiber and atom of which was for him equally alive and meaningful.

From these satires it is apparent that he could not begin to solve his problem because he could not quite state it. He felt, on the one hand, the need of an exact method in order to make headway in biological and psychological science; but, on the other hand, the existing methods could never interpret the events which they recorded. As he groped about, satirizing quantitative science under a pseudonym, he was at the same time carrying on exact research in the field of physics—was identified, for example, with investigations into the atomic theory. While teaching in the classroom the physics of the day, he was constantly trying to see a way in which satire could be replaced by a new understanding of the subject matter of science, an understanding which would make both the human soul and the objects which it knows equally accessible to methods by which real knowledge can be amassed.

During this period Fechner suffered from a progressively severe illness; perhaps it was the sort of illness that is now vaguely called a "nervous breakdown." He persisted in increasing his difficulties by undertaking the study of positive afterimages from bright stimuli, particularly the sun. Violent pain in his eyes and partial blindness resulted, from which he did not recover for several years. The earlier disorder, complicated by the inability to read, and apparently even the inability to think clearly without great difficulty, caused something verging upon a collapse. His wife, however, brought him through this difficult time, and he gradually recovered.

As the vigorous use of his mind returned to him, he began to ponder again the relation of mental to physical processes and the possibility of discovering a definite relation between them. One day the discovery burst upon him that there is one sort of quantitative relation observable in daily life: namely, the intensity of sensation does not increase in a one-to-one correspondence with an increasing stimulus, but rather in an arithmetical series which may be contrasted with the geometrical series which characterizes the stimulus. If one bell is ringing, the addition of a second bell makes much more impression upon us than the addition of one bell to ten bells already ringing; if four or five candles are burning, the addition of another makes a scarcely distinguishable difference, while if it appeared with only two its effect would be considerable. The effects of stimuli are not absolute, but relative; relative, that is, to the amount of sensation already existing. It occurred to him that for each sense modality there might be a certain relative increase in the stimulus which would always produce an observable intensification of the sensation; and this ratio would hold for the entire range through which the stimuli might be made to increase. We might say, for example, that sensations increase arithmetically, according to a formula in which we need only to know the constants which determine the rate of geometrical progession for the different sense modalities. This he stated as

$$S = C \log \frac{R}{R_0}$$

where S is the intensity of the sensation, C is a constant for each of the different fields of sense, R is the intensity of the stimulus, and R_0 is the intensity of the stimulus at the threshold.

We should note that Fechner's search and doubts were taking place at a time when European thinking was making significant new contacts with the Orient. The British had made contact with India before 1800; and soon contacts with Persia, China, and other great Oriental cultures were added. At a time when American sailing men were carrying American folk tunes and spirituals to Asian seaports and bringing back fragments of Asian lore, scholars were making their way toward the comprehension of Sanskrit poems. Schopenhauer and soon Nietzsche were glorying in the history of Oriental thought. Brett (1965, p. 582) wrote:

> From 1820 to 1830 Hegel delivered his annual lectures on the philosophy of history, and pictured to his audience the life of the East as "a dream, not of the individual mind, but of absolute spirit."

One of the first waves of this new movement to strike these American shores was Ralph Waldo Emerson's celebrated poem responding to the great epic of India:

> If the red slayer think he slays / or if the slain think he is slain, / they know not well the subtle ways / I keep, and pass, and turn again.

More broadly it may be maintained that a certain vast and powerful, though vague and imprecise, effort at "the meeting of East and West" was beginning in the first half of the nineteenth century, a movement carried magnificently forward by the huge system of translations of Oriental philosophy and religion edited by F. Max Müller (1879) under the title *The Sacred Books of the East*. Mysticism and a certain yearning for ultimate meanings became interwoven with the yen for things Oriental, even in such a crude form as Kipling's craving for a mystic vision in "The Road to Mandalay." During this time the West received from the East a good deal more than the East received from the West, for it was not until late in the nineteenth century that India, China, or Japan really assimilated the basic philosophical and psychological conceptions of the Western world.

In this same period Fechner published a sort of philosophy of nature of his own, entitled the *Zend-Avesta* (1851), its title reflecting the general incursion of Oriental thought during the middle of the century. The Persian system, with its fundamental dualism, in which good and evil center in personal beings, laid hold upon Fechner's imagination; through it the world could be seen to be really personal, really alive. It absorbed Fechner partly because it made possible the personal interpretation of the natural world, a world not seen, however, as an antithesis between natural and supernatural, but as natural and spiritual at once. This gave him the desired antithesis to the science of his day; it gave the universe a soul, or rather a plurality of souls. In the *Zend-Avesta* Fechner mentioned that he had recently discovered a simple mathematical relation between the spiritual and the physical world.

He now undertook a series of experiments on brightness and lifted weights, visual and tactual distances, to test his hypothesis regarding the relation of sensation intensities to stimulus intensities. Immediately after beginning these he happened upon the work of Weber, which had commenced a quarter-century before. Weber had shown that there appeared to be a definite law governing the relation between the intensities of stimulation and the ability to distinguish which of two stimuli was the greater. The "just noticeable difference" is a constant fraction of the standard stimulus. This principle, laid down by Weber, seemed to Fechner to be a mathematical generalization of great importance. He saw its relation to his own hypothesis. He seized upon it, made much of it, and proceeded to extend enormously the experimental work to confirm it. But the difference between Fechner's hypothesis and Weber's is immense. Weber had concerned himself with "just noticeable differences," but Fechner could be satisfied only with a mathematical statement of the relation of the physical to the spiritual world.

Fechner's formula had to be put to the test of long and arduous experimentation. He had, of course, to use two supplementary hypotheses: first, that sensations can be measured (for example, three units of loudness); and second, that there is a zero point for all sensation. Both points became the subject of endless controversy, but both, as Fechner realized from the beginning, were essential to the very core of his purpose. For in this measurement of sensation, as he explicitly stated over and over again, his one purpose was to find the quantitative relation of the objective to the subjective world. The longing to grasp the meaning of the world in terms which would articulate with the scientific methods of his day — that is, to find the relation between the qualities of experience and the quantities of science — was the thing which forced the treatment of qualities into the quantitative mold. If he laid a foundation for one great subdivision of experimental psychology, seeking to confirm his law in as many fields and through as many methods as possible, it was in the service of a struggle to find confirmation for his great conviction.

A closer examination of the most important of Fechner's psychophysical methods is necessary. Weber's law remained his guiding principle. He carried on his experiments, stimulated by Weber's discovery, for seven or eight years before he gave any account of his methods or his findings to the public. The first presentation of his work (1858) was a paper on mental measurement, a two-year forerunner of the *Elements of Psychophysics,* which appeared in 1860. In the *Elements,* psychophysics was defined as an exact science of the functional relations, or relations of dependence, between body and mind. Its sphere included sensation, perception, feeling, action, attention, and so forth. He selected sensation as most susceptible of measurement at that stage of the science and developed his methods on the basis of the fundamental principle that sensation is a measurable magnitude. That is, any sensation is the sum of a number of *sensation units,* and these units can be standardized by the aid of the correlated stimuli. The ideal of psychophysics is, of course, to measure the relation of subjective intensities to the bodily intensities which accompany them: for example, to compare sensations with brain changes. This realm of "inner psychophysics" was regarded by Fechner as free from those inconsistencies and errors which attend "outer psychophysics," in which the stimulus rather than the bodily response is compared with subjective intensities. Outer psychophysics was accepted only because it was more immediately practicable.

Fechner developed Weber's method of "just noticeable differences" during the course of his work on vision and temperature sensations.[1] He used Weber's method of presenting two like stimuli and increasing or diminishing one of them until a difference became noticeable. Fechner, however, recommended approaching the just noticeable difference from both directions and averaging the just noticeable differences obtained from the ascending and the descending approach.[2]

The method of "right and wrong cases," although originated by Vierordt (1852), was developed and established as a tool Fechner used in his elaborate work with lifted weights, involving over 67,000 comparisons. In contrast to the method just described, in which the stimuli vary and a constant judgment is sought (the judgment of the just noticeable difference), the method of right and wrong cases depends on constant stimuli and varying judgments. The aim of the method, according to Fechner, was to measure the difference between stimuli which was required to produce a given proportion of right judgments. Fechner found it possible, by the use of an intricate mathematical formula, to simplify the procedure of measuring sensitivity by this method. Thus, instead of arriving at the desired difference after experimentation with a number of differences, one small difference was decided upon with which the series of judgments was to be made. This difference was large enough to be recognized most of the time, but not large enough to be recognized invariably. The right, wrong, and doubtful judgments were computed to give the measure of the perceptibility of this chosen difference. The formula,

[1] Fechner's insistence on the psychophysical value of the method of just noticeable differences is not justified by the results of experimentation since his time, although the *psychological* value of the method remains almost undisputed. See Titchener (1901–5, Vol. 2, Pt. 2, p. cxiii).

[2] He did not sufficiently appreciate the value of making a carefully graded approach from a difference greater or less than the just noticeable difference. This modification was made by G. E. Müller (1878), who did not however make large use of the method. Wundt worked out the method with this modification of small gradations and extended its use under the name of the method of "minimal changes." Wundt insisted that judgments of just noticeable difference were determined under the cumulative influence of previous judgments and that their significance was therefore psychological rather than psychophysical (1873–74, pp. 295, 326 ff.). Wundt emphasized also the method of "mean gradations," in which the subject adjusts a stimulus so that it seems midway between two others.

based upon the theory of probability, then made possible the computation of the difference required to give the percentage of right cases desired.[3]

In cooperation with Volkmann, Fechner developed the method of "average error" (already in use in astronomy) for use in visual and tactual measurement. The procedure is based upon the recognition that errors of observation and judgment depend not only on variable factors in the situation or within the observer himself, but, most significantly, upon the magnitude and variability of the difference between stimuli required to be noticeable. This method involves the adjustment of a variable stimulus to subjective equality with a given constant stimulus. Under controlled test conditions the mean value of the differences between the given stimulus and the "error" stimulus (adjusted by the observer) will represent the subject's error of observation. When applied to lifted weights, the method is simply as follows: the subject takes an accurately measured weight as the norm and attempts to make a second (or "error") weight equal to it. When he is satisfied of the equality of the two weights, he determines his error by weighing the second weight. The errors through many experiments are averaged to give the "average error."

Although Fechner's confidence in the psychophysical significance of his methods was not shared by his successors, and although his methods have suffered devastating criticism and provoked endless controversy,[4] his contribution, as the real creator of psychophysics, was of immense importance. It was largely through these investigations that Wundt was stimulated to conceive of an exact science which should study the relations of physical stimuli to mental events. Indeed, Fechner's long and careful research did much to give Wundt and his contemporaries the plan of an experimental psychology (Titchener, 1901–5, Vol. 2, Pt. 2, p. xx).

When at last his *Elements of Psychophysics* (1860) was published, Fechner was beginning to turn to other fields of investigation in a way that would tempt one to think that he pretended to finality. As a matter of fact, however, the work went on and on. Through his contact with Wundt and the latter's

---

[3] G. E. Müller (1878) objected that Fechner did not distinguish between the measure of precision of the observer and the true difference required for correct judgments; he also objected to Fechner's method of disposition of the doubtful judgments by dividing them between the right and wrong judgments. He worked out formulae for the right, wrong, and doubtful cases, and measured both precision and sensitivity.

[4] "Those who desire this dreadful literature," said William James, "can find it; it has a disciplinary value; but I will not even enumerate it in a footnote" (1890, Vol. 1, p. 549). The historian cannot escape so easily. The principal criticisms by Müller (1878) and Wundt (1873–74) are already cited, but the following are also important: Müller (1903); Fechner (1877 and 1882). Additional references are to be found in Titchener (1901–05, Vol. 2, Pt. 2, p. xlvii) and Fröbes (1923–29). See also Boring (1950, pp. 275–95) and Woodworth and Schlosberg (1965). But the vast complexities of modern psychophysics do not belong here. One noted experimental psychologist (S. S. Stevens at Harvard) has become a professor of psychophysics.

laboratory investigations and publications, Fechner was constantly occupying himself with the writing of new articles and with answering objections.

In this period he began to concern himself with a further statement of his philosophical position and as time went on gave it more adequate expression. This statement he called "the day view opposed to the night view" (1879). In it appears an insistence upon the meaning and the value of all the known universe, expressed with a lyrical beauty which moved William James several decades later to an outburst of enthusiastic welcome to a most kindred spirit (1909, Chap. 4). The universe, said Fechner, is an organism with articulate parts, living and rejoicing in living. Each of the stars and planets, each stone, each clod of earth, has its organization, and organization means life, and life means soul. Everything is imbued with a consciousness of itself and a response to the things about it. This view Fechner carried into the foundations of a system of philosophy which is as utterly and absolutely monistic as the materialism of the nineteenth century, but as pantheistic as Hinduism. It is a far cry from this to that parallelism which says that mental processes and brain processes go on without relation, like two trains moving on tracks side by side. Fechner was assumed to be a parallelist. But for him the world had become one; the experience which men have as persons is of the very substance of the universe, all of which is throbbing with life and experience. This life we may, if we choose, study quantitatively; we may study it in the physical laboratory or in measuring the intensity of sensations.

Both experimentally and logically, therefore, Fechner's purpose seemed fulfilled. But he was not content, and, pushing forward to new worlds to conquer, he laid the foundations of the science of experimental aesthetics (1876). Just as he had protested against the vague symbolism of the "philosophy of nature," so he protested against the aesthetics "from above" which undertook to lay down the principles of beauty from which the beauty of the individual object might be deduced. He began to measure books, cards, windows, and many such objects of daily use, to find what quantitative relations of line are judged to be beautiful. He carried this into the study of the masterpieces of pictorial art, undertaking to find those linear relations which the artist had unconsciously used. This aesthetics "from beneath" was to offer the same humble but endlessly careful approach to the problem of beauty which the psychophysics had offered toward the mind-body problem.

His hopes were destined to remain unfulfilled. Time has gratefully taken his methods and his data and gone on with them, to be sure, to a rich harvest. The problem, however, to which he sought the key was not so easily solved. The modern temper finds the union of the mystical and the scientific difficult to understand. Yet Fechner's mystical grasp upon the unity of life and of the world lives on, and in each generation finds a welcome from a few.

Müller and Physiology

In 1833 Johannes Müller became Professor of Physiology at Berlin. As an experimentalist, especially in the physiology of the senses, he ranks among the greatest of the nineteenth century; but his enduring influence is due even more to his success as a teacher and as a systematizer of knowledge. Before his time physiological experimentation was carried on by physicians and teachers of medicine, partly in connection with clinical practice and partly as an adjunct to anatomy; Müller's career marked the emancipation of physiology from the practical demands of medicine.

He was interested in a number of specific problems in sense physiology, most of all in optics. The best known of his investigations are those which dealt with the external muscles of the eye and with the problem of space perception. His researches were inspired in part by Kant's doctrine of the innate character of space perception. Kant had laid down the principle that space perception is given to us by virtue of an innate capacity; space was for Kant a mode of experience beyond which we can never hope to go. But Berkeley had prepared the way for an "empirical" theory by asserting that the third dimension, as we know it, is built up through experience — it is necessary only that the different elements of the retina and the skin should be stimulated simultaneously — and Herbart had gone further, maintaining that the world of space is organized through the integration of a large number of specific experiences. The debate over "nativism" and "empiricism" which was to occupy much attention throughout the century was already in full swing when Müller approached the problem. No compromise between the two views seemed possible; they were stated in such arbitrary terms that no genetic analysis of the facts could be made. Müller put the problem in such a way as to make use of the arguments of both schools, and in a form to some extent experimentally verifiable. His position was as follows: we are endowed with a general ability to perceive space as such, but not with the specific capacities to judge distances, size, and position. We learn by experience whether a given object is within reach or not. But we could never learn such specific relations were we not endowed with a general capacity to perceive in spatial terms. Müller borrowed from Berkeley and Herbart the idea that we build up a spatial order through experience. Important in this connection was his study of binocular vision and of the nerve pathways in the chiasma.[5] We shall see later that the problem of the empirical derivation of the spatial order (learning to judge distances, learning to recognize at what point we are stimulated, and so on) was carried further by Lotze.

---

[5] Wheatstone's discovery of the stereoscope in 1833 gave a technique for the further investigation (notably by Helmholtz) of this problem. Müller had made at least one phase of the problem amenable to experimental attack.

Another striking contribution was the experimental study of reflex action. This was inspired partly by the teaching of Descartes, and, more immediately, by Bell's study of the functions of the spinal roots. The theory demanded experimental verification to support anatomical analysis. It was Müller who supplied the necessary data, from experimentation with frogs. He showed that reflex activity comprises three steps: (1) impulse from sense organ to nerve center via the dorsal root, (2) connection in the cord, and (3) impulse going out via the ventral root to the muscle.

The most important theoretical contribution which he offered was the doctrine of "specific energies" (1833–40, Bk. 5). Bell had suggested that each sensory nerve conveys one kind of quality or experience; visual nerves carry only visual impressions, auditory only auditory impressions, and so on. Müller saw the importance of such a view; if this were true, the whole nervous system could be regarded as a company of specialists, each performing its own task, but unable to take over the functions of another. Might it not be true, moreover, that the various *qualities of experience* can come to us only through the specific qualities or energies of particular nerves? Some nerves, for example, are specialized to give us vision; just as the eye is specialized to receive light, so the optic nerve is specialized to provide visual qualities in consciousness. No other nerve could ever take over these functions; these qualities in experience come from physical qualities intrinsic in the nerve tissue.[6]

It occurred to Müller that there is perhaps another way of defining specialization in the nervous system. Not the nerves, but the terminals in the brain, may give specific qualities. Perhaps the nerves function simply as a system of connections between the sense organs and the appropriate brain tissues, and perhaps the different parts of the brain are themselves specialized to provide the various qualities. Do visual qualities result directly from the stimulation of the optic nerve or, on the contrary, do they arise from the excitement of a specialized visual area in the brain, the optic nerve serving merely to transmit the various stimuli impressed on the retina? He believed both alternatives defensible, the evidence being inconclusive in favor of either. He decided, however, in favor of the theory of specific energies in the nerves themselves. This view experimental work has now disproved, but it seemed not unreasonable in Müller's time.

His whole approach was of the greatest significance for the generation which followed. It implied that the qualities of experience are given us not by the sense organs alone but by the very constitution of specialized parts of the nervous system. The reason why we have visual experience is that we have brains containing specialized tissues which give rise to that specific kind of experience. This view led to a physiological psychology in which

---

[6] Thus the doctrine reasserted the principle that the qualities of experience are not the qualities of an external world.

mind and body were even more intimately related than in the systems of Hobbes, Hartley, and Cabanis. It helped to drive from the field the doctrines of Cartesian dualism and its congeners, which were indeed already dying of inanition. Whereas earlier physiological psychologists had contented themselves for the most part with showing a correspondence between brain *connections* and mental associations or *connections,* Müller's reasoning sought to find in the brain the physiological basis for difference in the elementary *modes of experience.* Whichever of Müller's alternatives be emphasized, our variety of experiences must be due to the functioning of a variety of tissues in the central nervous system. Not, of course, that such a conception put an end to all dualism in psychology. Müller's own views, as we have seen, tended to differentiate *mental* from *physical* events. But the dualisms which have taken account of Müller's principle have necessarily narrowed the scope of the mental to a central governing principle, the particular varieties of experience being stated more and more in terms of physiological events. In modern times there has been much clinical and experimental work to show that affective experience (or "appetitive" and "aversive" experience) both in animals and in men is directly related to specific and finely localizable brain regions.

Few physiologists clearly grasped the fact that the problem of specific energies was very similar to that of local specialization within the nervous system as it had been stated by Gall and the phrenologists. Müller had seriously entertained the possibility that the different parts of the brain might have their specific qualities. We have seen that phrenology, in defending a rather similar position, fell on evil days. Flourens's experiments on the brains of pigeons (1824), leading to the conclusion that the brain acts *as a whole,* and that no local specialization exists, were generally accepted, to the discredit of phrenology; yet without in any sense dislodging either of Müller's versions of the principle of specific energies. Flourens's work put an end for the time being to what little reputation the doctrine of cortical localization enjoyed. But it did not affect Müller's position at all. He had, in fact, given preference to the alternative of specialization in the peripheral as against the central elements. His theory of specific energies remained as orthodox as did Flourens's view that the brain functioned as a whole. In the latter part of the century clinical studies led to a revival of the concept of cerebral localization, while physiological research served to discredit the doctrine of specific energies in the form preferred by Müller. Nevertheless the plasticity of the theory gave it long life, while its attempt at definiteness in the quest for neural foundations for sensory experience made it useful as a hypothesis in experimental psychology. Helmholtz's color theory (1856–66) and Blix's studies of cutaneous nerves (1884) are two familiar examples. We shall return to the localization problem later.

While Johannes Müller was devoting himself to special problems of this kind, he was also concerned with the relation of physiology to other sciences. It is interesting to see on the one hand the eagerness of his research and on the other hand the perfectly clear allegiance which he felt to Kant and to the philosophy of nature. He tried to reach a philosophical understanding of physiology. One of the clearest illustrations of this was his long and detailed discussion of the difference between the "mental principle" and the "vital principle." It is evident, he said, that the vital principle which distinguishes living from nonliving processes must exist not only in certain parts of the body but in all the body. But the mental principle is not so widely diffused. He was inclined to accept the mental principle as distinct from the vital principle, and as residing in the nervous system and not in the other tissues. The brain was the chief seat of the mental principle. His concern with this question is important for the light it throws upon the nature of some of the problems with which physiologists were still occupying themselves a hundred years ago. Müller was drawn into the maelstrom of the controversy concerning the nature of living matter and the whole problem of vitalism, for the excitement engendered by the discovery of electrical phenomena in the living body had gained rather than lost in intensity in the opening decades of the century. The prevalent vitalism, and the bold romanticism of the philosophy of nature, left their mark upon him.

Perhaps more important than any of these things was his production of the first great textbook of physiology since Haller's time. Müller's *Elements of Physiology* (1833–40) quickly became the international standard. Since it brought together all the notable results of European research in the whole realm of physiology, it was quite naturally translated into many tongues and served as an international storehouse and authority. From a modern viewpoint the book treats both physiology and anatomy. In fact, it is interesting to see the list of tissues and organs whose gross anatomy and histology Müller knew without knowing anything about their physiology. The description, for example, of the structure of the sympathetic nervous system and the glands of internal secretion reads much like that available in contemporary handbooks; but on many pages Müller contents himself, after describing the structure, with the brief statement that the functions are unknown. In view of the breadth of outlook and the eclectic spirit in which the book was compiled, it is futile to search in it for a rigid didactic outlook. Indeed, the very fact that Müller had an impartial avidity for all sorts of physiological data did as much as any other factor to turn German physiology in the first half of the nineteenth century from its abject position under the philosophy of nature to its independent magnificence in the hands of Helmholtz. It was indeed this quality which led men like Helmholtz and Du Bois-Reymond to study with him; it was this that made his work the point from which discussion began and from which research followed, and marked him as the great master by whom all others were to be measured.

Beneke

In Müller's era lived a number of psychologists who sought to instigate a rebellion against the prevailing transcendentalism. A prominent figure among them was F. E. Beneke, the title of whose work, *A Textbook of Psychology as a Natural Science* (1832), indicated the adoption of that spirit which had guided the English associationists. His central problem was to define how it is that the chaos of the newborn child's experience becomes organized into a coherent unity. There had been two traditional answers to this question. The associationists had maintained that all experience comes through the senses, and that elementary experiences are associated to make the more complex forms of experience. The "nativists," on the other hand, of whom Kant was the most illustrious spokesman, had emphasized the fundamental innate ways of knowing and thinking which are ours simply by virtue of being human. Beneke rejected both interpretations. A child begins life with a capacity for a great number of single activities, but not with the complex capacities of the adult; he manifests neither perception nor judgment, neither reason nor will. He is equipped only with very *elementary* capacities of mind and body. For example, he is not born with the ability to perceive space; he is born with many part functions ("fundamental processes") which are integrated in the total process through which space perception is achieved. The same method of approach characterizes Beneke's treatment of such traditional faculties as memory, reason, and will. Beneke may be reckoned a contributor to the dissection and hence to the disappearance of the "faculties" which still throve in German psychology.

Perhaps the chief *specific* contribution of Beneke was the doctrine of "traces." His view closely resembled that of Herbart, who had taught that the ideas lying outside the field of consciousness have a *tendency* to reappear in consciousness. Similarly Beneke postulated traces by which each idea is linked to another. He refused to state this in physiological terms and insisted on the right of psychology to treat of its laws without recourse to the data of another science. He made use of these traces to explain how an experience may be brought back into consciousness; that is, remembered. The disappearance of an idea from consciousness simply leaves a trace which serves as basis for the later revival of the idea. For Beneke it was all-important that memory as a faculty should be dethroned; the traces were for him a simple and empirical explanation of all memory phenomena. The value of his analysis is of less interest to us than his influence in undermining the complacency of the transcendentalists.

But Beneke's task was not an easy one. So solidly entrenched was the habit of recourse to the transcendental that Beneke's book on the "foundation of a physics of morality" caused the loss of his right to teach at the University of Berlin. The Prussian Minister of Instruction explained "that it was not single passages which had given offense, but the whole scheme, and that a philosophy which did not deduce everything from the Absolute could not be considered to be philosophy at all" (Merz, 1896–1914, Vol. 3, p. 208 n).

REFERENCES

Beneke, F. E. *Lehrbuch der Psychologie als Naturwissenschaft* [*A Textbook of Psychology as a Natural Science*]. Berlin: Mittler, 1832.

Blix, M. "Experimentelle Beiträge zur Lösung der Frage über die specifische Energie der Hautnerven." *Zeitschrift für Biologie*, 20 (1884), 141.

Boring, E. G. *A History of Experimental Psychology*. 2nd ed. New York: Appleton-Century-Crofts, 1950.

Brett, G. S. *A History of Psychology*. Rev. ed. R. S. Peters, ed. Cambridge, Mass.: M.I.T. Press, 1965.

Brown, T. *Lectures on the Philosophy of the Human Mind*. Edinburgh: Tait, Longman, 1820.

Delezenne, C. E. J. "Sur les valeurs numériques des notes de la gamme." *Recueil des Travaux de la Société des Sciences, de l'Agriculture et des Arts de Lille*, 1827.

Fechner, G. T. *Zend-Avesta*. Leipzig: Voss, 1851.

————. *Elemente der Psychophysik* [*Elements of Psychophysics*]. Leipzig: Breitkopf and Härtel, 1860.

————. *Das Büchlein vom Leben nach dem Tode*. Hamburg: Voss, 1866.

————. *Vorschule der Aesthetik*. Leipzig: Breitkopf and Härtel, 1876.

————. *In Sachen der Psychophysik*. Leipzig: Breitkopf and Härtel, 1877.

————. *Die Tagesansicht Gegenüber der Nachtansicht*. Leipzig: Breitkopf and Härtel, 1879.

————. *Revision der Hauptpunkte der Psychophysik*. Leipzig: Breitkopf and Härtel, 1882.

Flourens, P. J. M. *Recherches expérimentales sur les propriétés et les fonctions du systeme neurveux dans les animaux vertébrés*. Paris: Crevot, 1824.

Fröbes, J. *Lehrbuch der Experimentellen Psychologie*. Freiburg: Herder, 1923–29.

Helmholtz, H. L. F. von. *Handbuch der Physiologischen Optik* [*Treatise on Physiological Optics*]. Leipzig: Voss, 1856–66.

James, W. *Principles of Psychology*. 2 vols. New York: Holt, 1890. New York: Dover, 1950.

————. *A Pluralistic Universe*. New York: Longmans, Green, 1909.

Merz, J. T. *History of European Thought in the Nineteenth Century*. 4 vols. Edinburgh: Blackwood, 1896–1914. New York: Dover, 1965.

Müller, F. M., ed. *The Sacred Books of the East*. Oxford: Clarendon Press, 1879.

Müller, G. E. *Zur Grundlegung der Psychophysik*. Berlin: Grüben, 1878.

————. "Die Gesichtspunkte und die Tatsachen der Psychophysischen Methodik." In L. Asher and K. Spiro, eds. *Ergebnisse der Physiologie*. Strasbourg: Bergmann, 1903.

Müller, J. *Handbuch der Physiologie des Menschen* [*Elements of Physiology*]. 3 vols. Coblenz: Hölscher, 1833–40.

Titchener, E. B. *Experimental Psychology*. 4 vols. New York: Macmillan, 1901–5.

Vierordt, K. "Neue Methode der Quantitativen Mikroskopischen Analyse des Blutes." *Archiv für Physiologie Heilkunde*, 11 (1852), 26–46.

Weber, E. H. *De pulsu, resorptione, auditu et tactu*. Leipzig: Koehler, 1834.

———. "Der Tastsinn und das Gemeingefühl." In R. Wagner, ed. *Handwörterbuch der Physiologie*. 4 vols. Braunschweig: Vieweg, 1842–53.

Woodworth, R. S. *Experimental Psychology*. New York: Holt, 1938.

Woodworth, R. S., and Schlosberg, H. *Experimental Psychology*. Rev. ed. New York: Holt, Rinehart and Winston, 1965.

Wundt, W. M. *Grundzüge der Physiologischen Psychologie*. Leipzig: Engelmann, 1873–74.

NOTE: A list of further readings appears at the back of the book.

7

British Psychology in the Mid-Nineteenth Century

The sceptre of psychology has returned to this island.
JOHN STUART MILL (on reading Bain)

Associationism and the Scottish school had quarreled through the latter half of the eighteenth century without learning much from one another. The first half of the nineteenth century, however, found them borrowing so freely from one another that it becomes more and more difficult to be sure where the one stops and the other begins. This means, of course, the decline of the Scottish school and of associationism as self-contained systems.

We shall find some interesting parallels between Britain and Germany in this period. Germany had been dominated during the interval from the time of Kant and Hegel until the middle of the nineteenth century by two philosophical approaches. One was transcendentalism, its characteristic appeal being to reality beyond experience, and the other the philosophy of nature, its keynote being an attempt to interpret nature symbolically and spiritually. Here and there a man made his protest; but in psychology proper (apart, of course, from physiology) only two figures of note, Herbart and Beneke, had seriously shaken these systems. And physiology, too, as represented by Weber and Johannes Müller, was considerably influenced by the philosophy of nature and the accompanying vitalism. It did succeed in making headway on empirical lines, because physiology was an independent discipline with an objective research problem; another half-century was to pass before psychology was to have its independent position as an experimental science. Psychology as the German intellectual of 1830 knew it was a mixture of transcendentalism and the philosophy of nature. It was this psychology against which Beneke had, not very successfully, rebelled.

This same attempt to supplant the current philosophy of mind was going on in Scotland. Religious and ethical dogmatism was beginning to yield to associationism. The tendency, inaugurated by Brown, to borrow from the associationists was destined within a generation to bring an end to the independent existence of the Scottish school. Some steps in the process are suggested by the work of Sir William Hamilton.

Hamilton's Integration of Scottish and English Psychology

Sir William Hamilton (1859–60) began as a young man to be drawn toward contemporary German philosophy. He studied in Germany to acquaint himself in detail with the transcendentalist movement. This transcendentalist approach he succeeded in unifying with the spiritual and ethical tradition which had been a part of his heritage as one educated in the Scottish universities. In 1836 he became the most influential teacher of psychology in Scotland. His work was distinguished equally by his mastery of the history of philosophy and by his ability to grapple with the psychological problems of his contemporaries, especially those raised by the associationists. His lectures dealt with crucial problems which the Scottish school had in general neglected. Through his fusion of German and Scottish thought, and the critical spirit he imparted to the latter, he became an organic part of the idealistic tradition of the nineteenth century.

Accepting the faculty psychology in the form advanced by Kant, Hamilton held the first principle to be the unity and activity of the mind. He refused to admit the usefulness of either the analytic or the physiological assumptions of the associationists. For him the main problem was not to explain how integrated experience is formed from past impressions, but how the underlying unitary substance manifests itself in a variety of different situations. This position gradually fused with the tradition then taking shape, which we may characterize by the general title of "British idealism," later represented by T. H. Green and Bradley. The Scottish school came to an end with Hamilton, not because his ideas died, but because they became assimilated with another movement, the idealistic movement, which was interested in the conservation of the same spiritual values which we have seen in the Scottish school.

His greatest psychological contribution lay in a theory as to the nature of memory and association, a theory which showed in clear form the difference between Scottish and English traditions as they then existed. This conception, known as "redintegration," was to the effect that each impression tends to bring back into consciousness the whole situation of which it has at one time been a part. It will be recalled that orthodox associationists, from Hartley on, had maintained that when A, B, C, D are actual sensations following in a given order, the sensation A will, when later presented alone, be followed by the memory images B, C, and D. This meant that the only part of the field of consciousness with which the psychologists were concerned was that which lay in the center of attention.

Psychology, in its whole history from the Greeks onward, had ignored Aristotle's distinction between *having* an experience and *observing* an experience — a distinction closely related to the distinction between *fringe* and *center* of consciousness. British and French psychologists were inclined to regard the stream of experience as simply the stream of items attended to. German psychologists, however, from Leibnitz onward, stressed the role of apperception (see p. 24), with its reinterpretation of center and fringe of consciousness; and Herbart's system had been founded upon the reality of degrees of intensity of elements which are simultaneously active. From the vantage point of his study of the German tradition, Hamilton was able to formulate precisely a continuing weakness in associationism. It presupposed the existence of individual *parts* of the mind, each of which sets going another part of the mind without any unifying principle to make the parts hold together. (Brown had realized this difficulty when he objected to the term "association" because it implied that mere sequence could give organic unity.) Going further, Hamilton showed that in their statement of the sequence of mental events, the associationists had written as if the remembering mind contained (or rather, were) one *single* idea at a time. Hamilton taught that the process of perception is such that *any one* of the elements simultaneously experienced is capable, when presented later, of bringing back the *total* experience. If a person hears another pronounce a series of numbers he may, indeed, recall them in order; but he actually recalls many other details besides. Hours later, a whole constellation of memories comes back at once, as soon as the experiment with the numbers is mentioned. The subject redintegrates in memory the original situation; he recalls not a series but a pattern. Hamilton, like Leibnitz and Herbart before him, was trying to call psychologists away from their oversimplified schematizations. He saw that any given mental event is only part of a much larger whole.

Hamilton overworked his hypothesis, omitting, as Brett (1965) remarks, to explain the process of *forgetting*. Memory items not only often fail to bring back their whole context, but even fail to bring back anything recognizable. Associationism could not, of course, be dislodged with a single blow; and Hamilton had clearly gone too far in neglecting both the facts of serial association and the frequent ineffectiveness or absence of the redintegrating principle. Neither Hartley's nor Hamilton's position stated the whole truth. But we still know very little about either forgetting or remembering, and such insight as we have is in part traceable to Hamilton's doctrine that association operates not through a chain of elements, but, so to speak, through a system of interconnected aspects. Bain, James, and many others have insisted on the importance of Hamilton's contribution. Even aside from his theory of memory, his emphasis upon the whole of experience, rather than upon the center of attention alone, was a means of bringing into British thought one of the most vital contributions of German psychology. The Scottish school, as such, ceases to occupy us from this moment. After Hamilton's death the school survived only in admixture with idealism, associationism, or both.

James Mill, John Stuart Mill

James Mill (1829), though a true Scot, and brought up under Scottish influences, identified himself with the English school and attained the most complete and most rigorous expression of associationism.

His unity of thought, and the severity and rigor of his ethics and his logic, mark him as a very unusual personality (J. S. Mill, 1873). He studied theology, but he quickly found himself out of sympathy with the doctrines of the Church and became an agnostic.[1] Earning his livelihood as an editor and a writer concerned primarily with the economic and political problems of his time, he is better known as an economist and a historian than as a psychologist. His *History of British India* (1817) gave him a nation-wide reputation. His system of political economy was closely allied to that of Bentham, with whom he enjoyed the closest friendship. He borrowed Bentham's pleasure-pain philosophy, the doctrine that human actions are motivated solely through self-interest. He borrowed also his ethical conceptions, the view that the wise organization of society is that which brings about the "greatest good of the greatest number." In seeking to outline a comprehensive political economy, he thus included a treatment of ethical and psychological questions. In general, Mill and the utilitarians favored the principle of free exchange without government interference; they believed that individual self-interest would bring about social welfare if economic (that is, from Mill's viewpoint, psychological) laws were left to themselves.

Psychology and economics were indeed growing close together. Adam Smith, one of the great founders of economic theory, as represented in his monumental *Wealth of Nations* (1776), also made the human struggles for a generous and ethical social system intelligible with his *Theory of the Moral Sentiments* (1759). It was Edmund Burke, remembered in American history as one who sided with the colonists in the American Revolution, whose essay *The Sublime and the Beautiful* (1757) contained some of the clearest and most systematic expressions of Hartley's association principles as applied to the more complex attitudes and ideals of men and society. In the tradition of Locke, Hume, and Hartley he attempted to show that our more complex appreciation of things noble and sublime rests upon very simple

---

[1] He arrived at a complete agnosticism of a kind which was rare even among "freethinkers" —neither affirming nor denying the existence of Deity and convinced that "concerning the origin of things nothing whatever can be known."

foundations—in the growth of simple joys and sufferings as elaborated by words and built into us in the responses of persons and groups dominated by a common culture. If we think of James Mill more as an economist than a psychologist, it is helpful to remember that in this era of the Industrial Revolution and the American and French revolutions emerged the conception of "social science"—concerned with individual psychology on one hand and with the larger problems of a changing social order on the other. Mill's psychology was definitely influenced by these new currents, which helped him shape a coherent interpretation of all the significant intellectual events in his life.[2]

The agnosticism which had taken hold of him made him go further in his tendency to mechanistic theory than his discipleship to Hartley required. He reduced mental life to elementary sensory particles, conceding nothing to the claims of the soul. Perception was a process by which a number of bits are put together to make a single whole. At the same time, the process of association was regarded as passive. Sensations were presented in a certain order, and later, when one of these was presented, the others followed mechanically. Association depended wholly upon contiguity. There was no association by similarity or contrast. The reason why one tree makes us think of another similar tree is simply the fact that "we are accustomed to see like things together." His explanation of association by contrast was equally simple. "Dwarf" does not make us think of "giant" by virtue of contrast, but simply because both depart from, and are necessarily associated with, a common standard.

Another aspect of Mill's psychology, one destined to be of importance because of its influence on Bain, was his concern with the task of reducing complex emotional states to simple sensory terms. Following the suggestions of Hartley, he undertook a genetic and analytic study of such complex phenomena as conscience, religious attitudes, and the like. In him associationism and hedonism were thoroughly fused, and every experience was conceived to be reducible to sensory components under the guidance of the pleasure-pain principle.

Associationism thus came to maturity. The uncompromising rigidity and consistency of Mill's system gave much to Bain and Spencer, and much of it still lives in modern psychology. But its consistency showed where its weaknesses lay, and in the generation which followed the inevitable reaction set in. Mill, its most thoroughgoing advocate, was willing to face the most complicated aspects of life in terms of sensation and association. The pendulum swung strongly thereafter in the direction of emphasis upon activity

[2] The widespread suffering of the factory workers in the newly established industrial order served to make the ethical aspects of political economy particularly acute. Partly because of the migration of agricultural laborers into the cities, there was a disturbance in the food supply. An increase in the population augmented the difficulty. Practical political problems such as the repeal of the Corn Laws were considerably influenced by the agitation of the utilitarians.

and unity; and the evolutionary theory emphasized both of these principles. Though mechanism and associationism continued to make their voices heard, they were relatively submerged until the turn of the century. Then, experimental biology contributed to the renaissance of emphasis upon analytical method, and to a philosophy not far from the traditional atomism of Democritus (see pp. 9–10).

John Stuart Mill, born in 1806, and brought up by his father, James, was an example of association psychology put to work. He was given unstinted time, attention, pressure, inspiration, and unremitting schooling by a father who was motivated to give his son the benefits of all that was available; believing firmly in the rational, orderly, disciplined associationist approach, Mill taught his little son the basics that needed to be learned, and as early as possible. In view of the nobility and clarity of the Greek language, he was certain that John Stuart's mind must first be shaped by thorough schooling in Greek; his father provided him with an individual lexicon of Greek-English and English-Greek terms, which he mastered so early in life that he could not remember a time when he did not read Greek. Latin came later; then a very long and systematic training in literature and history, with critical analysis and evaluation of all he read. Order, clarity, and grace in the English language, as well as in the classics, were paramount. By the age of thirteen he was ready for long walks with his father, during which they discussed political economy.

This drilling of the mind had some effects which James Mill did not foresee. When John Stuart was in his late teens he became suddenly aware that all he valued, appreciated, and enjoyed were based on the associations his father had instilled in him. If the things that seemed right had been presented in another light by his father, would he not have believed the opposite of all he had accepted? It was poetry, which reminded him of the beauty and power of nature, that restored to him some of the more primitive ways of making real contact with real things. The association principle did work well: the three areas in which John Stuart Mill made a signal contribution were psychology, logic, and economics. In all three areas he was coached, guided, and inspired by his father. It was in the combination of these that he made his greatest mark: in his essays on the rights of oppressed peoples, the establishment of genuine equality for women, and the systematic justification of the doctrine of utilitarianism. Utilitarianism for him was not at all the crass justification of petty and momentary pleasures which many claimed it was; utilitarianism was the systematic cultivation of the doctrine that all men are entitled to welfare and that society can be so ordered that the welfare of all, with due checks and balances, can be maintained.

In considering his work as a psychologist only, the most obvious and important factor is his reaction against extreme analytical associationism in favor of a new conception of synthesis. This new conception arose directly from the advances in a new science, the science of chemistry, which had played little part as a model for the thinking of psychologists until this period. It was during the French Revolution and the era of Napoleon that the process of oxidation and the biological process of respiration began to be understood. At the beginning of the nineteenth century Dalton established an atomic base for chemistry, and quantitative research in chemical laboratories laid a foundation for the understanding of chemical compounds. So rapid was the gain that, as noted, a bridge from inorganic to organic chemistry was already being laid in Germany as early as the 1820s. In this climate a thoughtful, scientifically oriented psychologist could draw his analogies just as well from chemistry as his predecessor had drawn them from physics. John Stuart Mill noted the fact that chemical compounds often represent qualitatively new attributes which neither of the components, entering into the compound, possessed. There is nothing about hydrogen or oxygen to suggest what water will be like when they are properly combined. Mental chemistry was the name given by John Stuart Mill to the principle that psychological compounds are constantly being formed from simpler psychological elements. Earlier, Hartley had noted a similar principle when he said that the taste of a medicine was not simply the taste of the separate ingredients; but John Stuart Mill offered a more systematic formulation. This type of qualitatively new construction, as in chemistry, is a guiding principle for psychological integrations to qualitatively new compounds. Whereas physics was a good model for James Mill, chemistry was a better one for John Stuart Mill.

Bain

A man of greater significance for psychology than either of the Mills was Alexander Bain. He devoted much energy to grammar, rhetoric, and education; he spent much of his long life in administrative activities of one type or another; and his chief university position was a chair not of psychology but of logic. In spite of this scattering of his energies he mastered the Scottish and English, as well as much of the German, psychology and brought together a vast quantity of material, ably organized and with great originality of treatment. His two greatest works are *The Senses and the Intellect* (1855) and *The Emotions and the Will* (1859).

Bain's approach was through physiology, particularly the work of the German physiologists; he incorporated in his writings a great quantity of research material. We find, for instance, Weber's experiments on the two-point threshold and on the temperature sense. Although the titles of his two celebrated works suggest the continuation of the old subdivisions of *knowing, feeling,* and *willing,* these titles are but cloaks for associationism. It was, however, an associationism based upon physiological findings far more detailed than had been available for any previous scholar. In Bain we have physiological explanations sufficiently elaborate to be taken seriously. The

psychologist was beginning to think of experimental physiology as fundamental to his science. The sense organs, the sensory and motor nerves, the
brain, and the muscles were considered in detail. The reflex arc and the instincts were regarded as elements of behavior, and human acts were presented as wholes the parts of which had been studied by the laboratory
method.

His view of psychology was relatively comprehensive. Its most serious
gap lay in the neglect of material (then being collected by neurologists) which
showed the relations of abnormal mental processes to abnormal brain processes. But he furnished a rich and vivid picture of an immense variety of
mental states and processes, many of which lay within the field now defined
as social psychology. He concerned himself, as James Mill had done, with
the origin of those complex attitudes and sentiments which we call aesthetic,
moral, and religious; these he related to his physiological principles. We may
not unfairly illustrate the kind of associationism to which this method leads
by citing an extreme case, his explanation of the behavior of a mother fon-
dling her child (1859, pp. 126–40). It is clear, said Bain, that things which
are warm are pleasant; so also are things which are soft; hence maternal joy.
(William James suggested that lonely parents might be supplied with pillows
heated to the necessary temperature [1890, Vol. 2, p. 552].) This was of
course a logical end result of the whole approach from Hartley onward.
Bain was concerned simply with carrying out to its logical implications the
doctrine of association wherever it could work.

Bain was not one to deny inborn or original nature. He was, in fact, much
more concerned with "instinct," innate dispositions to action, than any previous associationist and was much interested in the mechanics of its function. Unfortunately, however, his chief contributions were written shortly
before the publication of Darwin's *The Origin of Species* (1859), and although he lived to see the spread of Darwinism, he never remodeled his
psychological conceptions upon Darwinian lines. Nevertheless he was,
throughout, thinking in terms of *inborn reaction tendencies,* tendencies
which came to be given a role of great importance by the Darwinians.

But the best known of Bain's specific contributions is his treatment of
learning and habit. Elaborating some suggestions of Spencer, he stated learning in terms of (1) random movements, (2) retention of acts which bring pleasant results, elimination of those which bring unpleasant results, (3) fixation
through repetition. His maxims on habit were quoted and elaborated by
James; along with some of Carpenter's observations they receive a very important place in William James's chapter on "Habit" (1890). This is but one
example of the position of authority which Bain enjoyed throughout the second half of the century, and the way in which his writings have been incorporated into the writings of others.

No one else had ever attempted, as he did, to cover the entire range of
normal human experience in a system of psychology. Among all association-

ists there were efforts to get universal principles, and with Brown an important list of secondary principles had been included; but no one before Bain had tried to analyze such a wealth of *particular* situations. Everything psychological, from the experience of a man jumping a ditch to the mental operations of a creative artist, was the perfectly legitimate concern of the psychologist. No other man had been so prolific in descriptions of human experiences, so serious in trying to give a colorful and exhaustive picture of mental life. It was as if previous authors had said, "Take these key principles and you may enter any room within the house of psychology." Bain said, "Here is the key to the study, with bookshelves that reach to the ceiling; here is the key to the conference room, with a long table surrounded by a dozen chairs." He was interested in providing not merely an entry into every mode of experience, but an analysis of its contents. This is the chief reason why he is so readable. Never had a psychologist been so widely read in his own day. He exerted as great a personal influence in psychology as did John Stuart Mill in political economy. Associationism became through him almost "popular." But in his interest in the living unity of the person, he reflected the spirit of the Scottish school. And he did not irritate his readers, as most of the associationists had done, by the apparent crassness of a mechanistic system. He made use of physiological principles for their practical usefulness, not for philosophical purposes. He was genuinely and consistently a psychologist; he might fairly be described as the first to write a comprehensive treatise having psychology as its sole purpose.

This work of Bain in the field of physiological psychology, if we may call it such, summed up and crowned the achievements of physiological as well as of introspective work up to the middle of the nineteenth century. Another great contribution of Bain was the founding in 1876 of a journal for the publication of psychological articles. Psychological writings before this time had for the most part appeared as independent books or pamphlets, or as contributions to general philosophical or physiological journals. The journal *Mind,* although of a philosophical cast, was from the first concerned chiefly with psychological material.

In the same era Carpenter's *Principles of Mental Physiology* (1874), and the writings of Maudsley (1867, 1884), served further to persuade the British reader that physiological conceptions were the groundwork of psychology. This idea was also becoming popular in France, especially through the writings of Ribot (1881, 1885).

But associationism — diluted, updated, and reorganized as it already was — had to undergo a further radical transformation. Immediately after this huge and successful synthesis by Bain, Darwin's *Origin of Species* was published. To British psychologists like John Stuart Mill 1859 was a turning point; and he thought it was too late for a man reared earlier in the century to make a complete change in outlook. Henry Adams compared the experience of living through Darwinism to the experience of a man undergoing seasickness for the first time. The evolutionary theory substituted for associationism two definite working concepts which radically changed the whole background of psychology: (1) the concept of *heredity* was important both for the under- standing of uniformities of mental structure and for the interpretation of per- manent and stable differences from one individual to another; and (2) the idea of the *adaptation* of the individual to his environment became basic for every psychological problem.

The biological outlook, emphasizing such concepts as the *functions* of an *organism,* had indeed been apparent in some quarters. But after Darwin the term "biological" became a symbol for a new way of thinking, in which every organ and function was understood in terms of its history and its relation to the life of the creature which displayed it. Such an approach could not have been made before Darwinian evolutionism and could not be avoided after it. These fundamental changes made associationism, as it flourished from Hartley to Bain, untenable. At the same time, the growing strength of the idealist philosophy (led by such men as T. H. Green), with its emphasis on the unity and activity of mind, was pressing associationism hard from an- other side. Associationism, in its weakened and beleaguered state, was at- tacked with equal vigor by those who thought it too biological and by those who thought it was not biological enough. Not that the central doctrines of the associationists have disappeared; and not that the wealth of their specific contributions has been forgotten. On the contrary, the attention given to memory and learning in all modern psychology has inevitably involved many associationist contributions. For example, students of the conditioned reflex and of modern American learning theory of a "behavioristic" cast have freely drawn upon associationist doctrines, while substituting for them a descrip- tion in terms of overt responses rather than of "ideas." Regardless of how much associationism is currently maintained in these more subtle ways, the classical doctrine, with its *explanation of all psychological events through the juxtaposition of sensory impressions,* may definitely be said to have died with Bain. All post-Darwinian psychologies have had to deal in one way or another with the unity of the living system, with the profound internal mo- tivating forces which appear in behavior, and with the basic problem of adap- tation to the environment.

Spencer

Herbert Spencer (1855) is sometimes regarded as sharing with Bain in the last defense of associationism; it is more nearly true to say that he was the first of the evolutionists. He does, indeed, seem much less important as a psychologist today than does Bain. But he had the advantage over Bain that he was an evolutionist before Darwin; as early as 1850 he had begun to write on evolution. His system attracted wide notice, so that when *The Origin of Species* was published, his own more speculative evolutionism drew strength from it. His evolutionary system has exerted more influence upon psychology than have the associationist principles which his own psychology embodies.

Spencer undertook to create a "synthetic philosophy," in which everything in the universe should be related to everything else, expressive of one developing totality. Development, whether of stars, of plants, of men, or of political institutions, involves *differentiation* followed by *integration*. In its earliest phase any growing thing is simple, uniform, homogeneous; in time there is differentiation, the emergence of recognizable and distinct parts; last of all comes integration, the articulation of the parts in a new functioning whole. Evolution is "change from incoherent indefinite homogeneity to coherent, definite heterogeneity," with constant adjustment of inner to outer relations. In the solar system, or in the embryo, or in the growth of nations, there is always a differentiation phase, then an integration phase. For psychology this meant that the increasing complexity of the nervous system was paralleled by an increasing richness and variety in the forms of experience and in the types of association. Together with increase in complexity of structure come higher and higher integrations of function. Association was regarded as an integrating mechanism by which a more and more complex type of experience becomes possible. Spencer's evolutionism was in the grand style. The all-encompassing philosophical spirit of Hegel's dialectical approach was supported by an essentially empirical anchorage in the physical and biological sciences of the mid-nineteenth century; and with the "down-to-earth" progressive emphasis on more and better achievement, more and better life for the individual and the group. This was characteristic of the new evolutionary thinking, as contrasted with the Absolute and the ultimately inscrutable cosmic foundations offered by Hegel.

Spencer was the first to elaborate the conception that the mind is what it is because it has had to cope with particular kinds of environment.[3] He laid great emphasis on the adaptive nature of nervous and mental processes, and on the notion that increasing complexity of experiences and of behavior is a part of the process of adaptation. This doctrine, though part of a speculative system, was singularly similar, as we shall see, to the conclusions which followed upon all the inductive work of Darwin. A more adequate and detailed application of evolutionary principles had to wait upon the accumulation of data by Darwin and his followers. Whereas Spencer's psychology never attained the vogue enjoyed by Bain's, his evolutionary teaching contributed to the widespread adoption by psychologists of biological conceptions, especially those relating to the principle of the adaptation of an organism to its environment.

One specific psychological doctrine of Spencer attracted attention and is still well known—his theory of the relation between mind and body. We may

[3] Though suggestions in this direction had been given by several: for example, Lucretius among the ancients, Schopenhauer among the moderns.

regard the mind, said Spencer, as a series of events, and the physical processes in the brain as a series of parallel events; but both of these arise from a deeper underlying reality. This is, of course, reminiscent of Spinoza's monism (see pp. 21, 23). The basic reality he regarded as unknowable. He was, for practical purposes, a parallelist, like those we have already had to consider. But, unlike Leibnitz, Spencer believed that mental and physical events were intimately and organically connected; not that either was the cause of the other, but that both sprang from the same soil.

REFERENCES

Bain, A. *The Senses and the Intellect*. London: Parker, 1855.

———. *The Emotions and the Will*. London: Parker, 1859.

Brett, G. S. *A History of Psychology*. Rev. ed. R. S. Peters, ed. Cambridge, Mass.: M.I.T. Press, 1965.

Burke, E. *A Philosophical Enquiry into the Origin of Our Ideas on the Sublime and the Beautiful*. London: Dodsley, 1757.

Carpenter, W. B. *Principles of Mental Physiology*. London: King, 1874.

Darwin, C. *The Origin of Species*. London: Murray, 1859.

Hamilton, W. *Lectures on Metaphysics*. London: Blackwood, 1859–60.

James, W. *Principles of Psychology*. 2 vols. New York: Holt, 1890. New York: Dover, 1950.

Maudsley, H. *Physiology and Pathology of Mind*. London: Macmillan, 1867.

———. *Body and Will*. New York: Appleton, 1884.

Mill, J. *History of British India*. London: Baldwin, Cradock and Jay, 1817.

———. *Analysis of the Phenomena of the Human Mind*. London: Longmans and Dyer, 1829.

Mill, J. S. *Autobiography*. London: Longmans, 1873.

Ribot, T.-A. *Les Maladies de la mémoire* [*Diseases of Memory*]. Paris: Alcan, 1881.

———. *Les Maladies de la personnalité* [*Diseases of Personality*]. Paris: Germer-Ballière, 1885.

Smith, A. *The Theory of the Moral Sentiments*. London: Millar, 1759.

———. *An Inquiry into the Nature and Causes of the Wealth of Nations*. 2 vols. London: Strahan and Cadell, 1776.

Spencer, H. *The Principles of Psychology*. 8 vols. London: Williams and Norgate, 1855.

NOTE: A list of further readings appears at the back of the book.

8

Physiological Psychology in the Second Half of the Nineteenth Century

It was the times that set the problems, but it was Helmholtz's genius that saw the problems and advanced their solution.

E. G. BORING

We return now to consider the progress of physiological psychology in Germany, which, in the hands of Weber, Fechner, and Johannes Müller had made such a magnificent beginning.

Helmholtz

Hermann von Helmholtz was the son of a Prussian army officer and was educated with a view to becoming an army surgeon. But the practice of medicine did not interest him, and he began to devote himself to physics and physiology for their own sake. Exposure to the "philosophy of nature" on the one hand, and to the exact scientific methods of his teacher Johannes Müller on the other hand, led to a rebellion against the former and an eager acceptance of the inductive and mathematical approach. Among Helmholtz's many experimental and theoretical contributions, which dealt with physics, physiology, and psychology, three are of chief interest to us: his investigations of reaction time, of audition, and of vision.

The reaction-time problem was old when he undertook it, though new as a field for physiological experiment. In the Royal Observatory at Greenwich, an assistant had lost his position because he and his chief consistently differed in recording the time of the passage of stars across the meridian. In 1822 a German astronomer, Bessel, noticed that such discrepancies held for all observers. Bessel and other astronomers found this individual variation in recording the times of transit an important source of error, and it became known as the *personal equation*. In the twenties and thirties a number of physiologists devised simple methods by which to measure such differences. The easiest explanation of the facts seemed to be that one individual reacted more quickly than another because his nerves conducted more quickly.

Not very much more than this was done until Helmholtz took hold of the problem. His first outstanding research (in the late forties) was upon the speed of conduction of nerve impulses. Little was known in this area; Müller, in fact, had thought that the speed of nerve conduction was comparable to the speed of light. Helmholtz found a method by which he could determine the speed of conduction in the motor nerves of the frog. In some experiments he stimulated a point on the nerve near the muscle, and in others a point farther away from the muscle. The difference between the time intervals from stimulus to muscular contraction in the two experimental series was the conduction time from the first point to the second. This method gave him fairly consistent results, indicating a speed of about 30 meters per second. Science was moving ever more rapidly from authoritative opinion to the ingenious discovery of precise techniques of control and measurement.

Carrying the problem further, he undertook with human subjects the study of the complete circuit from the stimulation of a sense organ to the motor response. By varying the point of stimulation he sought to ascertain variations in reaction time which would throw light on the speed of conduction in sensory nerves. These were the earliest "reaction-time" experiments as such. The results he obtained were so very inconsistent — showing enormous differences not only from one individual to another, but from one trial to the next in a given subject — that he abandoned the investigation altogether. What he was trying to do was to get a reliable measure of the speed of conduction in nerves. The individual differences which would have interested Galton so much were for him merely uncontrollable variables. Within the thirty years following Helmholtz's experiments more than a dozen investigators tried to confirm his work, reaching results most widely discrepant from one another and from Helmholtz's figures.

It was not Helmholtz, but Donders (1868), a Dutch physiologist, who grasped the psychological significance of the problem. He undertook in the decade of the sixties, in cooperation with De Jaager, a series of investigations which aimed at the discovery of the various factors intervening between stimulus and response. He realized the importance of some of those psychological factors which for Helmholtz had been a nuisance and a despair. The method of applying the stimulus and the nature of the task required of the subject were of capital importance. Donders used three methods. In the first, the subject made a specific movement as quickly as possible upon the presentation of a stimulus. This was called the *a* method. Next, he was shown two stimuli and instructed to react in one way if the first was presented and in another way if the other was presented. This was the *b* method. Then the individual was again shown two stimuli; he was to react if he saw one and *not to react* if he saw the other. This was the *c* method. The time in the *c* method (for example, reacting to red light, but withholding reaction to green light) was longer than that in the *a* method (simple reaction); Donders explained this on the hypothesis that the *c* method involved not only reaction but discrimination between red and green. He thought he could measure the discrimination time by subtracting the simple reaction time from that taken with the discrimination method. Finally, in the *choice* reaction between red and green (reacting, for example, with the right hand if he saw the red light, and with the left hand if he saw the green), the time was longer than in the mere discrimination reaction, so that by the same reasoning he undertook to calculate the speed of choice. If the simple reaction was 200 one-thousandths of a second, the discrimination reaction 300, and the choice reaction 375, the discrimination time was 100 and the choice time 75 one-thousandths. In view of the originality and the ingenuity of this first attempt to measure the speed of higher mental processes, it is astonishing to see the small amount of data upon which Donders based his judgments, thirty trials or less with some of his subjects. The influence of training was disregarded. The validity of the method of subtraction has never been accepted by most investigators. One can hardly say that one process exactly fills its assigned span of time and is instantly superseded by another process when it ceases. But the work of Donders is of permanent importance in two respects: first, he showed that some of the variability of results was clearly due not to simple differences in the speed of conduction, but to central processes; second, he laid the cornerstone for the analytic study of the time relations of mental processes. He found also that the reaction time for the different senses showed characteristic differences.

But to return to the researches of Helmholtz. Our next concern is with his epoch-making investigations of vision. His great treatise *Physiological Optics* (1856–66) drew together research findings and general principles from the physics, physiology, and philosophy of the time, and much fundamental new material discovered and interpreted by himself, in a coherent account of the process of visual perception. His part in experimental physiology and psychology is typically represented by the fact that new editions of his work, rather than new treatises, remained the dominant reference texts of later years. Among the most important experiments he performed were those in relation to the external muscles of the eye, and among his important theoretical contributions was the statement of the mechanism by which the lenses are focused by the internal eye muscles.

Helmholtz sponsored Young's theory of color vision (1807). According to Helmholtz, the receptors in the eye which make differential response to color are only three; separate stimulation of these three gives respectively red, green, and blue. Each type of receptor is stimulated to a maximum degree by a certain wave length, and to a lesser degree by wave lengths adjacent in the spectrum. A wave length of 526 millionths of a millimeter, for example, has a given stimulating effect on the "green" receptor, while wave lengths of 500 and 550 stimulate it to a lesser extent. But these wave lengths stimulate also to some extent the "red" and "blue" receptors. The sensation resulting from 550 is not a faint green, but a mixture perceived as a yellowish green. He showed that these three fundamental colors may be combined in various proportions to give the various colors of the spectrum; and, when properly balanced, to give white or gray. In this scheme Helmholtz made the far-reaching assumption that there is in the brain a specialization corresponding to these three elements in the retina. There must be three kinds of activity evoked in the cortex by the activities of the three receptors; combination is a central function. The doctrine of the *specific energies of cortical areas* (the alternative raised but rejected by Müller) was essential to Helmholtz's formulation.

The theory, of course, had various difficulties to encounter; for example, in the problem of color blindness (and of partial color blindness). It had been discovered long before Helmholtz's time that the colorblind individual of the type most commonly encountered lacks sensitivity to both red and green.[1] Why should red and green be lost together but leave the perception of yellow? But the difficulties were met by a series of physiological and psychological observations. For example, the facts of color contrast were ingeniously explained through a psychological principle. Take the case of a white patch seen against a colored background. This is viewed as if through a colored covering. It is not distinguished as independent, and simply as a white patch. Rather, we carry out an "unconscious inference" as to what its true color would have to be to make it look as it does through such a covering; and this would be the complementary color. Notwithstanding difficulties, the theory has proved exceedingly valuable and has in recent years served as the basis for new "three-color theories." The physical fact that three elementary colors can yield, in mixture, all color experiences has continued to influence the effort to find a theory agreeing with all psychological facts.

The conception of unconscious inference has proved to be very widely useful, implying that our percepts and judgments are in fact constantly influenced by the context in which each stimulus appears; and that we judge, or indeed receive, each stimulus "in the light of" or in terms "relative to" this context. The colors, the tones, the pressures, and so forth, are perceived as they would *have to be* if we explicitly drew an inference from the secondary sources of information which supply the context.[2] Basically, each

---

[1] The pioneer contribution coming from Dalton, who gave a paper before the Manchester Literary and Philosophical Society in 1794, entitled "Extraordinary Facts Relating to the Vision of Colours." Dalton was himself partially colorblind.

[2] See Helson's *Adaptation-Level Theory* (1964) for a comprehensive, systematic quantitative conception of the interrelations between stimulus values and response values in their relations to the level to which the organism is adapted. Also see Gibson's information-theory approach to all perception (1950); and the enduring conceptions of "apperception mass" which are still with us from the time of Herbart (1816).

fragment of a familiar whole, like a bit of a tune, or a fragment of a photograph, can bring back the whole and we "think we see" our friend approaching, or think we hear the footsteps of the sentinel who comes to relieve us. This is virtually Hamilton's theory of redintegration (1859–60). Why it should be acceptable in so many contexts but arouse so much hesitation when we encounter it in Helmholtz, we shall not attempt to say.

Helmholtz's work in acoustics is as substantial and as noteworthy as his work in optics (1863). The brilliance and the significance of his experiments are difficult to exaggerate. We may subdivide these investigations into the study of three problems: the perception of individual tones; the perception of combination of tones; and the nature of harmony and discord.

It had long been known that the pitch of a tone depends upon the rapidity of vibration of the sounding instrument. As regards the perception of individual tones, Helmholtz came to the conclusion that there is in the ear a mechanism capable of receiving all those individual variations of pitch which the hearer can discriminate. Experimentally determining the highest and the lowest audible pitch and the number of distinguishable tones between, he supposed that the rods of Corti were capable of vibrating "sympathetically" in differential response to all distinguishable tones. It was shown later by Hensen that the basilar membrane, lying in the inner ear in a conchlike form, meets the needs of the theory more adequately. It was only necessary to assume that each fiber responded sympathetically to a given wave length or pitch. For these fibers were just such as would be expected from the study of instruments with strings of different lengths corresponding to various pitches. But whereas the longest fibers in the basilar membrane are less than three times as long as the shortest, the highest audible pitch has many thousand times the vibration rate of the lowest. This point was studied by Ewald (1894–1903), who noted that we find frequently in sympathetic vibration a tendency for a body to vibrate not in sharply subdivided areas, but as a whole, and in a number of different patterns. Modern methods of mapping the areas of maximum sensitivity to pitch show that there is nevertheless a progression along the basilar membrane.

Helmholtz worked on the closely related problem of pitch discrimination; and upon a long series of studies in the physiology and psychology of experiences of pitch. One of his greatest experimental contributions was the discovery of what it is that makes the characteristic differences in *tone quality* or *timbre*. Everyone knew that the vibration rate of middle C on the violin was the same as that of middle C on the piano, but the difference in qualities was not understood. Helmholtz discovered the significance of the fact that every kind of musical instrument gives off not only a certain fundamental tone, but, in addition, certain overtones with vibration rates more rapid than those of the fundamental. With the use of resonators he showed that by varying the intensity of the overtones he could produce synthetically the characteristic quality of each instrument, thus establishing beyond doubt the correctness of his hypothesis.

He went on from this to a theory of discord and harmony. Discord he believed to be due to a familiar phenomenon known as "beating"—the production of throbbing sounds resulting from the simultaneous presentation of two tones of nearly the same vibration rate. Dissonance was due to the presence of beats, either between fundamentals or between the overtones of the two tones under consideration. He believed harmony was due to the absence of discord. Subsequent work showed that when the beats are "filtered out" from dissonant tone combinations they remain dissonant, and the theory is today discredited.

Helmholtz was much interested in the history of music. He showed that there had been consistent development (from Greek to nineteenth-century music) in the direction of a constantly greater complexity of relations between tones combined for purposes of harmony. To the simple octave there have been added progressively the fifth, the fourth, the major third, and the minor third; the mathematical relation of vibration rates has become more and more complex. Apparently when listeners are adjusted to one combination of tones, they are preparing for another with more complexity, so that harmony has inevitably become more and more complicated. The chief significance of the theory was its emphasis upon factors of habituation. The man who contributed most to the physiological approach to tone perception was not content to neglect the importance of educational and historical factors.

Hering

Several other German experimentalists contributed largely during the third quarter of the century to the establishment of a physiological psychology. Two are arbitrarily selected here who are known for specific contributions which still form part of the working principles of psychology as a science.

Ewald Hering contributed to several aspects of sensory physiology, including problems in the temperature sense and in optics. While Weber had taught that the *rising* or *falling* of the skin temperature is responsible for the temperature sensations, Hering attempted to show that it is not the rising or falling, but the relative temperature of the skin, whether below or above its own "zero point," that determines the appearance of sensations of warmth and cold (1879–80, Vol. 3). The familiar experiment in which one hand is immersed in warm water and the other in cold, and then both are plunged into lukewarm water, can be interpreted as well on Hering's as on Weber's hypothesis. Perhaps the skin of each hand has adapted itself to a given temperature, its "physiological zero"; the lukewarm water is below one zero point and above the other.

Hering is chiefly celebrated for the theory of color with which he opposed that of Helmholtz. He elaborated and systematized the suggestions of

Goethe (1810) and Aubert (1865) and introduced improved experimental methods for the study of such phenomena as contrast, afterimage, color blindness in the periphery of the retina. Goethe had argued that there must of necessity be four elementary colors (disregarding white and black). If, said Hering, we take white (or gray), as demonstrated by Newton, to be due to the mixture of all wave lengths, we encounter on any three-color theory serious difficulty in explaining cases where *two* primary colors give the same white or gray. If, for example, red and green mixed give white, the blue remaining should give us together with the white an "unsaturated" blue (a tint or shade, not a pure color). It seemed to Hering that while Goethe's hypothesis must be supplemented with more psychological detail, the four primary colors must be accepted. There must be two pairs. Red and green when mixed would give gray. Each, moreover, was the afterimage of the other as well as its contrast color (the color seen as a border around the stimulus color when shown on a gray field). Similarly, in the case of blue and yellow Hering assumed that as a pair of primary colors which are thus related in afterimage and contrast phenomena, they must, when mixed in the right proportions, give gray. Now it was known that blue and yellow when mixed do give perfect white or gray, but that many familar reds and greens when mixed give not white, but yellow. This forced Hering into the curious problem of constructing a red and green which when mixed *would* give white. The red and green thus selected are not the red and green which seem to most subjects to be pure and simple colors. We have, then, red and green, yellow and blue, together with white and black. These six primaries were regarded as having direct stimulating effect on the receptors in the eye.[3] To explain negative afterimages and color contrast, he assumed that blue and yellow light act upon one type of receptor, red and green upon a second, and white and black upon a third. In this he found an explanation for negative afterimages and color contrast. Each color was believed to produce a chemical change in the receptor just the reverse of that produced by the other color of its pair. Yellow light caused dissimilation or katabolism in the receptor; blue light caused assimilation or anabolism. Thus the same receptors might serve to communicate either blue or yellow to the brain, depending upon whether the chemical process within them is one of building up or one of breaking down.[4] In the same way, red and green, white and black, upset the chemical equilibrium in opposite directions. If any two of these opposed functions tend to take place simultaneously, we have

[3] The "duplicity" or "duplexity" theory, stated by Schultze in 1866, and generally accepted, asserted that there are in the retina receptors the stimulation of which gives color sensations, and other receptors whose stimulation gives colorless sensations.

[4] This assumption of anabolism in the functioning of a sense organ is overbold. Stimulation, as far as we know, regularly means katabolism. The doctrine of specific energies was likewise attacked by Hering's theory; a given type of nerve fiber could initiate either "red" or "green" impulses. So far as is known today, this is unsound.

gray; red and green cancel one another, leaving the gray which all light arouses through its action on the white-black substance. Blue and yellow similarly cancel. Negative afterimages were easily explained. If we gaze fixedly at red we overwork the process of katabolism and break down tissue, and the reverse process sets in, so that we experience green. The explanation of contrast was similar. Gazing at a red stimulus on a gray field causes katabolism in one retinal area and anabolism in the adjoining region.

One of the greatest successes of Hering's theory was its easy explanation of the fact that in color blindness red and green are usually lost together, as if dependent on one type of receptor. This conquest was pushed further by the experimental investigation of the zones of the retina; the outermost zone was shown to be responsive only to white and black, the second zone to blue and yellow as well, and the central zone to all six of Hering's primary colors. The formulation of a hypothesis by which blue and yellow, red and green, were linked together in all the main problems of their relation made it immediately acceptable to a large number of psychologists. It did after all bring an extraordinary amount of order into a very chaotic field.

The theory has, however, undergone many revisions, some of which differ so much as to be designated new theories. Research in the psychology of color has long since become a highly refined specialty within a specialty, and jejune new theories are usually unwelcome. Many of the issues have been preempted by biochemists and physiologists who ask complicated questions about receptors, afferent fibers, the localization of visual sensitivity in the brain—problems in which one can roam from a very small, precise specific brain activity to a very large problem in the integration of the central nervous system. One can thus make not the *eye* but the whole organism carry out the process of seeing; one may attempt to find how the local and specific excitations integrate into higher and higher levels of function. It is no longer as convenient as it once was to build a visual problem out of many local details. One begins to realize how, even in the era of Helmholtz and Hering, the strong feeling prevailed that perceptual responses were of great complexity and required understanding the whole living system; and there is more and more reason to espouse such a view in the light of what has been done in research since their time.

Lotze and Local Signs

In the psychological work of Rudolph Hermann Lotze there was an extraordinary synthesis of materials drawn from the biological sciences and from philosophy. He was in his day better known for his masterful handling of philosophical and biological problems than for the specific contribution which still bears his name in psychology. Lotze studied at Leipzig, took both Ph.D. and M.D., and became Professor of Philosophy at Göttingen in 1844. Within a decade he was well known as an author of both philosophical and medical works, especially of works which were *both* philosophical and medical. It was not the practice of medicine that interested him, but the knowledge of the body in its relation to the problems of the mind; it was this that enabled him to feel comfortable and competent in relation to the more complex psychological problems of personality, temperament, will, and the world of values. As a student of Fechner and his collaborator, Volkmann, he developed respect for and competence in the integration of the *Geistes-wissenschaften* (cultural sciences) and the *Naturwissenschaften* (natural sciences). The task of reconciliation appears to have been utterly genuine and, in its era, acceptable and productive. But most of the biologically minded and the culturally minded did not really want integration. One could wish that Lotze were still alive to speak to a generation which so frequently asks whether one has to give up one's values to be a scientist, or one's science to develop a world of values.

Like Bain, Lotze sought to unify physiological and psychological material in a coherent system in which justice should be done both to empirical findings and to the philosopher's demand for interpretation. Unlike Bain, he was a master of the physiology and the neuropathology of his day. At the same time he contributed powerfully to the elaboration of a form of philosophy which was destined to be of considerable significance in nineteenth-century thought. It influenced such men as Wundt and became in time a foundation principle for many psychological schools. Lotze insisted, in the first place, on the futility of trying to find mental processes which are not related to physical processes; in other words, he protested against those forms of idealism which sought to save a part of psychology from the encroachments of physics and chemistry. Psychology must deal with the organism. The nervous system and the mind must be seen in relation to each other. On the other hand, he maintained with equal definiteness that it was ridiculous to suppose that the mere existence of physical and chemical process was an "explanation" of mind. Exact science can give us no clue as to the ultimate nature of mental processes. In particular, said Lotze, the meanings of life, the significance of things about us, the reality of our pleasures and pains, the reality of our ideals and dreams, are not affected by the discovery of mechanical laws.[5] This approach helped clarify the problem for the psychologist. It gave courage to those who were seeking a formulation of psychological principles based upon the natural sciences; at the same time it cut the ground from under those who easily dismissed all problems of value as irrelevant and those who denied to psychology a subject matter of its own.

Lotze made two specific contributions in addition to this general one. He studied the psychology of the emotions and was one of the first to give a detailed statement of the nature of the expressive functions: the way in which the face and posture, as well as the pulse, breathing, and so forth,

[5] See William James, pp. 193–207.

behave in the various emotional states. He had, therefore, considerable influence in later formulations of the relation of emotions to bodily change (such as the James-Lange theory) and helped prepare the way for the experimental studies of emotion which became numerous toward the end of the century.

But he is chiefly known for his theory of "local signs" (1883, Chap. 4). This was an attempt to find a compromise between the opposed views on space perception which had been constantly reiterated since the days of Kant. Herbart had made the entire spatial order the product of experience. Johannes Müller had taught that the germ of space perception is innate but that the elaboration of the world of space, and its organization through the modes of perception known to the adult, have to be learned. He had advocated, as we have seen, a compromise view—that in spite of a primitive awareness of bodily extension much of the process of space perception depends on learning. But many who rejected transcendentalism held with Kant that space perception is purely innate. Müller's authority carried, of course, much weight. But he had not explained how a serial order is built up in the visual world so that each object is seen in a certain relation to each other object, above or below, right or left; nor had the problem of tactual space been seriously considered. These were the tasks Lotze imposed upon himself and solved so ingeniously that the outlines of his theory still remain influential in our analysis of space perception.

Beginning with vision, Lotze conjectured that each stimulus acting on the retina caused not only a characteristic nonspatial quality such as color, but a sensation specifically related to the point stimulated and differing qualitatively from sensations aroused by the same object when stimulating any other point on the retina. Each point on the retina had its "local sign." The nature of these local signs and of their organization into a continuum, to give the world of visual space, was stated in terms of the muscular sensations aroused when, upon stimulation, the eye turns so as to bring the stimulus to the point of clearest vision. A light striking the retina at any point causes the eye to swing reflexly to fixate the object. But the direction and the magnitude of the arc through which the eye must pass are different for each point on the retina. Corresponding to all stimulable points on the retina there is, therefore, an immense variety of "feelings of position," forming an orderly, graded series. In the course of time each visual stimulus arouses by association memories of the muscular sensations previously excited as the eye sought its fixation point. In this way stimuli which were at first nonspatial take on a spatial character.

There are likewise local signs in the skin. We need only to note that in addition to the nonspatial experiences of pressure, temperature, and so on, there are experiences which depend upon the region stimulated; the tension and the curvature of the skin vary from point to point. Each stimulus arouses, therefore, a number of distinct impressions, depending on location;

and these, through experience and association, come to form a coherent, graded series. The order thus constituted is now associated with the world of visual space. In the case of those born blind it is necessary to emphasize the orderly series of muscular sensations in making contact with objects at various distances and in various directions from any given starting point.

Both in visual and in cutaneous space the fundamental conception was that psychological space is built up from sensations which in isolation would not be spatial, but whose order of stimulation corresponds to transition of the stimulus from one point in physical space to another. The theory was not only highly important as an application of physiological findings[6] and associationist theory to an extremely complex and baffling problem; it marked one of the boldest and most fruitful attempts to make the muscular sensations play their part in mental life.[7] The analytic, atomistic, and associationist conceptions emphasized here were of course to be challenged, then swept aside, by the emphasis on organismic and especially Gestalt approaches to psychology, as by Wertheimer (1912). In Lotze's time the analytic method had to be pushed for all it was worth; the pendulum had to swing as far as it could before there was a chance for a countermovement. Little pendular movements like these, paced by big pendular movements, are parts of the "dialectical" approach which any history higher than a sheer chronicle must try to make clear.

In the middle of the nineteenth century, in spite of the work of such men as Helmholtz and Lotze, relatively little detailed information regarding the physiology of the nervous system was available as yet for psychological purposes. The hope of a physiological psychology, repeatedly uttered in the eighteenth century, had so far resulted in meager data of a type really useful in the explanation of specific psychological events. But from about 1860 on there occurred a series of discoveries in neurology which began to exert important influences on psychology.

Anatomy and Physiology of the Nervous System

It will be recalled that Johannes Müller (1833–40) had discussed the question of the localization of function within the cerebral cortex. Further studies during the twenties and thirties as to the definite localization of speech functions led in 1861 to the declaration by Broca that injuries to the third frontal convolution of the left hemisphere were the cause of motor aphasia, the loss of voluntary speech. This statement of Broca attracted attention and soon came into wide acceptance. This was the first case of definitely accepted cortical localization for a specific function, antedating

---

[6] In particular, Weber's data on the two-point threshold, which Lotze interpreted as indicating that local signs change more rapidly in some regions than in others.

[7] Lotze's emphasis on the muscle sense in connection with vision was welcomed and carried even further by many: for example, by Wundt and Münsterberg, a generation later.

by twenty years the definite location of any of the sensory centers and by ten years the *experimental* demonstration of the location of the motor functions, first in the dog, then in other mammals. In 1870 work was published by Fritsch and Hitzig (1870) on the localization of motor functions in the cerebrum of the dog. Stimulation of the region immediately in front of the Rolandic fissure was found to elicit movements of the limbs.

During the period of the seventies and eighties this work of mapping cerebral localization was carried on extensively. One of the most significant contributions was that of Ferrier (1876), who succeeded in working out the localization of motor functions in the brains of monkeys; this proved to be similar to that found for the dog. Ferrier did more than explore the motor area in order to find out how the subdivisions of the motor cortex were arranged; he and others began to contribute much to the localization of *sensory* functions. Not content with the mere tracing of sensory fibers through their devious paths to the cortex, they made use of the technique of cutting sensory fibers and determining whether the visual, auditory, or other functions were affected. Grunbaum and Sherrington (1903) were soon exploring the brains of anthropoid apes (Sherrington, 1906).

This kind of research made it possible to say in a general way that there are regions in the cortex which have specific functions. The whole problem of cortical localization stood in a new light as compared with the middle of the century. By 1885 or 1890 the main cortical centers for sensation and (voluntary) movement were worked out for mammals to the general satisfaction of most critics. Partly by the use of analogy, but chiefly through clinical studies and anatomical research, similar localization within the human brain won general acceptance. It became a matter of agreement that the area immediately in front of the fissure of Rolando is uniformly motor and that the post-Rolandic area serves the "general senses" of warmth, cold, touch, and pain. The visual center was assigned to the occipital lobe and the auditory to the temporal lobe. A region near the olfactory bulb was recognized as the olfactory lobe. The results from tracing fibers and those obtained from the extirpation and cutting of fibers were consistent.

Many writers carried cortical localization much further. Wernicke (1874) and others helped to define the types of aphasia on the hypothesis that there is a specific cortical localization for each type (disorders in reading, in writing, in talking, and in understanding spoken language). They described, for example, patients who had lost the ability to read—that is, to *understand* printed symbols—without manifesting any other language disturbance. This disorder was attributed to a specific lesion so circumscribed as to leave the rest of the brain unaffected. Hinshelwood (1900), among others, believed that the centers for visual memory are distinct from those for visual sensation. Destroy the visual center and the patient still has visual memories; destroy the visual memory region and the patient may have the capacity to see, without recognizing what he sees. While in general rejecting this simple localization of memory functions, many neurologists and psychologists came to the conclusion that certain lesions can disturb perception without affecting sensation. Hence the doctrine that perceptual functions are carried out not by the sensory centers themselves, but by regions adjacent to them. This fitted in well with the theory that coordinating or integrating centers for motor functions lie adjacent to the motor area in the pre-Rolandic region. Many clinical and anatomical studies were being made in this period, which seemed in general to confirm the view.[8]

Especially significant were the studies of J. Hughlings Jackson, a clinical neurologist, whose clinical and postmortem studies on various neural disorders led to exceedingly accurate localization of cortical areas with specific functions (Taylor, 1958). He had pointed out that higher cerebral centers exert controlling influence on lower centers and showed the behavioral signs of neurological disorders in this relationship. His studies form the basis for modern clinical neurology.

A closely related problem was that of tracing sensory fibers through the spinal cord and brain stem to the cortical sensory areas. Pathological cases helped greatly to clarify and interpret anatomical research; injuries to the nervous system could be directly compared with losses of specific sensory functions. Animal experimentation also added much; if certain fibers in the cord were cut and certain functions were consistently lost, it was possible to say with fair certainty what functions these fibers served. The discreteness of these functions seemed to call for the discovery of separate pathways serving their respective functions. Pain and temperature pathways, for example, were satisfactorily traced.

Significant contributions were made in neurophysiology by the Russian neurologist and physiologist Ivan Sechenov. He had studied or worked with many of the outstanding physiologists of the time during his various trips to western Europe, including Johannes Müller and Helmholtz. Sechenov (1863) advanced several original ideas regarding the reflex mechanisms of behavior, which came to full fruition in the later work of Ivan Pavlov. While working in the laboratory of Claude Bernard in France, Sechenov discovered that spinal reflexes are influenced, even to the extent of complete inhibition, by activities at higher neural centers. Starting from this observation he came to the conclusion that all neural activity should be understood in terms of the interactive processes of inhibition and facilitation. He proposed that the reflex act is the sole mechanism of associations and that both physiological and psychological reactions are to be understood in terms of reflex activity. He concluded that psychology is a subject matter for physiologists investigating the reflexes of the brain. It is under Sechenov's influence that most of the experimental investigations of behavior, which in the West are considered to be psychological, in Russia

---

[8] The evidence from postmortem examination was scarcely definite, in view of the extraordinary irregularity of lesions and the scarcity of "pure" aphasic types.

are undertaken even today in physiological laboratories; and that Sechenov and Pavlov are never referred to by their countrymen as psychologists. Although most of Sechenov's physiological work was known and incorporated into the body of science of his time, it is only currently, and largely through the efforts of the outstanding western representatives of the Sechenov-Pavlov tradition — Gregory Razran, Horsley Gantt, Howard Liddell — that the extent of his contribution to psychology is being fully acknowledged.

Another field of research important for psychology was the intensive study of the general anatomy and physiology of nerve cells. Histological methods, such as the staining of normal and injured nerve tissue, made possible not only the tracing of fibers but the observation and classification of many types of cells previously unrecognized. One of the most important steps taken in this direction was the method of staining used by Golgi, in Italy. A common view that the various parts of the nervous system are all anatomically connected did not seem to be confirmed by the evidence from staining, or from other methods utilized during the seventies and eighties. Staining methods seemed to indicate that nerve cells are anatomically distinct from one another; there appeared, at least in higher animals, no clear cases of fibers passing from one cell into another. This led students of the subject to gravitate toward the view that each nerve cell is in some way connected physiologically, but not anatomically, with other nerve cells. Cells are capable of influencing one another, but each cell carries on independently such functions as nutrition and self-repair. Other evidence to the same general effect was obtained from the embryological researches of His. The problem of His was to determine whether the nerve cells arise, so to speak, from one another, or whether each one pursues from the beginning an independent development. He showed that each nerve cell is from the time of its appearance until completely developed an *individual,* not sharing in the life of the other cells except in deriving its nutrition and so on from a common source. This was important in confirming the belief that the most significant relation between nerve cells was to be found not in their anatomical interconnections, but in the ways in which they might influence one another in function. This view, developing largely from the work of Ramón y Cajal, was named by Waldeyer the *neuron theory* in 1891. This was one of the most important neurological contributions for the history of psychology. It brought together numerous evidences as to the nature of nervous physiology which psychologists could use. Its central conception was the anatomical independence of nerve cells and their physiological interconnection at junction points or *synapses.*

We may best understand the influence of the theory upon psychology by considering briefly the kind of neurophysiology upon which psychologists had been relying. Many psychologists had exploited the nervous system as an explanatory principle for mental life, but explanation of the part played by the nervous system in *specific* mental processes had inevitably been extremely vague. Let us choose for illustration the work of one French and one American psychologist. Ribot in *Diseases of Memory* (1881) regarded these as the product of disordered brain functions. But he thought in terms of gross lesions, not in terms of the disorganization of microscopic or ultramicroscopic elements, such as connections between one nerve cell and another. Even the concept of the difference between organic and functional psychoses was at that time impossible; the importance of gross injuries to the brain was overemphasized, simply because the significance of ultramiscroscopic changes could not be clearly stated.

Similarly, a comparison of William James's chapter "Habit," in *Principles of Psychology* (1890), with statements of the physiology of habit current a few years *after* the acceptance of the neurone theory, shows how great was the revolution in the theory of learning.[9] James was trying to think in neurological terms. He sought to find how it was that a series of connections could be made between different parts of our bodies, one movement leading to the next; but he worked without any clear conception as to the mechanism by which one nerve cell might influence another. The same lack of definite neurological concepts with which to work is apparent in James's theory of association. In his chapter "Association," he offered a theory as to the neural functions involved in all the sequences of mental life. He suggested that if any two points in the cerebral cortex are simultaneously active, the two centers tend to "drain" into each other. Pathways are thus established, which later are traversed when either center is excited. If we *see* a man and at the same time *hear* his name, a linkage is established which later enables either experience to recall the other. *Successive* association was explained in similar terms, a hypothesis being added to the effect that when one area is excited immediately *after* another, the energy drained from the first to the second is greater than the quantity drained from the second to the first. This presupposed, of course, an "irradiation" of energy in the cortex which need not involve motor discharge; it was therefore a necessary supplement to James's theory of habit. But it did not tell *how* the disturbances in one nerve cell could affect another nerve cell.

The neuron theory gave both the theory of learning and the theory of association a much more definite and usable form. The theory teaches that each nerve cell is an individual which carries on its own life as regards nutrition and other metabolic functions. The connection between one nerve cell and another is, as we saw, by means of the synapse, or junction point. The synapse is not a fibrous connection, but a point at which the nervous impulse is relayed from one nerve cell to the next. But the terminal or end brush of a neurone A may be in close proximity to the receiving organs, or

---

[9] James borrowed a great deal from Meynert. Meynert's scheme postulated that habit was based upon the interconnection of brain areas, without making clear the mechanism of such connection.

dendrites, of *many* other neurones, B, C, D . . . so that according to the theory, the actual pathway A – B or A – C or A – D . . . depends upon the physiological properties of the synapse at the time. There may, of course, be synaptic connections so intimate that they cannot be broken by anything. Such would be cases of reflex action so firmly established as to be practically unmodifiable. Some of the reflexes of the spinal frog would, perhaps, represent the extreme of unmodifiability. At the opposite extreme, or limiting case, there may be synapses in which there is an equal predisposition for the impulses to go in any one of a great number of directions, the choice between the alternatives depending on slight and momentary factors, such as refractory phases or summation. These conceptions make possible a theory of learning in terms of modification of the synapse. Between these two extreme cases there are conceived to be behavior patterns less rigid than the one and less plastic than the other, so that an original disposition may have sufficient plasticity to permit the reorganization of nervous pathways as the result of experience. This view makes possible the formulation of the learning process in terms of the building up of resistance at certain points and the breaking down of resistance at others; and the patterned or organized functioning of many synapses jointly involved in a complex total. These aspects of the neurone theory, developed and systematized by many physiologists and psychologists, seemed to be of immediate value for the psychology of learning and for many other problems. They were rapidly accepted and came into general use in the first years of the twentieth century.

The next great step after acceptance of the neuron theory, in inducing psychologists to think in neurological terms, was the work of Sherrington during the opening years of the century, described in his *Integrative Action of the Nervous System* (1906). Fundamental conceptions for neurophysiology were defined and in many cases experimentally verified, frequently with reference to psychological implications. The experimental study of the reflex arc in normal and decerebrate mammals such as the dog underwent, with Sherrington, a series of refinements. When a single stimulus was too weak to elicit a motor response, the repeated application of the same weak stimulus was found to be capable, by "summation," of traversing the threshold, throwing the reflex into full swing. But simultaneous, as well as successive, stimuli might cooperate with or "facilitate" one another. When a stimulus at one point was too weak to set the reflex going, a stimulus at another point might, although itself also too weak, join forces with the first, evoking the response. In other cases, a stimulus which would ordinarily evoke a reflex response was found to be "inhibited" by another stimulus. Such "facilitation" and "inhibition," already familiar to physiologists,[10] were elaborately analyzed, and definite evidence was offered to show their relation to the functions of the synapse. Both processes seemed to

[10] Especially through the work of Exner (1882).

be effected by synapses intermediate between receptor and organ of response; on reaching a synapse two pathways might either aid or interfere with one another. "Reciprocal inhibition" was demonstrated in numerous instances; the innervation of extensor muscles involved not only the inactivity but the *lowered tonus* of the flexor muscles of the same limbs. The process by which one pathway was opened served also to block pathways leading to opposed action.[11]

The supposition that facilitation and inhibition are synaptic functions was greatly strengthened by Sherrington's study of the effect of fatigue and drugs. A bit of nerve tissue containing no synapses proved quite insusceptible to fatigue, whereas regions containing synapses could conduct only for a brief period without the occurrence of fatigue. Certain drugs were found to block off an impulse quite effectively if applied to a region containing synapses, while regions containing none were practically unaffected. Other drugs, instead of increasing, greatly reduced synaptic resistance.

All this work, then, confirmed for psychologists the extraordinary importance of the synapses for facilitation and inhibition in higher processes. The nature of synaptic function, however, was not disclosed by Sherrington's methods. An interesting line of inquiry was associated with the names of Nernst (1908), Lillie (1911, 1923), and Lucas (1917). Theoretical and experimental conditions alike suggested that the nerve current is a "wave of depolarization" which passes along the nerve fiber whenever a stimulus disturbs the delicate balance of positive and negative ions produced in the metabolism of the nerve. An instant after the depolarization at a given point, that point is in "refractory phase"; another instant later it is in a condition of "hyperexcitability." Each synapse was conceived to have its own refractory phase, resulting in inhibition; and its period of hyperexcitability. The hypothesis encountered many difficulties, the problem being highly complex, and several other theories later claimed the field (Fulton, 1938). Such a view was illustrative, however, of the advances of physiological chemistry and the growing insistence that the synapse should be conceived in such terms as to throw genuine light upon the phenomena of facilitation and inhibition. To such problems we must briefly recur at a later point, in the chapter on modern comparative and physiological psychology.

REFERENCES

Aubert, H. *Physiologie der Netzhaut*. Breslau: Morgenstern, 1865.
Broca, P. "Remarques sur le siège de la faculté du langage articulé, suivi d'une observation d'aphémie." *Bulletin Société d'Anatomie*, 2nd ser., 6 (1861), 330–57.

[11] McDougall's "drainage theory" of reciprocal inhibition (1905) held that when A – B and C – D are antagonistic reflexes, A – B, while functioning, draws off the energy of C, so that the response D is inhibited; fatigue in the pathway A – B makes possible the sudden activity of C – D, draining the energy from A.

Dalton, J. "Extraordinary Facts Relating to the Vision of Colours." Read October 31, 1794. *Memoirs and Proceedings of the Literary and Philosophical Society of Manchester*, 5 (1798), 28–45.

Donders, F. C. "Die Schnelligkeit psychischer Processe." *Archiv für Anatomie und Physiologie* (1868), 657–81.

Ewald, J. R. "Zur Physiologie des Labyrinths." *Archiv für die gesamte Physiologie*, 59–93 (1894–1903).

Exner, S. *Archiv für die gesamte Physiologie*, 28 (1882).

Ferrier, D. *The Functions of the Brain*. London: Smith, Elder, 1876.

Fritsch, G., and Hitzig, E. "Über die Elektrische Erregharkeit des Grosshirns." *Archiv für Anatomie und Physiologie* (1870), 300–332.

Fulton, J. F. *Physiology of the Nervous System*. London: Oxford University Press, 1938.

Gibson, J. J. *The Perception of the Visual World*. Boston: Houghton Mifflin, 1950.

Goethe, J. W. von. *Zur Farbenlehre*. 2 vols. Tübingen: Cotta, 1810.

Grunbaum, A. S. F., and Sherrington, C. S. *Observations on the Physiology of the Cerebral Cortex of Anthropoid Apes*. Liverpool: Thompson Yates and Johnson, 1903.

Hamilton, W. *Lectures on Metaphysics*. London: Blackwood, 1859–60.

Helmholtz, H. L. F. von. *Die Lehre von den Tonempfindungen als Physiologischer Grundlage für die Theorie der Musik*. Braunschweig: Vieweg, 1863.

———. *Handbuch der Physiologischen Optik [Treatise on Physiological Optics]*. Leipzig: Voss, 1856–66.

Helson, H. *Adaptation Level Theory*. New York: Harper & Row, 1964.

Herbart, J. F. *Lehrbuch zur Psychologie*. Königsberg: Unzer, 1816.

Hering, E. "Der Temperatursinn." In L. Hermann, ed. *Handbuch der Physiologie*. 6 vols. in 12. Leipzig: Vogel, 1879–80.

Hinshelwood, J. *Letter-, Word-, and Mind-Blindness*. London: Lewis, 1900.

James, W. *Principles of Psychology*. 2 vols. New York: Holt, 1890. New York: Dover, 1950.

Lillie, R. S. "The Relation of Stimulation and Conduction in Irritable Tissues to Changes in the Permeability of the Limiting Membranes." *American Journal of Physiology*, 28 (1911), 197–222.

———. *Protoplasmic Action and Nervous Action*. Chicago: University of Chicago Press, 1923.

Lotze, R. H. *Grundzüge der Psychologie*. Leipzig: Hirzel, 1883.

Lucas, K. *The Conduction of the Nervous Impulse*. London: Longmans, Green, 1917.

McDougall, W. *Physiological Psychology*. London: Dent, 1905. New York: Macmillan, 1905.

Müller, J. *Handbuch der Physiologie des Menschen*. 3 vols. Coblenz: Hölscher, 1833–40.

Nernst, W. H. "Zur Theorie des Elektrischen Reizes." *Archiv für die gesamte Physiologie*, 132 (1908), 275–314.

Ribot, T.-A. *Les Maladies de la mémoire [Diseases of Memory]*. Paris: Alcan, 1881.

Schultze, M. J. S. *Zur Anatomie und Physiologie der Retina*. Bonn: Cohen, 1866.

Sechenov, I. *[Reflexes of the Brain.]* St. Petersburg: Sushchinskii, 1863.

Sherrington, C. S. *The Integrative Action of the Nervous System.* New Haven: Yale University Press, 1906.

Taylor, J., ed. *Selected Writings of John Hughlings Jackson.* New York: Basic Books, 1958.

Waldeyer, H. W. von. "Ueber einige Neuere Forschungen im Gebiete der Anatomie des Centralnervensystems." *Deutsche Medizinische Wochenschrift,* 17 (1891), 1213–18, 1244–46, 1287–89, 1331–32, 1352–56.

Wernicke, C. *Der Aphasische Symptomencomplex.* Breslau: Cohn and Weigert, 1874.

Wertheimer, M. "Experimentelle Studien über das Sehen von Bewegungen." *Zeitschrift für Psychologie,* 61 (1912), 161–265.

Young, T. *A Course of Lectures on Natural Philosophy and the Mechanical Arts.* 2 vols. London: Johnson, 1807.

NOTE: A list of further readings appears at the back of the book.

9

The
Theory of
Evolution

*What a magnificent idea of the infinite power of the great architect! The
cause of causes! Parent of parents! Ens entium!*

ERASMUS DARWIN

The majority naturally perished, having too weak a constitution.

HIPPOCRATES

Though the idea of evolution is commonly traced to the ancients,
it must be granted that their primitive evolutionism, from Empedocles to the
great panorama of cosmic development that had been drawn by Lucretius,
has little to do with the modern theory of evolution. The latter emerged on
the heels of the Renaissance out of the conflicts and mutual influences of the
Judeo-Christian doctrines of revelation and creation and the emerging mechanistic philosophy and empiricism. The stable meaning and purpose infused
into the affairs of man by the Judeo-Christian doctrines of divine wisdom
were as important in the birth of scientific biology as was the new insistence
on their verification by hard facts.

Post-Renaissance empiricism spread to all, even to those who recognized
the threat posed by the new mechanistic philosophy for the established doctrines and social order; it was espoused by all sides in the growing struggle
of ideas. In fact, much of the early systematic description of nature, as in
John Ray's *The Wisdom of God Manifested in the Work of Creation* (1692),
or in the work of Linnaeus (1735), was aimed at demonstrating fully the immense wisdom and foresight of the Creator in providing man with a suitable
habitat. There was a great difference, therefore, between these new systematic accounts of nature and the work of Aristotle.

Aristotle systematized and described the known, but he did not have a
well-articulated and generally accepted universal theory. His search was not
guided by a single doctrine, nor his data measured by a single yardstick. Ray

and Linnaeus, on the other hand, collected and systematized in order to support and prove a single theory: the theory that the earth was created for the habitat of man by a divine will which remains the guiding force in the affairs of man. The post-Renaissance conceptions of evolution emerged from progressively refined efforts at classification and empirical examination of phenomena implied in Genesis and from the gradual resolution of the disagreements between facts implied and facts observed. When the collected data did not fit the theory, the theory was modified.

What were the facts implied by the "theory" of Genesis? They were a trinity, each implying observable, pertinent evidence: first, about the age of the world; second, the immutability of species; and third, a profusion of nature, divinely guided. It became evident that there was a contradiction between the postulate of law-bound matter in motion and the doctrine of divine guidance. This was resolved not by rejection but by modification, by the relegation of divine guidance to the primary act of creation. The infinite wisdom of the Creator, it was argued, emanated from the laws laid down at the time of creation, from the divinely fixed immutable laws of matter in motion.

By the time of Kant, Buffon, and Laplace, it became known that nature is not immutable—that while some stars are born others disappear and that it must have taken millions of years for the common forces of erosion to bring about the known changes in the earth's crust. There was a steady accumulation of huge fossil bones. Tusks and teeth clearly of animal origin were found, but their size did not match existing species. Fossilized bones of fish were located in unlikely places—on mountain slopes miles away from the water in which such fish could have lived. All these discoveries forced upon contemporary thinkers the idea of change. Change was accepted once again only as a modifier of the original doctrine of creation. Time, it was argued, slowly erodes an originally pristine and perfect world. This new theory of gradual deterioration was later amended by Cuvier's catastrophism, by the idea that the earth and its inhabitants had been exposed to catastrophic events. Having the Biblical deluge as prototype, these catastrophes were to account for the bones of extinct species and the by-then recognized great upheavals in the earth's geological structure. Georges Cuvier (1769–1832) lent a new lease on life to the old doctrine of creation. But under the ever-increasing pressure of discordant evidence, an entirely new explanation began to emerge; change began to be viewed as a process of progressive improvement rather than deterioration.

Meanwhile, the facts of change were pressing relentlessly into the daily affairs of man. Political and industrial revolutions resulted in profound upheavals in the lives of individuals and institutions. The new romantic philosophy of the period emphasized more and more the idea of diversification. Thus, Goethe, one of the most illustrious of the romanticists, found evolutionary conceptions useful in his studies of botany and indeed worked out his own theory of organic evolution. Among the French, Fourier constructed a theory of human destiny in terms of progressive improvement and the many thousands of years that must be spent at each stage of growth. The same tendency was expressed in Hegel's conviction that civilization had been worked out in progressive steps according to a universal idea.

During this period, two types of evolutionary teaching went on side by side: first, the theory of evolution of the inanimate physical universe, the study of inorganic evolution; second, the study of biological, or organic, evolution. Kant first suggested, and later Laplace developed in connection with his mechanics, the theory commonly known as the *nebular hypothesis.* This sought to explain the origin of planets through the interaction of gravitational and centrifugal forces in rotating nebulae. Buffon (1749–1804), in the middle of the eighteenth century, outlined a broadly speculative view of organic development, in which he argued that species, while created at the beginning of time, undergo chance variations and deteriorative modification from generation to generation. Erasmus Darwin (the grandfather of Charles Darwin) half a century later proposed that living things undergo a different type of progressive transformation.

Physician, biologist, and poet, Erasmus Darwin (1794–96) believed in the perpetual improvement of nature. The capacity to undergo progressively improving transformation in structures, needs, and functions was the peculiarity of living things, he argued. In agreement with the Scottish philosopher David Hume, he believed that the world as we know it was not created but generated. This was a new and complete readjustment of the original Biblical theory of purposeful creation, a new faith in purpose and progress of cosmic proportions.

Lamarck

Jean-Baptiste Lamarck elaborated Erasmus Darwin's conception in a system which became widely and controversially known. He had attempted to divorce the issues of evolution and purposeful creation from each other, but he succeeded only in introducing a new teleological puzzle through postulating needs, purposes, and a priori directions in living things themselves. The fact that he mastered both zoology and botany, and the fact that he had made elaborate studies and published dozens of volumes on different phases of organic life (which included his coining the word "biology"), gave weight to his views and demanded for them serious consideration. His was a theory which raised the question of why specific cumulative changes in organisms take place from generation to generation.

Lamarck (1809) assumed an internal, essentially psychological response by organisms to environmental change and argued that change in organic structures is guided by such internal responses. While advocating the inheritance of characteristics acquired in the process of responding to environmental change, Lamarck was somewhat confused about the nature of these acquired changes and the mechanisms of their guidance by internal responses. At times he related them to an inherent tendency of living things toward progressive complications, which of course could imply the same purposeful direction that had been celebrated by Erasmus Darwin. At other times he argued that both the internal responses and related organic changes are entirely due to local conditions.

Lamarck's theory involves three steps. First, in confronting the physical environment, the organism meets the situation with appropriate adaptive internal response. Second, this situation, demanding adjustment, results in the exercise of certain parts of the body. Third, the exercise of a given part of the body makes that particular part develop to the point sufficiently advanced to cause the change to appear in the offspring as an inherited characteristic. Whereas Buffon (1749–1804) explained variation by a process of degeneration or chance deviation from original forms, Lamarck, following Erasmus Darwin, reversed this process and argued that evolution started from simple beginnings and resulted in progressively increasing complexities of organic gains. His theory may be tossed lightly aside, but the basic issue of the role of tension, pressure, urge, purpose, or whatever the impulsive and creative factors had to be taken into account more and more seriously. While Lamarck's conception of the inheritance of acquired characters has fared ill in the light of the data accumulated by biologists, especially in our own century, a broader issue raised by Lamarck will not give up the ghost. The impulsive, or hormic, principle, which was divorced from the divine act of creation by Lamarck, kept reappearing in the work of philosophers of the stature of Bergson and Driesch, in the instinctivistic and purposivistic psychologies of McDougall, Tolman, and Freud, and more recently in the work of ethologists.

Shortly after Lamarck put forth this theory, a debate began between Saint-Hilaire and Cuvier. Saint-Hilaire championed Lamarck's doctrine of transmutation of species, though he differed from Lamarck as to its mechanisms. Cuvier refused to entertain an evolutionary doctrine on the grounds of the inadequacy of evidence that would contradict his own theory of "catastrophism." This debate was bound to be decided in scientific circles of the day in favor of Cuvier, because of Cuvier's immense prestige and because, although practically all ideas that later entered into Darwin's theory were already at hand, the time was not yet ripe; and the evidence, while certainly adequate for entertaining views different from the views of catastrophic and deteriorative change, was in fact inadequate to overcome the concentrated opposition from all corners of contemporary thought.

Meanwhile in geology, Lyell (1839) was making investigations (1830 to 1860) to show how rock strata were formed by series of changes in the earth. The late seventeenth and early eighteenth centuries had marked the beginnings of this type of research; by the early nineteenth century it could be demonstrated that the different strata had been built one upon another in a certain sequence, occupying definite periods of time. The various organisms whose fossil remains were found in these strata must necessarily have lived at different times, in periods corresponding to the strata where the fossils were found. Lyell enunciated the theory that the earth itself had gone through an orderly series of changes, in which a chaos of elements had gradually been superseded by differentiation and separation. Thus different kinds of rock had been formed and had become relatively fixed and immutable. This form of thought was as foreign to the idea of special creation as was the Darwinian theory itself; and Lyell, though a deeply religious man, had to face serious religious opposition. He had undertaken to show that the earth itself reveals stages requiring vastly greater time than the six days allowed in the Book of Genesis. Lyell was not the first nor the last, but, in terms of scientific as well as popular influence, he was by far the greatest of the geological evolutionists. He prepared the way for the habit of thinking in terms of progressive growth and change. Lyell's evolutionism was, indeed, a direct stimulus to the work of Charles Darwin.

Darwin

The task of gathering the data bearing directly on the reality of evolution, as well as on the mechanisms by which it was effected, are associated with Charles Darwin. Darwin's importance lay not in his being the first to think in terms of evolution but in his recognizing that the problem could be solved only by the accumulation of enormous and well-ordered masses of evidence. His monumental work forced a reluctant audience to abandon the belief in a stable world; his facts spoke of merciless, all-encompassing, unguided change.

Failing to discover at Cambridge what really interested him and reluctant to accept advice from his father, Darwin wandered and hesitated until the right opportunity dropped into his lap. Having been intrigued by the work of the naturalists and having conducted small informal studies of plants and animals, he accepted the position of naturalist in a research expedition on the *Beagle* through the South Seas (1831–36). This gave him an opportunity for observation and collection of plants and animals in a wide variety of geographical and climatic regions of the world. Having formed the excellent habit of taking notes on observations, he began to notice a marvelous adaptation of each form of life to the environment in which it appeared. In his notebook of 1837, he tells of his concern with the problem of selection. He had noted that out of every generation some individuals were eliminated, although apparently constructed much like their brothers and sisters. What made some die and others live? What was the mechanism of selection? How did nature choose from the many?

In 1838 he read Malthus's *Essay on the Principle of Population* (1798), a treatise written forty years before during the period of the first terrible impact of the Industrial Revolution on families transplanted to industrial cities from their farms, making their way of life one of long hours and disease. Malthus discussed the problem of the relation of the death rate to the birth rate, noting that societies tended to suffer from overpopulation or indeed from "population explosions." He asked whether the lot of the poor could be improved. Malthus had concluded that the improvement which might be made in the production of food would tend to follow an *arithmetical* progression, while increase in population would inevitably conform to a *geometrical* progression. If, for example, each family has four children and three of them live and have offspring, the number given by the geometrical ratio must, in time, surpass the number that can be fed. So long as one ratio is arithmetical and the other geometrical there must follow an *excess* of population. Some individuals must be eliminated in one way or another, through starvation and disease, or through war. There was no escape from these hard alternatives. It was a rather loosely worked out hypothesis, but it had the advantage of examining human society in biological terms. The hypothesis that the number of offspring is usually greater than the number that can subsist implied that there must be a struggle for existence, the elimination of some and the preservation of others.

The reading of Malthus's essay, interpreted in the light of Darwin's own observations, suggested an answer to his problem. He began to outline the theory of evolution which he later published. The theory was based upon the facts that there are considerable variations among individual numbers of species which may distinguish an individual member as more fit, or less fit, to cope with a given environmental demand and that in most species the total number is stationary although there are more offspring than parents. In fish there may be a hundred thousand eggs for each two parents; there must be an elimination of all but two individuals. This leads directly to the idea of the "survival of the fittest." An organism is "fit" if in a given environment it is well adapted to the task of getting food and warding off its enemies. It has to survive and to develop until it is able to reproduce its kind. But if there is survival of the fittest, and at the same time adaptation to the environment (which is the necessary condition of the survival itself), this adaptation to environment must mean survival of those which are fittest in the particular environment. If in each generation those which are fittest for the particular environment survive, and if over the years there are changes in the environment, it follows that there must be changes in the kinds of individuals which can survive. As a common stock drifts into different regions and the struggle for existence goes on generation by generation, individuals well adapted to each region will differ from the individuals adapted to other regions; there will be selection within each region, providing adaptation to the requirements of that region, of that "adaptive niche." Darwinism has meant many things to many men. One meaning — namely, adaptation to the environment — leaves open for the psychologist large questions as to the kinds of pressures which different kinds of environments place upon the development of the human species, and to the kinds of hereditary and early-growth processes which are responsible for man in society as we have known him.

After his first rough formulation of the theory, Darwin set for himself the task of collecting data on a scale large enough to permit the verification or refutation of the hypothesis, keeping a careful record of cases which seemed to count against his own view. By 1858 he had a large amount of material. In the meantime, he had achieved through a variety of publications general recognition as a naturalist. He was nearly ready to publish the book which was to advance his theory. In that year he received a letter and a manuscript from a young Englishman in the East Indies, Alfred Russel Wallace. Through an extraordinary coincidence, Wallace, while pondering Malthus's essay, had formulated a doctrine much like Darwin's. During an illness he had worked out in a few hours the main outlines of a very similar evolutionary theory. In sending his manuscript to Darwin he asked for his opinion as to its merit and whether he would help him to get it published. Darwin was in a difficult position; he must be fair to the man who had prepared a statement of the theory before his own appeared, yet Wallace's manuscript contained no such mass of data as Darwin had collected. So he submitted Wallace's work and an abstract of his own theory to Lyell. The latter decided that both must be submitted to the Linnean Society. Some portions of Darwin's forthcoming book were read, together with Wallace's manuscript (1858). In 1859, Darwin's *Origin of Species* was published.

Evolutionary theories were not, we must remind ourselves, new, and even the hypothesis as to the mechanism of evolution had been anticipated. The chief significance of the book lay in the mass of relevant data presented to show the reality of the transmutation of species and the compelling force with which they commanded serious attention. A general storm was precipitated and some of the most violent battles in intellectual history took place. Spencer had prepared the intelligentsia for such doctrine: Huxley was one of the greatest of those who took Darwin's side; Haeckel saw the whole world-view inevitably involved in the theory. Though much of the resistance to the theory was on religious grounds (because of its rejection of the principle of special creation), there was at first considerable acrimony even among scientists. Many were not ready to capitulate at once. Agassiz, probably the most eminent biologist in the United States, died without accepting the evidence. By the decade of the eighties, however, the last actual opposition to the theory of evolution as such disappeared among biologists.

Darwin had noticed already in the South Sea islands that certain species showed differentiation even on the same island; the struggle for existence had selected one type of individual for the shore, another for the interior. One species migrating into an environment that offers two mutually exclusive adaptive opportunities, might become, in time, two species. What caused the chance variations which were selected by the environment, Darwin did not profess to know. Nor did he offer a satisfactory explanation for the mechanisms of inheritance that would be congruent with both the observed chance variations in species and the inherited retention of variations in the selected progeny. In fact, the notion that hereditary differences blend on crossing, as Darwin assumed, was justly and powerfully criticized by Fleeming Jenkin,[1] a professor of engineering at Edinburgh University. If the chance variations blend at crossing, he argued, then any new variation would diminish in importance from generation to generation and could not last long enough to be subject to natural selection. Darwin mistakenly regarded this criticism as relevant to the idea of natural selection — rather than to the popular notion of blending inheritance — and gradually shifted horses back to the Lamarckian view of the inheritance of acquired characteristics. In fact, when Darwin discussed the evolution of the moral nature of man in *The Descent of Man* (1871), he resorted to the argument that various social instincts evolved as a result of "natural selection aided by inherited habits." Further discussions of natural selection versus inherited habit are so thoroughly confused that the reader can take his choice (see Darlington, 1959). Mendel's pertinent hard evidence, which demonstrated that hereditary differences do not blend but remain separate in crossing, was comfortably tucked away on the shelves of some obscure library. The evidence was at hand but the time was not ripe yet for understanding its significance.

In 1865, at the February and March meetings of the Natural History Society at Brünn, Austria, Gregor Johann Mendel read a paper which could have solved Darwin's problems. A year later the paper was published (1866) but did not attract attention until long after Darwin and Mendel were gone from the scene. Mendel studied the mechanisms of heredity by crossing various strains of peas. When, for example, he used pollen from a dwarf strain of peas and fertilized the flowers of a true breeding tall line, the resulting seeds bore only tall plants. The hereditary influence of the tall line was "dominant." But when he crossed these tall hybrids with dwarf plants, he observed that about half of the progeny were tall and half were dwarf. From numerous observations of this type, Mendel was able to conclude that hereditary influences do not blend upon crossing but are related to separate particles present in pairs, one from each parent, which obey specific laws of segregation and independent assortment. Mendel's brilliant experimental procedure and his innovative mathematical approach to the problem rank among the highest accomplishments of human reason. His paper was rediscovered in 1900, thirty-four years after its original publication.

By the 1880s and 1890s it became clear, through the work of Weismann and De Vries, that changes which occur from generation to generation can be explained not by the influence of acquired changes occurring in the body, nor by blending inheritance, but by the shifting of elements in the germ cells

---

[1] See a detailed exposition of this criticism in Darlington (1959).

—that the germ cells preserve a continuity of their own and that they are rather remarkably free from environmental influences. De Vries and others pointed out that the germinal material might undergo sudden mutations and that new species arise as a result of the selection of such germinal changes. The mechanisms and biochemical coding and decoding of information required for the transmission of specific characteristics from one generation to another remained one of the major questions of science throughout the first part of our own century. The search for such mechanisms culminated recently in the successful identification of specific molecular structures (RNA and DNA) and their mode of interaction, opening an entirely new chapter on the influence of evolutionary thought upon the science of behavior, the psychopharmacological study of information coding and behavioral genetics.

Evolutionism and the Birth of Comparative Psychology

The influence of Darwinism upon psychology during the last quarter of the nineteenth century probably did as much as any single factor to shape the science as it exists today. Psychology was to become consistently more biological; even the description of mental processes tended to be more and more in terms of the underlying brain mechanisms the functions served and the tasks accomplished in adjusting to the environment. The comparative viewpoint, although present here and there in the seventeenth and eighteenth centuries, could come into its own only when evolutionism had become the groundwork of psychological thinking. As a natural consequence, interest in animal psychology rapidly increased. Many books appeared which concerned themselves with the nature of instinct and with the phylogenetic study of intelligence. Studies of animal behavior appeared in psychological journals. The great gulf established by Descartes between human and animal psychology had been bridged. Human psychology was to be seen in relation to all the phenomena of life.

Early Comparative Psychology

While it is the theory of evolution that built the final bridge between man and animals, animal psychology is certainly older than the theory of evolution. Many among the early philosophers, especially among the atomists and primitive evolutionists (Democritus, Heraclitus, and Empedocles) and the Epicureans (Lucretius and Plutarch), believed in some form of continuity between human and animal behavior. Aristotle's differentiation between the two attributes of soul (*anima intellectualis* and *anima sensitiva*), however, paved the way for the subsequent categorical separation of man and animal which culminated in Descartes's dualism. Descartes, we should remember, relegated the entire puzzling issue of distinction and interaction between body and soul to the mechanistic properties of animal and human reflex behavior and to the rational attributes of the soul. He sharply divided man and animal by ascribing the presence of soul to man only and viewed animal behavior as rigidly mechanistic, devoid of the flexibilities and rationality of human mind—a position that was to be retained for a long time in the characterization of instinct.

First among the post-Renaissance observers of animal behavior were Ray's collaborator, Willughby (1678), and Pernau (see Streseman, 1947). Both were field ornithologists who observed and classified bird species and came to interesting discoveries regarding their behavior. They knew the phenomena of territoriality and described how bird song is used for attracting a mate to a secure territory. The most outstanding among pre-Darwinian animal behaviorists, however, was Leroy (1802). A well-educated keeper of woods and forests at the court of Louis XV, he kept abreast of the great ideas of his time and knew the significance of the observations he made on the behavior of animals. We may justifiably refer to him as the first comparative psychologist; he was the first to state explicitly that the study of animal behavior should be helpful in the understanding of human behavior. He believed that animals solve problems in a way comparable to human beings and was critical of the Aristotelian dichotomy of animal automaton versus human soul. His arguments that we should have complete biography of all species and that animals should be studied in their natural habitat are refreshingly modern.

Another great step in the development of the science of animal behavior was made by La Mettrie (1748). He rejected the opinion that "animals are pure machines" as being mere "play of wit," or "philosophical pastime," and believed that there are very few differences between human and animal souls. Such differences, whenever they exist, should be attributed to the differences between human and animal brains, he argued. Signs of some understanding of adaptation can also be detected in the writings of La Mettrie when he related animal instincts to needs and capacities for dealing with dangers in the environment.

Buffon, on the basis of the then available evidence, found it necessary to attribute feelings and consciousness to animals. However, he denied the faculty of memory and felt that animals are incapable of comparing different impressions. About eighty years later, the brother of Georges Cuvier, Frederic Cuvier, advanced a view of instincts that could be readily integrated with Darwin's theory of evolution. According to Frederic Cuvier, instincts are unalterably fixed and therefore are useful for taxonomic purposes. Such behavior patterns, he argued, are inherited and cannot be modified by experience; they are to be distinguished from learned behavior which he believed to be also present in animals. While not the first to experiment with animal behavior, Frederic Cuvier (1842) did undertake an experiment which supported his position on the nature of instinct. He had raised a beaver from birth in complete isolation from species members. When given the opportunity, this animal responded to twigs in a manner characteristic of beavers. It peeled them and used them in erecting structures characteristic of experienced beavers. Here was the first isolation experiment and the first experimental proof that animals do develop species-typical behavior patterns that are not dependent on prior learning experiences. The step to current ethological theories and research is a small one indeed from these early speculations and observations by Frederic Cuvier.

Darwin himself, in *The Descent of Man* (1871), emphasized the essential similarities between human and animal behavior. His *Expression of the Emotions in Man and Animals* (1872) suggested an evolutionary interpretation of the characteristic facial and postural changes during strong emotions. The expression of an emotional response characteristic of a critical life situation involves the activation of many organs and tissues. Fear, for example, is evidenced in irregular breathing, a pounding heart, a drying throat, and a vast array of inner psychophysiological responses — which serve a very definite biological function to the animal engaged in attack, or defense, or stress of almost any kind.

There are, Darwin suggested, three basic principles relating to the expressive aspect of emotions: (1) some expressive movements are weakened or simplified forms of a response, taking the place of fully overt actions, as when snarling or baring the teeth takes the place of aggressive fighting; (2) the communicative signal values of expressive movements enable organisms to react properly in a given stimulus situation without direct experience with the relevant external stimuli, as when the little movements around the nose and mouth show that the situation is essentially "sweet" or "bitter" for the individual experiencing its impact; (3) there is an exchange of social messages in expressive movements, as when vigorous, erect posture and clenched fist betoken aggressiveness and stooped shoulders and dropped arms indicate diffidence or surrender. The adaptive need for a quick, vigorous physical expression and communication remains the key to the whole range of emotional expressions from animals to man. Thus *The Expression of the Emotions* is a clue to Darwin's whole psychology; the behavior of each individual living thing bears witness to a long adaptive history and to the present encounter with an adaptive challenge. The students of animal behavior in the latter part of the nineteenth century spent a great deal of time assimilating this essential and all-important feature introduced by Darwin into the study of behavior.

As we saw, evolutionary ideas did not originate with Darwin, nor did the pre-Darwinian conception of evolution die with the publication of *The Origin of Species*. Unilinear conceptions of evolution and the arguments for identifiable and predictable progressively higher stages and steps in evolutionary development, especially those raised by the cultural and social evolutionists to be discussed in the next section of this chapter, persisted and drew temporary support from Darwin's data and theory. It was difficult, and still is difficult, to reconcile the promise and new faith in progress with the Darwinian evolutionary process based on chance events.

Romanes was the first to follow Darwin's path in the field of animal behavior and to investigate evolutionary continuities between animal and human behavior. He is credited with the first book of comparative psychology, entitled *Animal Intelligence* (1883), but has been much criticized for heavy reliance on anecdotal accounts and for an "anthropomorphic" position. Romanes had indeed perceived and interpreted animal activities with eyes trained for human self-understanding. Nevertheless, his was an extremely important book. He had espoused the new theory of evolution without reservation and attempted a systematic study of the phenomena implied by it, but the magnitude of the task and lack of precedent forced him to rely on a mixed bag of anecdotal and descriptive data. It was only a matter of time, and a short time for that matter, before the fallacies of his approach became apparent and the need for experimentation in comparative psychology was understood.

The job of dissecting and disposing of the anecdotal method befell another great evolutionist and animal behaviorist of the time, C. Lloyd Morgan (1890–91). He is best known to students and historians of psychology for his popular "Law of Parsimony" (1894, Chap. 3), or "Lloyd Morgan's canon," which states: "In no case may we interpret an action as the outcome of the exercise of higher psychical faculty, if it can be interpreted as the outcome of the exercise of one which stands lower in the psychological scale" (Boring, 1950, p. 474). The view expressed in this statement has been generally applauded because it pointed to the fallacy in Romanes's method. It should be of greater concern to us, however, that this "law" is deeply rooted in a pre-Darwinian conception of emergent evolution. Morgan's view of a psychological scale of lower to higher faculties and their implicit unilinear evolutionary progression remains a remarkable, though questionable, principle to our day.

Morgan relied on data he had collected personally, but his method was primarily descriptive and retained a subjective flavor. It was Loeb (1890, 1908) who first fully applied the experimental method in the comparative study of animal behavior. The approach in his work on tropisms was experimental and mechanistic. So were the experimental-descriptive procedures of Fabre (1879–1907), Forel (1891, 1908), and Bethe (1898), who studied the behavior of insects. These studies represent the continuity from the pre-Darwinian mechanistic views to post-Darwinian comparative psychology. But there were also other conceptions of an entirely different sort. Lubbock (1882) viewed the high order of insect "civilization" as indicative of a rudimentary kind of "mind." Hobhouse (1901) tackled the very difficult issue of "mind in evolution." The mechanistic experimental approach in the investigation of the fixed behavior patterns and the views of continuity of the mind throughout all living things set the stage for the next significant phase in the development of comparative psychology, which we will return to in the chapters dealing with the work of Thorndike, Pavlov, McDougall, Watson, Yerkes, Lashley, and other great contributors to modern comparative psychology.

Evolution and Human Behavior: Galton

Francis Galton was the first who attempted in a thoroughgoing way to apply the principles of variation, selection, and adaptation to the study of human individuals and races. He published in 1869, a decade after the publication of *The Origin of Species,* a book entitled *Hereditary Genius,* the aim of which was to show that individual greatness follows certain family lines with a frequency and a clarity that belie any explanation in terms of environment. These studies were, for the most part, investigations into family trees of eminent jurists, scientists, authors, and so on. He collected data to show that in each case these men not only inherited genius, as shown by a long line of persons before them, but that they inherited *specific* forms of genius. A great jurist comes from a family which has attained not only eminence, but eminence in the law. The theory presupposed that there have been, at some time in the past, variations within the human stock and that these variations have been able to survive. Galton believed that the Darwinian principle of accidental variation about the average or norm of the group applied as much to the general and specific gifts of man as to the length of a bird's wings or the length of a polar bear's hair and that these variations tended to persist.

Such *individual differences* had not been seriously treated before as part of the subject matter of psychology. Perhaps their neglect had been the most extraordinary blind spot in previous formal psychology. It was Darwinism, rather than the previous history of psychology, which brought about an interest in the problem. A few of the fragmentary studies of the subject in the nineteenth century, before Galton, may be noted. Thomas Brown had included, in his secondary laws of association, the factor of constitutional differences in persons. Herbart, about the same time, had written of differences in association accompanying various degrees of intelligence. Among experimentalists, Weber, Fechner, and Helmholtz had found individual differences but had not studied them systematically. Galton was the first important figure to explore the field.

Galton undertook also to compare the various human races with respect to their hereditary make-up and to show that the different races have been evolved because of their adaptation to their particular environment (1883). Darwin had pointed out instances in which the skin, the proportions of the limbs, and the like, are adapted to the mode of life of given races in a particular climate (1871). Galton held that not only do variations occur from one individual to another, but there may be widespread variation and selection, so that new races are evolved.

So profoundly challenging and stimulating an idea was bound to lead to exaggerations. Galton's faith in the all-importance of heredity could scarcely be better indicated than in the following two passages. After reference to anthropometric studies on the "criminal type," he proceeds to these generalizations:

> The deficiency of conscience in criminals, as shown by the absence of genuine remorse for their guilt, astonishes all who first become familiar with the details of prison life. Scenes of heart-rending despair are hardly ever witnessed among prisoners; their sleep is broken by no uneasy dreams ("Criminals and the Insane," 1883).

Galton assumed that all this was biologically conditioned; individuals are born not only to peculiarities of skull or feature, not only to genius or imbecility, but to intrinsic criminalism. This is perhaps the most extreme case of neglect of the *environmental* factors which we have to consider in all our studies so far, just as associationism in general represents the most extreme neglect of the hereditary factors. The second passage indicates an even more picturesque application (and abuse) of Darwinian principles:

> I may take this opportunity of remarking on the well-known hereditary character of colour blindness in connection with the fact that it is nearly twice as prevalent among the Quakers as among the rest of the community, the proportions being as 5.9 to 3.5 percent. We might have expected an even larger ratio. Nearly every Quaker is descended on both sides solely from members of a group of men and women who segregated themselves from the rest of the world five or six generations ago; one of their strongest opinions being that the fine arts were worldly snares, and their most conspicuous practice being to dress in drabs. A born artist could never have consented to separate himself from his fellows on such grounds; he would have felt the profession of those opinions and their accompanying practices to be a treason to his aesthetic nature. Consequently few of the original stock of Quakers are likely to have had the temperament that is associated with a love for colour, and it is in consequence most reasonable to believe that a larger proportion of colour-blind men would have been found among them than among the rest of the population ("Unconsciousness of Peculiarities," 1883).

After establishing in *Hereditary Genius* the pedigree method of studying mental endowment (a method quickly turned to account in the study of mental deficiency, beginning with Dugdale's *The Jukes,* 1877), Galton turned to the construction of more refined quantitative methods in prosecution of the same problem. In his *Inquiries into Human Faculty and Its Development* (1883) he outlined the procedure and results of two epoch-making studies. The first was his experiment on free association, the essentials of which he had already outlined (1879–80). Associationism had lived its whole life without any recourse to experimental procedure. Galton undertook to study quantitatively the appearance of various types of association.

He prepared a list of seventy-five words, each word on a slip of paper which he placed underneath a book. He looked at them one at a time, using a spring chronometer to measure the time it took to form two associations with the word thus drawn. The associations might come spontaneously and immediately, or only after a pause. Many of the associations were themselves single words, but there were many cases in which there came to mind not a word but a mental picture, an image; and this image had to be described. Either a word or an image satisfied Galton's definition of an "association," but all were reduced to verbal form. These associations were analyzed with reference to their probable origin in his experience; in particular, with reference to the time when the given association seemed to have been first established. One of the most definite of his discoveries related to the great frequency of associations from early boyhood and adolescence. An example of a boyhood association was the appearance of images recalling the scene of a laboratory where he had been allowed to dabble in chemistry. This was one of the earliest attempts to show the significance of very early life, particularly childhood, for adult personality and to demonstrate the amount of childish material that remains. But of greater importance was the whole fresh conception of an experimental study of association. Galton's association experiment was quickly adopted with greatly improved technique by Wundt, who had just founded his laboratory in Leipzig.

A second and equally significant contribution was the publication (also in the *Inquiries into Human Faculty*) of an extensive study of "mental imagery." [2] It was carried on by questionnaire rather than by experiment; it was, in fact, the first extensive psychological use of the questionnaire. Galton put before his subjects the task:

> Before addressing yourself to any of the questions on the opposite page, think of some definite object—suppose it is your breakfast-table as you sat down to it this morning—and consider carefully the picture that rises before your mind's eye. (1) *Illumination.*—Is the image dim or fairly clear? Is its brightness comparable to that of the actual scene? (2) *Definition.*—Are all the objects pretty well defined at the same time, or is the place of sharpest definition at any one moment more contracted than it is in a real scene? (3) *Colouring.*—Are the colours of the china, of the toast, bread-crust, mustard, meat, parsley, or whatever may have been on the table, quite distinct and natural?

One of the most noteworthy things about this study was its use of quantitative method. Images were arranged in serial order from 0 to 100, according to their intensity or likeness to sensation. Galton found evidence that some individuals have no imagery whatever within certain fields. Even some well-known painters reported little or no visual imagery. There were, however, some individuals for whom it was a common experience to have images

---

[2] The imagery of several individuals had been reported by Fechner (1860, Vol. 2, pp. 469 ff.).

nearly as intense as full-fledged hallucinations (Society for Psychical Research, 1894). The study of imagery lent itself, as the association experiment had done, to refinement as an experimental problem; before the close of the century the investigation of imagery became a standard problem in German and American laboratories. Imagery proved to be one of the richest fields for the study of individual differences. And the attempt to get statistical control of data that could not be measured by the yardstick was highly significant for psychology. Galton's chief interest in the problem of imagery, as in most other problems, lay in the attempt to establish hereditary resemblances; he showed, for example, that similarity between children of the same parent was greater than similarity between individuals taken at random.

Here, as elsewhere, the exclusion of the influence of differences in environment proved to be no easy matter. There was no way of excluding the influence of tradition in the family. Such environmental factors might cause resemblances even in such traits as imagery. Partially meeting the difficulty, Galton centered his attention upon the immensely significant fact of *twin resemblance* in the problem of heredity.[3] Though very little of the mechanism of heredity was then understood, Galton knew that twins inherit more in common than other individuals. He collected, indeed, some remarkable anecdotes about twins who were susceptible to the same diseases, or who, though separated for months, died on the same day.

He conceived the problem of "nature and nurture" as a practical social problem, and the eugenics movement was his personal achievement. Eugenics, as Galton formulated it, aimed not merely at the elimination of the unfit, but at the general and systematic improvement of the race through the study and use of biological laws. Spencer had discussed the future of humanity in social and moral terms, taking practically no account of biological factors. Darwin had made it clear that evolution involved not merely changes in species, but actual elimination of some stocks and increase in others. Galton asked whether it might not be possible to establish a new biological foundation upon which a more adequate social organization could be constructed. This eugenics program is still of small importance as far as its social accomplishment is concerned. But it has been significant in making thoughtful mankind more aware of the biological risks involved in the large-scale reproduction of handicapped persons, which may be accompanied by the relatively small-scale reproduction of gifted persons — trends calling for research worthy of the magnitude of the problem. In Galton's time, and indeed for the half century thereafter, it was often assumed that those favored in the dominant societies of the period were necessarily, intrinsically, and by heredity "superior" to other classes and races. For the past several decades research and opinion have challenged this belief in the superiority of

---

[3] Thorndike, Gesell, Newman, Gardner, and many others have realized Galton's ambition: to put the intellectual resemblance of twins into quantitative terms.

one large group over another but have tended to reinforce the belief in the enormous importance of *individual* variations within each human stock.

In all this work, as we have seen in several instances, Galton was thinking quantitatively; and one step of the greatest importance to psychology was his immense contribution to the science of statistics. Statistics may perhaps be said to have come into existence in the seventeenth century in connection with the tabulation of births, marriages, and deaths and to have been greatly advanced by the discoveries by Laplace, Gauss, and others of methods of ascertaining the likelihood of errors of various magnitudes. Nineteenth-century science, in pursuit of causal relations between variables, had had to make much use of the theory of probability, wherever causal relations of a one-to-one type were not apparent. There existed, however, no standard procedure for stating the degree to which two variables were related. The first step in the creation of such an instrument, "the coefficient of correlation," was the work of Galton.

Suppose he wished to find the relation between height and weight. The relation was, of course, not one of perfect correspondence; there were *some* men five feet eight inches tall who were heavier than *some* who were five feet nine. Yet he could predict, with small risk of error, that the average weight of a hundred men of the first group would be less than that of a hundred men of the second. Seeking to get the relation of such variables as height and weight into quantitative terms, he devised a primitive correlation method of measuring concomitant variations. He laid off the familiar x and y axes perpendicular to one another (as in analytical geometry) and marked off units upon both of these axes. Let us consider first an ideal case, a case of perfect correspondence between the two variables: if the units of measurement for the two variables are comparable, the recorded data when entered on our graph will give us a straight line at an angle of $45°$ from the x axis. If we find an increase in height, but no increase in weight, we record the addition of a number of units on the x axis and no units at all on the y axis; there is no correlation. Intermediate between those situations are those in which the observed amounts of x and y tend to vary together but not in a one-to-one fashion.

But the treatment of variables like height and weight is actually rather complicated. Among a hundred men there may be, for example, *several* men of the same height but of *differing* weights, and though greater height would in general mean greater weight, there would be many individuals below average weight but above average height. These exceptions to the general tendency would "lower the correlation." How was the relation to be precisely measured? Pearson, Galton's pupil, saw the application of Gauss's "theory of least squares" to this problem. He saw that in measuring a correlation we may take the products of the x and y deviations and add these products algebraically. Tending toward a positive or plus correlation is a man above average in both weight and height; tending toward a negative or minus correlation is a man above average in one and below average in the other. Pearson's formula, worked out in the last decade of the century, superseded Galton's graphic method and made possible the statement of correlations on a scale from -1 through 0 to $+1$. It permitted a quantitative statement of the degree of dependence between any two measurable variables, or, of course, of their dependence upon some other factor or factors.[4]

Evolutionism in the Social Sciences

Evolutionism profoundly affected also the sister sciences of anthropology, sociology, and economics in many ways, tending in general to bring their subject matter closer to the interests of the psychologists. In the social sciences, as in the physical and biological sciences, the idea of evolution was already familiar; it had been a current method of approach to the phenomena of social life long before Darwin. But Darwinism gave it a force, a rational basis, a mass of empirical data, and hence a prestige which it could not otherwise have attained.

Evolutionary thinking, to use the term very broadly, appears in the work of the German travelers Bastian and Ratzel. Ratzel's volumes, published early in the latter half of the century, described human customs as ways of adjusting to various environments. This work was followed by the world-wide assemblage of data, through many scattered collaborators, by Spencer (1873–85). His work, however, was hardly inductive; he was concerned rather to find support for a scheme of evolution through which he believed human institutions must pass. Spencer held that social institutions pass through a definite series of *stages;* fundamental laws of development conceived in terms of his general philosophical principle were supposed to lie behind changes in economic and social structure. This was the first clear evolutionary approach to anthropological data.

Lewis Henry Morgan (1877) put forth a related theory in which he argued that cultures evolve through progressive stages from barbarism to improved levels of civilization. This theory found particularly warm welcome from Marx and his followers, who took a similar position from a dialectical-materialistic point of view.

The work of Tylor expressed a somewhat less extreme evolutionism (1871). Tylor's central problem, and that which stands out as his greatest contribution, is connected with the doctrine that religion has evolved from certain attributes of primitive mentality. His theory of *animism* held that primitive man universally thinks of the world as a host of animated beings. The forces of nature, and all things perceived, are friendly or inimical to man; they are quasipersonal, animate, or "besouled." No difference is made between a man, a flower, a stone, and a star as far as their animate nature is

---

[4] It does not prove causal relationship, but it does measure the "concomitant variation" which must appear (though perhaps masked) if causal relationship exists.

concerned. If a man trips on a stone, giving himself an ugly fall, the stone is malevolent. Or if his fishing net brings a large catch, this must be due to the favor of some natural deity; he seizes upon the most obvious thing, perhaps the lake, to worship. Moreover, for primitive man human and animal souls are something separate from the body. Like wine which can be poured into or out of a bottle, the soul in dreams seems to him to pass into or out of the body. This animism was shown to be general among primitive people and to be important in their thinking. This was indeed an epoch-making contribution to psychological anthropology; religion and magic were given a simple and universal psychological interpretation. This doctrine of Tylor was accompanied by an emphasis upon a theory of cultural development known as "parallelism," which asserted that wherever cultures are at the same level of advancement, the same customs may arise independently among different groups. Wherever the environments of two tribes or peoples are similar, the peoples tend to develop the same adaptations.

Toward the close of the century a large amount of data came to hand whose effect was to undermine this more naïve evolutionary point of view. In particular, there was evidence to show that many of these cases of "parallelism" were due not to independent adaptation of different groups to similar environments, but to borrowing or "diffusion" between tribes.[5] The possibility of diffusion necessitated a more critical and inductive approach to each alleged instance. Another factor equally important in forcing a revision of anthropological evolutionism was the discovery that no definite series of stages through which societies pass can be found; the stages are different for different societies. The use of evolutionary conceptions had its value; its very weaknesses helped make clear the necessity of taking account of the extraordinary variety of cultural changes and helped make clear to anthropologists the direction in which their discipline must move if it were to become an inductive science. In our time, the cultural evolutionary point of view has been carried to new levels of sophistication, especially in the work of White (1949) and his followers.

Much of the same kind of development was going on in sociology. One of the first great figures was Auguste Comte. During the second quarter of the nineteenth century he became known for a simple but definite evolutionary theory associated with a philosophy to which he gave the name of *positivism* (1830–42). His viewpoint was, in part, a reaction against the "idealism" of French philosophers, a demand for empirical methods, for objectivity and definiteness. Comte became a colossal influence in social theory, chiefly through the efforts of John Stuart Mill. Comte's evolutionism can be summarized in a few words. There are three stages in human evolution: the theological, the metaphysical, and the positive. Social reconstruction is to be effected through the emancipation of mankind from metaphysics

[5] Moreover, many supposed cases of parallelism turned out on closer examination to involve only superficial resemblances.

in favor of the habit of direct appeal to experience. Terse as the doctrine was, it was important for social theory, allying itself easily with other forms of evolutionism and helping greatly to substitute dynamic for static conceptions of society. Comte also inveighed against introspective methods very much in the spirit of modern behaviorism; if he had offered a program of research, he might fairly be called the first behaviorist.

Another great social evolutionist was Karl Marx, a radical critic of the contemporary political economy. The *Communist Manifesto* (1848), in collaboration with Engels, and *Capital* (1867) were steps in the enunciation of the "economic interpretation of history," the view that social changes result primarily from the operation of economic laws, the development of new industrial arts, and the struggle of economic classes. Marx was one among many who gave expression before Darwin to what we may call "economic evolutionism." His importance for psychology, slight at the time, became great after the Russian Revolution.

The theory of evolution was also conspicuous in linguistic science. Max Müller stood out as one of the greatest products of the university system which, as we have seen, was the cradle of philological science in the late eighteenth and early nineteenth centuries. As an instance of German philological work in the nineteenth century may be mentioned Müller's study of the gradual differentiation of the Indo-European languages. Closely allied to such philological work was the study of the religion of early Aryan peoples and the stages in its development as exemplified in mythology and sacred writings.

Another social science, which concerns us more closely, is the "folk psychology" of Steinthal and Lazarus. In a journal appearing in 1860, they published much material relating to the folklore, customs, and religion of many peoples. Their work presupposed the existence of differences in the fundamental psychology of races, by virtue of which, for example, a Norwegian looks at things differently from an Italian or an American Indian. The elements which form the aggregate of what members of a race have in common psychologically they regarded as a social mind. They espoused, in fact, the theory of a "social mind" distinct from that of individuals in the social groups. They were concerned also with the problem of transition from one to another type of social mind, and the material they gathered contributed to the vast stream of evolutionary thinking. Their work was important also as background for the "folk psychology" and "social psychology" of the late nineteenth century, to be considered later.

In all, we may conclude that evolutionism was deeply rooted in the various understandings and approaches of nineteenth-century social science. Much of it, however, was pre-Darwinian evolutionism. Social scientists led the way in disseminating the idea of social change and progress. There was a feeling of certainty that man's lot could be improved by man in the here and now. New laws of progress were devised with the same fervor and same teleological certainty that had been accorded earlier to the ideas of special creation. But the postulates of Darwinian evolution, and the lessons of the historical development of evolutionary theory, were not thoroughly understood. The amalgam of new evolutionary ideas did not always take into account the continuous and intricate multidimensionality in the natural selection of random variations and, most importantly, the ways of science and scientific understanding of nature (including the understanding of human nature and social change), which evolve through the matching of ideas with facts — that ideas themselves are subject to gradual evolution.

REFERENCES

Bethe, A. "Dürfen wir den Ameisen und Bienen psychische Qualitäten zuschreiben?" *Archiv für die gesamte Physiologie,* 70 (1898), 15–100.

Buffon, G.-L.-L. de. *Histoire naturelle.* 44 vols. Paris: Imprimerie Royal, 1749–1804.

Comte, A. *Cours de philosophie positive* [*System of Positive Polity*]. 6 vols. Paris: Bachelier, 1830–42.

Cuvier, F.-G. *Recherches experimentales sur les propriétés et les fonctions du système nerveux.* Paris, 1842.

Cuvier, G. *Le Règne animale.* 20 vols. Paris: Fortin, Masson, 1769–1832.

Darlington, C. D. "The Origin of Darwinism." *Scientific American,* 200 (1959), 60–66.

Darwin, C. *The Origin of Species.* London: Murray, 1859.

———. *The Descent of Man.* 2 vols. London: Murray, 1871.

———. *The Expression of the Emotions in Man and Animals.* London: Murray, 1872.

Darwin, E. *Zoonomia or the Laws of Organic Life.* 2 vols. London: Johnson, 1794–96.

Dugdale, R. L. *The Jukes.* New York: Putnam, 1877.

Fabre, J.-H. *Souvenirs entomologiques.* Paris: Delagrave, 1879–1907.

Fechner, G. T. *Elemente der Psychophysik* [*Elements of Psychophysics*]. Leipzig: Breitkopf and Härtel, 1860.

Forel, A. . . . *Les Formicides.* Paris: Imprimerie Royal, 1891.

———. *The Senses of Insects.* Translated by P. M. Yearsley. London: Methuen, 1908.

Galton, F. *Hereditary Genius.* London: Macmillan, 1869.

———. "Psychometric Experiments." *Brain,* 2 (1879–80), 149–62.

———. *Inquiries into Human Faculty and Its Development.* London: Macmillan, 1883.

Hobhouse, L. T. *Mind in Evolution.* London: Macmillan, 1901.

Lamarck, J.-B. *Philosophie zoologique* [*Zoological Philosophy*]. 2 vols. Paris: Baillière, 1809.

La Mettrie, J.-O. de. *L'Homme machine* [*Man as Machine*]. Leyden: Luzac, 1748.

Leroy, C. G. *Lectures philosophiques sur l'intelligence et la perfectibilité des animaux.* Paris: 1802. London: Chapman and Hall, 1870.

Linnaeus, C. *Systema naturae.* Lugduni Batavorum, apud Theodore Haak, 1735.

Loeb, J. *Der Heliotropismus der Thiere und seine Ueberstimmung mit dem Heliotropismus der Pflanzen.* Würzburg: Hertz, 1890.

———. *Forced Movements, Tropisms and Animal Conduct.* Philadelphia: Lippincott, 1908.

Lubbock, J. *Ants, Bees, and Wasps.* New York: Appleton, 1882.

Lyell, C. *Elements of Geology.* Philadelphia: McKay, 1839.

Malthus, T. R. *An Essay on the Principle of Population.* London: Johnson, 1798.

Marx, K. *Das Kapital* [*Capital*]. 3 vols. Hamburg: Meissner, 1867.

Marx, K., and Engels, F. *Das Kommunistische Manifest* [*Communist Manifesto*]. London: Communist League, 1848.

Mendel, G. J. "Versuche über Pflanzenhybriden." *Verhandlungen des Naturforschenden Vereins Brünn,* 4 (1866), 3–47.

Morgan, C. L. *Animal Life and Intelligence.* London: Arnold, 1890–91.

———. *An Introduction to Comparative Psychology.* London: Scott, 1894.

Morgan, L. H. *Ancient Society.* New York: Holt, 1877.

Ray, J. *The Wisdom of God Manifested in the Work of Creation.* 2nd ed. London: Smith, 1692.

Romanes, G. J. *Animal Intelligence.* New York: Appleton, 1883.

Society for Psychical Research. "Census of Hallucinations." *Proceedings of the Society for Psychical Research,* 10 (1894).

Spencer, H. *The Principles of Sociology.* 8 vols. London: Williams and Norgate, 1873–85.

Steinthal, H., and Lazarus, M. *Zeitschrift für Völkerpsychologie und Sprachwissenschaft,* 1–30 (1860–90).

Streseman, E. "Baron von Pernau, Pioneer Student of Bird Behavior." *Auk,* 64 (1947), 35–37.

Tylor, E. B. *Primitive Culture.* London: Murray, 1871.

Wallace, A. R., and Darwin, C. *Linnean Society Journal* (1858). (Joint essay read July 1, 1858.)

White, L. A. *The Science of Culture.* New York: Farrar, Straus, and Young, 1949.

Willughby, F. "The Ornithology of Francis Willughby." *Wherein All the Birds Hitherto Known Are Accurately Described.* J. Ray, ed. London: Martyn, 1678.

NOTE: A list of further readings appears at the back of the book.

10

Psychiatry from Pinel and Mesmer to Charcot

Canst thou not minister to a mind diseased?
SHAKESPEARE

The story of psychiatry belongs primarily to the history of medicine rather than to the history of psychology; but both disciplines reflect common origins in the intellectual development of western Europe and in the tumultuous rise of the modern research spirit. The unavoidable inertia of medicine, an applied profession as old as man's first perception of "illness," and the relative lack of concern with application in the experimental and theoretical innovations of the new psychology entailed huge gaps at the outset which have not been entirely bridged to this day.

The descriptions and classifications of the forms of mental disease had been rich during the eighteenth and nineteenth centuries. Despite the fact that clinical observations pointed more and more clearly to the role of the brain in psychopathology, no great discoveries pointed specifically to the role of anatomical or biochemical factors in mental disorders. The mentally afflicted were thrust into jails and almshouses, or wandered about as curiosities or object lessons, for a public who would as soon see a "madman" in the stocks as a thief. The instruments of constraint and punishment (by the lash, by chains, by incarceration in small boxes, and so on) would startle us were it not for the fact that instruments of the same sort, in use only a few decades ago, are still to be shown in our psychiatric museums. The insane and the defective were not often regarded as medical problems. They belonged to no one, except perhaps to the moralist, the buffoon, or a sadistic keeper at "Bedlam," the Bethlehem Royal Hospital in London.

With this background, the more astonishing appears the merciful note, the humanitarian note. Some of the great teachers in France, Britain, and the United States tried to find naturalistic approaches — ways of conceiving what it might mean to be insane, or epileptic, or frantically disturbed. By the time of the French Revolution, the humanitarians had prepared the soil. It is not accidental that immediately upon the outbreak of the French Revolution a widespread change in attitude — toward fundamental human nature in the quest for naturalistic causes — began rapidly to spread. At the same time the great Pinel struck off the chains of the insane at the Bicêtre, he developed a mode of classification of the physical causes of mental disease. Sweeping aside the remnants of demonological psychiatry — the belief that demons caused mental disorder — he looked for naturalistic sources and modes of operation of physical causes. His successor, Esquirol, refined this classification. At the same time we find, to our surprise, that what we would call today *psychological* interpretations of mental disease (Burton, 1621; Moreau de Tours, 1840) were being made and that a psychiatry was coming into existence which tried to describe the psychology of various types of disorders.

During the time of Esquirol's dominance in France, German psychiatry began to appreciate the significance of the work done, and there arose during the second quarter of the century a number of German physicians who contributed to the work on classification. Chief among them was Griesinger, whose work was elaborate and detailed. He conceived of mental disease in the definite terms of physical pathology. Throughout the remainder of the century emphasis alternated between somatic factors and psychic factors. The importance of the somatic conception lay not only in pointing to the etiology of some of the "organic psychoses," but also in awakening physicians to the fact that insanity was *their* problem. In the generation which followed, new systems of classification were legion. (Of course the classifications took account for the most part of gross symptoms rather than of etiology.) We find, for example, good descriptions of the condition known as mania: the patient is excited and agitated, talks incoherently, and is frequently elated. Such problems as the average duration of such conditions, the existence of intellectual disorder remaining after recovery from the attack, and the like, were very inadequately treated. Griesinger's work was followed by more and more subdividing of clinical types. Among his followers, the subdivision of clinical types into subheads bearing new names went so far that some classifications listed as many as three hundred mental disorders. In the third quarter of the century the pendulum began to swing back. By the end of the century psychiatry was tending, under Kraepelin's influence, to settle down to the recognition of about twenty main types of psychosis. Remarkably enough, there was throughout the nineteenth century very little recognition among physicians that normal psychology had anything to offer and very little recognition among psychologists that mental disorder could teach them anything.

This is more astonishing when considered in the light of the fact that many of the philosophers who devoted themselves to psychological problems held medical degrees (this was true in Germany, France, and Britain) and that some of the ablest systematic thinking about mind and body was couched in terms of "medical psychology" as represented, for example, by Lotze (1852), Ribot (1883), and Maudsley (1884). The inertia of medicine could not as yet be influenced by these new efforts at a systematic psychology, nor could the efforts of systematic psychology be very much concerned with psychopathology or with medical problems of any sort—except insofar as the life sciences themselves, independent of their applications, could be regarded as fundamental to psychological effort. We have thus in the work of Helmholtz a constant preoccupation with problems of physics and of physiology, but not a medical approach; and in Lotze, despite his medical degree, a preoccupation with life science as science, but not with medicine as one of its applications. Nevertheless, many mental diseases gradually became recognized as physical entities. For example, by the middle of the century many of the gross pathological changes in the nervous system in dementia paralytica (general paresis) were definitely known from post-mortem examinations. In this field, as in that of classification, German work overtook the French.

The movement for humane treatment of the insane was paralleled by progress in neurology. This was of extraordinary importance for psychiatry, because the increased knowledge in neurology provided the chief justification for taking the insane from the hands of jailers and almshouse-keepers and giving them into the care of physicians. Before the middle of the nineteenth century, institutions for the insane were few and far between. Private institutions were pitifully inadequate, and society was not sufficiently interested to support public institutions. Public conscience recognizing the obligation of society to care for the insane was created first in the United States, and then in almost all of the countries that had been touched by the Industrial Revolution. It was chiefly the work of one person: Dorothea Dix.

A woman subject to long illnesses and interruptions, but of extraordinary personal gifts, Dorothea Dix became interested about 1840 in the condition of prisoners and made visits to the prisons and jails of her own state, Massachusetts. The conditions prevailing were unspeakable, one of the worst abuses being the incarceration of many insane and feeble-minded together with criminals of "normal" make-up. From this beginning her work extended into two fields, one the reform of institutions for criminals, the other the creation of public institutions for the insane. Her method was the arousal of public conscience and the persuasion of legislative bodies. Massachusetts, as a result of her efforts, appropriated funds for an institution for the insane; nearby states quickly followed. Miss Dix traveled down the Atlantic coast and into the southern states, sweeping everything before her; legislature after legislature capitulated. Within thirty years twenty states had established such institutions. Always in delicate health and realizing the necessity of avoiding a breakdown, she went to England. But finding that there were no public institutions for the insane in Scotland, she proceeded to get an Act of Parliament to provide for them. "She extended her work into the Channel Islands, and then to France, Italy, Austria, Greece, Turkey, Russia, Sweden, Norway, Denmark, Holland, Belgium, and a part of Germany. Her influence over Arinori Mori, the Japanese *chargé d'affaires* at Washington, led eventually to the establishment of two asylums for the insane in Japan" (*Encylopaedia Britannica,* p. 346). There are few cases in history where a social movement of such proportions can be attributed to the work of a single individual.[1]

Mental Deficiency

In 1798 a group of French sportsmen found in Aveyron a boy about ten years old who could not talk and who appeared to be living "wild" without human contacts. (Many such "feral" — animal-like — children are known to history.) He was taken to Paris and turned over to Itard, an expert in the methods of training the deaf (1894). Itard was under the influence of associationist psychology, whose principle, it will be recalled, was that experience is the basis of all mental capacity and that from experience is to be explained all mental growth. Adult intelligence is built up through the accumulation of sensory experiences. Itard saw the opportunity to put the theory to the test. Here was a boy who obviously had very little intelligence, very few ideas. Perhaps if he were given more ideas his intelligence would be raised. Itard set to work and for five years labored to make a social being out of this pathetic foundling. He did not succeed and reported sadly to the Academy that the boy was practically untrainable. The great Pinel had foreseen this outcome, predicting that Itard would be successful only if the boy were free from intrinsic mental defect. But the Academy refused to regard Itard's work as a failure; they were much impressed with the definite progress which he had made in helping the boy to form a number of useful habits. Itard continued to interest himself in the problem of the subnormal, until there came under his influence a young man, Seguin, who was destined to be the greatest figure in the century in the training of mental defectives. During the thirties Seguin became known for his own achievements. His emphasis was chiefly upon what he called a "physiological method," the development of the sensory and motor functions. The child was to be educated first through stimulation by bright colors, insistent sounds, and the like. He was to be trained in motor control by being made to walk along lines, upon ladders, and so on. Seguin realized that there was no hope of bringing the feeble-minded to normal intelligence; the aim must be to develop what capacities they had. In 1842 he became the head

[1] Her many other extraordinary achievements — prison reform, cooperation with Howe in the work for defectives, service as Chief Nurse of the Union Armies, 1861–65 — are described in Tiffany's *Life of Dorothea Lynde Dix* (1890).

of an institution which had been established in Paris in 1828 for the training of the feeble-minded, but unfortunately he soon got into administrative difficulties and had to give up his position.

It so happened, however, that there was a large opportunity for his work elsewhere. Dr. Samuel Howe, of the Perkins Institution for the Blind in Boston, had found that blind children suffering from mental defect could not be trained by the same methods as blind children of normal intelligence. He recognized that Seguin would be a suitable person to bring to the United States to give instruction in methods of training the feeble-minded. Seguin accepted the call and for two decades contributed abundantly both to the improvement of methods and to the movement for the establishment of institutions for mental defectives. Then, with the assistance of Miss Dix and other philanthropists, Howe succeeded in 1848 in getting an appropriation for the training of a few feeble-minded children. Institutions for the feeble-minded spread rapidly through the United States.

Following the lead of the French, a similar movement was spreading in Europe. Switzerland is of particular interest in this connection because of the prevalence along its southern frontier of the special type of mental deficiency known as cretinism. Napoleon had tried unsuccessfully to extirpate the condition (arising from thyroid defect) by the transplanting of families. The serious problem of cretinism called forth the devoted efforts of a young physician, Guggenbühl, who undertook in 1842 the systematic study and instruction of these defectives, in a colony of buildings high up in the mountains. Cretinism is not found above a certain altitude. This was the beginning of the now widespread "colonial" system of caring for defectives. Saegert, in charge of an institution for deaf-mutes in Berlin, encountered a problem similar to that which Howe had had to face; mental defectives among the deaf required special methods of training. He not only worked out methods of instruction but succeeded in founding in Berlin in 1845 an institution for the feeble-minded, which led to the rapid establishment of similar institutions in many of the German states. In Britain a home for mental defectives at Park House, Highgate, in 1848, was quickly followed by other publicly endowed institutions. The movement for the public assumption of responsibility for the care of mental defectives made rapid gains during the third quarter of the century and still continues.

The Birth of Psychosomatic Medicine

Despite the gap, noted above, between medicine and psychology the development of the physical and biological sciences during the latter half of the nineteenth century began to give physicians an increasing hope that they could control mental disease through understanding physical causes. They were thus inclined to a somewhat more optimistic view than that which had prevailed in the previous century. Yet in their preoccupation with physical causes they were seldom inclined to look systematically for concomitant psychological causes for medical problems. Psychological reality could be a *result,* but not a *cause,* of a medical problem.

The whole theme is brilliantly lighted by the struggle over "animal magnetism" in the eighteenth and early nineteenth centuries. The physician and astronomer Paracelsus (1490–1541) believed that he had found a relation between the heavenly bodies and magnetism and that these relationships could be used in the promotion of human health. Van Helmont taught that an "animal magnetism" can be directed by one man to another. In the seventeenth century the itinerant healer Greatrakes drew great crowds to observe his "magnetic" cures. Reputable science was not ready to be influenced. No one thought that Greatrakes or Van Helmont's cures could be "psychological." They were either physical or they were nothing. This sets the scene for the appearance of Mesmer, an Austrian physician, who had read Paracelsus about 1760 and was apparently quite willing to go along with the belief that there were magnetic influences from the heavenly bodies (1766). About 1770 he witnessed a demonstration of cures apparently effected by the use of magnetized plates. In 1776 he encountered the demonstrations of a priest named Gassner, who convinced him that the human hand was as effective a means of magnetizing as were metal plates. The term "animal magnetism" designated this magnetic influence of the human body. Mesmer went to Paris, where, as the intellectual center of the world, all eyes were turned upon anyone who had some new idea to disseminate. He quickly attracted the patronage of patients suffering from all sorts of diseases. "Mesmerism" became a fad.

The center of his practice was the *baquet,* a tub containing magnetized iron filings around which his patients sat. Metal bars reached out from the tub in different directions. The magnetic influence was supposed to pass from the filings through the iron rods to the bodies of the patients. We have a few descriptions of what happened to these people. Some of them had "fits" or crises. After these crises a large number of them got well, at least well enough to keep Mesmer's prestige at a great height.

He was shortly confronted with severe opposition from the medical profession, which branded him as a quack. A royal commission was organized to inquire into the value of his work. This commission included the great chemist Lavoisier and Benjamin Franklin, the ambassador of the newly constituted United States. The commission, after studying Mesmer's work, did not controvert the claims of cure; they concentrated their attention upon the theory of animal magnetism. The cures, they said, were due not to magnetism but to the patients' "imagination." As a result of this negative report, Mesmer was forced to leave Paris. But the therapeutic use of magnetized metal and of the hands continued.

The chief of Mesmer's followers was the Marquis de Puységur, who made the important discovery that it was possible to throw the patient into a quiet sleeplike state, from which he emerged to find his condition bettered. Puységur found, at Soissons, that not only human hands, but trees, could be "magnetized." If patients stood beneath these trees, cures were effected. Then Franklin tried the experiment of telling peasants that certain trees had been magnetized. Some stood under them and were cured as effectively as those beneath Puységur's magnetized trees. This was, to Franklin's mind, good evidence that "imagination" was a sufficient explanation. The followers of Mesmer, however, went on with their work.

Shortly after 1820 another period of intense popular interest in mesmerism led to a second medical investigation. The movement had spread, in the meantime, to Germany, England, and the United States, and popular demonstrations were given everywhere. Mesmerism became an international problem, from the medical viewpoint an international nuisance. The new committee spent several years studying the mesmeric methods and their results. They reported that the cures were genuine and, moreover, that there were a number of extraordinary phenomena which far transcended the scope of existing medicine: the transference of thought from one mind to another without a word spoken, the reading of letters so sealed that no normal reading of them was possible, the "transposition of the senses"—seeing with the tips of the fingers, and so on—and other similar phenomena of the kind studied later by psychical research. The committee, however, drew no definite conclusion as to the nature of "animal magnetism." This report provoked the most violent dissent, not only because of its emphasis upon the genuineness of the cures but also because of the marvels that had been reported—telepathy, clairvoyance, and the transposition of the senses—which objectors regarded as cases of imposture. The simplest way to explain the cures was to say that they were all based on fraud or illusion. A third committee was appointed, which came to a conclusion more in conformity with the opinions of medical men, with emphasis upon the statement that "animal magnetism" itself was a hoax. Mesmerism fell into even more serious disrepute. It had never succeeded in getting a standing, and now it was thrown into outer darkness.

Not that it lost its popular appeal. Among British mesmerists the leading figure was Elliotson, a physician who was convinced of the value of the method and struggled to obtain a fair hearing for it from medical men. He had such faith in the mesmeric cures that he willingly submitted the phenomena to tests by skeptics. He would "magnetize" a coin; then the coin would be applied to the body of a patient, and the patient would feel better. He gave a demonstration before one of the editors of the *Lancet*, who tried an experiment closely similar to Franklin's. It was reported that the only necessary condition was the patient's *belief* that a coin had been "magnetized"; Elliotson's "magnetization" made no difference. Mesmerism had fallen low, but it dropped to a still lower ebb through its association with phrenology. Since the hands had magnetic influence, it was argued that when they touched a particular part of the skull, the brain area beneath that spot would be called into function. This union of mesmerism and phrenology was defended in Elliotson's journal, the *Phreno-magnet.*

While Elliotson fought unsuccessfully for the recognition of mesmeric therapy, word reached England regarding the hundreds of successful operations performed in Ceylon by Esdaile through induction of the mesmeric trance, a procedure already used by native surgeons. Here was support for the lonely Elliotson. Yet, as it happened, the reports synchronized closely with reports from the United States of successful operations under general anesthesia (both chloroform and ether came into use in the forties), and general anesthesia, being easier to accept and to control than was mesmerism, preempted the field.

But a turning point came with the work of Braid, a surgeon of Manchester. He witnessed demonstrations of mesmerism in 1841, which started him off on a long series of reflections, doubts, and experiments. He later gave a vivid account of a young woman who while in the mesmeric trance gave ample demonstration of these wonders.

> Under "adhesiveness and friendship" she clasped me, and on stimulating the organ of "combativeness" on the opposite side of the head, with the arm of that side she struck two gentlemen (who, she imagined, were about to attack me) in such a manner as nearly laid one on the floor, whilst with the other arm she held me in the most friendly manner. Under "benevolence" she seemed quite overwhelmed with compassion; under "acquisitiveness" stole greedily all she could lay her hands on, which was retained whilst I excited many other manifestations, but the moment my fingers touched "conscientiousness" she threw all she had stolen on the floor, as if horror-stricken, and burst into a flood of tears (1843, pp. 135–36).

Braid was at first skeptical about the reality of the whole cycle of psychological effects which the mesmerists seemed to induce. Through his own experimentation he became convinced, however, that there were genuine phenomena to be explained, not in magnetic, but in *physiological,* terms. He experimented with various methods of inducing the sleeplike state which mesmerists induced and found that such physiological factors as muscular fatigue served a useful purpose. This physiological emphasis, coming from a surgeon in good repute who had once been a complete skeptic, was just what was needed to win the attention of the medical public. The word "hypnotism," with its emphasis upon as common and natural a thing as sleep, marked the shift in outlook; and by experimental demonstrations Braid invited the skeptic to make his own tests. Hypnotism began, shortly after the middle of the century, to be accepted by medical men. Even fifty years after Puységur's experiments, reputable physicians had been few who would accept any explanation for mesmeric phenomena other than fraud on the part of experimenter or subject or both; after Braid, the existence of a genuine hypnotic state came to be generally recognized. Yet Braid himself came in time to see the inadequacy of the physiological hypothesis and emphasized psychological factors, such as suggestion.[2]

The next great step to be taken was by Liébeault of Nancy (1866), whose celebrated clinic demonstrated therapy through suggestion over a long span of years. For Liébeault and his pupil Bernheim, "suggestion" was a name for the process by which ideas were accepted by the patient in such a way as to lead directly to new beliefs, attitudes, and conduct. Not only could temporary changes in the patient be produced, but, through belief in the hypnotist's suggestion of health, the patient seemed in many cases to be cured. Bernheim emphasized especially that hysterical symptoms (functional blindness, functional paralysis, and the like) could be understood through supposing that the subject was suggestible in respect to his inability to perform functions which no known organic condition prevented; as suggestion caused the trouble, so it could cause the cure. A man who has been in a railroad accident is amenable to the suggestion that his legs are injured; the suggestion may be given him by another person or by associations within his own mind. Paralysis of the legs ensues. These views became the cornerstone of the "Nancy school." The Nancy school developed hypnotic methods which emphasized the direct *suggestion of sleep* as a means of inducing the hypnotic trance, in place of the physiological methods initiated by Braid. Verbal suggestion was the chief method by which experimental study of hypnotic phenomena, as well as the treatment of patients, was carried on. Bernheim systematically studied a wide variety of hypnotic phenomena, such as functional anesthesias and paralyses, amnesias and hallucinations, and showed that in many patients all these effects can be produced by suggestion in the waking state.[3]

But the physiological viewpoint was not to be dislodged so easily. A few years after Liébeault's work, Charcot, at Paris, advocated a conception of hypnosis which was in clear conflict with the theory of the Nancy school (1872–87). For him, hypnosis was a physiological phenomenon to be understood as one manifestation of hysteria; and hysteria was a disease of the nervous system to be compared and contrasted with various other nervous disorders. Hypnosis was, from Charcot's viewpoint, a condition peculiar to hysterics and a method par excellence of investigating the hysterical predisposition. Charcot's eminence as a director of two great hospital services for mental disease in Paris was augmented by his introduction of clinical

[2] The theory of suggestion had been outlined over twenty years before by Bertrand. But he never succeeded in attracting attention to his views; for this reason Braid rather than Bertrand is of chief historical significance.

[3] About the turn of the century the school came under the influence of the concept of "autosuggestion." The term marked a rebellion against the assumption of the all-importance of rapport between hypnotist and patient, insisting that all suggestion is imposed by the patient upon himself. This conception marks the transition from the "Old Nancy school" to the "New Nancy school," of which Coué (1912) was the best-known exponent.

methods, which gave him an opportunity to become one of the greatest teachers of neurology in the nineteenth century. Thus, a century after Mesmer's arrival in Paris, hypnotic technique became a method in the study of clinical neurology at the French capital. The position of Charcot in French psychiatry and psychology is one of such prominence that we shall return to him in our survey of French psychology toward the close of the century.

Charcot and his great pupil Pierre Janet developed a consistently medical point of view, which was at the same time both physiological and psychological. From the basic organic make-up of the individual developed failures of adaptation. Janet, for example, sees the individual as either well or loosely put together; and if the latter, various components like seeing and hearing and remembering and thinking and willing may fall apart, so that in a "psychogenic" crisis he loses his memories or his ability to see or to make decisions. There is a place in such a system for a psychological and a physiological study of the strengths and weaknesses of each individual patient. As Janet says, life is like a balance sheet, with the patient's resources sometimes equal to the demands or the stresses placed upon him and sometimes not. From this relatively simple and straightforward viewpoint it was possible to study the constitutional factors, the proneness to stress, the actual life difficulties of the patient, and the devices by which the physician may assess and use the weaknesses and strengths of each patient (1919).

But hypnosis had another use — namely, as a device for recovering forgotten stressful episodes. As we shall see, Freud and his followers emphasized, then abandoned, this use of hypnosis in the recovery of stressful experiences; but the combination of hypnosis and psychoanalytic procedures, known as "hypnoanalysis," became important in the psychopathology of the post–World War I era. While many other factors were pointing to the importance of conflict and unconscious dynamics, the availability of hypnosis as theory and as practical tool materially influenced the directions taken by dynamic psychiatry at the end of the last century and the beginning of the present century.

The full story of the contribution of medical theory and practice to systematic psychology cannot be told here. We shall refer to this theme later when speaking of the development of a modern psychology of personality, when we look at the development of physiological psychology and its relation to psychopathology, and when we reopen and consider more fully the intimate relation of medicine to science.

REFERENCES

Braid, J. *Neurypnology*. London: Churchill, 1843.

Burton, R. *Anatomy of Melancholy*. Oxford: Cripps, 1621.

Charcot, J.-M. *Leçons sur les maladies du système nerveux* [*Clinical Lectures on Diseases of the Nervous System*]. 3 vols. Paris: Delahaye, 1872–87.

Coué, É. *La Maîtrise de soi-même par l'autosuggestion consciente; conférence fait par M. Coué à Chaumont.* 1912.

Encyclopaedia Britannica. "Dorothea Lynde Dix." 11th ed. Vol. 8. 1910.

Itard, J. M. G. . . . *Rapports et memoires sur le sauvage de l'Aveyron.* Paris: Bureaux du Progrès Médical, 1894.

Janet, P. *Les Medications psychologiques.* Paris: Alcan, 1919.

Liébeault, A.-A. *Du sommeil et des états analogues.* Paris: Masson, 1866.

Lotze, R. H. *Medicinische Psychologie* [*Medical Psychology*]. Leipzig: Weidmann, 1852.

Maudsley, H. *Body and Will.* New York: Appleton, 1884.

Mesmer, F. A. *De planetarum influxu.* Vienna: Ghelen, 1766.

Moreau de Tours, J.-J. *Études psychiques sur la folie.* Paris: Lacour, 1840.

Ribot, T.-A. *Les Maladies de la volonté.* Paris: Alcan, 1883.

Tiffany, F. *Life of Dorothea Lynde Dix.* Boston: Houghton Mifflin, 1890.

NOTE: A list of further readings appears at the back of the book.

11

Wundt and the Spread of Experimental Psychology

The full tide of successful experiment.
JEFFERSON

Physiology was assuming by the mid-nineteenth century much of that systematic structural form, that solid organization of data provided by a mature conception of method, which characterizes the conception of science. The biologist began to realize that he must use his laboratory as much as possible; even when the evolutionary theory became central to the biological sciences, the laboratory methods of the physical sciences were being used. Thus biochemistry, endocrinology, and, ultimately, genetics and molecular biology developed essentially along the lines of the physical sciences. When asked what his profession was, Selig Hecht replied, a "biophysicist; that is, a biologist who works in the physics building." He meant by this that the biologist could surround himself by all the methods which enabled his biology to become articulate with his physics.

Many of those looking at the structure of modern psychology have seen matters very differently. Many have expected that the evolutionary theory would give perspectives and guidelines to *all* of modern psychology; that the biological conceptions of clinicians working with people in life situations would deliver a clear message to psychologists as to how they should construct their science. From this viewpoint, experimental psychology was belittled by many who believed sciences should be based on field observations and not upon laboratory experimentation. Indeed, to them laboratory experimentation was a narrow and hyperspecialized approach, with scant concern about fundamental problems.

Unfortunately, this issue has become central in professional controversies. Naturalists have often had much to complain about in the methods of experimentalists, and vice versa. It is not surprising that even today those who see the experimental laboratory as central in the structure of science are those who have been so trained. The others, trained within a more liberal "history of ideas" tradition, see the laboratory approach as "specialized," perhaps even "provincial." Who is right? Neither, we think. The way of science is to formulate predictive theories and to test them by empirical data. The issue is really part of the problem of how to formulate testable theories and paradigms: how a specific empirically proven, or disproven, hypothesis may reflect on a theory and on the larger body of knowledge that constitutes a field around that theory; and what constitutes empirical proof or disproof. All these issues in turn belong to the even larger considerations of the "sociology of knowledge" and will not be settled by sheer arguments.

Wundt

The story of Wilhelm Wundt and his work is primarily the story of a physiological psychologist who succeeded so well in turning psychology into a laboratory-based science that since his time all other aspects of psychology have suffered from feelings of second-class citizenship.

Wundt was probably the most comprehensive expression in his time of the scientific forces that were remaking psychology. His position as founder of the first laboratory for experimental psychology, and his huge influence as teacher of those who flocked to study there, arose largely from the fact that he was one of those men who grasp the intellectual forces that are developing about them, realize where they are tending, and undertake to bring them to fruition.

We have seen that much of the psychology of the mid-nineteenth century was incorporated within experimental physiology. The latter included such psychological problems as seeing and hearing, comparisons of "sensation intensities" in the Weber-Fechner work, and the various studies of reaction time. All these types of investigation were carried on in physiological laboratories but were beginning to be colored by a psychological cast of thought. There was in progess, on the other hand, the development of genetic method, due more to Darwin than to any other man. An evolutionary outlook had led, through Galton, to the empirical investigation of association and imagery; evolutionism also encouraged the tendency to emphasize not only cognitive processes but affective and volitional processes as well. These various tendencies were synthesized in the work of Wundt.

Wundt took his degrees of Ph.D. and M.D. at Heidelberg and was for a time laboratory assistant to Helmholtz. He went in 1874 to the University of Zürich. He was shortly thereafter called to Leipzig as Professor of Philosophy and there remained until his death in 1920.

In 1873–74 he published his monumental *Principles of Physiological Psychology,* containing the foundations of much of his later work. The term "physiological psychology" meant for Wundt a psychology investigated by *physiological methods.* Its emphasis was on certain aspects of the method of the physiological laboratory. A genuinely psychological experiment involved an objectively knowable and preferably a measurable stimulus, applied under stated conditions and resulting in a response likewise objectively known and measured. But there were certain intervening steps, which were known through introspection, sometimes supplemented by instrumentation. In this formulation Wundt radically broke with the introspective psychologists from Hobbes onward. For no matter how much emphasis had been given to behavior, and to stimuli causing behavior, by such psychologists as Hobbes and Hartley (and even by men who, like Bain and Lotze, made large use of physiology), no one had grasped in its entirety the scientific implications of stating mental events in relation to objectively knowable and measureable stimuli and reactions. Nevertheless, introspection, which had been present in rudimentary form in the experimental program of Fechner and Helmholtz, became with Wundt a primary tool of the experimental psychologist. To Wundt, the keystone of all total adjustments of the organism was a psychophysical process, an organic response approachable through both physiology and psychology. What, then, was the relation between the psychological factors and the physiological factors? The physiological psychologist was concerned with the whole series of excitations from stimulation of sense organs, through sensory neurones to lower or higher centers in the central nervous system and out from these centers to muscles; but parallel with the physiological activities of the higher centers ran the events of mental life, known through introspection. We must therefore have psychology and physiology side by side, always beginning with a stimulus and following through to a response. Physiological psychology was, throughout, an empirical science; it was a union of the long-established introspective methods with methods borrowed from nineteenth-century physiology.

It is not an exaggeration to say that the conception of an experimental psychology was very largely Wundt's own creation. Many psychologists had insisted on empiricism, and many physiologists, as well as philosophers and physicists, had experimentally approached psychological problems. But five years after Wundt went to Leipzig — in 1879 — this conception of psychological method took definite form in the founding of a laboratory for psychology independent of the laboratory for physiology. This was of no great consequence so far as its immediate technical results were concerned, but it was of very great consequence in its effect on psychology. Shortly afterward, in 1883, Wundt began to publish a periodical, *Philosophische Studien,* containing some theoretical articles but devoted largely to reports on the problems of the laboratory. The yearly tables of contents give a fair indication of the interests of Wundt and his school. These interests, though widely varied, were for the most part identified with problems already generally known to physiologists.

We may classify Wundt's specific contributions under two heads: first, his work as a "systematic psychologist"; second, his work as an experimentalist. His psychological system, his point of view, and the edifice which he created are presupposed throughout his detailed theoretical contributions and in his organization and interpretation of experiments.

In accordance with his physiological viewpoint, Wundt found a place for inherited physiological mechanisms serving reflex and instinct. As far as consciousness was concerned, he assumed a one-to-one correspondence, a parallelism between an excitation of the cerebral cortex and a "corresponding" form of sensory experience. Sensations were ultimate or elementary forms of experience. Sensations were aroused when a sense organ was stimulated and the incoming impulse reached the brain. They were classified according to their modality (seeing, hearing, smelling, and so on), or intensity, or other special features, such as duration and extension. There was no fundamental difference between sensations and images. These latter were also associated with local excitation within the cortex. In addition to these two groups of elements there were qualities known as *feelings*. Under this head were to be included all qualities of experience which did not come from any sense organ, nor from the revival of sensory experiences. Just as there was a vast number of possible elementary sensations, one might not say how many possible feelings there might be. But feelings can be classified. In the fourth edition of the *Physiological Psychology,* in 1893, appears the "tridimensional theory of feeling," to the effect that the feelings may be classified as pleasant or unpleasant, tense or relaxed, excited or depressed. A given feeling might at the same time be pleasant, tense, and depressed.

Another type of elementary experience was accepted by Wundt in his early work. This was the feeling of innervation, the feeling we have when we set going a nervous impulse to a muscle — an experience to be differentiated from kinesthetic experience (the sensations from muscles, tendons, and joints). Wundt abandoned this conception in later writings, because of the lack of introspective evidence for it. His empirical attitude was reflected in his willingness to change his mind with each new volume or edition.

Sensations carry with them feeling qualities, and when sensations combine to form more complex states, a certain feeling quality results from the total. This total may again combine with another total, a new feeling resulting from this higher compound. These feeling qualities are arranged not only in patterns, in cross sections of experience in time (the experience at a given *instant*), but in certain *sequences;* feelings follow certain regular orders, and these regular orders of feelings are called *emotions*. Emotions cannot be understood in terms of mere cross sections at given moments; they are characteristic sequences. In rage, for example, there is a characteristic series of feelings, giving a temporal pattern distinguishable from the patterns of other emotions.

Usually emotions lead into acts of *will*. Will, like emotion, is characterized by a special temporal pattern of feelings. Will itself is a series of feelings in which at first emotional elements, together with ideas, are present; then ensue peculiar feelings of "resolution," from which the overt act follows. A particular series of feelings, therefore, constitutes the act of will. The line between emotion and will is purely arbitrary, except that volition includes some feelings never found elsewhere.

The question then arises, from our genetic viewpoint, as to which of these various processes are fundamental—reflex acts, sensations, images, simple feelings, emotions, or acts of will. Wundt approached this problem from an evolutionary point of view, emphasizing the essentially adaptive nature of reflex acts (the term "adaptive" here summarizing the conception of biological adjustment). Acts which, ages ago, were the direct expression of the animal's wants have in time become mechanized, so that their essentially voluntary character is overlooked. Reflex acts, from the simplest to the most complicated, do, in the long run, what the organism needs to do; therefore reflex acts were, for Wundt, "purposive."

One feels here the influence of Schopenhauer, who had made the will the central point in his philosophy. Schopenhauer's most important works were written early in the second quarter of the century, but it was not until past the middle of the century that his influence reached its peak. He had taught that life is essentially a struggle in which every satisfaction leads to a new struggle, implying, therefore, the impossibility of achieving happiness. The world was a center of striving before it became an object of knowledge. With evolutionism it became easy to think of the will as the thing that adapts us to situations, that drives us when we are not adapted.[1] With Schopenhauer the will was absolute and primal; and intelligence had been evolved simply as a means to give what the will demanded. The conception is similar to Bichat's distinction between "animal" and "vital"; later came emphasis on the control of central nervous activities by visceral and autonomic processes and then its theoretical use by psychologists and psychiatrists. Cravings were the ultimate mainsprings of conduct.

Schopenhauer had undertaken to show that will need not be regarded as a conscious function; Wundt utilized the conception and adapted it to his own system. For Wundt the will was primal, but in evolution its activities had in some cases degenerated into the reflex response. Wundt was heart and soul a voluntarist, a believer in the purposive nature of all life, from the most primitive ameboid movement to the most abstract intellectualism. The will, though known to introspection as a *compound,* is of the very life of the organism. The feelings were indeed coming into their own in this period. Horwicz had constructed a psychology upon the basis of the affective life (1872–78). Bain and Maudsley represent the same emphasis in British psychology.

So far, we have Wundt's elements, but what of the integrating power of the organism? The first answer lies in the characteristically Wundtian doc-

[1] Lamarck had stressed this point; Darwin's theory, despite its different emphasis, made wide secondary use of Lamarckian principles.

trine of apperception. Leibnitz had distinguished between obscure perceptions and those clearly apprehended or "apperceived." French and British psychologists had in general ignored such observations and had for the most part contented themselves with the study of focal consciousness (that which chiefly occupies attention). With Kant and with Herbart, however, apperception had been the process of assimilating and interpreting new impressions. Wundt used the term "apperception," with slightly different emphasis, to describe the process by which the elements of experience are appropriated or laid hold of by the individual — that is, drawn into clear introspective consciousness. From such appropriation follows the necessity of a term to describe the process of relating the various elements in a unity; the process was designated "creative synthesis." [2] Many elementary experiences — sensations, images, and feelings — are organized into a whole by the process of creative synthesis. We have in all psychological processes the following necessary steps: first, stimulation; second, perception (in which the experience is present in consciousness, nothing more than that); third, apperception (in which the experience is identified, appropriated, and synthesized); finally, an act of will which sets going the reaction. Wundt's apperception enjoyed a prominent position in German psychology for decades, though vigorously attacked by Ziehen and those of a more mechanistic turn of thought; its influence was less profound and of shorter life outside of Germany.[3] Everywhere, however, Wundt's doctrine helped awaken psychologists to the necessity of distinguishing between focal and marginal events — in other words, to a more serious study of the nature of attention. The term "apperception" has in general been discarded, while many features of Wundt's description of apperception are still current under the caption of "attention." Wundt's emphasis upon unity and activity represents, moreover, the same point of view that we saw in John Stuart Mill in the reaction against his father's extreme associationism and atomism. Wundt held that it is of the very nature of human experience to give itself organization.

In the early years of Wundt's laboratory it was chiefly he who set the problems for experimental psychology. Wundt, like Nestor, was "alive on the earth with three generations of mortal men." Born in 1832, and living until 1920, he grew up in the atmosphere of Hegel and Schopenhauer and the new experimental physiology which came to flower in the work of Helmholtz; he lived to dominate the psychology of the late nineteenth century, perma-

---

[2] The necessity for such a relating process had been recognized by Lotze, who in fact described it as "creation."

[3] Though Herbartian apperception still found favor in many educational circles, James's gentle cynicism regarding all "apperception" (1899) seems to be shared by most contemporary psychologists. The term is best known today in connection with the concept of "thematic apperception" and the well-known clinical instrument, the Thematic Apperception Test of Morgan and Murray (see p. 434), offering the patient or subject the opportunity to make up a story as he looks at a picture including human figures; his way of apperceiving the picture indicates his way of viewing all of life.

nently impressing his empirical spirit upon it, and to witness in his old age the extension of his experimental methods to a range of problems vastly beyond the scope of his own somewhat limited conception.

For Wundt believed that experimental psychology must concern itself, at least for the time being, with problems which had already been attacked and reduced to more or less quantitative form. He did not occupy himself greatly with *new* kinds of experiments. Most of his laboratory problems can be classified under a few main heads which are already familiar to the reader. First came the psychology and physiology of seeing and hearing, and, to some extent, of the lower senses; much of his work in optics (latent time of the retina, studies in eye movements, and the like) represented a continuation of Helmholtz's work.

A second concern of Wundt was the reaction-time experiments, as taken from Helmholtz and Donders. In this he thought he possessed a method of showing experimentally the three stages which he believed to be present in all responses to a stimulus: perception, apperception, and will. When the stimulus is presented to the subject, he first perceives it; he then apperceives it; finally, he wills to react, and from this the muscular innervation follows. The hypothesis was not well supported by ongoing research at Leipzig and elsewhere; but another aspect of the reaction-time experiment, which proved more productive, was the discovery by Ludwig Lange (1888) that some subjects attend to the stimulus, others to the response; the latter were found capable of quicker reactions.

Third, Wundt encouraged in every way the experiments in psychophysics to which Fechner was still giving attention and to which G. E. Müller had made important methodological contributions (1878). Psychophysics, in the hands of Wundt, continued to present quantitative problems. He did, however, disagree with Fechner on one crucial point. It is indeed possible, he held, to say that two stimuli seem to be of equal intensity or that one is just noticeably different from another. But he could not admit that sensations could be measured; measurement, strictly speaking, applied only to the *stimuli*. Instead of seeking the relation between the physical and psychical worlds, Wundt was content to regard the psychophysical method as a means of studying the relation between sensation intensities and the process of *judgment*. Stimuli have to differ to an extent which makes possible a correct judgment as to their relative magnitudes. Wundt adopted a purely psychological interpretation of Weber's law, which was for him simply an example of the psychological law of relativity.

The fourth field of experimentation in which Wundt worked was the analysis of association, begun by Galton. In 1880, Wundt adapted this experiment to the needs of the Leipzig laboratory. Galton had made use of single words as stimuli but had recorded his responses in different forms; some were single words, but others were descriptions of images of varying complexity. In the latter case a genuine classification of the responses was difficult, and their time relations were not susceptible of exact measurement. Wundt simplified the experiment, and made it a more accurate instrument, by requiring his subjects to give each response in the form of a *single word*. In conformity with his whole conception of experimental psychology, it was now possible to examine in each case the relation between stimulus word and response word.

Wundt and his pupils worked out devices for the uniform presentation of word stimuli in visual form. Auditory presentation was sometimes substituted. The desire for exact and uniform methods of presenting the stimuli, and of recording and measuring the responses, led to the use of the lip key and of the Hipp chronoscope (measuring one-thousandths of a second) and made possible a precision in time measurement which has seldom subsequently been thought necessary. Wundt then proceeded to classify the types of word association discovered when one-word stimuli were presented; they were so classified as to afford keys to the nature of all verbal association. Since Hartley there had been scores of attempts to classify the types of association; these were uniformly worked out so as to constitute a system intellectually satisfying to the psychologist. Even Thomas Brown, the most gifted of those among the moderns who attempted such analysis, never realized the simple wisdom of finding out inductively, as Wundt and his pupils now did, what the common types of association might be in that world of heard and spoken language which plays so great a part in the structure of thought. Wundt recognized that Galton had hit upon a method all-important for inductive psychology.

He subdivided all word associations into two grand categories, *inner* and *outer*. The *inner* association is one in which there is an intrinsic connection between the meanings of the two words. Definitions, for example, are inner associations; the meaning of the response word is identical with or closely similar to that of the stimulus. Supraordination is a second type of inner association; when the stimulus "snake" evokes the response "reptile," the subject has emphasized an aspect of the meaning of the stimulus word and has given it the form of a generalization; similarly, subordination (snake — viper) and coordination (snake — lizard) involve meaningful relations; so also do noun-adjective associations (snake — venomous); adjective-noun associations (slippery — snake); contrasts (white — black); and many others. Sharply distinguished from all these, the *outer* associations are those in which a purely extrinsic or accidental connection exists between stimulus and response. Contiguity in time and space are found here; if the stimulus "candle" evokes the response "box" or "Christmas," the cause is presumably to be found in the subject's habits of buying candles by the box, or of seeing them at Christmas time, rather than to any inherent similarity between the meanings. When the stimulus word itself, rather than its meaning, evokes the response, as in the case of rhymes, the association is classified as outer; so also with the very common "speech-habit" group, in which the response word completes some catch phrase of ingrained verbal habit (dog—days, fire—fly). The elaboration of Wundt's system of classification was undertaken by Trautscholdt (1883).

Experimental Psychopathology

Among Wundt's pupils in the early days was Kraepelin, a physician who saw the possibility of extending Wundt's experimental method to the related field of psychopathology. Not only were mental abnormalities to be studied through experiment, and their phenomena stated in quantitative terms whenever possible, but mental abnormalities of the milder type were to be experimentally *induced*. The association method was applied by Kraepelin (1892) and his pupils to groups subjected to the effects of fatigue, hunger, alcohol, and other disturbing influences.[4] All these agencies increased the number of "superficial"—that is, outer—associations; it was as if a disorder of attention had been produced. Kraepelin's laboratory yielded also much valuable material on the curve of work, both in relation to fatigue and in relation to other factors making for increase or decrease of efficiency. These and many other investigations, notably those upon the effect of a great variety of drugs, have not only fulfilled his hope that much could be done toward the establishment of an "experimental psychopathology," but have directly furthered the course of experimental psychology itself.

Folk Psychology

To folk psychology Wundt devoted some of his best energies (1900–1914). Believing that "cultural products," as well as introspective reports, are a legitimate subject matter for psychology, he undertook a systematic psychological interpretation of the data of anthropology and history. His studies on the psychological interpretation of language are perhaps his best-known contributions. He emphasized the interpenetration of psychical and physiological factors in linguistic structure, protesting against that naïve psychologism to which phonetics was a mere incident and, with equal explicitness, against that merely philological approach which had sought to explain all linguistic change in terms of the laws of vocal utterance. But he gave the weight of his authority to that trend which aimed toward the understanding of each social group through the analysis of its language, believing that the very vocabulary and grammar of a people reveal its psychic constitution—a view later repudiated, then again revived, by later students of language.

In consequence of his vast learning and the many problems on which he worked, Wundt gave a unity to the field of psychology such as no one else in his day conceived. Before Wundt published his *Physiological Psychology*

---

[4] Bekhterev and his pupils were carrying on similar investigations in the same period.

(1873–74) and established his laboratory, psychology was little more than a waif knocking now at the door of physiology, now at the door of ethics, now at the door of epistemology. In 1879, it set iself up as an experimental science with a local habitation and a name. Although he was unqualified to handle many phases of the new science, Wundt tried to bring together experimental psychology, child psychology, animal psychology, folk psychology; nothing that was psychology was foreign to him. He poured his energies into examination of nearly every corner of mental life. When he failed as an experimentalist, as he frequently did, he stimulated much research which led far beyond anything he was himself capable of imagining; and when his theories proved to be inadequate, as they frequently did, they could and did undergo transformation through laboratory work. He saw no great new vistas, as did, for example, Freud and Wertheimer; but it was after all largely through Wundt's vision that the conception of an independent inductive psychology came into being. Such a synthesis and the establishment of such an experimental movement were, of course, the natural outcome of the development of the biological sciences, especially within the German universities. Wundt was the fulfillment, not the origin, of the movement with which his name is associated. But to bring such a movement to its fulfillment, and to outline with vigor and earnestness the conception of an experimental psychology which should take its place among the natural sciences, was an achievement of such magnitude as to give him a unique position among the psychologists of the modern period.

It may seem today that to bring together these four great areas — sense perception, reaction time, association, and psychophysics — was an obvious thing to do. Actually, these different problems were either parts of physiology or were loose, disjointed elements, which had no organic relation to one another. The very considerable scholarly background in medicine and philosophy, and the integrative tendencies current in German biology and philosophy in the era, enabled a bold and imaginative physiologist to conceive experimental psychology. It is true that the experimental method, which for Wundt meant experimental physiological method, dominated the scene. Allan Fromme wrote a comment on an earlier version of this present study:

> Some comment ought to be made on the domination of experimental technique over psychological subject matter, typical of German experimental psychology. I think Wundt tried to do something about this but was too steeped in the tradition to be successful. Even William James — a far more imaginative person — failed to synthesize many of the currents he was exposed to and, like Wundt, tended to close an era rather than open one.

There were many signs reflecting the narrowness of the new experimental psychology. When Ebbinghaus (1885) introduced his experimental methods into the study of memory, Wundt repudiated the new approach and when, years later, Külpe (1893) introduced experimental methods into the study of the thought processes, again Wundt rejected the newcomer; so did Titchener. These signs of resistance show that the evolution of science is subject to all sorts of selective forces, only part of which originate from a thirst for more knowledge and better understanding. Indeed, much of the "new psychology" was caught up in the enthusiasm for experimental method as applied to those specific areas that had been already worked out. Countless similar examples can be found in the twentieth century. Despite the fact that experimental methods in the study of attitudes, temperament, cognitive style, creativity, stress tolerance, and so on, have crowded upon us in recent decades, there is still a tendency to regard the term "experimental psychology" as applicable only to a few broad areas, most of which had already been staked out at the time of Wundt. When new fields emerge around new paradigms, such as those initiated by Pavlov and elaborated by his followers in the study of the learning process, they tend to create their own forces of resistance against modification.

Cattell

The close relation between Wundt and his immediate followers has been emphasized; one cannot really distinguish between what Wundt himself did and what his pupils did. When we speak of the Wundtian laboratory we have to think of a group of individuals, drawn from many nations and speaking many languages, catching the master's enthusiasm for the creation of an experimental psychology, free both from its sister sciences and from philosophy. This viewpoint of Wundt inspired directly or indirectly a very large amount of research; and in discussing the work of individuals in the school it is a matter of opinion how far we should regard them, during their stay at Leipzig, as pursuing investigations in their own right. Work with the association test illustrates the point. Some of Wundt's pupils, however, began even while still with him the study of problems which were both envisaged and prosecuted with originality and relative independence.

J. McK. Cattell may be chosen here as an exceptionally original and productive member of the Wundtian group of experimenters, while a later chapter will consider the furtherance of Wundt's systematic approach by Titchener. Cattell's work brilliantly exemplified the spirit of the school. He succeeded in winning wide respect for the point of view and the methods which he had seen at Leipzig; he was also conspicuous for the versatility and volume of his own work and the significance of the problems and results associated with his name. Attention will be given to his work at this point, both before considering the development of experimental psychology in Germany outside of Wundt's laboratory and before looking broadly at American psychology; in this way perhaps the conquests and the long-range significance of the Wundtian approach can be most effectively brought out.

Going to the Leipzig laboratory in 1880, Cattell later became Wundt's assistant. Partly on his own initiative and partly as a result of suggestions from Wundt, he performed a series of experiments which are cornerstones of subsequent research. His return to the United States in 1888, as Professor of Psychology at the University of Pennsylvania, marked no interruption in his life as an experimentalist.

Of Cattell's many contributions the most elaborate and extensive was his investigation of reaction time (1885, 1885a). At Leipzig he not only studied elaborately some physiological aspects of the problem, but gave close attention to introspective analysis. Nothing could show more clearly than this that Wundt's point of view as to the nature of psychology constituted a large part of the background of Cattell's work. The study of reaction time led to two elaborations, one the measurement of the speed of perceptual processes of various degrees of complexity, the other the use of classification methods in the association experiment—another of Wundt's favorite children. Another important contribution to the study of the time relations of mental processes was Cattell's investigation of the "span of attention" (1886).[5] He found that a subject could correctly name the number of lines shown in a brief exposure if the number did not exceed four or five; the span for letters was about the same; and it was not appreciably less for short words. For the study of the speed of perception under a variety of different conditions, Cattell made use of the gravity tachistoscope (which makes possible the sudden exposure of an object through a slit in a screen) and in conjunction with it the gravity chronometer. He measured the length of time during which a colored stimulus must act on the retina in order to be perceived as color.

He proceeded to study the speed of perception of letters and words. Problems in the latter field led to the invention of another method of exposing stimuli. This was a revolving drum behind a screen containing a slot which enabled the subject to read letters pasted on the drum; the speed of rotation of the drum determined the rapidity of presentation of the various letters. Cattell found that in order to name the letters correctly when they were presented one at a time as single objects, almost half a second was required. On the other hand, if he enlarged the slit so that one letter could be seen while the preceding one was being named, the time was from one-third to one-fifth of a second. In fact, as the slit was enlarged until three, then four, and then five could be seen, for the majority of the nine subjects there was a steady improvement in speed. This pointed conclusively to the factor of *overlapping:* that an individual could not only carry on simultaneously a perceptual and a motor response, but could deal at the same time with various stages in the total response to several stimuli. Cattell used the same approach in experiments on the perception and naming of colors, showing that

[5] The problem had been approached experimentally by Bonnet (1760) and by Sir William Hamilton.

the time required to give a color its name was shortened if the subject was allowed to have a new color in view before naming the preceding one; over-lapping was again present. This recognition of the measurable nature of over-lapping processes is one of Cattell's most significant achievements. As we shall see later, Bryan and Harter demonstrated the applicability of this con-cept to the learning process.

These studies were part of a systematic attack on the problem of reading. Cattell presented words as well as letters, noting the variation in reading time as the words became longer and less familiar. In this work he found that the perception of whole words of moderate length took no longer than the perception of single letters; in fact, letters frequently took longer. Here he recognized that such perceptual responses need not involve the serial per-ception of elements present in the pattern. This principle of the organization of "higher units of response" was much utilized later in experiments on learning. Illustrative also of his studies of reading was his demonstration that an individual could read his own native language at far greater *speed* than other languages which he could speak and write virtually as well. Ger-mans, even if very familiar with English, actually read it more slowly than German; in the same way, although several experimental subjects were well trained in the classics, the speed of reading Latin and Greek was very much less than that for the native tongue. This showed that even such associa-tions as were regarded as absolutely fixed and mechanized were capable of quantitative differentiation.

In the association experiment Cattell and Bryant employed the classifi-cation method as described above (1889). In the major contribution in this field there were about five hundred subjects. The responses were classified according to the frequency of each response word given. In relation to each stimulus, each response word was shown to have a certain degree of com-monplaceness. This was the first *frequency table,* an instrument elaborated and widely used in later investigations. Sommer utilized it for psychiatric purposes, believing that the presence in a patient's associations of a large number of rare associations was characteristic of certain disorders (1894).[6]

The word-association method led naturally to the investigation of *con-trolled association,* in which the subject was required to give not simply *any* one word, but a word bearing a specific relation to the stimulus word. De-spite Hobbes's and Brown's recognition of the problem, associationism had in general neglected the factor of control through the subject's attitude and the situation accompanying the chief or more obvious stimulus; experimen-talists like Galton and Wundt had quite naturally failed to see the importance of such control. In these experiments Cattell made use to some extent of Wundt's classification of association. He required the subject in some cases to give a contrast word, in some a supraordinate, in others a subordinate,

---

[6] Cattell's and Sommer's methods were carried further by Kent and Rosanoff (1910) with 1000 normal and 247 psychopathic subjects, using 100 stimulus words.

and so on. Cattell showed that in general such controlled association was quicker than free association. He also found that some types of controlled association were regularly quicker than others; for example, supraordinates took less time than subordinates. This was apparently because the habits of classifying — passing from a species to a genus — are in general more firmly established than are connections from a genus to any one species within it. To classify "pine" as "tree" was easy and familiar; but "tree" might arouse a variety of subordinate responses, each of which tended to inhibit all others. And just as this matter of interference delayed response, so it was easy to see why free association, offering such a wide variety of possible response, was in general slower than controlled association. The same principle emerged even more clearly in naming, for instance, a country to which a city belonged and a city to which a country belonged. Given the stimulus word "Rome," the subject quickly replied "Italy"; whereas "Italy" might tend to arouse "Naples," "Venice," and so on, with almost equal facility.

A natural outcome of all these experiments of Cattell, in which subjects differed markedly from one another, was the tendency to pass beyond the formulation of general rules and to define quantitatively the nature and significance of *individual differences*. But Wundt's concern was regularly with principles, not with questions of degree; and it was not until the nineties that the field of individual differences, which had been originally explored by Galton, became, through Cattell, a prominent part of experimental psychology. Galton, an ardent evolutionist, saw the importance of individual differences in all studies of organisms, and the inspiration of assisting Galton for a few months at the South Kensington Museum apparently made a deep and lasting impression upon the younger man. Cattell's first elaborate exploration of individual differences, as aside from the determination of general laws, was in the use of the freshman (and senior) tests conducted at Columbia in 1894 (Cattell and Farrand, 1896). This was the first battery of "psychological" tests ever given to a large number of individuals. Among these tests were measures of free and controlled association, and of simple perceptual processes, reaction time, and memory. The improvement of statistical methods in the handling of results was much needed, and methods of studying central tendency as well as variability engaged Cattell's attention.

Another field in which Cattell saw the possibilities of a new mathematical treatment was psychophysics. This work he carried out in conjunction with Fullerton, in the years immediately after returning from the Leipzig laboratory. They devised a substitute for the Weber-Fechner law. Collecting a mass of data by a variety of psychophysical methods (1892), they proceeded to formulate a mathematical generalization (1893). It postulated that the organic response to a stimulus must vary as the square root of the intensity of the stimulus. Errors of observation are included among such organic responses, and as the stimulus increases, the factors which produce errors in observation increase not directly, but as the square root of the stimulus.

"The usual increase of the error of observation with the magnitude of the stimulus is accounted for in a satisfactory manner by the summation of errors." This work of Fullerton and Cattell was close enough to the general trend of psychophysical findings to be taken very seriously, but not close enough to be generally accepted.

Prominent among the later researches of Cattell were studies in the "order of merit" method (1903, 1903a) and the practical use of the method in the study *American Men of Science* (1906), which attracted attention to methods of ranking and rating personal qualities difficult to measure in the laboratory. Throughout all these investigations Cattell was clearly working further and further away from the confinements of the Wundtian method. He might be regarded as a pupil of Galton as much as of Wundt. He did, in fact, to an extraordinary extent reconcile and interweave the Helmholtz-Wundt tradition with the extramural psychology of Galton. Next to his versatility, perhaps the most striking of Cattell's characteristics as a psychologist was his constant effort to reduce everything to quantitative terms, in which general principles and individual variability won equal attention.

Parallel Developments in German Physiological Psychology

To return now to Germany. The movement begun by Wundt in 1879 to separate experimental psychology from physiology, and the founding of journals to disseminate psychological material, went on apace. Most of the larger universities soon had psychological laboratories. Except as expressed later in the thriving laboratory at Vienna, the movement never reached large proportions in Austria. This was due partly to the fact that there were in Austria at the time several great psychologists whose interests were chiefly philosophical; they were less concerned with experimentation.

And a great deal of psychological experimentation continued to be done in laboratories of physiology. In spite of Wundt's declaration of independence, the physiological tradition represented by such names as Weber and Helmholtz was continuing and constantly contributing psychological data of which psychologists had to take serious account. Physiologists and physicists were, in fact, contributing a great deal of important material on sensory functions. Thus in the eighties König and Brodhun published systematic work on psychophysics as such, showing that Weber's law holds for a middle range but is quite unsatisfactory for low and high intensities (1888–89). The exploration of the sensory functions in the skin is another instance. At the time of the founding of Wundt's laboratory, no systematic exploration of the cutaneous senses had been undertaken. Wundt and his followers recognized, of course, that there was no such thing as a sense of touch in general, but it was not until the eighties that the sensations from the skin were studied intensively. This work was begun by Blix (1884) and carried further by Goldscheider. The latter is responsible more than anyone else for the existing technique for ascertaining the points on the skin which are sensitive to warmth, cold, touch, and pain. He heated a stylus and moved it from point to point, demonstrating that receptors for warmth are scattered irregularly throughout the skin. Similarly, cold, pressure, and pain had their sensitive "spots." Parallel with the study of the skin senses, anatomical and physiological studies were published on the kinesthetic senses, through which receptors in the muscles, tendons, and joints enable us to determine the position of our limbs (1898). Whereas the work of Wundt, centering in such questions as reaction time and association tests, set the main problems for many psychologists, these studies in the lower senses, conducted outside the Wundtian school, became by the end of the century standard laboratory investigations wherever the introspective analysis of experience was dominant.

And physiological and experimental psychology, despite Wundt's prowess and prestige, continued to be advanced by many workers who were not dependent upon him. Stumpf's *Tonpsychologie* (1883–90), for example, and his other studies of music, placed him second only to Helmholtz in the realm of psychological acoustics. Much original experimentation was accompanied by ingenious interpretation. Stumpf's theory of consonance and dissonance won special favor (1898–1924). He emphasized the fact that tones an octave apart seem to "fuse" into one psychical unity and that such fusion involves musical consonance. But when one tone is sounded together with another a semitone higher, the hearer is keenly aware of the distinctness of the two tones, and at the same time finds the combination highly discordant. The degree of fusion between tones was regarded by Stumpf as the basis for musical consonance. The fact that the increasing complexity of vibration ratios is in general accompanied by decreasing consonance fits well with the theory; but Stumpf's emphasis on "fusion" makes it distinctly not a physical but a psychological theory.

Another great figure in the era of Wundt, whose best work is in no sense a reflection of Wundt's influence, is Lipps. The study of optical illusions led him to the conclusion that the observing subject tends to project himself into the pattern. A vertical line, for example, gives the observer the sense of contending against gravity, while the angles and curves of many illusions make the subject expand, bend, or whirl. The theory has very important consequences for aesthetics. A man "feels himself into" the material of visual art (1897),[7] and the nature of the tension or relaxation which he experiences determines many aspects of his aesthetic response. A column, for example, must not have too large a capital, because this would oppress the observer with an insufferable burden; too small a capital would give him the sense of great strength devoted to a trifling task.[8]

[7] The term *"Einfühlung"* ("empathy") has in fact come into general psychological use; one "feels oneself into" a tree, or a client, or a character in a novel.

[8] For a systematic exposition of the modern psychology of visual perception as related to the arts, see Arnheim (1954).

With regard to the experimental psychology of the United States, it may be said without hesitation that in the first few years of its development it was primarily Wundtian in its outlook and approach. American psychology had hitherto been saturated with the spirit of the Scottish school; it had been dogmatic in its approach, disregarding both physiological and experimental methods. Prior to 1880, the only important American contributions were a few articles by William James during the seventies.[9] But now American psychology began suddenly to be captured by the experimentalists' enthusiasm. The new psychologists who came back from Germany as pupils of Wundt carried everything before them. Chronologically, the first of these was Stanley Hall, who was also a pupil of several other physiologists and philosophers. Returning from Leipzig, he went in 1883 to Johns Hopkins,[10] establishing the first American psychological laboratory which followed the small beginnings by James in 1875. Hall did not carry out any important original experiments during his six years at Johns Hopkins; but by founding the *American Journal of Psychology* in 1887, he gave the adherents of the new psychology not only a storehouse for contributions both experimental and theoretical, but a sense of solidarity and independence. When Clark University was founded in 1889, Hall was called to be its president. Two years later, he founded a journal dealing with child psychology, the *Pedagogical Seminary* (now the *Journal of Genetic Psychology*). Hall played a leading part in founding the American Psychological Association in 1892.

Münsterberg was called by James to take over and develop the Harvard experimental psychology laboratory in 1892, and Titchener began his career at Cornell in the same year — where Frank Angell had established a Wundtian laboratory and had gone on to found another at Stanford. In 1894 an inquiry made into the experimental psychology of the United States revealed twenty-seven laboratories. In the same year was founded the *Psychological Review*. The laboratories and journals, and the Association, furnished good opportunities for the intercommunication of ideas and for personal contact. The most important single factor in saving American psychology in this period from becoming essentially a branch of Wundt's laboratory was the influence of William James. American psychology, as the early journals show, was indeed interested in many problems not strictly experimental; but it was James who did most to give psychologists a broad and flexible definition of their field, in which the whole wealth of human exper-

---

[9] The task of conquering the soil and devising means to utilize its vast resources, the possibilities for the acquisition of land, and an absorbing commercial activity had kept philosophy and pure science at a low level. The United States had made some significant contributions to physical science (for example, through Franklin and Henry), but mostly in relation to its application to industry. It would probably not be forcing the point about practicality to recall that whereas psychology as a science had amounted to very little in this country, the practical task of care for mental defectives and the insane had offered through Howe and Dix an opportunity for American leadership.

[10] His pupils there included Jastrow and Dewey.

rience was welcomed for investigation. Before long we shall be considering James's contributions in greater detail.

French Psychology

While the new spirit of psychological experimentation spread with the speed of a brush fire and led to the proud, independent identity of "psychology" and "psychologists" in Germany and the United States, French psychology continued to remain hidden in the field of psychiatry and medicine. The great figures in French psychology were, in fact, physicians, the dominant names being Ribot and Janet. The most prominent exception in the era of the late nineteenth century was Taine (1870), advocate of the new associationism. The primary field of research was hypnosis. Richet, as early as 1870, had reported that consciousness may be split, one conscious activity being out of contact with another conscious activity in the same person (1875). This was a part of the new French psychology of personality to which Binet later drew attention.

As we saw, the great clinician and clinical teacher Charcot emphasized the relation of hypnotic suggestion to the phenomenon of hysteria, while the Nancy school taught that hypnosis was a special case of normal suggestibility.

Among Charcot's pupils, Janet was especially interested in dissociation, the splitting of personality (1892, 1907). This led to a systematic conception of personality as an integration of ideas and tendencies. In normal personality the integration is relatively stable and constant; hysteria is characterized by imperfect integration, lowered "psychic tension," which in extreme cases may result in the cleavage of the individual into two or more "alternating personalities." During the eighties and thereafter, Prince and others began to make the French work popular in the United States (1885), while William James incorporated much of it in his writings. In Britain, Braid had already prepared the way, and the work of the Paris and Nancy schools was easily assimilated.

A dominant figure, alert to all the newer British and German trends and fully expressive of the medical and psychiatric approach of French psychology, was Ribot. Though a contributor to many fields, Ribot is perhaps best known for his writings on psychopathology, especially the *Diseases of Memory* (1881) and *Diseases of Personality* (1885). He represented the fusion of two streams, psychiatric practice and mechanistic theory. The mechanistic physiological psychology inaugurated by Hobbes and La Mettrie had deeply colored medical and psychological thought. Exemplified by Ziehen (1891–1914) in Germany and by Maudsley (1867, 1884) in Britain, it took vigorous form in the writings of Ribot, who made brain physiology and brain disease the basis of personality and its disorders. Ribot's desire for an empirical psychology, and his familiarity with the German work, made him a logical candidate for the position of director of the first French psychological laboratory at the Collège de France, to which, a decade after the founding of the Leipzig laboratory, he was appointed.

This was followed immediately by the establishment of a psychological laboratory at the Sorbonne. Here Binet began his career (Varon, 1935). He was in his early years a student of hypnosis. He and Féré published a series of experiments on animal magnetism (1887), in which the chief interest lay in the investigation of hyperesthesia during hypnotic trance. The importance of the work lay mainly in the separation of hypnotic practice from its clinical surroundings, opening the way toward its utilization by experimental psychologists. Binet served later as editor of the *Année Psychologique,* founded in 1895. He was a lifelong student of personality, making pioneer studies of individual differences — for example, in the response to suggestion (1900) and of abnormalities portrayed in handwriting (1906) — and became best known for his studies of the thought processes. His *Psychology of Reasoning,* with Féré (1886), was followed by a long series of empirical studies of specific kinds of thinking; for example, the thinking of mental defectives, and of chess players and lightning calculators (1894). The experimental investigations of thinking, in which his two little daughters served as subjects (1903), belong to a period when his rigid associationism was being washed away by evidences of unity, activity, ego function, in normal and abnormal alike. It was his feeling that instead of approaching the big and the complex through the little and the simple, it was imperative to confront the big and the complex directly. It was in this spirit that he conceived the problem of testing intelligence; we shall return to this task of his later years.

Binet's collaborator, Féré, made other notable contributions in this period. In 1888, he discovered the electrical phenomena in the body associated with emotion, to which the name *psychogalvanic reflex* was applied. He also conducted important experiments on fatigue, devising the first ergograph for the measurement of muscular energy expended. The latter experiments are associated with his celebrated doctrine of dynamogenesis (1887), which emphasized the function of stimuli in liberating energy within the organism; muscular contractions were increased even by apparently irrelevant stimuli. We may say that by the end of the century French experimental psychology, though still far behind the German, had displayed its own intrinsic genius through several men of the first caliber.

Psychology in Italy in this period was modeled to some extent upon that of Germany and never attained proportions to make it comparable with Italian neurology and psychiatry. Few laboratories were founded. Child study, however, as we shall see later, made new strides. Considerable work was done on the physiology of the emotions. Though much of this was of a purely descriptive character, Mosso was one of the first to study physiological changes experimentally induced by fear and excitement (1884). The Netherlands, Belgium, Switzerland, and the Scandinavian countries were responsive to the new trends; new laboratories reflected the Wundtian outlook. But French psychiatric interests were strong at Geneva, where Flournoy significantly contributed to the study of dissociation and suggestion (1900). He had a broad and deep interest in philosophy, the psychology of personality, and psychical research, as exemplified, for example, in long, thoughtful conversations and much correspondence with William James (LeClair, 1966).

Experimental Psychology in Britain

Experimental psychology was received slowly, and with little enthusiasm, in Britain. In spite of Galton's genius, and his marked influence upon Wundt and Cattell, British psychology made at first rather limited use of his methods. It was not until the appearance of Pearson (1897) that there was any Galtonian psychology to speak of; and with Pearson and his school, Galton's *statistical* methods enjoyed much greater favor than his *experimental* methods. British psychology became vigorously evolutionary, emphasizing the problems of instinct and intelligence, the phylogenetic approach, and the problems of adaptation to the environment, with a sprinkling of good animal experiments and systematic treatises on psychological development. Such an approach fused well with those philosophical schools which emphasized the unity of human experience and behavior rather than the traditional associationist piecemeal approach, or, as the British saw it, the fragmentary and disjointed findings from the new German psychological laboratories. The earlier German emphasis upon activity and unity had, as we saw, come to life in the new dynamic philosophy of the school represented by James Ward, a school which we should be inclined to call today "idealistic" but which could more appropriately be called "personalistic" in the sense in which, at a later time, William Stern used the term. In his article on psychology in the 1886 edition of the *Encyclopaedia Britannica* he summarized the dominant British viewpoint in questioning whether "association should be regarded as the bedrock of all mental complexity and unity, or whether it was a minor affair dependent upon some larger and deeper conception of unity" (Brett, 1965, p. 229). Thus the term "psychology" in Britain may legitimately be applied to the continuing philosophical approach that descended from the Scottish school and from associationism, or it may with equal justice be applied to the new evolutionary psychology expressed in the observations of Lloyd Morgan and Romanes. Such animal experimentation as was done was inspired much more by Darwin than by Wundt. Evolutionism became, in fact, the dominant tendency. The first British psychological laboratory was at Cambridge; here C. S. Myers attained eminence as an experimentalist. Other laboratories followed from time to time, but laboratory studies made up only a very small fraction of the psychological output of the period.

This total picture shows rather wide geographical differences, some of which remain today. German and American psychology at the end of the nineteenth century were emphasizing the experimental approach; French psychology, the psychiatric; British psychology, the evolutionary and comparative. In later chapters it will become evident that these national differences in emphasis have tended to become less clear-cut but that they are still of importance.

REFERENCES

Arnheim, R. *Art and Visual Perception*. Berkeley: University of California Press, 1954.

Binet, A. *La Psychologie des grands calculateurs et joueurs d'échec*. Paris: Hachette, 1894.

————. *La Suggestibilité*. Paris: Schleicher, 1900.

————. *L'Etude experimentale de l'intelligence*. Paris: Schleicher, 1903.

————. *Les Révélations de l'écriture d'après un contrôle scientifique*. Paris: Alcan, 1906.

Binet, A., and Féré, C. *La Psychologie du raisonnement* [*The Psychology of Reasoning*]. Paris: Alcan, 1886.

————. *Le Magnétisme animal*. Paris: Alcan, 1887.

Blix, M. "Experimentelle Beiträge zur Lösung der Frage über die specifische Energie der Hautnerven." *Zeitschrift für Biologie*, 20 (1884), 141.

Bonnet, C. *Essai analytique sur les facultés de l'âme*. Copenhagen: Philibert, 1760.

Brett, G. S. *A History of Psychology*. Rev. ed. R. S. Peters, ed. Cambridge, Mass.: M.I.T. Press, 1965.

Cattell, J. McK. "Über die Zeit der Erkennung und Benennung von Schriftzeichen, Bildern und Farben." *Philosophische Studien*, 2 (1885), 635–50.

————. "Über die Trägheit der Netzhaut und des Sehcentrums." *Philosophische Studien*, 3 (1885a), 94.

————. "Psychometrische Untersuchungen." *Philosophische Studien*, 3 (1886), 305–35, 452–92.

————. "A Statistical Study of Eminent Men." *Popular Science Monthly*, 57 (1903), 359–77.

————. "Statistics of American Psychologists." *American Journal of Psychology*, 14 (1903a), 310–28.

————, ed. *American Men of Science*. 1st ed. 1906. (Cattell edited six editions, from 1906 to 1938.)

Cattell, J. McK., and Bryant, S. "Mental Association Investigated by Experiment." *Mind*, 14 (1889), 230–50.

Cattell, J. McK., and Farrand, L. "Physical and Mental Measurements of the Students of Columbia University." *Psychological Review*, 3 (1896), 618–48.

Cattell, J. McK., and Fullerton, G. "On the Perception of Small Differences." *University of Pennsylvania Publications, Philosophy Series*, Vol. 2 (1892).

————. "On Errors of Observation." *American Journal of Psychology*, 5 (1893), 285–93.

Ebbinghaus, H. *Über das Gedächtnis*. Leipzig: Duncker and Humblot, 1885.

Féré, C. S. *Sensation et mouvement*. Paris: Alcan, 1887.

Flournoy, T. *From India to the Planet Mars*. New York: Harper, 1900.

Goldscheider, A. *Gesamelte Abhandlungen, Physiologie des Muskelsinnes*. Leipzig: Barth, 1898.

Horwicz, A. *Psychologische Analysen auf Physiologicher Grundlage.* Halle: Pfeffer, 1872-78.

James, W. *Talks to Teachers.* New York: Holt, 1899.

Janet, P. *L'État mental des hysteriques.* Paris: Ruell, 1892.

———. *The Major Symptoms of Hysteria.* New York: Macmillan, 1907.

Kent, G. H., and Rosanoff, A. J. "A Study of Association in Insanity." *American Journal of Insanity,* 67 (1910), 37-96, 317-90.

König, A., and Brodhun, E. "Experimentelle Untersuchungen über die Psychophysische Fundamentalformeh in Bezug auf den Gesichtssin." *Akademie der wissenschaften (Berlin) Sitzungberichte* (1888-89), 917-31.

Kraepelin, E. *Ueber die Beeinflussung Einfacher Psychischer Vorgänge.* Jena: Fischer, 1892.

Külpe, O. *Grundriss der Psychologie.* Leipzig: Engelmann, 1893.

Lange, L. "Neue Experimente über den Vorgang der Einfachen Reaction auf Sinnesreizen." *Philosophische Studien,* 4 (1888), 479-510.

LeClair, R. C., ed. *Letters of William James and Théodore Flournoy.* Madison: University of Wisconsin Press, 1966.

Lipps, T. *Raumaesthetik und Geometrisch-Optische Taüschungen.* Leipzig: Barth, 1897.

Maudsley, H. *Physiology and Pathology of Mind.* London: Macmillan, 1867.

———. *Body and Will.* New York: Appleton, 1884.

Mosso, A. *La Paura.* Milan: Fratelli Treves, 1884.

Müller, G. E. *Zur Grundlegung der Psychophysik.* Berlin: Grüben, 1878.

Pearson, K. "Mathematical Contributions to the Theory of Evolution: Regression, Heredity, and Panmixia." *Philosophical Transactions,* 187 (1897), 253-318.

Prince, M. *Nature of Mind and Human Automatism.* Philadelphia: Lippincott, 1885.

Ribot, T.-A. *Les Maladies de la mémoire [Diseases of Memory].* Paris: Alcan, 1881.

———. *Les Maladies de la personnalité [Diseases of Personality].* Paris: Germer Baillière, 1885.

Richet, C.-R. "Du somnambulisme provoqué." *Journal of Anatomy and Physiology,* 11 (1875), 348-78.

Sommer, R. *Diagnostik der Geisteskrankheiten.* Vienna and Leipzig: Urban and Schwarzenberg, 1894.

Stumpf, K. *Tonpsychologie.* Leipzig: Hirzel, 1883-90.

———. *Beiträge zur Akustik und Musikwissenschaft.* 9 parts. Leipzig: Barth, 1898-1924.

Taine, H.-A. *De l'intelligence.* 1870. 2 vols. New York: Holt, 1871.

Trautscholdt, M. "Experimentelle Untersuchungen über die Association der Vorstellungen." *Philosophische Studien,* 1 (1883), 213-50.

Varon, E. "The Development of Alfred Binet's Psychology." *Psychological Monographs,* 46 (1935), 207.

Wundt, W. *Grundzüge der Physiologischen Psychologie [Principles of Physiological Psychology].* Leipzig: Engelmann, 1873-74.

———. *Völkerpsychologie.* 4 vols. Leipzig: Engelmann, 1900-14.

Ziehen, T. *Leitfaden der Physiologischen Psychologie.* 16 vols. Jena: Fischer, 1891-1914.

NOTE: A list of further readings appears at the back of the book.

12

Early Studies
of Memory
and Learning

*We clearly understand by this what memory is. It is nothing else than
a certain concatenation of ideas, involving the nature of things which
are outside the body, a concatenation which corresponds in the mind to
the order and concatenation of the modification of the human body.*

SPINOZA

The decade of the eighties marked the first systematic experimental investigation of learning and memory. There had indeed been a little fragmentary investigation of memory and allied processes before that; a close approach to experimental work on memory was Galton's comparison of his own childhood and adult associations. There had been a little animal experimentation in the field of learning, concerned, for example, with the attempt to find out whether certain acts were instinctive or learned. The material was inadequate to establish any general principle regarding the learning process. In general, psychologists were thinking in terms of learning versus forgetting, making a sharp line between what was learned and what was not learned, between what was forgotten and what was not forgotten. They were not yet thinking in quantitative terms; they took no account of degrees of learning and degrees of forgetting.

Ebbinghaus

The whole character of the problem was changed by Hermann Ebbinghaus, who from 1879 to 1884 subjected both learning and forgetting to quantitative treatment (1885). This was one of the greatest triumphs of original genius in experimental psychology. For the first time, moreover, experimental psychology undertook, with an attempt to introduce the safeguards and precautions of scientific procedure, a psychological problem which was not

181

simply an adjunct to physiology.[1] The great bulk of Wundt's experimental procedure had been borrowed from physiologists. The field of experimental psychology changed immediately when Ebbinghaus entered it; his conceptions and methods came in time to be as characteristic of the "new psychology" as were those of Wundt.

Glancing through the offerings of a Paris bookstall, he had happened upon Fechner's *Elements of Psychophysics* (1860) and had been electrified by it. What Fechner had done through strict and systematic measurements for a science of psychophysics, he would do for memory study. His first step was the adoption of certain statistical methods through which the accuracy of observation was to be gauged by the extent to which various observations agreed (that is, the study of variability about the mean). This principle, furthermore, was stated in terms of the symmetry of the curve of errors. Such symmetrical curves, said Ebbinghaus, give us reason to believe that we are dealing with variable errors, not with constant errors. Variable errors can be disregarded; for if observations are sufficiently numerous, such errors in one direction from the mean should cancel those in the opposite direction. Bringing this method into psychology, he reduced psychological material to that department of the language of science which speaks in terms of averages and probable errors of observation.[2] In so doing, he atoned in part for the fact that he made use of only one experimental subject, himself. He got rid, to a large extent, of variable errors. Of course, the *constants* due to his own personal idiosyncrasies remained.

His second great innovation was the elimination of another group of variable errors which may be called qualitative rather than quantitative – the *meanings* of things learned. We cannot by any possible process of analysis take account of the varieties of meaning that attach to words as they are learned and forgotten. Ebbinghaus wished to find materials entirely or at least relatively free from meaning. One can do this more effectively in German than in English; over two thousand nonsense syllables can be constructed in German by the utilization of two consonants separated by a vowel. At one stroke Ebbinghaus solved a problem which had confused students of psychology, particularly associationists, for centuries.[3] The extraordinary complexity of factors which make for meaning was in considerable measure excluded. These nonsense syllables were of unequal "difficulty," but when combined in groups their differences could be treated as variable errors of the type described.

---

[1] Psychological experiments performed outside the physiological laboratory had inevitably been amateurish and crude; even Galton's association experiment illustrates the point.

[2] Fechner's psychophysical methods had expressed the closest previous approach to such a conception, but Ebbinghaus borrowed not so much from Fechner as from contemporary physical science.

[3] "It is not too much to say that the recourse to nonsense syllables, as means to the study of association, marks the most considerable advance, in this chapter of psychology, since the time of Aristotle" (Titchener, 1909–10, pp. 380–81).

Whereas Galton and Wundt had measured the time relations of the process of association initiated by a single verbal stimulus, Ebbinghaus devoted himself to the formation of *series* of connections. Instead of studying associations already formed, he investigated the steps in the formation of associations; he presented for memorization a series containing many syllables which were to be learned in their order. An important contribution here was the standardization of the rate of presentation. This was set at two-fifths of a second per syllable.[4] Throughout his experiments he made the general conditions of the experiment as constant as he could, experimenting at the same hours from day to day and keeping his regimen and habits as regular as possible. The reader who takes cognizance of the vast quantity of work to which he subjected himself may well inquire whether his interest remained constant throughout; the Herculean task has never been fully repeated.

One of his first problems was the effect of varying the length of the series to be learned, finding how the number of readings necessary for memorization increases with the length of the list.[5] He found that under ordinary conditions he could learn seven, frequently eight, nonsense syllables at one reading. This was the first systematic measurement of the "memory span." A sudden and immense increase occurred in the time required as he increased the number of syllables to nine, ten, and beyond. For example, instead of merely increasing 25 per cent in passing from twelve to fifteen syllables, the labor required was much greater.

Ebbinghaus suffered from an intellectual blind spot which is comprehensible when one recalls the cardinal tenets of associationism. Associationists, with few exceptions, had disregarded the possibility that mind is anything more than a series of impressions contributed by experience, the possibility that it may *actively* adjust itself to its tasks.[6] Ebbinghaus made no distinction between mere rereading on the one hand and the process of active recall on the other. He read through the lists passively until he thought he knew them; he then forced himself to recall them, and wherever necessary he prompted himself. In some of these series he knew the list perfectly without prompting, and in other cases he might prompt himself several times. We cannot tell to what extent he made use of forced recall of material. He was saved from failure only by his statistical method, which, with so much material, presumably caused this factor of active recitation to operate (at least in most of his problems) as a variable rather than as a constant

---

[4] In spite of the many systematic variations of procedure, he failed to study the effect of varying the speed of presentation.

[5] Memorization was construed in his first experiments as that to the point of two perfect repetitions; in the later series, to the point of one perfect repetition.

[6] Herbart had, indeed, explicitly recognized *activity*, yet he failed to utilize the concept so as to draw a distinction between what is actively recalled and what is effortlessly brought back by new stimulation. For him, activity belonged to *ideas;* the distinction between active and passive *learning* was disregarded.

error. It must, however, have tended in general to shorten the learning time. Not until the early years of the present century was the importance of this principle of active recitation recognized.[7]

Ebbinghaus's next problem was the influence of repeated reading after the attainment of the capacity for perfect repetition; that is, the influence of *overlearning*. He wished to know what happened when, after he had learned a series completely, he continued to study it. This involved his conception of memory as a matter of *degree;* he sought to measure the *strength* of the connections established between observed items. Instead of relying upon the distinction between learned and unlearned material, he introduced the celebrated "saving method," which undertakes to measure how much labor is necessary to bring back what has once been known. Suppose we learn two lists of forty-eight syllables each, and then allow twenty-four hours to pass. We may then find that from the first we can recall two-thirds of the syllables but that it takes twenty repetitions to regain the whole list; from the second list we may recall the same number of *items,* but it may take thirty repetitions to complete the series. Ebbinghaus realized that he could get a better test of retention by measuring the amount of work needed to relearn than by measuring the gross amount of material recalled. There is, of course, room for difference of opinion as to the best single test of memory in any given case; in fact, Ebbinghaus's methods did much to make it clear that memory is not a single process, and that a variety of methods is needed because of the variety of problems presented.

The use of the saving method made possible also a determination of the value of various amounts of overlearning, by measuring the relation of overlearning to saving. If it takes twenty repetitions to get the list of syllables, how many more repetitions are necessary to retain it twenty-four hours? Ebbinghaus recognized that there is not only a stage just below the point of knowing the material, but a stage just *above* knowing it, so to speak. These are the convex and concave sides of the same problem; the formation of linkages between terms is not an all-or-none matter, but a question of degree. Now the amount of overlearning was compared directly with the amount of saving manifested in relearning. Knowing how much work would ordinarily be required after a given interval to relearn material which had been just learned and no more, it was possible to show how much more quickly the material could be relearned if it had in the first place been overlearned. The ratio of overlearning to saving turned out, in Ebbinghaus's data, to be roughly a straight-line relationship. Additional units of overlearning produced, after a twenty-four-hour interval, fairly uniform amounts of saving. With nonsense material under the conditions stated the number of repetitions saved was

[7] The "memory-span" experiment was a direct development of Ebbinghaus's study of the influence of varying the length of a series. In 1887, Jacobs published a further investigation of the memory span with a number of subjects, the first intensive study of the problem. The method was adopted by Cattell and others and has been in wide use ever since.

consistently about one-third of the number of repetitions in overlearning.[8]

One of the great triumphs of the saving method was the quantitative examination of the process of forgetting. From a standard mass of memorized material, decrements due to the lapse of various intervals of time could be computed. Having learned a list, for example, requiring fifteen repetitions, Ebbinghaus could find how much work it took, say twenty-four hours later, to bring back that list to the point of perfect repetition, so that he could go through it without aid. In this way he obtained the material for his "curve of forgetting," which showed that forgetting was extremely rapid in the first few minutes, considerably less rapid in the next few hours, and even less rapid in the next few days. It became at last almost a straight line, asymptotic to the x axis upon which time intervals were measured. This method established definitely a quantitative basis for the study of forgetting and therefore of retention. The curve was extremely simple mathematically, stated in a form of very general validity. The exact form of the curves of forgetting, plotted by Ebbinghaus for his own data with himself as subject, has not, of course, proved adequate for other data and for other observers. These qualifications do not, however, affect the general form of the curve, which has been abundantly verified: an initial drop, gradually becoming less steep in asymptotic form.

The method was capable of application to meaningful material, and Ebbinghaus later compared this with nonsense material in order to determine whether the form of the curve still held good. He memorized many stanzas from Byron's *Don Juan* and ascertained the amount of material retained after varying intervals, using the saving method. The same *general* shape of the curve was found for the meaningful as for the nonsense material, though the fall was less rapid throughout. He went back to this problem twenty-two years later and relearned many of these stanzas, having in the meantime given them no further rehearsal. Comparing these with new stanzas memorized, he found an appreciable difference in learning time; the saving method revealed some retention over the twenty-two-year period (1902, Vol. 1). This result could scarcely be explained on the basis of mere familiarity with particular words in the text. For in another connection he directly attacked the question whether the familiarity of elements in memory material altered the form of the curves or not. He made up lists in which each syllable was familiar to him and found that the lists were just as hard to learn as lists of equal length containing unfamiliar syllables. It seemed to be the *connections* which were significant in the learning process. It appeared then that connections established in meaningful material enjoy very long life.

Another of his contributions which has been recognized and used on a large scale was the study of the most effective distribution of working time — the question of whether a given amount of time yields a larger return when

---

[8] This linear relation held up to sixty-four repetitions; the nature of the curve above that point was not ascertained.

given uninterruptedly to the memorizing of material or when broken up into shorter periods with rest intervals between. Is it better, for example, to give an hour all at once to incessant repetition of a task, or to break it into periods of two half-hours separated by an interval, or into four fifteen-minute periods? Ebbinghaus found that "spaced" repetition was decidedly to be preferred to continuous and "unspaced" repetition. He did not ascertain the optimum interval between work periods; but such evidence as we have indicates that the twenty-four-hour interval, which he used, was a good choice.

Finally, he sought to answer the question whether associations are ever formed according to any other pattern than A − B − C − D, the letters repsenting items learned and the dashes associations or linkages. Hartley had asserted that if a series of elements A, B, C, D is learned, there is a tendency for A to recall faint images, B, C, and D, which are memories of the original elements. Now, said Ebbinghaus, we know from Herbart's work and his mathematical formulae (which Ebbinghaus almost alone of all psychologists took rather seriously) that there are associations not only from A to B, but also from A to C and from A to D. There are ideas rising into consciousness and disappearing again; there may be several present above the threshold at once. There may be in the process of learning more than two items undergoing linkage at a given moment; several terms, A, B, C, D, may be in consciousness at once. At a given moment A may be about to disappear from consciousness while B is, so to speak, at its zenith; C is rising into clear consciousness while D is only vaguely present. Hence there may be not only remote forward connections such as A − C and A − D, but backward associations such as D − C and even C − A. Ebbinghaus undertook to find out whether connections were actually formed as the theory demanded. Taking nonsense lists which had once been learned, he constructed from these *new* lists in which every *second* syllable was used: A, C, E, G. Similarly, lists were formed by taking every third item of a learned list A, D, G . . . , and so on, to the point of selecting every eighth syllable. Now he found that he could learn the new list (made up by skipping every second syllable and so on) more rapidly than comparable nonsense material that was new. For him this proved that when he had originally learned the list A, B, C, D he had actually formed associations not only from A to B and from B to C, but from A to C, and the like. Herbart was vindicated. By the saving method Ebbinghaus showed that the linkage of A with C was more effective than that of A with D and that the strength of the linkage consistently decreased with the number of syllables skipped until, with the skipping of seven syllables, the curve approached the base line.

Similarly, he constructed lists of nonsense syllables in an order the reverse of the one used in the original learning. He found that he could learn these more quickly than comparable material which was new, thus apparently showing that when learning the list in the first place he had established connections also from B to A, from C to B, and so on. And he constructed lists in which both backward association and skipping were to be tested—such as E, C, A. Even these lists were more effectively learned than was new material. Various objections have been raised, but it is by no means certain that these objections dispose of the problem.

The place of Ebbinghaus in the history of psychology is not, however, confined to the issue of finding ways to investigate memory. His determination to develop a refined technique, to control everything that could be controlled, and to reduce everything to quantitative form vividly exemplified the incursion of the physical-science methods into psychology; it set a new direction for psychology as dramatically and as clearly as did anything in the era.

The Expansion of the New Program

Ebbinghaus's memory work inspired a great deal of further investigation. G. E. Müller, working now with one and now with another collaborator, improved some of the methods of Ebbinghaus and attacked many new problems. Müller and Schumann (1893), for example, devised a method for the uniform presentation, upon a revolving drum, of nonsense syllables for memorization, so that the rate of presentation could be systematically varied. An exposure slot makes it possible for the subject to observe one syllable in one unit of time. Another improvement in Ebbinghaus's methods was the devising of lists of nonsense syllables which were found in practice to be of approximately equal difficulty.

While such modifications in method were being made, Müller and many others contributed new experiments and results. It was found by W. G. Smith in 1896 that early and late syllables were fixated much more quickly than those in the middle of a series. Steffens discovered shortly thereafter (1900) a principle which has been much utilized. She demonstrated the futility of trying to break up long passages of meaningful material into short passages for memorizing; material was found to be better learned when read through from beginning to end than when learned in parts and pieced together. The task of fitting together the different parts when learned separately was very wasteful of time. The experiment has been repeated by many students, the majority of whom have confirmed the reality of this advantage of "whole learning" over "part learning" in most individuals.

One of the most important of these extensions of Ebbinghaus's procedure consisted in the study of individual connections or linkages; emphasis was withdrawn from "serial" learning and given to association between pairs of elements. To this end, Calkins devised a method of presenting, both visually and auditorily, *pairs* of items, the items having no obvious meaningful relation; for example, a pair might consist of a word and a number (1896). Her first use of the method was to study the influence of primacy, recency, frequency, and vividness. By demonstrating the influence of these factors in assisting her subjects to recall the second item of each pair, she gave experimental confirmation to some of those "secondary" laws of association which Thomas Brown had enumerated three-quarters of a century before. Pairs early and late in the series were compared with those in the middle; frequently presented pairs were contrasted with those less frequently shown; variation in size and color of type gave to some items special vividness. The method was shortly afterward adopted and developed by Müller and Pilzecker (1900). Performance was measured in terms of the number of cases in which the second term could be recalled when the first term was presented. The new method of "paired associates" was applicable to a study of many sorts of variables appearing with each association to be formed.[9]

During the twenty years which followed the experiments of Ebbinghaus, research was dominated by his concepts and concerned primarily with the extension of his methods. Nevertheless, it began to be more and more evident that a simple associationism could not account for what happened. It was discovered that the way in which the individual learned depended on his attitude or purpose. The task the individual undertook determined the manner of learning: if, for example, the syllables were simply read through without the purpose of learning them, very little connection between them was formed.

Indeed, one main result of the long series of memory studies, especially those of Müller, was to reveal the great variety of devices spontaneously adopted by the memorizing subject to facilitate his difficult task. Rhythmical and other groupings, similarities and other relationships observed, even in nonsense materials, and meanings of all sorts read into the material, make the memorizing process very different from a passive or receptive establishment of contiguities.

Motor Skills

In the closing years of the nineteenth century and the opening years of the twentieth, the problem of the acquisition of motor skills was vigorously studied. Memory as Ebbinghaus had conceived it had proved amenable to quantitative examination, but it now became apparent that other forms of the learning process could be approached in the same experimental spirit as the functions of memorizing and forgetting syllables and words.

Bryan and Harter undertook a study (1897, 1899) of the stages in learning to send and receive telegraphic messages. Curves of learning were constructed, indicating the stages of progress toward mastery of the task over a period of many months. The "learning curves" thus plotted indicated that progress was more rapid at first than later. Progress being measured in terms of the number of units which could be handled in a unit of time; the

[9] Ebbinghaus himself later introduced the "prompting method" for this purpose (1902, Vol. 1, p. 648). The subject is prompted whenever he falters.

time devoted to learning yielded gradually less return as the task went on. But the two men found the learning process to be not a regular, even progression, but a series of jumps. Learning to receive telegraphic messages was frequently interrupted by periods of no progress; in these intervals the learning curve presented very roughly a horizontal line, to which the name "plateau" was given.[10] No uniform duration of the plateau or uniform interval between plateaus was apparent.

Following the principle of "diminishing returns" noted above, the learning curve was found also to reach a point where no further gains were apparent; practice merely kept the subject up to his acquired standard. This last stage was entitled the "physiological limit." But the horizontal line of the physiological limit seemed to differ psychologically from the plateaus; the plateaus did not appear to be genuine periods of *no progress*. They seemed to be periods in which the subject had reached the maximum attainable *with a given method;* but after practice had continued for a time, he was able to take advantage of a new and more efficient type of response, for which he would previously have been unprepared.

But just what is being practiced during a plateau? In one instance, the subject has learned how to receive each letter of the alphabet; he handles each word as the sum of the letters composing it, interpreting the symbol for one letter and then, after a brief pause, the letter which follows. He is in the "letter-habit" stage. When the letters have been practiced long enough, the subject passes rapidly to a new system of habits in which words are grasped and received as integrated units. The subject has entered the "word-habit" stage, and the learning curve again rises. The word is a "higher unit," similar to the higher units discovered by Cattell in his investigation of word perception. When the word habit has been mastered, the subject may pass to the phrase habit or even to the sentence habit. Some expert telegraphers were found to follow more than two hundred clicks behind a message to which they listened; they were taking in great masses of material in the form of higher units.

In connection with this matter of higher units, or organization into groups or wholes, the work of Bryan and Harter showed that two or more responses might go on at once, in such a way that the first "overlapped" the second. This had been found also by Cattell in the reading of letters and words; a word might be perceived before the previous word had been enunciated. So, in receiving a message and transcribing it on a typewriter, experts were found to follow from six to twelve words after the message; higher units and overlapping were present in conjunction. The messages were received and typed not letter by letter, but phrase by phrase, or even sentence by sentence. The subject could begin a new activity while waiting to complete a higher unit.

---

[10] Such plateaus were not clearly demonstrable in the curves for "sending."

Similar studies in the acquisition of skill were made within a few years by Swift (1903, 1905) and Book (1908). While in general confirming the conclusions of Bryan and Harter, and discovering similar plateaus, their interpretations of the significance of the plateau differed. Swift pointed out that higher units may be in the process of formation even during the plateau. Book, studying the acquisition of skill in typewriting, found that subjects frequently showed loss of interest at the beginning of the plateau and, further, that physiological observations (for example, of the pulse) indicated a lax or depressed state, which in itself seemed sufficient to account for the absence of progress. Book suggested that the plateau, far from being a period of hidden progress, was actually wasted time. Book's plateaus, similar to those of Bryan and Harter, seemed to correspond to the passage from lower to higher units.

One of Book's most important contributions is related to the process of overlearning. Ebbinghaus had shown that additional memorizing beyond the amount needed for a perfect recitation at the time has a marked effect in facilitating the task of relearning — in fact, that the whole curve of forgetting for overlearned material falls off much more slowly than that for just-learned material. Book's subjects, after acquiring considerable skill in typewriting — in which, of course, a great many reactions were overlearned — dropped it for four months. Upon resuming practice they regained in a few days the same level of skill which had at first cost them several weeks. Book concluded that something had occurred which illustrated James's suggestion ("from an unknown German scientist") that we may perhaps learn to skate in the summer and to swim in the winter; the period of disuse was credited with "the disappearance, with the lapse of time, of numerous psycho-physical difficulties . . . interfering habits and tendencies, which, as they faded, left the more firmly established typewriting associations free to act." Though this conclusion has not commanded universal assent, the data did at least clearly demonstrate the vast importance of intensive overlearning. In terms of Ebbinghaus's "saving method," the loss during four months of no practice was exceedingly slight.

REFERENCES

Book, W. F. "The Psychology of Skill with Special Reference to the Acquisition of Typewriting." *University of Montana Publications in Psychology* (1908).

Bryan, W. L., and Harter, N. H. "Studies in the Physiology and Psychology of the Telegraphic Language." *Psychological Review,* 4 (1897), 27–53.

———. "Studies on the Telegraphic Language: The Acquisition of a Hierarchy of Habits." *Psychological Review,* 6 (1899), 346–75.

Calkins, M. W. "Association." *Psychological Review,* 3 (1896), 32–49.

Ebbinghaus, H. *Über das Gedächtnis.* Leipzig: Duncker and Humblot, 1885.

———. *Grundzüge der Psychologie.* 2 vols. Leipzig: Veit, 1902–11.

Fechner, G. T. *Elemente der Psychophysik* [*Elements of Psychophysics*]. Leipzig: Breitkopf and Härtel, 1860.

Jacobs, J. "Experiments on 'Prehension.' " *Mind,* 12 (1887), 75–79.

Müller, G. E., and Pilzecker, A. *Experimentelle Beiträge zur Lehre vom Gedächtniss.* Leipzig: Barth, 1900.

Müller, G. E., and Schumann, F. "Experimentelle Beiträge zur Untersuchungen des Gedächtnisses." *Zeitschrift für Psychologie,* 6 (1893), 81–190, 257–339.

Smith, W. G. "The Place of Repetition in Memory." *Psychological Review,* 3 (1896), 21–31.

Steffens, L. "Experimentelle Beiträge zur Lehre vom ökonomischen Lernen." *Zeitschrift für Psychologie,* 22 (1900), 321–80.

Swift, E. J. "Studies in the Psychology and Physiology of Learning." *American Journal of Psychology,* 14 (1903), 201–51.

———. "Memory of a Complex Skillful Act." *American Journal of Psychology,* 16 (1905), 131–33.

Titchener, E. B. *A Text-Book of Psychology.* New York: Macmillan, 1909–10.

NOTE: A list of further readings appears at the back of the book.

13

William James

He always left the impression that there was more; that he knew there was more; and that the more to come might, for all one knew, throw a very different light on the matters under discussion. He respected his universe too much to believe that he could carry it under his own hat. These saving doubts arose from the same source as his tolerance and respect for his fellow man. The universe, like one's neighbor, is never wholly disclosed to outward view, and the last word must be a consent that the other should be itself.

R. B. PERRY

America after the Civil War was characterized by the great realities of the frontier in the West and the industrial development in the East. The new evolutionary thinking was concordant with the vast developments in the land, with the surging exploratory spirit of Walt Whitman. The proud achievements of Thomas A. Edison belonged to this world. But whenever there was leisure and a chance to reflect, there was hunger for the letters, arts, and science of Britain, France, Germany, and Italy.

From a fortune made in Albany (New York) real estate — as the Erie Canal carried men and goods to western settlements — came the prosperity of the James family. The writer Henry James was one member of this family. He made his way to England — to spend most of his life as a reflective and analytical student of the inner, subjective world. His older brother, William James (1842–1910), was also familiar with the rich culture of western Europe. William James made repeated trips, sometimes with the James family and later alone or with his wife and children, to Britain, France, Switzerland, Germany, and Italy. He was absorbed by painting, music, philosophy, and literature; having first decided to become a painter, he spent several years as an artist in the colony at Newport, Rhode Island; but soon he turned to science. His training at Harvard, combined with an inordinate amount of independent hard reading and endless discussions, prepared him for the M.D. degree in 1869. While he was a medical student in 1865, James had the opportunity to join Louis Agassiz in collecting scientific specimens near the Amazon. There he contracted a tropical fever, which was the first in a long series of physical ailments. Another trip to Germany led to backaches and other troubles. His attempts at a cure in resort towns, through the spas that the Europeans thought could help him, only led to discouragement.

In this period of doubts and difficulties he read the French philosopher Renouvier, a disciple of Kant. Renouvier taught that the *will* could restore a man's course in life. A man could remake his path. For James this meant that he could, by an act of will, achieve good health. The effect, his family reported, was immediate and profound, which, together with his happy marriage and a tiny teaching post at Harvard University in 1872, started his life on an upward course. At Harvard he taught and demonstrated anatomy and physiology; but his reading and his ambitions, as his letters show, were broad and deep; and he was writing.

The journal *Mind,* founded in 1876,[1] contained in its first volume an article from his pen. In the next ten years a series of articles under his name appeared in this and in other magazines. Much of this material was destined to be incorporated later in the *Principles of Psychology* (1890). From these studies and from his letters (Henry James, ed., 1920) it is not hard to see what major forces were acting on his thinking. He was a terrific reader, attaining a very unusual degree of erudition and range of information. He was deeply absorbed in the Scottish and the associationist psychologies and in that mixture of the two which flourished in Britain in the middle of the century. Here, as elsewhere, his voracious and restless spirit seized what it could use.[2]

German experimental work also influenced James enormously, in spite of his animus against what he called "brass-instrument" psychology. Notwithstanding his feeling that the laboratory method tended to become the dissection of dead minds, he devoted nearly two hundred pages in his *Principles* to the newest experimental findings. It is clear that James regarded the Leipzig movement as a source of much usable material; but not, as the Wundtians considered it, as offering a new Constitution for Psychology. Of the three experimentalists — Helmholtz, Fechner, and Wundt — he was least partial toward Fechner; he was deeply appreciative of Fechner's *philosophy,* but he held the upshot of his experimental work to be "just nothing." He was interested enough in the methods of Helmholtz and Wundt to invite Münsterberg, a representative of the new experimental psychology, to become director of the Harvard psychological laboratory. In spite of James's acknowledged prejudices, he did seek empirical material wherever he could.

[1] By Alexander Bain; Wilhelm Wundt's *Philosophische Studien* was founded in 1883.

[2] His father's religious earnestness (for example, his devotion to Swedenborg) profoundly influenced him; a curious combination of personal mysticism and New England matter-of-factness is apparent throughout his work.

One has the feeling that just as he adopted the German experimental methods and results, he was determined to learn and to use every bit of psychological material that existed anywhere. The chapter "The Perception of Space" (1890, Vol. 2) reads like the work of a man who finds an immense and demanding task to be done and marshals every effort to measure up to it. Many of these new problems were ones which could hardly have been undertaken, he said, in a country "whose natives could be bored"; but experiments yielded facts and, ardent empiricist that he was, he had to have facts wherever they lay. To the Hegelian movement and other idealistic trends James reacted with strenuous and prolonged protest. To him they seemed wordy and without substance; they represented the "thin" rather than the "thick" in philosophy (1909a, p. 136). German philosophy accentuated his inclination toward "radical empiricism." His psychological outlook was a protest against both German and British "absolute idealism."

The same reverence for factual material which James showed in relation to German psychology was liberated and given new life by French psychology. He thought something really important had been discovered by French psychiatric research. He was deeply interested in the work of Charcot, Janet, and others who had studied hysteria, hypnotism, and dissociation; he believed that such studies had something fundamental to teach about the structure of personality. He gave much attention to Janet's evidence that there may be parts of personality functioning unknown to our introspective consciousness (1890, Vol. 1, pp. 227 ff.). This discovery seemed to James to be of great moment, indicating that personality is not the little circle of events upon which the light of introspection is thrown, but represents various levels or strata which may be as genuinely psychological as the superficially apparent. He felt that dissociation, or splitting of personality, made it possible to study at different times elements in personality which take their turns in controlling individual conduct. The mental events which go on outside the patient's consciousness might as a rule be regarded as "secondary personalities," real selves distinct from the self which is at the time in control. There are, nevertheless, James believed, *some* mental events outside of personal awareness which are not a part of any *self:* Janet's "organic memories." These questions of subconscious or unconscious mental life seemed to James to be among the central issues for psychology.

So much for the academic influences. At least as important were the personal and social influences: the progressivism and optimism of an America grown strong and turbulent; the warmth and the deep comradeships which at every time in his life were his in all his family relationships; the semi-invalidism, the heartbreaking long periods of bad eyes, aching back, nervous fatigue, which made him seek — and find — a philosophy of spontaneity, of free creativeness, in which healing could be achieved. Of all the nineteenth-century currents most fundamentally congenial to him, because so closely related to such needs, the most important was evolutionism; an evolutionism which meant creativeness through struggle, the primacy of the immediate task to be done over any abstraction which is a step removed from life.

"The Principles of Psychology"

The contract for *The Principles of Psychology* (1890) was signed in 1878, when James was thirty-six years old; he was forty-eight when the book was published. Several of the chapters, in the meantime, had appeared in periodicals, but *The Principles* burst upon the world like a volcanic eruption. Both he and his brother Henry had been under great stress for a number of years to establish themselves at the vanguard of the profession each represented. In 1890, as James's *Principles* lay on the desk of Henry Holt, the publisher, in New York, James wrote his brother: "With that work, your *Tragic Muse* and . . . my *Psychology* all appearing in it, the year 1890 will be known as the great epochal year in American literature." But what he wrote his publisher was a little different. The message with the manuscript of *The Principles* said: "A loathsome, distended, tumified, bloated, dropsical mass, testifying to nothing but two facts: first, that there is no such thing as a *science* of psychology and second, that W. J. is an incapable." The verdict of the public was, of course, much closer to what he wrote Henry James than what he wrote Henry Holt.

In commenting upon his extraordinary book, there is a temptation to introduce it as a new "system" of psychology. Perhaps, however, the term "system" is misleading; for just as Wundt was the systematic psychologist par excellence, so James might be called the *un*systematic psychologist par excellence. He was very much less occupied with the problem of creating order and system than with the task of giving the reader something to feed upon. The chapters of *The Principles* are not built into a structural unity; that James was fully aware of this is clear from his Preface. We can tell which chapters were borrowed from British sources (note, for example, the relation of Bain and Carpenter to James's chapter "Habit"). The three chapters on "perception" (the perception of time, space, and things) were taken largely from German sources. "The Emotions," "Will," "The Stream of Thought," "Consciousness of Self," and "Necessary Truths," while utilizing contemporary material, were in large part original.

Having emphasized the fact that the chapters do not set forth a true "system," we shall not have to ask about the *elements* from which, according to James, the mind is composed; he was not interested in such a question. Wundt had taught that experience was composed of three main types of elements: sensations, images, and feelings — three categories which survived in the psychology of the "structuralists." But the term "feeling" had no sharply definable meaning for James. Dozens of "feelings" appear in connection with James's discussion of instinct, emotion, will, and indeed the rational processes; but there is no simple analytical psychology of the basic feelings as there is in the work of Wundt.

James was profoundly antianalytical. The analytic method, in fact, seemed to him to be unwarranted. Experiences simply are what they are—and not groups of elements which we can constrain ourselves to detect through introspection (1890, Vol. 1, pp. 157 ff.). The introspective discovery of discrete elements does not prove that they were present *before* their observation occurred. For Locke, father of structuralism, the taste of lemonade would have consisted of sourness, plus coldness, plus sweetness, plus tactual sensations from the tongue, and so on. Even for Wundt (in spite of "creative synthesis") there were components—sensations, images, feelings—to be combined. James thought this whole approach sterile. When confronting experience, the psychologist reads into his experience, James said, what he thinks his theory requires. If a man is sipping lemonade we may regard it as our scientific responsibility to assume that he is experiencing sour, sweet, and cold as sensory elements. But it is improbable that the man's experience is really reducible in this manner. Suppose a tea-taster trains himself to discriminate in a flavor those elements which to most observers are fused into an unanalyzable blend. From James's viewpoint, the fact that this individual taster can analyze his experience does not prove that the separate analyzed elements are present in the consciousness of everyone who tastes the compound. To make such an assumption is to be guilty of the "psychologist's fallacy."

Just as we cannot break up a given mental content into pure sensory elements, the attempt to subdivide consciousness into a series of temporally distinct phases is unwarranted. We cannot talk about one thing leading by association to the next, as one clock tick succeeds another. There is, on the contrary, a continuous flow, a "stream of thought," and each of the entities ordinarily studied by psychologists is nothing more than a cross section arbitrarily taken out of the stream. James Mill, Spencer, and Bain had all emphasized the constant flux of consciousness, believing that it was quite impossible to describe a momentary cross section of experience except in terms of the stages just preceding it. Bain had written: "To be distinctly affected by two or more successive impressions is the most general fact of consciousness. We are never conscious at all without experiencing transition or change" (1864, p. 325). James, accepting and elaborating this view, held that the process of analyzing experience into temporal pigeonholes is just as absurd as the psychologist's fallacy. Mental life at any time is a unity, a total experience, flowing and changing as does a stream.

A great deal in this stream of consciousness is not easily grasped in introspective terms; much of it is vague, incoherent, intangible. A large part of it is marginal. James made much of what he called *transitive* as opposed to *substantive* states. Thought contains not only stopping places that are easily observed, but transitional states so vague and fleeting that they have escaped the attention of most psychologists. Psychologists have taken cross sections of the stream of thought at the substantive points; they have neglected the vague, the fleeting, the indefinite. If, for instance, we should say, "Substantive states do not constitute the entire subject matter of psychology," probably the word "of" would play a transitive, not a substantive, role. James suggested here that one of his tasks was to restore to psychology the vague, indefinite, and unsubstantial. But he was not alone. The same conception was apparent in other revolts against structuralism (to which we shall devote attention a little later) and soon became a subject for experimental study.

The evolutionism, the dynamism, the creativeness that pervade James can best of all be portrayed in his own words as he grappled with one of the problems closest to his heart: the nature of the will. The following is from his account of the will and his classification of the *types of decision* (1890, Vol. 2, pp. 531–34).

> The first may be called *the reasonable type.* It is that of those cases in which the arguments for and against a given course seem gradually and almost insensibly to settle themselves in the mind and to end by leaving a clear balance in favor of one alternative, which alternative we then adopt without effort or constraint. . . . In this easy transition from doubt to assurance we seem to ourselves almost passive; the "reasons" which decide us appearing to flow in from the nature of things, and to owe nothing to our will. . . . In the *second type* of case our feeling is . . . that of letting ourselves drift with a certain indifferent acquiescence in a direction accidentally determined *from without. . . . In the third type . . .* it . . . often happens, when the absence of imperative principle is perplexing and suspense distracting, that we find ourselves acting, as it were, automatically . . . in the direction of one of the horns of the dilemma. . . . "Forward now!" we inwardly cry, "though the heavens fall."

The fourth form of decision

> comes when, in consequence of some outer experience or some inexplicable inward charge, *we suddenly pass from the easy and careless to the sober and strenuous mood. . . .* The whole scale of values of our motives and impulses then undergoes a change . . . all "light fantastic" notions lose their motive power, all solemn ones find theirs multiplied manyfold.

In the fifth

> we feel, in deciding, as if we ourselves by our own wilful act inclined the beam. . . . The slow dead heave of the will that is felt in these instances makes of them a class altogether different subjectively from all the three preceding classes. . . . Whether it be the dreary resignation for the sake of austere and naked duty of all sorts of rich, mundane delights, or

whether it be the heavy resolve that of two mutually exclusive trains of future fact, both sweet and good . . . one shall forevermore become impossible, while the other shall become reality, it is a desolate and acrid sort of act, an excursion into a lonesome moral wilderness.

For James, the will is, moreover, a crucial point at which all mechanistic interpretation fails. Psychology as a science must proceed on the assumption of a causal (determinist) principle; but there are other principles — philosophical principles — to be considered. James has been accused of inconsistency regarding the mind-body relation. It is true that he repeatedly asserted that psychologists must dispense with the soul as a datum for their science; but on the other hand we find him saying that there seems to him some integrating and organizing force beyond the separate experiences, which looks like personality or soul, holding in cohesion and in integrated action the many disparate functions (1890, Vol. 1, p. 181). The inconsistency is in fact quite apparent if we contrast the treatment of "The Stream of Thought" with the discussion of "Will." In the former, thought is, so to speak, self-propelling — the self appearing as an experienced entity but not necessarily as a reality beyond experience. In the latter, volition exhibits in certain cases the intervention of an entity not explainable in terms of the elements preceding the decision.[3] James's heart was plainly in the doctrine of interaction between soul and body. He tried most of the time to think in monistic terms, using a neurological terminology, but did not believe such an approach to be ultimate. We shall see later, in connection with his studies of religious experience, other instances of his disbelief in the finality of mechanistic, or in fact of any rationalistic, methods.

The most celebrated and influential of James's theories (and he was prolific in theories) had to do with the emotions. Since the publication of Lotze's *Medical Psychology* (1852), a great quantity of descriptive work on the physiological aspects of emotion had been published. Such descriptions were inevitably rather sterile, most of them being based on no carefully controlled data and presented without reference to any distinct and verifiable hypothesis. Little critical thinking had been done as to *what emotions were:* popular terms like "fear" and "rage" served as starting points for detailed description of what various parts of the body do in such states. In a first critical endeavor to determine the relation between what was called emotion on the one hand and its physiological expression on the other, James published in *Mind* in 1884 an article on this problem, which was included six years later in *The Principles of Psychology* (1890, Vol. 2, p. 449). In this article he undertook to bridge the gap between emotions and the expressive movements which attend them; he sought to show that emotions have no existence whatever apart from such physiological changes. Each emotion, he held, is nothing but a product of the reverberation of physiological changes in the

---

[3] His position was more fully stated in his essays "The Dilemma of Determinism" and "The Will to Believe" (1897).

body. This was a flat contradiction of the common assumption that emotion precedes physical expression. Whereas it is customary to think that "we lose our fortune, are sorry, and weep; we meet a bear, are frightened, and run," James maintained that we lose our fortune, cry, and are sorry; see the bear, run, and are afraid. And not only does the arousal of physical responses precede the appearance of the emotions, but our feeling of bodily changes as they occur *is* the emotion.

"Emotion" is a name for certain experiences which are produced by vigorous bodily response, especially response of viscera and muscles. In James's first statement of this he was unfortunate in stressing the *somatic* muscles, particularly the gross changes involved in such acts as running when we are afraid; but his whole treatment showed that he meant to include and to emphasize visceral changes too. (In most of the many elaborations of the theory by other writers, visceral factors have been given great prominence.) James urged that if we analyze out the various bodily reverberations in emotion—the tension of muscles, the fluttering of the heart, the coldness of the skin, and the like—there will be nothing left of the emotion. His view was epoch-making, not only in that it reversed the order in which emotion and physiological changes were said to occur, but in its reduction of emotion to a problem whose core is physiological. He sought in clinics and in hospitals the evidence which might favor his view and found a few cases in which a disorder of visceral processes did indeed present anomalies of emotion. But the evidence was not satisfactory. Objectors to the James theory run into the hundreds; but we have here a view destined to be of enormous influence among psychologists, the starting point for nearly all modern theory regarding the emotions, as well as the stimulus to much research.

In 1885 a strikingly similar view was independently offered by the Danish physiologist Carl Lange, who described the physiology of fear, rage, and the like, and arrived at the conclusion that emotions are based simply and solely upon such physiological changes (1885).[4] For him, the nineteenth-century distinction between mentally aroused and physically aroused emotions was meaningless; in fact, it was difficult to find any emotions which were not "physically aroused." Bodily changes, especially those of the vascular system, not only gave rise to, but wholly determined, the nature of each emotional state. The general similarity of this to James's view led to the habit of designating as the "James-Lange theory" the assertion that emotions are simply the manifestations in consciousness of a tide of sensory impressions from skeletal muscles, viscera, and other organs.

James's theory of memory is also historically important. There had been two dominant theories of memory since the seventeenth century. The first was the faculty psychologists' notion that memory is an ultimate power

---

[4] Lange's theory was in large part derived from Malebranche (1674), who was in turn indebted to Descartes.

of the soul or mind. If you cultivate your powers of memory, you can have better memory for *everything*. The second, that of the associationists, held that memory is simply a name for the process by which experiences are reinstated usually through reexcitement of their physical basis in the brain. Most associationists would say that each person's memory for a given event is a straightforward result of associative laws: frequency, recency, vividness of associations, and so on. In the faculty psychology memory was one unitary function; in the association psychology memory was a loose name for an indefinite number of separate events by which an indefinite number of experiences might be reinstated through association. James suggested a view intermediate between these extremes. Retentiveness, he suggested, is a general property of brain structure and varies from one individual to another. On the other hand, retention of a given item depends not simply upon the individual brain, but also upon practicing a *specific* brain pathway. And he conducted a series of experiments (1890, Vol. 1, pp. 666 ff.) to find out whether the memorizing of certain kinds of poetry would improve the memory for poetry in general — whether the practice of some memory functions would aid others, as was assumed by those who argued that the classics, or ancient history, would "strengthen memory." He came to the conclusion that general retentiveness could not be improved by training; practice in learning one sort of material was of no value in learning other material. This pioneer investigation was followed shortly by a variety of similar inquiries, the majority of which supported James's contention that there is, in the strict sense, no such thing as general memory training. The problem as to the unity or multiplicity of memory functions had been brought to clear focus. This was the only historically important *experimental* investigation which James carried through.

James's evolutionism has been emphasized; the theory of the emotions made phylogenetic sense, and all human processes were conceived of in terms of their inheritance from an animal ancestry. Symptomatic of the evolutionary point of view was James's catalogue of the instincts. The first catalogue of human instincts and reflexes made on a careful empirical basis was that of Preyer (1882). James accepted and greatly extended Preyer's list of human instincts. He included such widely separated things as hiccoughing and hunting. Protesting against the view that man, by virtue of his reason, is but poorly equipped with those instincts that impel animal life, James asserted that man has more instincts than any other animal. In the years since James's list of instincts was presented a great number of similar catalogues have been compiled.[5]

But one contribution, which has not received much attention from psychologists, is especially interesting as an illustration of the much more profound and radical way in which evolutionary principles had taken hold

[5] Another era in the problem was marked by McDougall (1908).

of James's thinking. It is the last chapter of *The Principles*, entitled "Necessary Truths and the Effects of Experience." In this he maintained that there are two ways in which experience may give us what we call knowledge. Some things are imposed upon us arbitrarily; in the strict sense, we "learn" them. We learn, for example, that water freezes at 32° Fahrenheit. The freezing point might as well be 28°; in fact it does vary from one region to another. Such facts are arbitrary. They are dinned into us by their regularity and inevitableness. The child has to collect such knowledge step by step. On the other hand, there are many things which "have to be" so, because of the very structure which evolution has given our minds. Geometrical relations and logical principles are of this sort. The logical structure is what it is because of the structure of the universe and because of the nature of the minds which have developed in creatures living within it.

This points to a fundamental cleavage in our mental processes between those constructed in the evolution of the species and those arising in the lifetime of an individual. The necessary truths that seem to us so inevitable are inevitable only because our minds cannot transcend their biological constitution.[6] They are not inevitable in any absolute sense. Here is evident the effect of the evolutionary teaching that mind is the product of adaptation to environment. James works out here for us in some detail the view that our minds are biological weapons, given to us because through countless ages our ancestors were selected by virtue of their possession of certain modes of reaction to the universe. But for truths which are not thus "necessary" a plastic nervous system is needed, which will enable us to learn the arbitrary facts of every day. James did not, perhaps, fully realize the implications of his point of view. Non-Euclidean geometry had been under construction for over half a century; from it and from new movements in physics and logic have arisen in recent years grave questions as to just what these "necessary truths" are. That mind is biological seems true enough, but just what limits are set upon it by this fact it is extremely difficult to define.

We cannot attempt here a further account of the great variety of brilliant passages of description and analysis given in *The Principles*. We shall, however, return to James's treatise from time to time as we consider recent developments which owe much to him.

"The Varieties of Religious Experience"

As he worked on *The Principles*, James was clearly turning more and more to philosophical pursuits, but he continued through the nineties an active interest in new psychological developments, especially in medical psychology. His own health, always delicate, was clearly a factor in his constant

[6] See Fries (1820–21).

effort to understand how psychological factors can work for health and illness. After an injury to his heart in 1898, and a recurrence of a period of abysmal fatigue, he set sail for Europe in 1899, aiming to prepare and deliver in Scotland the Gifford Lectures on "natural religion." On the ship he broke down, and in Europe he passed through a long and terrible twilight of half-life before he gradually regained the ability to speak and to write. At last, in 1901, came the lectures *The Varieties of Religious Experience* (1902).

The "psychology of religion" had begun to take shape a few years before, the child of cultural anthropology and of the new study of individual growth to which Stanley Hall gave such an impetus. A primary factor had been the collection, by Starbuck (1899), of a mass of manuscripts on religious experiences, especially religious conversion. This intensive study of the psychology of conversion formed a part of the groundwork upon which James developed his lectures. James used also much historical material on religious experience, particularly records of the lives of great mystics and religious leaders.

He began with a challenge to those who delighted in probing the relation of the morbid to the religious. He took serious account of the work of authors who had emphasized the frequency of mental abnormality among religious leaders; but he insisted that the question of mental instability throws no light upon the *value* of experience – the existential approach to religion leaves open the question of its significance.[7] As a problem in psychology, George Fox's aberrations have nothing to teach us regarding the beauty and power of his message. The intense and dynamic person, though ill-balanced, may be a genuine leader, and in a field where emotion is such a vital factor, disintegration may alternate with significant achievement. The achievement may be worth more than the cost of the neuropathic signs that come with it. There is, however, a deeper significance in this relation of religion to psychopathology. James was concerned to show that our whole system of values in regard to social experiences has been woefully narrow; that if we are going to understand civilization at all, we must stop the uncritical use of the terms "normal" and "abnormal" and abandon the tendency to fling aside things that do not harmonize with smooth, easy-rolling, everyday experience. He constantly protested against the habit of making stability of mind the criterion of social worth.

James outlined two fundamental types of religious experience. The first is the religion of "healthy-mindedness," in which the world is taken as a joyful place to live in and all that appears evil is incidental or irrelevant in the face of fundamental goodness. This religion of healthy-mindedness cannot understand misery and despair; it is in accord with the widespread nineteenth-century movement of mental healing through belief in the *unreality*

---

[7] He was frankly and deeply interested, for example, in the use of drugs in inducing mystical states; the physical factors did not for him involve the exclusion of the claims of mysticism.

of sickness.[8] He expressed little respect for this attitude, believing that it involved direct rejection of undeniably real and omnipresent anguish. "Civilization is founded on the shambles." If we refuse to recognize this fact, we blind ourselves to deep and terrible realities.

In contrast with healthy-mindedness is the religion of the "sick soul." The personal narratives of disillusionment and despair which he quotes remind one of those morbid states in which the individual feels that something is fundamentally wrong not only in his own inner life, but in the world itself. This view, James urges, is more comprehensive than that of the healthy-minded; it faces the whole of life and finds a need for some kind of conquest of evil or some reconciliation in which evil can somehow be made to contribute to the good. The sick soul cannot understand why the same universe creates both kindness and bitterness, but it struggles both to understand the universe and to grasp the relation of himself to the world. He finds himself striving toward the attainment of happiness or the happiness of his fellows; yet he commits acts which cause distress to himself or to those whom he loves. He finds himself in a tortured relation both with his world and with his own nature. Wherever the self conceives the powers controlling the universe in personal terms, the evil within one's individual nature is felt to be a violation of one's relation with the universe; sin inflicts suffering upon God Himself. The conflict within the self must somehow be resolved. The soul feels itself torn into two parts and must be integrated. It tries in vain to find satisfaction in "the senses." This leads to a crisis, and this crisis necessarily takes the form of a struggle involving the ejection of some parts of the personality from the realm of consciousness.[9] Suddenly a solution is reached in which the individual *identifies himself* with what he feels to be good, abandoning his interest in all those dominating satisfactions which appear to be in conflict with his new purpose. Conversion represents a transformation of the self, in which petty aims are subordinated. Conversion, therefore, is the unification of the self through absorption in one group of ideals which evoke such profound devotion that conflicting forces lose their potency.

The last third of *The Varieties of Religious Experience* is devoted to a study of mysticism. James regarded mysticism as that form of experience in which we come into contact with elements in the universe which we cannot

[8] James appears to have appraised the strength of the movement more justly than his contemporaries; witness the extraordinary wealth in recent years of popular psychology which "radiates sunshine" and the conviction that health is to be had for the asking. The vogue of the New Nancy movement seems largely attributable to the same source. The urge for a "healthy-minded" denial of the existence of evil has, to be sure, spread far beyond the limits of religion as such; methods which in the nineteenth century were largely tinged with religious coloring have in recent years become methods of "strengthening one's will," or making one's personality "magnetic" with a view to practical success.

[9] The concept of the subconscious had been so widely heralded by Carpenter, Von Hartmann, Janet, Myers, and James's own earlier writings that the assumption that disturbing tendencies were forced into the subconscious was a matter of course.

grasp through sensory or intellectual processes. As James puts it, it is a window into an invisible world, a way of seeing into realities which are ordinarily hidden. After describing several aspects of mystic experience — such as the fact that to the mystic it is ineffable and that it takes on the character of complete and absolute reality — he comes to two generalizations as to the content of these states. First, mystic experiences are regularly optimistic, not in the carefree manner of the healthy-minded, but through the *conquest* of despair; they reveal the universe as ultimately good. Second, they represent the world as *unified*. To be sure, James goes on in characteristic fashion to give exceptions, describing the mysticism of despair and conflict. But this typical optimism and sense of unity are for him crucial in determining both the claims of mysticism to validity and the significance of mysticism for the world of values. These aspects of mysticism serve to show that notwithstanding the multitude of religious backgrounds from which mysticism arises, mystics do nevertheless seize upon something which is more than the product of time and place. They achieve for the individual a sense of grasping the meaning of the whole universe, and hence an authority which is absolute. James went the whole way in maintaining that the mystic experience is a genuine, valid way of getting into touch with aspects of the world that one cannot otherwise apprehend. But though the authority of the experience is absolute for the individual, and though full sympathy may be extended to those who live with such a faith, James regards such experiences, by virtue of their very ineffability, as authoritative only for those to whom they directly come.

Interest in Psychical Research

In 1882 there was founded in England the Society for Psychical Research, which was to investigate alleged supernormal psychic phenomena, such as telepathy and clairvoyance, hauntings, and communications with the dead. James played a large part in the founding in the United States of an organization for the same purpose in 1884; he was active for many years in the examination of evidence for telepathy and for communication with the dead and acquainted himself at first hand with a great variety of psychic manifestations. This interest, which absorbed his eager attention throughout his life, resulted in some of the most earnest writings he ever penned; indeed, few of his philosophical or psychological writings surpass in vigor and personal self-realization his "Report on Mrs. Piper's Hodgson-Control" (1909b) and his review (1903) of Myers's *Human Personality and Its Survival of Bodily Death* (1903). He was early convinced of the reality of telepathy, or communication from one mind to another by other means than the mediation of the senses, and wrote of it in "What Psychical Research Has Accomplished" (1897). Whether we can have communication with the dead remained with him a purely open question, while he constantly insisted on the legitimacy and great importance of the matter.

James's Philosophy

The distinction between psychology and philosophy was never sharp for James, and even when he was working on *The Principles of Psychology* he was making philosophical history; but after the publication of *The Principles* most of his energies went into problems with which American psychologists, proud of their new science, had rather little commerce. Some of his studies dealt with the analysis of the ultimate basis of knowledge: how it is that our minds can know anything; how we can get in touch with reality. The popular notion of the correspondence between an external and an internal world seemed to him misleading. He found at various times three different solutions to his problem. He became identified with three schools of thought, all of which have ventured upon a theory of knowledge and have had something to say also of the mind-body relation. His *Pragmatism* (1907) and *The Meaning of Truth* (1909), though expressly representing a compilation and a revision of earlier teachings rather than a new school, mark the beginning of that contemporary pragmatist school which places its emphasis upon the relativity of knowledge, the impossibility of obtaining absolute truth, and the essentially adaptive nature of all thought. Another school which is heavily indebted to James is neorealism. In his essay "Does Consciousness Exist?" James puts forward the view that the world, insofar as we can ever know it, consists simply of things that are perceived; mind is not an independent function which knows these things, but comprises the same entities (1904). Mental events and physical events are distinguishable only through the fact that the order in which events are perceived depends not simply upon the events at a given point in space but upon the life of the organism. This view, already sketched by Mach (1886), offered no escape to those who had admitted Mach's premises; it followed that "consciousness" does *not* exist, but is simply a loose name for the fact that events are related not only to time and space but to the life of the experiencing organism. Nor can "consciousness of" events change their character. But usually two persons take part in different events, and in this their personal identity consists. Neorealism, which arose chiefly among a group of American philosophers early in the present century, has developed these conceptions to take account of many corollaries which James was disposed to neglect. Among the difficulties which have engaged closest attention are the problem of error (especially in relation to hallucinations, illusions, and delusions) and the analysis of mental events which do not at first blush seem to be identical with physical events: for example, feeling and will. Behaviorism, as we shall see, naturally found in this doctrine much that was congenial. Holt succeeded in defining consciousness itself in terms of an adjustment of the organism (1914) and in subsuming both cognition and volition under the head of muscular response. The behaviorist's dismissal of all "mental" events was most easily supported by the adoption of the neorealist contention that there really were no events to be added to the events of which physical science had already taken account. While behaviorists have in general declined to enter into discussions of epistemology, they have often tacitly (Watson, 1919), and sometimes explicitly (Holt, 1915), affiliated themselves with this form of psychophysical monism.

Another solution for the mind-body problem was offered by James in the form of a new variety of dualism (1898). The interaction of soul and body had been recognized in *The Principles*. The brain, he suggested, may be not the *basis* for mental life, but merely the agency which *transmits* psychic realities into the terms which organisms use in their relations to their environment. The idea that psychic events have a genuine domain of their own, not explicable through biological concepts, appears again, as we noted, in his discussion of mysticism. He felt that something of immense value could be learned from phenomena which appeared to him to indicate that the organism comes into contact with superbiological forces. The relation of man to reality seemed to include much that was not to be found in the biological structure of personality.

In evaluating James's place and influence, account must be taken of his role as teacher and of the American and European readiness to respond to his writings. During his period of service as Professor of Psychology at Harvard until 1897, and during the following years, in which his chief energies were given to philosophy, he enjoyed as pupils a large number of those who have become eminent as psychologists in the present century.[10] In every corner of the globe where psychology was known, his name was one to conjure with. Tens of thousands read *The Principles* and hundreds of thousands, as college students, the one-volume *Briefer Course*. For a long time it seemed silly to remark that James was America's greatest psychologist; for in the judgment of scholars and of laymen alike, any second to him was a poor second. But it must be remembered that even at the height of his powers he rejected the trends that were most popular in American psychology; and to the later popular trends, such as that toward the measurement of intelligence, he turned a deaf ear. It is not surprising that as the ocean of time has closed over him he has become one of the immortals, one of the eternal spirits, rather than a presiding genius moving with the newer trends. European psychologists, reading fewer things and rereading them more times, less concerned with being up-to-the-minute, very much less concerned with

[10] Among his pupils were Angell, Calkins, Healy, Sidis, Thorndike, Woodworth, Yerkes, and many others.

the winning of prestige by performing beautiful experiments like those of the biologists, have in recent decades known James better than his countrymen; they have always invited his spirit to the feast when any great new psychological venture, empirical or theoretical, was to be broached. To many Americans, he remains "back there," framed in time; to most Europeans, he marches on. Some may feel that European psychology is too somnolent to take note of anything that has occurred in the field since 1890; others, that American psychology is too immature, too gadget-minded, to be resonant to its greatest figure. There is, of course, some measure of truth in both judgments. Putting it all less invidiously, the research tools which he distrusted have become the chief keys to a technical world for which he had no taste. Whatever the reasons, his pages speak to a generation of American psychologists whose interests and problems are in large part foreign to his own. Today they feel they should read him as a "classic." How he would have hated that word!

All this is vaguely sensed by those thoughtful Americans who are not professional psychologists: artists, physicians, men of affairs; the writers and the readers of novels, essays, plays; those who roam widely and speculate freely upon the infinite fullness, complexity, subtlety of human experience. It has become a part of our desperately solemn growing up to put away the yen for these wider horizons. As it learns to walk, science must attend to the "hayfoot, strawfoot," its ordered mastery of the terrain just ahead. But the question is whether, in forgetting the vistas, the feet are necessarily planted in a direction that leads to major discoveries. In forgetting James one may feel that one's scientific conscience may come to rest. Yet it would be worthwhile, sometime, for the general historian of science to tell us just what happens when science forgoes the concern with the teeming richness and immediacy of personal experience.

REFERENCES

Bain, A. *The Senses and the Intellect*. Rev. ed. London: Parker, 1864.

Fries, J. F. *Handbuch der Psychischen Anthropologie*. Jena: Croker, 1820–21.

Holt, E. B. *The Concept of Consciousness*. New York: Macmillan, 1914.

———. *The Freudian Wish and Its Place in Ethics*. New York: Holt, 1915.

James, H. *The Tragic Muse*. Boston: Houghton Mifflin, 1890.

———, ed. *The Letters of William James*. 2 vols. New York: Little, Brown, 1920.

James, W. *The Will to Believe*. New York: Longmans, Green, 1897.

———. *Human Immortality*. Boston: Houghton Mifflin, 1898.

———. *Principles of Psychology*. 2 vols. New York: Henry Holt, 1890.

———. *The Varieties of Religious Experience*. New York: Longmans, Green, 1902.

———. "Review of *Human Personality and Its Survival of Bodily Death*." *Proceedings of the Society for Psychical Research*, 18 (1903), 22–23.

James, W. "Does Consciousness Exist?" *Journal of Philosophy, Psychology, and Scientific Method,* I (1904), 477–91.

———. *Pragmatism.* New York: Longmans, Green, 1907.

———. *The Meaning of Truth.* New York: Longmans, Green, 1909.

———. *A Pluralistic Universe.* New York: Longmans, Green, 1909a.

———. "Report on Mrs. Piper's Hodgson-Control." *Proceedings of the Society for Psychical Research,* 28 (1909b), 1–121.

Lange, C. G. *Om Sindsbevaegelser.* Copenhagen: Lunds, 1885.

Lotze, R. H. *Medicinische Psychologie [Medical Psychology].* Leipzig: Weidmann, 1852.

Mach, E. *Die Analyse der Empfindungen und das Verhältnis des Psychischen zum Physischen [The Analysis of Sensations].* Jena: Fischer, 1886.

Malebranche, N. de. *De la recherche de la vérité.* . . . 1674. 4th ed. Amsterdam: Desbordes, 1688.

McDougall, W. *An Introduction to Social Psychology.* London: Methuen, 1908.

Myers, F. W. H. *Human Personality and Its Survival of Bodily Death.* 2 vols. London: Longmans, Green, 1903.

Preyer, W. *Die Seele des Kindes.* Leipzig: Grieben, 1882.

Starbuck, E. D. *The Psychology of Religion.* New York: Scribner, 1899.

Watson, J. B. *Psychology from the Standpoint of a Behaviorist.* Philadelphia: Lippincott, 1919.

NOTE: A list of further readings appears at the back of the book.

Part Three

GATEWAY
TO THE
PRESENT:
PSYCHOLOGICAL
SYSTEMS
IN THE
TWENTIETH
CENTURY

14

Structural and Functional Psychologies

At all events [say the Stoics] an image is contemplated in a different light by a man skilful in art from that in which it is viewed by a man ignorant of art.

DIOGENES LAERTIUS

As we turn now to the psychology of the twentieth century, in which the wealth of material will require that each topic, considered individually in its turn, be brought up to the present period, it will be well to get a brief overall view of the forces that were at work or in the making. A short sketch of national differences in psychological interest was given in commenting on the rise of the laboratory movement; here we may attempt a more specific characterization of men and their projects and, instead of simply summarizing what was said earlier, make mention of many other figures hitherto unnamed who, already at work in 1900, belong primarily to the twentieth century. Imagine an observer on a high parapet above the world, armed with a telescope which could pick out all the psychological doings as the twentieth century began. What could the observer have seen?

In the German universities, many eager devotees of the new experimentalism: Wundt at Leipzig, at sixty-eight going strong and delving into folk psychology as he kept an eye on the young experimentalists; Ebbinghaus at Breslau, ardent associationist, concerned with memory and with intelligence and its testing; G. E. Müller at Göttingen, likewise indefatigable student of memory, dean of psychophysicists; Stumpf at Berlin, experimental analyst of music; Stern at Hamburg, who was destined to create a great new place for child psychology and for psychological applications to law and industry; Külpe at Würzburg, about to launch a new experimental movement dealing with attitudes and thought processes. Everywhere the new experimentalism could be seen creeping into education, too, and into

211

psychiatry. If the man at the telescope was not too rigidly and narrowly an experimental psychologist, he would also have discerned many other lively figures whose reflective energies served to define new psychological problems: men like the physicist Mach, who asked searching questions about sensations; the philosopher Dilthey, who rejected associationism and stressed the unity, the structural wholeness, of the process of *understanding;* over the border, in Austria, the former priest Brentano, who saw in psychology the study of psychological *acts* rather than of *states;* and sitting behind his patient's couch, the thoughtful physician Sigmund Freud, for whom dark and unspeakable things were becoming both clear and communicable.

Glancing northward to the Scandinavian lands, our observer would have noted the scholarly philosopher Höffding, and the active laboratory worker Lehman, at Copenhagen, and a few very limited beginnings elsewhere. Turning eastward to the Russian Empire, he would have espied an occasional idealist philosopher continuing some of the German traditions and two indomitable and hard-driving physiologists, Bekhterev and Pavlov, whose studies of reflexes were soon to make history. In northern and central Italy he would have seen a few drawing their inspiration from Wundt; he would have seen Mosso and his physiological colleagues concerned with fatigue and with the emotions; Lombroso and the anthropologists concerned with body types related to personality. Madame Montessori was building educational practice around the stimulation of the senses and the encouragement of activity. In German-speaking Switzerland were psychologically minded psychiatrists; in French-speaking Switzerland the traditional concern for educational psychology was expressed by Claparède, who was active also in the laboratory; while Flournoy made pioneer studies of dissociated states and strange utterances in the "language of Mars" and gave psychical research his sustained attention.

In France, while medical men in the provinces contributed occasional psychological papers to hospital gazettes, and hypnotic practice continued at Nancy, almost everything psychological was centered in Paris. There Ribot interpreted British and German psychology to his countrymen and carried on the great tradition in medical psychology; Janet had achieved eminence through his sustained and judicious study of hysteria and his many contacts with physiological, experimental, and social psychology; Binet was delving into the nature of dissociation and suggestibility of the thought processes and of intelligence. In Belgium a research interest in child psychology was already apparent; in the Netherlands the laboratory movement was supplemented, in the person of Heymans, by interest in the general psychology of individual differences.

In the same matter of individual differences, Galton, across the Channel, was finding in Pearson a worthy successor, where biometric and statistical prowess so greatly influenced psychology that a whole new branch of quantitative work—factor analysis—came into being. English and Scottish universities interpreted the associationist, evolutionist, and Scottish traditions in their own ways. Ward was busy studying deep dispositions unknown to consciousness. F. W. H. Myers, in the last years of his life, was struggling with the theory of the "subliminal self," with the nature of genius and the creative; Stout was lucidly portraying psychology as the study of the processes of knowing, feeling, and striving; and the young physician McDougall, rebelling against associationism, was beginning to ask whether Darwinian evolutionism and the primitive strivings of all animal life could receive justice in a psychological system. Sully was writing of child psychology; Hobhouse and Lloyd Morgan of animal intelligence, instinct, and learning.

As he turned his instrument toward the Western Hemisphere, he would have noted dozens of new American laboratories where preoccupations were similar to those he had seen in Germany. Among the persons and centers of activity typical of the new era were the scholarly Titchener and his Cornell laboratory, with its rigorous experimental studies of introspective problems; Stanley Hall and genetic psychology at Clark; Baldwin and genetic psychology at Princeton; Cattell, at Columbia, turning more and more from Wundtian studies to studies of individual differences; and across the street at Teachers College the young Thorndike, fresh from Harvard, with his new curves and theories to show how his cats had learned to solve problems; Calkins, experimentalist and student of the self, at Wellesley; Jastrow at Wisconsin and Pillsbury at Michigan, interested in studies of the cutaneous and kinesthetic senses. At Chicago John Dewey taught a James-like philosophy of wholeness of activity and of adjustment. At Yale, Ladd, a philosopher who had written *Elements of Physiological Psychology* (1887) in the new mode, had brought in Scripture as experimentalist just as James had brought in young Münsterberg to run the Harvard laboratory. At the University of Pennsylvania an observer would note a new thing in the world, a "psychological clinic" for the study of the psychologically handicapped. In Canada he would have seen British traditions loyally followed; in the rest of the New World he would have seen psychology still an aspect of philosophy and of education, with much reliance on French sources. In India, China, and Japan he would have found huge masses of psychology embedded in the ancient systems of wisdom, but not as yet distilled into a form with which the research-minded Occident could easily cope.

But what about the general spirit, the basic credo of all the new psychology, as contrasted with all the old? Must we necessarily remain content with this piecemeal geographic or panoramic view of men and enterprises; is there no possibility of seeing the forest despite the trees, no means of grouping and articulating these impressions? Grouping and organizing is indeed possible, and it shall be attempted. The only danger is that the reader will attach too much importance to one rather than another equally legitimate method of organizing.

There is some reason to believe that the *best* (but not by any means the *only possible*) takeoff point is to ask how psychologists conceived the fundamental task of psychology as a science. It may be legitimate to say, in the broadest possible terms, that most psychologists who were concerned with such questions were influenced primarily by the methods and concepts of the physical sciences as they then existed. Now the traditional method of the physical sciences was to discover, by analysis, the particles of which wholes are composed and then to formulate laws relating to the interaction of such particles. The atomic theory in chemistry had powerfully confirmed the belief that this is the method of science par excellence. A psychologist who wanted to be a scientist would inevitably find in the sensationist and associationist traditions a close parallel to the world view of the physical sciences. If introspection reveals sensations and other mental elements, and if the study of association, or memory, or attention can reveal the form of the interrelation of such elements, the scientist's program is mapped out. And it is not the fact of individual differences, but universal laws like the laws of physics, that interest the scientist.

To many psychologists, however, such questions about *elements* and *interconnections* had taken on a completely new meaning after Darwin. It was not that there was anything wrong with seeking elements and connections, but that everything looked very different when one asked about *functions,* especially the functions of whole things such as animals and plants, which, in the evolutionary struggle, have survived not as organs, nor as tissues, but as going concerns about which one always has to ask: How is this activity related to adaptation and to survival? Here individual differences achieve fundamental importance. The issue could not be resolved by debate. The issue of loyalty to the method of analysis, as contrasted with loyalty to the evolutionary approach, was likely to be decided by reference to different conceptions of science and to orientation to different kinds of facts. Indeed, as Hollingworth (1928) suggested, such issues regarding which facts are *basic* are decided partly by the predispositions of psychologists toward one rather than another form of sense experience.

By and large, the people who, about 1900, wanted to write a psychology in terms of primary forms of experience and the interrelations of sense experience were called *structuralists,* though later their dominant figure preferred to write *existentialists;* those who stressed adjustment and adaptation were known in those years as *functionalists.* These two psychological schools, in the extreme form noted here, were American products; Europe was destined to yield new psychological schools at a later period.

Titchener and Structural Psychology

The acknowledged leader of the structuralists was E. B. Titchener (1898, 1899, 1909–10), whose system and whose experiments have been generally recognized as constituting him the spiritual successor to Wundt. Completing his training at Leipzig and coming to the United States, he became at Cornell in 1892 the director of a psychological laboratory which served as a model in the study of those problems which Wundt had attacked. The unlimited erudition of his four-volume *Experimental Psychology* (1901–5) was paralleled by the systematic training which taught students how to introspect and to make systematic reports on events introspectively observed. For psychology dealt with experience as reported by the subject himself.

Titchener's structuralism may be regarded as a rigorous simplification of Wundt's. Mental states are made up of sensations, images, and feelings. But the only "simple" feelings are pleasantness and unpleasantness, other feeling states being in reality compounds or "sense feelings." "Apperception" is discarded, but "attention" is the process by which sensations or images take on greater "clearness." "Meaning" is simply the context in which a mental structure appears; if it has any further signification, the problem concerns logic and not psychology. Among the main problems of such structuralism are the elements and their attributes, their modes of composition, the structural characteristics of familiar types of compounds, the nature and role of attention. These problems appear in the work of Titchener's laboratory, work which, though constantly inspired and directed by his interests, has been published under the names of his pupils. The list of Titchener's personal publications gives, therefore, no suggestion of the wealth of material produced. His pupils established themselves at many universities; many of them came together with him annually to exchange research reports.

A few specific problems may serve to indicate the range of Titchener's interests and contributions. Here we find several systematic studies of sensations from skin and viscera (1915). He was concerned with the question of "mixed feelings" (1908): the question of whether pleasantness and unpleasantness may exist in consciousness at the same instant. He was much interested in the later report by Nafe (1924) that feelings are essentially sensory, not as independent and distinctive as they seem to be.

Geissler examined the various degrees of clearness involved in attention (1909). Is there in attention a gradual transition from maximal to minimal clearness, or are there a number of definable "steps"? The reports of some subjects indicated two distinct levels, focal clearness and marginal clearness. Other subjects reported several levels of clearness. Here, as elsewhere, subjects trained in introspection were used; Titchener took seriously only the testimony of subjects who had learned to introspect: that is, to observe and describe accurately the mental states experienced. And while individual differences between subjects were sometimes revealed in introspection, Titchener remained convinced that science was concerned with general laws, not with individual differences.

It must not be concluded that all the Cornell material relied upon the adequacy of verbal report. This is evident in an ingenious experiment dealing (in part) with the relation of percept to image. Perky (1910)[1] seated her sub-

---

[1] The experiment described is preliminary to a comparison of memory images with those of imagination.

jects in a dark room before a screen. She asked them in some experiments to "project" upon a screen images of familiar objects named to them, such as apple, banana, knife. Unknown to them, in some experiments she threw a faint picture upon the screen. The subjects were usually unaware that a "real" picture had been added; some of them made the comment, in such cases, that their imagery was especially good that day. In another series of experiments, a picture was actually projected and the subjects were asked to observe it. Unknown to them, the illumination of the faint image was sometimes reduced to zero, so that no objective picture remained. Nevertheless, most subjects continued to "see" the picture, quite unaware that no illumination came to them from the screen. Not one of the twenty subjects could consistently differentiate between images and faint sensations. The desire to find clear points of difference between sensation and image must apparently be tempered by the recognition that under special conditions the two phenomena may be indistinguishable (Read, 1908). Such a result as this objective failure in reporting the presence or absence of an external object is of interest to all experimental psychology, whether it stresses introspection or not.

Functionalism

In contrast to such emphasis upon the problems of mental structure, there had arisen long before 1900 a widespread demand for a more intensive study of problems of function. We have seen that James was unsympathetic toward the attempt to analyze states of consciousness into elements. He was but one of a large number who in the closing years of the nineteenth century expressed the feeling that "mind" should be not a structural but a dynamic concept. Many psychologists began to shift their emphasis from states to processes. In fact, the change of emphasis was followed by a change in the whole conception of what psychology is. In place of the analysis of experience, many sought to substitute statements of the ways in which the mind functions, especially in relation to the life of the whole organism. So many individuals toward the close of the century exhibit these tendencies that this book can give only a kaleidoscopic view of the transition, arbitrarily selecting elements from the writings of several whose systems are widely divergent.

British psychologists in this era were primarily interested in functional problems; Ward and McDougall were prominent examples. Stout's *Manual of Psychology* (1899) illustrates the same division of mind into a few main ways of *acting* rather than a few main types of *experience,* as noted in the case of Höffding; the process of cognition, for example, overshadows the analysis of cognitive *states.* Stout gives a discussion of memory in many ways similar to that of Herbart and Beneke, emphasizing the *disposition* of experiences to return into consciousness after a period of eclipse. When material has been memorized, the appearance of the first item in consciousness creates a disposition for the others to recur. Emphasis is not upon the structural similarity between an experience and its reproduction, but upon the tendency of experience to reinstate itself. As we have seen, associationism had suffered decline and fall largely because of the structuralism inherent in it. Stout is representative of the general tendency in late nineteenth-century British psychology to make mental activity, rather than the analysis of consciousness, the central problem. His emphasis upon conation, or striving, an emphasis shared by many other leaders in twentieth-century British psychology, is perhaps an even clearer indication of the trend toward dynamic conceptions.

The same tendency is strikingly apparent in the schools of physiological psychology. Münsterberg, who came to the United States in 1892, formulated an ingenious theory as to the nature of psychological events, in which an ultimate type of process, rather than an ultimate type of structure, was emphasized. The "action theory" of Münsterberg was a clear-cut doctrine as to the physiological unit which corresponds to the simplest act in experience (1900). The theory states that when the stimulation of a sense organ leads to a conscious event and a motor response, the sensation arises not in connection with the mere excitement of a sensory area of the brain, but with the passage of the neural impulse from sensory to motor regions.

Structuralists had in general assumed that the neurological counterpart of psychological elements is the excitation of particular points in the cortex. The experience of pain when the finger is burned had been correlated, for example, with the specific local excitement in the general-sense area of the cortex. In visual hallucination we may perhaps suffer from something acting directly on a point within the visual area in the cortex, although neither the sensory nor the motor neurons of the usual neural pathway have been brought into action. Münsterberg asserted, in contrast to this, that all life is impulsive, tends to action. We know nothing about sensory experiences of a purely passive nature. Says Münsterberg, every experience means not simply the excitation of a sensory region in the cortex, but the passage of that excitation through the motor centers and out to the motor response mechanisms. The more open the path for motor discharge, the more clearly conscious the sensation (or other experience). Münsterberg insisted that consciousness occurs only when there is a *complete circuit* from sense organ to motor response. This theory does not necessarily exclude a structural approach to consciousness; but logical consequences are not the same as historical consequences, and the view was one of many which turned attention from states to activities, seen as a part of the behavior of the whole individual. Many whose conception of psychology differed radically from Münsterberg's have agreed that the whole sensorimotor arc is the true physiological unit for each psychological event.

Serious objections were immediately offered to that part of the theory which stated that the more open the pathway, the more conscious must be the mental process attending it. Münsterberg's neglect of reflex action was serious; for these pathways, as especially "open," ought, according to the theory, to involve clear consciousness. Another serious objection was the fact that the passage of the impulse becomes easier and easier as a habit is formed. Something which requires much effort, and is at first very clearly conscious, becomes gradually easy and smooth-running but less and less conscious. The action theory would demand the reverse. Montague (1908) consequently suggested that the degree of consciousness is not in direct but in *inverse* ratio to the openness of the pathway from sensory to motor elements in the cortex.

A compromise between these two positions was offered by Washburn. She suggested:

> Consciousness accompanies a certain ratio of excitation to inhibition in a motor discharge. . . . If the amount of excitation either sinks below a certain minimum or rises above a certain maximum, consciousness is lessened. . . . The ·kind of consciousness which we call an "image" or "centrally excited sensation," such as remembered or imagined sensation, also depends on the simultaneous excitation and inhibition of a motor pathway. The "association of ideas" depends on the fact that when the full motor response to a stimulus is prevented from occurring, a weakened type of response may take place which we shall call "tentative movement" (1908, pp. 25–26).

From such conceptions, Washburn built up a "motor psychology," which, while making abundant use of introspective material,[2] was of a consistently dynamic character.

Holt (1915), in the same era, suggested that consciousness is simply a name for a specific kind of sensorimotor adjustment to an object. To be conscious of an apple is to adjust one's eye muscles and so on to it. Consciousness is the bringing of an object into a particular relation with the organism; this specific relation is one kind of adjustment of the muscles to it. This view derives from the neorealist belief that objects outside consciousness have the same qualities as those within consciousness; cognition does not *create* the qualities which appear in experience, but simply relates them to the life of the organism. Consciousness is not something "rolled up in the skull." This concept is perhaps more radically dynamic than any heretofore named.

These are but a few illustrations to indicate that the increasing emphasis on *motor discharge* contained enough dynamite to lead to a great many explosions. The emphasis on process as opposed to structure became very evident not only in theory but in the experimental laboratory. Külpe, trained in Wundt's methods, early came to the conclusion that the relatively simple

---

[2] This hypothesis did not in any sense involve an *attack* upon structural psychology; Titchener himself was not averse to such physiological hypotheses.

type of conscious association to which both British associationists and Wundt had given emphasis was not sufficient to explain the great variability in the types of volition found in the same individual from one experiment to another. The subject's behavior in the experimental situation depended not only upon elements in consciousness, but upon adjustments or attitudes, which might operate decisively although not present to introspective analysis. These findings regarding the reality of unconscious determinants to action undermined to some extent the structural assumptions which had come down from associationism. Even in relation to the mere reproduction of learned material, such a view was significant. But in relation to the task of adjusting to a new situation, the discovery that the course of mental life could not be understood in terms of its predecessors in the introspective consciousness involved the necessity of admitting as a real problem for psychology the study of processes outside of consciousness, and, inevitably a shift of emphasis to more dynamic conceptions. Simply because in many cases they could not be introspectively analyzed, attitudes had to be treated as functional units.

Külpe's recognition of all this led to important consequences in the field of systematic psychology in the twenty years which followed. From it followed the experimental study of both the conscious and the unconscious aspects of "attitudes," with a view to determining to what extent the language of structuralism can describe, analyze, and classify them. This field of investigation was explored in Külpe's laboratory at Würzburg by men whose training and outlook were essentially structuralistic; and many of their findings were accepted and utilized as enrichments to structural psychology. But in accepting these findings, structuralism itself tended, so to speak, to become more functional; statics already had begun to give way to dynamics.[3] And this new department of introspective psychology, while analyzing the elements of thought, showed very clearly the need of a more adequate knowledge of the functional relations subsisting between these elements. We shall soon be looking more carefully at Külpe's work.

Shortly after Külpe's first recognition of the role of adjustment in volition came the development of the "functional psychology" of the United States. The sources of the movement are quite complex. A factor of importance had been the emergence of John Dewey in the eighties and nineties.[4] Borrowing from the general revolt against associationism in the late nineteenth century, and most of all from William James, he turned his attention chiefly to the organism's ways of adjusting to environment (1896). At the University of Chicago in the early years of this century, when his

---

[3] A summary of the later conception of structuralism is given in Titchener (1909), in which sensation itself is treated genetically. And Titchener insists that his psychology, like Wundt's, differs from the psychology of the associationists in making sensations *processes* rather than *states*.

[4] *Psychology* (1886) was his earliest book in the field.

thought was concerned primarily with social problems and with the philosophy of education, Dewey had considerable influence upon a group of younger psychologists. His junior colleague Angell (1904) soon became well known. With the help of kindred spirits, including Judd (1907), who had studied with Wundt and had served in Ladd's department at Yale, a distinctive school developed, whose chief contribution lay in emphasis upon adjustment and, specifically, in a genetic treatment of attitudes.[5]

From the standpoint of today there seems to have been scant logical necessity for this gulf that separated structuralists and functionalists. The structuralist recognized problems of activity and adaptation; the functionalist agreed that consciousness was interesting and important. Differences of opinion about the nature of science, and the investment of many an ego in the issue, kept the schools apart.

Functionalism did not long maintain itself as a school; but some of its emphasis lived on in behaviorism and in the increasing tendency to ask less about consciousness, more about activity—a tendency already evident in such men as Cattell and Thorndike. Structuralism, or existentialism,[6] was eloquently defended in Titchener's posthumous volume *Systematic Psychology: Prolegomena* (1929), a volume showing that he never abandoned his primary beliefs. But the chief issue today is how to integrate structural and functional data in relation to each psychological problem. Just as it had been evident to Aristotle that *awareness* is not necessarily the same thing as *psychological activity,* so the evolutionary psychology of today strives to conceive of awareness as one kind, but not the only kind, of adaptive psychological response.

REFERENCES

Angell, J. R. *Psychology.* New York: Holt, 1904.

Dewey, J. *Psychology.* New York: Harper, 1886.

———. "The Reflex Arc Concept in Psychology." *Psychological Review,* 3 (1896), 357–70.

Geissler, L. R. "The Measurement of Attention." *American Journal of Psychology,* 20 (1909), 473–529.

Hollingworth, H. L. "Sensuous Determinants of Psychological Attitude." *Psychological Review,* 35 (1928), 93–117.

Holt, E. B. *The Freudian Wish and Its Place in Ethics.* New York: Holt, 1915.

[5] The treatment of motor phenomena in Judd gives a summary and classic statement of the doctrines of the school. Mental processes were brought into relation with muscular adjustments which were stated not in introspective but in functional terms. The whole question whether such muscular adjustments *can* be introspectively approached will be present with us in the next chapter.

[6] The very different modern use of the term "existentialism" is considered below on pages 303, 475–76.

Judd, C. H. *Psychology*. Boston: Ginn, 1907.

Ladd, G. T. *Elements of Physiological Psychology*. New York: Scribner, 1887.

Montague, W. P. "Consciousness, a Form of Energy." In (Colleagues at Columbia University) *Essays Philosophical and Psychological in Honor of William James*. New York: Longmans, Green, 1908.

Münsterberg, H. *Grundzüge der Psychologie*. Leipzig: Barth, 1900.

Nafe, J. P. "An Experimental Study of the Affective Qualities." *American Journal of Psychology*, 35 (1924), 507–44.

Perky, C. W. "An Experimental Study of Imagination." *American Journal of Psychology*, 21 (1910), 422–52.

Read, C. "On the Difference Between Percepts and Images." *British Journal of Psychology*, 2 (1908), 323–37.

Stout, G. F. *A Manual of Psychology*. London: Hinds, Nobel and Eldredge, 1899.

Titchener, E. B. "The Postulates of a Structural Psychology." *Philosophical Review*, 7 (1898), 449–65.

———. "Structural and Functional Psychology." *Philosophical Review*, 8 (1899), 290–99.

———. *Experimental Psychology*. 4 vols. New York: Macmillan, 1901–5.

———. *The Elementary Psychology of Feeling and Attention*. New York: Macmillan, 1908.

———. *Lectures on the Experimental Psychology of the Thought-Processes*. New York: Macmillan, 1909.

———. *A Text-book of Psychology*. New York: Macmillan, 1909–10.

———. "Sensation and System." *American Journal of Psychology*, 26 (1915), 258–67.

———. *Systematic Psychology: Prolegomena*. New York: Macmillan, 1929.

Washburn, M. F. *Movement and Mental Imagery*. Boston: Houghton Mifflin, 1908.

NOTE: A list of further readings appears at the back of the book.

15

The Würzburg School

Shall we not, then, as we have lots of time, retrace our steps a little, and examine ourselves calmly and earnestly, in order to see what these images in us are?

PLATO

We have given some attention to the revolt against the fundamental tenets of that modern structuralism which had begun with Locke and had been perfected by associationism, by Wundt, and by Titchener. One phase of the revolt must now be more closely considered.

One of the great leaders was Brentano (1874), who built up a psychology in which the "act" rather than the content of experience was central. His distinction between the content of any experience and the act of experiencing, a distinction stated in a few words, is really quite involved; and to grasp it we must go back at least as far as Leibnitz's doctrine of apperception, the process by which we become conscious of our experiences. Kant and Herbart, though with personal additions to the theory, had emphasized the *activity* of mind in taking hold of the elements of experience which would otherwise have no relation to the self; we may have experience without cognizing the fact that the experience is there, and the quality of the experience is distinct from the act by which it is recognized. In Brentano's hands this conception took a more radical form. Instead of drawing a distinction between an experience and the act of recognizing that we have it, Brentano held that the distinction is to be made between the experience as a structure and the experience as a way of acting. For example, in the case of sensation there is a difference between the quality "red" and the *sensing* of "red." The true subject matter of psychology, said Brentano, is not, for example, "red," but the process of "experiencing red," the act which the mind carries out when it, so to speak, "reddens." The experience as we look

222

at a red object is a way of behaving, and this way of behaving is to be distinguished from the quality of redness as such, which is a purely passive thing. For Brentano, the content of mind points to something outside itself ("intentionality") within the framework of the act, and mind can never be reduced to content.

Mach (1886), though a structuralist, also contributed to the same movement. He held that the world of physics and the world of psychology are the same world but that psychology must take account of certain sensations which correspond not to individual physical objects but to relations obtaining between them. If, said Mach, we see three separate spots, to each of which we react by perception, there is in our experience something more than one spot plus another, plus a third.[1] There is a spatial relation present between them, and that spatial relation is just as much a quality of experience as any of the independent spots before us; the spatial quality by which we get triangularity is just as observable introspectively as any of the other elements. If we arrange the dots in different ways we get different "sensations of space." Mach was structural in his way of thinking, but his emphasis was on the inadequacy of the traditional categories of sensory experience.

Following upon Mach came the work of Von Ehrenfels (1890) and the conception of *Gestaltqualität* (a word which we may roughly define as "the quality conferred by a pattern"). He maintained that in all perception qualities appear which are something more than separate sensory entities, something added by the subject: namely, the quality of the configuration or form or pattern or melody presented. For example, the quality of triangularity or the quality of squareness is typical of *all* perceptual reactions in that all percepts involve qualities dependent on the way in which sensory elements are integrated. This doctrine was in contrast to the Wundtian systematic psychology. Wundt had, indeed, recognized "creative synthesis," but the products created had to be stated in terms of the synthesis of the elements assumed in his system. Von Ehrenfels undertook to show that the process of meeting a situation is more than the sum total of the elements presented by the separate parts of the situation; it has a quality given by the form of perception.

None of these contributions in the seventies, eighties, and nineties was expressly experimental. It remained for Külpe, as director of the experimental laboratory at Würzburg, to subject some of these viewpoints to an experimental analysis. Külpe (1893) himself had contributed to the analysis of factors which steer or drive volitional processes; these factors might be either conscious or unconscious (this is the concept now often called "mental set" or simply "set").[2] Külpe's school began, at the beginning of the present century, a series of epoch-making experiments which contributed

---

[1] The point had been made by Laromiguière nearly a century earlier.

[2] His view had in several respects been foreshadowed by others. See the summary in Titchener (1909, pp. 162 ff.).

much to the antistructuralist movement we have just sketched. His laboratory at Würzburg became the center for research on problems which the structuralism of Wundt's school had disregarded.

First of all came the studies of Marbe (1901). In these studies the subject was required to form a judgment about a situation (as in determining which of two weights was heavier) and to report on the processes that intervened between stimulation and report. His judgment was to be given in the form of a verbal report or an overt act which could be labeled by the experimenter as right or wrong; but attention was given to the thought processes which preceded the act.

Next came a method, introduced by Watt (1905) and Messer (1906), of utilizing the association test to find out what thought processes occurred between the presentation of a word and the word response. These (and similar) investigations led to scattered and incoherent masses of introspective material in which there constantly appeared evidences of preoccupation with elements of experience that to the subjects did not seem to be capable of description in sensory terms. This material, though heterogeneous, indicated the existence of a kind of experience closely similar to the transitive states which James had discussed in his chapter "The Stream of Thought" — something to be contrasted with the substantive, the relatively discrete and independent bits of experience. These rather vague and indefinite experiences that were found to occur in the thought processes were given a name which we may roughly translate "conscious attitudes" (*Bewusstseinslagen*, the word suggested by Marbe). These states of consciousness were not reducible to simple sensations or images or feelings. Here, early in the Würzburg work, we have the emergence of elements of experience which appeared to have been disregarded by the entire school of experimental psychology under Wundt's leadership, and whose existence had been generally ignored ever since the structuralism of Locke. They bore a certain resemblance to the "imageless thoughts" which Stout had mentioned in 1896. These conscious attitudes included, for example, experiences of doubt and of certainty, of affirmation and of dissent. Watt emphasized also the *Aufgabe* (task or problem) which, though not necessarily present in *consciousness*, exercises a controlling influence upon the judgment or act of thought.

The Würzburg school advanced, however, to new problems. Ach (1905) proceeded to analyze the process by which decisions are reached, classifying individuals into "decision types" on the basis of their introspections. He found that there are, in addition to the conscious attitudes preceding a decision, many predispositions which, although outside of consciousness, operate to control the course of thought and to steer toward a decision. This discovery seemed to verify one of Külpe's conceptions which was mentioned above, and it emphasized in the field of volition entities very similar to the *Aufgaben* found by Watt in the study of judgment. To these agencies, so important in the process of volition, Ach gave the name "determining tendencies." Recognition of such determining tendencies was closely related to the theory of meaning. Ach outlined a theory to the effect that consciousness of meaning may be carried entirely through unconscious mechanisms. If a given imaginal content of consciousness is meaningful, it is because a number of associated ideas are subexcited though not actually brought into consciousness. Meaning itself depends on such subexcitation of associated ideas. In addition to consciousness of meaning, Ach recognized consciousness of *relation* and certain intermediate stages between these two groups of nonimaginal experiences.

There followed a new period in the Würzburg school, beginning with the investigations of Karl Bühler (1907). These were not essentially different in purpose from Woodworth's. In fact, Bühler used a method already employed by Woodworth—that of stating a question which required reflection before an answer could be given and recording the steps involved in reaching the answer. The important thing for Bühler was the reality of nonsensory *thought* processes, a finding which had been hitherto only an aspect, not the essential purpose, of the Würzburg investigations. Bühler's work necessitated a very long period (say 5 to 20 seconds) between problem and answer, so that introspective reports were necessarily subject to much error. Largely on this score, Wundt attacked such work as undeserving of the designation "experimental." But an important difference between Bühler's work and similar Würzburg investigations lay in the fact that the shock of conflict with the Wundtian methods and concepts came out much more clearly. It was Bühler, more than anyone else, who served to bring out the apparent evidence for the existence of items of experience which are not sensory.

It may be hard to see why this should have provoked a storm, in view of the fact that the school of *Gestaltqualität* had long emphasized the relational elements in experience. But there is a new feature in Bühler's work. For all the previous psychologists the relations, after all, were only relations.[3] Even in the case of Mach's quality of "triangularity," a sensationist could say that such a spatial relation is simply a logical name for the way we react, not a name for a new quality of experience; or he could, in fact, accept Mach's description of these as *sensations of space*. But Bühler asserted explicitly that psychology must take account of new kinds of structural elements: namely, thought elements. He was trying to import into the precincts of introspective consciousness elements whose credentials had repeatedly been refused. Furthermore, these were vital elements and served in large measure as the content of the process of thinking. An American pupil of Külpe, Angell (1904), had taken a somewhat similar position.

In 1909 came Titchener's series of lectures incorporated in his book *The Experimental Psychology of the Thought-Processes* (1909). The position

---

[3] Some of them were, in fact, identified with some of Wundt's "feelings."

here taken is of considerable historical importance. The Würzburg school had been very much on the defensive as a result of Wundt's scathing denunciation. Every student was alert to hear what a scholar of great erudition, and long experience with introspective method, had to say. His verdict was that as regards their activities in relation to determining tendencies, the defendants were innocent; indeed, he commended highly their ingenuity, versatility, and inventiveness. But on the charge of introducing methods and terms which could never form a part of systematic psychology, they were guilty. Titchener found no reason to change his view that the only elements in consciousness are sensations, images, and feelings; there was no such thing as an imageless thought. Moreover, the "conscious attitudes" of the early members of the Würzburg school, and the thought elements of Bühler, which had been expressly stated to be nonsensory, were reduced to the familiar terms of structuralism. The "conscious attitudes" were classed as highly complex integrations of sensory components, which faulty introspective technique had failed to recognize, and, insofar as nonsensory meaning elements were really found, they were the concern of logic, not of psychology. Titchener did, as a matter of fact, repeat Woodworth's experiments, finding that his own subjects did not confirm the statements of Woodworth's subjects; the experience of Titchener's observers was described in the accepted language of structuralism.

Titchener maintained that when introspection yields no clear result, the only way to get at obscure states is through a genetic study – an inquiry as to how they arose. If we go back to the earliest experience of the individual to find how conscious attitudes and thought elements began, we find that they arose largely from muscular adjustments and hence are of kinesthetic quality. Our muscular sensations or images may be difficult to recognize, but they are all-important for the psychology of thought. The genetic approach is legitimate as an adjunct to the analytical method. The muscular nature of many attitudes is apparent if we study an individual who confronts a strange object for the first time. Attitudes and thought elements are really the last vestigial form of groups of kinesthetic and organic sensations.

The effect of Titchener's verdict was naturally to center attention on the main point of difference between his own and the Würzburg positions. The Würzburg school interpreted Titchener's lectures as indicating that they had not given enough evidence that there were such mental states as they had described. They rallied to the defense of what they had come to regard as their cardinal doctrine. An instance of the labors of the Würzburg school to defend their position was the examination by Moore (1915) of the relation of meaning to image. He presented a series of words both visually and auditorily to nine subjects. In one presentation, he gave the instructions that the subject was to lift his hand from a telegraph key as soon as the given word evoked meaning. In other experiments, the subject was to lift his hand from the key as soon as an image appeared in response to the word. Except in the case of one subject, it was found that the meanings came more quickly than the images. The time for evoking images averaged nearly a second, that for meanings about half that period. Moore concluded that meaning and image are distinct psychological elements. He therefore proceeded to postulate a structural psychology in which there were not three but four independent elements — sensation, image, feeling, and *meaning* — in consciousness.

A few words must be added about the subsequent history of the Titchenerian method. For Titchener this structural viewpoint and the exclusion of meanings became, as the result of the Würzburg investigations, even more vital than before. It became acutely necessary for him to instruct his pupils to distinguish between immediate experience (sensations, images, and feelings) on the one hand and meanings or interpretations on the other hand. The subject must avoid the "stimulus error": namely, the tendency to talk about the object which is stimulating him rather than to describe the observed content of experience. The subject must not say he is "angry," for this is but an interpretation of his mental state. A true description would deal simply with such elements as the kinesthetic sensations experienced and the feelings accompanying them. The all-important distinction made by Titchener and others between experience and meaning was elaborated with the use of the German *Beschreibung* ("description") and *Kundgabe* ("meaning").[4]

A few words may be said by way of evaluation of the Würzburg movement as a whole. The concepts of attitude and set have greatly influenced all psychology. While the effort to make experimental studies of volition and thought was obviously an appropriate one, the new investigations did not provide methods which could completely fulfill the promise. Even with regard to simple sensations, images, and feelings, it was already proving difficult to get incontrovertible evidence from introspection. As to imageless thought, we have already mentioned differences between Woodworth's and Titchener's observers; and there were instances in which Titchener's pupils, working in later years in other laboratories, reported data at variance with Titchener's formulation (Young, 1932). Introspection may be adequate to block out the main contours of mental events and yet fail as a precision instrument; there may be a region beyond which it is helpless to catch the delicate and fast-moving processes of thought.

None of all this, however, has in any way interfered with experimental study of thought processes from a functional viewpoint; the nature of thought may be revealed by its works. There has followed, since Bühler's time, a substantial experimental literature on many aspects of the thought processes: the formation of concepts; symbolism; the quest for missing terms or relations; the solution of mathematical, logical, aesthetic, ethical problems — all conceived in terms of necessary steps to be taken and the

---

[4] The terms were proposed by Von Aster (1908).

conditions governing each such step. Some of this work, like the *Denkpsy-chologie* of Selz (1922), was in the Würzburg tradition; but much of it has a very different ancestry.

Studies of Learning in Relation to Attitude and Thought

The controversy which arose long ago regarding the Würzburg results has in no way prevented Külpe's movement from participating with other move-ments in giving rise to a rich and solid experimental psychology of thinking. Such a psychology of thinking, however, has as a rule been conceived more and more in developmental terms; or it has tended to ask more and more ur-gently how each kind of thinking arises in the individual history and thus to link the problem to questions of growth and of learning. There still remains a place for the kinds of questions which Külpe's school raised, insofar as introspection can be sharpened to permit reliable answers; but on the whole these questions appear today to belong rather in the context of a psychology of learning, very broadly conceived, a psychology of the total process of coping with and solving a life problem.

Research upon the thought processes had in the meantime been carried on independently by Binet in France and by Woodworth in the United States. Binet had been interested in the thought processes for twenty years. In 1886 he had published *The Psychology of Reasoning,* which from the association-ist viewpoint he then held suggested that reasoning is a sort of continually changing perception. In 1903 he published a study of the thought processes, a report of experiments in which his two little girls had acted as subjects. He had asked them to solve simple problems and then to report on the mental steps taken. They told him what thoughts passed through their minds, and he came to the conclusion that there was in their experience much which could not be reduced to simple sensory terms. Woodworth, in a series of ex-periments published four years later and continued several years thereafter, came to the same general conclusion. Woodworth's chief emphasis was upon the reality of thought that was not of imaginal structure and upon "feelings of relation." Not contenting himself with the statement that the experiences were not reducible to the traditional structural terms, he emphasized the reality of two distinct forms of meaningful consciousness, forms closely similar to those described by Ach.

Importance must be attached to the experiments of Ruger (1910), who of-fered partial confirmation of the trial-and-error theory of thinking and made extensive use of the German and American studies of "attitudes." He studied the process of solving mechanical puzzles, in which the subject had to dis-entangle and remove some part through a complex series of manual move-ments. In this process it was usually necessary for the subject to go through random movements or trial-and-error activity similar to that shown by Thorndike's cats. Ruger found much of this random exploratory behavior in his twenty-five subjects; a large proportion of the first solutions were genuinely accidental. Further, the subjects' reports showed that, in addition to such *overt* behavior, much *mental* trial-and-error activity was going on. But he found frequently a sudden and permanent drop in the time for learning an act, corresponding to a successful lead which the subject grasped clearly and continued to utilize. Such sudden drops were often caused by noticing the *locus* of a difficulty.[5] In other cases, the drops corresponded to more complex instances of analyses of the nature of the problem. Ruger was interested in those complex mental states in which the process of "analysis" occurred: that is, recognition of similarities and differences; observation of the relation between movements hitherto disconnected; and the like. Such responses suggested "insight" — a term soon widely used by Gestaltists (see p. 262). The effectiveness of the subject's analysis was found to depend largely upon his attitude. The conception of attitudes, while specifically borrowed from the Würzburg experimentalists, was not, as with them, that of a new kind of *structure* but that of a way of *facing* the situation. Among these attitudes, by far the most effective was the "problem attitude," in which the subject forgot his self-consciousness and the desire to make a good showing and became interested in the problem itself. The problem attitude was the one most favorable to the emergence of sudden and useful insights. Even here, however, Ruger's data showed that such insights were likely to depend on similarities between the new task and a previous task successfully mastered. Sudden insight, far from overthrowing the trial-and-error conception, seemed often to go hand in hand with it — arising from the reappearance of a response tendency which in a previous situation had given successful results.

Binet had shown certain striking similarities between perception and reasoning. Ruger and others ventured in the same direction. The reports of Ruger's subjects, as well as those of the Würzburg school, had in fact revealed many processes which might be classified equally well under perception, reasoning, or learning. The traditional distinctions seemed to be shaken. In the case of the German investigators the new tendency took the form of reducing the reasoning processes, in some instances, to sequences of "attitudes." Ruger, and the American "functionalist" school, made attitudes equally important for reasoning and for perception. Indeed, theoretical and experimental studies of the learning process threw such light on perception and reasoning as to make both processes seem to be classifiable as subheads under learning.

We find ourselves in the midst of the study of the transfer of training. It was often naïvely assumed that any faculty — memory, or will, or motor skill — is generally strengthened through use. But would a careful measurement actually reveal that anything is "strengthened" except the specific

[5] The same fact, in chimpanzee learning, had been noted by Woodworth in 1902-3. See Ladd and Woodworth (1911, pp. 552–53).

habits practiced? The earliest careful study of transfer in motor functions[6] was made by Scripture and his collaborators, who in 1894 trained subjects to carry out various movements with the right hand and measured the degree of improvement in the same movement with the left hand. They found a large degree of transfer in such "cross education."

Thorndike and Woodworth, in 1901, trained subjects in such tasks as the estimation of geometrical areas and of the magnitude of weights. When larger areas and weights were substituted for those used in the practice series, the transfer effects from training were slight. Such effects as did appear were interpreted as due to "identical elements" present in the practice and in the final series; these identical elements included specific habits and attitudes involved in adjustment to the task. Conclusions were stated in terms of the absence of general training in the functions involved; the elements trained were specific habits which played a part only because of the close similarity between the situations encountered. This interpretation was in accordance with Thorndike's stimulus-response psychology, and in particular with his view that learning consists in the alteration of specific bonds. Much discussion of the whole conception of identical elements ensued.[7] Ebert and Meumann (1904) undertook an experiment closely similar to that of James, testing the effect of a practice period of memorizing upon the efficiency of memorizing other material. Their results seemed to show decided improvement as the result of memory training. It was pointed out by Dearborn (1909) that sufficient account had not been taken of the influence of the test material given before the practice period. Repeating their initial and final tests without the practice period, he found a high level of attainment in the final tests, which was attributable to the effect of the initial test. The implications of all this for the theory of "formal discipline" were clear; "perception" and "reasoning" seemed scarcely likely to be general functions capable of direct training, but names for very complex groups of activities, each activity being understood in terms of specific habits acquired by the individual.[8] Perception and reasoning were no longer clearly separable from the learning process.

The work of Fracker (1908) is of special interest, because of his success in getting rid of obvious similarities between practice material and test material. He presented to his subjects a series of musical tones in groups of four. Immediately afterward, before allowing them to reproduce what they had heard, he gave four more tones and asked them to reproduce, in order, the first group of four. Of course there was much interference, which in-

[6] Fechner (1858) had reported that learning to write with one hand facilitated the process with the other hand. Volkmann had shown experimentally that the reduction of the "two-point threshold" in certain regions through training lowered the threshold in other regions (1858).

[7] Bair (1902) found that the curve of a skilled act showed, from its beginning, the influence of practice in another skilled act which had some elements in common with it.

[8] For an example of the early experimental evidence indicating some transfer from one school subject to another, when closely related, see Dallam (1917).

volved the necessity that each subject should find a mnemonic device, some scheme by which to fixate the tones so as to permit recall. Most of the subjects were able to learn to reproduce the first series in spite of interference from the second; they had improved their performance by virtue of a specific technique and not as the result of formal memory training. Many other studies of transfer have served to confirm the Thorndike-Woodworth conclusions as to identical elements,[9] although strong opposition to the view has been a prominent feature of the Gestalt psychology. The identical elements were often, but not necessarily, of a sensory and motor sort; they included specific attitudes to the task and way of going to work on a new and challenging problem.

Another field of investigation, usually treated in the same spirit, is *interference,* or the decrease in efficiency which is observable in some activities in consequence of participation in other activities. Müller and Pilzecker (1900) found that when a given pair of items, A and B, had been learned in conjunction, and an attempt was then made to link A with C, the connection A–C might prove peculiarly hard to establish because of interference from B. This was a statement of the problem of interference in terms of specific connections or linkages. Similar interference has been found in the study of overt motor acts. Münsterberg (1889–92) conducted the simple experiment of changing his watch from one pocket to another and noting how many times a day he put it into the "wrong" pocket. He and subsequent investigators have reported that imperfectly formed habits tend to interfere with one another, while more thoroughly practiced acts cease to do so.

An aspect of interference which has engaged much interest is *retroactive inhibition* (Müller and Pilzecker, 1900). If immediately after a learning period the subject is confronted with a new task, his recall of the learned material is appreciably less efficient than is his recall of material followed by a rest period. The amount of interference depends on the similarity between the learned material and the task which immediately follows, but all tasks exert some inhibitory effect.[10]

But much evidence came to hand to show that the learning process could not be regarded *merely* as a relation between stimuli and responses. The internal condition of the organism was of major importance. Thorndike emphasized "readiness." Müller and Schumann showed that the reading of nonsense syllables need not result in learning their *order,* but that when the subject's attitude is altered through the instruction to learn the syllables in order, rapid learning follows (1893). The new attitude was called the "will to learn" (Ebert and Meumann, 1904). For some, this suggestion vied with Külpe's movement in sweeping away the debris of the associationist tradition; for others, the newly emphasized attitudes were themselves as-

---

[9] See, for example, Sleight (1911). It must, however, be remembered that the term "element" is still hard to define.

[10] See, for example, Robinson (1920).

sociations. The trend in all modern work is in the direction of showing the significance of the attitudes taken, the "control" or the "mental set" determining the formation of new associations.

A fertile field of research bearing on this question of the will to learn has been the problem of "incidental memory": that is, memory for material which has never been consciously learned.[11] As early as 1895 this was investigated by Cattell. He gave a series of questions to Columbia undergraduates about things they had recently seen. The results pointed to the great unreliability of casual everyday observation, showing that many things frequently seen had failed to make an impression definite enough to permit recall. Moreover, individuals were often certain of much which had no basis in fact. This experiment was repeated by Jastrow with confirmatory results (Bolton, 1896). Binet, using suggestion, obtained corroboration for Cattell's thesis (1900). The study took quantitative form in the work of Stern (1903),[12] who ascertained the increase or decrease in the number of items reported with the lapse of time after the presentation and found a decrease in the accuracy of testimony as time elapsed. He was interested in the "psychology of testimony" as a practical problem; hence not only defective memory, but the unwitting tendency to fabricate material to take the place of what was forgotten, was important. Claparède (1906) found that with the lapse of time there was a tendency to neglect the unusual and the contingent and to testify in the direction of the "probable." Of course these studies, unless especially planned to meet this difficulty, leave open the question of whether the results are due to failures of recall or to the failure to *notice* items in one's surroundings.[13] The question frequently appears to be not how good a man's memory is, but whether items were ever observed.

The Revision of Associationism

But traditional associationism was to suffer even more serious rebuffs than these. In 1907 Witasek discovered that the mere passive reading and rereading of printed matter was decidedly less efficacious than reading followed by "active recitation" in which the subject forced himself to recall what he had read. This statement was reduced to clear quantitative form by Gates (1917), who not only confirmed Witasek's conclusions, but showed

[11] The problem has generally been so defined as to include many questions which have only one thing in common: the search for mental connections established without deliberate purpose.

[12] See also Stern (1903–4), in which the decrease of suggestibility with age was demonstrated.

[13] Whatever bugbears arise when "attention" is mentioned, it would appear that the understanding of these results can come only through further investigation of the functional significance, if not, in fact, of the nature, of attention. We need to know not only the relation of attention to learning, but to the entire curve of forgetting in the case of material learned with varying degrees of thoroughness.

that both the rate of learning and the amount retained were increased by devoting larger and larger percentages of the learning time to recitation; even the use of 80 per cent of the time for recitation was more effective than smaller percentages. It was clear that learning was at least something more than the indiscriminate formation of linkages; the ways in which such linkages were formed called aloud for investigation.

Another experiment necessitating a revision of classical associationism was the study of the role of the image in relation to the fixation and recall of complex visual stimuli. The experiments of Judd and Cowling (1907) were designed to find how a picture was recalled after it had been briefly exposed. They found that the subject made definite attacks on the task; he would look at different points and immediately afterward recall those details that he had noticed. Each time the picture was presented, he would name a few more things observed. But there was no process by which he mentally saw the picture all at once and then read off from his "mental picture" a series of details. Results equally damaging to the interpretation of memory in terms of simple imagery were obtained by Fernald (1912). She put before her subjects an arrangement of letters in both vertical and horizontal lines so as to form a square (Binet letter square). Having asked her subject to get a complete visual image of this letter square, she removed the letters. The letters could then, indeed, be named by some subjects; but when instructions were given to read, for example, from the lower right-hand corner vertically to the upper right-hand corner, or to read letters from right to left, confusion and error resulted. By rehearsing the whole series, the subject might be able to perform even such tasks, but evidently he was not reading from a clear memory image. The contrast between the reproduction of the letters in the *order learned* and the reproduction of them in any *other* order was so great as to indicate that the square was not recalled primarily in terms of mental images. The visualizer may, indeed, "see" individual letters, but he can scarcely make good his claim that he continues to see the square. Adherents to the theory of imageless thought found here much comfort. All this is independent, of course, of the special case of those possessing that vivid type of imagery known as "eidetic" (Klüver, 1932); such images may persist for hours.

Into the chaos of theories resulting from such studies came an illuminating suggestion from Woodworth (1915). He described perception as a form of response; the "perceptual-reaction" theory postulated a process above and beyond the arousal of a group of sensations or images. It supposed that brain areas outside the sensory regions *react to* the separate sensory items in a way which the items themselves could never determine. In every perceptual experience there are sensory elements, but they do not constitute a percept unless the organism makes such a perceptual reaction. Woodworth had read to a group of subjects a series of words, instructing them to learn the words in such fashion that the first word of each pair, when presented, would recall the second. But he presented the stimuli at a constant rate; the interval between A and B was identical with that between B and C. Associationists in the tradition of Hartley and James Mill might expect that the linkage from B to C would be as firmly established as the linkage from A to B. But the tendency for the first term of a pair to recall its second term was actually eighty-five times as great as the tendency of the latter to recall the first term of the next pair. Woodworth concluded that the *perception of A and B as a pair* served as a basis for the connection between them. Not their proximity, not the formal will to learn, not any special attitude, but the act of perception itself established the connection. Perception was interpreted not as a state within which sensation exists, but as a reaction. "Imageless thought" might appear whenever a perceptual experience was revived without the revival of the sensory constituents.

One more departure from Hartleyan associationism must be noted in the emphasis upon total experience and its "redintegration" rather than more serial arrangement of *items* of experience. Hamilton's doctrine, adopted and used by Bain and James, and undergoing various vicissitudes in the hands of Bradley (1883) and Semon (1904), has served as the starting point for much modern discussion of learning. Hollingworth (1926) used the term "redintegration" to describe not the process by which an element *brings back* its context, but the process by which it *functions for* the situation of which it was once a part; the part acts for the whole. It is evident that association (or "associative shifting") is not the *key* to such a process, but rather a special case of a principle of wide application.

More broadly, the Würzburg school may be regarded either as an attack upon associationism or as a supplement to it. Certainly it was a gateway to new ideas, especially those of Gestalt psychology. Binet and Woodworth, in this light, were primarily empirical researchers, eager to report their findings but not essentially revolutionaries, nor system builders. The highly influential conception of transfer of training through "identical elements" and related analytical studies were a support to associationism, although soon the Gestaltists, including Lewin (see p. 264), were objecting to the "atomism" of such studies, and even to Bühler's "thought elements." American functionalism was still within the associationist tradition.

REFERENCES

Ach, N. *Ueber die Willenstätigkeit und das Denken*. Göttingen: Vardenboek, 1905.
Angell, J. R. *Psychology*. New York: Holt, 1904.
Aster, E. von. "Die Psychologische Beobachtung und Experimentelle Untersuchung von Denkvorgängen." *Zeitschrift für Psychologie*, 49 (1908), 56–107.
Bair, J. H. *The Practice Curve, Psychological Review Monograph Supplement*, Vol. 5, No. 19 (1902).

Binet, A. *La Psychologie du raisonnement* [*The Psychology of Reasoning*]. Paris: Alcan, 1886.

———. *La Suggestibilité*. Paris: Schleicher, 1900.

———. *L'Étude expérimentale de l'intelligence*. Paris: Schleicher, 1903.

Bolton, F. E. "The Accuracy of Recollection and Observation." *Psychological Review*, 3 (1896), 286–95.

Bradley, F. H. *Principles of Logic*. London: Kegan Paul, Trench, 1883.

Brentano, F. *Psychologie vom Empirischen Standpunkte*. Leipzig: Duncker, 1874.

Bühler, K. "Tatsachen und Probleme zu einer Psychologie der Denkvorgänge." *Archiv für die gesamte Psychologie*, 9 (1907), 297–365.

Cattell, J. McK. "Measurements of the Accuracy of Recollection." *Science*, n.s. 2 (1895), pp. 761–66.

Claparède, É. "Expériences collectives sur le témoignage." *Archives de Psychologie*, 5 (1906), 344–87.

Dallam, M. T. "Is the Study of Latin Advantageous to the Study of English?" *Educational Review*, 54 (1917), 500–3.

Dearborn, W. F. "The General Effects of Special Practice in Memory." *Psychological Bulletin*, 6 (1909), 44.

Ebert, E., and Meumann, E. "Über einige Grundfragen der Psychologie der Übungsphänomene im Bereiche des Gedächtnisses." *Archiv für die gesamte Psychologie*, 4 (1904), 1–232.

Ehrenfels, C. von. "Über Gestaltqualitäten." *Vierteljahrschrift für wissenschaftliche Philosophie*, 14 (1890), 249–92.

Fechner, G. T. "Beobachtungen Welche zu Beweisen Scheinen dass Durch die Uebung der Glieder der Einen Seite die der Andern Zugleich mit Geübt Werden." *Berichte der königlich-sächsischen Gesellschaft der Wissenschaften zu Leipzig mathematisch-physische*, 10 (1858), 70–76.

Fernald, M. R. *The Diagnosis of Mental Imagery*. *Psychological Review Monograph Supplement*, Vol. 14, No. 58 (1912).

Fracker, G. C. "On the Transference of Training in Memory." *Psychological Monographs*, 9 (1908), 56–102.

Gates, A. I. "Recitation as a Factor in Memorizing." *Archives of Psychology*, No. 40 (1917), 104.

Hollingworth, H. L. *The Psychology of Thought*. New York: Appleton, 1926.

Judd, C. H., and Cowling, D. J. *Studies in Perceptual Development*. *Psychological Review Monograph Supplement*, Vol. 8, No. 34 (1907).

Klüver, H. "Eidetic Phenomena." *Psychological Bulletin*, 29 (1932), 181–203.

Külpe, O. *Grundriss der Psychologie*. Leipzig: Engelmann, 1893.

Ladd, G. T., and Woodworth, R. S. *Elements of Physiological Psychology*. New York: Scribner, 1911.

Mach, E. *Die Analyse der Emfindungen und das Verhältnis des Psychischen zum Physischen* [*The Analysis of Sensations*]. Jena: Fischer, 1886.

Marbe, K. *Experimentell-psychologische Untersuchungen über das Urteil, eine Einleitung in die Logik*. Leipzig: Engelmann, 1901.

Messer, A. "Experimentell-psychologische Untersuchungen über das Denken." *Archiv für die gesamte Psychologie*, 8 (1906), 1–224.

Moore, T. V. "The Temporal Relations of Meaning and Imagery." *Psychological Review*, 22 (1915), 177–225.

Müller, G. E., and Pilzecker, A. "Experimentelle Beiträge zur Lehre vom Gedächt-niss." Leipzig: Barth, 1900.

Müller, G. E., and Schumann, F. "Experimentelle Beiträge zur Untersuchung des Gedächtnisses." *Zeitschrift für Psychologie,* 6 (1893), 81–190, 257–339.

Münsterberg, H. *Beiträge zur Experimentelle Psychologie.* 2 vols. Freiburg: Mohr, 1889–92.

Robinson, E. S. "Some Factors Determining the Degree of Retroactive Inhibition." *Psychological Review Monograph Supplement,* Vol. 28, No. 28 (1920).

Ruger, H. A. "The Psychology of Efficiency." *Archives of Psychology,* 15 (1910), 88.

Scripture, E. W., Smith, T. L., and Brown, E. M. "On the Education of Muscular Control and Power." *Studies from the Yale Psychological Laboratory,* 2 (1894), 114–19.

Selz, O. *Zur Psychologie des Produktiven Denkens und des Irrtums.* Bonn: Cohen, 1922.

Semon, R. W. *Die Mneme.* Leipzig: Engelmann, 1904.

Sleight, W. G. "Memory and Formal Training." *British Journal of Psychology,* 4 (1911), 386–457.

Stern, L. W. "Zur Psychologie der Aussage." *Zeitschrift für die gesamte Straf-rechtswissenschaft,* 23 (1903), 56.

———. *Beiträge zur Psychologie der Aussage.* Leipzig: Barth, 1903–4.

Stout, G. F. *Analytic Psychology.* New York: Macmillan, 1896.

Taine, H.-A. *De l'intelligence.* 1870. 2 vols. New York: Holt, 1871.

Thorndike, E. L., and Woodworth, R. S. "The Influence of Improvement in One Mental Function upon the Efficiencies of Other Functions." *Psychological Review,* 8 (1901), 247–61, 384–95, 553–64.

Titchener, E. B. *Lectures on the Experimental Psychology of the Thought-Processes.* New York: Macmillan, 1909.

Volkmann, A. W. "Über den Einfluss der Übang auf das Erkennen räumlicher Distanzen." *Berichte der königlich-sächsischen Gesellschaft der Wissenschaften zu Leipzig, mathematisch-physische,* 10 (1858), 38–69.

Watt, H. J. "Experimentelle Beiträge zu einer Theorie des Denkens." *Archiv für die gesamte Psychologie,* 4 (1905), 289–436.

Witasek, S. "Über, Lesen und Rezitieren in Ihren Beziehungen zum Gedächtnis." *Zeitschrift für Psychologie,* 44 (1907), 161–85, 246–82.

Woodworth, R. S. "Non-Sensory Components of Sense Perception." *Journal of Philosophy, Psychology, and Scientific Method,* 4 (1907), 169–76.

———. "A Review of Imageless Thought." *Psychological Review,* 22 (1915), 1–27.

Young, P. T. "The Relation of Bright and Dull Pressure to Affectivity." *American Journal of Psychology,* 44 (1932), 780–84.

NOTE: A list of further readings appears at the back of the book.

16

Behaviorism

Dismiss therefore every idle fancy and foolish conjecture of those who confine the intellectual activity to particular locations in the body.

GREGORY OF NYSSA

The growth of the biological sciences in the nineteenth century was something of a struggle between the physicalist conception (in which events can move in any direction) and the developmental conception (in which they take a direction and tend to maintain it). There were a good many attempts to dissolve the opposition between the two and to create a sort of unidirectional physical universe, in which life should be viewed after the manner of physics, yet as developing essentially from simple to complex. The mechanistic conception of life developed in the ancient world by Democritus and Epicurus, revived and given huge vitality by Hobbes and by La Mettrie, had come into eighteenth- and nineteenth-century thinking under the form of "materialism," which was to make life a special expression of forces which in their inwardness consisted simply of incessant and purposeless reorganizations of material particles. In general, despite many ingenious efforts to do away with oversimplification of the problem, those who concerned themselves with the nature of life, and of mind, found themselves forced into monistic interpretations of Democritus's type, or dualistic interpretations such as those of Plato and Descartes. Stating the problem in this guise, it gradually became more and more obvious that scientific method and the scientists' struggle to make order and clarity out of the universe pushed one, more and more, into the "materialistic" camp; efforts to preserve the traditional dualism resulted inevitably in one's being classified as a devotee of religion rather than of science in an era in which the "warfare of science and theology" became ever more acute.

Studies of life processes all through the nineteenth century—studies dealing with embryology and histology as well as with gross anatomy—came more and more to give coherence and conviction to this viewpoint. Helmholtz's disgust with the "philosophy of nature" was typical of the general nineteenth-century movement of the exact sciences away from dualisms of every type, and in support of a conception of life which placed it squarely within the orbit of ordinary natural — that is, physical — law, and of mind within the scope of the law of life.

We have, therefore, the conditions which led inevitably in the late nineteenth century to a triumphant "materialism," or "mechanism," in which the problems of mind were no longer to be tolerated as such, but were to be reduced to the form of general physical problems. The phrase "mental physiology," coined by the British physician Carpenter (1874), and the pessimistic view of man's higher aspirations (as reducible essentially to brain mechanics, or even brain pathology), as formulated by Maudsley (1884), are characteristic of the movement. In the same era dogmatic mechanism flourished in Germany, notably among the pupils of Haeckel; in France and in Italy such mechanistic trends, joined with other anticlerical forces, had of course been well known since the eighteenth century, particularly since the French Revolution.

All these predisposing factors were ready to be drawn suddenly into a new creative process, the construction of a "psychology without a soul" — indeed, a psychology which would systematically fulfill the promise of Hobbes and La Mettrie. This was to be a psychology of action rather than of thought, a psychology of physiological processes based upon the physics and chemistry of the response of living tissue. It would inevitably differ from earlier mechanistic psychology in that there would be ready at the disposal of the theorists far greater masses of material regarding the dependence of mental processes upon physiological action patterns, and it would find itself placed in a cosmic scheme following the essentially purposeless pattern of a Darwinian struggle for existence and survival of the fittest.

New Mechanistic Conceptions

It was Loeb, more than any other one person, who finally formalized a mature and complete mechanistic psychology in the closing years of the nineteenth century. The notion which gave this the specificity, the vivid concreteness necessary to win the allegiance of eager investigators was that of the *tropism* (1890). Just as water moves downhill, so the roots of a plant, activated by a more complex physicochemical necessity, find their way toward the center of the earth. Instead of speaking of the "lust for life" which leads the living thing to reach down toward the great mother and source of all living substances, the root is said to be essentially coerced by physical and chemical relations obtaining between it and the soil about it. There is at the same time a tendency for the portion of the plant lying above the earth to make its way upward away from the earth and toward the sun. There are, moreover, lines of conduction within the plant which carry substances and energies from one point to another. We begin to think of the living system as physically one with the environment — not only at its periphery but at its very core. If one thoroughly understood light, warmth, acidity, gravity, and other elementary things which actually are the core of the plant's being, we should have no essential difficulty in explaining its growth, reproduction, distribution over a large area, and ultimately its whole evolutionary position in nature, in reference to the "forced movements" which its environment imposes upon it. The tropism, or turning process — turning toward or away from specific objects in the environment — becomes the key to instinct and to life in general.

Many kindred spirits in the biological sciences eagerly grasped the new theory and proceeded to develop a science of objective behavior in which the traditional problems about the nature of life were stated in terms of the tropism. Just as La Mettrie had concluded that man differs in no essential way from the lower animals, so the mechanists concluded that the "forced movements" of simple animals differed in no essential way from those of plants and that one might, if one wished, extend the interpretation upward to include man.

Many others, who declined to accept *mechanistic philosophy* as such, proceeded nevertheless to formulate the problems of response to the environment in terms of a similar emphasis upon physical factors. The turning of the eyes or of the head, or indeed the running of the animal toward or away from the sight or sound which at the moment stimulated it, was to be conceived without any reference whatever to problems of seeing or hearing or associating or learning. Indeed, one could write a psychology in terms of the tropism theory and make it as systematic as one liked. With the departure of Loeb from Germany to take up a post at the Rockefeller Institute in New York, it became possible to speak compactly of those who expressed this outlook in Germany as the "German objectivists"; the greatest names were those of Bethe, Beer, and Von Uexküll. They were interested in a biochemistry and biophysics of the living system in which it would be possible to describe the response to sound without saying anything about hearing, or the response to light without saying anything about seeing. It was sufficient to write of phonoreceptors and photoreceptors. The fact that they were not mechanists in La Mettrie's sense was the reason why Watson noted that they remained "orthodox parallelists"; that is, they admitted a place for mental processes as running parallel to physical processes. It should be stressed, however, that their positive program lay entirely within the area of objective study of observable responses to observable stimulation.

The great bulk of the early animal experimentation was being done by physiologists, German work being especially abundant. The physiologists were concerned with part-functions, relatively little with total adjustments. Studies in reflex action were numerous. Some experiments dealing with perceptual and instinctive functions were performed by British and American students (Lubbock, 1882). In 1876 Spalding sought an answer to the question of whether swallows fly instinctively or *learn* to fly. Swallows were placed in a small cage as soon as they were hatched; when liberated at the normal flying age, some flew without assistance. But perhaps the most conspicuous studies of animals were those of Lloyd Morgan (1891), pursued, for the most part, by the method of collecting observations rather than by controlled experiment. Galton, too, familiarized himself with the ways of wild animals. The observations of Lloyd Morgan and Galton are imbued with the evolutionary spirit, and are among the most obvious reverberations of Darwinian influence. Animals, they held, are equipped with innate mechanisms of reaction which make possible their adaptation to environment. In most of this work there was no quantitative analysis of instinctive behavior, very little experimental isolation of variables, and no thorough analysis of animal learning. It is therefore no exaggeration to say that Thorndike's quantitative experiments on animal learning (see p. 314) awakened psychologists to the conception of an experimental animal psychology. But behaviorism emerged as an independent school of psychology from the laboratories of Pavlov, Bekhterev, and Watson.

Conditioning: Pavlov and Bekhterev

If a small child whimpers when he sees a white coat the bystander is likely to say: "He must have been in the doctor's office recently." Perhaps a "shot" had hurt him, and the white coat that went along with the shot touches off the whimpering; it is as if the white coat were implicit in, or a part of, or "associated with" the shot.

This simple and ancient principle of learning is not even explicitly noted, so far as we can find, in Greek or Renaissance psychology.[1] Psychology, as the science of soul or mind, made *use* of such a learning principle but assumed conscious operations which are not evident to the observer; the raw phenomenon of the triggering of a response because of the nearness of a response-engendering situation and a signal made the principle too simple for the kinds of psychology that existed.

Aristotle, of course, had talked about association by contiguity, and in the context he is plainly thinking about the world of memories, judgments, and thoughts. Association by contiguity belongs to this higher mental life. Augustine and Aquinas had a place for association in this sense. Hobbes made much of it: "From Peter the mind runneth to a stone." Locke came closer. The association of ideas, as we saw, appears to have come to him as an afterthought. He does, however, grasp clearly that an act (not just an idea) may be touched off by a signal which would not innately have the capacity to

---

[1] But as J. H. Arjona and W. A. Bousfield (Bousfield, 1955) have pointed out, the Spanish playwright Lope de Vega was already "somewhat of an authority on classical conditioning" in 1615, when he described in one of his plays the entire process of conditioned avoidance training, purportedly undertaken by Saint Ildefonso in his unsaintly efforts to save his food from marauding cats.

touch it off. A couple dancing in a large hall had to swing about to avoid a trunk and did so regularly. In a later dance, when the trunk had been removed, they still swung at the point where the trunk had stood. The "avoiding response" had been "conditioned to" one part of the room. Hartley explicitly noted that acts as well as ideas are associated and gives a straightforward, modern, scientific account of the elicitation of motor responses by stimuli associated with those which originally elicited them. These were not really central principles in his association psychology, which continued to work with conscious events rather than with acts; but he grasped the issue clearly. Spencer did so likewise in the nineteenth century. It did not seem to be a very important issue until a system of forces within psychology began to push toward objectivity, in the strict sense of avoiding all assumptions about consciousness and turning to the explicit description of the relations between stimulating situations and the responses to them.

In the last years of the nineteenth century this issue came suddenly into sharp focus. Loeb described such responses by the term "associative memory" and was plainly concerned both with association and with memory in objective behavioral terms. The German objectivists had already begun to sketch out their position. But it was the Russian physiologist Sechenov who had first pointed to the reflex act as the cardinal element of behavior, and Ivan P. Pavlov, at the turn of the century, made it explicit in his principle of the *conditioned reflex* response.

In a long train of investigations of the physiology of digestion (which brought him international prestige and a Nobel prize), Pavlov (see also Chapter 23) began to ask what elicited the flow of the digestive juices (1897). The salivary glands especially interested him. Severely objective and quantitative, he encountered direct physical and chemical excitants to the salivary response; but he noted also that indirect auditory stimulation—the footsteps of the experimenter across the floor—would have the same effect if such footsteps had been heard previously in association with feeding. It was not necessary to say that the dog associated the footsteps with the meat powder, but only to say that salivation in response to footsteps was conditional upon this dog's experience with both stimuli, the footsteps and the food, at about the same time.

Many such conditioned responses soon came to be recognized. They were at times called "psychic" reflexes, but with sharp emphasis upon the fact that the term "psychic" connoted only the physiological realm of discourse familiar to the students of Sechenov. The problems, moreover, were conceived in terms of the physiology of the reflex, especially the salivary reflex system. It was soon noted that a number of functional laws could easily be described, indeed described in quantitative terms. Study of the relation of the amount of meat powder to the amount of salivation was followed by the problem of the time relations of the signal (the "conditioned stimulus") and the response. The disappearance of the response, if the signal was given but no food followed, became known as "extinction," and a system of quantitative laws emerged relating to the dependence of extinction upon the history of the establishment of the reflex in the animal (1912). There was also "reinforcement," by which the extinguished response was brought back, and under certain conditions there was "spontaneous recovery" of the extinguished response. Of great importance was generalization, or carry-over, of the response to situations not identical with those under which the response was first acquired. A whole spectrum of interesting physiological problems emerged.

An example of the straightforward manner in which a traditional psychological problem was redefined in the physiological laboratory was the problem of differentiation between stimuli. Such differentiation was a classical problem in ancient and modern psychology, and of course, was at the heart of the whole world of psychophysics. If Pavlov had sounded a tuning fork at 256 cycles per second before feeding the dog and had thus established a conditioned response to the tuning fork, he would have found that different vibration rates would also have touched off the response. But he did not stop there. Whenever 256 was sounded the dog was fed, but when 400 or 150, and so on, was sounded the dog was not fed. Now the higher tone was reduced, say to 350, and the dog not fed, but again fed at 256; thus, by progressive reduction of differences, the experimenter got to the point where, let us say at 260, there would be no salivation, but the original 256 continued to elicit the response. Somewhere between 256 and 260 a point was found at which there was a diminution of the salivary flow from the maximum established at 256. If there was no such diminution, the dog was not objectively "differentiating." One reached the point, in fact, at which there was no difference in his response to 256 and a nearby tone like 258; he had reached his limit. Similar methods of differentiating between visual stimuli were developed, and the whole psychology of differential response seemed to be on the way to being experimentally clarified.

The conditioned reflex provided a tool with great power in deductive inquiry. The studies on the limits of sensory differentiation, for example, soon led to the problem of experimentally induced behavioral disorders. One of Pavlov's students, Shenger-Krestovnikova, discovered that a progressively refined discrimination task may at points of extreme difficulty result in disturbed behavior. She trained dogs to make finer and finer discriminations between a circle and an ellipse by reinforcing the response only to the circle and making the ellipse more and more circular. In some animals the lack of ability to make the progressively refined discrimination was expressed in the appearance of highly irregular and abnormal behavior; the animal refused to cooperate with the experimenter and became incapable of making even the simplest discrimination. Such a subject could not be used in further experimentation. It showed what Pavlov later referred to as "experimental neurosis." This simple information arrived at in the study of discrimination learning provided the basis for a long series of studies on experimentally induced behavioral disorders and their mechanisms.

In addition to the various aspects of the experimental situation which made a difference in the establishment, differentiation, or extinction of the conditioned responses, there were factors inside the experimental animal. Some of these seemed to do with excitability or passivity. One might say that responses in general were subject to types of facilitation and inhibition which were not uniform in all dogs of a given breed, but highly individualized. This led to various theories of typologies (see p. 394), and indeed of constitutional predispositions, in the field of conditioning.

Now, of course, the conception of attaching an old response to a new stimulus was very familiar. Loeb had clearly described this mechanism in *Physiology of the Brain* (1899), calling it "associative memory" and describing it quite objectively. Hobbes, Locke, and Spencer, among others, had described some cases of association in terms nearly objective enough to pass for descriptions of conditioned responses. What Pavlov's work accomplished in time was to suggest more fully how, upon this base, a more generalized theory of behavior could be constructed in terms of objective physiological phenomena. For Pavlov was determined to avoid all psychological problems connected with "association" and with learning as it had come down through the ages as a psychological problem. He contented himself with the formulation of what he called "conditioned reflexes": that is, reflexes conditional upon the history of association between adequate stimuli, such as meat, and associated stimuli, such as footsteps. He rejected all appeals regarding the formulation of psychological problems and warned his students to keep away from psychology. Though he had become within a decade a hero of the rapidly developing psychology of objective behavior study, his response to an invitation to attend the International Congress of Psychology in 1929 was that he doubted whether psychologists would really be interested in what he had to say. Persuaded at last, in his old age, he met many of those who for years had been his devoted disciples.

Imbued with the same objective spirit was the indefatigable Russian physiologist and neurologist Vladimir Bekhterev, pioneer in half a dozen research areas, who in the opening years of the century was studying human learning and thought processes with objective techniques. His cardinal concept was the reflex, and the objective avenue to all higher phenomena lay in the fact that reflexes are elicited not only by the few stimuli which are in themselves adequate (for example, electric shock for retraction of the finger), but by many others which are associated with these. He showed, for example, that sights and sounds present at the time the reflex occurred could soon elicit the reflex without the presence of the original stimulus. The associationists would have regarded this as a mental process; for Bekhterev, as for Pavlov, it remained a reflex. Reflex responses of the striped musculature received chief emphasis. He suggested that more complex habits might involve the compounding of such motor reflexes, and that the thought process itself, depending on inner activities of the musculature of speech, was essentially of the same character. It finally became his conviction that all the problems of psychology could be handled in this way. The theory was presented in *Objective Psychology* in 1907, parts of which appeared later in German (1913) and in French (1913a). A decade later he used the term "reflexology" (1917). Proceeding in this way, he extended his studies to include experiments on interaction in the social group, to which he gave the name "collective reflexology" (Bekhterev and Lange, 1924).

Bekhterev's whole concern was with the positive problem of writing a description of behavior in which the language of physiology would suffice. While Pavlov worked slowly and systematically in the development of a precise laboratory technique, and only after some twenty years allowed himself to be drawn into a broad systematic exposition of the nature of conditioned reflexes, Bekhterev rapidly sketched out a theory of learning through conditioning which made it possible to formulate acts of a high degree of complexity as compounds of conditioned responses. Attaching special importance to response to symbols, and emphasizing the acquisition of verbal symbols as a key to the development of the world of thought, imagination, and volition, Bekhterev constructed a complete system. A great deal of this broad system of psychology consists of special pleading for a monistic approach to the mind, as an expression of bodily activity; but it is buttressed by a great deal of experimental and clinical material. As a plea for a point of view, his book would probably have attracted no special attention. As a cornerstone, however, of a new psychological system, in which all the higher processes were to be systematically reduced to *symbolic responses based on conditioning,* it was certainly the most original effort at monistic psychology that had appeared in the post-Darwinian era.

The aspect of the new approach which first attracted the attention of American experimentalists was the salivary-reflex method of approaching the psychology of discrimination. Yerkes and Morgulis brought this to their colleagues' attention in a general review of Pavlov's work in 1909. The use of the new discrimination technique did not, however, carry with it Pavlov's scorn for subjective analysis, nor did it eliminate from American work the discussion of the subjective side of the animal's responses. Washburn, in *The Animal Mind* (1908), devoted considerable attention to the analysis of the probable conscious states attending observed behavior. Yerkes (1916), the most prolific in research among American experimentalists in the first years of this century, continued to employ many terms from the study of consciousness, discussing, for example, "ideational" behavior.

Watson

Now, in the spirit of the whole trend away from the concern with consciousness, an independent movement began in the work of J. B. Watson.[2] He was impelled, on the one hand, by his recognition of the fertility of the many new objective methods of animal psychology to explore more and more into the nature of the learning process as a problem in the modification of *behavior*. And on the other hand, he was much disgusted by the inability of introspective psychologists, such as Titchener, Angell, and Woodworth, to demonstrate a finality with respect to imageless thought. There seemed to be great unreliability in the testimony of human subjects as to their imagery, and this seemed to give ground for doubt as to the possibility of using the image as a datum for psychology. The whole conception of consciousness, as Watson understood it—a stuff to be introspectively analyzed— seemed to him to involve dualism of mind and body. As an avowed materialist, Watson decided to throw overboard the entire concept of mind or consciousness and to make both animal and human psychology the study of behavior. Modifications of behavior were to be studied in terms of stimulus-response situations, not at all in terms of conscious concomitants or neurological assumptions.

A first formulation of a behaviorist system of psychology was presented to a seminar at the University of Chicago in 1908. In 1912 came an opportunity to lecture at Columbia, on Cattell's invitation, and the result was the paper which appeared in the *Psychological Review* in 1913: "Psychology as the Behaviorist Views It." Here we have the beginnings of a psychological system which has a place for receptor functions, effector functions, and learning, but none for sensation, image, or feeling. The gauntlet was thrown down dramatically the following year in the first chapter of his new textbook, *Behavior: An Introduction to Comparative Psychology* (1914), in which it is perfectly plain that not animal psychology alone, but all psychology, can achieve the status of science by objective definition of all its problems. The same volume affords numerous concrete examples of the concepts which he believed must be pruned away. In the "law of effect," for example, Thorndike had maintained that if an animal does something which brings about *satisfaction,* the result is an improvement in the conductivity of the neural connections leading to the performance of the act. Acts which cause annoyance involve a decrease in neural conductivity tending to the elimination of the act. Watson objected not only to the concepts of satisfaction and annoyance. but to the claim that there was here a factor not taken account of by the principles of frequency and recency. If a cat obtains food immediately

[2] Watson believed that Thorndike stimulated him much more than did the "objectivists," whose "parallelism" he contrasts with his own monistic system. (See the Preface to *Psychology from the Standpoint of a Behaviorist,* 1919.)

after the movement of releasing the bolt of a puzzle box, this movement is the *last* act of all that occurs in the cage. Furthermore, whereas unsuccessful movements are legion, there is but one successful movement; over a number of trials the successful movement will therefore be repeated more *frequently* than any other.[3]

Some extraordinarily interesting things happened to the theory early in 1916. Watson's presidential address to the American Psychological Association in December, 1915, had stressed the possibility of studying discrimination by the differential-response technique (1916). But conditioning received no mention as a general clue to the learning process. That winter, however, Watson got hold of the French and German translations of Bekhterev and saw that here was just what he wanted. He began to see that his own objective psychology might well stress conditioning as the clue to all learning and to all higher processes. So rapidly did he think out the implications that a new approach to psychopathology was offered within a few months: What we have called a sick mind is the result of a training process. The "psychopathological" dog will eat decayed meat, will avoid fresh meat; but the mystery disappears if we know the punishments which fresh meat bring him. So too, if we knew the history of our human maladjustments, we could explain them all in terms of conditioning.

With these new vistas before him, Watson turned energetically to human problems, especially to problems in infant psychology. He and J. J. B. Morgan sketched in 1917 the possibility of a psychology of personality based on early conditioning. In the winter of 1916–17 a small grant and an opportunity to work at the Phipps Clinic in Baltimore had led Watson to studies of reflexes and instinctive behavior in the newborn.

Publishing in 1919 a general textbook of psychology, Watson went forward with studies of infant conditioning. In collaboration with Raynor (1920), he first ascertained that furry animals caused no fear in children about a year old, then noted their fear of the clanging sound of a hammer on a metal bar, and then struck this bar whenever the child touched the furry animal. Fear in response to the animal, without the bar, was soon evident. Despite its crudeness, this experiment immediately had a profound effect on American psychology, for it appeared to support the whole conception that not only simple motor habits, but important, enduring traits of personality, such as emotional tendencies, may in fact be "built into" the child by conditioning.

While the first definitions of behaviorism were stated in rather negative terms — in terms of the exclusion of parts of the subject matter of contemporary psychology (1913) — the movement was rapidly developing a system of positive assumptions and working these into a psychological system. Even

---

[3] To this it was retorted that in many cases one successful movement was promptly learned, while an unsuccessful movement, *though repeated several times in the same trial,* was eliminated. See Thorndike and Herrick (1915).

in his earliest work, Watson emphasized the right of the behaviorist to think of "mental" processes as *internal* forms of behavior, the relation of language to thought being especially stressed. Indeed, one of Watson's most important theoretical contributions was the suggestion, and as time elapsed the insistence, that all the phenomena of "inner" life are in reality the functioning of mechanisms which are as objective, though not as observable, as gross muscular contractions. In particular, imagination and thought have been stated in terms of "implicit" muscular behavior, especially the behavior of the speech organs and other mechanisms which symbolize lines of overt conduct. The study of language is therefore of paramount importance for the formulation of behaviorist theory.

It is necessary, of course, to distinguish between "passive language habits" (the response to words) and "active language habits" (the use of words). The interpretation of passive language habits in behavior terms turned out to be very simple. Holt (1915), a neorealist (one who believes that we respond to things *as they are* rather than merely "interpret" the sensations they arouse) who early declared himself a behaviorist, put the matter well. Words, acting as substitutes for situations, *evoke the same responses* that the situations themselves would elicit.[4] The "meaning" of a word is *nothing but* a conditioned response to that word. We can see this plainly in the case of movements which have arisen in the history of the individual in relation to specific objects; for example, in the act of reaching. If the child reaches for a bottle and the word "bottle" is repeated many times in connection with it, the word "bottle" will in time produce in the child the specific kind of appropriate reaching movement; a conditioned response has been established. What the word "bottle" *means* is the behavior in reference to it. If bottle, glass, and pitcher have to be grasped and manipulated in different ways, the meanings are provided by the different motor responses.

But active language was a larger problem. To this problem Watson addressed himself in a paper presented to the International Congress of Philosophy and Psychology in 1920;[5] his view was later set forth in the second edition (1924) of his *Psychology from the Standpoint of a Behaviorist* and in *Behaviorism* (1924a). Beginning with the random babblings of the child, any sounds that cause other persons to minister to the child's needs tend in the long run to be repeated more often than sounds which bring little or no result.[6] Consequently, the child develops, purely through such trial-and-error variations, sounds which, by approximating genuine words, bring

[4] This obvious fact was of course not put forward as a new discovery, but the grasping of its implications for behaviorism was important.

[5] Though Watson was not present, his paper became the subject of much discussion.

[6] This would, of course, be cited by Thorndike's followers as a case of the "law of effect." From the Watsonian viewpoint we are dealing simply with the elimination of irrelevant responses.

quicker and better results. No mechanism of learning need be supposed other than those manifest in the rat's learning the maze, or the cat's learning to escape from the puzzle box. The child learns to say "da-da" and later "doll" by the same mechanism. If the word "da-da" is used and is understood by others to mean doll, it serves the purpose; the only thing necessary is that it should work. Whenever it fails to work, further trial and error occurs until "doll" is uttered.[7]

So far, we have the process by which the chief terms used in thinking — namely, words — are learned as separate units; they are now integrated, in like manner with other forms of behavior, into "higher units." The next step is to show how this overt language is replaced by internal language: that is, how we learn to talk to ourselves instead of talking aloud. Watson suggests that the child's vocalization is eliminated through social pressure, so that children in talking to themselves no longer talk aloud, but in a whisper (1919, pp. 343 ff.). Only one modification is necessary to change ordinary speech to a whisper: namely, that the vocal cords should be relaxed instead of being active. All the rest of the speech mechanism works as before. Finally, whispering itself is eliminated, yet speech movements continue; "implicit" language activity continues in the form of constant changes in tension among the various speech mechanisms, which are duplicates of the movement involved in overt speech.

It will be recalled that several authors had described thinking in terms of mental experimentation and had shown the close similarity between thought and overt trial-and-error behavior. Ruger had shown that a good deal of this trial-and-error activity exists in the thought processes involved in solving new and complicated problems. Now the trial-and-error mechanism, as

---

[7] In the view just stated, the *imitation* of words can be explained only by assuming an extraordinary amount of random activity which develops, step by step, a child's ability to duplicate what it hears or sees. But observation of the degree of successful imitation present in the second year of life suggested the need of an explanation which will not insist upon the laborious process just described, yet will avoid recourse to the theory of the "instinct of imitation." Allport (1924) utilized for the purpose a doctrine developed by Baldwin (1895): the "circular reflex." Baldwin had asserted that the constant repetition of a movement might be due to the fact that each movement serves as a stimulus for its own repetition; as, for instance, when a monkey was observed to slap a surface of water over and over again. Allport assumed that the child's random utterances stimulate its auditory brain area while its motor-speech centers are still active; a connection is thus established which may lead to almost endless repetition of a sound. Such a reaction having been established between the hearing of a sound and the uttering of it, the utterance of a sound by another individual may cause, immediately, the child's repetition of it. This view seems really a supplement to the Watsonian view rather than a direct contradiction of it. Imitation itself is regarded not as the perception of the utility of duplicating an observed act, but as a type of behavior which appears only as motor mechanisms have been practiced, ineffective acts having been rejected and effective ones gradually selected. As the sparrow *gradually* learns to approximate the songs of the canaries with which he is caged, but can, after such learning, copy a trill with sudden and dramatic success (Conradi, 1905), so all imitative conduct is based on the previous mastery of the necessary elements.

described by Ruger, consisted, to a large extent, in the manipulation of ideas or attitudes. These processes lend themselves to construction in terms of language mechanisms. Thinking consists, therefore, for the behaviorist, of speech movements made on a very small scale and substituted for overt acts.[8] Trial and error goes on in implicit language behavior, each word or phrase in the thinking process serving as a substitute for some act. No longer do we find "ideas," but speech movements, as the elements involved in thought.

Behaviorism, therefore, had stated the thought processes in terms of language, which, through the conditioned response, serves in place of similarly conditioned overt acts. To be sure, there must be forms of thinking which are not verbal, and these are stated by the behaviorists in terms of gesture, of movements of the hands, feet, neck, trunk, and especially of the eyes.[9] The elaborate study of eye movements, begun by Helmholtz, had been continued by many experimenters. The relation of these movements to the reading process had become a fertile field of inquiry early in the present century, and it was easy for the behaviorist to press such studies into his service by suggesting that memory for verbal material, as well as for events observed, may be in part the repetition of the eye movements which have occurred before, repeated in abbreviated form. Slight ("implicit") gestures and delicate eye movements cooperate constantly with speech movements in the complex processes of thought. Though the brain remains a connecting station, it is for the behaviorist no more intelligible to say that we think with the brain than to say that we walk with the spinal cord.[10]

In place of the classical doctrine of the association of ideas, behaviorism substitutes the conception of an ordered series of *motor* responses. The center of gravity is moved, so to speak, from the cortex to the periphery. The facts pertaining to "mental set," or the "motives" which give direction to the thought process, occasion no difficulty. Such mental sets are themselves, in part, a matter of verbal organization which plays its part in the total conditioning, while motives are intraorganic stimuli—"visceral tensions" or other disturbances which may give rise to verbal trial and error.

[8] Bain, Ribot, and others had described speech movements which occur in the process of thinking; but the *identification* of such movements with the thinking process is the work of Watson.

[9] But behaviorists insisted that speech movements can rarely be wholly eliminated. Children seldom, if ever, succeed in completely eliminating the tongue and lip movements associated with the original printed word. The deaf and dumb use their fingers to think with: Watson, in fact, reminded the incredulous that Laura Bridgman could be observed to talk in her sleep by means of her fingers.

[10] The associationists, from Hartley on, although writing of the "association of ideas," had with few exceptions assumed that the real basis for mental connections lies in brain connections. Behaviorism undertook to get rid not only of "mental" connections, but of emphasis upon the mechanisms of cortical connection. If the neurologist wishes to study brain connections, well and good; the psychologist is concerned with observable behavior.

They set going implicit activity just as they set going overt muscular trial and error, until some act puts an end to the tension.[11]

Spread of the Conditioned-Response Method

In the meantime, the conditioned-response *method* was beginning to be widely applied in human psychology, with profound consequences for psychological theory,[12] both within and outside the behaviorist movement. Lashley (1916), for example, demonstrated that the conditioned salivary reflex could be elicited in human beings through the sight of chocolate candy, a small cup against the parotid gland collecting quantities of saliva which varied with the nearness of the stimulus. Continuing the conditioning studies with infants initiated by Krasnogorskii (1907), Mateer (1918) demonstrated conditioned opening of the mouth in response to tactual contact, comparing rate of learning with intelligence level (mental age).

New possibilities of the method were also shown by Cason (1922, 1922a), who found that the pupillary reflex can be conditioned by the simultaneous presentation of visual and auditory stimuli. A sound may in time produce those pupillary contractions which resulted originally from light. It was inevitable that profound changes in the definition of the learning process should follow from all these new studies and that they should lead toward a restatement of the whole problem as to the mechanism by which connections between stimuli and responses are altered. They helped greatly in the effort of Watson and his followers and intellectual comrades to see their way clear to utilize these simple doctrines in the construction of the new systematic psychology which was to reduce such time-honored problems as perception, judgment, intelligence and reasoning, emotion and personality to the more elementary forms of response. For one result of such intensive study of the conditioned response, and of the recognition of its importance for the theory of learning, has been the tendency of behaviorists to believe that *all* learning is simply conditioning and that the conditioned response is the true *unit* of learned behavior.[13] The first formulation of behaviorism, as we saw, relied in no way upon conditioning; but it became the core, and for

---

[11] As regards experimental evidence for the behavioristic theory of the process of thinking, many investigations (for example, Reed, 1916) have indeed shown a relation between the movements of the tongue and the thinking process, indicating that in some cases of silent thought the tongue actually traces the form of overt speech. The evidence seems to indicate, however, that the identity of form between "uttered" and "thought" syllables is at least very far from universal (Thorson, 1925). The rejoinder of the behaviorists lays stress on variations in muscular tonus too delicate to be observed and on symbolic movements executed by other parts of the speech mechanism, or indeed of the whole body. See also Max (1937) and Jacobson (1938, pp. 327–45).

[12] An early summary and bibliography appears in Cason (1925).

[13] In addition to Pavlov and Bekhterev, Watson (1924a) and Smith and Guthrie (1921) are forerunners of this view.

some psychologists the chief criterion, of behaviorist theory. No less important for behaviorism has been the consistent exclusion of the concept of "ideational" behavior and of the claim that animals and men are capable of sudden "insight" into situations in terms other than those of previous learning and the operation of trial and error. And emphasis on the genetic method leads the behaviorist always to inquire regarding the organism's previous conditioning.

The popularity of behaviorism in the United States became so great that a multitude of objective experiments, as well as a multitude of theories, were loosely termed "behavioristic," although little indeed of the behaviorist system was involved. Behaviorism has become in some quarters not so much a research program as a name for mechanistic psychology (essentially in accord with La Mettrie's conception of the mechanistic) [14] or has been reduced to a mere *emphasis* upon objective, as opposed to subjective, data. The description of experience known only to the subject, as in dreams, is admitted even by Watson, the interest lying ostensibly in the sleeper's implicit behavior and in his verbal reports. Indeed, the proportions of the movement would be greatly understated were we to confine the term to a set of experiments or to the program of 1914. Accurately or inaccurately, "behaviorism" means to many psychologists today any of the following:

1. The biological approach to animal and human psychology, promising that psychology shall one day make itself as objective as physical science.
2. A mechanistic or materialist view of psychology.
3. Watson's personal combination of (1) and (2).
4. The totality of behavior-centered systems.
5. The more recent behavior-oriented system of Skinner (see pp. 325 ff.).

In other words, the progeny of the behaviorism of a half a century ago are already very diverse in appearance and in disposition.

REFERENCES

Allport, F. H. *Social Psychology.* Boston: Houghton Mifflin, 1924.
Baldwin, J. M. *Mental Development in the Child and the Race.* New York: Macmillan, 1895.

[14] "To me the essence of behaviorism is the belief that the study of man will reveal nothing except what is adequately describable in the concepts of mechanics and chemistry, and this far outweighs the question of the method by which the study is conducted" (Lashley, 1923, p. 244). Such quotations might be multiplied indefinitely. For many, the term "behaviorism" simply summarizes the whole trend toward "natural-science" psychology and, in particular, the trend away from psychophysical dualism. Probably the most coherent statement of *behaviorist theory* is Weiss (1925), who combined objectivism and mechanism; yet it was not coherence, but simple intelligible experiment, that was in chief demand. A systematic integration of objective concepts and of Gestalt concepts was achieved by Kantor (1924–26).

Bekhterev, V. M. *Objektive Psychologie*. Leipzig: Tuebner, 1913.
———. *La Psychologie objective*. Paris: Alcan, 1913a.
———. [*General Principles of Human Reflexology.*] 1917. 3rd ed. Leningrad: GIZ, 1926.
Bekhterev, V. M., and Lange, M. W. "Die Ergebnisse des experiments auf dem Gebiete der Kollektiven Reflexologie." *Zeitschrift für Angewandte Psychologie*, 24 (1924), 305–44.
Bousfield, W. A. "Lope de Vega on Early Conditioning." *American Psychologist*, 10 (1955), 828.
Carpenter, W. B. *Principles of Mental Physiology*. London: King, 1874. New York: Appleton, 1874.
Cason, H. "The Conditioned Pupillary Reaction." *Journal of Experimental Psychology*, 5 (1922), 108–46.
———. "The Conditioned Eyelid Reaction." *Journal of Experimental Psychology*, 5 (1922a), 153–96.
———. "The Conditioned Reflex or Conditioned Response as a Common Activity of Living Organisms." *Psychological Bulletin*, 22 (1925), 445–72.
Conradi, E. "Song and Call-Notes of English Sparrows When Reared by Canaries." *American Journal of Psychology*, 16 (1905), 190–98.
Holt, E. B. *The Freudian Wish and Its Place in Ethics*. New York: Holt, 1915.
Jacobson, E. *Progressive Relaxation*. 2nd ed. Chicago: University of Chicago Press, 1938.
Kantor, J. R. *Principles of Psychology*. 2 vols. Bloomington, Ind.: Principia Press, 1924–26.
Krasnogorskii, N. I. ["Artificial Reflexes in Young Children."] *Russkii Vrach*, 6 (1907), 1245.
Lashley, K. S. "The Human Salivary Reflex and Its Use in Psychology." *Psychological Review*, 23 (1916), 446–64.
———. "The Behavioristic Interpretation of Consciousness." *Psychological Review*, 30 (1923), 237–72, 329–53.
Loeb, J. *Der Heliotropismus der Tiere*. Würzburg: Hertz, 1890.
———. *Einleitung in die Vergleichende Gehirnphysiologie und Vergleichende Psychologie* [*Physiology of the Brain*]. Leipzig: Barth, 1899.
Lubbock, J. *Ants, Bees, and Wasps*. New York: Appleton, 1882.
Mateer, F. E. *Child Behavior*. Boston: Badger, 1918.
Maudsley, H. *Body and Will*. New York: Appleton, 1884.
Max, L. W. "Experimental Study of the Motor Theory of Consciousness. IV: Action-Current Responses in the Deaf During Awakening, Kinaesthetic Imagery and Abstract Thinking." *Journal of Comparative Psychology*, 24 (1937), 301–44.
Morgan, C. L. *Animal Life and Intelligence*. London: Arnold, 1891.
———. *Animal Intelligence*. Psychological Review Monograph Supplement, Vol. 2, No. 8 (1897).
———. *Animal Behavior*. London: Arnold, 1900.
Pavlov, I. P. [*Lectures on the Work of the Principal Digestive Glands.*] St. Petersburg: Kushnereff, 1897.
———. ["Principal Laws of the Activity of the Central Nervous System, as They Find Expression in Conditioned Reflexes."] *Russkii Vrach*, 11 (1912), 1507–11.

Reed, H. B. "The Existence and Function of Inner Speech in Thought-Processes." *Journal of Experimental Psychology,* 1 (1916), 365–90.

Smith, S., and Guthrie, E. R. *General Psychology in Terms of Behavior.* New York: Appleton, 1921.

Spalding, D. A. "Instinct and Acquisition." *Popular Science Monthly,* 8 (1876), 310–15.

Thorndike, E. L. *The Mental Life of the Monkeys. Psychological Review Monograph Supplement,* Vol. 3, No. 15 (1899).

————. *Educational Psychology.* Vol. 1. New York: Lemcke and Buechner, 1903. Vol. 2. New York: Teachers College, Columbia University, 1913. Vol. 3. New York: Teachers College, Columbia University, 1914.

————. *The Elements of Psychology.* New York: Seiler, 1905.

Thorndike, E. L., and Herrick, C. J. "Watson's Behavior." *Journal of Animal Behavior,* 5 (1915), 462–70.

Thorson, A. "The Relation of Tongue-Movements to Internal Speech." *Journal of Experimental Psychology,* 3 (1925), 1–32.

Waldeyer, H. W. von. "Ueber einige neuere Forschungen im Gebiete der Anatomie des Centralnervensystems." *Deutsche medizinische Wochenschrift,* 17 (1891), 1213–18, 1244–46, 1287–89, 1331–32, 1352–56.

Washburn, M. F. *The Animal Mind.* New York: Macmillan, 1908.

Watson, J. B. "Psychology as the Behaviorist Views It." *Psychological Review,* 20 (1913), 158–77.

————. *Behavior: An Introduction to Comparative Psychology.* New York: Holt, 1914.

————. "Behavior and the Concept of Mental Disease." *Journal of Philosophy,* 13 (1916), 589–97.

————. *Psychology from the Standpoint of a Behaviorist.* 1919. 2nd ed. Philadelphia: Lippincott, 1924.

————. "Is Thinking Merely the Action of Language Mechanisms?" *British Journal of Psychology,* 11 (1920), 87–104.

————. *Behaviorism.* New York: Norton, 1924a.

Watson, J. B., and Raynor, R. "Conditioned Emotional Reactions." *Journal of Experimental Psychology,* 3 (1920), 1–14.

Weiss, A. P. *A Theoretical Basis of Human Behavior.* Columbus, Ohio: Adams, 1925.

Yerkes, R. M. "Ideational Behavior of Monkeys and Apes." *Proceedings of the National Academy of Sciences,* 2 (1916), 639–42.

Yerkes, R. M., and Morgulis, S. "The Method of Pavlov in Animal Psychology." *Psychological Bulletin,* 6 (1909), 257–73.

NOTE: A list of further readings appears at the back of the book.

17

Gestalt
and
Field
Theory

Nature is neither kernel nor shell; she is everything at once.
GOETHE

. . . to range the faculties
In scale and order, class the cabinet
Of their sensations, and in voluble phrase
Run through the history and birth of each
As of a single independent thing.
Hard task, vain hope, to analyse the mind.
WORDSWORTH

As one dips into the works of psychologists in any period, from the pre-Socratic to the present, one may run across phrases which deny the possibility of explaining wholes by a study of their constituent parts. It is a futile enterprise to try to specify who first got hold of the general principle of Gestalt psychology; and it is particularly futile to try to guess which of the Gestalt writers were influenced, consciously or unconsciously, by this or that earlier formulation of doctrines of wholeness or structure.

It is, however, worthwhile to note that relationships, or modes of organization, are repeatedly stressed by early Greek thinkers, many of whom decried the tendency to find a primordial stuff of which the world was made and looked rather for a law of arrangement, a principle of synthesis or order. In general, the Pythagorèan answers were the most successful; and the history of science has shown them to be the most generally followed by men of later eras. It was, in other words, the mathematical approach to the problem of structure or organization that stood in the most fruitful and dynamic opposition to the various types of atomism or elementarism. The Platonists, of course, had enthusiastically taken over the emphasis upon mathematics as a clue to structure, and Platonism contains many passages which may reasonably enough be regarded as suggestive of a Gestalt theory.

In modern times — to remind the reader of a few examples already cited — Hartley had pointed out that tastes and smells may not only combine in such a way as to give new qualities, but may be experienced in such a way that the original elements are no longer observable at all. The elements are literally lost to view. John Stuart Mill had later made a profitable use of this conception. For Bain there is no starting or stopping; there is constantly a dynamic readjustment in the structure of a complex experience, which makes mechanical types of analysis peculiarly unfruitful.

William James was positively obsessed with this problem and returned to it on every possible occasion. The best known of his philippics against the atomistic view is the discussion of the "psychologist's fallacy," which is simply the assumption that when one has reduced a complex to its supposed parts, the parts must have been there all the time and must have been the real key to the complex. James seldom worked out his position from an initial protest to the calm and positive assertion of a system; in fact, one feels that he would have knocked down the system if he had ever succeeded in building one. But insofar as Gestalt psychology is a protest against elementarism or atomism, this celebrated passage of James's is a clear enough forerunner.

The protest against atomism was not limited to psychology. Indeed, both atomism and the protest against it continued in the physical and biological sciences. With the development of appropriate tools at the beginning of the nineteenth century, the chemists and biologists had discovered elements and cells. The physicists and biochemists of the twentieth century, with their x-rays of crystals and their double helix formation of DNA-RNA structures, give us the sense of a Gothic cathedral reduced to an almost infinitesimal droplet of physical reality based ultimately upon knowable and describable systems of relationships.

One may think of the elegant structure of DNA, built up of long, definable strands of nucleic acid, as examples of atomism or as examples of supra-summative properties.[1] One may regard a Gothic cathedral as a collection of stones and glass put together in a particular way or as a totality in which the parts are almost utterly meaningless without the whole; and in the same way, we may think of the genetic code in terms of the strands of nucleic acids or in terms of the biological structure or wholeness in the light of which the details are understood.

In psychology it was evident, from Lotze to Wundt, that elementarism could have its central position *only* if it were willing to yield an equally central position to an integrative or creative principle. It was an unhappy

---

[1] We owe this sentence to E. R. Hilgard.

but, for the time being, workable alliance between atomism and a doctrine of order.

However, the alliance became less and less workable. One difficulty was that the elements discovered by introspection seemed to vary with the training of the observer and with the instructions given by the experimenter. Another difficulty was that the evolutionary principle required emphasis upon adaptation of the whole living individual, and the sensory functions needed to be seen in relation to this evolutionary requirement. The third, and perhaps most compelling, difficulty was that the problems which the new psychology discovered for meaningful attack in the laboratory were largely problems of what the organism was *doing:* whether perceiving, or recalling, or thinking, and so on. There was always room for introspective reports on the life of sensation, image, and feeling; but these seemed to lead into a more and more intricate and ever darkening tunnel, and the daylight seemed to beat in upon problems of adjustment and adaptation. This was evident, for example, in the experimental work of Cattell and Thorndike.

This combination of forces demanding a more functional emphasis came to a head in a brilliantly conceived essay by John Dewey in 1896: "The Reflex Arc Concept in Psychology." Here the whole psychological act of response to an environmental situation is considered as a unit. There is a place for perceptual, integrative, interpretative, decision-making, and action phases, in which it is impossible to understand the sensory aspects without carrying through to the motor aspects; and impossible to understand the motor aspects except in the light of the ongoing situation in which the fresh sensory components are also present. Not only were sensations alone irrelevant to the understanding of the biological meaning of the response; the units of the reflex arc itself were similarly without meaning except in their biological context.

But Gestalt psychology arose in Germany. Here we may follow Helson (1925, 1926) in noting the importance of Mach, who grappled so brilliantly with the "analysis of sensations" in the eighties. While Mach had come to the conclusion that the world of sensations with which the physical scientist deals as he takes note of lights, sounds, and temperatures is identical with the world of lights, sounds, and temperatures with which the psychologist is concerned, he did note certain relational problems which seemed to disturb the symmetry of this beautiful analysis. He noted, for example, that the arrangement of elements—say, for example, the arrangement of lines in geometrical figures—causes the emergence of different totals which are reported as squares, diamonds, and so on. He had therefore resorted to the doctrine that there are "sensations of space," sensations which, while not pointing directly to the elements of the original experience, must be taken jointly with them if we are to explain the structured total.

This tour de force was followed a few years later by the more radical and adequate formulation of von Ehrenfels. In a paper in 1890 von Ehrenfels noted that melodies must consist of something other than a sequence of tones, since obviously one sings or recognizes the melody in other keys; and indeed (with the very dubious exception of instances of absolute pitch) one makes no absolute use at all of specific tonal *elements* which enter into the melody. One may, moreover, encounter the same "element" (say middle C) in different melodies played in different keys and find that they differ utterly. If we can have the same elements and get a different result, and have different elements yet get the same result, where are we with regard to the reduction of experience to fixed components? Von Ehrenfels went on to conclude that over and above various sensory ingredients there must be qualities belonging to organized forms and coined the term "form quality" — *Gestaltqualität* — to describe that which a melody or a painting or a sonnet possesses which is not given in the component tones, colors, or words. Though this is more like a real psychological theory than is Mach's, it is extraordinary that von Ehrenfels did not really undertake to solve, any more than did Mach, the question of what to do with the *new* elements — in this case new qualities — which he had thrown into the picture. One might accuse both Mach and von Ehrenfels of buttressing up a tottering elementarism by throwing new elements into the situation rather than by noting the nature of the architectural problem. If there are sensations of space, then what is the relation of the sensation of space to the other sensations already present? So also with regard to von Ehrenfels: As we specify *qualities* to be added to sensory *elements,* why do we not need to specify other qualities which result from the relations of the first qualities to the sensory elements? If qualities or relations of any sort *between elements* are to be added to primary elements, do we not find ourselves lost in an infinite regression? Indeed, if there are form qualities which go with certain sequences of tones (melodies), these must candidly be regarded as new elements in experience.

Moreover, the von Ehrenfels solution makes one begin to wonder whether it means anything to say that *the same melody* sounds different in different keys. Just what do we mean by "the same"? If a voice on one occasion and a violin on another occasion carry an air, and we note the same form quality, we have the quality reappearing when no one of the original elements is there, a resultant without any component forces. Our problem has not really been solved; all we have done is to name a quality given by each structural total so that to all intents and purposes their number is unlimited. If it is replied that this is a new structural conception, one may simply note that unless form can be more fully defined, one has no more help in explaining and predicting the outcome of a new combination of ingredients than one would have if one simply let the ingredients try to do their own work without such aid. Certainly the von Ehrenfels principle is an honest recognition of a grave difficulty, and there can certainly be no quarrel with its statement of the facts; perceptual wholes are not made up of the kinds of sensory elements that had traditionally been described as their ingredients. But just what form actually is and what its laws are remain indeterminate.

Wertheimer

That is where the problem stood during the time of the Würzburg investigations of attitude and thought, described above. Eagerly prosecuting such studies of higher mental processes, Max Wertheimer and two of his experimental collaborators, Köhler and Koffka, came upon a radically different way of viewing the whole problem. It was Wertheimer's formulation of what occurred that led in Frankfurt in 1912 to the formal inauguration of the Gestalt psychology—the psychology of form.

The problem was the perception of motion. When light is thrown through a small slit placed vertically, and a moment later through a slit inclined 20° or 30° to the right, the interval separating the two presentations may be so chosen that the shaft of light appears to *fall* from one position to the other. Wertheimer proceeded to work out quantitatively those time relations which would give (1) two simultaneous illuminated slits, (2) the experience of motion from A to B, and (3) the sense of temporal succession, the first being followed by the second, but no movement being involved. The central problem was the nature of the experience of movement, the *phi phenomenon*.

Now a rather good elementaristic explanation of movement had been developed by Lotze some three decades earlier (1882). For Lotze, the visual perception of motion depended upon the sequential stimulation of points on the retina and hence the sequential stimulation of brain regions; a moving object caused a track of light to be made upon the retina. If, however, there is no such track of light when the eye is stationary while being stimulated successively by two lights as in the Wertheimer experiment with the phi phenomenon, Lotze's interpretation collapses. The perception of motion, argued Wertheimer (1912), is an experience organically different from the perception of stationary lights, and no kind of serial arrangement of static stimulating points can give us this unique type of experience. The very essence of the experience is the manner in which temporal organization of two stimulations occurs. Wertheimer developed, therefore, the conception of "cross-processes" in the brain, dynamic *interactions* between the various cortical excitations which follow from the two stimulations.

Not being content with the insistence upon the reality of the experience of motion as something dynamically distinct from the awareness of position and of temporal succession of such positions, Wertheimer proceeded at once to a reformulation of the theory of wholes and parts. Just as Fechner (1876) had protested against the procedure of the philosopher from above to below, so Wertheimer protested against the general modern scientific movement from below to above. We shall never achieve an understanding of structured totals by starting with the ingredient parts which enter into them. On the contrary, we shall need to understand the structure; we shall need to have insight into it. There is then some possibility that the components themselves will be understood.

This leads immediately to two laws which follow inevitably if the relation of whole to parts has been properly stated. The first is the law of membership character. The tones in a melody do not have their several fixed qualities, to which a form quality is somehow added; rather, each such tone manifests qualities which depend upon the place of the tone in the context. Such attributes, depending on the place of an identifiable component in a structure, permit no use of the conception of elements which when compounded into totals remain what they were before. Similarly, a patch of color in a landscape, far from being an ingredient in a total, depends for its value upon the context which nature, or the artist, supplies; we are working from above rather than from below. The Gestaltist insists that the attributes or aspects of the component parts, insofar as they can be defined, are defined by their relations to the system as a whole in which they are functioning.

A simple laboratory demonstration is offered by a red cross on a gray field which after twenty seconds' fixation in fair light will elicit a green border, according to the familiar dynamics of contrast. Cut out, however, a tiny notch in one of the arms of the cross. What color will the space within the notch yield to our observation? Green, says the traditional elementarist theory, for it is a part of the gray border which must take on a contrasting hue. Red, says the Gestaltist, for a cross is one of those organized wholes which forces the component materials within it, as a result of membership character, to take on the attributes supporting the structure. The Gestaltist predicts more accurately than the elementarist what will actually occur.

Proceeding further, however, Wertheimer noted that there are certain directions in which one can predict the emergence of structured wholes. Instead of simply saying with Von Ehrenfels that there is always something more than the parts, Wertheimer notes that if unstable equilibrium and unstable structure are given, which manifest certain types of inner relationships, one can predict from a knowledge of the laws of structure what kind of organization must supervene. It will be that kind of organization which is most orderly, most comprehensive, most stable, most free of the casual and the arbitrary; in a single word, that which is most good. Goodness or, as he preferred to say, *Prägnanz* is the dynamic attribute of self-fulfillment, intrinsic in all structured totals. Glancing back at the example of the notched cross, one sees immediately that the stable, rugged, definite outlines of the arms have a far higher degree of *Prägnanz* than the chaotic, and one might even say rather irrational, lines of the notch, which disturb the simple, orderly, and stable pattern presented. These two laws, the law of membership character and the law of *Prägnanz,* are typical of many which rapidly evolved in Wertheimer's thinking. They are in general representative of

Gestalt laws as a whole, laws in which one works not with an infinite number of tiny particles arranging themselves more or less independently, but with a limited, finite number of possible modes of stable organization, which because of their orderly, rationally intelligible form are capable of being discovered and their dynamics understood.

The first task of the perceiver, then, is not to create, but to apprehend the order and meaning which is there objectively in the world. This is, so far, essentially like Platonism. There are, however, many forms or structures to be found, not all of which are of equal relevance to the perceiver. Just as perception moves from the incomplete toward that which is more nearly complete, so there is continuous dynamic selection and integration of forms. We have thus a direct transition from the psychology of perception to the psychology of thought, without involving the need of any essentially different principles. We need to grasp, first of all, the order lying in nature and waiting for our apprehension; and second, that internal order which the thinker manifests as he passes from one to another orderly form, creating new order in the succession and in the integration. The psychology of thinking already implicit in Wertheimer's earlier work became more and more important both in his own work and in that of his pupils. It was the process of thinking which intrigued Köhler (1917) in his comparison of men with apes. It was thinking which intrigued Koffka (1921) as he first ventured to conceive of educational psychology as the successive realization of levels of complexity, growing out of the capacity of the individual to move ever toward higher integrations rather than simply to acquire piecemeal one new response at a time. It is not in any sense accidental that during those last years of his life, when Wertheimer was endlessly burdened with the task of adapting to a new environment (after 1933 he taught at the New School for Social Research in New York), the book upon which he labored was a book on productive thinking (1945).

The basic conception which runs through this struggle to lay bare the dynamics of thought was the conception of *recentering:* the discovery of new forms of figure-ground organization in which an inadequate and ultimately disorderly mode of centering or focusing is thrust aside in favor of a newly recentered pattern—insightful and correct in the sense of mediating contact with reality, because the center as apprehended by the observer corresponds with a natural center in the objective event waiting for such discovery.

From the new viewpoint the entire domain of cognitive processes—processes of perception, learning, thinking, imagining—was to be systematically redefined in terms of the conception of Gestalt. In practice, moreover, cognitive phenomena were to be studied alongside the phenomena of affect. Emotion came to be viewed, for example, as a response involving the entire living system, rather than as a local response of the midbrain, after the manner of Cannon (1915). And impulse, instinct, and will were treated ultimately as processes involving the entire community of various aspects of a bodily tension system and presenting no possibility that a segmental act of impulse or will could be mapped out and independently studied.

At this point, one turns inevitably to our major source of information regarding the total activity of the human brain: namely, the study of brain disorder resulting from disease or from industrial or military catastrophe, and in particular the cases classically known as aphasia. Here the results obtained in England by Head (1923), and in Germany a few years earlier by Gelb and Goldstein (1920), led to a converging philosophy of neural function. Head found himself unable to use effectively Broca's conception of specific localization and specific functions in specific brain areas and found himself drawn to a conception of relations between certain broad types of speech activity and certain ways or forms of brain activity. In the same way, Gelb and Goldstein, studying the brains of men suffering from gunshot wounds in World War I, found that the whole visual field would be recast if a slight injury was inflicted upon the visual area. It was not a question of cutting out, so to speak, one part of the visual field; rather, it was a question of forcing upon the impaired organism a completely new way of giving structure to the perceived world. If, for example, the brain area supposedly serving the region of the fovea is shot away, the result is not the loss of foveal vision, but rather the development of a "pseudo-fovea" in another region. There must be focusing, there must be sharp figure-ground differentiation, if anything like human seeing is to go on. What is seen, moreover, must be meaningfully organized. Suppose a man has suffered a local "micropsia," so that part of the world appears abnormally small. When looking at a cross which lies partly in the area of micropsia, he does not see *part* of the cross reduced in size, but sees all of it large or all of it small. Organizing tendencies dominate any punctiform activities which may be going on here and there.

In the same way, in the case of intellectual functions Goldstein showed that specific errors do not necessarily follow upon local injury; rather, the shattered or broken individual reduces the level of his activity, attempts less, and finds a way of coping with life at a reduced level. The organism must always "come to terms" with the environment. Instead of reacting "mosaic-fashion" to specific brain losses, the organism makes a patterned response in a qualitatively distinct mode of adjustment.

Köhler and Koffka

The new doctrine was broadened and deepened and carried to the world by Wolfgang Köhler and Kurt Koffka. In Köhler's posthumous statement, presented to the American Psychological Association in 1967, it was clear that from his youth his enthusiasm for the epoch-making new concepts of Planck on quantum theory and "field physics" had been the breath of life and the permanent central sustaining force in all his thought and work. It was not only the *method* of physics; it was the conceptual scheme leaping out from the ingenious new experiments which pointed the way for the young psychologist. Köhler had made his commitment to Wertheimer and to the Gestalt principle in psychology in 1912, but, in a sense, the Gestalt conception was for him a psychophysiological and, indeed, a physical principle; with this emphasis upon his period with Planck as our background, it is clear why the principle of "isomorphism" meant so much to him: the principle that not mere analogy, but basic *identity of form,* brings psychology into the most intimate relation to physics. Psychology, because it is a lawful expression of the organism, and because the organism is a lawful expression of a physical universe, must reveal the quantum, the field physics, the basic at-last-discovered dynamics of the world. Later Köhler's effort to bring the psychosocial and the sociocultural world into alignment with the basic realities is seen in his lectures *The Place of Value in a World of Facts* (1938).

Though Koffka's survey article "Perception: An Introduction to the *Gestalttheorie*" had appeared in the *Psychological Bulletin* in 1922, the viva voce introduction of Gestalt psychology into the United States occurred at the Christmas meetings of the American Psychological Association in that year, through a paper read by Ogden. The response was quite hesitant and uncertain: What was this Gestalt psychology? Was it just one more foggy German philosophy? It soon became evident, however, that masses of experimental materials, highly ingenious and challenging, were waiting to be assimilated along with the new theory. Through extraordinary good fortune for the movement, both Koffka and Köhler were soon available to explain, at every interested American university center, what the new movement was all about and to show its revolutionary implications. The vivid personalities and good-tempered debating tactics of Koffka and Köhler led quickly to a widening interest in the new school, and soon everybody was taking Gestalt psychology in his stride.

Fortunate indeed for the spread of the Gestalt doctrine was the series of circumstances which led Koffka and Köhler into the public eye. Marooned in the Canary Islands during World War I, Köhler had carried out a series of ingenious studies to test the Thorndike hypothesis that animal learning depends simply upon trial and error and upon the stamping in of the correct responses. Working with the anthropoid apes at the Teneriffe research station, Köhler presented a series of simple problems in which the animal had to discover a way of reaching a suspended banana by placing boxes underneath it and climbing up on them, or by fitting together sticks which, when thus fitted together, would make it possible to reach the food. Köhler strove to demonstrate that apes, no less than men, come to solutions all at once by a process of integration or insight, in which not a series of separate clues taken in series, but an integrated system of clues, is responded to all at once. His reports appeared in German in 1917 and in English in 1924, as *The Men-*

tality of Apes (a translation of the German title would read *Intelligence Tests on Anthropoid Apes*).

Köhler's middle and later years were spent mainly in extending and systematizing the theory, as through the experiments on "figural after-effects" (Köhler and Wallach, 1944) and on the basic nature of the time error as expressions of anchoring tendencies. He thought his data exemplified direct currents in the brain (a controversial issue in which he was involved in debate with Lashley; but Köhler continued with his direct-current model).[2]

Wertheimer continued to be the originator, the philosopher, the logician, the ethicist, and Köhler continued to be the physiologist and the physicist of the movement. Koffka became the most complete systematizer and organizer of theory, authoritative selector and integrator of all the experimental evidence. Originally known to psychologists through his study *The Growth of the Mind* (1921), he continued to be the student of cognitive-perceptual development and to be the systematizer of the relation between perception, thought, affect, and action (*The Principles of Gestalt Psychology,* 1935).

With the development and exposition of the principles of wholeness, closure, *Prägnanz,* and membership character, there remained for the Gestaltist primarily the problem of systematic applications of the doctrine to complex human situations, for which, as they saw it, only piecemeal approaches had been available. Outstandingly creative in this regard is the work of the Gestaltists in the arts: especially in music, in literature, and in the visual space arts (representative arts). Arnheim, early a student under Wertheimer, concerned himself with experimental studies in recognizing personality from handwriting. The time came for the systematic presentation of the entire dynamic system of concepts available from Gestalt psychology to the world of painting, drawing, sculpture, and architecture. Here, in *Art and Visual Perception* (1954), spatial (and at times temporal) organization is considered in full systematic relationship to Gestalt principles; motion, shading, color, and the more complex symbolic aspects of visual art are developed.

While still working under Wertheimer, Werner Wolff (1943) began to conceive of a way of looking at the expression of personality in Gestalt terms; he noted posture, gesture, and stride, for example, as observable and recordable human movements which, as in the early work of Klages, made possible a consideration of personality in time-space-organized form. His documentation of his point was particularly clear when it was shown that the individual might have grave difficulties in recognizing his own expressive movements, perhaps for reasons of defense, in the psychoanalytic sense. From such studies developed a systematic integration of Gestalt with psychoanalytic conceptions. Parts of the early work of Wolff were replicated by Huntley, at Harvard, under Gordon Allport's direction, and other parts were repli-

---

[2] See also *Dynamics in Psychology* (1940).

cated and extended after Wolff's arrival in the United States in the late thirties. Personality study, in the sense of time, space, and dynamic interrelations between the components of expression, and between such systematic expressive behavior and an inner core or radix, became the fulfillment of an early Gestalt hope that personality might quite literally be seen as a dynamic whole.

It is within this frame of reference, with the developments in physics in the late nineteenth and early twentieth centuries, that one must understand the development of field theory in psychology. Indeed, as early as 1920 Köhler, in a volume dealing with "physical Gestalten," specifically called attention to those experiments in physics in which the local event is determined by the entire context; in which it is impossible to specify any detail which, defined in and for itself, can then be placed in the total situation and be found to remain what it was before. So far, this gave background for Gestalt psychology; Köhler was describing Gestalten in the physical world which were analogous to perceptual responses.

Lewin and Field Theory

In this period the young student of mathematics and physics Kurt Lewin, who had recently returned from army service, became a vigorous and intensely creative member of the Gestalt group at the University of Berlin. He rapidly qualified himself for the role of colleague of the three senior Gestaltists already named: Wertheimer, Köhler, and Koffka. At Berlin he carried out a series of studies of the dynamics of memory, in which he showed that items are linked together in memory not by virtue of "association," but by virtue of the way in which each word or nonsense syllable expresses the field organization of the experimental task as a whole.

But feeling a need for a fuller utilization of what the physicists were doing, he began to think of psychological problems more and more in terms of events occurring in a kind of space which had something in common with physical space and to think of psychological activity as a progression from one point to another within this life space, or psychological space. Here he felt the need for more adequate mathematical tools and gave himself intensely to that branch of mathematics which deals with such types of space as are of interest for their own intrinsic spatial attributes and not for their quantitative relationships. He found what he needed in the branch of mathematics known as topology, in which one is concerned with regions and their boundaries and subdivisions, the modes of progression which are possible within them, and the possibility of transformation of such portions of space as a result of weakening or strengthening barriers. Instead of the formal quantitative laws of the individual organism conceived as a biological system, we find ourselves confronted with *psychological motion toward goals within defined regions of life space* (1935, 1936).

Our interest in quantitative problems here becomes secondary; our interest turns rather to goals toward which psychological motion occurs, the tension systems or needs which appear as vectors expressing such motion, the barriers which interfere with it, the subdivisions into subregions of life space which occur (as in the absent-minded or the dissociated), the new integration which may occur under therapy, and so on. He thus simultaneously solved two problems: first, that of transferring the field mode of thought into psychology; and second, that of representing graphically rather than verbally the nature of psychological impulsions, the resistance to such impulsions, and the resulting transformations in movement toward goals.

A very simple illustration of the Lewinian mode of thought and expression: a child wants to go to a party; upon adamant refusal of his parents he "goes out of the field" by withdrawing into a daydream; he sets up a substitute field at another level in which the barrier becomes porous, and he imagines ways in which parents can be persuaded or circumvented; finally he reaches the goal at the imaginative level.

Utilizing his dynamic approach in experimental psychology, Lewin set going two lines of research which soon became especially popular and influential. Both express the vitality of the conception of psychological needs as tension systems: that is, as systems of interrelated forces within a bounded field capable of being conceptualized as the bases for locomotion in one or another direction. The first is the study of what happens to a tension system when a reduction in tension level is permitted. The pioneer study is that of Zeigarnik (1927), who, after administering a series of tasks to her laboratory subjects, allowed them to complete some tasks but interrupted others before completion. She later found that the subjects were on the whole able to recall the unfinished tasks more easily than the completed ones. Subsequent research has shown that the tensions in such situations may be various and complex, but it has clearly confirmed the importance of thinking of the tension system as continuing until a means for its reduction is available. This shows, in other words, that things do not just "die down," or peter out, but remain until something new supervenes. It is only when the task is completed that the artificially induced tension state (the "quasi-need") is put to rest. This "Zeigarnik effect" on the nature of the factors which may reduce tension has been the subject of many later investigations.

In the same years Hoppe (1930) and others set for their subjects tasks which were somewhat difficult to achieve and studied the many factors tending to raise or lower the expectation of the individual as to what he would be able to achieve—his "aspiration level." In time, notably in the work of Frank (1935), who worked with Lewin at Cornell, it became customary to think of aspiration level as a definite quantitative gauge of the person's expectation regarding his own future performance; and it became the habit to treat the difference between his aspiration and his present view of himself (his ego level) in terms of "difference scores." Such difference scores have been brought into relation to many sorts of personal variables; and it has been found, as by Gould (1939) and others, that a rather accurate picture of the individual's struggle for status and his struggle to find an acceptable self is portrayed in his endless jockeying with the aspiration level so that it will neither be so high as to leave him in a perpetual state of frustration nor so low as to be overeasily attained and hence to lose its zest. Indeed, level of aspiration, like several other Lewinian concepts, has become a widely acknowledged method of studying personality (Rotter, 1942).

A more detailed illustration, taken from the research of Lewin and his associates after his coming to the United States in 1932, will serve to show the radically empirical, and at the same time theoretically rich, nature of the approach. The hypothesis set by Barker *et al.* (1941) was that the Freudian conception of regression may be restated in topological terms: regression is the loss of differentiation; therefore one may refer to "*de*differentiation." Lewin conceived of the mind of the newborn as essentially an undifferentiated whole. A bare circular outline may be used to portray this. Gradually, sensory components take shape as the child becomes aware of objects about him which he can recognize; and at the same time motor components, habitual acts, make their appearance. These events going on during the opening weeks are followed by the development of an inner world of memories, images, values, and purposes; in this inner world, then, we have a series of differentiations going on which make the adult infinitely more specific and at the same time more rigid than the child. The process of dedifferentiation consists of losing such differentiated subregions and reverting to the infantile condition. Now we should assume in general that frustrations, if intense enough, will cause such dedifferentiation. We have then the hypothesis: frustration will produce a regression, meaning specifically a measurable reduction in the differentiatedness of behavior.

To test this hypothesis, children of nursery-school age, whose behavior had been rated on scales indicating the degree of their "social constructiveness" while playing with a set of toys, were given a chance to observe some new and fascinating toys and to play a few minutes with them and were then led back to the old, familiar playroom equipment. Between the child and the new toys a large wire-mesh screen was pulled down and padlocked. The behavior of most of the children in the subsequent period of observation consisted, in good measure, of responses of a rather undifferentiated sort which they had shown when much younger. Thus a child who before this experiment had used a toy telephone to carry on a conversation proved after the frustrating experience to lose this "mature behavior" and simply used the telephone as a rattle. A child who had been "writing a letter" went back to sheer scribbling. The hypothesis seems verified. A topological change occurs, in the sense of a reduction in the number and the firmness of the boundaries within the system as a whole—a dedifferentiation.

Lewin emphasized social psychology more and more, making a series of notable contributions during the thirties and during the war years, and thereafter, until his death in 1947, playing an especially large role in new ways of conceptualizing life space and interpersonal and intergroup patterns within it. We shall take up this theme in Chapter 25. Here it is mainly necessary to emphasize the emergence of Lewin as a vital member of the Gestalt group at the University of Berlin and the impact of his field theory upon American psychology, especially with respect to ways of establishing field situations productive of new insights and stimulating new research efforts.

The Spread of Gestalt Psychology

There is no doubt that the enthusiasm over Watson's behaviorism as a system was a factor challenging all his opponents to discover a countersystem which had the same vitality. It was also no doubt true that the various experimental studies being carried out in laboratories charged with the maintenance of the introspective tradition called loudly for some vivid systematization that would give them the crisp and compelling form which was felt to be wanting in Titchener's rather cold and arid system. Integrations of Gestalt psychology and behaviorism were likewise attempted. In the same period appeared Kantor's organismic psychology (1924–26), in which the interdependence and formal unity of all organic responses is noted, but with an emphasis upon objectivism.

By the mid-thirties Gestalt psychology had become a complete system, with all the cardinal areas and problems of psychology undergoing redefinition in terms of the theory of form. These doctrines were coming into applied psychology, likewise notably into psychiatry and education, and were being heard of and used by social scientists such as anthropologists and sociologists. In 1933 the movement was solidly established in Germany and in the United States (hardly known elsewhere). It then became centered in the latter country, owing to the departure from Germany of Wertheimer and numerous other proponents of Gestalt doctrines and, upon their arrival in the United States, to the appeal of the message which the expanding group of laboratory and clinical people brought to these shores. One encountered, particularly on the Eastern seaboard, dozens of young research psychologists who had learned to think in Gestalt terms and who could talk interestingly, in or out of academic situations, regarding the promise of this approach; likewise, literally hundreds of clinical workers who had combined the Gestalt approach with psychoanalytic concepts in one guise or another. Gestalt psychology, then, came to be a vital new phase of American psychology, rapidly moving West as the doctrines were published and distributed in American journals and as the eager young refugees themselves showed what a difference it made whether one did or did not utilize these new ideas.

It is not meant to imply that Gestalt psychology disappeared in Germany, or that it won an uncontested triumph in the United States. What happened in Germany after the departure of the leader and many of his followers was that the general emphasis upon wholeness and structure (which, as we saw, had been increasing for several decades) went on increasing and various types of applied psychology, such as graphology and the Rorschach method (already saturated with theories of wholeness), were given a larger and larger place in the various types of clinical assessment of individuals. German psychological warfare itself made extensive use of personality testing based upon various theories of structure. That was, however, at best a rather diluted form of Gestalt psychology, when it was Gestalt psychology at all; and the amount of original experimental work done under the aegis of such studies of wholeness was apparently trivial. Gestalt psychology was reduced to a very minor position in the German university system.

In the United States, the most general tendency, except among German-trained scholars who came here as complete adherents to the system, was to regard Gestalt psychology as an interesting and valuable, but not a final or complete, solution to primary problems. Sometimes the theory was diluted to mean simply that there must always be a consideration of the multiplicity of factors working toward any given response; sometimes it was meant to signify a study of relationships obtaining between various stimuli present in the stimulus field, or various responses going on successively or simultaneously (so much, of course, any associationist would have granted). Sometimes it came nearer to the Wertheimer doctrine by emphasizing membership character and the futility of dissecting out supposedly independent elements. Occasionally it meant going the whole way, insisting that conscious or behavioral responses are intelligible only as structures or systems and that all aspects or phases of such wholes, with their membership character, express cross sections in a dynamic flow oriented toward the completion of some purposive act.

If such a characterization is at all adequate, it means that in general Gestalt psychology has been gratefully received and grafted upon existing systems but that it has not, except here and there on a very small scale, been espoused by American psychology as a final or fundamental solution of psychological problems.

Particularly characteristic of American psychology has been the effort, through countless experiments and clinical observations, to show that *both* piecemeal *and* organized responses occur—just as, in response to behaviorism, the prevalent tendency has been to say that both consciousness and behavior need to be studied. Typical of dozens of studies is Durkin's generalization (1937) that in problem-solving the responses made by her subjects ranged all the way from blind poking about until pieces happened to fall into a correct position to those responses in which a large number of separate pieces suddenly seemed to leap together into one meaningful and adequate total. There are, then, according to Durkin, and a great many of the middle-of-the-roaders, not only two basic ways of thinking—the associationist way and the insightful way—but all the possible theoretical intervening points on a continuum.

That aspect of Gestalt psychology which seems to us most fundamental and at the same time most incompletely worked out is the definition of membership character. At times one discovers in the Gestalt literature the conception that all the elements or component parts of a total need to be seen in their interrelations in order to understand the structure. On another page, however, one discovers that there *are* no elements or component parts. Each aspect or phase of the total manifests those attributes which each must possess if it is to stand at a particular point and function in a particular role; attributes which belong *to the elements themselves* are not definable. If this second statement is true, then obviously the first is far from the mark. Surely if membership character in so fundamental a sense dominates not only the locus but the very character of every ingredient, then there are no parts or elements or components, and it means nothing to say that the relations between them must be studied. The Gestaltist sometimes tries to have his cake and eat it too as he maintains that there are components which enter into structures and also that there are no components. The issue seems to stand about as it stood forty years ago. The theory of membership character and the whole ultimate theory of the atomic or nonatomic character of psychological events remains unresolved—both as to clear theoretical treatment and as to answers from crucial experiments.

Yet every nook and cranny of psychology has been invaded with the conception of structure, or system, or interdependence; every theoretical system today either rejects atomism or admits its incompleteness, or at least apologizes for it. So huge a tidal wave cannot be "met" by a countermovement of any sort; it will have its effect. Since in general the trend is clearly in accord with general trends in physics toward fields and wholeness, and general trends in biology toward the actualization of evolutionary patterns involving the interdependence of organs, of whole individuals, and of species, this movement in psychology is fully in the modern spirit.

REFERENCES

Arnheim, R. "Experimentell-Psychologische Untersuchungen zum Ausdrucksproblem." *Psychologische Forschung,* 11 (1928), 1–132.

———. *Art and Visual Perception.* Berkeley: University of California Press, 1954.

Barker, R. G., Dembo, T., and Lewin, K. "Frustration and Regression: An Experiment with Children." *University of Iowa Studies in Child Welfare,* Vol. 18, No. 1 (1941).

Cannon, W. *Bodily Changes in Pain, Hunger, Fear and Rage.* New York: Appleton, 1915.

Dewey, J. "The Reflex Arc Concept in Psychology." *Psychological Review,* 3 (1896), 357–70.

Durkin, H. "Trial-and-Error Gradual Analysis, and Sudden Reorganization: An Experimental Study of Problem Solving." *Archives of Psychology,* No. 210 (1937).

Ehrenfels, C. von. "Über Gestaltqualitäten." *Vierteljahrschrift für wissenschaftliche Philosophie,* 14 (1890), 249–92.

Fechner, G. T. *Vorschule der Aesthetik.* Leipzig: Breitkopf and Härtel, 1876.

Frank, J. D. "Individual Differences in Certain Aspects of the Level of Aspiration." *American Journal of Psychology,* 47 (1935), 119–28.

Gelb, A., and Goldstein, K. *Psychologische Analysen hirnpathologisher Fälle auf Grund von Untersuchungen Hirnverletzter.* Leipzig: Barth, 1920.

Gould, R. "An Experimental Analysis of 'Levels of Aspiration.' " *Genetic Psychology Monograph,* 21 (1939), 3–115.

Head, H. *Aphasia and Kindred Disorders of Speech.* 2 vols. Cambridge: Cambridge University Press, 1923.

Helson, H. "The Psychology of Gestalt." *American Journal of Psychology,* 36 (1925), 342–70, 494–526.

———. "The Psychology of Gestalt." *American Journal of Psychology,* 37 (1926), 25–62, 189–223.

Hoppe, F. "Erfolg und Misserfolg." *Psychologische Forschung,* 14 (1930), 1–62.

Kantor, J. R. *Principles of Psychology.* 2 vols. Bloomington, Ind.: Principia Press, 1924–26.

Koffka, K. *Die Grundlagen der psychischen Entwicklung; eine Einführung in die Kinderpsychologie* [*The Growth of the Mind*]. Osterwieck: Zickfeldt, 1921.

———. "Perception: An Introduction to the *Gestalttheorie.*" *Psychological Bulletin,* 19 (1922), 531–85.

———. *The Principles of Gestalt Psychology.* New York: Harcourt Brace Jovanovich, 1935.

Köhler, W. *Intelligenz-prüfungen an Menschenaffen.* Berlin: Springer, 1917. *The Mentality of Apes.* Translated by E. Winter. London: Kegan Paul, 1924.

———. *Die Physischen Gestalten in Ruhe und im Stationären Zustand.* Erlangen: Weltkreisverlag, 1920.

———. *The Place of Value in a World of Facts.* New York: Liveright, 1938.

———. *Dynamics in Psychology.* New York: Liveright, 1940.

Köhler, W., and Wallach, H. "Figural After-Effects: An Investigation of Visual Processes." *Proceedings of the American Philosophical Society,* 88 (1944), 269–357.

Lewin, K. *A Dynamic Theory of Personality.* Translated by D. K. Adams and K. E. Zener. New York: McGraw-Hill, 1935.

———. *Principles of Topological Psychology.* Translated by F. Heider and G. M. Heider. New York: McGraw-Hill, 1936.

Lotze, R. H. *Grundzüge der Psychologie.* Leipzig: Hirzel, 1882.

Ogden, R. M. "The Gestalt Hypothesis." *Psychological Review,* 35 (1928), 136–41.

Rotter, J. B. "Level of Aspiration as a Method of Studying Personality." *Development and Evaluation of a Controlled Method,* 31 (1942), 410–22.

Wertheimer, M. "Experimentelle Studien über das sehen von Bewegungen." *Zeitschrift für Psychologie,* 61 (1912), 161–265.

———. *Productive Thinking.* New York: Harper, 1945.

Wolff, W. *The Expression of Personality.* New York: Harper, 1943.

Zeigarnik, B. W. "Über das Behalten von erledigten und unerledigten Handlungen." *Psychologische Forschung,* 9 (1927), 1–85.

NOTE: A list of further readings appears at the back of the book.

18

Sigmund Freud and Psychoanalysis

Well-educated physicians, at any rate, say that we should pay close attention to dreams. . . . The most skilful interpreter of dreams is he who can discern resemblances. . . . As the picture in the water, so the dream can be similarly distorted.

ARISTOTLE

I bid you, mock not Eros,
He knows not doubt or shame,
And, unaware of proverbs,
The burnt child craves the flame.
CHRISTOPHER MORLEY

The physicians of the Renaissance had Galen to lean upon. There was no good theory, but there were hundreds of rule-of-thumb empirical principles. The story goes that when a steel splinter got into Michelangelo's eye and he was in terror of losing it, a celebrated physician killed a few pigeons whose blood trickled over the eye, and the steel splinter was quickly extruded. It was, of course, partly hit-or-miss. When George Washington fell ill, he was bled and died. But that was in the same era in which Jenner, and then Catherine the Great, made massive and successful attacks on smallpox through "experiments in immunization." As the great nineteenth-century schools of medicine arose, they began to systematize genuine knowledge of histology, embryology, pathology—even, in the hands of Pasteur, immunology and the art of prevention. Medicine was beginning to be based on the firm principles of the newly established sciences.

This was, then, the situation with regard to physical disease. It was for the first time being systematically studied in terms of the new sciences of physics and chemistry, and the biological sciences pyramided upon these. *Mental* diseases, however (psychosis, neurosis, character disorders), though considered the reponsibility of the physician, were refractory to treatment. The sufferings of a nervous man were brilliantly portrayed in literature but were not medical triumphs. We learn, in William James's letters, of the horrible backaches for which he sought relief in the mud baths of Teplitz in Bohemia; and in Freud's account of his early days as a physician, he tells us that helio-therapy, hydrotherapy, and many another type of physical therapy was being used on the "nervous sufferers" of those years and that the patients some-times felt better or even got well. Some attributed the cures to "suggestion." Freud remarked that he, too, would have attributed the cures to "suggestion" had he, in fact, seen any cures!

In these paragraphs we have tried to indicate the stark and difficult di-lemma of the physician of the last half of the nineteenth century. He wanted, above all, to be a scientist; and at the same time he wanted, above all, to get results. Results were being claimed right and left; in fact, they were to be seen achieved through many methods other than those of exact science. Here and there some concrete physical intervention would appear to help. Sometimes the "psychological approach" to "psychological disease," which had been demonstrated by the Mesmerists and indeed by a school of "psy-chogenic" interpretations (for example, Moreau de Tours, 1840), was making brief sallies into this vast realm of suffering and defeat. But psychology was itself poorly systematized and difficult both to formulate and to apply. If you happen to believe — as the authors of this book believe — that the major achievement of Freud was to develop a systematic psychological approach to mental disease, then it will be self-evident that biographical detail is im-portant and that the personality of this inventive spirit needs very much more than cursory attention. As a matter of fact, the stories of the "uncon-scious before Freud" and Western psychiatry in the nineteenth century have been well told many times. Freud himself wrote three different autobiograph-ical sketches (1901a, 1925, 1935) of his life as psychiatrist and psychoana-lyst, and several dozen biographical studies worth taking seriously have been offered, capped by the three-volume biographical study by Jones (1953–57). The present narrative offers no astounding new insights. Its aim is to show the situation which Freud confronted; the steps in his growth, learn-ing, and struggle which made possible his series of discoveries; and the im-pact which his work made upon followers and colleagues and ultimately upon Western thought as a whole.

To look for cultural contexts for psychoanalysis in the German-speaking world of the latter half of the nineteenth century, one would begin with the medical schools — especially a few great schools like those at Berlin, Leip-zig, and Vienna — with their very rich cultivation of both the sciences and the philosophies of the mind. It would mean examining what was happening in the intellectual tradition among the professional groups, which were prac-ticing and giving clinical demonstrations in the fields of their specialization, as well as giving university lectures. It would also mean paying close atten-tion to the Jewish community, which in that era struggled against professional ostracism, yet somehow pushed hard enough and met the competitive demands so well that a vigorous Jewish contingent was to be found in medical practice, while a few German universities here and there actually had a place for Jewish professors.

In the small Bohemian town where Freud was born in 1856, the family business went well and, in time, justified their moving to Vienna. In Vienna a talented son would be sure to find vigorous support and encouragement from the family as a whole. We find that Freud, as a very bright boy, met the standards, went ahead through preparatory school, and was assigned by the family a study all to himself, the better to pursue his university work! His achievement of the medical degree offered an opportunity to work in the laboratory of Brücke, one of the great men in embryology and histology; Freud's first published work was an evolutionary embryological study of the eel (1877).

Though in later years he systematically destroyed every letter, every purely personal record, everything by which an inquisitive biographer might like to tease out a portrait of the genius "as a young man," Freud did read so much, think so much, accumulate so much experience to which he later felt impelled to look back that we do get a picture of him.

The picture does not conform to Freud's idea that he was only important because of his work as an analyst and that everything else about him was of no importance. We do indeed know that he was profoundly concerned with philosophical issues; that he sided, for example, vigorously with Brücke and Du Bois-Reymond in the staunch belief that physics and chemistry had the answers to the questions of the life sciences; and that he eschewed the vague vitalism of the "philosophy of nature." We know also that he was full of a poetic and, in the literal sense, an artistic conception of life and personality. Winning the Goethe Prize was precious to him, and his journey to Italy, to steep himself in Renaissance majesties such as Michelangelo's exquisite statues of Moses and David, meant as much to him as the plaudits of the great in the world of science. We know also that he fell very intensely in love and that intellectual brotherhood and his later role as patriarchal and benign guide of younger men meant more than sheer "professional solidarity." The family was intense, and he was intense in response to it. The bitterness that came from his estrangement with some of his early colleagues was part of the general sensitivity and intensity of a very vital man with very powerful loves and hates.

He had, of course, to make a decision as to whether he would go on doing embryological and neurological research. Vienna was full of nervous sufferers. Income and prestige were on the side of medical practice rather than research. The difficult decision was made, and he associated himself with a well-known family physician, Josef Breuer, who had been making use of the hypnotic techniques with hysterics, as used by Charcot in Paris (1888–94). Hysteria was conceived to be a mental disease peculiarly amenable to direct hypnotic suggestion, and the two men had apparently some success in utilizing this approach. Freud felt, however, the need for a more direct contact with the best the method had to offer, and in 1885 he went to Paris to hear Charcot's lectures and witness his demonstrations. Charcot was a stellar figure in French medicine whose work, especially his study of the diseases of the liver (1877), had given him a great reputation. He believed it possible to demonstrate that a nervous sufferer—let us use the term "hysteric" in the rather inexact sense in which the term was then used—could be directly freed of a symptom, or that the symptom could be brought back again, by hypnotic suggestion. Hypnosis, as a standard practice, involved relaxation, a sleeplike state, and suggestibility. It was necessary to induce the state by verbal emphasis upon the act of sleeping; then, while the patient was in the sleeplike state, the suggestion would be given that a symptom would disappear. For example, in the case of a hysterical paralysis, Charcot would utter the phrase *ça passe*—"that is going away"—and the paralysis would be gone. It could be brought back again. Indeed, the patient could be, as it were, molded into or out of one symptom complex after another. The conclusion seemed to be clear: *an idea can cause a physical symptom.*

However trite and obvious this may seem today, it must be recalled that in the era of Charcot this was a precise illustration of what a "hard" scientist must *not* believe. Whatever the philosophical confusions and supposed spiritual or materialistic implications, the physician wanted to find an "organic" cause, that is, a microscopic or directly visible lesion or region of specific pathologic function. Here was Charcot making and breaking disease patterns through verbal, that is, ideational, manipulation. This made its mark upon Freud. He apparently knew all this before, but he knew it now in a new way. He knew it as a fact of medicine in a medical setting: uttered and demonstrated in direct terms and capable of acting as a new pivot upon which to swing a whole medical conception of mental disease.

He went back to Vienna and resumed collaboration with Breuer. By modern standards, the work went on at a leisurely pace. Though he published some neurological papers during the early nineties, his basic observations of hysteria, published with Breuer's name first, appeared only in 1893–95. This celebrated study is often regarded as the beginning of psychoanalysis as such. The reason lies not in the fact of the psychological rather than the organic approach to hysteria, but rather in the matter of method Breuer and Freud discovered together. (Freud generously gave the whole credit to Breuer for initiating the method.) It consisted in studying the psychology of the hysterical condition not by direct manipulation, but by letting the patient talk freely about his condition, especially allowing him to talk when in a drowsy, or dreamlike, or dissociated state, in which he would ramble over the area of his difficulties and much besides and talk about episodes distressing to him which had been sealed off, or repressed, or made unavailable to recall.

Thus, a governess who was very much on her good behavior in a well-to-do home had observed a dog drinking from a glass of water and had been disgusted. This, like all details, seemed trivial. But she had to *master* her disgust, and the whole episode involving the dog came back only in a relaxed talking-out session in which, as it came back, she manifested the disgust which had been repressed. From one event to another, more and more disagreeable, repulsive, or blameworthy episodes crowded in. It began to be evident, as Freud said later, that "our patients are suffering from reminiscences." So much for the etiology. The cure lay not in driving the symptom away by exhortation; rather, the symptom would appear less threatening when recounted to the physician in this specific professional relation of sharing memories regarding troublesome pasts. Freud discovered, moreover, that relaxation was an important aspect of the technique which brought memories back and was soon thereafter beginning his lifelong use of the analytic couch, which allowed the patient to relax and reminisce and did not require that the physician and the patient look at one another during the analytic interchanges. It became more and more evident from Freud's use of these methods that the emotional quality of the interchange, the "transference," was a fundamental part of the newly developing "psychoanalytic" method. The patient *transferred to the physician* the feelings — especially the feelings of love, fear, and hate — which he had originally had toward the parents. The patient was recapitulating the emotional relations of child and parent which somehow had planted the seeds of many later difficulties.

As we describe these events we find ourselves moving from the discussion of the work of Breuer and Freud to the discussion of the work of Freud alone. This is what has to happen in any record of the development of the psychoanalytic method. Whether Viennese medical circles could face it frankly or not, women patients began, in these therapeutic situations, to fall in love with the physician, in an obvious or a furtive way. Breuer, as a family physician, felt the situation was too hot to handle. Freud felt that important medical facts were coming to light and that they needed to be faced. This was the parting of the ways.

We have mentioned Charcot and Breuer, but a third important medical figure should be mentioned. In the 1860s a clinic had been established at Nancy (see p. 156), in northeastern France, at which a straightforward psychological approach to suggestive therapeutics was offered by Liébeault (1866), and later by his celebrated successor Bernheim (1891). In contrast to the Paris school under Charcot, and its belief that the hysterical condition was basically rooted in a physiological or constitutional predisposition, Liébeault and Bernheim were content to look for the psychological origins of psychological conditions. They appear, moreover, to have been extraordinarily skilled hypnotists. A very large proportion of their clinic patients were helped. Freud had an opportunity to observe Bernheim at work, using, for example, the following simple demonstration technique: while in the hypnotic trance the patient would be told that at a signal given him after his awakening he would go to his umbrella and put it up over his head. The physician would ask why he was putting up the umbrella indoors. The patient always had a "good reason" for what he did: "I wanted to see if it had a hole in it" or "By looking inside I could be sure it was my own." This, however, was not the *real* reason. The physician would then say: "But tell me the real reason." The patient might be embarrassed or he might delay, but he would soon enough come to the point and say: "Because you told me to." The implications for suggestive therapeutics, and also for the understanding of the etiology of such types of self-deception, become plain: the patient does not know why he does what he does, but under a little pressure from the physician he can recover these blocked memories. Freud took this seriously to the point of spending the time to translate the French of Bernheim into German.

We have seen that there was a good deal having to do with unconscious mental operations in the work of all three of these men — Breuer, Charcot, and Bernheim. Only in the case of the work with Breuer, however, had Freud had an intimate, first-hand opportunity to observe what actually went on in the emotional transactions between patient and physician, and to this point more attention needs to be given. The falling-in-love episodes which he had witnessed seemed to be related to phenomena of sexual pathology of various sorts, about which medical men were beginning to read. (It was the era of Krafft-Ebing, and soon came the impact of Havelock Ellis upon medical thought, and indeed upon all Western thought.)

Most physicians, however, did not seem to be facing these observations with complete candor. One day after a lecture, one of Charcot's audience had asked about a difficulty which he did not understand. Charcot replied with great animation: "This always has to do with the sexual zone — always, always, always!" Freud said to himself: "But if he knows this, why does he never say so?" Later on, the gynecologist Chrobach, in Vienna, had retracted a reference to the sexual in psychopathology, stating that he had never made it, and apparently Breuer himself was unwilling to be reminded of what he had said to the same effect. Freud felt alone; and indeed, to all intents and purposes, he *was* alone. We have the extraordinary story of his confrontation with the Viennese Medical Society, the *Gesellschaft der Ärzte*. He had been asked to present some medical observations. As he finished and looked up from his paper, he found that a good part of the audience had gone to the rear seats as if not to be contaminated by this evil man. No one congratulated him on his findings. No one even shook hands. He determined from that time henceforth, he says, to seek from every patient the sexual origin of his neurosis.

Freud had, then, an area of specialization — the neuroses; a method — the talking-out method; and a leading theme — the problem of disguised, inhibited sexuality. He could see his path and he must tread it alone.

The Psychoanalytic Method

Freud proceeded to develop this new method. He told the patient simply to attempt a narrative of his free associations; the origin of his symptoms would gradually become clear. To be sure, this necessitated the consecutive overcoming of resistances at points where the patient said that he could not think of anything more, or that he was thinking of something absurd or ugly which he hated to mention. At these points there seemed to be not so much a genuine failure of memory, through time, as an effect of the same mechanism which had been involved in the repression: namely, a resistance to the free expression of an impulsive tendency. Freud learned by experience that resistances were vitally important and that it was at these very points that something illuminating could, through the patient's perseverance in the task, be disclosed. Resistances were especially evident where associations of a sexual nature appeared.

The "psychoanalytic" method was this use of free association; with this method, psychoanalysis as such began. Through the patient's gradual recall of the emotional episodes which precipitated the conflict, and, in particular, through the free recognition and release of pent-up emotion,[1] the struggle could sometimes be terminated and the patient's mental health restored. More adequate cooperation was secured than was possible through hypnosis, for instead of dealing with a passive subject (and all hypnotic subjects who merely follow the suggestion of the hypnotizer are passive), he had the patient's active assistance toward revealing the deeply submerged tendencies in personality.[2]

At this period (the last decade of the century) Freud had not succeeded very far in relating specific types of symptoms to specific types of conflict; nor had he any clear notion as to the period in life at which such psychopathic dispositions were at first formed. There was no reason to suppose that they necessarily involved anything more remote than emotional experiences such as were apparent in cases like that of the girl unable to drink from a glass of water. He was not as yet concerned to show an earlier origin, some predisposing cause, for such manifestations in the life of the patient. But the cure of a symptom was sometimes followed by new symptoms, and it became necessary to penetrate deeper; that is, to go farther and farther back into the patient's personal history. Adult experience seemed to call for emphasis upon the importance of childhood conflicts as basic for adult maladjustment.

[1] *Abreaktion,* a part of the "cathartic method" already developed by Breuer and Freud in conjunction with hypnotic technique.

[2] Such spatial and mechanical metaphors are prominent throughout the history of psychoanalysis. James, in discussing closely similar material, said "in the end we fall back on the hackneyed symbolism of a mechanical equilibrium" (1902, p. 197). The metaphors were surely helpful at first; but with time their value has been more and more seriously challenged.

Freud did, moreover, encounter many psychoneuroses in *children*. A boy, for example, was afflicted by a strange compulsion; before he could go to sleep he had to arrange a row of chairs beside his bed, pile pillows on them, and turn his face toward the wall (1896). The study of the case showed that he had been the victim of a sexual assault which had so terrified him that ever afterward a barricade must be placed between the bed and the open room, and his face averted. Thus the symptoms were *symbols* of the conflict. A great variety of such symbolic symptoms were presented in Freud's essays.

A clear divergence is apparent between Freud's interpretation of symptoms and the interpretation offered by Janet (1892). Janet had indeed emphasized the reality of aspects of personality which were so dissociated as to be no longer capable of conscious control; but with Freud emphasis was laid especially upon the *dynamics* of such dissociation. The ultimate forces at work were provided by instinct; and the energy coming from instinctual forces operated outside consciousness as it did inside the conscious field. It was, he believed, only by conflict that any element or impulse could be kept outside personal awareness. But just as conflict was the explanation of dissociation, so it was held to be the clue to the particular *form* which the dissociation took and consequently to the nature of the symptoms. The symptoms were, in a broad sense, symbols of the repressed tendencies, symbols to be understood through examination of the course of the disease. Janet had himself thought that symptoms arose from "subconscious ideas" and that amnesia involved the narrowing of the field of consciousness; but he had left the dynamics of the process almost untouched. For Freud this conception was eminently unsatisfactory;[3] in a host of cases like those already mentioned, the symptom seemed clearly to be a symbol of a specific conflict.

After the joint labor with Breuer, finally published under the title *Studies on Hysteria* (1893–95), Freud began to work alone and to cultivate his new method and his new system of ideas in a bold, swift-moving stream of creativity. To this period belongs the extraordinary correspondence which he carried out with his friend Fliess (1887–1902), with whom he shared many ideas regarding the philosophy of personality and of mental disease — work which never saw the light until long after his death. To this period also belongs a remarkable document, *Project for a Scientific Psychology* (1895), which embodies a thoroughgoing scheme for reference to the central nervous system and its function as the basis for the understanding of psychopathology. The rich period of neurological and neurophysiological investigations, dominated by such heroic figures as Ramon y Cajal and expressed in the "neuron theory" of Waldeyer (1891), offered Freud the possibility that specific anatomical and physiological detail, such as the diameters of the axons of nerve cells, might hold the secret of memory and forgetfulness, facilitation and inhibition in the functioning of the pathways. The goal of

[3] For Janet himself it was only a provisional, and not in any sense an explanatoty, formulation.

Helmholtz, Brücke, and Du Bois-Reymond of stating psychological events in the language of physics and chemistry might be reachable.

But he never published the *Project.* Indeed, the story of the *Project,* and Freud's putting it aside, is another bit of clear evidence that Freud was really basically concerned with building a psychological system, not with dabbling in speculative neurophysiology. He did indeed look forward to the day when the great neurologists might "shake hands" with the great psychologists, but he decided that that day was not very near. The Fliess correspondence and the *Project* were not available to the historian of the mid-twentieth century. We ourselves may benefit from the work of those who made possible the discovery and reexamination of this evidence; but as far as the history of the psychoanalytic movement as a whole is concerned, it is mainly a history of psychodynamics and not of psychophysiology, and it moves smoothly forward from the talking-out method through a series of great steps in psychological medicine.

The next step was the interpretation of dreams, a labor intensively cultivated during the last years of the nineteenth century. Freud made himself familiar with classical dream theory, with its emphasis upon symbolism, as represented in the quotation from Aristotle at the beginning of the chapter. Dreams show symbolically, according to the theory, what has happened, or is happening, or will happen. It was, however, Freud's belief that the dream portrays the world as the dreamer wishes it to be. The cognitive life is largely molded in a form required by human needs. The dream emanates basically from physiological tensions which are the substrate of the dreaming process as known psychologically. From this deeply unconscious wish or system of wishes (the "latent dream") there develops a pictorial schema of events meaningful to the dreamer. The pictographic process is controlled not by a realistic series of procedures which would fulfill the wish; rather the wish indirectly and symbolically incorporates the longed-for fulfillment. This is the "primary process" character of the dream; the dream represents what is desired. Of course, it must do this without blatantly representing wishes which are taboo, particularly those having to do with sexuality and, in Freud's later emphasis, aggression, too. As in all earlier dream theories, symbolism is given wide scope. It is only in the narration of the dream to the physician, together with the series of "free associations" which arise when the dream has been recounted to him, that it begins to be evident — perhaps first to the physician and later to the patient — what is really being portrayed. The process by which the latent dream is converted into a dream which can be remembered in the morning and repeated to the physician is the "dream work," and the daytime remembrance of the course of the dream is the "manifest dream."

Here we encounter a major redirection in the course of psychology. From the time of Aristotle onward, thoughts had been regarded as basically different from motives, drive, impulses. Hobbes had mentioned the role of "design" (purpose) in thought, but psychologists and philosophers were rather deaf to this approach. Freud seemed to be finding that thoughts were first of all the embodiment of wishes. In their *primary* form, thoughts tell what we immediately *wish*. But in time they are partially replaced by an inclination to *delay* gratification so as to give attention to reality — the process of "reality testing." This is *secondary process*. But *primary process*, the initial guidance of thought by the impulse of gratification, is a central key concept for the understanding of psychoanalytic dynamics. There are indeed instances in which the immediate fulfillment of a wish, the immediate realization of the pleasure principle, is impossible. All along, the dreamer pursues a tortuous course, avoiding too direct an expression of his wishes. The realization of the dream is partially blocked by a process of "censorship" (*die Zensur,* in German) — an impersonal process depending ultimately upon the balance of intrapsychic forces which may, under certain circumstances, allow a disguised version of what is really going on.

The dream may contain any combination of primary- and secondary-process thinking. After listening to the dreamer's "free associations," the analyst's conception of the language of the dream — what it is that the dreamer is really saying — is offered as an interpretation, which then may be wholly, or partly, or not at all acceptable to the patient. There may, of course, be many dreams over many weeks, or months, or years, together with similar multiple episodes of free association with regard to daily activities which seem to bespeak some unrealized strivings or some expression of conflict on the part of the patient.

Dream interpretation is not carried out independently of the general course of psychoanalytic therapy. In the early establishment of rituals to which Freud adhered the rest of his life, and to which most analysts adhere, it was agreed that the patient would make a fixed appointment, usually for five times a week, come in, lie down, free associate with reference to a dream, or any recent event, or anything whatever which occurs to him, and talk or be silent, as he sees fit, while the analyst listens, or interprets, or reminds the patient of earlier free associations, or helps the patient to think back to conflictful material which he believes must be held responsible for the patient's painful situation. And since *resistance* and *transference* are so central, the analyst is necessarily concerned with analyzing, and understanding — and to some degree resolving — resistances and in analyzing the transference itself; the patient is ultimately set free from the deep dependence which, for a while, must characterize his relation to the therapist.

During these early years of psychoanalysis, the broadly defined sexual energies already noted, called the libido, were held to be in conflict with a group of ego demands or drives which sought social acceptability. The ego demands lay behind the processes of censorship and the maintenance of an acceptable social pattern of life through the control of the motor outlets of speech and acceptable overt behavior. The tracing backward of adult conflict situations to those of earlier and earlier years led to more and more attention to a conception of infantile sexuality. In a series of papers appearing shortly after *The Interpretation of Dreams* (1900), notably in *Three Essays on the Theory of Sexuality* (1905), Freud undertook to show that adult sexuality is not by any means the only form of sexual expression, but that from infancy onward there are multiple expressions of the sexual impulse, involving diffuse sexual preoccupations with the body as a whole and with specific erogenous zones. Later, during the latency period (between infancy and puberty), and during puberty itself, they are redirected from a homosexual to a heterosexual form.

This conception of psychosexual stages made it possible to believe in various normal developmental levels involving relatively smooth transitions from one level to the next but also to take account of the fact that there might be a fixation at any stage which might result in difficulty in completion of the normal course of development. It might, in fact, lead to chronic infantilism of various sorts, or to perversions, or to incomplete passage to the heterosexual form of adaptation.

Two other works of this first decade of the twentieth century need, likewise, to be noted here for their theoretical importance: one is "The Psychopathology of Everyday Life" (1901), an extraordinary contribution carrying out the dynamic conception that the course of thought is by no means primarily rational, but that perception, and memory, and thought, as well as impulse, are constantly guided by unconscious wishes. We say what we "do not mean to say." We get caught in a compromise between the aggressive or insulting remark that we would *like* to make and the remark *required* by the situation and say something absurd—sometimes fairly well hidden, sometimes rather transparent. We forget our keys when starting out on a journey and cannot unlock our trunk. Did we really want to go on the journey? The concluding chapter takes to task the classical (Aristotelian) conception that there are "accidental" events as contrasted with lawful events and strongly suggests, under the term "determinism," the conception of a dynamic unity in which all that happens psychologically is as systematically regulated as is that which happens in the physical world.

The other contribution, *Jokes and Their Relation to the Unconscious* (1905a), pursues essentially the same theme in showing that wit is an expression of suddenly released energies. The pun, or play on words, says a great deal with a little effort, and there is energy to spare; and many a witty remark contains likewise an expression of veiled aggression as well as obvious "passes" at the religious, sexual, and other taboos which control public utterance.

We have then, by 1910, a reasonably well coordinated conception of unconscious dynamics, based essentially upon sexual energies which go through a complex metamorphosis during the growth period but are constantly held under restraints owing to parental and other social controls.

All this suggests the obvious importance of the relation of the little child to his parents. One of the primary strokes of genius here lay in demonstrating the intensity of child-parent erotic response, which had, as a matter of fact, been quite well known in many quarters and has been independently emphasized in systems other than the Freudian, but to which Freud gave heavy and continuous emphasis during this entire period. The Greek myth of Oedipus, who unwittingly carried out a baleful prophecy according to which he would slay his father and marry his mother, is supplemented by a number of other Greek myths and tragic themes illustrating that there is essentially no escape from the intense demand of the little child for the parents, especially for the parent of opposite sex, and noting that uneven development and frequent interference with the primitive demands for reciprocated love make human life intrinsically a tragedy from which no ultimate solution is to be expected. Elaborate methods for deflecting sexual energies through sublimation are offered by the arts and sciences.

Putting aside for the moment the defection of his primary adherents and followers, Jung and Adler, in 1911, we may say that by the outbreak of World War I Freud had wrought a coherent system and was going forward to the applications of libido theory and dream theory to many outlying regions. He had delivered at Clark University, in 1909, the epoch-making *Origin and Development of Psychoanalysis* (1910) and was becoming broadly known as the prophetic founder of a vastly significant conception of human development. The break with Jung and Adler gave a poignant expression to his autobiographical essay "On the History of the Psychoanalytic Movement" (1914), which may be regarded as the milestone marking the end of the first great phase of psychoanalysis.

Psychoanalytic Ego Psychology

The second great phase, according to the judgment of many, lies in the development of a new theory of the ego, dating from the paper "On Narcissism" (1914a) and including *Group Psychology and the Analysis of Ego* (1921), *The Ego and the Id* (1923), and *Inhibitions, Symptoms, and Anxiety* (1926).

"On Narcissism," like several early papers, seeks a cross-cultural and poetic context in which to place a simple clinical observation: the fact of absorption in oneself. In Ovid's beautiful story of Echo and Narcissus, the youth cannot find the beloved creature from whom the sweet voice in the forest is coming, but he seeks out a pool, in the clear surface of which he hopes to find his beloved. He looks into the water and sees his own reflection and is forever trapped in this intense, undeflected self-adoration. Even so, Freud says, the little child—perhaps even before birth, and certainly in the opening weeks of postnatal life—is preoccupied with himself. He never indeed does give up the precious image. Although he may manipulate his body and may seek to derive pleasure from its topography, more is involved; it is the rhythms and cadences of his own voice, and the rhythms and cadences of his own muscular activity, later on the preoccupation with his own thought processes, that keep him oriented to himself as the first and final love object. One of his primary problems is to find a way of reducing the intensity of this outpouring libido and to discover worthy fixation points for his needed "object love" without which human life, in family or out of it, is impossible.

The self, then, has begun to be perceived, and the libido has been "invested" in it. For this concept of investment in the self, or in objects, or in activities of many sorts, the translator expects us to use and accept the term "cathexis," the Greek term suggesting "taking hold." The term "investment," however, is a direct translation of Freud's term used here, and we shall use it.

But it became necessary for Freud to say more about the relation of the primal energies of life to the ego. This he spelled out first in *Group Psychology and the Analysis of the Ego,* aimed at problems of crowd (and mob) behavior. He showed that organized groups, such as the church and the army, make most of a brother-to-brother and also of a son-to-father relation. Crowds are not held together by "suggestion" alone. It is really the deep generic libidinal tie that expresses itself in the interdependence of people in the crowd and polarizes them toward the leader who is a father surrogate. Men are even more dependent upon the father surrogate than they are upon one another. Stable social structures like the church and the army are full of similar symbolism: the great commander in the field is a "father to his men"; the members of monastic orders are "brothers" and "sisters"; often there is a "Mother Superior," and, above all, there is a papa or Pope.

Upon the heels of this volume, defining the libidinal basis of the social order, followed a small, simple, spare little volume—*The Ego and the Id*—which developed the energy relationships so important for responsible membership in society. We learn that the blind, tumultuous energies of life, invested in one's own person or one's object relations, lead to a consolidation of forces related to control of the environment (the "executive functions" already noted). The possibility of delay becomes involved in a complicated way with processes of "identification" with those who are near and dear, especially the parents. By this process of "identification" one brings within oneself, or "introjects," the image of the parent. Up to this point we may speak of forces which are consolidating the response of the individual to his own body, his own person, and this can be observed in the development of an ego orientation to life, an orientation concerned with reality testing, delay, and executive functions.

So far, we might simply continue to say that the ego is conscious and that it regulates the blind and unconscious forces of the unconscious. At times, however, this definition runs into serious contradictions. Let us take, for example, the case of a man who suffers from a hysterical complaint: he lies in bed, and while the muscles of his legs are normal, he cannot stand upon the floor or walk—he crumples up. This is a case of "astasia abasia" (Greek for "not standing, not walking"). We find from the man's free associations that he cannot touch the floor because "floor" (*Boden* in German) means also "ground" or "Mother Earth": he must not touch mother. The Oedipus theme stands out clearly.

But how in the world could the ego simply be consciousness? The man does not know what he is doing to himself. The ego, in its unconscious functioning, is overwhelmed with guilt and will not allow him to make contact with the floor—as if he had planned it. This conscious operation which says that he may not stand or walk is actually fully replaced by an *unconscious* operation—he does not know why he shows this behavior. From this way of thinking Freud developed a way of thinking about the ego which allowed it to have both conscious and unconscious aspects and indeed, in between the two, a preconscious aspect. The raw instinctual urge, the id system, has supplied all the energy which has appeared in this ego system.

But then a further factor becomes evident: in the development of identification with the parents the individual has identified with them in their *loving role* and in their *disciplinary role*. One can observe in the "ego ideal" that cultivation of goodness, decency, humanity, and generosity which bespeaks the parent in the loving role; while in identification with the disciplinary role, one builds into oneself a conscience, a form of ego control which arises in and is differentiated out of the ego and has become, as Freud says, a superego—*über ich*. The movement is from the simple and primitive to the complex and socially sophisticated. But the id, the raw energy, is the source of it all.

We begin, then, with the riderless horse, the pure energy. George Groddeck put it well by saying: "We do not live. We are lived." From the total life process, however, the controlling system—the ego with its identification and its executive functions—is differentiated off.

One more book belongs to this series—*Inhibitions, Symptoms, and Anxiety*—in which Freud, changing his mind from the earlier years, views the development of anxiety as an ego function. "Signal anxiety," as he states it, is the anxiety which the ego produces to warn against dangerous regions and to defend itself from getting caught in utter helplessness. We may say, then, that the ego has gradually become focal, central, never further to be avoided in any mature statement of a psychoanalytic proposition. "Psychoanalytic ego psychology" makes use of the whole system of psychoanalytic concepts and methods, but it places the ego in a central theoretical position. In therapy, too, this is the aim. "Where id was, there shall ego be."

During the period between the two world wars these systematic steps taken by Freud were followed, in general, by development of psychoanalysis in the German-speaking world and in Britain and the United States. On one major theme—Freud's belief in a pure aggressive or death instinct, the inherent force of which was to destroy—a very considerable resistance to his ideas appeared, but this did not prevent the essential coherence of his group of followers. They clung together through psychoanalytic meetings planned in international terms and through publications which maintained the outlook and the integrity of the founding father. This is the more remarkable because of the inherent complexities and difficulties of maintaining a simple discipline where ideas of formidable power are involved. One must also remember his illness: a malignancy of the mouth requiring a hard replacement object for the lost soft tissues—the "monster," he called it—which was there to remind him, along with surgery, that there appeared to be no escape. Finally, as the Nazi system took over Germany and then Austria, it became evident that he should flee, and almost at the last moment he and the family made their escape to Britain where, in the months just before the outbreak of World War II, he died.

We have left out, in this presentation, not only the far-flung philosophical goals which were quite precious to Freud, but even the "metapsychology," the system of principles by which we always look for genetic or developmental explanations and for economic, dynamic, topographic, and adaptive principles, too. At times, even for clinical purposes, all of these different approaches, these different aspects, must be used.

There were minor defections from Freud as soon as his system became a system: that is, as soon as the fortnightly psychoanalytic meetings, with the black coffee and the black cigars, led to seriously entertained divergences of opinion. Psychoanalysis was, however, its founder's child, and he alone had serious responsibility and capacity to carry it forward. The rate of his productivity was so astounding that it would have been pointless to make a great issue out of detailed disagreements. Simultaneously, psychoanalysis became known through many cities in central and western Europe. There began to be, notably in Berlin and in London, strong outlying psychoanalytic schools from which ultimately psychoanalytic training institutes developed. Freud was, of course, grateful for this rapid and widespread response. He was quite aware of the fact that most of his strong support came from Jewish physicians and was explicitly gratified to have the support of the non-Jewish Jung of Zürich. There were also strong men in the Viennese circle, such as Stekel, who differed about dream interpretation, and Adler, who thought that constitutional inferiority and compensation for it were more important realities than Freud had grasped. We shall consider the doctrines of these "deviants" in a moment. Here, rather, our hope is to suggest a general principle about the need for and the consequences of great defections in the establishment of the profoundly new and challenging doctrine.

There are many close parallels for the establishment of a strongly structured way of thinking which can stand up against disintegrative tendencies. Catholic theology is the most obvious illustration in the West. When, after a long defensive struggle from the thirteenth to the sixteenth centuries, serious threat to Catholic orthodoxy appeared, the splinters flew fast and far until there were nearly as many Protestants as there were Roman Catholics in northern Europe. Catholic doctrine had to be clear and its discipline firm to protect itself against utter disintegration.

Marxist ideology, which took shape in the late nineteenth century, was finally welded into a powerful engine by Lenin despite permutations of doctrine and discipline through subsequent Secretaries of the Communist party within the Soviet Union. There has had to be tight and firm structure, and an iron discipline. This reminds us of serious lawful principles regarding the nature of human innovations; and the fact that psychoanalysis is a psychological system—a system of interpretation—does not exempt it from being subject to an objective and independent analysis. Freud's great power of thought, and his strongly resolute manner of developing his system, made it possible for minor deviants to be dropped and ignored; but when a serious split was threatened, there appeared a full mobilization against it.

It is of the utmost importance, as one speaks of "deviant schools" in modern dynamic psychology, to keep in mind this difference. Largely it was a question of adherence to the great central principles, such as the principles of resistance and transference, as Freud said; partly it was a question of the depth of personal loyalty, allowing just so much, but no more deviation. We may say, from this point of view, that Jung's ideas about schizophrenia, in 1907, and Abraham's rather similar ideas, in 1908, were regarded as legitimate and praiseworthy extensions of psychoanalytic theory. A few years later it became clear to the naked eye that Jung's ideas led off in a threatening direction but that Abraham's ideas were related to the budding new (but Freudian) psychoanalytic ego psychology.

Similarly, Erikson's extraordinary skills in developing a psychoanalytic ego psychology and social psychology built on cross-cultural diversities (as among American Indian tribes) and on racial, political, and military strife in the modern world were in general acceptable and warmly hailed as contributions to psychoanalytic ego psychology. It is too much to expect absolute agreement on such issues. It is, however, important to stress that some of the most powerful psychoanalytic writers of modern times, such as Horney, Sullivan, and Fromm (see pp. 298 ff.) have, by common consent, been extruded from the Freudian system, while others, notably Kris, Greenacre, Rapaport, and Erikson, have in general been regarded as "within" rather than "without." The reasons are not arbitrary, nor are they obscure. They need to be considered with whatever detachment can be marshaled, rather than denied, or applauded, or regretted.

Specifically, in the very year of Freud's death, 1939, a major new departure appeared in Hartmann's essay on adaptation (see p. 304). If it is really true, he points out, that evolution means the development of organisms adapted to their environments, there must be, in human nature, some basic capacity to make real contact with the physical and social worlds; there must be more than blind instinct, however well it may be related dynamically to the service of life needs. There must be capacities to make genuine and effective use of the equipment which serves perception, memory, and thought; there must be action which is rooted in external reality, not solely in conflict, evasion, escape, or denial; there must be, in fact, "conflict-free ego spheres" — spheres of autonomy. Psychoanalysis had appeared to be paying too much attention to the role of conflict in engendering distortions of perceiving and thinking. The reality principle, emphasized by Freud as far back as *The Interpretation of Dreams* (1900), must be emphasized. In the same spirit, Kris (1952) was prepared to show that the ego is often in control, and in the midst of conflict there is regression in the service of the ego and effective ego control in the creative life of man even when libidinal energies, in sublimated forms, appear to be dictating the outcome in the arts and sciences.

REFERENCES

Abraham, K. ["The Psycho-sexual Differences Between Hysteria and Dementia Praecox."] *Zentralblatt für Nervenheilkunde und Psychiatrie,* 19 (1908), 521–32.

Bernheim, H. *Hypnotisme, suggestion, psychothérapie.* Paris: Doin, 1891.

Breuer, J., and Freud, S. [*Studies on Hysteria.*] Leipzig: Deuticke, 1893–95. (*SE,* Vol. 2, 1955.)[4]

Charcot, J.-M. *Leçons sur les maladies du foie, des voies biliaires et des reins.* Paris: Bureaux du Progrès Médical, 1877.

———. *Oeuvres complètes.* Paris: Bureaux du Progrès Médical, 1888–94.

Erikson, E. H. *Childhood and Society.* New York: Norton, 1950, rev. ed. 1963.

———. "The Problem of Ego Identity." *Journal of the American Psychoanalytic Association,* 4 (1956), 56–121.

Freud, S. ["Observations on the Formation and More Delicate Structure of the Lobe-Shaped Organs of the Eel, Described as Testicles."] *Akademie der wissenschaften Sitzungsberichte,* 1 (1877), Abt. 75 (4), 419–31.

———. [*The Origins of Psychoanalysis. Letters to William Fliess.*] N.p., 1887–1902. (*SE,* Vol. 1, 1966.)

———. [*Project for a Scientific Psychology.*] N.p., 1895. (*SE,* Vol. 1, 1966.)

———. ["Further Remarks on the Neuro-Psychoses of Defense."] *Neurologisches Zentralblatt,* 15 (1896), 434–48. (*SE,* Vol. 3, 1962.)

———. [*The Interpretation of Dreams.*] Leipzig and Vienna: Deuticke, 1900. (*SE,* Vols. 4–5, 1953.)

---

[4] Freud's works are listed with the original dates and translated titles, followed by their location in the *Standard Edition.*

Freud, S. ["The Psychopathology of Everyday Life."] *Monatsschrift für Psychiatrie und Neurologie*, 10, No. 1 (1901), 1–32; No. 2, 95–143. (*SE*, Vol. 6, 1960.)

——. ["Autobiographical Note."] In J. L. Pagel. [*Biographical Lexicon.*] Berlin, 1901a. (*SE*, Vol. 3, 1962.)

——. [*Three Essays on the Theory of Sexuality.*] Leipzig: Deuticke, 1905. (*SE*, Vol. 7, 1953.)

——. [*Jokes and Their Relation to the Unconscious.*] Leipzig and Vienna: Deuticke, 1905a. (*SE*, Vol. 8, 1960.)

——. [*The Origin and Development of Psychoanalysis.*] Leipzig: Deuticke, 1910. (*SE*, Vol. 11, 1957.)

——. [*Totem and Taboo.*] Leipzig and Vienna: Heller, 1913. (*SE*, Vol. 13, 1955.)

——. ["On the History of the Psychoanalytic Movement."] *Jahrbuch der Psychoanalyse*, 6 (1914), 207–60. (*SE*, Vol. 14, 1957.)

——. ["On Narcissism: An Introduction."] *Jahrbuch der Psychoanalyse*, 6 (1914a), 1–24. (*SE*, Vol. 14, 1957.)

——. [*Group Psychology and the Analysis of the Ego.*] Leipzig, Vienna, and Zurich: Internationaler Psychoanalytischer Verlag, 1921. (*SE*, Vol. 18, 1955.)

——. [*The Ego and the Id.*] Leipzig, Vienna, and Zurich: Internationaler Psychoanalytischer Verlag, 1923. (*SE*, Vol. 19, 1961.)

——. ["An Autobiographical Study."] *Die Medizin der Gegenwart in Selbstdarstellungen*, 4 (1925), 1–52. (*SE*, Vol. 20, 1959.)

——. [*Inhibitions, Symptoms, and Anxiety.*] Leipzig, Vienna, and Zurich: Internationaler Psychoanalytischer Verlag, 1926. (*SE*, Vol. 20, 1959.)

——. *Postscript to an Autobiographical Study.* New York: Norton, 1935. (*SE*, Vol. 20, 1959.)

Hartmann, H. ["Ego Psychology and the Problem of Adaptation."] *Internationale Zeitschrift für Psychoanalyse und "Imago,"* 24 (1939), 62–135.

James, W. *The Varieties of Religious Experience.* New York: Longmans, Green, 1902.

Janet, P. *L'Etat mental des hysteriques.* Paris: Rueff, 1892.

Jones, E. *The Life and Work of Sigmund Freud, 1856–1900.* 3 vols. New York: Basic Books, 1953–57.

Jung, C. G. [*The Psychology of Dementia Praecox.*] Halle: Marhold, 1907.

Kris, E. *Psychoanalytic Explorations in Art.* New York: International Universities Press, 1952.

Liébeault, A.-A. *Du sommeil et des états analogues.* Paris: Masson, 1866.

Moreau de Tours, J.-J. *Études psychiques sur la folie.* Paris: Lacour, 1840.

Waldeyer, H. W. von. "Ueber Einige Neurer Forschungen im Gebiete der Anatomie des Centralnervensystems." *Deutsche medizinische Wochenschrift*, 17 (1891), 1213–18, 1244–46, 1287–89, 1331–32, 1352–56.

NOTE: A list of further readings appears at the back of the book.

19

The Response to Freud

A man lives not only his personal life, as an individual, but also, consciously or unconsciously, the life of his epoch and his contemporaries.
THOMAS MANN

Immediately upon the appearance of Freud's *Interpretation of Dreams* (1900), C. G. Jung of Zürich became greatly interested and put himself eagerly in touch with the new movement. He was especially interested in the possibility of integrating the new method with the methods which had developed in the psychological laboratories of the German-speaking world.

Jung

Jung thus conceived the possibility of a large-scale objective and experimental testing program relating to certain aspects of Freud's theory and, in collaboration with Riklin and others, undertook systematic investigations of unconscious dynamics by means of the association test, combined with various physiological methods which would reveal unconscious conflict. Starting with classical association theory, Jung undertook to define submerged mental contents very much as Herbart had done, with emphasis upon those clusters of emotionally toned ideas which had been shown by Freud to be the source of continued suffering. To these clusters Jung gave the name *complexes*. One of his methods, then, was to use a systematic association test in the exploration of repressed complexes. In hysteria, for example, words were presented which led not to simple everyday associations, like *black-white,* but to marked delay in response, or to repetition of the stimulus word, or to coughing, sighing, blushing, stammering, or other

289

"complex indicators," the true nature of which would become evident to the psychiatrist either through further probing with the test or through the familiar psychoanalytic procedure. Jung believed that an experimental technique such as the association test would serve as a starting point for certain analyses, or as a method for short-cutting the length of the analytic procedure. Jung gave sustained attention also to the question of personality typing in the association test, undertaking to show how hysterics differ from normals and indeed how educated people differ from uneducated, mature from immature, men from women.

By far the best known of these many studies with the association test were those which dealt with the detection of crime. The theory was very simple. A group of accused persons may all be frightened during the period of police examination, but, so to speak, only the guilty know *exactly* what to be frightened about. On the occasion of a theft at one of the Zürich hospitals, words representing the objects in a stolen purse, mixed in with words of indifferent affective value, were presented serially to the various suspects. In the case of only one individual there was repeated evidence that words referring to the specific contents of the purse elicited a type of response which other "indifferent" words in the test did not elicit. Dramatically, the culprit, a nurse, confessed as soon as she became aware of the results of the test.[1] The primary meaning of such results, as far as psychologists are concerned, has been that the types of unconscious motivation and of blockage described by psychoanalysis have become amenable in some degree to experimental examination.

Parallel to these extensive experimental studies, Jung gave his attention to the application of basic psychoanalytic theory. As early as 1907, he formulated a conception in which physiological and psychoanalytic factors were studied in intimate association. It had been evident that Freudian theory would sooner or later lead to a full characterization of dementia praecox as a faulty form of investment of the libido. Jung in 1907 (and Abraham in 1908) stressed the inward turning of the libido, the development of a morbid attitude of self-absorption, from which would follow an inability to make normal social contacts. For Jung, however, the psychoanalytic formulation was simply the first step in a more comprehensive theory. Faulty adjustment to life demands leads, Jung suggested, to a biochemical disorder, so that in time the morbid absorption in oneself leads to a deterioration of bodily processes, involving toxic effects injurious to the central nervous system. The actual deterioration of many patients in later stages of dementia praecox thus becomes a *psychosomatic* expression of a pathological libidinal process. This approach was hailed by Freud.

Immediately after this contribution, we find Jung joining Freud in the symposium at Clark University at Worcester, Massachusetts, organized by G. Stanley Hall in 1909 and marking in fact the introduction of the Ameri-

---

[1] "Crime-detection" techniques have become common, partly as demonstrations in psychology courses and partly as an adjunct to police-court procedures.

can public to psychoanalytic theory. Here, after Freud had outlined "The Origin and Development of Psychoanalysis" (1910), Jung spoke on "The Association Method" (1910), making clear and vivid the use of the association test and the integration of psychoanalytic and experimental techniques. Upon returning to Europe after this occasion, Jung was invited again to speak in the United States and accepted; Freud in the same period declined a similar invitation. Freud spoke with asperity in later years about a letter Jung sent to him from the United States in which it was made clear that the American public was eager to accept psychoanalysis when freed of its "over-emphasis" upon sexual factors. This was, of course, one of various early intimations that Freud had regarding Jung's unwillingness to accept the psychoanalytic system as Freud saw it.

A number of other factors contributed to a break between them. One that Freud himself emphasized was bad feeling over the presidency of one of the international congresses. Another, stressed by Jung, was a difference of opinion regarding the ultimate definition of the libido and of its relation to early trauma. For Freud, in those years, the libido was sexual, and when injury to the infantile libidinal impulse was experienced, there was trauma or shock, involving lifelong consequences. Jung disagreed on two counts. First, he came to believe that the libido was simply a life process taking different forms at different periods—taking, for example, the nutrient form in infancy, the form of play and casual friendly interaction in subsequent years, and a heterosexual form only after puberty. Second, he came to the opinion that trauma is of no real importance in itself but is used by the individual patient as a device for compelling attention and pity, or whatever it is that the patient wishes to achieve. If we understand the present needs of the patient, and the purposes which, as a living system, he is fulfilling in consequence of those needs, we shall find that the trauma is simply one of many items in his experience which he plays up or plays down in the service of these purposes. A girl, for example, who had behaved hysterically when she heard a team of horses on the road—rushing ahead of them instead of quietly withdrawing to one side—proved upon analysis to be behaving hysterically as a device for being picked up and taken to the nearest house, where there was every reason to believe that she would be cared for by a man whom she loved (1914–15). These two changes in orientation, together with personal factors, led to a sharp break and the setting up of an independent system of therapy known thereafter as "analytical psychology."

One fundamental difference between Freud and Jung lay in the approach to individual differences. With Freud, the attempt was made from the very beginning to find universal dynamics applicable to each case. Interest in individual differences was secondary; indeed, it did not come sharply into focus until the time of his study of character types in the middle of the first decade of this century and never became the center of his system. Despite the recognition of heredity in predisposing toward one or another character type, Freud was always concerned primarily with a conception of instinctual life and the dispositions of energies applicable to all human experience. With Jung, on the other hand, there was a prominent place for that heavy emphasis on typology, that grouping of persons into basic types, which was so characteristic of nineteenth-century philosophy.

On the basis of such conceptions Jung early turned the libido theory to account (1921). There were for him two fundamental types, the extravert and the introvert, who were congenitally predisposed to the outer and the inner manifestations of the libido. The extravert was primarily concerned with social relationships in which a rich fulfillment of libidinal needs could be found; the introvert, preoccupied with his own inner world of fantasy and bodily activity, was relatively incapable of such outgoing social participation. This conception, which "caught" like wildfire in psychiatry, in psychology, and in the mind of the general reading public, was shortly elaborated by means of a subdivision of mental operations into four fundamental activities: sensing, feeling, thinking, and intuiting—operations into which the libido may flow, in such a way that each of these four processes may be brought into relation either to external or to internal objects. There may thus be a sensing extravert, and a sensing introvert, and so on.

Comparable to the polarity of the extravert and the introvert is likewise the polarity of true and of make-believe individuality, the *persona* and the *socius,* what one might call the inner self and the social pose. There is likewise the polarity of the essentially masculine and the essentially feminine, the animus and the anima, found (in accordance with the theory of bisexuality) in all individuals, the man unconsciously expressing feminine and the woman masculine attitudes along with those attitudes which are accepted at the conscious level.

As regards therapy, and education with a therapeutic cast, there is again fundamental cleavage between Jung and Freud. Freud remained to the end essentially a medical practitioner operating on the basis of natural science. However speculative his doctrines might be, they proceeded from nineteenth-century monistic conceptions of the mind-body relation and regarded mental processes in all their aspects as expressions of an evolutionary reality residing in the tissues of the living organism. For Jung, however, emphasis on the conception of spiritual forces and a spiritual destiny became prominent in the early years, and became more and more prominent as the decades went by. The title of one of Jung's most influential books, *Modern Man in Search of a Soul* (1931), indicates quite exactly the direction in which he made his own protest against the naturalism of Freud—expressed in caustic language by Freud himself in earlier years in a reference to the period in which Jung was a psychoanalyst and did not yet aspire to be a "prophet." Jung replied to this, and all other implied accusations, by an extraordinary chapter in which he said that it is right for each investigator to tell the world candidly what he finds in his own soul; and that just as Freud has so faithfully described the dark forces he finds in his own, so he, Jung, has the obligation to report the high aspirations which he and many of his patients have experienced.

Judgment as to the degree of importance to be attached to emotional cleavages as profound as this becomes, of course, partly a question of individual temperament and taste. It would be a mistake, however, to imply that for purposes of world psychology the naturalistic is the *only* important trend visible to the naked eye, or that the philosophical controversy of nineteenth-century naturalism and idealism is at an end. The naturalistic outlook is still an item of faith rather than just the forced acceptance of a simple fact, and in a number of important works, such as Müller-Freienfels's *The Evolution of Modern Psychology* (1935), it is made clear that one can find as much in support of, as in opposition to, Jung's conception that the really important forces lie outside the sphere to which biology (or economics) possesses the keys. There has been a continuous hammering by numerous physicists at the same issue in recent years. The problem is the general direction of the long-range philosophical trend of a society which has gone through paroxysmal changes in ideology in the last few centuries; and it is only here and there, as among the Watsonian behaviorists and among the Marxists, that one is willing to predict with finality what the scientific outcome must ultimately be.

As the years went by, it became more and more evident that Jung could not be defined simply in terms of his relation to Freud. He was not one more psychoanalyst; he was not even one more depth psychologist. He was something different—as different, let us say, as Rorschach, or Piaget, or even Pavlov. He did indeed receive massive inspiration from Freud at the turn of the century. He did continue, after the break with Freud in 1911, to use many Freudian concepts, especially those relating to conflict, the unconscious mechanisms of defense, and the importance of conscience and the ego ideal. In some of these matters he continued to use ideas which Freud had formulated, and in some, such as these relating to the world of the ideal, he had expressed himself before Freud found it timely to make his own statement. But he was more than all this.

Jung was a prophetic figure. The term is not used either in terms of adulation or of denigration. Certainly, however, in the broadest sense, both Freud and Jung were prophets, and they were prophets with very different messages. Freud, the agnostic, found the world impersonal, inscrutable, "oceanic" both in its gift of joy and in its exquisite cruelty. But to try to make the world personal seemed to him to be just part of man's hopelessly and helplessly biased outlook on an impersonal cosmos. As prophet, he saw the sweep of vast forces by which man was caught and against which he could make only a Job-like protest. For Jung, however, there was an increasingly large place for intuitive contact with the majestic and the divine, a willing encouragement of the patient and of the doctor to move freely and without resistance in the direction of mystical aspirations. As these two men appear reflected, distorted, refracted through modern literature in seemingly endless quotations, paraphrases, and reinterpretations, one may perhaps conceive the one as a staunch figure confronting the bleak, though · tremendous, force of an alien universe against which man may offer local and limited defenses; and the other as a guide to a sublimely challenging world to which man is genuinely attuned. If this is a fair way of stating the matter, it would follow that modern psychology, with its severe addiction to an impersonal scientific approach, will be bound to find much more that it can use in Freud than in Jung; by the same token, it would follow that the protesting humanistic and existential psychologies, breathing the spirit of Kierkegaard in the West and the *Bhagavad Gita* in the East, are closer to Jung.

Adler

Among the young medical men who joined Freud's seminar in the earliest years of this century was Alfred Adler, who apparently from the beginning regarded himself as a junior colleague rather than as a disciple of the master. Drawn early by the strictly biological aspects of Freud's doctrine, he sought to expand and develop one cardinal thesis which Freud had already defined: the nature of the process of *compensation*. In the case of incomplete sexual development, Freud had noticed a basic need to compensate for the deficiency. The individual might become in some ways more "masculine" or more "feminine" than anatomical or physiological factors could warrant.

Why not, said Adler, extend this doctrine of defect, and of compensation for defect, to cover every type of constitutional limitation? He drew attention to the tendency for a lung or a kidney to do extra work if the corresponding organ was injured; the tendency of one eye to become more acute if the other was defective; the tendency to develop a hypertrophy of function, a secondary acuteness, wherever sense organs fell short of normal adequacy. But among all the organs of compensation for civilized man there is a primary emphasis upon the central nervous system, for man's adaptation to social living is largely a question of learning how to cope with the demands of others and with social requirements. Whereas, therefore, compensation at the biological level appears in animals, most of the significant types of compensation in man are conscious or unconscious efforts to make good where one is socially inadequate.

The thesis up to this point, appearing in a publication entitled *A Study of Organic Inferiority and Its Psychical Compensation* (1907), was accepted by Freud and his followers as a significant contribution to ego psychology. For four more years Adler went on developing this conception, showing more and more devices by means of which inadequacy — physical, intellectual, or social — was "compensated for" through overt behavior, through symptoms, or through a broad technique for dominating a hostile environment. He developed the thesis to a point where compensation became not a peripheral, but the central, clue to neurosis.

In 1911, according to Wittels (1924), and Freud appears to endorse the story, Adler requested of the seminar the opportunity to develop an orderly thesis regarding the role of compensation. Consent was given and several consecutive meetings of the seminar were devoted to this purpose. At the end of the last presentation, one of Freud's followers offered a motion to the effect that since Dr. Adler was "not in sympathy with psychoanalysis," he be asked to withdraw from the seminar. Apparently the motion was formally seconded and passed, and Adler together with nine of his associates (in a total group of perhaps thirty-five physicians) withdrew. Immediately there-after Adler formally established his school of *individual psychology,* which began to develop its own postulates and to publish its own journal.

Individual psychology, as defined, is founded first upon the conception that the experience of life in the newborn child is one of weakness, inade-quacy, and frustration. He finds big, strong, active people who go marching about; who decide what they want to do and do it; upon whose tenderness or pity he must rely if he wants to be nursed or picked up or dried or amused. He is a little, helpless object, to whom this or that specific want, such as that for food or for a maternal embrace, is altogether secondary to the primary want to control one's own activity, to be oneself and liberate oneself from the domination of this big, inscrutable world. Power, in other words, is the first good, just as weakness is the first evil; and compensation becomes sim-ply a name for the struggle of the individual in the direction of power. It is relatively easy for the child to discover the things that endear him to his par-ents or the things that shock them, and it is not surprising, in view of the bi-ology of sexuality, that both the tendency to be pleased and the tendency to be shocked are manipulated by the child very much as the analysts describe. The essential clue, however, is compensation for inferiority.

The child develops, as a rule, a rather consistent and workable method of compensating—a method depending upon his own situation, the personal-ities of his parents, their age and economic status, the presence and attri-butes of brothers, sisters, grandparents, and so on, in the home. Later the nature of neighborhood and community pressure determines what it takes to get over being a helpless little baby; determines whether one is to become a brat, a braggard, a delinquent, a mamma's boy, a poor little thing for whom everyone is sorry, and so on. Individual personality takes shape as a device for coping with the frustrations of infantile experience.

The essential technique of each individual for coping with such difficulties becomes more and more generalized and consolidated and becomes the "style of life" destined, as a rule, to persist. If the parent for whose sake the device is developed suddenly dies, or if one moves to a neighborhood in which the early technique can no longer be used, one may have to abandon the established style of life and begin all over again; and from this fact serious difficulties — everything from blushing or stammering to a psychotic episode — may develop. Running through all this description is the basic assumption of continuity of purpose. The power objective of the individual may take on different masks from time to time, but it remains the real generator of every specific activity. Since this is the case, it follows that in a long-drawn-out psychoanalysis the patient is playing a game to hoodwink the physician. Free associations on a couch are usually less painful than admission that one is out for power; but they serve the purpose. By costing the family a good deal of money, one can dominate them too. For Adler all that was necessary was that physician and patient sit vis-à-vis and face realities directly.

Especially interesting among Adler's specific contributions to individual character study are those which have to do with position in the family: that is, with order of birth, and with the relations of siblings. The "only child" not only dominates the father and mother during the entire growing-up period, forcing them to adapt their previously rather free existence to his own needs, but also carries over into the school and the community a number of the habits which have worked well at home. This may mean that some of the frustrations are peculiarly acute when it proves impossible to handle the teacher as one handles one's parents; but at the same time it may mean that a number of the same techniques which prove capable of transfer — such as hyper-intellectualism and hypermaturity, a readiness to get along with grownups rather than with children, and so on — become consolidated as a permanent personality attribute. The second-born child has at first the experience of dominating the household which was originally the privilege of the eldest, but in addition he is capable of dethroning the first-born from a position of both power and affection, and instead of mastering two people, he finds a way to master three. The youngest child in a rather large family not only enjoys at first a rather large domain in which his control can be exercised, but learns with peculiar poignancy the satisfactions of being little, helpless, cute, and perhaps even pitiful. One is permanently the baby of the family, and in addition one reminds the parents continually of the days when they had little children and draws them back to their youth with an appeal few can resist.

These brief paragraphs perhaps show how far we are from the biological emphasis of Freudian psychology and from the biological orientation of Adler's own earlier work. More and more the nature of the social pattern of which the growing individual is an aspect comes into focus. It is hardly surprising to learn that individual psychology became during the twenties essentially a theory of group action, a theory applied to delinquency, to the classroom situation, and to social movements. To two of the social movements Adler devoted special energy: feminism and socialism.

Rejecting root and branch the entire Freudian conception of basic masculine and feminine psychology, Adler pointed to the fact that biological differentiation is relatively unimportant until it has been exploited for the purposes of power. Just as Veblen in *The Theory of the Leisure Class* (1899) had developed the conception of masculinity as essentially a social rather than a biological phenomenon, the basis of which he calls the "predation" of one individual upon another, so Adler undertook to show that masculine and feminine psychologies are sheer artifacts of a social order in which patriarchal family status is accompanied by military, economic, and political power. The struggle of the modern woman in the direction of masculinity has nothing whatever to do with anatomical deficiencies or compensatory activities of the sort which he himself would have stressed in 1907. It has everything to do with the dislocation in traditional feminine roles and the double pressures upon contemporary woman to enter the existing masculine orbit and to remain at the same time in the earlier wifely and motherly orbit, with high probability that the satisfactions from neither will be really complete.

Socialism, in the same way, became for Adler a direct and necessary expression of response to a fundamental frustration which falls to the lot of most people living in an industrial civilization. For most men and women removed from the immediate satisfactions of contact with the soil or the artisan's delight in seeing the labors of his own hands, there is a world of routine, mechanical activity which is intrinsically meaningless, and during which one is dominated either by a man whom one does not know or by a machine whose function and ultimate objective one does not understand. There is no escape except in full democratic participation in the planning and in the control of processes of production. We constantly find ourselves emerging with an essentially socialistic conception regarding the incompatibility between human nature and the existing social order. It might be argued, of course, that man can adapt himself to any kind of a social order; but with Adler the experience of weakness and the need for power as a compensatory device is so fundamental that there is only one means of satisfaction: a social order in which each man's compensatory struggle can be integrated effectively with that of each other man. Men would thus collectively dominate some natural difficulty; through "social feeling" rather than through hostility they would achieve a livable social reality.

It became rather obvious that insofar as the Marxists of central Europe were concerned with psychology at all in the period between the two world wars, they would incline to Adler rather than to Freud or Jung. It was not simply that Freud had himself written caustically on the matter of Marxism; it had a strong positive basis in the fact that Adler's was the first psychological system in the history of psychology that was developed in what we should today call a social-science direction. While much effort has been evident in the gradual adaptation of Freudian psychoanalysis to the findings of cultural anthropology, and the resultant struggle to align a biological scheme with a system of compelling social forces, the Adlerian system slipped so casually and easily into a social frame of reference that one would never think it necessary to write a book showing how individualistic and social-science conceptions are to be reconciled.

Fromm and Horney

But even within the heart of psychoanalytic practice with patients in our own culture, there has occurred an active movement against the biological assumptions of Freudian psychoanalysis and an effort to conceive psycho-analytic problems in terms of social dynamics. Those who represent this tendency have come to feel that the primary factors operative both in neuroses and in the shaping of the normal personality are those which spring from conflicting cultural pressures, or from demands upon the individual in response to which nothing really satisfying and adequate can be done.

It is difficult to specify at what point this "left-wing" movement in psychoanalysis began. It is different from the many splinter groups which developed within the Freudian system itself in earlier years. Many of these splinter groups were concerned with differences in the technique of dream interpretation. Others, such as the strong group led by Otto Rank, asked whether analysis should go on until the patient wanted to stop it or should stop at a point specified in advance by the analyst. Rank was especially concerned with the patient's attitude (for example, his activity or passivity) and with the analyst's determination to study and rectify the *relationships,* the social world, of the patient. Such questions were questions of method; they were not centered in the question of Freud's biological theory. But the new movement with which we are now concerned arose from the basic conviction that the Freudian system of biological assumptions was ill adapted to the study of men in industrial society, that it was much less effective in contemporary American urban centers than it had been in the Vienna of half a century ago — or even of twenty years ago — in which the patriarchal family still supplied most of the background with which the individual analyst had to deal.

It was Erich Fromm who sketched, in the middle thirties, a theory of "authority and the family," which challenged the postulates regarding the father-son relationship so prominent in the Oedipus complex. Fromm began to raise questions regarding the cultural diversities of expression, and even regarding the ultimate cultural origins of various types of character formation. Believing that the psychoanalytic mechanisms would be of real value in the study of all cultures — that is, that all cultural groups would show the basic phenomena of repression, projection, rationalization, and so on — he maintained that the specific content of the neurosis, and indeed of the individual personality pattern, depends largely upon the type of social pressure first applied in early life. Fromm made these ideas the common property of a series of seminars and of other groups of physicians and psychologists with whom he was associated.

Contemporaneously, Karen Horney began to stress, as a staff member of the New York Psychoanalytic Institute, the role of various social factors in neuroses and began to challenge the biographical functions of the Freudian system (1937, 1939). She and her pupils felt themselves stifled in the orthodox atmosphere; the system departed so far in the social direction that it experienced, as had Adler's thirty years earlier, a need to strike out on its own path. Horney and her associates, accordingly, began openly to carry out analysis without an instinct theory, and without any assumptions regarding the inevitable rise of an ego and a superego as a result of instinctual repressions and conflicts, and began to emphasize the nature of urban industrial society and the broader contributions of our whole culture as a basis for the "neurotic personality of our time." In consequence partly of a wide therapeutic following and partly of a series of vivid and compelling publications, Horney found herself the leader of a social school of psychoanalysis in which the psychoanalytic tools and psychodynamic assumptions are retained insofar as one can retain them without laying any stress whatever upon fixed biological trends or instincts. She did not deny, any more than Adler had, the reality of the life of instinct. But she stressed, as did he, the social form which the instincts are given and the fact that they are made to conflict with one another not through the operation of inevitable forces, but because society plays them against one another.

From what has been said, it should be clear why the Adlerians accuse Horney of plagiarism and why she in turn insists that Adler's method (which, as we have seen, makes short shrift of the whole psychoanalytic technique and procedure), while it may make many right guesses, is superficial and lacks the solid foundations required of theory and practice in the study of personality. It is sufficient for present purposes to indicate that Horney, with all the weapons of psychoanalysis, has been treading the path of social interpretation upon which, more naïvely and impulsively, Adler had ventured in earlier years. It goes almost without saying that the yield from the Horney technique is richer; it also goes without saying that a certain blunt simplicity, as exemplified in Adler, may have been of great value in its time in calling attention to neglected realities.

But, as many psychiatrists have pointed out, the orthodox and the newer statements are two aspects of a reality which need not be so hopelessly obscure. Perhaps all human beings develop quite early in life some preoccupation with their own bodies, some need to defend the body against injury, and at the same time a primitive capacity for warm, outgoing response which inevitably is bestowed upon one's own person just as it may be upon any other available object. The result would be a need to enhance and defend the self (see Sullivan, 1940). Sometimes these primitive tendencies are frustrated, and very complicated and devious means of defense must be found.

Ultimately, however, the mainsprings of what Adler calls compensatory activity may be traced to these simple mechanisms. In the same way the main outlines of the psychoanalytic system may be reduced to the perpetual struggle to enhance and defend the self. The one difficulty which the socially oriented analyst would find in this formulation would lie in its oversimplified statement of the nature of social frustrations to the process of self-enhancement. One might therefore quite appropriately accept their suggestions by spelling out in considerable detail the different ways in which different societies frustrate primitive self-enhancing tendencies, and the various ways in which the lovable picture of the self which the child has had a chance to build up is mutilated by reproof or by social ostracism. In the meantime everything that has been discovered by Freud regarding methods of plumbing unconscious dynamics can continue to be used — and joined with data from experimentation and projective methods — in a socially oriented psychoanalysis.

It appears likely, moreover, that what had already happened in psychiatry, in psychiatric social work, and in the deep-level study of our own society by sociologists and group workers will in time happen in the more academic formulation of personality problems: namely, the various systems will be forced to shed some of their dogmatic trappings and be reduced to a relatively orderly and uniform pattern in which the primary role of the self, and of activities centered around it, will be placed in the central position which Freud, as early as 1913, suggested it might require. This, of course, foreshadowed the end of naïve "drive psychology" and its replacement by an "ego psychology" oriented toward the study of conflict and of the means of escaping it and achieving integration.

In perspective, it would appear that psychiatry has become deeply concerned with the predicament of man in a sick society — that especially Fromm (1955), Horney (1937, 1939), and Sullivan (1953) gained ascendancy partly because of the broad social-science perspective in which they have tried to describe the loneliness, the alienation, the social hungers of modern man, his need to live in and through his society with "consensual validation" for his own personal appraisals; and partly because the preoccupation with the social isolation of the schizophrenic has become a sort of central preoccupation of all psychiatry. One might almost say that the neuroses, which were central in Freud's thinking, have been partly replaced by schizophrenia and schizophrenia-like psychotic or borderline responses as the interesting, cogent, central themes of contemporary psychiatry. Sullivan thought and taught in those terms. One may, in fact, say that Adler, Horney, Fromm, and Sullivan have all ridden on the same great crest of concern for the social aspects and social meaning of mental disease. Judging by the frequency of public and private discussion, by books and articles, and by predilections of psychiatrists, psychologists, social workers, and the lay public, one would have to conclude that these "deviant schools" (deviant from Freud) have constituted various competitive threats to the orthodox Freudian movement. This depends, however, upon criteria. Nose-counting is not the answer, nor are prestige-bearing posts, income, or volume of publications. We said that psychoanalysis is here to stay. We add that non-Freudian analysis seems also here to stay.

But before we leave the problem of the impact of Freud upon our era, a few more words may be said about the constraint of the individual by society: the problem of discipline. The modern world has been undergoing a fabulous — or catastrophic — reconsideration of the fixed rules, the lawful codes, by which civilized human beings are to live. Whether it be feeling bound to follow the impersonal "lonely crowd" (Riesman, 1950), or whether it be student protest, or sit-in, or wild racial strife, or nervous inquiry about the ground rules related to sexual, political, economic amenities, decencies, codes, and laws, there can be no doubt that modern man has seen, in a few decades, a "terrible swift sword" of disintegration — with great uncertainties regarding the restoration of the old order. The grand new freedoms, the "brave new world" of the pioneer and the frontiersman, the freedom of thought and of press, assembly, and speech have not led to utopia. Psychoanalysis appeared just as the rising tide of the demand for freedom swept through the Western world. It was construed to be saying that strife, hate, crime, failure — the ugliness of life generally — are largely due to dishonesty, evasion, self-deception; and that the opening, the clarification, of modes of observing oneself, and of the social code, will give a healing peace in which new perspectives may be gained, and new orientations defined. Actually, since World War II it seems to have become less and less evident that direct confrontation and expression of primitive strivings — sexual, aggressive, or whatever — can be credited with an increase in individual freedom. Just possibly something has always had to sit on the trembling lid; and even though past methods may have been savage and stupid, it may be that the new situation, after repressions are removed, will involve even more chaos until new controls can be forged, tested, and applied. Civilized man has, in a sense, been caught short, with his assumption that seeing deep into the volcanic pit automatically leads in utopian directions.

Freud, of course, was intensely aware of the issue. In *Civilization and Its Discontents* (1930) and *The Future of an Illusion* (1927), he made plain enough for the record the uncertainties for the future as to any likely escape from uncontrolled wild beasts. His possible solution, in the often-quoted and remarkable phrase "Where id was, there must ego be" leaves us with the hope of an ever greater rationality and a rationality working through a disciplined control that is based not only upon repression but upon parental love. Issues regarding techniques of psychoanalysis appear rather petty in contrast to this massive question regarding the possible salvation of man through an increasing amount of love and of rationality.

"Humanistic" Psychologies

Academic psychology has shown great reserve in response to almost all new "schools" of thought suspected of having philosophical pretensions. Yet for vitality, and for sheer volume of thinking, clinical practice, and research, the newer existentialist, phenomenological, and humanistic psychologies – sometimes catching the fire of psychoanalysis, sometimes striving to extinguish it – need to be noted here.

Since the early nineteenth century the direct appraisal of the "human condition" in terms of immediate experiences of helplessness, or sinfulness, or failure to achieve the ideal has been a concern of religious philosophies that considered themselves psychological. Catholic, Lutheran, Calvinist, and various categories of evangelical theologians have emphasized the fall of man, his utter helplessness, the unlovely human image which emerges from historical and cross-cultural pictures of man's inhumanity to man. In general, the Christian theologies as a whole made much of the evil in man and his need for help. New movements, such as Christian Science and the Church of the Latter-Day Saints, were representative of a fresh yearning for a redefinition of God's plan for man. At the philosophical level, man's tragic condition, as described by the suffering Kierkegaard, called into being an "existential" psychology, a psychology of confrontation of man's actual state. A religious atmosphere dominates much of contemporary humanistic thought – in the Protestant theology of Tillich, the Jewish tradition in the Israeli philosopher Buber, and the cosmic or even theological spirit awake in the revivalist mood of many encounter groups. For some the religious, the philosophical, and the psychological are not really distinguishable. For others, such as Carl Rogers and A. H. Maslow, the scientific is well defined and sharply focused and may carry religious implications; but the implications may be pursued in varying degree and in varying directions by different adherents to the humanist approach. American humanistic psychology is close to the optimistic or confident tone of the psychologies of "healthy-mindedness" described by William James (see p. 202), while the European humanistic psychology has much more heavily stressed the sorrow and helplessness of man's state.

During the 1960s the influence of Maslow became great, especially because of his broad background in comparative, developmental, and social psychology. He made a clean separation between what he regarded as the dry, narrow, and dehumanized character of "scientific psychology" and a new psychology which could be based upon taking human life exactly as it is, with all its unfulfilled potentials and vast aspirations, a psychology of self-actualization. Just before his death he had published a remarkable volume, *The Psychology of Science,* in which he had undertaken to show the full vision of human life which must be the guide to the serious investigator rather than the system of abstractions derived from the physical sciences.

Rogers, who had made ⸂ huge reputation in nondirective "client-centered" therapy, became responsive to the new thrust of the humanistic psychology and a new approach swinging somewhat away from the "one-to-one" relationship between therapist and client; he came to believe strongly in the humanistic approaches of the group-centered sort, to which "encounter group" has become more and more the standard descriptive term. This term and the whole conception of group therapy are of course loosely defined in the humanistic movement. Like all enthusiastic movements, it is still hard to define, especially with respect to the limits of classification and the rubrics within which psychologists are to be placed.

A second historical source of preoccupation with *experience* as a clue to psychology lay in the attempt at a more and more refined view of the *world of consciousness as directly confronted*. It became evident by the end of the nineteenth century that the dissection techniques of the armchair introspector and of the new laboratory psychologist alike yielded snippets of sensations, images, and feelings but not the actual world of experience. Among the many who moved toward the description of the inner world, emphasis must be given especially to Husserl, who, in 1900, described a "phenomenology" which should be nothing less than an unbiased confrontation of the whole inner world, seeking to view, rather than to analyze or classify, the full contents of experience as given.

If, now, we used the term "existentialism" very broadly to cover the movement from Kierkegaard forward toward the full recognition of man's helplessness and unworthiness, and the system of Husserl, concerned with a full and honest picture of the world of experience as a scientific task, we might say that the two movements were to some degree bound to flow together and that during the period between the two world wars they were patently flowing together both in the scholar's study and in the clinician's office. There was another movement ready to join them: the philosophical message of existentialism as worked out as a personal philosophy by Sartre (1940) during the 1930s.

In the meantime, both before and after World War II, German psychiatrists became impressed with the value of the full phenomenological account of the patient's inner world and with the possibilities for a therapeutic program which should be true both to the existentialist and to the phenomenological demands. After World War II, existentialism, containing important phenomenological components, invaded the thinking of American psychiatrists and psychologists — and almost at the same moment the thinking of the general lay public. There was a great wave of phenomenology and existentialism, often fused together in the 1950s. Of course many who represented phenomenology were but little concerned with the problem of human misery and with the problems of therapy; they were concerned with the adequacy of psychological descriptive records as represented, for example, in Barker and Wright's study (1966) of the world of a boy growing up in a small Kansas town. The greatest impact, however, of the new phenomenological movement was in psychotherapy, where it rapidly became evident that there was a need for the constant assimilation and digestion of new ideas relating to the emotional color and meaning of the therapeutic encounter.

It soon became common practice to refer to this newly emerging integrative psychology and its offshoots as "humanistic." The movement took on such proportions that one would have to count not by the dozens, but by the hundreds, the number of academic centers in which humanistic psychology is being pursued informally, if not formally; and in terms of thousands the number of those attending conferences of humanistic psychologists and sharing in a spirit of hope, comradeship, and ready "encounter," which sweeps almost everything before it. The movement is well epitomized in the word "humanistic," which will serve well enough to denote the many trends concerned not with behavior analysis as such, but with the human experience. Though there are many efforts to cut it down to size, this interrelated group of humanistic psychologies is already making a considerable dent in the thinking of both the academic and the nonacademic worlds.

Erikson and Identity

But it may be asked at this juncture whether there is no dominant figure still giving life and leadership to the cultural message of Freud himself. Is it a question of Freud's world, which came to an end in 1939, struggling to maintain its existence against the competition of Fromm, Horney, Sullivan, and such Jungian and Adlerian representatives as still ply their trade and write their books? Is there no strong figure to represent the Freudian movement as we now move into the last third of the twentieth century? Replies will vary, of course, but it appears to us that the issue can be divided into two questions: What is the cutting edge, the new message, of Freudian psychology in the modern era? Who most adequately represents this cutting edge? The answer to the first question appears to be plainly psychoanalytic ego psychology. Nothing very new and important about instinct theory, libido theory, symptom formation, or metapsychology seems to have appeared except this one central and fundamental problem of psychoanalytic ego psychology.[2] This can be regarded as beginning with the papers by Freud, named above (see p. 282), or with Anna Freud's interpretations and integrations of psychoanalytic findings in *The Ego and the Mechanisms of Defense* (1936), or with Hartmann's emphasis upon adaptation and "con-

[2] Other more specific and more technical problems, for example, the problem of "object relations," would very likely be mentioned here by those in the midst of psychoanalytic practice. Our own judgment is based on an effort at a broad perspective on the psychoanalytic movement as a whole.

flict-free ego spheres" which give the ego direct contact and control so that the environment really becomes relevant to the inner psychological world (see p. 298). Or, if one takes all this for granted and looks for more recent contributions, one may place today's emphasis upon Erik Erikson.

Erikson was a young painter in Vienna in the twenties. Solely on the basis of his personal attributes — not his training — he was sent to Anna Freud as a likely possibility for analytic work. Soon he was a member of the inner circle of Freud and his daughter.

Three seminal ideas appear in his early work (1930): (1) the conception, developed by Freud and by Abraham, that life energies express themselves through special zones and that ultimately they may be freed of the specific zonal or regional quality, while retaining their basic character as intrusive or extrusive, as ordered in space and time in a dynamic fashion which transcends the particular zone in which they appear; (2) the conception of the role of the body in the world of fantasy as one studies the unconscious representations of the body in drawing, or block-building, or the arrangement of miniature life toys; (3) the conception of "identity" as something more than a process of infantile identification with the parent, but involving the deepest and fullest psychoanalytic insights as to the nature of one's own individuality, one's relation to family and neighborhood figures, and one's ultimate achievement of uniqueness in the fulfillment of a rich ground of potentialities. These are thus not just biological stages in growth, but psychosocial stages of development.

Coming to the United States in the early thirties, Erikson found, in the dramatic play constructions of college freshmen (asked to make up a "dramatic scene" with miniature life figures) and, later, in the child's play (1937), in the configurations as he represents his body, more material for interpretation. He continued to develop the doctrine of zones and modes — for example, the concern of the child in preliterate society with the important object relationships in his life, the conflicts regarding his own body, and leading on into his conception of identity. He was helped by psychologists and psychiatrists to see these processes in American children and youth, and by anthropologists, notably by Margaret Mead and Kroeber, to see these processes in the Sioux (1939) and Yurok Indian tribes (1943). He found, for example, the human alimentary canal psychologically assimilated to the river in which the salmon literally bring life to the tribe. Experiences with submarine crews, with political leaders — notably with the world of Mahatma Gandhi — and with alienated college youth of the contemporary scene have led to an exceptionally rich conception of personal identity as a central problem for psychiatry, for education, and indeed for the evaluation of the whole civilization. *Childhood and Society* (1950), his first integrative work, now in a revised edition, brings into systematic patterning these many concerns.

Erikson's emphasis upon identity expresses a sweeping cross-cultural orientation through passing from American Indian tribes, through the

Soviet Union, through industrialized America, through the sixteenth-century Germany of Martin Luther, and through the heroic leadership pattern of Mahatma Gandhi. All this is in documentation of a thesis regarding eight stages of psychosocial growth which, like the Shakespearean stages, give personality a temporal rather than simply a cross-sectional status in a general psychology in response to man's deeply social needs. Psychoanalysis has, through these modern movements, passed beyond the clinical psychology, the one-to-one relation between patient and therapist, and has become, as Freud dreamed, in 1913 (*Totem and Taboo*) and 1921 (*Group Psychology and the Analysis of Ego*), a preoccupation with all that is human. There is, of course, some reluctance among many of the orthodox group to note this development in the direction of "sociology" rather than "clinical dynamics," but there is so much empirical material, both normal developmental material and clinical material in the reports cited, that one must definitely include this series of contributions as profound psychoanalysis — and indeed psychoanalysis within the Freudian fold. To the question who represents the cutting edge of psychoanalytic ego psychology in the world of today there seems to be very little reason to doubt that it is Erik Erikson (Coles, 1970).

We have said little about the negative or hostile response to Freud except insofar as the protest of Jung, Adler, and later clinicians implied that Freud missed the boat, overlooked the really important and creative forces at work in human personality. There were, however, negative responses of a very different sort (Bailey, 1965, for example) — responses of shock and vigorous rejection of the postulates of psychoanalysis as speculative fancies not controlled by rational and orderly experimentation; rejection on the grounds that psychoanalysis lacks all awareness of the general world of science, that it lacks any understanding of the content and method of science. The objections, however phrased, were difficult to meet and reply to in the heat of emotional fireworks displayed on both sides. Freud's hostility toward those who criticized him and his system, of course, seemed to support the general insistence that his was not the way of science. But in the meantime most psychoanalytically oriented psychiatrists and psychologists kept on with their work, and, by and large, responded with a shrug. In our judgment the pros and cons are not yet stabilized. Psychoanalysis seems to be currently moving a little closer to the general structure of science; it will have gained a lot when and if this movement is completed. But it may very well lose its separate identity in the process. Science, on the other hand, may also gain, in the ways of an expanded horizon of valid and pertinent subject matters, when it succeeds in fully incorporating within its evolving structure the heritage of Freud and his followers.

REFERENCES

Abraham, K. ["The Psycho-Sexual Differences Between Hysteria and Dementia Praecox."] *Zentralblatt für Nervenheilkunde und Psychiatrie,* 19 (1908), 521–32.

Adler, A. [*A Study of Organic Inferiority and Its Psychical Compensation.*] Berlin: Urban and Schwarzenberg, 1907.

Bailey, P. *Sigmund the Unserene.* Springfield, Ill.: Thomas, 1965.

Barker, R. G., and Wright, H. *One Boy's Day.* Hamden, Conn.: Shoe String, 1966.

Coles, R. *Erik H. Erikson: The Growth of His Work.* Boston: Little, Brown, 1970.

Erikson, E. H. "Die Zukunft der Aufklärung und die Psychoanalyse." *Zeitschrift der Psychoanalyse,* 4 (1930), 201–16.

———. "Configurations in Play – Clinical Notes." *Psychoanalytic Quarterly,* 6 (1937), 139–214.

———. "Observations on Sioux Education." *Journal of Psychology,* 7 (1939), 101–56.

———. "Observations on the Yurok: Childhood and World Image." *University of California Publications in American Archaeology and Ethnology,* 35 (1943), 257–301.

———. *Childhood and Society.* 1950. 2nd ed. New York: Norton, 1963.

Freud, A. *The Ego and the Mechanisms of Defense.* Rev. ed. New York: International Universities Press, 1967.

Freud, S. [*The Interpretation of Dreams.*] Leipzig: Deuticke, 1900. (*Standard Edition,* Vols. 4–5, 1953.)

———. [*The Origin and Development of Psychoanalysis.*] Leipzig: Deuticke, 1910. (Standard Edition, Vol. 11, 1957.)

———. [*The Future of an Illusion.*] Leipzig, Vienna, and Zurich: Internationaler Psychoanalytischer Verlag, 1927. (Standard Edition, Vol. 21, 1961.)

———. [*Civilization and Its Discontents.*] Vienna: Internationaler Psychoanalytischer Verlag, 1930. (*SE,* Vol. 21, 1961.)

Fromm, E. *The Sane Society.* New York: Holt, Rinehart and Winston, 1955.

Horney, K. *The Neurotic Personality of Our Times.* New York: Norton, 1937.

———. *New Ways in Psychoanalysis.* New York: Norton, 1939.

Jung, C. G. [*The Psychology of Dementia Praecox.*] Halle: Marhold, 1907.

———. "The Association Method." *American Journal of Psychology,* 31 (1910), 219–69.

———. "The Theory of Psychoanalysis." *Psychoanalytic Review,* 1 (1914), 1–40, 153–77, 260–84, 415–30; 2 (1915), 29–51.

———. [*Psychological Types.*] Zürich: Rascher, 1921.

———. [*Modern Man in Search of a Soul.*] Zürich: Rascher, 1931.

Maslow, A. H. *The Psychology of Science.* New York: Harper & Row, 1966.

Müller-Freienfels, R. [*The Evolution of Modern Psychology.*] Translated from German typescript by W. B. Wolfe. New Haven: Yale University Press, 1935.

Riesman, D. *The Lonely Crowd.* New Haven: Yale University Press, 1950.

Sartre, J. P. *L'Imaginaire: Psychologie — phenomenologique de l'imagination.* Paris: Gallimard, 1940.

Sullivan, H. S. "Conceptions of Modern Psychiatry." *Psychiatry,* 3 (1940), 1–117.

———. *The Interpersonal Theory of Psychiatry.* New York: Norton, 1953.

———. *Schizophrenia as a Human Process.* New York: Norton, 1962.

Veblen, T. *The Theory of the Leisure Class.* New York: Macmillan, 1899.

Wittels, F. [*Sigmund Freud, His Personality, Teaching, and School.*] Leipzig: Tal Varlag, 1924.

NOTE: A list of further readings appears at the back of the book.

Part Four

CURRENT
TRENDS
AND
DISCIPLINES
IN
PSYCHOLOGY

20

Psychology of Learning

There can be indefinitely more "mind" accumulated as time goes on, now that we have the trick.

JAMES HARVEY ROBINSON

Much of nineteenth- and early twentieth-century psychology revolved around various conceptualizations of the observable and measurable in mental life and behavior. Earlier ideas of the mind gave way to arguments that the mind be reduced to its elements, that mental be reduced to behavioral and behavioral to physiological. There were those who believed that psychology must contend with the purely psychological, and others who insisted that explanation in psychology will have to go hand in hand with explanation in biology, anatomy, and physiology. The learning process occupied a focal point in these arguments.

The achievements of nineteenth-century neurology and neurophysiology, as we have seen in Chapter 8, had greatly influenced the growth of psychology as an experimental science, but the first "physiological" and "anatomical" theories of learning had long antedated these advances. When Plato [1] described the mind as a block of wax into which sensory experiences can be imprinted, he referred, even if only by way of analogy and for the purpose of refutation, to organic correlates of memory. Similarly, when Locke reintroduced this argument (the *tabula rasa* hypothesis) into modern psychology, he too sought to understand memory by figurative reference to organic factors. Long before this time, Aristotle had already changed this approach to the organic by analogy in his proposal of specific anatomical location and physiological mechanisms for memory. He believed that experience is transmitted by the blood and that memory is stored in the heart. It was but a short step from this to Galen's suggestion that memories are stored in the brain, which, stripped of the reference to ventricles of the brain, remains the foundation of neuroanatomy and neurophysiology to our day.

[1] See Hamilton and Cairns, eds. (1961, 191c, 193b–196a).

Descartes also devoted a great deal of attention to the specific anatomical location of the mind and body interaction; he believed it to be the pineal gland. Movements in this gland, he argued, correspond to sense impressions; they send "animal spirits" through the pores of the brain and deposit traces for later recall. From Descartes on, there has been a close relationship between theoretical advances in leading natural sciences and ideas in explaining the learning process. The brain became firmly established as the anatomical seat of memory and the transmission of sensory information, and the functional processes of memory storage within the brain became a central conception.

Hartley (1749) applied the Newtonian theory of moving particles to the problem and suggested that vibrations in the white medullary substance of the brain form the basis for memory. He believed that sensations modify natural vibration patterns — repeated identical sensory experiences resulting in retention of modified patterns. With Hartley, the psychology of learning arrived at the issue of functional relationship between practice and retention and the issue of specific neurophysiological correlates of learning and memory. These issues have remained with us ever since.

With nineteenth-century advances in neuroanatomy and neurophysiology, the problems of a functional division in the brain and of the conducting properties of neural tissue became central to the study of learning. Bain (1855), for example, declared that every habit, sensory impression, or chain of ideas is associated with growth at the nerve junction. The neuron theory (see p. 120) led the way, from earlier speculative postulates on the location and mechanisms of memory, to specific neuroanatomical and neurochemical studies of neural-impulse transmission — particularly at the point of junction between discontinuous neurons. The possibility of experiential modification of impulse conduction at the synaptic junction provided the central model for subsequent psychological and physiological theories of learning. We will return to the latter in Chapter 22, with a discussion of historical backgrounds and current developments in comparative and physiological psychology. Now we turn to the recent history of psychological conceptions of the learning process.

All "schools" and systematic viewpoints of early twentieth-century psychology necessarily took a position regarding the learning process. More-or-less complete expositions of "learning theories" can be found in the work of the later adherents to practically all the major psychology systems outlined in the preceding chapters of this book. It may be argued that Freud, and psychoanalysis in general, neglected learning theory. If so, this is largely because Freud's approach to affect, fixation, transference, and so on, and his use of the developmental method, emphasized areas neglected by most previous psychological schools. Psychoanalysis made its richest contributions where other systems were silent. It had, so to speak, entered the psychology of learning by the back door. Gestalt psychology, which began in the perception-cognition field, also invaded learning theory through the back door; and only because Köhler and later Koffka, and later still Wertheimer, found that the whole contemporary conception of learning was, from their point of view, rotten-ripe for radical reconsideration. Phenomenology and humanistic psychology continued to remain, in general, impatient with learning theory, because most learning theory had placed emphasis on details which appeared to them basically irrelevant to the essentials of the human way of approaching reality.

Learning theory has become a major component in that part of contemporary systematic psychology which arose from early associationism and behaviorism. Nevertheless, the contemporary psychology of learning cannot be confined within the limits of a single school, or approach, or system. Having an extensive many-sided experimental literature, of which even the compressed summary (Hilgard and Bower, 1966) is a large book-length undertaking, the contemporary psychology of learning incorporates many of the leads hinted at by the various schools early in our century and branches out into a myriad of conceptual and methodological subsystems.

We see today a progressively accelerating trend, in which the polarized schools of an earlier era have all but disappeared. They are being replaced by well-circumscribed experimental disciplines, which are centered in limited behavioral areas, methodological approaches, and theoretical issues. In this book we are trying to show the recent historical origin and contemporary state of understanding of the learning process. We will draw, with necessarily large and unfinished strokes, the picture of contemporary issues and approaches that comprise the current field as one aspect of the totality of modern psychology. At first we will look at those major psychologists who shaped, during the first half of our century, the various psychological approaches to the problem of learning: Thorndike, Guthrie, Tolman, Hull, and Skinner.

As Thorndike early in this century had made clear, and as Guthrie later emphasized, the facts of the learning process are facts about a process of "connections." The making and breaking of connections are the essential observable facts that have to be explained. For the most part, throughout the history of psychology the S-S (sensory impression to sensory impression) connection was of most interest; but usually with a comfortable place provided for the S-R (stimulus-response), as, for example, in Locke and Hartley. Pavlov, considering himself a physiologist rather than a psychologist, nevertheless also caused reflexes to be produced by adventitious stimuli in new S-R patterns. Gestalt psychology, objecting strenuously to the apparent automatism of the S-R relation, used a conception of S-S thinking arrived at in Köhler's insight experiments. But the Gestaltists made the response essential to the functioning of the S-S pattern, just as Guthrie used the concept of "movement-produced stimuli" and Tolman and others used "feedback" concepts to maintain the cycle of action from one S-R pattern to the next.

"Connectionism," Thorndike's preferred word, is not far from a bull's-eye definition of what modern learning theory is about. Throughout the history of psychology, as Guthrie (1952) has reminded us, psychologists have emphasized connections: connections between situations and acts; connections between acts and other acts; connections between perceptions and other perceptions; connections between thoughts and other thoughts. Psychologists have also noted the peculiarly intimate and important relations between these connections and their affective qualities of delight and distress—the relationships between the acts which these associations prompt and the joys or woes to which they lead. In other words, associationism and psychological hedonism have always been with us. Within the womb of associationism has been the connectionism of Thorndike and Guthrie, the free association and primary-process dynamics of Freud, the formal systematic learning theory of Hull, the structured insight learning of Köhler, and the sign-Gestalt learning of Tolman. Some of these theories, most notably Guthrie's conditioning by contiguity, are pure associationism. Others, like Freud's and Köhler's, subordinate the connection principle to other principles. But all need the principle of connections, because just as the impulses within the nervous systems are connecting and integrating, so do all systems at the psychological level call loudly for the recognition of the role of connection.

Thorndike's Reinforcement Theory and Guthrie's Conditioning by Contiguity

The British evolutionist C. Lloyd Morgan lectured at Harvard to the students of William James. There, the young and alert E. L. Thorndike caught the message as it was related to animal learning processes. His first experiments were upon chickens, dogs, and cats. Shortly afterward he improvised an animal laboratory at Columbia University, where, with Cattell's approval, the work continued.

The problem most extensively studied was the nature of the animal learning curve. A cat was placed, for example, in a cage which could be opened only by striking a latch or button, and a piece of fish was placed outside. Biting, clawing, and scurrying ensued, followed at last by the accidental movement which set the animal free. On a later trial the same general behavior followed, and so on in each new test. However, the total time required to get out, though fluctuating, showed a consistent tendency to decrease. When the number of practice days was indicated on the x axis and the number of minutes required to complete an act on the y axis, the learning curve was found to fall rapidly at first, then more and more gradually, until a limit, a horizontal line, was reached, indicating the animal's complete mastery of the task. Such a curve obviously corresponded to the learning curves for telegraphy previously reported by Bryan and Harter (1897). The latter, though measuring in terms of accomplishment per unit of time rather than in terms of time per unit of accomplishment, had pointed to the same conclusion: the principle of diminishing returns with practice. Both curves were, in respect to this principle, similar to Ebbinghaus's curves of forgetting.

It appeared clear from Thorndike's curves that sudden insight into the nature of the task was rare or indeed entirely absent. There was no sudden and permanent drop in the curve indicating that the cat had "solved" the problem. The cat started with random movements, which were gradually eliminated as practice went on; the time taken to strike the latch necessarily decreased. Thorndike saw, as had Spencer and Bain before him, the importance of such "random" movements in leading to the discovery of the "right" response. For this kind of behavior the term "trial and error" was soon in general use. Even in the monkey, Thorndike reported learning to be of this general type. He found no clear cases of insight or imitation.[2]

Thorndike did not himself concentrate on the physiological process underlying learning. The general physiological conceptions of the time, arising from the neurophysiological discoveries in the late nineteenth century, and from Pavlov's work on conditioning, were nevertheless utilized by Thorndike in his formulations of a variety of psychological laws of learning. These were offered in *The Elements of Psychology* (1905) and later elaborated upon in *The Psychology of Learning* (1913), and later still in *The Fundamentals of Learning* (1932). Perhaps the most noteworthy among these laws was Thorndike's *law of effect,* which deals with the strengthening or weakening of connections as a result of experience and reinforcement. Satisfaction following an act was said to strengthen a bond, resulting in the higher likelihood of the new occurrence of response; whereas *annoyance* tended to weaken the bond, hence diminishing the likelihood of response. The *law of readiness,* an accessory to the *law of effect,* stated the circumstances under which an act is satisfying or annoying. The *law of exercise* stated that use strengthens and disuse weakens established bonds between sensory impressions and impulses to act. This law was later modified in the light of new evidence which showed that practice influences learning only because it brings into play other more direct mechanisms, such as the effects of reward and punishment. During the later period in his career Thorndike concentrated almost exclusively on the law of effect. He took the position that reward and punishment influence not only the reinforced stimulus-response connection but "spread" to the adjacent ones both preceding and following the primary connection. While relinquishing some of his earlier accessory laws, such as the law of exercise, he made a new concession to the Gestalt approach by acknowledging the role of stimulus membership, *belongingness,* in connection formation.

One of the relatively minor laws in Thorndike's system, the *law of associ-*

---

[2] We do, of course, know from the later work of Köhler and others that there are such things as imitation and insight in the monkey, or for that matter in organisms as lowly as the rat (see p. 318).

ative shifting, stated that when two stimuli are present and one elicits a response, the other acquires the capacity to elicit the same response. This law is very close to the Pavlovian classical conditioning paradigm and became the single central postulate in the learning theory of Guthrie.

Guthrie was a systematizer of the Watsonian tradition (see p. 245), who abhorred anything even slightly suggesting an interpretation in terms of mental, conscious, or subjective phenomena. Association of stimulus and response by contiguity was the central thesis in Guthrie's system. Upon this he built a learning theory and managed to avoid not only the use of mentalistic concepts, but also of the concepts of drive, reward, and punishment as well. Even the obvious influence of practice upon learning was disposed of by Guthrie; he argued that a stimulus-response association gains full strength on its first full occurrence. Increases in the number of such associations alone, not the strength or weakness in the individual bond, explain observable increases in performance after practice, he argued. What about drives and reinforcement, the readiness of the organism to act, and the influence of the outcome of an act in leading to satisfaction or pain? All these, and some other factors that must be taken into account in the study of learning, were explained by Guthrie in terms of movement-produced internal stimuli. It should be recalled that this was Watson's device also in dealing, and not very successfully we may note, with the complex processes of speech.

Since, according to Guthrie, there is nothing to weaken or strengthen an established associative bond, naturally there can be no forgetting either. What then with the clearly observable decrease in performance after prolonged disuse or lack of practice? These, Guthrie argued, are due to the formation of new bonds which are incompatible with the original bond. Motivational states, dealt with by Thorndike in his *law of readiness,* were retained in Guthrie's system only as accessory influences; they were believed to influence learning only indirectly, through increasing the frequency and vigor of movements. Reward was regarded by Guthrie as relevant only to the mechanical arrangement of stimulus presentation. Reward removes the organism from a stimulus situation at the end of a series of acts, he argued, and thereby preserves the contiguity between the last act and last stimulus by preventing formation of new incompatible associations.

Guthrie presented his mechanistic conceptions of learning in numerous publications. He was a master at illustrating his points with colorful examples from complex situations of human learning. Perhaps it was because of the contradiction between his insistence on hard, simple, mechanistic, and all-encompassing principles and his absorbing interest in complex forms of human behavior that he never offered a single concise summary of his learning theory. This was undertaken by one of his students, Virginia Voeks (1950).

Tolman's Sign-Gestalt Theory of Learning

The purposivism of McDougall and the behaviorism of Thorndike and Guthrie made their mark on E. C. Tolman, who began in the 1920s, as a student of animal learning, to formulate a systematic "purposive behaviorism." This envisaged in all animal and human learning a basic goal-seeking trend. With the white rat as his subject, he maintained, for thirty years at the University of California at Berkeley, a vigorous program of pursuing the role and development of "cognitive maps," "sign learning," and "intervening variables," which were part of a bold cognitive psychology far indeed from both its earlier behavioristic and purposivistic origins.

While it is fairly easy to classify students of learning into the two main groups, those accepting the associationist tradition and those rejecting it in favor of some Gestalt-like principle, the classification breaks down in the case of Tolman (1932). Agreeing with McDougall as to the need for a *purposive* approach and with the behaviorists as to the need for objective observations, he emphasized, in a long-range program in comparative psychology, the structural aspects of the learning situation: the capacity of the organism to respond purposefully and selectively to its environment. He gave reason to believe that the organism perceives various objects as means toward goals; in fact, that its cognitive life is complex, orderly, and saturated with meanings, exactly as the Gestalt psychologists had maintained. Between stimuli and observed responses it was necessary (as with Hull) to interpolate a series of "intervening variables" in the light of which responses became intelligible. The nature of these variables had to be tested by experiment. But these factors were very different from those postulated by most behaviorists. They are not easily summarized. Note, for example, that "behavior-supports" are "characters in the environment required by behavior acts in order that they may go off without disruption."[3] More specifically, behavior-supports divide into discriminanda, manipulanda, and means-end relations. Organisms are constantly responding not just to stimuli, but to *sign-Gestalts;* and a sign-Gestalt is a "complex behavior-support, consisting of a sign object, a signified object, and a signified means-end relation." All these concepts are systematically employed in devising crucial experimental tests and in integrating earlier work.

Clearly, then, stimuli do not simply *act upon* the organism; the organism is oriented to use them. Far from admitting that sheer satisfyingness automatically stamps in behavior, Tolman offered a long series of experiments to show that goals serve to give meaning to the various objects in the environment. Electric shock, for example, may serve as an "emphasizer." The explanation of learning in terms of conditioning was attacked by Tolman on

[3] Disruption is "a breakdown and upset in behavior produced when some change, not previously met, is introduced into a given environment."

various grounds: he pointed to the fact that the responses to the conditioned stimulus need not be at all the same as the response to the original unconditioned stimulus. Eating is an appropriate response to food, but not to an alley in a maze; the rat does not eat the alley, but enters it. Conditioning, according to Tolman, is not simply the establishment of a new stimulus-response connection; it is the building up of a "sign-Gestalt expectation." Outstandingly important in the Tolman approach has been the insistence that living organisms set up expectations and that they are capable of *inventive* learning. Especially influential here was the early suggestion of Krechevsky (1932) that even a rat sets up "hypotheses" about ways to solve his problem and that it tests the hypotheses as it proceeds. Though failing to convince fully the behaviorally oriented, such a conception did much to emphasize the possibility that the cognitive life of animals, as well as their motor behavior, needed to be brought into experimental contact with the psychology of human beings.

Enough has perhaps been said to show why Tolman's approach was neither ordinary purposivism nor ordinary behaviorism, and why he said that despite his own need for "*analyzed* variables," he would have been proud to join the Gestaltists' fold. He was a "molar," not a "molecular," behaviorist; he sought objectivity in the study of purposive wholes. His associationism certainly belongs with the behaviorist trend; it rejected introspection as a method for psychological analysis. The unity of mental events, however, played a significant part in it through the device of intervening variables, which were to be inferred from and correlated with observable environmental and behavioral events. Tolman insisted that behavior has its distinct characteristics, which can be identified (even if by inference) and described independent of the underlying neural, muscular, or glandular processes in the organism. In this also, of course, Tolman belongs to the behaviorist school, whose adherents had long emphasized that behavior is to be understood in its own terms, rather than in terms of reduction to anatomy or physiology. Like Thorndike and Guthrie before him, Tolman was not against using neural conceptions as analogies. But it is clear that they all talked about psychology, not physiology—about impulses to action and about connections between observed or inferred psychological units of overt and covert behavior.

While Tolman's system was purposivistic, he went to great pains to avoid any hint of teleological implications. His purposivism simply implied that behavior is regulated by observable, objectively describable end products which, however, did not imply for him any reversed order of causative determinants. In a more recent perspective, Tolman should be regarded as first among those who recognized essential differences between functional and antecedent-causative explanations. Many current issues of feedback-loop and cybernetic models can, in a sense, be traced back to Tolman. Not all the possible problems of teleology have been eliminated from the psy-

chology of today, but the considerable advances that have been made originated mainly in Tolman's system. The Tolman left behind the purely mecha-
nistic-deterministic behaviorism of Watson and Guthrie, and even the hedonistic behaviorism of Thorndike, precisely by perceiving the possibility
of an objective approach to goal-seeking aspects of behavior and by recognizing the overriding importance of feedback from an accomplished act
upon the formation and the strengthening of behavior.

Tolman may also be regarded as the founding father of cognitive psychology. His emphasis upon intervening variables resounded widely through
the whole world of learning theories of his time. The paper by MacCorquodale and Meehl (1948) made clear that a great deal was at stake in the use of
such variables. The execution of a response may be conceptualized as a
simple S-R connection, or as having a complex intervening pattern of "hypothetical constructs" rooted in identifiable physiological variables or "intervening psychological variables" which demand no concrete physiological
identification. This is part of what Hilgard means by saying that a special
language, a special system of constructs, has come into the psychology of
learning which is usable by most psychologists who wish to study learning in
the laboratory, and that the battle between the "schools," so intense during
the twenties and thirties, is greatly muted today.

Hull's Reinforcement Theory

The early years of the twentieth century offered two formidable systematic psychologies of the learning process, both associationist in spirit
and reductionist in style. The Pavlovian conditioning paradigm provided the
tool for a deductive method in which the operation of higher neural mechanisms and neurophysiological processes were to be inferred from controlled,
objective, observable stimulus-response associations. Thorndike's law of
effect combined earlier hedonistic principles with systematic approaches of
the early twentieth century, and, buttressed with the great achievements of
experimental deductive method, it resulted in Hull's work – in a tight system of specific definitions, theories, and postulates. It is impossible to do
justice here to an elaborate theory of this type.

Clark L. Hull's system was presented in three major publications: *Principles of Behavior* (1943), *Essentials of Behavior* (1951), and *A Behavior
System* (1952). There are seventeen postulates and seventeen corollaries in
the final form of this system, which define, as symbolic interacting units:
(1) unlearned stimulus-response connections and sensory capacities that the
organism brings to a situation prior to learning; (2) processes of motivation
and drive state that enable effective reinforcement of behavior to occur; (3)
laws of habit formation; (4) factors outside the associative process which
influence the elicitation of responses; (5) reactive and conditioned inhibition
of response tendencies; (6) factors that complicate both habit strength and

response tendencies when more than one stimulus has been associated with the same response through reinforcement; (7) factors that complicate the excitatory properties of stimuli when more than one stimulus is presented at a time; (8) variations in the constants employed in learning formulas due to individual differences.

A principle of reinforcement is the cornerstone of this system. In its initial form Hull's reinforcement hypothesis stated that a response is strengthened by the satisfaction of a basic need or drive. Later, under the influence of Miller and Dollard's emphasis on the drive stimuli (1941) rather than the drive states themselves, Hull shifted the argument from satisfaction of basic needs to manipulation of drive stimuli. Thus, in avoidance-learning the avoidance of painful sensation, rather than the satisfaction of an underlying need to escape injury, became the important response reinforcer. Both drive state and drive stimuli were regarded by Hull as intervening variables. They were fed into the system as symbolic units to be treated in elaborate mathematical formulas of functional relationships between stimulation and responses. These symbolic units were not conceived to refer to physiological or biochemical mechanisms, but rather to psychological factors inferred from observable input/output variables. Tight mathematical use of such symbolic units formed the basic logic of the system.

Hull's approach dominated psychological conceptions of learning for nearly thirty years, and his system was applied to the investigation of practically all the known problems of learning. Spence (1940, 1956), for example, was very successful in applying this system to the problem of discrimination learning. Here the issue revolved around the question of whether learning to discriminate between two stimuli is based primarily on *continuity* between past and present associative processes, or whether there is a break of continuity in learning as the organism shifts from one systematic mode of behavior to another and achieves in the process a new level of integration—a new insight. The latter position had been defended by Tolman and his followers, especially Krech. But Spence took the position of continuity; through ingenious application of the Hullian principles he arrived at a complex but highly predictive theory regarding the interaction of generalization gradients and reinforcement-related excitatory and inhibitory potentials in discrimination learning. Despite such successful efforts, Hull's approach was not uniformly respected. The irreconcilable differences between the then-current systems, particularly the persisting differences between the Gestalt and behavioristic interpretations of behavior, prevented the emergence of a single generally acceptable theory of learning. Hull's system received criticism from various quarters on various grounds. There were criticisms aimed at Hull's insistence on the role of reinforcement and at his emphasis on a drive-reduction principle. There were also objections from those who unequivocally accepted the use of symbolic units, rational constructs, and mathematical approaches in psychological theorizing. For them Hull was not mathematical enough; his mathematical approaches and symbolic constructs did not amount to more than the mere fitting of available data to empirical curves of limited generality. This did not satisfy the new demand for true rational constructs of wide mathematical generality and independent manipulative power. Time moved on and bypassed Hull's mechanistic mathematico-deductive approach to psychological phenomena. There are no extensive experimental programs today based on Hull's system, a system which only two decades ago was at the very heart of learning psychology.

But time has also shown that, while not entirely amenable to the rigorous symbolic treatment of the kind attempted by Hull, behavior is a proper subject matter for refined mathematical approaches; and that, at the same time, the study of behavior can make significant strides even in purely data-oriented, antitheoretical approaches, such as the one put forth by Skinner. Furthermore, current ethological and comparative psychological researches began to show that adaptation is a very complex process indeed, which is influenced by the intricacies of phylogenetic "history" of organisms as much as by ontogenetic history; that the myriads of ways evolution has dealt with environmental problems may not permit uniform cross-species treatment of a general "learning process." Hull's system, we may state with reasonable certainty, has already receded into the world of "historical significance." It made its dent in the development of psychology by providing an approach to emulate; but its specifics have already lost their former challenge.

However, Hull's central emphasis on drive reduction in the learning process persisted for some time and underwent several modifications. The first was Miller and Dollard's switch of emphasis from drive states and drive reduction to experimental manipulation of drive stimuli, which, as we have seen, was incorporated into the later form of Hull's system. Another significant modification was introduced by Mowrer, who argued that the drive-state principle is relevant only to instrumental learning, to trial-and-error learning in which an emitted response is manipulated by reinforcement. He argued that classical conditioning can be fully accounted for by stimulus substitution and associative shift. The resulting categorically different learning processes (*sign learning* for stimulus substitution and *solution learning* for the reinforced trial-and-error processes) and their relationship to general theories of behavior were examined by Mowrer in great detail and force in *Learning Theory and Behavior* (1960) and *Learning Theory and the Symbolic Processes* (1960a). Much of the argument and experimental material examined in these books is still too recent to establish a proper historical perspective for our present context. Similar significant replacements and alternatives to the Hullian approach are being currently developed in the area of mathematical theories and by the Skinnerian approach of operant conditioning.

Mathematical Models and Theories of Learning

The conception of a hypothesis to be tested, so fundamental in the experimental psychology of half a century ago, has gradually taken on new meanings related on the one hand to Fisher's *Design of Experiments* (1935) and on the other to the field-theoretical approach imported from the physical into the biological sciences. It was gradually agreed upon that hypotheses constitute a fraternity of cognitive tools which belong in a system by which a "theory" can be tested. Sometimes "hypothetical constructs," as in Hull's system, or axiomatically accepted working principles, were regarded as underlying the theory which was to be empirically tested. In any event, it was plain that there was need for a method of abstracting and describing the system of interrelated operations that had to be carried out in the process of theory formulation and theory testing. During the period following World War II, usage rapidly consolidated in favor of "mathematical models" in describing the psychological *systems of observables*. The use of the universal language of science—mathematics—required a uniform abstraction and measurement of psychological data. It required a certain maturity of psychological data collection to allow the application of mathematical thinking. At the same time, the application of appropriate mathematical manipulation excluded certain types of problems from the immediate research program. Among those which were amenable to such treatment, precision and consistency became the hallmarks of the effective use of this new tool.

The oldest quantitative data in psychology—as those from perception, from psychophysics, and especially from the learning and forgetting processes—lend themselves actively to this approach. One could ask not only whether the learning curve of nonsense syllables and meaningful material were identical but, going much further, whether the acquisition of knowledge and skills, the removal of interferences, the achievement of insights, all exemplified the same basic curve; whether, if not the same, there were at least available "families" of curves. One could ask what types of mathematical generalizability existed among all learning curves, or indeed among all curves representing functional relationships between environmental aspects and organic activities. The most general questions regarding adaptation, learning, adjustment, growth, and so on, became relevant and symbolically treatable.

Hull's system was certainly the most extensive and most widely acclaimed symbolic approach to problems of learning, but it had not evolved beyond the point of manipulative constructs inferred from observed data. Recent mathematical theorists (Estes, 1950; Bush, 1960) compliment Hull for his efforts to make psychology a hard science; but they also criticize his deficiencies as a mathematical theorist. Hull's was essentially a curve-fitting procedure which dealt with simple exponential functions. He is criticized for his empirico-deductive approach and for the lack of concern in his system for the many mathematically treatable details of learning data.[4] Interestingly, Skinner's objection to Hull was that psychology was not yet ripe for formal theorizing and that there were not enough data as yet for such an exact approach. This position was rejected by many, inside and outside of the field of mathematical theories, with the argument that the primary role of theory is to specify what data should be collected and why, and not the other way around.

Since Ebbinghaus's first systematic treatment of the learning process, there have been many attempts at symbolic formulation of one type or another in a broad effort to establish a generalizable picture of functional relationship between experience and learning performance. Objective measurement of the various factors that enter into learning, and the qualitative mathematical treatment of these factors, were always the focal points in these attempts. It was Thurstone, in 1919, who first undertook the task of establishing a systematic mathematical function between an objective measure of experience and an equally objective measure of learning performance. The available experimental data suggested a learning curve of monotonically increasing function having an asymptote that corresponds to best performance. This is, of course, the same curve Hull later dealt with. The initial attempts at fitting such a general learning curve to available data gradually led, again first in the work of Thurstone, to deriving a function from purely rational-mathematical tools employed here.

Rashevsky's work (1951) in mathematical biology also offered new models for learning. But perhaps because Rashevsky's primary emphasis was on the biological and physiological material, his approach did not appreciably influence those whose interest lay with psychological data. Estes stands out prominently among the latter. The developments he had initiated grew into a sizable field of mathematical approaches to learning and other psychological processes. He put the emphasis on the characteristics of stimulus populations in relation to elicited and acquired responses. The major axiom in his mathematical theory of learning is that the probability of occurrence of a response is equal to the number of available stimulus elements conditioned to that response, divided by the total number of stimulus elements sampled. As Guthrie had before him, Estes assumed a one-trial attachment of a response to a sampled stimulus at the first contiguous occurrence.

The questions that may be raised about Estes's mathematical theory are also in many ways similar to those that have been raised regarding Guthrie's interpretation of learning. The inviting simplicity of the approach may not

---

[4] A similar attitude can be detected also toward Kurt Lewin, who, while introducing a new symbolic approach (field theory) and several new mathematical concepts to psychology, did not himself attempt to use these in a rigorous mathematical approach.

necessarily reflect parsimony, only a limited applicability. It is, of course, by the goodness of fit between the offered theoretical functions and the collected empirical data that the value of this approach is determined. However, in the present form Estes's system seems to leave untouched many problems of individual and cross-species variations. The abstraction of learning as a uniform process (which all current mathematical theories make), independent of minutely differentiated species-typical, developmental, and ecological variables in adaptation, is a brave undertaking indeed. Its promise is as old and as great as Fechner's first thoughts in psychophysics, but it is not without pitfalls.

Mathematical models may be regarded as extensions of the principle of generalization, in two respects: (1) looking for the same formal system of relationships in quite different areas of observation, and (2) stripping the basic functional realities of all contaminating or disturbing features of "concreteness," or of "appeal," to the observer or conceptualizer. They allow highly complex exercise in pure mathematics. They offer, moreover, the possibility that a "general systems theory" may find the same basic model requirements at different levels, from the cellular to the sociological level, or from very simple individual function as exemplified in the "fatigue decrement" in reflex action to the satiation effects in listening to music, or even more broadly to the raising of thresholds or the establishing of higher stimulus barriers in consequence of successive stimulations. Generalization is one of the things that mathematics regularly induces in those who intelligently use it.

It follows therefore that there may be highly generalized psychological or behavioral laws which, when handled in terms of mathematical models, will lead back immediately to similar laws which are patently applicable to the functioning of the central nervous system as such. It is quite possible that mind-body theories, even double-aspect theories, or isomorphic form theories, may actually be advanced by the ways of thinking which develop among the model-builders. Examples appear in Rashevsky's general dynamics of the central nervous system, which is essentially a generalization beyond Köhler's isomorphism of perception and cortex identity of form.

Here we encounter another illustration of the role of a tool or a method upon the extension of a conceptual system. The fact that electronic high-speed computers are now available for the solution of countless intricate problems in organic function means that hundreds of important problems about psychophysiology, and even about the ultimate philosophy of mind-body relations, are coming within the shadow of computer possibilities and mathematics. Programs are already being written for the disentangling of basic psychophysiological functions which, a few years ago, were obscured behind too many "disturbing" variables to be observable. Thus, with a "computer of average transience," one can quickly lay bare a recurrent functional relation between "psychological" or "physiological" phenomena, which must occur under certain conditions but had not been clearly shown until now because of inadequate experimental and conceptual approaches to the control of all relevant variables. Mathematical models move therefore with the tide of progressive instrumental simplification of reality through the removal of such contaminating or disturbing variables, and move back again with the tide when new psychophysiological principles acquire fresh mathematical conceptualization. Models are the handmaids of experiments, and a moment later experiments become the handmaids of the models. Severe devotion to modes of thinking borrowed from physics continues at this writing to strengthen the interdependence of mathematical models and experimental design. There will be some discussion later regarding a variety of protests against this marriage. Here, however, we witness the wedding taking place; the atmosphere in which it is to be judged will depend on the quality of the issues which result.

Skinner's Operant Conditioning

B. F. Skinner is a scion of the tribe of the Galtonians who combined psychological creativeness with an inventor's genius for contriving situations in which new principles can suddenly emerge charmingly and cleanly from the underbrush of complications. Early he combined the delight in seeing what made animals and children tick with a literary ambition which in his late teens he tried hard to satisfy. The fusion of these interests appears in this autobiographical note: "The literary magazine called *The Dial,* to which I subscribed, was publishing articles by Bertrand Russell, and they led me to Russell's book, *Philosophy,* published in 1925, in which he devoted a good deal of time to John B. Watson's *Behaviorism* . . . and in the bookstore in New York I read the store's copy of his *Psychological Care of Infant and Child* between customers" (Skinner, 1967, p. 397). His intense interest in language and literature remained. His *Walden Two* (1948) is a Utopia based on the right habits, written with both scientific accuracy and stylistic charm.

But his main bent was plainly toward an experimental and analytical approach to behavior problems. At Harvard, and later at the University of Minnesota, he produced a behavior system upon which all his subsequent work over thirty years has been premised. One cardinal achievement is the conceptual disentangling of the Pavlovian from the Thorndikian type of learning. Responses are *emitted* or *elicited;* and for most purposes the *elicited* responses pale into insignificance in comparison with the *emitted* responses.

In this behavior system, it is not the explanation, or even the understanding, of the original biological forces within the organism from which the behavior manifestations arise that we seek. Rather, we wait until a specific and clearly defined act occurs, and then we reinforce this act by some carefully predetermined reinforcing agent. For example, we construct a box (the

"Skinner box") that contains simply a horizontal bar which the animal can depress, releasing from a magazine a pellet of food; and now we study not the attachment of a conditioned stimulus to an unconditioned response, but the definable laws under which reinforcements of various sorts operate and the time relations of emitted behavior which enable us to attack problems of the nature of the learning curve, the generalization curve, the extinction curve. All of this is best done by extreme simplification of the environment. Much of the work has been done with the pecking response of the pigeon, which can be very precisely controlled; the pigeon quickly learns to peck at a stimulus, or to discriminate between the stimuli, when the pecking at the right stimulus is reinforced, and a grain is picked up by the pecking. It is the simplicity of the approach and the generalizability of the principles so obtained which drew most admiration.

Two of these broad principles, which were implicit already in Thorndike's conception of learning, were now brought clearly to light: the principle of "schedules of reinforcement" and the principle of "shaping." It was discovered that the rapidity of learning, the generalization of the learning to new situations, and the extinction of the learned response depended directly and predictably upon the schedule of reinforcement (for example, whether the reinforcement was given after *each* act, such as bar-pressing or pecking, which had been selected as the response to be acquired, or whether there were to be periodic reinforcements, such as reinforcement after two, or five, appropriate emitted responses, the rest of the responses being unreinforced, or whether irregular and "unpredictable" reinforcement schedules were to be used). The rat or pigeon was often induced to hold to a habit for a very long time if reinforcements were not invariably attached to the specific rewarded act. A higher control of the learning and extinction processes had been achieved. The principle of "shaping," already stressed by Thorndike and in wide use among animal trainers, stated that reinforcement is not held back until the desired act has occurred, but is given for anything related to or part of the desired response. To put this in the vernacular, "If you want to teach a seal to play baseball, you don't wait until he knocks a home run and then toss him a bit of fish; every time he lunges toward the bat or rolls his eyes at the ball, the bit of fish is his." Patterns are built. The components are molded or sculptured into the desired or remotely imagined goal response. Skinner's system is full of flexible extensions of these two principles.

It is largely for these reasons that among normal children, as well as disturbed, defective, and other groups of children, the learning process has been expedited by "operant-conditioning" procedures. It proved relatively simple to deal with unfortunate habits by reinforcement schedules in which candy, chewing gum, cigarettes, or a kind word ("social reinforcement") replaced the routines and the lectures, scoldings and punishments ordinarily available for children or youth who misbehave. Operant-conditioning programs became widely used in institutions for defective and disturbed children and for mentally disturbed adults.

But the main concern was really not with troubled children but with the ordinary range of normal children and youth whose learning can be made enormously more agreeable and enormously more effective. Settings can be so planned that children can attack the problems in which they are interested, getting either external satisfactions or the intrinsic satisfactions of doing what they can do, and be "promoted" by going on to the next task. They can, in this way, receive not mechanized but individualized or personally "programmed" instructions. The use of "teaching machines," offered earlier by Pressey (1926), finds here a sympathetic note of response, for Skinner has been one of the imaginative inventors of teaching machines —not primarily as a labor-saving device, but as a device for building in satisfactions, that is, reinforcements, at appropriate points, to permit less misery and blockage, more palatable and effective work.

If the issues had remained at this level, Skinner would be generally regarded as one of the great benefactors not only of psychology but of the human race. Unfortunately, as seen at least from the present vantage point, the issue has been sliding back to the old questions of whether man is in fact a machine and of whether the use of rewards and punishments will work better in this sophisticated form than it can in the older ways. It was John Stuart Mill's father who taught him by a strict and systematic reinforcement schedule. As mentioned earlier, the question ultimately arose for Mill of whether arbitrary satisfactions from external rewards could ever take the place of deep preoccupation with the mainsprings of conduct. For Skinner there is no legitimate question about such deep mainsprings; one waits for the response, inscrutable as it may be, and then reinforces it. There also arises incidentally the question here of who decides to reward what. These issues remain, since no one knows what ultimate human nature is or who should decide what would be satisfaction for it. Even in a purely scientific perspective, the questions remain: How and why should a clever technological manipulation of the learning process replace its theoretical understanding? In Skinner's hands behavioral engineering and the implementation of practical know-how acquired an overriding legitimacy. But the cultish antitheoretical chorus of his followers is something else again; it is already laden with a suffocating air of irrelevance.[5]

Many an evaluator can, however, allow himself a word of positive response to Skinner. His conception of "shaping" offers profound possibilities in planning and moving from an unfortunate and frustrating situation to a fortunate and satisfying situation. It is Skinner, unafraid of competition with

[5] Skinner's latest and widely discussed book (*Beyond Freedom and Dignity*, New York: Knopf, 1971), which appeared after these lines were written, leaves us still wondering about the answers to these questions.

simple men, who has pursued this magnificently sensible idea to the point of suggesting a way to a more comfortable manner of acting. If the same wisdom went into the problem of contriving a goal worth attaining, a goal worthy of the fine imagination of *Walden Two,* and related to the intrinsic human needs which will remain after all current learning theories are gone, it would be excitingly worthwhile.

American psychology during the period between the two world wars was ready to use both behavioral research tools and the behavioristic approaches to a general philosophy of the organism. Pavlov's ideas were a bit simplistic, and Watson had not done very well in making classical conditioning a *vade mecum* to the world of psychology. But Skinner was a symbol, very generally respected, and many hoped for a richer approach to human nature than either Pavlov or Watson could offer. The appearance of Skinner's *The Behavior of Organisms* in 1938 produced more than enthusiasm; it was soon obviously serving as a pacemaker for all who had objectivist or, to speak more philosophically, behavioristic inclinations. Widely read psychologists were soon quoting Skinner right and left, and with the advent of successful textbooks such as the one by Keller and Schoenfeld (1950), the Skinnerian system was ready either to preempt the field or act as guide wherever the individual instructor felt able to follow. As had been the case with Watson, Skinner had to carry the responsibility for specific research concepts and methods, but he also had to carry the onus or the glory, as one sees it, of representing "materialism," "mechanism," or "hardnosed science," or whatever one likes to call this pole of modern psychology, in opposition to the personalists or humanists or broadly intuitive, as represented, for example, by C. R. Rogers, G. W. Allport, or A. H. Maslow.

What is new, then, in the learning psychology of the last quarter century? The articulation of learning theory with all of systematic psychology led to the elucidation and experimental analysis of many problems regarding hypothetical constructs and intervening variables. But, as the strict polarization of schools and systems gave way both to a growing eclecticism and an increasing specialization in the concern with issues common to all, so did the systematic but polarized concerns with intervening psychological variables give way to the new search for and discoveries regarding the role of the nervous system in learning. At the same time, the vigorous development of reinforcement theory, especially of schedules of reinforcement and shaping techniques, though long known to animal trainers in a rudimentary way, has been raised to the dignity of a systematic position. Next in importance comes the very sophisticated analytical and experimental work on quantitative psychological parameters of the learning process as expressed in the world of mathematical models. Likewise there are new social perspectives (see pp. 339, 411) in which it is recognized that the deep cultural and personal readiness or unreadiness to learn depend heavily on the perceptual and affective learning experiences in early life, which make a great deal of difference to the learner's capacity to adjust to a learning situation. We will return to these issues later in the chapters on development and on perceptual and cognitive functions; and in the chapter on comparative and physiological psychology we shall try to show how the functions of the nervous system are conceived to be related to the principles of learning.

REFERENCES

Bain, A. *The Senses and the Intellect*. London: Parker, 1855.

Bryan, W. L., and Harter, N. "Studies in the Physiology and Psychology of Telegraphic Language." *Psychological Review,* 4 (1897), 27–53.

Bush, R. R. "A Survey of Mathematical Learning Theory." In R. D. Luce, ed. *Developments in Mathematical Psychology*. Glencoe, Ill.: Free Press, 1960.

Estes, W. K. "Toward a Statistical Theory of Learning." *Psychological Review,* 57 (1950), 94–107.

Fisher, R. A. *Design of Experiments*. Edinburgh: Oliver and Boyd, 1935.

Guthrie, E. R. *The Psychology of Learning*. Rev. ed. New York: Harper & Row, 1952.

Hamilton, E., and Cairns, H., eds. *The Collected Dialogues of Plato*. New York: Pantheon, 1961.

Hartley, D. *Observations on Man, His Frame, His Duty and His Expectations*. London: Johnson, 1749.

Hilgard, E. R., and Bower, G. H. *Theories of Learning*. 3rd ed. New York: Appleton-Century-Crofts, 1966.

Hull, C. L. *Principles of Behavior*. New York: Appleton-Century-Crofts, 1943.

———. *Essentials of Behavior*. New Haven: Yale University Press, 1951.

———. *A Behavior System: An Introduction to Behavior Theory Concerning the Individual Organism*. New Haven: Yale University Press, 1952.

Keller, F. S., and Schoenfeld, W. N. *Principles of Psychology*. New York: Appleton-Century-Crofts, 1950.

Krechevsky, I. " 'Hypotheses' in Rats." *Psychological Review,* 39 (1932), 516–32.

MacCorquodale, K., and Meehl, P. E. "On a Distinction Between Hypothetical Constructs and Intervening Variables." *Psychological Review,* 55 (1948), 95–107.

Mill, J. S. *Autobiography*. London: Longmans, 1873.

Miller, N. E., and Dollard, J. *Social Learning and Imitation*. New Haven: Yale University Press, 1941.

Mowrer, O. H. *Learning Theory and Behavior*. New York: Wiley, 1960.

———. *Learning Theory and the Symbolic Processes*. New York: Wiley, 1960a.

Pressey, S. L. "A Simple Apparatus Which Gives Tests and Scores – and Teaches." *School and Society,* 23 (1926), 373–76.

Rashevsky, N. *The Mathematical Biology of Social Behavior*. Chicago: University of Chicago Press, 1951.

Skinner, B. F. *The Behavior of Organisms*. New York: Appleton-Century-Crofts, 1938.

———. *Walden Two*. New York: Macmillan, 1948.

Skinner, B. F. *Science and Human Behavior.* New York: Macmillan, 1953.

———. "B. F. Skinner." In E. G. Boring and G. Lindzey, eds. *A History of Psychology in Autobiography.* Vol. 5. New York: Appleton-Century-Crofts, 1967.

Spence, K. W. "Continuous Versus Non-Continuous Interpretations of Discrimination Learning." *Psychological Review,* 47 (1940), 271–88.

———. *Behavior Theory and Conditioning.* New Haven: Yale University Press, 1956.

Thorndike, E. L. *The Elements of Psychology.* New York: Seiler, 1905.

———. *The Psychology of Learning.* (*Educational Psychology,* Vol. 2.) New York: Teachers College, Columbia University Press, 1913.

———. *The Fundamentals of Learning.* New York: Teachers College, Columbia University Press, 1932.

Thurstone, L. L. "The Learning Curve Equation." *Psychological Monographs,* 26 (1919), 1–51.

Tolman, E. C. *Purposive Behavior in Animals and Men.* New York: Appleton-Century, 1932.

Voeks, V. W. "Formalization and Clarification of a Theory of Learning." *Journal of Psychology,* 30 (1950), 341–62.

Waldeyer, H. W. von. "Ueber Einige Neurere Forschungen im Gebiete der Anatomie des Centralnervensystems." *Deutsche medizinische Wochenschrift,* 17 (1891), 1213–18, 1244–46, 1287–89, 1331–32, 1352–56.

Watson, J. B. *Behaviorism.* New York: Norton, 1924.

———. *Psychological Care of Infant and Child.* New York: Norton, 1928.

NOTE: A list of further readings appears at the back of the book.

21

Sensory, Perceptual, and Cognitive Functions

. . . sensation is nothing but a direct connection of the mind with the external world; it is the transformation of energy of external excitation into a mental state.

LENIN

Among the scenes which are deeply impressed on my mind, none exceed in sublimity the primeval forests undefaced by the hand of man. No one can stand in these solitudes unmoved, and not feel there is more in man than the mere breath of his body.

DARWIN

The concepts and methods of a sensory psychology have been with us since Aristotle. While sensing, perceiving, judging, and remembering were greatly stressed by early Greek psychology, notably by the atomists, it was Aristotle who explicitly differentiated between sensory and motor functions, asked what sense organs are, defined the difference between the sensory and perceptual functions, and went on to suggest that sensory modalities of information about the environment are transcended by percept and thought. He described sense organs and their functions in many forms of life. He saw the relation of imagination, and therefore of reproductive thinking, to the residues of sense impressions: "Imagination is decaying sense," he stated. Hobbes, Locke, and Hartley presupposed the sensory basis of the contents of consciousness. Quite aside from what man can *do* with sensations or their residues (the images), most psychologists have held that we must *begin* with them, essentially as did Condillac.

This kind of sensory psychology was enriched by the nineteenth-century studies of the sense organs from an anatomical, physiological, and psychological point of view. The first great journal of psychology was the *Zeitschrift für Psychologie und Physiologie der Sinnesorgane,* the journal for the psychology and physiology of the sense organs. The study of the senses was the labor of anatomists, physiologists, embryologists, histologists, zoologists; all, whether they were psychologists or not, began with the primordial stuff, conscious qualities which the senses bring. They were all concerned with the contact which living things make with their environments through specialized receptor cells, grouped and housed in appropriate form to bring into the organism kinds of energy which could be adaptively useful. This meant that the evolutionary theory, greatly strengthened, gave context to and supported the perspectives of a sensory psychology.

One other younger biological science of our own century which should be freshly stressed here is biochemistry, for it was the chemistry of environmental action upon receptor cells, and of the nerve impulse generated inward from such stimulation, that made possible the more refined quantitative study of the relation of stimulation to response. It made possible the study of the specific receptors which mediate specific qualities of experience, supplying new context for the "specific-energies" doctrine (see p. 89). It made possible the determination of thresholds for excitation and for awareness of stimuli. In the chemical senses, for example, we have learned to relate concentrations of chemical substances to the detection of particular stimulus agents, with just concern for anatomy and physiology in the same analysis.

"Sensory psychology" has not gotten lost back there in the nineteenth century; it continues to deliver extraordinarily significant knowledge for the understanding of adaptive functions. The movement of a bat in a dark room has been related to the use of ultrasonic receptor functions, while Frisch's (1954) studies of the signaling system of bees has made it possible to show the evolutionary role of very refined responses to very refined stimulus movements from other individuals of the species. Recently the emphasis has been switched from the "qualities of experience" to the "information supplied" by sensory signals. Parallel to relatively simple phylogenetic comparisons of the sensory systems of different species there has gone on a series of increasingly more sophisticated studies which have shown that human sensitivities are vastly more delicate than could have been imagined even a few decades ago. With the study of the response to very faint visual, auditory, tactual, and other exteroceptive stimulation, there has come about an awareness of man's utter need for continuous messages of considerable complexity. He is, as it were, bathed in a sea of sensory stimulation without which he is incapable of normal functioning.

Sensory Deprivation and Enrichment

The issue was first brought boldly before the scientific world by studies under the direction of Hebb (see p. 354) and a research team at McGill

University (Bexton *et al.*, 1954), which studied men in isolation booths. They wore goggles which permitted no visual perception; their ears and nostrils were stuffed; heavy cardboard splints and heavy boots permitted little by way of joint and foot movements; they sat alone. After a few hours they might hallucinate, they might begin to be nervous, or they might become frightened. The experience of being cut off from sensory stimulation proved to be anything but restful. Most of them refused, indeed, to go back. From this study onward, dozens of investigations of sensory isolation have been carried out — sometimes allowing a good deal of normal activity (reading, thinking, and so on); sometimes involving the extreme restriction and isolation of confinement in a respirator; sometimes allowing the subject to keep track of time; sometimes providing no ti.ne anchorage points at all. The results are too complex to be summarized here. They tend, however, to indicate that a man isolated, even in this sense, is no longer completely a man. We can think of mariners drifting for weeks in the South Pacific, of the radio and radar crews in the Arctic, of prisoners in solitary confinement, and even of such relative isolation situations as those of the submarine and the spaceship. All of the studies on sensory isolation have begun to make clear how heavily we rely upon the mass of known or even unknown stimulation, and how, together with this reliance, we send out, as it were, messages for feedback of information from the world outside of the body.

From this point we can travel to the sensory deprivation studies by Krech and his collaborators (1966) and to sensory and social isolation studies by Harlow (1961). We can begin to think of the evolutionary series as furthering the development of a very rich system of receptor functions which make possible continuous contact with the environment and, at the same time, promoting the presence of vastly more stimulation than can be handled or processed at one time. Thus arises the problem of "overload," or "breaking through the stimulus barrier." It begins to appear that normal function depends upon both amount and balance of the sensory constituents that are hammering continually upon the many sensory doors.

In the same way we can go on to studies of *sensory enrichment* and their apparently extraordinary consequences for intellectual functioning. In the Krech experiments (1966), while *deprivation* resulted in reduction of the thickness of the brain cortex and reduced the value of cholinesterase activity, a specially *enriched* and challenging environment resulted in increased thickness of brain cortex and increased values of cholinesterase activity. There was apparently even some transfer of training to new tasks: that is, a heightened "intelligence" in the confrontation of new tasks.

This type of information, coming today from many sources, allowing rather exact experimental control, may be at least usefully compared with the studies of sensory deprivation and sensory enrichment among infant and preschool children. A number of contemporary studies indicate that a kind of sensory-cognitive pushing may make its mark for at least some months or years, while in a somewhat larger theater of observation it has likewise been shown that sensory enrichment can stimulate affective, impulsive, and other functions as well as the perceptual-cognitive interests; it can alert, brighten up (perhaps through reorientation), make available to the organism a larger variety of appeals to curiosity. Here the rich curiosity research program of Berlyne (1954) appears to join hands with the sensory enrichment studies. The question arises as to whether we have another instance here in which affect and sensation turn out to be not so utterly different. There appears to be a kind of stirring up and enrichment through a stimulus which stretches through the gamut of sensory and affective appeals; it could be compared with *arousal* (see p. 352), except that we are here dealing with long-range effects (days, months, perhaps years) rather then with short-range effects (seconds, minutes).

Sensory Cues and Perception

What has been happening about the ancient problem of the relation of sensation and perception? The Gestaltists managed for a few years to sidetrack a number of traditional and persistent problems by appearing to demonstrate the membership character (see p. 259) that appears in all perceptual situations, which requires us to give up the use of pure sensation as a useful concept. Before long, however, it began to be insisted that this type of analysis, or even atomization, was scientifically necessary, and as new techniques of mechanical, electrical, and biochemical stimulation became available, there was more and more effort to try to get the sensations themselves in the most refined and pure form possible.

Without abandoning the ancient view that perceiving must depend upon sensory cues, the emphasis still lies largely on the study of the cues available and what the organism does with them. Clearly, they are used not in a sheer summative way, but in terms of a texture, as defined in the studies by J. J. Gibson (1950). E. J. Gibson and R. Walk, in studies of the "visual cliff," have shown that human infants draw back from a visual pattern which includes "depth"; they do not need "learning" to see the "third dimension."

The *conflict of cues,* in turn, has been used by Ames (1955), who developed a series of demonstrations of the influence of visual context upon monocular and binocular perception.[1] He produced surprising, indeed startling, effects — like seeing one's friends changed to giants and dwarfs, and red spots on playing cards change to black — because of sheer congruity and the need for internal unity. Objects were made to appear nearer or farther away, larger or smaller, by placing them in a distorting room, such as, for example, a room with tilted walls or floor or ceiling. Under conditions of monocular vision, and under conditions in which the subject assumes the room to be a hollow cube, the human figure takes on the proportions required to fit the

[1] Ames was probably influenced by Gestalt psychology, but even more by John Dewey's emphasis upon the interaction or "transaction" between inner and outer world.

space. There are affective factors and factors of long-term habituation, as in the "Höni effect"; persons recently married are at first reported somewhat immune to the general distortion effect, but in the course of a year "habituate" to the spouse. Under certain conditions one may much more rapidly habituate. Here the older materials of Helmholtz come to life, conjoined with the perceptual learning evidence from the Gestalt group. Here also we find ourselves turning to the conception of differentiation within the perceptual field, as developed by Werner (Werner and Wapner, 1949), and as very notably developed into a whole new conception of human growth by Witkin and his collaborators (1954). Perception as synthesis takes on new meaning as the parts to be synthesized are more closely reviewed and as the modality of their synthesis is brought into relation to basic neural function.

Kilpatrick (1954) had his subjects look with one eye through a peephole into a small room which appeared to be a hollow cube. They bounced a ball within this space. Since, however, the room was really a small "distorting room," the bouncing of the ball soon betrayed the realities, and within less than an hour the room had moved into a new perceptual character, being seen as it was, an inverted truncated pyramid. Then the subject, having learned the nature of such illusory responses, was asked to look through a peephole into *another* small room which he then saw in the character in which he had learned to perceive this kind of visual stimulation; he saw it as an inverted truncated pyramid, although it was actually a cube. Perceptual habits of either kind can be made and broken.

Roughly parallel with this period of response to Ames's work came the impact of the work at Graz by Kohler (1951). These studies took their cue from the early work of Stratton (1897) on vision with glasses which inverted the visual field and went on to a variety of new types of lenses which, after a training period of adjustment, made possible normal perception of the world despite the profoundly altered relation of the stimulus field to the behavior requirements. In Kohler's work, moreover, the adaptation of the subject to new optical conditions was pursued for a matter of weeks without taking the glasses off. Blue lenses which at first, of course, made the world blue were soon bringing the normal color world to the individual. After some weeks, when the lenses were removed, the world was seen as yellow, that is, in complementary color terms. A series of rich dynamic problems have arisen which seem strongly to support the view that even such elementary sensory realities as hue must be seen in *contextual terms* — if not in the terms of Gestalt psychology, then in other terms equally complex. It is evident that the world of sensation and perception is a world of integration and of potential conflict, a world of structure and of integration.

We are reminded here once again of Werner's developmental system (1957) in which components that are more or less melted indiscriminately into one another at a primitive level may, at a higher level, become differentiated (Witkin *et al.,* 1954) and then at a still higher level may become integrated or given structural unity very different from the diffuse unity found at the lowest level. Problems which are conceived by Kohler in terms of the integration and conflict of cues can be conceived almost exactly as if they were phenomena of motor interference; in fact, in a study by Snyder and Pronko (1952), as well as in the studies of Kohler, it is clear that in learning to adjust to inverting lenses, the subject goes through conflict and integration of sensory cues at the behavior level and, at the same time, at the perceptual level. These are among the phenomena which have led many psychologists to the view that the perceptual system is an action system, that it has its own problems of focusing and fringe, of internal conflict, resolution, and integration. Perhaps, indeed, the whole range of laws of motor learning, developed by Thorndike, Hull, Skinner, and other contemporary learning theorists, may apply quite exquisitely and intimately to the phenomena of perception and perceptual learning, too.

A powerful new weapon is information theory, which, with its conceptions of "signal" and "noise," provides for the loss of function in a channel that has previously been providing information. J. J. Gibson has freshly surveyed the whole field of the relation of sensory to perceptual activity in a notable study utilizing information theory, tilting vigorously against the traditional conception that bits of sensory experience are fed in through sensory channels. He has presented an evolutionary view of perception, with emphasis upon the information-yielding rather than the sensation-yielding role of the senses: *The Senses Considered as Perceptual Systems* (1966) emphasizes what information is needed from the environment and how the senses mediate such information. From this point of view, the piecing together of bits of sensory stuff seems to be a long way indeed from the functional role of information supply, which, in the evolutionary series, the senses have to carry out.

There is, indeed, not only strong position-taking and theory-defending as a normal part of the growth of science, with incomplete data constrained to serve the experimenter's urgent professional needs, but beyond all that, there are actually research findings at all levels of solidity, supporting both the atomistic view and the fine-structured Gestalt view, and many intermediate and tangential positions in an area which is not all ready for a clear and final scientific assessment. Gibson's thesis of the importance of information, as contrasted with sensory content, is highly impressive, but so is Kohler's evidence (1951) that specific qualities are brought to experience by specific kinds of stimulation. And so, also, is Kilpatrick's evidence (1954) clear that perceptual learning may move massively away from the information-bearing role which has been central. There are, of course, in general biology, thousands of examples of functions which serve most of the time for effective adaptation but which, under various conditions, are nonadaptive or even antiadaptive. Perception is the name for a complex series of functions. Other such names — thought, will, affect, emotion — cut across psychological realities. The faculty psychology which assumes that names refer to psychologically homogeneous processes is still very much alive, and while being displaced bit by bit here and there in specific research areas, it quietly preempts the field again as new terms are coined to deal with new kinds of findings. There is always a segmental factor and always a comprehensive integral factor, and it is the business of the psychological historian to emphasize the perennially unfinished character of all clean and effective solutions.

Nativism and Empiricism in Perception

For the Greeks and for the people of India, perception was an inborn capacity. It might lead to misinterpretations of reality; but for a world too big and complicated to be understood, it was still a window into the world. For the most part the Greco-Roman tradition had based the capacity to confront the world upon perception first and then upon thought. There was no problem of "learning to perceive." Perception was conceived as almost reflexlike in its inherited character. Plato belittled the truth-yielding qualities of perception, but Aristotle restored them in his organic conception of true (though occasionally malfunctioning) use of the senses to make contact with the world. The distinction between primary and secondary qualities made by Democritus was preserved in varying forms to the time of Kepler. For Locke, percepts as well as serial associations depended upon individual past experience; in Hartley's writings, for the first time, the principle of experience became heavily emphasized, and the world of structured perceptual response to the environment was clearly enunciated. For Kant and Herbart, as well as for the English school following Hartley, perception was directly accessible to empirical study; it was no longer a faculty; it was a series of contingencies, dependent upon the vicissitudes of individual life history. The Germans and the English differed in one very important respect: Kant, Herbart, and most other German writers still believed in a native capacity to perceive, a basic capacity of the soul, while the original perceptual faculty was no longer needed by the English group.

The theory of evolution of course changed all this, as it changed everything else. A natural history of the process of perceiving began to be written in terms of progressive complexity of the central nervous system. The enormous research activity upon the functions of individual cells within the laboratories of histology and embryology in the German universities were brought into relation to elementary sensory functions; while with the neuron theory and the studies of aphasia, perception was conceived in terms of complex neurophysiological patterns. Localization and extirpation studies with animals were related to human clinical findings from brain injury. Several decades of concern with the organic totality of brain function were followed by a return swing to relative emphasis upon precise localization. Especially telling were the studies of Penfield (1952), showing that direct electrical brain stimulation of patients under local anesthesia yielded precise memories, both visual and auditory, and that repeated stimulation of the same region, with certain patients at least, brought back the same memories.

But the evolutionary point of view involves the conception that cortical tissue, like all other tissue, indirectly reflects the whole history of the previous life, including the life of the genus and the species. The human brain, like every brain, reveals differentiated and integrated functions which are phylogenetically determined, so that specific *ways* of perceiving are distinctly human, not perception in general. It is not just a question of finer sensitivity of one species compared to another, for there seem to be both general qualities of perceiving and specific phylogenetically and ontogenetically differentiated forms of perceptual responses.

This would mean, then, that in infancy there are distinctively human albeit primitive, ways of perceiving. These include a selectivity in attending, as, for example, in attending to the structured rather than the unstructured, and a rapid development in the early weeks of perceptual discrimination of particular stimuli, like mother's face or voice, or the structure of one's own body. Piaget (1961), on the one hand, and Bruner and his colleagues (1966), on the other, show how the world is brought in or assimilated, and how it, in turn, is modified, "accommodated," to the influx of new information. Because of the extremely active investigation since World War II, we see empiricism at work everywhere, yielding a rich harvest.

At this point, however, we find many experiments which show that at least some forms of perception do not require prior training. The visual cliff experiments of Gibson and Walk (1960) demonstrate that depth is a fear-evoking and avoidance-eliciting stimulus in the inexperienced neonate of a wide variety of species, man included. Also of great theoretical importance are the studies by Riesen *et al.* (1951), who isolated infrahuman primates in totally unilluminated living quarters and observed that associations not formed in the early months can never be adequately formed later. Similarly, the maternal and social deprivation studies of Harlow (1961) show the tremendous impact on primates of early sensory and affective experiences. Though not experimentally controlled, we must note the great impact of current observations of sensory and cognitive deprivation in human infants under conditions of economic or general social isolation (Spitz, 1965). There are also a few reports of successful surgery with children born blind but not operated on until the preadolescent period, which show that even the seemingly simplest human perceptual responses are molded into their final almost reflexlike form by long tedious processes of experience (Senden, 1932). But the evidence is that at least some primitive forms of perceiving, such as the perception of depth, of colors, of certain patterns, and even of complex stimulus patterns releasing specific species-typical responses (see

p. 361), are inherent in the phylogenetic organization of the sensory and nervous systems and that the lower the species on the phylogenetic scale, the more such phenomena may be found.

Internal Dynamics of Perception

All the systems, or models of contact with the environment, considered so far are essentially pertinent to the problem of perception. But we have to consider now the fact that perceptual and affective components are not easily distinguished. In this modern era, let us say since about 1900, an ancient and persistent problem has reasserted itself more and more vigorously: the problem of whether there really is a sensory, or perceptual, or cognitive life which can be studied in its own right, independently of the life of affect, feeling, impulse, or volition. Freud, as we saw, raised the problem of primary versus secondary process thinking. He suggested that at an early stage children see, hear, remember, and think in terms of what they want and only slowly learn to delay satisfactions while getting more information to permit a broader assessment of the situation. Bleuler distinguished between realistic thinking and "autistic" thinking, or thinking which is guided directly by the wish to perceive and think in a way satisfying the impulse toward a goal. The ancient process of seeing as one needs to see — and "none so blind as those that will not see" — becomes the cliché of "wishful thinking."

While this is ordinarily recognized both by psychologists and by laymen when the thought processes or even memory are involved, it has been much more difficult to convince the professional psychologist that the world of sense perception is itself directly involved in this type of "contamination" by wishes or drives, or, for that matter, fears, hates, or any other kind of affective or impulsive dynamic. The extensive literature on "subliminal perception" or subception under conditions of varying motivation overlaps here the extensive experimental literature on the role of affect in controlling or limiting perceptual possibilities. Two illustrations will serve to indicate the kinds of issues to be resolved: (1) the work of Bevan and Pritchard (1963) indicates that stimuli below threshold can influence judgments of loudness; and (2) a series of studies with the autokinetic effect (Farrow *et al.,* 1965) indicates that a stationary light perceived as moving will "keep out of" a region which has been associated with electric shock. What is taken for granted in a clinical situation (as, for example, with the Rorschach Test or the Thematic Apperception Test, in which wishes and fears write their story into the protocol of the responding subject) is offered in the laboratory with much more elaborate controls. It seems fair at this time to generalize. If we follow Hochberg's arrangement (1956) of the perceptual-cognitive life on a continuum from the externally given perceptual phenomena to the conceptually given responses of the thinking subject, psychologists can in turn be arranged on an attitude continuum in which some would emphasize the role of "autistic" factors in perception, and others would altogether deny the existence of solid evidence of such factors in perception though admitting them in the region of a higher cognitive life.

The issue is, of course, related to the traditional *physiological* issues as to the distinguishability of *affective* components from *sensory* or *cognitive* ones. It is partly a question of the still unresolved intricacies in the interrelations of the central and autonomic nervous systems, and partly a question of the introspective difficulty of finding any consistent hallmark by which an affect can be differentiated from a sensory component.

It has often been said that sensation in and of itself is without *meaning* but that perception has *meaning*. The reason given is that the sensation is embedded in other sensations, and that the resulting context supplies the meaning (Titchener's context theory). Sometimes the meaning is conceived to follow from *action* which follows upon the stimulation: the meaning of "up" and "down" is given by action away from or toward the earth. The problem of meaning, however, has proved to be one of those philosophical problems which have not been easily domiciled in psychological laboratories. It illustrates what Boring had in mind when he said that psychologists can neither embrace philosophy nor get rid of it.

A modern illustration will nevertheless be useful as we try to compare the problems of sensation, perception, affect, and cognition. This is the work of Schachter and Singer (1962). The problem is what really makes the difference between different affective states. The long-drawn-out battle over the James-Lange theory has left us unclear as to where the differences between say fear, rage, and distress lie in the differentiable conscious states which result from different visceral and proprioceptive input. Schachter and Singer administered hormone injections which gave rise to affectively rich conscious states. These were sometimes called rage, sometimes fear, sometimes surprise, and so on. When, however, the experimental atmosphere led the subject to *expect* rage, the welter of internal messages "meant" rage, even though the same system of experimentally controlled messages meant, for other subjects or even for the same subject, fear or surprise under conditions leading to expectation of fear or surprise. The meaning of the situation took the amorphous messages from within the body and shaped them, so to speak, to convey whatever the centers "wanted" to receive or were "predisposed" to receive. Perhaps this was because cognitive messages were dominant over visceral messages, at least within the intensity ranges used here. Perhaps, as in the dominance theory of Ukhtomskii, one component in a response system can give character to the system as a whole, can suppress competing components, or can even force them to deliver the same message which the dominant or victorious components are delivering.

While modern dynamic psychiatry took its start largely from emphasis upon the affect-impulse component in the perception-cognitive life, experimental psychology was slow to grasp the issues. Rorschach (1921) had seen clearly the role of the affective life in the structuring of percepts, but it was not until Bartlett (1932) that perception and memory were seen systematically in these terms. Bartlett was followed in the mid thirties by H. A. Murray (1938) at Harvard Psychological Clinic where, in collaboration with R. N. Sanford and others, he systematically studied the role of needs, presses, and themes, not only upon perception of the pictures used in projective tests (TAT; see p. 435), but in a variety of laboratory settings. These studies were modified and extended in the City College laboratories in New York and later at the Menninger Foundation by Murphy and his associates, while a "new look" movement, launched by Bruner and Postman (1949) at Harvard, soon spearheaded some scores of studies on the role of "value" and related concepts in structuring the perceptual and cognitive life. In the great majority of these cases, a clinical cast of thought was evident which finally took the center of the stage, with the emphasis on conflict and particularly on "dissonance." There was often, however, a feeling in the midst of all this perception research that to bring *affect* into the orderly world of *perceiving* and *thinking* was a bit indecent. We can see the issue clearly in Sherif's emphasis upon impulse and Murray's emphasis upon needs yielding to Festinger's emphasis (1957) on "cognitive dissonance"; when the field of perception and the field of thought are dissonant, the trouble is at the cognitive level — not, as Murray and Sherif had supposed, at the motivation level. A central issue remains: When do cues conflict because they give discordant information, and when do they conflict because they arouse antithetical impulses?

If there are ways in which perception becomes more orderly or more confused, or if, indeed, there are different ways in which the integrative role of perceiving can be individualized, there arises the problem of "perceptual-cognitive style" — the problem of the way in which the same perceptual task is resolved by different subjects who, in fact, both see different things and, even without illusion, see things in their own unique ways. These problems intrigued Klein (1949) in the same period when Bruner and Postman were launching the "new look" approach; perception with the "new look" is an expansion of the whole person, including drives and attitudes, not just stimulus presentations. Soon Schlesinger (1954) and Gardner and Holzman and their collaborators (1959) at the Menninger Foundation were using the classical experimental methods, especially those of the Marburg laboratory (with its emphasis on individuality in response to those experimental dimensions of perception, memory, and thought), to investigate personal styles of perceiving and ways of responding to illusions, showing "leveling and sharpening," "intolerance of ambiguity," "field articulation" — all these individual diversities were being measured and treated by factor analysis to yield broad general attributes of individual personality style.

Much of the problem of style proved to be closely related to or even directly dependent upon ways of attending. This is particularly clear in the work of Gardner and Moriarty (1968), especially as it relates to the work of Piaget (1961), as, for example, the process of centration involves ways of attending, over and over again, to certain parts of a figure and being thus overinfluenced by them.

Such studies as these suggest that there still are affective components which can be identified. They may be classified according to traditional systems or to any number of modern systems; or we may, if we like, arrange affect on a single dimension of pleasantness-unpleasantness, and, like Titchener, subsume all other affects under sensory categories. Perhaps it would not make any real difference whether there are anatomically distinct receptors for affect; the phenomenological or introspective problem would remain.

This issue is changing somewhat as a result of directions taken in recent years regarding the problem of "localization" within the central nervous system of the "centers" for various types of affective experience. Following the gross localization of sensory and motor centers recognized at the end of the nineteenth century, a more and more refined stimulation (by electrodes with exposed tips) has made possible the demonstration of divisions and subdivisions within the sensory centers, and near them centers which seem to serve specific perceptual and specific memoric functions (see, for example, Neff and Diamond's work on cats, 1958). Now, by essentially similar thinking, Olds and Milner (1954) have found it possible to stimulate, in animal subjects, regions in the basal ganglia which lead to the animal's acting as if it were "overjoyed"; supplying it with its own controlling system, the animal self-stimulated itself hour after hour. One may, if one likes, think of a "pleasure center." Similarly, Delgado (1969) found "unpleasantness" centers which, when stimulated, led to a sharp discontinuation of the activity and no further readiness of the animal to administer such stimulation. Some incomplete but rather convergent evidence from human subjects (Heath, 1964) suggests that we are dealing here with true affective responses varying in quality as well as in intensity. Perhaps there is a wide variety of affective centers, each with its own qualities, each having its own definite geography and capable of consistent mapping for the species or indeed for the individual.

Feedback and Internal Stimuli in Perceptual Learning

To say, as all these modern studies say, that the environment and organism are richly intertwined in the development of a perceptual whole may seem at first self-evident; but this is different from the classical conception of perceiving as a mark made upon a passive receptor surface, a white paper or *tabula rasa*. There have been hints, in all the modern work so far described, that the perceiver goes to meet the situation, that he is selectively or attentively utilizing the cues available—indeed, that he is making something for himself, call it a behavioral environment, or an ecology, or a source of information, or a world to live in. The old problem of the *activity of the perceiver* and thinker, as we saw it in Leibnitz, has been very much to the fore in all the years of the present century, and especially since World War II. This is an enriched utilization of the Helmholtz principle of "unconscious inference," for there is "feedback" from the adaptive act to the brain processes in which perception of the environment goes on. We see the consequences of our reaction or, within limits, we see our own reaction itself, our own movement of hand or head against a relatively stationary context.

The conception of behavior as a continuous series of feedback loops with suitable mathematical treatment burst upon the world in Norbert Wiener's *Cyberneties* (1948). It began to be grasped that there is much to be *done* whenever we see or hear or smell or taste or touch. There is sniffing, cocking the head, tightening muscles here, relaxing them there, placing the eyes in a better position, or using their movements to permit quicker or more complete return information.

The process of *attending* is basically a way of mobilizing more points of contact, or mobilizing them more continuously or more effectively. We cut a course through life, sending out as it were radar messages and getting fresh return information. Perceptual learning, from this point of view, has to be in considerable measure individualized; with eye movements and language playing a highly responsible role in this total array of activities. Of course, even the simplest reward-punishment learning involves feedback, and of course motor learning, as in Guthrie's reference to "movement-produced stimuli," has brought the striped musculature of voluntary motor activity into a prominent place.

It has been shown by Miller (1969) and his associates (as had earlier been suggested by a large amount of Soviet psychophysiological research) that autonomically controlled organs and tissues are likewise capable of acquiring learned responses. The organism can be considered constantly engaged in both striped muscle and unstriped muscle activities which bring further information as to what is going on, including what is going on *inside itself.* The perceptual learning process involves partly learning to perceive the outer world, but also partly learning to respond to what goes on within. When autonomically controlled responses are reinforced by stimulation of the "pleasure centers" (Olds and Milner, 1954), the organism must be capable of responding to its own activities. The organism is not only registering but also integrating registered impressions regarding the outer world, regarding itself, and regarding the relations between the two. This is a complexity for which the older theories were unprepared. But from an evolutionary point of view it is obvious that the tasks are necessary ones, that the complicated machinery which evolution has supplied is ready to be used, and that its use can be learned.

It is equally clear that the voluntary control of striped and smooth muscles can lead, without gross change in technique, to the development of skills for the control of our own brain activities. We need only a clear and dependable source of feedback information. Kamiya (1969) asked his subjects to respond when the alpha rhythm of the EEG was present; finding that they could do so, he went on to teach them—with an auditory symbol activated by the alpha—to get voluntary control of the alpha. Brown (1970) used *visual* signals for the same purpose. We can, in this way, quickly acquire voluntary control of our own brain waves, at least in the alpha and beta region. It would appear that the world of perceptual learning is leading into a world of inner self-discovery, somewhat like the inner self-discovery of Yoga and Zen Buddhism; in fact, recent studies (Green *et al.*, 1970) suggest that persons thoroughly trained in these Oriental systems are undergoing brain-wave changes comparable to those which the very relaxed Western observer undergoes during states which have something in common with the "meditation," the "Samadhi," and the "Satori" of the East. Perceptual learning and the discovery of an internal world turn out to be intimately related processes and seem currently to open a new door for a combination of the new hard scientific experimentation and the method of introspection brought back from an earlier era.

The Thought Processes

As we have noted, there are two great traditions in psychology relating to the thought processes. One of these deals with the chainlike arrangement of ideas as expressed by Democritus, Aristotle, Hobbes, and modern associationists. The other, looking for dynamic sources of associative processes, has been most vigorously expressed by Herbart. In recent decades, the two traditions have tended to coalesce somewhat, though the distinction between them is still visible. A few milestones along the way to a modern theory of thinking may be briefly noted here.

James's ideas on "the stream of thought" (1892, Chap. 2) became a model for direct introspective and retrospective study of the content and the directing forces within the thinking processes. His emphasis was on continuity—on the rich and complex guiding forces, frequently unconscious, which give shape to explicitly conscious or "substantive" factors embedded within a flowing matrix. James was greatly influenced by the thought of his Cambridge University friend F. W. H. Myers (1903). Myers had developed a rich and highly influential theory of the "subliminal" dynamic factors involved in all cognition and in all complex expressions of personality; notably in a creative act which represents a "subliminal uprush" of new ideas at points of major insight or illumination. Gertrude Stein was a pupil of James at Harvard at the turn of the century, and the "stream of thought" school of drama and fiction owed much to her, and through her to William James.

The Würzburg school and Binet were also working on the thought processes at the opening of the twentieth century. With the advent of the Gestalt school after 1912, Wertheimer with his conception of productive thinking, emphasized reorganization or "recentering" of thought as a total configurational process, allowing for some low-level associative phenomena, but with emphasis upon the intact new restructuring process (see p. 260). In the meantime, fresh empirical work emerged on the complexities of the process of concept formation related to memory processes and to the search for common factors. A group of new materials, permitting the definition of an abstraction, were emphasized by Vygotskii (1962),[2] by Bruner and his collaborators (Bruner and Goodman, 1947; Bruner *et al.*, 1956), and by Bartlett (1958).

It became evident in all these studies that the process of thought frequently assumes bewilderingly complicated forms whether approached in the laboratory or the clinic, or whether reconstructed by the individual thinker from his recent or remote memories. This view has also been expressed by current analysts of the thought processes, who are familiar with advanced computer technology. Thought processes are enormously more complicated than any of the experimental models available to the computer; and our experimental work on the thought processes does not as yet enable us to get to a point at which we would really make adequate use even of the available computer modalities.

Perhaps because of the same problem of complexity, professional psychology also neglected the question of creative thinking from which all great contributions, including the contributions of science, have come. Psychology was challenged by the problem of creativity and its relation to thinking, as, for example, in Guilford's work (1964) on creativity and in his distinction between "convergent" and "divergent" thinking (1959), but it had not as yet produced a massive response. There have been sporadic concerns with creativity at various levels and in various forms: as it appears in imaginative productions of school-age children, and as it flashes through the minds of the great pioneers in the arts and sciences. Creativity is often a process of "rearrangement," and there are many remaining questions as to how, when, why, and by whom the new and old raw materials, like tones and words, get shuffled about; and under what conditions the original, the unpredictable, the psychologically new, and socially important appear. Many have dealt with the properties of the individual creative personality (MacKinnon, 1962). Many have been concerned with the properties of the individual creative act (Barron, 1969). Clinical thought, especially psychoanalytic thought, has also frequently been mobilized in relation to the problem (Rapaport, 1951), while the members of the Gestalt group have endeavored to show that perception is in itself a creative act (Arnheim, 1954). The increasingly sensitive current studies of "altered states of conscious-

[2] Vygotskii is sometimes transliterated Vygotsky, as in this 1962 citation.

ness" (Tart, 1969) may throw new light on the "concentrated" or "distracted" or "frenzied" or utterly "open" states, in which an object or an idea of supreme worth is sought by the creative thinker.

REFERENCES

Ames, A., Jr. *An Interpretive Manual for the Demonstrations in the Psychological Research Center, Princeton University: The Nature of Our Perceptions, Prehension, and Behavior.* Princeton: Princeton University Press, 1955.

Arnheim, R. *Art and Visual Perception.* Berkeley: University of California Press, 1954.

Attneave, F. "Perception and Related Areas." In S. Koch, ed. *Psychology: A Study of a Science.* Vol. 4. New York: McGraw-Hill, 1962.

Barron, F. *Creative Person and Creative Process.* New York: Holt, Rinehart and Winston, 1969.

Bartlett, F. C. *Remembering.* London: Cambridge University Press, 1932.

——. *Thinking: An Experimental and Social Study.* New York: Basic Books, 1958.

Berlyne, D. E. "A Theory of Human Curiosity." *British Journal of Psychology,* 45 (1954), 180–91.

Bevan, W., Jr., and Pritchard, J. F. "The Effect of Subliminal Tones upon the Judgment of Loudness." *Journal of Experimental Psychology,* 66 (1963), 23–29.

Bexton, W. H., Heron, W., and Scott, T. H. "Effects of Decreased Variation in the Sensory Environment." *Canadian Journal of Psychology,* 8 (1954), 70–76.

Brown, B. B. "Recognition of Aspects of Consciousness Through Association with EEG Alpha Activity Represented by a Light Signal." *Psychophysiology,* 6 (1970), 442–52.

Bruner, J. S., and Goodman, C. C. "Value and Need as Organizing Factors in Perception." *Journal of Abnormal and Social Psychology,* 42 (1947), 33–44.

Bruner, J. S., Goodnow, J. J., and Austin, G. A. *A Study of Thinking.* New York: Wiley, 1956.

Bruner, J. S., Oliver, R. R., and Greenfield, P. M., *et al. Studies in Cognitive Growth.* New York: Wiley, 1966.

Bruner, J. S., and Postman, L. "Perception, Cognition, and Behavior." *Journal of Personality,* 18 (1949), 15–31.

Delgado, J. M. R. *Physical Control of the Mind.* New York: Harper & Row, 1969.

Farrow, B. J., Santos, J. F., Haines, J. R., and Solley, C. M. "Influence of Repeated Experience on Latency and Extent of Autokinetic Movements." *Perception and Motor Skills,* 20 (1965), 1113–20.

Festinger, L. *A Theory of Cognitive Dissonance.* Palo Alto, Calif.: Stanford University Press, 1957.

Frisch, K. von. *The Dancing Bees.* London: Methuen, 1954.

Gardner, R. W., Holzman, P. S., Klein, G. S., Linton, H. B., and Spence, D. P. "Cognitive Control." In G. S. Klein, ed. *Psychological Issues.* New York: International Universities Press, 1959.

Gardner, R. W., and Moriarty, A. *Personality Development at Preadolescence:*

Explorations of Structure Formation. Seattle: University of Washington Press, 1968.

Gibson, J. J. *The Perception of the Visual World.* Boston: Houghton Mifflin, 1950.

———. *The Senses Considered as Perceptual Systems.* Boston: Houghton Mifflin, 1966.

Gibson, J. J. and Walk, R. D. "The Visual Cliff." *Scientific American,* 202 (1960), 64–73.

Green, E. E., Green, A. M., and Walters, E. D. "Voluntary Control of Internal States: Psychological and Physiological." *Journal of Transpersonal Psychology,* 2 (1970), 1–26.

Guilford, J. P. "Three Faces of Intellect." *American Psychologist,* 14 (1959), 469–79.

———. "Some New Looks at the Nature of Creative Processes." In N. Frederiksen and H. Gulliksen, eds. *Contributions to Mathematical Psychology.* New York: Holt, Rinehart and Winston, 1964.

Harlow, H. F. "The Development of Affectional Patterns in Infant Monkeys." In B. M. Foss, ed. *Determinants of Infant Behavior.* New York: Wiley, 1961.

Harlow, H. F., and Harlow, M. K. "The Effect of Rearing Conditions on Behavior." *Bulletin of the Menninger Clinic,* 26 (1962), 213–24.

Heath, R. G. "Pleasure Response of Human Subjects to Direct Stimulation of the Brain: Physiologic and Psychodynamic Considerations." In R. G. Heath, ed. *The Role of Pleasure in Behavior.* New York: Harper & Row, 1964.

Hochberg, J. E. "Perception: Toward the Recovery of a Definition." *Psychological Review,* 63 (1956), 400–405.

James, W. *Textbook of Psychology: Briefer Course.* New York: Holt, 1892.

Kamiya, J. "Operant Control of the EEG Alpha Rhythm and Some of Its Reported Effects on Consciousness." In C. T. Tart, ed. *Altered States of Consciousness.* New York: Wiley, 1969.

Kilpatrick, F. P. "Two Processes in Perceptual Learning." *Journal of Experimental Psychology,* 47 (1954), 362–70.

Klein, G. S. "Adaptive Properties of Sensory Functioning." *Bulletin of the Menninger Clinic,* 13 (1949), 16–23.

Kohler, I. *Über Aufbau und Wandlungen der Wahrnebmungwelt.* Vienna: Rohrer, 1951.

Krech, D., Rosenzweig, M. R., and Bennett, E. L. "Environmental Impoverishment, Social Isolation and Changes in Brain Chemistry and Anatomy." *Physiology and Behavior,* 1 (1966), 99–109.

MacKinnon, D. W. "The Nature and Nurture of Creative Talent." *American Psychologist,* 17 (1962), 484–95.

Miller, N. "Learning of Visceral and Glandular Responses." *Science,* 163 (1969), 434–45.

Murray, H. A., *et al. Explorations in Personality.* Oxford: Oxford University Press, 1938.

Myers, F. W. H. *Human Personality and Its Survival After Bodily Death.* 2 vols. London: Longmans, Green, 1903.

Neff, W. D., and Diamond, I. T. "The Neural Basis of Auditory Discrimination." In H. F. Harlow and C. N. Woolsey, eds. *Biological and Biochemical Bases of Behavior.* Madison: University of Wisconsin Press, 1958.

Olds, J., and Milner, P. "Positive Reinforcement Produced by Electrical Stimulation of Septal Area and Other Regions of Rat Brain." *Journal of Comparative and Physiological Psychology,* 47 (1954), 419.

Penfield, W. "Memory Mechanisms." *AMA Archives of Neurology and Psychiatry,* 67 (1952), 178–98.

Piaget, J. *Les Méchanismes perceptifs.* Paris: Presses Universitaires de France, 1961. Translated by G. N. Seagrim. *The Mechanisms of Perception.* New York: Basic Books, 1969.

Rapaport, D. *Organization and Pathology of Thought.* New York: Columbia University Press, 1951.

Riesen, A. H., Chow, K.-L., Seemes, J., and Nissen, H. W. "Chimpanzee Vision After Four Conditions of Light Deprivation." *American Psychologist,* 6 (1951), 282. (Abstract.)

Rorschach, H. [*Psychodiagnostics: A Diagnostic Test Based on Perception.*] Bern: Huber, 1921. Translated by P. Lemkau and B. Kronenberg. New York: Grune and Stratton, 1942.

Schachter, S., and Singer, J. E. "Cognitive, Social and Physiological Determinants of Emotional State." *Psychological Review,* 69 (1962), 379–99.

Schlesinger, H. J. "Cognitive Attitudes in Relation to Susceptibility to Interference." *Journal of Personality,* 22 (1954), 354–74.

Senden, M. von. *Raum-und Gestaltauffassung bei Operierten Blindegeborenen vor und nach der Operation.* Leipzig: Barth, 1932.

Snyder, F. W., and Pronko, N. H. *Vision with Spatial Inversion.* Wichita, Kans.: University of Wichita Press, 1952.

Solley, C. M., and Murphy, G. *Development of the Perceptual World.* New York: Basic Books, 1960.

Spitz, R. A., in collaboration with Cobliner, W. G. *The First Year of Life.* New York: International Universities Press, 1965.

Stratton, G. M. "Vision Without Inversion of the Retinal Image." *Psychological Review,* 4 (1897), 341–60.

Tart, C. T., ed. *Altered States of Consciousness.* New York: Wiley, 1969.

Vygotskii, L. S. *Thought and Language.* Translated by E. Haufman and G. Vakar, Cambridge, Mass.: M.I.T. Press, 1962.

Werner, H., and Wapner, S. "Sensory-Tonic Field Theory of Perception." *Journal of Personality,* 18 (1949), 88–107.

Wiener, N. *Cybernetics.* New York: Wiley, 1948.

Witkin, H. A., Lewis, H., Hertzman, M., Machover, K., Meissner, P. B., and Wapner, S. *Personality Through Perception.* New York: Harper, 1954.

NOTE: A list of further readings appears at the back of the book.

22

Comparative
and
Physiological
Psychology

Here in the length of half a millimeter are encompassed all of the major problems of dynamic psychologies.

K. S. LASHLEY

The two great concerns to be grasped and reconciled by biologically minded psychologists are the implications of evolutionary process and of the physical sciences for the study of behavior. The development of physics and, in particular, of electronics in the early decades of this century led rapidly to two new trends in psychology: (1) the living system was conceived less in terms of anatomy and more in terms of refined analysis of tissues, transcending classical histology and involving molecular biology, electrophysiology, and biochemistry; (2) the rapid development of new techniques permitted more exact localization of physiological responses and direct experimental intervention in physiological and biochemical events. Both trends have, of course, greatly influenced our philosophical conceptions of the organism; it appears that a whole new approach and experimental methodology for the life sciences are being rapidly and dramatically implemented.

Experimental intervention formerly meant discovering what nature is doing in her own private way; today it means eliciting responses from organisms that were never thought to reside in those organisms, with the idea of getting down to a deep physiochemical level at which the nature of life process is more closely glimpsed—just as the recent space experiments and sensory deprivation studies subject man to conditions which could not occur except in hitherto unexplored or newly created environments. This is a part of the way in which techniques, available at a particular time in the development of science, so alter the scientist's methods that in time they bring him to see what he would not have seen, and, as a result, force changes in his most basic conceptions.

Physiological Basis of Behavior

The intensive work of the nineteenth and early twentieth centuries brought about an increasing understanding of the fundamental organismic mediator of behavior, the electrochemical propagation of nerve impulses within and between cell elements of the neural tissue. It became known that electrical impulses do not simply jump from one nerve cell to another; instead, the arrival of an impulse at the end of an axon initiates the release of neuro-humoral substances, which in turn spread across the synaptic gap and initiate new impulses in the next cell. It became known also that the propagation of electrical impulses within the nervous tissue is not entirely dependent on continuous external stimulation; there are clearly detectable *spontaneous electrical activity patterns* in the brain. In the late twenties, Berger (1929) discovered that it was possible to detect and amplify potential changes in various parts of the human cerebral cortex and record them in the form of visible waves. These "brain waves," sensitive and complex as they were, soon yielded to systematic study. Electroencephalographic, or EEG, responses could be picked up from the skull and under certain special conditions directly from the cortex itself. It was soon learned that particular regions tended to yield specific kinds of waves; for example, the occipital cortex in the relaxed subject yielded "alpha" waves of 8 to 15 per second frequency, while faster waves, such as "theta" and "delta," could be picked up in other regions. In the case of each psychological response which might give variation to an observable EEG response, it was always, therefore, a problem to determine the region, the rate and form of the wave patterns, and the specific external and internal stimulus conditions which brought them about. Many changes of state, such as sleep, drowsiness, relaxation, alertness, concentration, gave their own characteristic pictures. It has become possible to think of particular psychological conditions as having their characteristic complex expression at the EEG level and also at the level of the electromyographic, or recorded muscle, response. It begins to be possible to think of consciousness as related in a clear, constant, organic way to particular time-space patterns of electrical potential changes in the cortex and of individual differences in EEG as related to personal idiosyncrasies in ways of thinking, feeling, or deciding.

The study of relationships between overt behavior and these gross electrical rhythms in the brain is but one step, though surely a very significant step, in the long search for specific impulse-conducting processes in the brain. We should recall (see p. 118) that Fritsch and Hitzig elicited, as far back as 1870, movements by direct application of electrical current to the brain. This was followed by a long series of studies in which the "irritability" of Swammerdam [1] and the "animal electricity" of Galvani took precedence over the old doctrine of "animal spirits." Ever more refined techniques of electrical stimulation of the brain, together with clinical and experimental studies of localized brain injury and a broad application of the general technique in which spontaneous or evoked electrical potentials are recorded from the brain, led to minutely detailed anatomical and physiological description of the various structural and functional properties of the brain, including minute localization of cortical sensory, motor, and associative functions.

The use of improved electrodes during the last few decades has made possible the excitation of very specific regions and subregions of the cerebral cortex and subcortical areas, eliciting functions far more precisely localizable than had generally been believed possible. Even some of the more wild and vague notions of the mid-nineteenth century, associating specific psychological activities with individual nerve cells, appear in the newer perspective as not so wild, not so vague. Recent concrete localization of reward and aversion systems (Olds, 1960) in minutely defined areas of the brain, for example, is as challenging to the neurophysiologist as it is to the biopsychologist who works on the old hedonistic principle with the help of these new insights and tools.

Studies of the sensory systems showed in minute detail the mechanical, neurochemical, and electrochemical mechanisms involved in the initiation of sensory impulses by specific quantitative and qualitative variables of external stimulation. Such studies led to redefinition of earlier theories of vision and audition and to the findings that even the smallest changes in external stimulation, corresponding to a single quantum of light energy or to minimum possible mechanical displacement of particles, may initiate sensory impulses in finely differentiated receptor systems; and that sensory impulses activate equally differentiated localizable projection areas in the cerebral cortex.

We have learned much about the complexity of the reflex arc, which, in higher organisms, appears to be based almost invariably on multidimensional connections and complex neurochemical relationships of excitation and inhibition. Sensory impulses can be initiated at any point of receptor surface, but they are not based on passive reaction to external stimulation, since, in all sensory systems, there are fibers descending from the brain which control the activity of the receptors through complex feedback impulses. Furthermore, organisms respond to environmental changes not only through neural excitation and muscular activities but also by internal secretion of highly specialized chemical substances, *hormones,* which are essential in the maintenance of internal metabolic and neurophysiological balance. There is, so

---

[1] Jan Swammerdam (1637–80), a Dutch naturalist, experimented with nerve-muscle preparation of the frog and collected the first conclusive experimental evidence against the Cartesian notion of animal spirits.

to speak, a dramatic orchestration of neural, hormonal, and behavioral regulating processes by which the organism maintains its internal and external environment within surprisingly narrow "homeostatic" limits of effective functioning (Cannon, 1939).

It had begun to be clear more than thirty years ago (see Duffy, 1934) that all psychological responses can be graded in terms of the degree of intensity of response from deeply inactive to most intensely active. Moruzzi and Magoun (1949) and their collaborators were able to show that the "reticular activating system" of the brain stem is directly related to the overall activation pattern. This general arousal system has been shown to exercise a controlling influence on both the receptor mechanisms and the cortical synthesis of impulses arriving at the brain and thereby to participate in the general processes of behavioral and physiological homeostasis. It became possible to think of each perception, each emotion, each act of recall or imagination, as having its place on an activation continuum. Consequently, there was a shift of interest from local changes associated with the execution of such acts toward the definition of the nature of the activation process. This led many to think of waking, alertness, attention, drowsiness, and other "psychological states" or "states of consciousness" as determined, in considerable measure, by the activation responses.

Molecular biology has also gone far in analyzing genetic material that might influence behavior, and obtained electromicroscopic confirmation of what had been worked through at the level of chemistry in defining the exact structure, the double helix, of the DNA. When studies of this type relate to problems of cortical localization, protein chemistry, and the learning process, physiological psychology becomes almost a new science. With the help of refined methods and continuous accumulation of new information, earlier hypothetical variables and hypothetical constructs for psychological phenomena can now be tested in the concrete process of neurophysiology and biochemistry. We shall now turn to an area where such experimental testing is in full swing.

Physiological Theories of Learning

Organismic and physiological thinking long antedated purely psychological approaches to learning, but, despite great advances in neurophysiology and neuroanatomy, the essential questions regarding the learning process — namely, how learning takes place and where memory is stored — remain the same as before. Every new finding gives new hope that a physiological solution is just around the corner. But more often than not it results only in the introduction of still another complexity. The unfolding search for the right answers to these questions, however, promises to be one of the most exciting chapters in man's understanding of nature and himself.

The recognition of the nerve cell and synaptic junction between nerve cells has quickly led to conceptualizations of the learning process in terms of neural-impulse conduction, specifically of facilitation and inhibition of neural impulses at the synapse as a result of learning. Ever since Tanzi's early theory (1893), a steady stream of hypotheses have come forth, all dealing, one way or another, with experience-induced changes at the synaptic junction between two or more neurons. Neuronal growth has been assumed by many to result in resistance changes at the synapse, thereby forming the physical basis for memory. There have been a variety of different conceptualizations, mostly based on information gained by studies of the growth of embryonic nervous systems, regarding the question of how such neuronal growth may take place.

Kappers (1917) argued that the specificity of the embryological growth of neuronal tissues can be explained by electrical attracting forces. His postulate of "neurobiotaxis" stated that the activity of neurons generates electromagnetic fields, which in turn influence the direction of their growth; electrical negativity in a group of active nerve cells exerts attraction for the growth of neighboring neurons. Kappers related these growth processes to problems of postnatal learning. He argued that similar electrical field forces may be generated during conditioning and may result in altered synaptic conduction at the time of learning. This argument, however, was not borne out by subsequent empirical studies.

Others had proposed random mechanical guidance along directional pathways and points of least resistance in the growth of nervous tissues. Still others, Ramon y Cajal (1911) the most influential among them, proposed chemotropic processes in which chemical substances in the neuronal environment exert directive forces on the growth of neurons. This theory continues to receive attention (Sperry, 1958) in the light of new evidence about neurochemical secretory processes.

Coghill (1929) extended the many available observations on prenatal development of the neural tissues to postnatal behavior and argued that although the growth and development of neuronal tissue may slow down at maturity, it does not stop but continues throughout the life of organisms. Continuous neuronal growth, he believed, results in an increased number of potential synaptic connections between neurons and thus forms the basis for behavioral plasticity in higher organisms. Experience and learning do not strictly influence these growth processes, according to Coghill; rather they create functional connections and systems out of the myriad of potential synaptic connections. This conceptualization of a functionally connected neuronal net, resulting from experience, has remained central in later physiological theories of learning, which have continued to seek the explanations of the learning process in synaptic changes and functional integration of individual nerve cells.

Holt (1931) further developed Kappers's notion of neurobiotaxis in relation to the problem of learning. He proposed that experience is as relevant in the prenatal development of the nervous system as it is influential in postnatal behavioral development and learning. Holt suggested that synaptic resistances vary randomly at first, and the initial conduction pathway is determined by chance; neuronal growth is determined by the activity-related biotaxic process proposed by Kappers and results in nonrandom integration of a functionally connected system under the directive influence of experiences. Thus Holt introduced the idea of randomness to the understanding of neuronal development and learning. This idea exerted considerable influence on a variety of later conceptualizations in comparative psychology.

Development of behavior has been regarded by many, under the influence of Holt, as an "epigenetic process" in which there is nothing inherently or instinctively determined except some elementary neonatal response tendencies to the source of stimulation and some species-typical directive trends in experience. The most notable among the current epigenetic theories is that of Schneirla (1959), who developed an elaborate epigenetic-developmental explanation based completely on initial approach-withdrawal responses of the neonate, which he held to be under the sole control of stimulus-intensity levels.

The many theories and arguments regarding neuronal growth and resistance changes at the synaptic junction, however, did not solve the problem of how specific neurons are selected and become integrated into functional systems. Nor did they deal satisfactorily with the question of how lasting alterations in synaptic resistance may take place as a result of brief conducting activities in neurons. Hebb (1949), utilizing earlier reverberatory concepts (Lorente de Nó, 1938; Hilgard and Marquis, 1940), tried to solve these problems with his notion that synaptic resistance changes result from prolonged reverberatory activities of functionally connected nerve cells. He proposed that the stimulation of a sensory cell sets up neuronal circuits in cortical association areas, leading eventually to the return of the impulse to the originating sensory area neuron and resulting in prolonged reverberation of impulses within a functionally connected neuronal net. He believed that the reverberation of such impulses continues beyond the point of cessation of the internal or external excitatory agents that brought the first neuron into activity. The repeated passage of neural impulses through this functionally connected circuit was said to result in specific and gradual neuronal growth and in a related lasting alteration of the resistance at the synaptic junction, which was said to form the basis for learning. The resulting "cell assemblies" could thus remain, thanks to the lasting synaptic alterations. This theory, like the others before it, implied that learning takes place and memory is stored by the establishment of specific functionally connected neuronal circuits.

Eccles (1961) proposed a similar hypothesis, also dealing with the influence of reverberatory excitation and the alteration of synaptic resistance. But, as Grossman (1967) notes, Eccles's great knowledge of neurochemistry and neural-impulse propagation was not fully matched by an equal sophistication in psychological understanding of the learning process. The study of learning seems to demand now a high level of cooperation among the practitioners of biopsychology, biochemistry, electrophysiology, and bioelectronics. The complexity and amount of knowledge within each of these fields are such that it is practically impossible to be fully competent in all.

A number of additional physiological theories of learning have been proposed, all primarily dealing with the problem of impulse propagation and changes in synaptic resistance. Konorski (1950), for example, followed the general postulates of Pavlovian physiological psychology, but at the same time he incorporated new information regarding the physiology of neuronal elements in the brain. Penfield (1952) proposed rather precise localizations of memory traces, on the basis of his clinical observations that long-forgotten memories in man can be brought back to consciousness by localized electrical stimulation of the brain.[2]

All these theories are aimed at better understanding the anatomical and neurochemical changes that take place at the synapse and at other localized areas of the brain. Localizations are conceptualized either in terms of functionally integrated cell assemblies through which neural impulses can reverberate, or in terms of identifiable cortical or subcortical areas which uniquely serve learning and storage of memory. None of these views, however, has yet been borne out fully by available empirical evidence; although each is based on some form of available data.

While the full application of electrophysiological technique has made dramatic differences in the contours of the physiological psychology of learning, the role of biochemistry has been at least as dramatic. The chemistry of the action current and, in particular, the discharge of adrenergic and cholinergic substances in the course of neural-impulse propagation have tended to force the psychologist to think of learning and emotions more and more in terms of basic chemistry. There have also been changes in stains, dyes, and so on, for the more exact observation of tissues involved. The new field of psychopharmacology has come to concern itself with alterations of mood, arousal level, and "states of consciousness." Even the central role of neural-impulse transmission and synaptic resistance in learning is beginning to be challenged at present in the light of structural characteristics of the brain and molecular biology. Galambos, for example, proposed in 1961 that it is not the resistance change at the neuronal junction but the specific biochemical changes in glial tissue that may be the key to learning and memory. In view of the current evidence on the molecular mechanisms of the coding of genetic information, the proposal of possible neurochemical interaction between neural and glial tissues and of the unique interaction of molecular-

---

[2] According to him, neurophysiological activities in the hippocampal and periamygdaloid areas of the brain are related to learning and memory.

neurochemical systems in coding and storage of behavioral information at areas other than the synapse itself is indeed very attractive.

In the sphere of drugs and toxins the meaning of chemistry for psychology has been rapidly becoming evident. Psychopharmacology had been but a small chapter in physiological psychology during the nineteenth century, and, despite the strange consequences of opiates and other "hallucinogenic" drugs, it was not until Kraepelin at the end of the century that systematic attacks on the psychological implication of drug use were developed. A great wave of excitement followed the discovery in the 1950s of new "psychoactive" drugs (relaxing and antidepressant drugs particularly). Albert Hofman had discovered, in 1943, the extraordinary psychological consequences of his synthesis of a lysergic acid derivative (LSD). He, and many subjects who took the drug, reported a psychoticlike state. In a few years it became clear that LSD, together with mescaline and other hallucinogenic agents, could produce a great range and complexity of states. These involved altered perception, memory, imagination, self-awareness, and much that had been earlier attributed mainly to the action of special physiological training, such as that used in yoga and Zen Buddhism. A new chapter of research on such psychedelic drugs has been written, which seems, to some, to give new support to the old reductionist notion that life and behavior are matters of biochemistry.

Phylogenetic Conceptions of Behavior: Comparative Psychology and Ethology

Once the evolutionary view is assimilated, one tends to see homologies and analogies everywhere and to ask by what specific course of development an organ or a function has taken a specific form. These questions acquired major significance in psychology almost immediately after Darwin put forth his theory of evolution. Since that time a growing emphasis has been placed on compilation of data from a variety of species, with the assumption that every bit of information is necessary and relevant in the development of cross-species theories regarding behavior. In this sense, then, the entire psychology of the late nineteenth and early twentieth centuries can be regarded as comparative psychology. Even those who were interested in the behavior of only one species, whether of the white rat or of man, drew large and free analogies from the behavior of other species. The Darwinian concept of adaptation revitalized psychology and provided the ultimate justification for experimental procedures in the study of the human mind.

Post-Darwinian psychology gradually began to regard itself as a biological science. It began to draw models from the life sciences rather than from the physical sciences, which had dominated psychological conceptualization prior to Darwin. This process, however, is not completed yet, for the model of science developed by astronomers, physicists, and chemists still holds a strong sway over the younger "social scientists," even as the former more and more look to the latter for inspiration and new models of relevance. We will now turn to those areas of psychology in which the theory of evolution became the single and central paradigm, to comparative psychology and ethology. Practitioners in these fields followed Darwin in the recognition that the phenomena of life and behavior are too complex to be fully fathomed by the simple methods and tools evolved in the study of the inorganic world, however successful these may have been in their original context.

We discussed in Chapter 9 the immediate impact of the theory of evolution on psychology. Romanes's anthropomorphic approach to animal behavior led quickly to the opposite and extreme mechanistic approach of Loeb (see p. 137) and various others. Jennings (1906) was perhaps the first modern comparative psychologist to emerge from the synthesis of these extreme positions. He had undertaken the study of behavioral development in a wide variety of lower organisms and, while rejecting the Romanes approach, insisted that Loeb's simplistic tropism does not account for all the different forms and complexities of behavior, even at their very lowest manifestations. McDougall's hormic theory (1930) also represented a revolt against the simplistic approaches of tropism and Pavlovian conditioning. McDougall was in strong opposition to all mechanistic conceptions prevalent around the turn of the century.

But Pavlov's conditioning approach and Watson's behaviorism can also, of course, be regarded as part of comparative psychology. A large variety of different species and organisms have been investigated by their procedures. In the Soviet Union, and in this country through the efforts of Razran (1965, 1971), who responded mainly to Soviet research materials, a new "evolutionary psychology" has been developed on Pavlovian principles. This psychology views each learning process and each growth process as an expression of adaptive requirements under specific ecological conditions. The psychology of learning looks very different indeed when conceived in terms of such phylogenetic and ecological orientation and when the emphasis is put on the learning of what, why, under what adaptive stress, by what kind of an organism. This way of thinking has not yet fully "sunk in" to American experimental psychology; although here, too, there are exceptions (Bitterman, 1965; Skinner, 1966) and definite signs of forthcoming change. So heavily had the experimental psychologist relied upon the white rat—and so few were those who objected to this single-species approach and its underlying physical-science model—that it seemed to be hard even to frame properly the question of whether the basic learning phenomena, so thoroughly studied in the rat, appeared in all rodents, or in all mammals, or in all animals. In a widely influential address, Beach ("The Snark Was a Boojum," 1950) reminded his colleagues of this situation. Psychology had been trying so hard to achieve a general sense of the specifics that the boojum, among others, had been forgotten.

In an endeavor initiated by Yerkes (1916) and Köhler (1917) to get a picture of more complex functions, some comparative psychologists turned to primate research. But the questions still had to be asked: Are rhesus monkeys like spider monkeys? Or among the apes, are gibbons essentially similar to chimpanzees? And finally, where does man stand in all this? Even the studies of many species, including many primate species, have had to round out the evolutionary question of whether these species do, in fact, live in comparable habitats, and what in their phylogenetic history, ecology, behavior, and physiology is specific to them, or common to some, or to all. Detailed descriptive studies of the behavior of many primate species in their natural wild habitat (see De Vore, 1965) will resolve many of these issues. Modern comparative psychology and ethology have made their major contributions precisely by concentrating on such issues and by protesting against restricting behavior experiments to a few species and to environments which are not natural to these species.

These issues, as we have seen, were largely disregarded in the development of American experimental psychology. Of course, there were exceptions. The most remarkable of these was Lashley (1938), who cannot be properly classified either as a behaviorist, a physiological psychologist, or a comparative psychologist; for he had devoted a great deal of attention to problems of behavior and neurophysiology, as well as to species-typical differences in behavior and physiological mechanisms associated with evolutionary adaptation of species. During the period between the two world wars, much of American comparative psychology outside of Lashley's influence seemed to be preoccupied with the synthesis of a *tabula rasa* conception of behavioral development and the Darwinian conception of adaptation. The intellectual mentor of this trend was Holt (1931), who argued that the prenatal as well as postnatal functional organization of the nervous system is based on intrinsically random growth processes and nonrandom influences of experience. This view was greatly bolstered by Kuo's series of papers (1932) on prenatal behavioral developments, which supported the notion that experience is a decisive factor in the prenatal development of behavior. More recent investigations of prenatal behavioral development (Gottlieb, 1968; Hamburger and Oppenheim, 1967; Kovach, 1970), however, show some shortcomings in Kuo's primarily descriptive procedures and indicate that his environmentalism may have been overstated.

The experiential and epigenetic conceptions of Holt and Kuo were further supported by the similar positions taken in Maier and Schneirla's influential book, *Principles of Animal Psychology* (1935). A strong group of "epigeneticists" arose in the wake of these efforts, their work and interests centering on the proposition that evolutionary psychology must be based on an epigenetic conception of behavioral development, in which the primary emphasis is put on the environment and experience (including prenatal environment and experience arising from self-stimulation) and on the phenotypic expression of inheritance. Invigorated by a newly emerging understanding of environmental and developmental influence in the phenotypic expression of a morphological genotype, this approach grew into a powerful force in the evolutionary study of neurophysiological and behavioral development. The achievements and current state of affairs in this area are best exemplified in the volume of essays published in the memory of T. C. Schneirla, *Development and Evolution of Behavior* (Aronson *et al.,* 1970).

Meanwhile, others followed Lashley's path in taking neither the extreme environmentalist nor the extreme constitutionalist point of view. Nissen (1958), for example, concentrated on the basic categories to be used for behavioral comparison of species in an evolutionary comparative psychology. Beach's major interests lay with a comparative analysis of sexual behavior and its hormonal mechanisms (1964). It is safe to say, however, that even in these cases experientialistic and environmentalistic approaches were central; and that, in contrast to the primarily constitutionalistic emphasis of European ethologists (a group of naturalists and zoologists, whose interests lay with the behavior of organisms in their natural habitat), epigenetic conceptions of behavioral development continued to dominate American comparative psychology. It is not surprising, therefore, that when the European ethological and the American comparative psychological ideas finally evolved to the point of possible synthesis, there was a crash head on. Lehrman (1953) heaped criticism on ethology on the grounds that it is finalistic; that it fails to take into account the proper influence of experience; that it uses teleological concepts which are not subject to proper empirical study; and so on. Much of this criticism, of course, was justified and has been resolved by gradual modification of ethological thinking. But the impact of European ethology on comparative psychology in North America, and in the Soviet Union, has been at least as great and as forceful as the impact of American comparative epigenetic approaches were on ethology. Their synthesis, as exemplified in Marler and Hamilton (1966) and more recently in Hinde (1970), is being carried to a point of fusion within a single comparative evolutionary discipline for the study of animal and human behavior.

Ethology's early pioneers were Whitman (1919), Heinroth (1910), Craig (1918), and Lorenz (1935). All were highly sensitive and competent naturalists concerned with minute details in species-typical differentiation of behavior. Many of their early explanations were centered on "instinctive behavior": on those highly complex adaptive behavior patterns which are exhibited by animals without any trace of rational understanding, and, in many instances, without the requirement of elaborate prior training (such as a beaver building a dam, or a bird migrating over thousands of unchartered miles from one exact spot on the globe to another).

Lorenz, the acknowledged dean of contemporary ethology, proposed a theoretical scheme of variable energy levels (action-specific energies) which were said to be related to instinctive behavioral acts and subject to release by well-defined external stimulation (releasers). He argued that both the behavioral act and the recognition of its releasing stimuli are innate, requiring no prior experiential shaping, and that action-specific energies are being continuously produced and stored in the central nervous system. The releaser was said to remove specific internal inhibitory factors and thereby release energy and action. In the absence of such stimulation, Lorenz argued, a continuous accumulation of energy takes place and, as a result of overflow, an instinctive act may appear even in the absence of proper external stimulation. This notion was supported by observations of the so-called vacuum activities, in which identifiable instinctive movements appear under conditions of stimulus deprivation and out of any useful functional context.

Tinbergen (1951) further elaborated on this system and postulated that instinctive behavioral acts and their internal releasing mechanisms are organized, within the central nervous system, in hierarchical fashion. We should note that this postulate dates back to one of the founders of modern neurology, J. Hughlings Jackson (see Taylor, 1958, pp. 422–43). Its application to so-called instinctive behavioral acts opened the door for the neurophysiological inquiries of Holst (1937) and others. It soon became apparent, however, that neither Lorenz's energy concept nor Tinbergen's hierarchical organization of instincts would fully withstand detailed logical and empirical scrutiny.

There was a great deal of argument about the proper conceptual status of energy in the field of ethology and in the study of behavior (Kennedy, 1954). The issues here resemble in many ways the difficulties in the use of energy concepts within the Freudian system and in the mixing of causative and functional explanations in Pavlovian psychology, which we will discuss in the next chapter on Soviet psychology. It became clear that experience and feedback from behavioral acts may be as important in the development of species-typical "instinctive" behavior patterns as they are in the development of everything else in behavior.

While there were very finely differentiated species-typical capacities found which had apparently evolved within the context of highly specific ecological conditions, the behavior patterns considered in the early days of ethological thinking to be genetically fixed and free of learning have not been shown free of all experiential influences. The history of an experiment by Tinbergen, which has been frequently cited as an example of innate perceptual schemata and innate releasing mechanisms, clearly shows both the strengths and weaknesses in early ethological thinking. Tinbergen (1948) found that an artificial hawk-goose model elicited alarm and avoidance responses in fowl when the pattern was flown overhead in one direction only — in the direction in which it resembled the flight of a hawk. When the direction was reversed so that the model resembled a flying goose (moving in the direction of the longer protrusion that had been the *tail* in the hawk flight pattern but now became the *neck* of the goose), there was no response at all. The hawk pattern was said to constitute the proper "releaser" for the instinctive escape response. A number of investigators tried to replicate this experiment and found no results similar to Tinbergen's; there was either no response to the model or the response was not differentiated according to the hawk versus goose characteristics of the model. At first the issue of "species-specificity" was raised, but subsequently more carefully collected evidence indicated that any flying object overhead may elicit avoidance and fear responses in the naïve neonate of some avian species, regardless of shape or flight pattern.

The controversy seems to be resolved at this point by the conclusion (Schleidt, 1961) that the differences in the responses to the hawk-goose model found by Tinbergen were not caused by highly specific differentiation in innate perception, but more likely by prior habituation and learning for which there was no proper control in his study. The common flight of geese overhead in Tinbergen's natural environment may have resulted in partial and stimulus-specific habituation of natural fear responses to objects flying overhead; the response to geese disappeared while the response to hawks remained. There appear to be general and specific species-typical perceptual patterns which result in unique response tendencies: any object flying overhead may elicit escape in some naïve fowl, and some configurational properties may in fact be more effective than others (Hess, 1962). These, however, do not appear to be as minutely specialized or as free of experience as had been assumed in earlier ethological thinking. Ethology made its contribution by calling attention to the great species-typical variations in behavior and to the need for examining behavior in the natural environment of species. Experimental and comparative psychology made their contribution by pointing to the fact that experience is important at all levels of behavioral development.

We should note that there is a considerable amount of current ethology-related work in the Soviet Union today (Kovach, 1971). The leader of this group is Slonim (see p. 391), who, together with a number of other Soviet investigators, works on problems of species-specific and ecological variables in the development of behavior. A rich Soviet literature is now available on maturational and ecological adequacy of stimulation in conditioning, which make earlier notions of a uniform "learning process" (to be studied in a single species and in uniform laboratory environment) more and more outdated.

Behavioral Development: Instincts, Motives, and Imprinting

The full impact of ethological thinking reverberated in the entire field of psychology, primarily through the concept of and research on imprinting. Imprinting is a quick early-learning process in which lasting social attachments and preferences become firmly established.

So great was the strength of "associationistic" tradition before the emergence of this new line of research that for a long time all tastes and preferences, deeply ingrained loves and hates, codes and values and ideals by which man lives were conceived to be molded entirely by the association of ideas. When Edmund Burke wrote his classic essay "On the Sublime and the Beautiful," he had before him the association theory of Hartley. When James Mill brought 'up his little son in rectitude of taste as well as belief, he did it by following a tradition older than even that of association psychology. The concept of "acquired tastes" was an implicit part of education even before the Book of Proverbs, or Plutarch's *Lives,* or Cicero's *Discourse on Old Age.* The conditioning formula of Pavlov provided a new approach to the same problem; and the acquisition of preferences, and of tastes and values, was quickly wrapped up within the conditioning scheme. It is remarkable how many attempts were made, and are being made, to rectify the "associationist" and "Pavlovian" formulations of the problem of early behavioral development. But the concept of imprinting has engaged fresh experimental thinking. Its appeal was immediate for the experimental as well as the clinical psychologist, because of its unmistakable relevance to an age-old problem — to the problem of how experience, especially early experience, can permanently modify not only a specific S-R connection but also a host of motivationally and cognitively related processes in environmental and social interaction. We shall now review briefly some of the earlier efforts related to this problem and examine some of the work undertaken before the concept of imprinting was formulated and adequately documented.

In *An Introduction to Social Psychology,* McDougall (1908) noted that drives do not function in the same way before and after their elicitation by a specific adequate stimulus. The drive is elicited by the stimulus, and thereafter solid habits can be shown to have developed out of it. One then continues to prefer the specific stimulus or the specific activity which has undergone this process of elicitation and attachment. According to McDougall, usually several "instincts," such as love, admiration, fear, and obeisance, are elicited in a kind of cluster. The term "sentiment" was then applied to a constellation of "instinctual energies" invested in this way in a specific object. Freud, of course, had already developed the theory of the investment of instinctual energies and its significance in the relative firmness of normal character. For McDougall, the sentiments, rather than the raw instincts, were the prime movers of social life.

A few years later, Woodworth (1918) devoted a lecture series to an analysis of McDougall's concepts. He reached the conclusion that instincts do not actually underlie or constitute a core of continuing habitual activities; rather, habits which have mediated the way to a goal may become intrinsically motivating in their own right. A somewhat similar doctrine, in the context of Allport's sophisticated conception of the unity of personality, was offered under the term "functional autonomy"; for Allport (1937), systems of human values or preoccupations, regardless of their origin, may achieve functional autonomy and become central in the guidance of relevant meaningful behavior. No reference need be made to the origin of such values if one wished simply to study the actual dynamic of its present occurrence. Several other doctrines were developed early in the twentieth century, breaking away from both the purely associationistic model and the use of Pavlovian conditioning formula as explanations for deeply ingrained, strongly motivated action patterns. The canalization hypotheses of Holt (1931) and Murphy (1947) should also be mentioned here. According to these hypotheses, the combined influence of initial preferences and learning experiences will exert directive influence on the behavioral selectivity for and developmental influences of subsequent experiences, and thus they will lead to progressive channeling of behavioral development.

In the meantime, much research material, heretofore neglected, began to be recalled; and new concepts emerged. It had been shown by Whitman (1919) that in hand-raised doves and pigeons sexual behavior may be elicited by the experimenter's hand and indeed that such behavior may become a habit sufficiently structured to interfere with the bird's normal sociosexual behavior. From this followed an observation by Lorenz (1935) which emphasized the early association of a specific adequate stimulus with a particular innate response. The Graylag gosling, for example, which usually follows its mother, was found to follow any moving object present in its field of view during a particularly early period of sensitivity; as a result, on reaching sexual maturity it showed preference for the early stimulus as the focal object of sociosexual interaction. The experimenter, if he moved briskly forward when the goslings were at the right age, could become the adequate stimulus for this early social interaction and remain "imprinted" for the rest of the goslings' lives. This simple observation elicited a great deal of interest and excitement about imprinting which has not yet subsided. The possible formative influence of phylogenetically determined predispositions and brief early experiences led to many questions about the formation of behavioral and drive patterns and of lasting social bonds—questions which were not properly answered by the old associationistic model nor by the later concepts of acquired autonomous drives.

Much of Lorenz's early data on imprinting was gathered by naturalistic observations. He relied heavily on a concept of instinct which is no longer acceptable to the majority of contemporary ethologists and psychologists

(Lehrman, 1970). The problem of imprinting, however, was quickly brought into the laboratory. Fabricius (1951) in Sweden devised the first imprinting apparatus in which artificial inanimate models elicited following behavior in young precocial birds. Later, primarily through the efforts of Hess (1959), the significance of imprinting for all of psychology became known and widely acknowledged. Hess, together with a still growing number of researchers, subjected the imprinting phenomena to meticulous studies. In these studies specific stimulus preferences and strictly limited sensitive periods for early following behavior and social attachment were demonstrated. However, no general agreement has emerged from these studies as to whether the imprinting process can be reduced to a general associationistic model (Moltz, 1960) or is a truly independent phenomenon.

The recent history of imprinting research once again shows the importance of standardized procedures in the definition of a phenomenon and in testing its paradigmatic significance. In comparative psychology the importance of specific procedures was first demonstrated by Pavlov's conditioning technique, and later by the Yerkes alley, the Lashley jumping stand, the Skinner box, and the like. The imprinting techniques of Fabricius (1951), later Ramsay and Hess (1954), and later still Kovach *et al.* (1969) led to a proliferation of imprinting studies and a more precise definition of what imprinting is all about. This in turn led to ever broadening studies of neonatal behavioral development through the use of imprinting procedures. The early theoretical formulations of imprinting by Lorenz (1935) are seriously questioned today (Schneirla, 1967), but imprinting is here to stay as a major experimental technique for the investigation of early behavioral development—especially for the study of how "inherited" preferences and response tendencies interact with maturation and experience in early life and how these result in lasting influences on behavioral development.

The imprinting principle elicited immediate interest from experimental psychologists, clinicians, and psychoanalysts. Clearly, there was something here which was closely related to the clinical problems of cathexis and fixation. Experimental evidence of imprinting in man, however, has proved to be difficult to establish. There is so much Pavlovian and operant conditioning in infancy, and the cultural and individual differences are so huge, that it is difficult to find clear examples of the imprinting principle sufficiently uniform and compellingly different from what is already explicable on some other basis. But the most important potential contribution of comparative psychology to the understanding of human behavior is not in the identification of uniform cross-species mechanisms, but rather in the creation of new models by which new areas and new variables, species-general or human, can be examined. The imprinting conceptualizations and research have proved invaluable in this effort.

It is also in the light of heuristic models that some current ethological approaches to human behavior should be evaluated. The extreme forms of these approaches reached the laity through the popular publications of Lorenz (*On Aggression,* 1966), Ardrey (*The Territorial Imperative,* 1966), and Morris (*The Naked Ape,* 1967, *The Human Zoo,* 1969). The general thesis in all these books is that man is not free from the phylogenetic heritage given to him by his primate ancestry; and that factors of social instincts, territoriality, aggression, and so on, which can be seen and tested in animals, are significant phylogenetically given determinants of human behavior. There can be, of course, no denial that man is not free of a highly specialized phylogenetic history, but the specifics of these interpretations and their heavy generalizations from the behavior of lower organisms to human behavior may not be justifiable. Nor do popularized publications — and their necessarily partisan emphasis on one or another from a myriad of equally important variables — represent the proper forum for establishing how ethology and comparative psychology may contribute to the understanding of human behavior. The significance of ethological contributions does not lie with such popularizations, but with the definitive studies which show that there are indeed critical stages in behavioral development in practically all species; that species-typical ecological conditions and related constitutionally given phylogenetic derivatives of neural and somatic functioning do indeed significantly influence the development of behavior; and that both phylogenetic and ontogenetic factors in behavioral development are subject to proper conceptualization, description, and experimental study. These are the truly significant and important issues that ethology has contributed and continues to contribute to psychology.

In the perspective of the many overstated generalizations from man to animal, or from animal to man, we again and again encounter the curious problem of enormous changes in the human brain in the brief moment, geologically speaking, since man passed the manlike, or hominid, level and became man. Against the backdrop of geological time it is extraordinary that a mere two million years have tripled the size of his brain, altered his posture, developed the usable hand with good eye-hand coordination, altered his relation to tools of creative and aggressive capacity, and catapulted him into the world of symbols and concepts. We seem to be caught here between two equally unserviceable ideas: (1) that his learning ability or his thought capacity makes no difference to his basic jungle nature; he will be just as wild and as mean as before but more clever in the implementation of his jungle drives; and (2) that he will soon creep away from his animal inheritance and live in a symbolic world filled with its own imaginative possibilities. The truth or, better still, the empirical reality is somewhere between these two extreme formulations. It is in the unraveling of the myriad of factors in this zone of in-between that the ultimate contribution of ethology and comparative psychology will lie.

Genetics and Behavior

The issues we have just discussed, of course, are inseparably intertwined with another pervasive product of evolutionary thinking—the field of behavioral genetics. Galton (1899) had seen the broad contours of the issue and had stressed both species heredity and individual heredity. Pearson (1904) developed a biometric and statistical aspect of parent-child and other blood kin relationships, and Thorndike (1905), always present where there were quantitative issues to be defined, had done twin-resemblance studies. Simple Mendelian relationships were pushed far, and feeble-mindedness and other pathologies were even regarded as simple Mendelian characteristics. The discovery of the gene, and the examination of its exact biological and biochemical settings with simple species like the fruit fly, led, on the one hand, into more and more biochemical analysis of the nature of the work done by the gene and, on the other hand, to problems of complex phylogenetic determination and degrees of "penetrance," that is, degrees to which a genetic effect may succeed in expressing itself at the observable phenotypic level. Students of psychology, in awe before the rapid and sure completion of a skeletal structure of modern genetics by Morgan (1911), went along with the prevailing modes of thinking. Wherever problems of behavior forced them to the challenging issues of "behavior genetics," psychologists gave up looking for simple Mendelian factors and became interested in complex polygenic effects. The gradual disappearance of the classical nature-nurture problem, and its replacement by various complex issues of interdependence between organism and environment, required more sophisticated use of behavioral analysis, including the complex mathematical models and statistics of Morganian genetics.

Two illustrations of this modern research may be allowed: one to show the outcome of straightforward Mendelian thinking, the other to show the complexities. On the basis of a pedigree study of a large number of persons with phenylketonuria (phenylpyruvic acid in the urine), a simple Mendelian recessive was identified. In certain family lines phenylketonuria was accompanied by mental and behavioral defects. Elaborate biochemical work showed a series of steps by which the original operation of the gene generated a condition in which damage was done to the central nervous system. On the basis of further chemical analysis, it was discovered that a proper diet given very early in life might avert or reduce the severity of the mental defect. Thus, what was a straightforward Mendelian hereditary effect could nonetheless be approached in environmental terms, provided that the chemistry was well understood and that the treatment was administered at the proper critical early stages of development.

Somewhat similar thinking went into the discovery by Hall (1947) that "audiogenic seizures" in mice in response to a loud sound (in which death from seizures almost always supervened) allowed a genetic analysis. Ginsburg (1963) went on to contrive a biochemical program to buffer the effects of the genes that were involved so that they could produce mice that did not have convulsions and mice whose convulsions did not lead to death, all behaving as straightforward gene theory would predict.

The complexities of these issues were highlighted by the massive experiments of Tryon (1942). His genetic study with rats was carried on over many generations of breeding the "bright" with the "bright" and the "dull" with the "dull," until he had produced almost nonoverlapping strains with respect to brightness in maze-learning problems. It looked as if "intelligence" were a polygenic capacity that could be distilled by genetic selection. Further work (Searle, 1949) showed, however, that the "bright" in the maze were not especially bright in other types of learning tasks, and it appeared doubtful whether general intelligence was really involved. In fact, it began to look as if drive, or motivation, or interest, or some other type of affective variable could be responsible for most of the effects. It became apparent that concentration upon gross behavioral capacities (such as the learning capacity of Tryon's selection experiments) has to be broken down to smaller intermediate units for meaningful genetic or behavioral analysis. The so-called "Tryon effect" (the lack of significant differences between the learning-trait variances of F_1 and F_2 hybrid crosses of selected lines, and its implication that the selected traits were highly polygenic) militated against refined structural-genetic analysis. On the behavioral side, the difficulty of identifying the primary variable (or variables) influenced by genetic selection prevented a thorough understanding of the investigated "learning capacity." But the mere recognition that genetic factors are important in the development of behavior, and that these factors are subject to experimental investigation, provided the impetus for the birth of a new field: the field of behavior genetics. The significance of this field in introducing the latest biological outlook into psychology is matched by a truly extensive research output during the past two decades.

As happened in other fast-growing scientific disciplines, the recognition of a central issue (of the role of genetic factors in behavior) quickly led to methodological and conceptual subspecializations for tackling it. These subsections of behavioral genetics may be categorized under the following interrelated headings: (1) *structural genetics of behavior,* the area which emphasizes identification of specific genetic factors relating to behavior; (2) *structural-physiological genetics of behavior,* the area which focuses on biochemical and neural mechanisms that mediate between identified genetic factors and overt behavior; (3) *psychogenetics,* the area which emphasizes genetic manipulation of some major behavioral mechanisms (such as learning, activity, emotion, drive, and so on); and (4) *genetics of behavioral development,* the area which emphasizes strain and genotype dependent differences in the process of behavioral development. In the light of the huge research output produced by these subareas, the issue that genetic factors are involved in behavior became a point of departure rather than a focus in itself.

The four major procedures used in structural behavior genetic studies are (1) artificial selection for specific behavioral traits; (2) crosses between lines selected for specific behavioral traits and analysis of the F_1 and F_2 hybrid variances and their backcrosses to parental strains; (3) analysis of intra-family and interfamily correlations of specific behavioral traits; and (4) multiple intercrosses and diallel crosses in situations where relatively clear genotype-behavior trait relationships are established. The majority of structural genetic studies emphasized the genotype-behavior relationship and focused on behavioral phenomena which are by and large marginal to the full picture of behavioral development, such as audiogenic seizure susceptibility (Hall, 1947; Ginsburg, 1963), alcohol preferences (McClearn and Rodgers, 1959; Fuller, 1964), locomotor abilities (Thompson, 1953; McClearn, 1959), hoarding behavior (Stamm, 1954), and so on. The particular structural genetic emphasis in these studies was also apparent in the use of species which are well suited for genetic analysis, especially the *Drosophila*. Particularly significant in this area were the studies of Hirsch (Hirsch and Boudreau, 1958; Hirsch and Tryon, 1956) of the phototaxic and geotaxic responses in the *Drosophila* and the mass selection procedure developed by him for effective and quick identification of behavioral traits in large populations. Such behavioral analyses were necessary for an effective genetic selection of behavioral traits and effective structural-genetic analysis of the selected traits (for heritability estimates, possible Mendelian mechanisms, epistatic effects, chromosomal linkages, and so on).

Regarding the directions of structural-physiological genetics of behavior and psychogenetics, two major points have been made. Ginsburg (1958) argued that genetically produced enzymatic variations should be used as the natural bridge between structural genetics and behavior. Fuller and Thompson (1960), on the other hand, argued (without negating the value of genetic psychochemistry) that the "natural units of behavior must be defined at a behavioral level, not in terms of genetics, chemistry, or neurology." However, in view of some more current investigative frameworks, the answer seems to reside in the relationships between natural units of behavior, their mediating mechanisms at the physiological-morphological levels, and their determinants in the genotype-environmental interaction process. Thus the issue appears to be not one of separation of different levels of inquiry, but rather of their integration. It is an issue of identifying units of behavior which are subject to clear genetic manipulation, finding the relevant variables in morphological mediation, and relating them to both ends of the continuum: to the genotype and to the behavioral phenotype. This investigative approach is now being implemented in several laboratories. Perhaps the most noteworthy among these is the work by Krech, Rosenzweig, and Bennett (see Rosenzweig, 1969), who investigated brain cholin-esterase activity in relation to visual learning in Tryon's maze-bright and maze-dull strains and found a positive relationship.

But regarding the theory of behavior and the introduction of a basic bio-logical outlook into the field of psychology, perhaps the most important area of behavioral genetics is that which concerns itself with the develop-ment of behavior. Here both sides of the coin discussed in the preceding section appear simultaneously. Some of the work concentrates on marginal behavioral phenomena but provides thorough genetic-developmental analy-sis, while in others genetically influenced differences are demonstrated in central behavior-developmental processes, the complexity of which does not allow refined structural genetic analysis. The former is characterized by the studies of the influence of auditory priming during early developmental stages upon the phenotypic expression of audiogenic seizures (Henry and Bowman, 1970) and by studies of genetic-developmental influences in brain cholinesterase activity and related learning. The latter approach appears in studies of strain differences in early socialization processes (such as those by Scott and Fuller, 1965). These demonstrate clear genetic influences (strain and breed differences) in early socialization and related critical develop-mental stages and show that no single testing age is appropriate for full appreciation of the joint effects of environmental input and genetic determi-nants in behavioral development. All these studies show the complexity of developmental interactions between heredity and environment. The dis-cipline of many such studies has been teaching psychologists the enormous difficulties of achieving sharp and clear thinking regarding heredity.

A large number of twin studies in schizophrenics and other psychiatric groups have also inched ahead and produced evidence that the blood rela-tives of schizophrenics are more likely to be schizophrenic than are random controls, even when elaborate exclusion of environmental affects is achieved. Current studies (Kety, 1970), especially in the Scandinavian countries, have shown that the chances of becoming a schizophrenic remains great even when the offspring is removed from schizophrenic parents in early infancy. However, the almost endlessly reiterated issues regarding the "inheritance of schizophrenia" have not yet received full accreditation.

The brilliance of the work in basic genetics done by Watson and Crick (1953), of Nobel fame, has made genetics, to use the term comprehensively, an exact science. The sequence of steps from triumph in molecular biology to the inheritance of schizophrenia, or to sibling resemblances in the white rat, or to inherited tendencies in imprinting proneness of the Japanese quail, is a long and complex one. But genetics and behavioral genetics have made a significant contribution to the entire field of psychology in addition to their successes in solving immediate empirical issues at hand. They have taken the lead in showing that typological thinking (Mayr, 1965) is not the proper way for the life sciences and psychology; that thinking in terms of abstract categories and classes within which an individual event is regarded as having meaning only as a representative of a class or category leads to the neglect of the much more important problems of experiential and hereditary individuality. Recent volumes in behavioral genetics, such as those by Fuller and Thompson (1960), Hirsch (1969), and Manosevitz, Lindzey, and Thiessen (1969), have been important in establishing the field as a mature discipline and in pointing out some major fallacies in the prevalent typological mode of thinking in psychology. The leadership of Hirsch (1969) is of particular importance in this respect. He calls for a complete reorientation of psychology back to its legitimate roots in the life sciences, back to the recognition of the tremendous role of hereditary and experiential individuality in everything organismic and behavioral. This of course does not mean a return to the era of instinctivistic preoccupation of some four or five decades ago. Current evidence (Denenberg, 1967) shows that in organisms even as lowly as the rat subtle influences of early experience in the parental generation may be retained by succeeding generations through unknown channels of social communication and learning. This kind of evidence is as significant in the new biopsychological outlook as are the demonstrations of phylogenetic derivatives and hereditary components in the behavioral adaptation of all species and organisms. A deep concern with the complex and fine interplay between phylogenetic and ontogenetic adaptation, between unfolding genetic potentials and individual experiences, is at the center of this newly emerging biological outlook in psychology.

Research on Stress

A huge amount of research in the last few decades has been organized on the concept of "stress." This psychophysiological problem permits both clinical and experimental analysis. In its simplest forms, stress can be regarded as a high degree of stimulus "overload" on the organism, which may break the organism's protective barriers. One may think of stress in terms of a high level of activation and note that beyond the critical point at which activation is facilitated, hyperstimulation may become disruptive and disorganizing. Such stresses may produce permanent organic damage. The stress-damage relationship has become prominent in psychosomatic medicine. Chronic and severe stresses are often not understood by the patient, nor are the processes of activation and entanglement of internal signals which bring about a confusing internally maintained stress pattern. These issues have become very important in psychoanalysis.

A distinction must be made, of course, between general stress levels and their specific symptomatic expressions (Alexander, 1950). The latter can be conceptualized as cathexis upon certain organs or parts of the body leading to effective reaction to threat directed toward this organ or part. Stresses of this sort can be aroused experimentally and handled experimentally, as

Grinker and Spiegel (1945) and their multidisciplinary team have done. They have looked at the biochemical, physiological, psychoanalytic, cross-cultural, and so forth, aspects of experimentally induced stresses. Sometimes the whole life history was surveyed, as by Binger and his collaborators (1945), to understand the onset of the stress and its psychosomatic expression at a particular time and place. Clinical and experimental methods were combined by Wolff (1953), who worked with a patient sustaining an injury to the esophagus. This subject had to be fed through a gastric fistula and was therefore observable in a hospital setting at all times. Emotional stress of this patient immediately became visible in heightened blood flow, hydrochloric acid flow, and hypermobility. With Selye (1950) the chief emphasis has been on a "general adaptation syndrome." He was concerned not only with episodic responses but with the course of responses in time under conditions of increasing stress—with the development of stress responses from initial periods of adaptation to breakdown in normal functioning.

All these studies, from the minute examination of the neurochemical mechanisms of nerve-impulse propagation to concepts like Selye's "adaptation syndrome" or the ethological concern with behavior in its total ecological setting, leave us with some unresolved and perhaps unresolvable questions of analytic-reductionistic versus holistic conceptions of organic functioning and behavior.

The research and conceptualizations we have described here may leave one with the feeling of piecemeal and disjointed work. This is a function of the progressive specialization at both conceptual and methodological levels, in which controlled technological progress plays a dominant role. From this viewpoint it is not surprising that a vast array of modern psychophysiological knowledge is obtained with instruments which were discovered or perfected only a few years, or a few months, ago. In fact, there are complaints that the journals carry much that is out of date, much that has been superseded by still unpublished papers. To try to balance such fragmentation, there is a growing interdisciplinary struggle for synthesis: for example, when the cultural anthropologist notes blood pressure and biochemical factors which differentiate between subcultural groups that vary in the level of their competitive achievement drives. Concepts lead to the application of new techniques, and new techniques change the flow of concepts.

No human or animal capacity can nowadays be considered exempt from analysis in terms of anatomy, physiology, and biochemistry. The psychologist has long wanted to know what goes on in the individual cell. Now with suitable electronic and biochemical techniques he can indeed peer inside a cell, and he is beginning to see what happens as the organism remembers or forgets. Moreover, with laboratory animals at his command, he can carry out finer and finer anatomical analyses of the specialized regions for specialized functions. Using powerful biochemical aids he can at last talk meaningfully about learning and memory as chemical processes. Improved research techniques have enabled the psychologist to move easily and freely from anatomical to physiological and to biochemical levels of analysis, so that he can easily regard a function as a "thing" to be identified in time and space, and measured, and weighed. This has been particularly striking in the conceptualization of memory as a block or load of matter, much like the memory bank of a computer. In this passage from the dynamic view of behavior to the structural, we are reminded of the earnest concern of a few years ago: the concern not to "reify," that is, to make a thing or a substance out of a process. The ground rules for "reification" are beginning to depend today less on a priori logic than on instrumental possibilities.

REFERENCES

Alexander, F. *Psychosomatic Medicine*. New York: Norton, 1950.

Allport, G. W. *Personality: A Psychological Interpretation*. New York: Holt, 1937.

Ardrey, R. *The Territorial Imperative*. New York: Atheneum, 1966.

Aronson, L. P., Tobach, E., Lehrman, D. S., and Rosenblatt, J. S., eds. *Development and Evolution of Behavior*. San Francisco: Freeman, 1970.

Beach, F. A. "The Snark Was a Boojum." *American Psychologist*, 5 (1950), 115–24.

———. "Biological Bases for Reproductive Behavior." In W. Etkin, ed. *Evolution of Social Behavior*. Chicago: University of Chicago Press, 1964.

Berger, J. "Über das Elektrenkephalogramm des Menschen." I, *Archiv für Psychiatrie und Nervenkrankheiten*, 87 (1929), 527–71.

Binger, C. A., Ackerman, N. W., Cohn, A. E., Schroeder, H. A., and Steele, J. M. "Personality in Arterial Hypertension." *Psychosomatic Medicine Monograph*, 8 (1945).

Bitterman, M. E. "The Evolution of Intelligence." *Scientific American*, 212 (1965), 92–100.

Cannon, W. B. *The Wisdom of the Body*. Rev. ed. New York: Norton, 1939.

Coghill, G. E. *Anatomy and the Problem of Behavior*. New York: Macmillan, 1929.

Craig, W. "Appetites and Aversions as Constituents of Instincts." *Biological Bulletin*, 34 (1918), 91–107.

Denenberg, V. H., and Rosenberg, K. M. "Nongenetic Transmission of Information." *Nature*, 216 (1967), 549–50.

De Vore, I., ed. *Primate Behavior*. New York: Holt, Rinehart and Winston, 1965.

Duffy, E. "Emotion: An Example of the Need for Reorientation in Psychology." *Psychological Review*, 41 (1934), 184–98.

Eccles, J. C. "The Effects of Use and Disuse on Synaptic Function." In J. F. Delafresnaye *et al.*, eds. *Brain Mechanisms and Learning*. Oxford: Blackwell Scientific, 1961.

Fabricius, E. "Zur Ethologie junger Anatiden." *Acta Zoologica Fennica*, 68 (1951), 1–175.

Fritsch, G. T., and Hitzig, E. "Über die Elektrische Erregbarkeit des Grosshirns." *Archiv für Anatomie und Physiologie* (1870), 300–332.

Fuller, J. L. "Measurement of Alcohol Preference in Genetic Experiments." *Journal of Comparative Physiology and Psychology*, 57 (1964), 85–88.

Fuller, J. L., and Thompson, W. R. *Behavior Genetics*. New York: Wiley, 1960.

Galambos, R. "A Glia-Neural Theory of Brain Function." *Proceedings of the National Academy of Science*, 57 (1961), 129–36.

Galton, F. *Natural Inheritance*. London: Macmillan, 1899.

Ginsburg, B. E. "Genetics as a Tool in the Study of Behavior." *Perspectives in Biology and Medicine*, 1 (1958), 397–424.

――――. "Causal Mechanisms in Audiogenic Seizures." *Colloques Internationaux du Centre National de la Recherche Scientifique*, No. 112 (1963), 217–25.

Gottlieb, G. "Prenatal Behavior of Birds." *Quarterly Review of Biology*, 43 (1968), 148–74.

Grinker, R. R., and Spiegel, J. P. *Men Under Stress*. Philadelphia: Blakiston, 1945.

Grossman, S. P. *A Textbook of Physiological Psychology*. New York: Wiley, 1967.

Hall, C. S. "Genetic Differences in Fatal Audiogenic Seizures Between Two Inbred Strains of House Mice." *Journal of Heredity*, 38 (1947), 2–6.

Hamburger, V., and Oppenheim, R. "Prehatching Motility and Hatching Behavior in the Chick." *Journal of Experimental Zoology*, 166 (1967), 171–204.

Hebb, D. O. *The Organization of Behavior*. New York: Wiley, 1949.

Heinroth, O. "Beitrage zur Biologie, Nahmentlich Ethologie und Physiologie der Anatiden." *5 International Ornithologisches Kongress* (1910), 589–702.

Helson, H. "Adaptation Level Theory." In S. Koch, ed. *Psychology: A Study of a Science*. Vol. 1. New York: McGraw-Hill, 1959.

Henry, K. R., and Bowman, R. E. "Behavior-Genetic Analysis of the Ontogeny of Acoustically Primed Audiogenic Seizures in Mice." *Journal of Comparative Physiology and Psychology*, 70 (1970), 235–41.

Hess, E. H. "Imprinting." *Science*, 130 (1959), 133–41.

――――. "Ethology: An Approach Toward the Complete Analysis of Behavior." In R. Brown *et al.*, eds. *New Directions in Psychology*. New York: Holt, Rinehart and Winston, 1962.

Hilgard, E. R., and Marquis, D. G. *Conditioning and Learning*. New York: Appleton-Century, 1940.

Hinde, R. A. *Animal Behavior: A Synthesis of Ethology and Comparative Psychology*, 2d ed. New York: McGraw-Hill, 1970.

Hirsch, J. "Behavior-Genetic, or 'Experimental,' Analysis: The Challenge of Science Versus the Lure of Technology." In M. Manosevitz *et al.*, eds. *Behavioral Genetics: Method and Research*. New York: Appleton-Century-Crofts, 1969.

Hirsch, J., and Boudreau, J. C. "Studies in Experimental Behavior Genetics: The Heritability of Phototaxis in a Population of *Drosophila melanogaster*." *Journal of Comparative Physiology and Psychology*, 51 (1958), 647–51.

Hirsch, J., and Tryon, R. "Mass Screening and Reliable Individual Measurement in the Experimental Behavior Genetics of Lower Organisms." *Psychological Bulletin*, 53 (1956), 402–10.

Hofman, A. ["Psychotomimetic Drugs."] *Acta Physiologica et Pharmacologica Neerlandica*, 8 (1959), 240–58.

Holst, E. von. "Vom Wesen der Ordnung im Zentralnervensystem." *Naturwissenschrift*, 25 (1937), 625–31, 641–47.

Holt, E. B. *Animal Drive and Learning Process: An Essay Toward Radical Empiricism*. New York: Holt, 1931.

Jennings, H. S. *The Behavior of the Lower Organisms.* New York: Columbia University Press, 1906.

Kappers, C. U. A. "Further Contributions on Neurobiotaxis. IX. An Attempt to Compare the Phenomena of Neurobiotaxis with Other Phenomena of Taxis and Tropism. The Dynamic Polarization of the Neurone." *Journal of Comparative Neurology,* 27 (1917), 261–98.

Kennedy, J. S. "Is Modern Ethology Objective?" *British Journal of Animal Behavior,* 2 (1954), 12–19.

Kety, S. S. "Genetic-Environmental Interactions in the Schizophrenic Syndrome." In R. Cancro, ed. *The Schizophrenic Reactions.* New York: Brunner/Mazel, 1970.

Köhler, W. *Intellegenzprüfungen an Menschenaffen.* Berlin: Springer, 1917.

Konorski, J. "Mechanisms of Learning." In *Physiological Mechanisms in Animal Behavior.* Society for Experimental Biology, Symposium No. 4. New York: Academic Press, 1950.

Kovach, J. K. "Development and Mechanisms of Behavior in the Chick Embryo During the Last Five Days of Incubation." *Journal of Comparative Physiology and Psychology,* 73 (1970), 392–406.

———. "Ethology in the Soviet Union." *Behaviour,* 39 (1971), 237–65.

Kovach, J. K., Callies, D., and Hartzell, R. "An Automated Procedure for the Study of Perceptual Imprinting." *Perceptual and Motor Skills,* 29 (1969), 123–28.

Kuo, Z. Y. "Ontogeny of Embryonic Behavior in Aves. I: The Chronology and General Nature of the Behavior of the Chick Embryo. II: The Mechanical Factors in Various Stages Leading to Hatching." *Journal of Experimental Zoology,* 61 (1932), 395–430, 453–89. "III: The Structure and Environmental Factors in Embryonic Behavior. IV: The Influence of Embryonic Movements upon the Behavior After Hatching." *Journal of Comparative Psychology,* 13 (1932), 245–72; 14 (1932), 109–22.

Lashley, K. S. "Experimental Analysis of Instinctive Behavior." *Psychological Review,* 45 (1938), 445–71.

Lehrman, D. S. "A Critique of Konrad Lorenz's Theory of Instinctive Behavior." *Quarterly Review of Biology,* 28 (1953), 337–63.

———. "Semantic and Conceptual Issues in the Nature-Nurture Problem." In L. P. Aronson *et al.,* eds. *Development and Evolution of Behavior.* San Francisco: Freeman, 1970.

Lorente de Nó, R. "Analysis of the Activity of the Chains of Internuncial Neurons." *Journal of Neurophysiology,* 1 (1938), 207–44.

Lorenz, K. Z. "Der Kumpan in der Umwelt des Vogels; die Antgenosse als Auslosends Moment Sozialer Verhaltungsweisen." *Journal of Ornithology,* 83 (1935), 137–213, 289–413.

———. "Companionship in Bird Life; Fellow Members of the Species as Releasers of Social Behavior." In C. H. Schiller, ed. *Instinctive Behavior.* New York: International Universities Press, 1957.

———. *On Aggression.* New York: Harcourt Brace Jovanovich, 1966.

Maier, N. R. F., and Schneirla, T. C. *Principles of Animal Psychology.* New York: McGraw-Hill, 1935.

Marler, P., and Hamilton, W. J. *Mechanisms of Animal Behavior.* New York: Wiley, 1966.

Mayr, E. *Animal Species and Evolution.* Cambridge, Mass.: Harvard University Press, 1965.

McClearn, G. E. "The Genetics of Mouse Behavior in Novel Situations." *Journal of Comparative Physiology and Psychology,* 52 (1959), 62–67.

McClearn, G. E., and Rodgers, D. A. "Differences in Alcohol Preference Among Inbred Strains of Mice." *Quarterly Journal of Studies of Alcohol,* 20 (1959), 691–95.

McDougall, W. *An Introduction to Social Psychology.* London: Methuen, 1908.

———. "The Hormic Psychology." In C. Murchison, ed. *Psychologies of 1930.* Worcester, Mass.: Clark University Press, 1930.

Moltz, H. "Imprinting: Empirical Basis and Theoretical Significance." *Psychological Bulletin,* 57 (1960), 291–314.

Morgan, T. H. "The Origin of Five Mutations in Eye Color in *Drosophila* and Their Modes of Inheritance." *Science,* 33 (1911), 534–37.

Morris, D. *The Naked Ape.* London: Cape, 1967.

———. *The Human Zoo.* New York: McGraw-Hill, 1969.

Moruzzi, G., and Magoun, H. W. "Brainstem Reticular Formation and Activation of the EEG." *EEG Clinical Neurophysiology,* 1 (1949), 455.

Murphy, G. *Personality.* New York: Harper, 1947. Also New York: Basic Books, 1966.

Nissen, H. W. "Axes of Behavioral Comparison." In A. Roe and G. C. Simpson, eds. *Behavior and Evolution.* New Haven: Yale University Press, 1958.

Olds, J. "Approach-Avoidance Dissociation in Rat Brain." *American Journal of Physiology,* 199 (1960), 965.

Pearson, K. "On the Laws of Inheritance in Man: II. On the Inheritance of the Mental and Moral Characters in Man, and Its Comparison with the Inheritance of Physical Characters." *Biometricka,* 3 (1904), 131–90.

Penfield, W. "Memory Mechanisms." *Archives of Neurology and Psychiatry,* 67 (1952), 178–98.

Ramón y Cajal, S. *Histologie du système nerveux de l'homme et des vertébrés.* Vol. 2. Paris: Maloine, 1911.

Ramsay, A. O., and Hess, E. H. "A Laboratory Approach to the Study of Imprinting." *Wilson Bulletin,* 66 (1954), 196–206.

Razran, G. "Russian Physiologists' Psychology and American Experimental Psychology: A Historical and a Systematic Collation and a Look into the Future." *Psychological Bulletin,* 62 (1965), 42–64.

———. *Mind in Evolution: An East-West Synthesis of Learned Behavior and Cognition.* Boston: Houghton Mifflin, 1971.

Romanes, G. J. *Mental Evolution in Animals.* London: Kegan, Paul, Trench, 1884.

Rosenzweig, M. R. "Effects of Heredity and Environment on Brain Chemistry, Brain Anatomy, and Learning Ability in the Rat." In M. Manosevitz *et al.,* eds. *Behavioral Genetics: Method and Research.* New York: Appleton-Century-Crofts, 1969.

Schleidt, W. M. "Reaktionen von Truthuhnern auf fliegende Raubvogel und Versuche zur Analyse ihrer AAM's." *Zeitschrift für Tierpsychologie,* 18 (1961), 534–60.

Schneirla, T. C. "An Evolutionary and Developmental Theory of Biphasic Processes Underlying Approach and Withdrawal." In M. R. Jones, ed. *Nebraska Symposium on Motivation, 1959.* Lincoln: University of Nebraska Press, 1959.

Scott, J. P., and Fuller, J. L. *Genetics and Social Behavior of the Dog.* Chicago: University of Chicago Press, 1965.

Searle, L. V. "The Organization of Hereditary Maze-Brightness and Maze-Dullness." *Genetic Psychology Monograph,* 39 (1949), 279–325.

Selye, H. *The Physiology and Pathology of Exposure to Stress.* Montreal: ACTA, 1950.

Skinner, B. F. "The Phylogeny and Ontogeny of Behavior." *Science,* 153 (1966), 1205–13.

Sperry, R. W. "Physiological Plasticity and Brain Circuit Theory." In H. F. Harlow and C. N. Woolsey, eds. *Biological and Biochemical Bases of Behavior.* Madison: University of Wisconsin Press, 1958.

Stamm, J. S. "Genetics of Hoarding. I. Hoarding Differences Between Homozygous Strains of Rats." *Journal of Comparative Physiology and Psychology,* 47 (1954), 157–61.

Tanzi, E. "I fatti e le induzione nell'odierna istologia del sistema nervoso." *Rivista Sperimentale di Freniatria,* 19 (1893), 419–72.

Taylor, J., ed. *Selected Writings of John Hughlings Jackson.* New York: Basic Books, 1958.

Thompson, W. R. "The Inheritance of Behavior: Behavioral Differences in Fifteen Mouse Strains." *Canadian Journal of Psychology,* 7 (1953), 145–55.

Thorndike, E. L. *The Measurement of Twins.* New York: Science Press, 1905.

Tinbergen, N. "Social Releasers and the Experimental Method Required for Their Study." *Wilson Bulletin,* 60 (1948), 6–52.

———. *The Study of Instinct.* Oxford: Oxford University Press, 1951.

Tryon, R. C. "Individual Differences." In F. A. Moss, ed. *Comparative Psychology.* Englewood Cliffs, N.J.: Prentice-Hall, 1942.

Watson, J. D., and Crick, F. H. C. "A Structure for Desoxyribose Nucleic Acid." *Nature,* 171 (1953), 737–38.

Whitman, C. O. "The Behavior of Pigeons." *Carnegie Institute of Washington Publication,* 257 (1919), 1–161.

Wolff, H. G. *Stress and Disease.* Springfield, Ill.: Thomas, 1953.

Woodworth, R. S. *Dynamic Psychology.* New York: Columbia University Press, 1918.

Yerkes, R. M. "The Mental Life of Monkeys and Apes: A Study of Ideational Behavior." *Behavior Monograph,* No. 12 (1916).

NOTE: A list of further readings appears at the back of the book.

23

Soviet
Psychology

The central physiological phenomenon in the normal work of the cerebral hemispheres is that which we have termed the conditioned reflex.
PAVLOV

Soviet psychology poses particular problems for a historical survey. The magnitude of its existing and potential impact on the entire body of modern psychology makes the customary discussions of a few major figures and ideas especially superficial. Nor can we justifiably accord the limiting status of a "school" or a "system" to all of psychological work in the Soviet Union. Such misleading conceptions of Soviet psychology are born in the all-absorbing brevity and categorical generalization demanded from that faithful servant of science, the textbook writer. They are perpetuated by linguistic and ideological barriers which stand between Western and Soviet psychologists.

Soviet psychology interlocks in a diverse way with the entire body of contemporary psychology. Why, then, this single chapter on Soviet psychology? Why not present the contributions of Soviet psychologists in their relevant international context? It is because the Soviet work cannot be properly evaluated without highlighting first the essential turning points in its growth, without discussing the major sociohistorical and ideological conditions which fostered some healthy developments and stifled others. The aim of this chapter, therefore, is *neither* to present a thorough summary of Soviet psychological ideas *nor* to convey the impression that Soviet psychology is an independent school or system, but rather to provide the necessary historical background for some major psychological ideas developed in the Soviet Union and to show the points of struggle between a modern science and a modern ideology.

We are fortunate that able men, especially Gregory Razran and Josef Brozek, have devoted considerable time and energy to interpreting developments in Soviet psychology for Western audiences. We are also fortunate

377

in having the recent *Handbook of Soviet Psychology* (edited by Cole and Maltzman, 1969) in the English language. This work contains not only articles by practically all the current leaders of Soviet psychology but also an excellent historical survey of the major events that shaped the development of psychology in the Soviet Union. It is more up to date and in many ways more informative than the original Russian language handbook from which it departs (*Psikhologicheskaia Nauka v SSSR,* 1959–60). Nevertheless, even this English language handbook may leave the uninitiated reader at a loss when he tries to understand the major conceptual, philosophical, and ideological approaches that are taken for granted by Soviet contributors. For example, the opening article in the Russian language handbook, written by Leont'ev (1959, Vol. 1), a Lenin prize laureate who appeared to be at that time the major ideological mentor of Soviet psychology, is devoted to problems of the acquisition of "sociohistorical experiences," which is, of course, a central theme in Marxist ideology. The same topic by Leont'ev reappears in the English language handbook, but only in a relatively colorless chapter in which the earlier unmistakable ideological message is obscured by empirical considerations on the training of auditory abilities in man. The reader is not alerted to the fact that he may be reading the current chief ideologist of Soviet psychology, although Leont'ev is still the single most frequently cited author in the handbook. Is this to mean that there is a current shift or relaxation in the ideological grip over psychology in the Soviet Union? Or have the editors missed some important aspects of the interaction between ideological prescriptions and scientific aims in the growth of Soviet psychology? These difficult questions would be of minor concern to us here but for the fact that Soviet psychology is unique only because of the unique ideological demands imposed upon all who have practiced it. The first step in understanding the development of Soviet psychology, therefore, is to examine the sociopolitical background and nature of these ideological demands and to see how Soviet psychologists have coped with them.

Sociopolitical Events That Influenced the Growth of Soviet Psychology

As we have indicated in the preceding chapters, the three outstanding progenitors of Russian psychology were Sechenov, Pavlov, and Bekhterev (see pp. 240 ff.). Their work was very much in tune with the general developments of late nineteenth- and early twentieth-century psychology and physiology; their influence on Western psychology has been as great as it has been on the development of prerevolutionary Russian psychology. The October revolution in 1917 created a new climate in Russia, which, despite the great hardships during the ensuing civil war, was at the outset congenial to the development of all sciences, including psychology. Pavlov continued to practice his inferential approach and physiological reductionism. His influence, however, was by no means dominant at this time. There were those who followed the Gestalt approach and still others who espoused the general behavioristic outlook that was gaining momentum everywhere during the twenties. Bekhterev's reflexology was particularly influential among the latter. It soon became apparent, however, that the central Marxist propositions on the theory of knowledge and the various current psychological postulates on man's contact with reality are closely and dialectically related. New demands emerged: first for their synthesis and shortly thereafter for the reformulation of psychological ideas in terms of the basic Leninist-Marxist postulates.

Kornilov (see Razran, 1958) was the leader of the synthesizers. Before the revolution he worked in the laboratory of Chelpanov, who was the leading Wundtian psychologist in prerevolutionary Russia. He rose to prominence quickly after the revolution and by 1924 became the director of the leading psychological laboratory in the Soviet Union and the leader of a semi-independent school which he named "reactology." His popular *Textbook of Psychology from the Standpoint of Dialectical Materialism,* first published in 1926, was an attempt to reconcile behaviorism with the philosophical tenets of Marxism, as he understood them both. However, stripped of the generous overlay of socioeconomic and class considerations, Kornilov's reactology had little new to offer beyond the then-popular mechanistic conceptions for the study of behavior and the rejection of consciousness as a proper subject matter in psychology.

The 1920s marked the beginning of Sovietization of Marxist philosophy and the growth of a central ideological control over all intellectual activities in the young state. These developments were not characterized by a thrust for logically tight and consistent postulates; rather they were forced and concentrated efforts to provide a functional system of concepts to be used in the proclaimed task of transforming society. Transformation of society and creation of a new "Soviet man" have remained the major objectives and ideological prescriptions throughout the Soviet era.

When applied to the immediate task of the industrialization of a backward multinational empire, Marxist philosophy quickly became the instrument of uniform and absolute political control. It is not surprising, therefore, that Kornilov's sincere but premature efforts at synthesizing Marxism and current psychology were judged wanting. Reactology's demise was as quick and as complete as its rise. It disappeared from the scene by 1930, together with practically all the various trends and disciplines that flourished during the twenties. Kornilov remained a leading figure, until his death in 1957, in the renewed efforts to interpret psychology in terms of dialectical materialism.

The first drastic change in the development of psychology is generally attributed to the appearance of Lenin's philosophical notebooks, a posthumous collection of marginal comments and notes on a variety of philosophical treatises (mainly on those by Hegel) which was probably not intended for publication (see his *Collected Works,* 1933–47). But looking at the tremendous social upheavals and dislocations that once again began to take place after the relative quiet of the NEP[1] period, Lenin's notebooks seem to have been the tool, not the cause. From this time on, it was the Stalinist version of Marxism which dictated the ups and downs of Soviet psychology. Thus a 1936 decree[2] of the Communist party's Central Committee on "pedological distortions" legislated psychological testing and practically all other psychological activities out of existence – after the fact, however: all psychological journals, for example, which came into existence during the twenties had ceased publication long before this decree, somewhere between 1932 and 1934. The few psychological studies that remained found publishing outlets only in educational journals. It is clear from the wording, "pedological distortions," that even the field of education was not a safe haven for psychologists. Interestingly, Pavlovian physiological psychology was left alone at this time. Pavlov's system may not have been in full agreement with dialectical materialism, but neither were there open conflicts between them.

Apart from Pavlovian work, there was very little psychological material published between the middle of the 1930s and the late 1940s. The research activity during this period had no systematic outlet and was preserved mostly in unpublished notes from various research establishments and in rare publications under the auspices of educational institutions. The single book worthy of note, Rubinshtein's *Foundations of General Psychology* (1940), went through several editions. It represented another effort at formulating psychological issues, especially the issue of consciousness, in terms of Marxist ideology. We will return to the problem of consciousness in the following section on dialectical materialism and the science of behavior. Here we should note only that consciousness was treated by Rubinshtein as the highest form of matter in motion, which is an attribute of man's higher nervous activities and is the historical product of his social interaction, language, and labor. By 1947, Rubinshtein's attempt at reconciling Marxism and psychology also fell into disfavor and was subjected to severe criticism. He was accused of an inadequate understanding of the new condition of labor and social realities which form the "new Soviet man" and of a heavy reliance on Western psychology.

The next significant turn of events took place in 1949, with the celebration of the hundredth anniversary of Pavlov's birth. This marked the beginning of Pavlov's elevation to the sanctity of Soviet classics. In the following year, a joint congress of the Academy of Sciences and the Academy of Medical Sciences was held on the teachings of Pavlov, and a new program was put forth for complete Pavlovization of behavioral and physiological sciences. The official organizers of this congress were Bykov and Ivanov-

---

[1] Lenin's New Economic Policy, which brought some measure of relaxation in the centralized economic and political control during the twenties.

[2] See the editors' introduction in Cole and Maltzman (1969).

Smolenskii; the latter received the Stalin prize for his interpretation of Pavlov's system (Ivanov-Smolenskii, 1954).

Razran (1958a) argues that there was nothing in the Pavlovian system that would have been uniquely suited to dialectical materialism. The elevation of Pavlov's theories into a position of dogma, he argues, is explainable only by Stalin's aims at Russofication of all Soviet sciences; Pavlov fitted the bill because he was both Russian and internationally prominent. This argument, however, needs qualification. There is nothing intrinsically contradictory between dialectical materialism and the Pavlovian system; there are, in fact, considerable similarities between the two. Both the dialectical materialistic and the Pavlovian system lack a clear conceptual differentiation between the factual and the inferred, and both are marked by a confusion of, and free interchange between, explanation in terms of specific adaptive functions and in terms of antecedent causal links.

The 1950 joint congress and some of its consequences were in many ways comparable to the happenings which had taken place only two years earlier as a closing chapter in the complete eradication, under the infamous leadership of Lysenko,[3] of all but Lamarckian (of the Michurin variety) genetics in the Soviet Union, including the actual annihilation of those who stood by Mendelian genetics. One might argue that the Lamarckian view of genetic inheritance (which was made an official Soviet dogma in the forties and was included as the proper course for the development of biological sciences as late as 1961 in the program of the Communist party of the Soviet Union)[4] is more in agreement with the basic tenets of dialectical materialism than with Mendelian genetics. This, however, is almost irrelevant to our present discussion because the forced synthesis of Marxist ideology and science in the Soviet Union always seemed to have been overshadowed by an arbitrary subordination of both ideology and science to a centralized and absolute political power. There can be no question, for example, that the major problem in Soviet economy, the constant lag in agricultural output, could have been alleviated by the application of the findings of Mendelian genetics, as happened in Western agriculture. It is equally clear that purely ideological considerations *alone* could not have suppressed the wealth of data supporting the Mendelian and Morganian interpretations of inheritance and their promise for improved agricultural output. It is the ruthless control over the entire society by one man, Stalin, with the corrupt servitude of a few pseudoscientists like Lysenko and Ivanov-Smolenskii that one can give as the sole explanation for these happenings. No historian can explain them in any other way; no current Soviet scientist would want him to explain it in any other way.

Concluding this brief summary of major historical events in Soviet psy-

[3] For a detailed account, see Medvedev, 1969.

[4] The relevant sentence reads: "It is essential to develop more broadly and deeply the Michurin line in biology, which is based on the proposition that conditions of life are primary in the development of the organic world" (Dmytryshyn, 1965, p. 518).

chology, we should point out a new, more encouraging trend. Stalin's death resulted in a slow but steady reversal in the Pavlovization of Soviet psychology. All those who were forced to self-criticisms and admission of deviation from the then-correct Marxist line (Anokhin, Orbeli, Beritashvili, Kupalov) regained their leading positions. The appearance of the new journal *Problems of Psychology,* in 1955, and the publication of the first *Handbook of Soviet Psychology,* in 1959 and 1960, marked psychology's coming of age in the Soviet Union. More recently, in 1968, a decree by the Council of Ministers for the first time officially recognized psychology as an independent scientific discipline and authorized the granting of higher degrees in this field (Brozek, 1970). There is presently a great creative turmoil in Soviet psychology, hinting at a bright and promising future.

Dialectical Materialism and the Science of Behavior

Biriukov (1963) stated in a paper dealing with the philosophical problems of the study of higher nervous activities that "Soviet investigators are in possession of such advantages as the objective method of experimentation worked out by Pavlov, the application of Marxist philosophy, and the theory of evolution." It is no accident that he mentioned these three factors in a single breath, for they are indistinguishably and uniquely intertwined in the official Soviet philosophy of behavioral science. The following four propositions form the fundamental Marxist basis for the latter:[5] (1) that motion is the mode of existence of all matter; (2) that the motion of matter provides the key to understanding the historical continuity between inorganic, organic, and human-social matter; (3) that the reciprocal influence of things in motion necessarily contains contradictions which in historical-developmental processes form the basis for a dialectical thesis-antithesis-synthesis paradigm; (4) that the thesis-antithesis-synthesis paradigm is both explanatory and predictive, in that it results in identifiable and qualitatively different steps and stages along single historical continua. These propositions, combined with the emphasis on the implementation of social change in accord with "well-established laws of history" rather than in terms of an evolving understanding and continued elaboration of such "laws," form the basis for the unique ideological control that has been imposed on Soviet psychology.

The central tenet in Marxist conceptualization of historical stages as they occur in the behavior of inorganic, living, and social matters is the concept of "reflection,"[6] which is also a central theme in the dialectical material-

[5] The best exposition of these propositions is to be found in Engels's *Ludwig Feuerbach and Herr Eugen Dühring's Revolution in Science.*

[6] The understanding of the concept of reflection is of particular significance for students of Soviet psychology and officially sanctioned epistemology. It does not mean "reflection" as in "meditative reflection," but rather as in "reflection by a mirror." The best exposition of the use of this concept in Leninist-Marxist dialectical materialism is to be found in Lenin (1927).

istic theory of knowledge. A considerable part of Biriukov's paper, for example, on the fundamental philosophical problems in the evolutionary physiology of higher neural activity, is devoted to this very issue. Biriukov first cites Lenin as saying: "It is logical to state that all matter possesses a quality which in fact is related to sensation; namely the quality of reflection"; he concludes that this statement by Lenin not only takes care of the relationships in the behavioral manifestation of matter in all its forms, but also implies successive developmental steps in "reflective capacity." He then goes on to point out that this capacity, while related to the phenomena of reflection in the inorganic world, is quite different in living systems for which the outstanding characteristic is the presence of a nervous system. Landygina-Kots (1956) goes a step further in using this mixture of epistemology and dialectics. She states: "Living matter in comparison to nonliving matter possesses a unique form of reflection, namely excitability on the basis of which during the process of evolution progressively higher forms of reflection emerge, such as sensation, perception, imagination, and thinking."

Such insistence on a dialectical-historical progression, and on identifiable qualitative steps and stages within this progression, leads directly to an interpretation of experimental data in which there is a subtle fusion of explanation by reference to adaptive functions and to antecedent causes. It is precisely at this point—at the lack of appreciation of the fundamental differences between questions demanding functional explanations (why, what for, what aim is accomplished?) and those demanding causative explanations (how, where from, by what causal links does it come about?)—that the Pavlovian system was open for an embrace by dialectical materialism.

This issue is also at the heart of the theory of knowledge in Soviet philosophy of science, as it is best exemplified in the following oft-quoted statement by Lenin: "Sensations of time and space enable men to orient in a biologically goal-directed manner. This is possible only because of the fact that his senses reflect the objective external reality since man could not adapt to his environment if his senses did not give him an objectively correct picture of it." The issue here, of course, is as old as philosophy itself: What constitutes reality, and what is man's contact with it? Lenin's "common sense" argument proposes a causal link (that the senses reflect objective reality) and a functional proof (that the senses reflect objective reality because this leads to successful adaptation).

There are two fundamental difficulties with this argument: (1) it perpetuates confusion between causal and functional explanations, and (2) it neglects the scientifically all-important issues of operational and statistical definition and linguistic communication of the observed "objective external reality." While these difficulties do not negate the materialistic outlook Lenin defended in his argument, the lack of consideration of these difficulties and the uncritical acceptance of Lenin's position may have created persistent problems in Soviet psychology.

The dialectical emphasis on interactive reflection of the environment by the organism, of course, also may explain the remarkable endurance of Lamarckism in Soviet biology and social sciences even after Stalin's death. Reflection and synthesis of the environment in ontogenetic and evolutionary development is, after all, the central thesis of Lamarck as well as of Marx. The works and influence of the latter, however, further complicated Soviet scientific approaches to behavior because of an unguarded eagerness of Soviet biologists and psychologists to apply focus on society and his concepts of social change to the biological realm. Another quotation from Biriukov (1963, p. 359) will illustrate the point:

> There is hardly anyone who would take it upon himself to reject the significance of *individual internal changeability* (author's italics), which has the broadest relevance. Having been fixed by the way of genetic transmission, this changeability may exercise the deepest influence on society as a whole. After all, approaching man from the point of view of his most appropriate measure, from the point of view of society, we are interested not so much in man's perspective as a species as in his social perspective.

Similar sentiments are expressed in Leont'ev's discussion of the problems of human acquisition of sociohistoric experiences (1959). The Lamarckian flavor of this argument is currently toned down, but the major emphasis on the socioeconomic conditions and social factors which may lead to creation of the "new consciousness" of the "Soviet man" remains.

The active principle of "consciousness" has been retained in Soviet psychology ever since the rejection of Kornilov's reactology in the late twenties. Consciousness is defined as the highest state of reality reflection, characteristic only of man. It is said to be brought about by the dialectical processes inherent in man's communal labor, social interaction, and language. There are, however, no methodological tools offered for investigating "consciousness" other than those implicit in the functional analysis of linguistic and social interaction, which necessitated in the first place the active principle of consciousness, or those implicit in Pavlovian physiological reductionism.

If we accept the position that neither a philosophy nor a scientific theory leads to immutably correct information regarding objective reality, or to absolute procedures for comprehending reality, then the relationship between empirical data, scientific theory, and philosophy becomes a matter of intricate reciprocal influences. Theory testing in the realm of empirical phenomena must be inseparably linked with theory modification and theory replacement, which in turn must be reflected in a more precise formulation of philosophical knowledge. Furthermore, it can be argued that one of the most important functions of a given conceptual scheme (philosophical, ideological, theoretical, or paradigmatic) is to provide a well-circumscribed historical framework for scientific activity (Kuhn, 1962). The Marxist conceptual system has certainly provided a working framework of considerable value for collecting scientific data, yet it has been a restrictive framework. While data of high quality and value have been collected within it, it has also strictly limited the number of focal points in scientific activities, the mode and style of operation within acceptable areas, and the avenues open for modification and replacement of available theories.

The restrictive influence of the prevailing philosophical and ideological climate has been reflected in the following characteristics of Soviet psychology: (1) a confusion between functional and causative explanation; (2) a retention of an active principle of consciousness without provision for methodological procedures in its scientific analysis; (3) practically no direct research or interest in areas covered by such Western concepts as drive and motivation, and an intense hostility toward hormic, especially the Freudian, explanatory schemes; and (4) an intense preoccupation with stages and steps within the historical processes and organization of psychological and physiological phenomena, the investigation of which has preceded primarily along the single line projected by Pavlov.

There has been, however, an upsurge in new psychological ideas. While Pavlov's work is still considered central for the development of Soviet psychology, there is hardly anyone among the current major figures (with the single outstanding exception of Asratyan, 1969) who would follow completely the orthodox Pavlovian system outlined in the late forties by Ivanov-Smolenskii.

Pavlov's System Within the Framework of Dialectical Materialism

As we have seen in Chapter 16, the conditioned reflex is both the empirical tool and the theoretical basis in the Pavlovian system. It has provided the central experimental approach for inferential analysis and theoretical interpretation of the higher neural activities and neuropsychological mechanisms of the brain.

Early in his work on conditioning, Pavlov differentiated between physiological and psychic experiments. The "physiological experiment" consisted of presenting a stimulus, such as food or acid placed on a dog's tongue, which resulted in immediate unconditional elicitation of a reflex response, such as salivation. In the "psychic experiment" a *neutral* stimulus, such as the sound of a bell, was presented together with an unconditional stimulus (acid or food placed on the tongue). Through such associated presentation the originally neutral stimulus was shown to acquire the capacity of eliciting the response on its own. The elicitation of such a response was said to be "conditional" on previous association of the two stimuli, the bell and the acid. It is an unfortunate accident of mistranslation that Pavlov's terms "unconditional" and "conditional" became known in the English language as "conditioned" and "unconditioned." The latter carry the connotation of completed accomplishments, whereas Pavlov referred only to the differentiating circumstances of his physiological and psychic experiments.

Realizing the possible subjective connotation of the term "psychic," Pavlov soon relinquished its use. By 1911 he had established a rule that a fine be imposed on workers in his laboratory who made the mistake of using it. The concept and word, however, were once again resurrected in the Sovietized Pavlovian system. The reader will recall that consciousness, defined as the highest level of matter in motion, and as a principle in man's active participation in reality reflection, is a fundamental postulate in dialectical materialism. Kornilov's reactology was disposed of as adhering to "vulgar materialism," precisely because his system regarded the organism as a passive reactor rather than an active participant in the behavioral reflection of external reality. By contrast, Rubinshtein's treatment of consciousness was rejected on the grounds that it did not fully define the new consciousness of the "Soviet man" as a reflector of the new Soviet reality.

The methodological issues raised by the behaviorists and Kornilov regarding the study of consciousness, however, were not solved by this outright acceptance of consciousness as a scientifically valid concept. Physiological inference and reductionism do not solve these issues, for they get rid of consciousness as a subject matter of scientific analysis (as Pavlov knew already in the beginning of the century), in the same way as psychological inference and reductionism of the behaviorists did. The notion of differentiated levels of reality reflection, with consciousness on top, provided a useful analogy but did not solve the problem either. As the experience of Western psychology teaches us, there are simply no two ways about the problem of consciousness: the cake either has to be eaten or to be kept as a cake; and, for that matter, to be kept as a cake whose function of "to be eaten" may set the limits, but it does not give an explanation of the taste, or color, or weight, or calorie content, or any other content.

Returning to the Pavlovian system, it is the spatial and temporal relationships in the association of the CS (conditioned stimuli) and the UCS (unconditioned stimuli) and the establishment of the CR (conditioned response) that were taken as the fundamental inferential tools in the understanding of higher neural activities. The spread of cortical excitations and inhibitions were inferred from these variables. The temporal relationship in which the CS always precedes or coincides with the presentation of the UCS, if it is to acquire the proper CS status, led to the conceptualization of "signaling function." The CS was said to reflect, by signaling, the objective reality of a forthcoming UCS. The biological significance of the CS was its signaling function. When it was not followed in a lawful temporal order by the presentation of a UCS, it became a "false signal" and eventually resulted in active inhibition of the previously established CR. The failure of the CS in this interpretation was a functional failure, while the postulated relation of this "false signal" to the cortical spread of active inhibition was causal. The dialectical materialistic theory of reflection sat in the middle and obscured the issue of feedback control that is required for a purely causal analysis of the proposed purposivistic signaling function of stimuli.

Pavlov's system has been criticized by many on the grounds that its inferences of the cortical spread of excitations and inhibitions conceives of the neural tissue as a homogeneous energy transmitter and neglects the known separation and multidimensional connections of individual nerve cells. We should remind ourselves that Pavlov's system of inferences from observed overt response patterns to physiological activities of the cerebral cortex belongs to MacCorquodale and Meehl's category of hypothetical constructs (see p. 319). It provides a useful description of a broad spectrum of behavioral phenomena and supplies hints for possible physiological and neural models to be unraveled by direct physiological inquiry.

While intervening psychological variables, such as those covered by Western concepts of drive and motivation, were rejected outright by the followers of Pavlov, even these variables reentered the system through the back door of physiology. Ukhtomskii's physiological theory of dominance is a good example (1923). It states that the dominant neural center of cerebral excitation acquires controlling and self-perpetrating functions; this center draws into itself excitations occurring in other centers and thereby increases the excitation of the dominant center and decreases the excitation of subordinate centers. When we consider that such a dominant center may be under the control of a variety of internal stimuli (which received a great deal of investigative attention in the Soviet Union primarily from Bykov and his colleagues), we can see clearly that Ukhtomskii's theory of the "dominant" has much in common with Western concepts of drive and motivation and the ethological concept of appetitive behavior. In addition to the implicit hormic principle in Ukhtomskii's theory, the orienting reflex and second-signal system are also conceptualized as physiological processes which provide the general and basic energizing circuits within the system.

The Orienting Reflex and the Second-Signal System

It was evident that the acquisition and extinction of conditioned responses of whatever type occur in the midst of a continuous, restless stream of exploratory activities. Organisms constantly show "orienting reflexes"—as Pavlov said, "the what-is-it reactions." Pricking up of the ears, turning of the head, or, in man, puckering of the forehead muscles, or changes in the blood supply to various parts of the body betoken a system of responses quite different from conditioned responses. Such orienting responses pass off as the animal actually achieves adaptive orientation. From then on, the conditioning responses can be built up. This "orienting reflex" was taken as the basic energizer in the Pavlovian conditioning paradigm; systematic psychophysiological laws relating to orienting reflexes had been stressed by all adherents of the Pavlovian system (see Sokolov, 1959).

In man this energizing function was said to be supplemented by language.

Language in turn was said to be based on Pavlov's notion of a *second-signal system*—a system in which words acquire a second-order signaling function through association with first-order signals, the conditioned stimuli. Elements of speech were conceptualized as second-order signals for a compound of first-order conditioned stimuli and thus as being only indirectly related to associative experiences with the UCS. Through these mechanisms, it was argued, human speech permits a fuller reflection of reality than can be obtained in animal behavior. It was argued also that language in man takes over the leading role in psychic development, in which social cooperation and work are the major significant causal elements. Reflection of reality through speech was thus viewed as a collective and historical undertaking, in full agreement with related Marxist postulates. However, explanation lapsed from the causative to the functional once again. It was stated that human interaction requires a high degree of coordinated signaling functions which cannot be met alone by the first-signal system and its primary energizer, the orienting reflex.

The concept of a second-signal system may certainly be regarded as helpful in analyzing man's contact with the objective external world. But even apart from the flaws relating to its functional definition, this concept also opened up as yet unexplored avenues for reality distortion and reality manipulation. Language is said to be based not on the objective reality of elicited UCRs, but merely on the associative connections to compounds of changeable first-order signals for the UCRs. The potential answer to this problem seems to reside in the elaboration of specific neural functions and currently emerging neural feedback conceptions.

Conceptions of Neural Functioning and Feedback Mechanisms

The sociopolitical conditions of the thirties and forties resulted in the elimination of major segments of psychological activity but did not set the officially sanctioned clear course for the activities that remained. Rejection of Kornilov's and Rubinshtein's efforts specified the errors and deviations from the "correct" line but did not specify the particulars of the correct line itself, except in broad generalities. In many ways, psychology was on the fringe of major events of the time. Urgent pragmatic considerations, first of collectivization, then of preparing for and winning the war and rebuilding society from the devastation of the war, absorbed the energies of all—the ideologist and the psychologist. It was only after the war that the ideological interpretations and aims could evolve to the point at which detailed directives for the "shoulds" as well as the "should-nots" were outlined. The result was the Pavlovization of psychology in 1949 and 1950. In the meantime a number of original contributions on neural functioning appeared—most within the Pavlovian framework and some under various Western influences. These formed the basis for the spectacular recovery of Soviet psychology after Stalin's death.

Ukhtomskii's theory of the "dominant" (see p. 387) was perhaps the most significant among the earliest original contributions. It has introduced a conceptual framework for the problem of motivation and drive within the Pavlovian system. But the most revolutionary among all Soviet formulations in relation to the central Pavlovian system were those put forth by Bernshtein, Beritashvili, and Anokhin.

Bernshtein (1969) was the first among Soviet investigators to recognize the need for the type of objective purposivistic considerations introduced to Western psychology by Tolman, and to point out the importance of feedback mechanisms in understanding behavior. He has dealt directly with the problem of the purpose and future consequences of behavior and has proposed a synthesis of these issues and the Marxist philosophy of science.

Beritashvili (1969) is the major figure who disagreed from the earliest times with the Pavlovian system. His methods and experiments also bear close resemblance to the cognitive-learning techniques and explanations of Tolman. However, he went a step beyond Tolman in providing a physiological theory for the cognitive map. From the earliest times, he was concerned with learning situations in which the animal is allowed to exercise free movements; in this his work bears close relationship to American behaviorists. He made strict differentiation between inherited "instinctive" behavior patterns and learned behavior, much as some Western ethologists have done, especially Lorenz (1965). He believed that *innate* behavior patterns are fully determined by the constitutionally given organization of the central nervous system and *acquired* behavior by functional reorganization of the central nervous system as a result of repeated perceptual experience with the external world. In acquired behavior, he emphasized the development of images of external objects and stated that the presentation of the image of a biologically important object will elicit goal-directed behavior, the image eliciting the same behavior as the perception of the object itself. Furthermore, he also used a basic hedonistic principle in his conceptualizations. He argued that each behavioral act is related to emotional excitation, which in turn reflects satisfaction or creation of an organic need. He provided specific neurophysiological models for exploring these emotional excitations, as well as the postulated image forming mechanisms in the cortex.

Anokhin (1969) pointed out that a reflex act cannot be considered an identifiable unit separate from: (1) the afferent input; (2) its central synthesis; (3) the efferent output; (4) the results to which the efferent output leads; and, most importantly, (5) the reafferent feedback from such results. In addition to being in tune with current Western and Soviet developments in the field of cybernetics — and offering a solution to the causative-functional dilemma we have discussed above — Anokhin's conceptualizations also placed the problem of need-specific arousal and motivational states of the organism on more solid ground than Ukhtomskii's theory of "dominance" had done before him. Anokhin insisted that afferent selection and synthesis of stimuli are determined by specific states of the nervous system, which are caused by hormonal, cyclical, situational, and environmental variables; and that feedback from a behavioral act will set the limits for the subsequent afferent synthesis and elicitation of subsequent responses. Furthermore, it was Anokhin who first put forth the idea that unconditioned and conditioned responses always become integrated during behavioral ontogeny and exert reciprocally controlling and modifying influences on each other. This postulate became a central theoretical theme in the field of ecological physiology, the Soviet field for evolutionary study of animal behavior (Kovach, 1971). Research currently being undertaken in Anokhin's laboratory employs sophisticated physiological and biochemical techniques in the study of afferent synthesis and the role of afferent signals in neural functioning and behavior.

Ecological Physiology

The Soviet evolutionary psychology of animal behavior is commonly referred to by the term "ecological physiology." It may be roughly divided into the following two interrelated areas: (1) Pavlovian ecological physiology of behavior, which retains an essentially unmodified Pavlovian conception of behavior but emphasizes internal and external ecological variables; (2) currently emerging broader naturalistic-biological approaches to behavior, which are the closest in their concepts and interests to Western comparative psychology and ethology.

The major representatives of the essentially Pavlovian ecological physiology are Bykov (1942), Biriukov (1963), and Kalabukhov (1963). They have demonstrated in numerous experiments that the naturalness and functional relevance of a stimulus, within the normal internal and external ecology of a given organism, is positively related to its effectiveness in eliciting unconditioned reflex responses and establishing temporary stimulus-response associations. Most of Bykov's work, for example, has been in the area of what he termed "cortico-visceral physiology." He dealt with the specific factors of external and internal environments and the homeostatic variables that influence conditioning. Using interoceptive conditioning procedures he had succeeded in establishing systems of acquired connections between events at various points inside the body.

Much experimental ingenuity went into surgically connecting and disconnecting various visceral regions. He demonstrated, for example, that warm water in the stomach could become a "conditional stimulus" for another vegetative response at another part of the body not ordinarily associated with it. Exteroceptive stimulation such as sight, hearing, and touch were also cross-connected with these interoceptive responses. In the same way, the striped muscle system was brought into connection with both interoceptive and exteroceptive systems, and proprioceptive conditioning became very important in later studies of feedback. In fact, we encounter in Bykov a systematic concatenation of components all over the body in a manner very similar to the behavior stream paradigm of Watson.

The broader naturalistic-biological approach to animal behavior is one of the promising new developments in Soviet psychology. Its major current representative is Slonim (1967, 1969). He follows the line initiated by Anokhin (1949), Promptov (1956), and Khrushinskii (1962), which is based on the following basic propositions: (1) that the unconditioned reflex is inborn; (2) that the unconditioned reflex is permanent while the conditioned reflex is temporary; and (3) that the complex chains of species-typical behavioral acts almost always incorporate unconditioned and conditioned reflexes in variable proportions (corresponding to variable environmental demands) and in accordance with the species-typical internal and external ecology of organisms.

An example of the type of experimentation on the development of feeding behavior in a variety of species will illustrate the approaches and evidence in this field. These investigations show marked species-typical variations in the development of behavior. In some species, such as the rabbit investigated by Klimova (1958), the development of the adult feeding pattern appears to be dependent upon unconditioned reflex responses to natural food, which are retained throughout the entire life cycle of these animals. Rabbits that have been raised on artificial food until adulthood responded to their natural food, to grass, immediately upon the first given opportunity. In other organisms, as shown by Uzhdavini's studies of the unconditioned reflex responses to meat in puppies (1958), such inborn responses appear only during critical stages of development and thereafter disappear when not used in normal context of natural feeding. Uzhdavini's puppies had shown definite approach and salivary response to meat upon the first encounter with this food, but when raised on milk alone for up to nine months and beyond, the initially present unconditioned reflexlike responses to meat became unstable, and in some instances completely disappeared. In still another species (sheep investigated by Rakhimov, 1958), the development of natural feeding does not seem to depend at all on native unconditioned reflex responses to natural food, but rather on imitative behavior and learned responses. Lambs will not respond to grass upon first exposure to normal grazing conditions, but will imitate the grazing of sheep around them and will gradually learn how to graze.

All these studies emphasize the great differences in the behavioral development of different species. All bring into focus the difficulties psychologists must face in developing general cross-species theories of behavior. The problems these studies point to are the same as those we have discussed in the preceding chapter, in the section on ethology and comparative psychology: they point to the need for considering the great differences in the ecological variables and phylogenetic derivatives of somatic, neural, and behavioral functioning of different organisms.

Conceptions of Human Development

From the earliest time Soviet psychology emphasized the essentially social nature of human development and differentiated between the development of animal behavior and the development of human behavior by attributing consciousness (social consciousness) only to the latter. Vygotskii (1934, 1956) argued, for example, that the formation of a complex of new behavior patterns in animals is always based on individual experiences, whereas the mental development of man demands a social mastery of a broad range of human experiences through the acquisition and indirect processes of language.

Of particular concern for Vygotskii was the process of concept formation. He developed an experimental procedure for its study, in which he presented the subject with an assortment of objects: blocks varied in size, shape, volume, height, and color. The subject was instructed to sort these objects into different categories according to some generalizable attributes. Unknown to the subject, each object was identified by an artificial word (nonsense syllable) printed on the bottom of the block and not visible to the subject at the time of sorting. Each of these words represented one of the possible attributes for sorting. Whenever the subject made a mistake in sorting, the nonsense syllable of the misplaced object was revealed to him. He was then allowed to continue the sorting procedure. In this way, in the process of abstracting appropriate categories and sorting the objects accordingly, the subject was allowed to discover and learn the artificial verbal referents (nonsense syllables) of the categories to which the objects could be classified; the experiment dealt with the process of concept formation.

Vygotskii studied the developmental sequence of concept formation at a given time within a given individual. He also investigated subjects at different ages by this procedure and arrived at some very interesting conclusions regarding the development of concept formation in children. At the earliest stages of the child's development, words were not found to play a significant role; they were totally subordinated to the influence of immediate attentions and sensory impressions in the environment. The very young child did not sort the subjects according to clear categories; rather, he collected and grouped together those objects which fell within his field of vision, with no apparent selectivity. During a more advanced verbal stage of development, the child was found to be more selective, but he was inclined to use a family of concepts in which he combined different attributes and grouped a family of multidimensionally related objects. Thus, a large red cube, for example, may have been put into a single category with all red objects, all cubes, and all large objects. The next stage, according to Vygotskii, is brought about by systematic training; the selection of each object in the experiment quickly becomes dependent on clear, though subtle, relationships between the identifying artificial word and the abstract attributes of the object. Abstract meaning now becomes the guiding principle and criterion for the completion of sorting.

Another area that significantly involves verbal development is semantic conditioning. Here the relationships between the generalization of a conditioned response initially attached to a specific word were studied. The words presented in a generalization test have either related meanings but different phonetic properties, or closely related phonetic properties but different meanings (such as in the relationship between the Russian words *doktor* and *vrach,* both meaning in the everyday use of language a medical doctor, and between *doktor* and *diktor,* the first meaning "doctor" and the latter "announcer"). It was found that under normal conditions the conditioned response is generalized to meaning but not to phonetic similarity. Under the influence of certain drugs, however, the situation was reversed.

This type of work indicates that there are complex relations present in each word and that, as Razran has argued (1952), the second-order-signal system of Pavlov, referring to language, should not be equated with the straightforward one-to-one relationships of second-order conditioning. Rather it should be equated with the relationship of a single verbal signal to a compound of interrelated associative response connections.

Studies of Vygotskii (1956) and El'khonin (1958, 1959) have also concentrated on the development of speech and the relationship between written and spoken language. The idea of special training and upbringing seems to be especially related to the written language, necessitating the identification and separation of individual words from the totality of living language and also requring conceptual treatment of the phonetic properties of words and sentences.

Of particular importance here is the Russian concept of *vospitanie,* which encompasses more than either of the two corresponding English dictionary translations of "education" or "upbringing." Within the concept of *vospitanie* the emphasis was put on cooperation and communal effort in the specific tasks of academic education and personality development. *Vospitanie* came to be regarded as the decisive variable in personality development—as the most significant factor of social conditioning that mediates between the conventional psychological variables of "nature" and "nurture."

One of the fundamental reasons for intensive and systematic studies of childhood conditioning lies in the laws relating to the acquisition and use of language. As we have seen, language was very important to the early Pavlov and became more and more important with the Sovietization of the Pavlovian system. The Marxism of Lenin and of the Soviet educational system placed great stress upon language as a cultural vehicle by which behavior patterns were passed on from adults to children; indeed, the values and attitudes so heavily stressed in Marxist education were, of course, conceived to be transmitted and modulated mainly through the language system. Pavlov's conception of the second-signal system made it clear that the laws of human thought and communication are, in many respects, essentially *different* from the laws of animal communication, or indeed all prelanguage levels in both the animal and the small child.

The sociocultural aspects of language as consolidator of attitudes and values were investigated by Vygotskii (1956) and, later, by Luria (1961). Luria also worked on a variety of problems on the physiology of higher nervous activity of man. His major assumption was that the cortex is organized, as a result of social experience, into integrated functional systems which are not necessarily identical with clearly localizable cortical activities. Thus damage or destruction of specific cortical areas may, according to him, interfere with the existing functional system. But through proper training new identical or similar functional systems can be developed, which once again will successfully mediate the affected psychological activity.

Apart from this type of neurophysiological work and theory, there has also been a widespread interest in the application of conditioning procedures in human education and human behavioral development. There has been a great interest in conditioning studies with children, almost from the beginning of work in conditioning laboratories. Conditioning was seen as a way of giving the child a new response repertory; if the concepts of inhibition were properly applied the child might also be freed of undesirable tendencies. Such work has continued and increased in complexity since the beginning of the century, from studies of the simple avoiding responses to the intricate studies of interacting conditioning patterns which offer insight to the higher nervous activity in man (as in Krasnogorskii, 1954).

Zaporozhets (1969), a student of Vygotskii, is one of the current leaders of child psychology in the Soviet Union. His sensory-training procedures are aimed at developing ways through which children sense, perceive, and form graphic ideas. These studies are based on conceptions of Vygotskii, Leont'ev, and Rubinshtein, in which sensory training is viewed as resulting in a new development of processes and abilities which a child does not have at the time of birth, but which can be brought about by careful training.

Typology

Some Western observers have assumed that the Pavlovian system, and indeed all Soviet psychology, would be subject to the heavy hand of environmentalism and to denial of hereditary individuality. This, however, is far from the truth. It is true, in line with consistent Marxism, that the environment has been more greatly emphasized than in some corners of Western psychology, but a concern with constitutional capacities has always been present as a dominant theme in Soviet psychology. Typology (Teplov, 1964) has become of major importance within this context.

From the earliest days of his work, Pavlov was intrigued with the great individual variations in conditioning performances of different individuals. He proposed that these are due to some essential constitutionally given differences in their nervous systems. He had adapted the Hippocratic classification (choleric, melancholic, sanguine, and phlegmatic) in referring to individual differences in the relative balance of what he regarded as cortical inhibitory and excitatory processes. "Excitation" was defined by the relative vigor of responses to a positive conditioning signal, while the withholding of responses to a negative signal indicated "cortical inhibition." Both of these definitions were established by measured indicators of conditioning performances, especially in learning to discriminate between a positive and negative stimulus and in related stimulus generalizations. The term "balance" referred to the relative predominance of inhibitory or excitatory processes within a given individual. The term "strength" referred to the capacity of the nervous system to resist excessive excitation. Individuals were classified along the measure of strength according to their capacity to maintain a normal conditioning performance in the face of an interfering excitation of increasing magnitude and complexity. "Mobility" referred to the nervous capacity to respond quickly to proper stimulation, particularly to changes in the signaling significance of conditioned stimuli, as in stimulus-discrimination situations in which the negative and positive signals were reversed. There is a practically infinite variety of combinations possible along these measures, but Soviet investigators concentrated, by and large, on only the four categories roughly corresponding to those adapted by Pavlov. Thus a lively ("sanguine") type would score high on strength, balance, and mobility; the impulsive ("choleric") type would score high on strength but would show imbalance toward excitation; the sedate ("phlegmatic") type would score high on strength and balance but low on mobility; and, finally, the inert ("melancholic") type would be low on strength and mobility and would be imbalanced toward inhibition.

In reference to the typology of human personality, an additional category was added. This was the relative balance in the dependence on the second-signal system. Thus the "thinking type" was characterized as having high dependence on the second-signal system (more inclined toward abstract thinking), whereas the "artistic type" [7] was characterized as having primary dependence on the first-order-signal system (more direct contact with the environment). Ordinary mortals could occupy any points representing combinations of these two extremes; the majority, of course, would be somewhere in the middle.

In addition to this type of interest in constitutionally given typological differences among individuals, there is also considerable current interest in critical stages of human behavioral development which is said to be dependent on both maturation and experience. Gal'perin (1969), for example,

[7] It should be noted that this conception of the artistic type follows closely the dictates of socialist-realism.

has outlined a sequence of ontogenetic changes which must occur for the development of normal cognitive functions. In recent years Gal'perin's theory has been applied in the implementation of programed teaching techniques in an effort to make best use of the environment in individual development.

Environmentalism, of course, has often meant, in practice, the utilization of the environment to bring out leadership potential, just as the Soviet educational system as a whole has looked for early methods of assessing gifts which can be cultivated for the benefit of the state. We see very powerful nationalistic forces at work here: pride in the great achievements of Sechenov and in the spectacular international role of Pavlov; pride in the strength and flexibility of the laboratory and educational systems which have everywhere given the Pavlov method such scientific prestige on the one hand and apparent practical applicability on the other. Such nationalism, combined with the problems of ideological control we have discussed above, makes the Pavlovian system considerably different from the comparable conditioned-reflex systems and psychological approaches in the West. Still, Soviet psychology is not a closed system; nor is it in an unresolvable disharmony with Western psychology.

REFERENCES

Akademiia Pedagogicheskikh Nauk RSFSR, Institut Psikhologii. *Psikhologicheskaia Nauka v SSSR*. 2 vols. Moscow: APN-RSFSR, 1959–60.

Anokhin, P. K. [*Problems of Higher Nervous Activity*.] Moscow: AMN-SSSR, 1949.

———. "Cybernetics and the Integrative Activity of the Brain." In M. Cole and I. Maltzman, eds. *A Handbook of Contemporary Soviet Psychology*. New York: Basic Books, 1969.

Asratyan, E. A., *et al.* "Classical Conditioning Research and Theories." In M. Cole and I. Maltzman, eds. *A Handbook of Contemporary Soviet Psychology*. New York: Basic Books, 1969.

Beritashvili, I. S. "Concerning Psychoneural Activity of Animals." In M. Cole and I. Maltzman, eds. *A Handbook of Contemporary Psychology*. New York: Basic Books, 1969.

Bernshtein, N. A. "Methods for Developing Physiology As Related to the Problems of Cybernetics." In M. Cole and I. Maltzman, eds. *A Handbook of Contemporary Soviet Psychology*. New York: Basic Books, 1969.

Biriukov, D. A. ["Fundamental Philosophical Problems of Evolutionary Physiology of Higher Nervous Activity."] In AN-SSSR, Institut Physiologii, ed. [*Philosophical Problems of the Physiology of Higher Nervous Activity and Psychology*]. Moscow: AN-SSSR, 1963.

Brozek, J. "Soviet Psychology's Coming of Age." *American Psychologist, 25* (1970), 1057–58.

Bykov, K. M. [*Cerebral Cortex and Internal Organs.*] Kirov; AN-USFSR, 1942.

Craig, W. "Appetites and Aversions as Constituents of Instincts." *Biological Bulletin,* 34 (1918), 91–107.

Dmytryshyn, B. *U.S.S.R.: A Concise History.* New York: Scribner, 1965.

El'khonin, D. B. [*Development of Speech at the Preschool Age.*] Moscow: APN-RSFSR, 1958.

———. [*Features of the Intersection of the First and Second Signal Systems in Children of Preschool Age.*] Moscow: APN-RSFSR, 1959.

Gal'perin, P. Y. "Stages in the Development of Mental Acts." In M. Cole and I. Maltzman, eds. *A Handbook of Contemporary Soviet Psychology.* New York: Basic Books, 1969.

Ivanov-Smolenskii, A. G. *Essays in the Patho-physiology of the Higher Nervous Activity.* Moscow: Foreign Language Publishing House, 1954.

Kalabukhov, N. I. ["The Significance of Certain Factors in the Behavior of Rodents for the Maintenance of Energy Balance in Their Organism."] In [*Physiological Bases of Complex Behavior*]. Moscow and Leningrad: AN-SSSR, 1963.

Khrushinskii, L. V. *Animal Behavior: Its Normal and Abnormal Development.* New York: Consultant Bureau, 1962.

Klimova, V. I. ["Ontogeny of Reflex Responses to Natural Food Stimuli in Dogs and Rabbits."] In [*Problems of Comparative Physiology*]. Leningrad: AN-SSSR, 1958.

Kornilov, K. N. "Psychology in the Light of Dialectical Materialism." In C. Murchison, ed. *Psychologies of 1930.* Worcester, Mass.: Clark University Press, 1930.

Kovach, J. K. "Ethology in the Soviet Union." *Behaviour,* 41 (1971), 237–65.

Krasnogorskii, N. I. *Studies of Higher Nervous Activity in Man and Animals,* Vol. 1. Moscow: Gosizdat, 1954.

Kuhn, T. S. *The Structure of Scientific Revolutions.* Chicago: University of Chicago Press, 1962.

Landygina-Kots, N. N. ["The Development of the Forms of Reflection in the Process of Organic Evolution."] *Voprosi Filosofii,* 4 (1956), 94.

Lenin, V. I. *Materialism and Empiriocriticism: Critical Notes Concerning a Reactionary Philosophy.* Moscow: Lenin Institute, 1927.

———. *Collected Works.* Moscow: Lenin Institute, 1933–47.

Leont'ev, A. N. ["On the Historic Course in the Study of Human Psyche."] In Akademiia Pedagogicheskikh Nauk. *Psikhologicheskaia Nauka v SSSR.* Vol. 1. Moscow: APN-RSFSR, 1959.

Lorenz, K. Z. *Evolution and Modification of Behavior.* Chicago: University of Chicago Press, 1965.

Luria, A. R. *The Role of Speech in the Regulation of Normal and Abnormal Behavior.* London: Pergamon Press, 1961.

Medvedev, Z. A. *The Rise and Fall of T. D. Lysenko.* New York and London: Columbia University Press, 1969.

Promptov, A. N. [*Essays on the Biological Adaptation of the Behavior in Passarine Birds.*] Moscow and Leningrad: AN-SSSR, 1956.

Rakhimov, K. R. ["Materials on the Study of the Formation of Natural Feeding Reflexes During Ontogeny in Ruminants."] In [*Questions of Physiology and Pathology of the Nervous System*]. Moscow and Leningrad: AN-SSSR, 1958.

Razran, G. "Experimental Semantics." *Transactions of the New York Academy of Sciences,* 14 (1952), 171–77.

———. "K. N. Kornilov, Theoretical and Experimental Psychologist." *Science,* 128 (1958), 74–75.

———. "Russian Physiologists' Psychology and American Experimental Psychology: A Historical and a Systematic Collation and a Look into the Future." *Psychological Bulletin,* 62 (1965), 42–64.

———. "Soviet Psychology and Psychophysiology." *Science,* 1958a, 128, 1187–94.

Rubinshtein, S. L. *Foundations of General Psychology.* 1940. *Fundamentals of General Psychology.* Moscow: AN-SSSR, 1946.

Slonim, A. D. [*Instinct: Puzzles of Inherited Behavior.*] Leningrad: Nauka, 1967.

———. "The Ecological Physiological Approach to Problems of Animal Behavior." In M. Cole and I. Maltzman, eds. *A Handbook of Contemporary Soviet Psychology.* New York: Basic Books, 1969.

Sokolov, E. N., ed. [*The Orienting Reflex and Problems of Higher Nervous Activity.*] Moscow: APN-RSFSR, 1959.

Teplov, B. M. "Problems in the Study of General Types of Higher Nervous Activity in Man and Animals." In J. A. Gray, ed. *Pavlov's Typology.* New York: Pergamon Press, 1964.

Ukhtomskii, A. A. ["Instinct and Dominants."] In *Collected Works.* Vol. 1. Moscow: Nauka, 1923, 1950.

Uzhdavini, E. R. ["On the Formation of Natural Reflex Responses to Food During Early Ontogeny in Dogs."] In [*Experimental Investigations of the Regulation of Physiological Functions*]. Vol. 4. Moscow and Leningrad: AN-SSSR, 1958.

Vygotskii, L. S. *Thought and Speech.* Moscow: Sotsekgiz, 1934.

———. [*Collected Psychological Investigations.*] Moscow: APN-RSFSR, 1956.

Zaporozhets, A. V. "Some of the Psychological Problems of Sensory Training in Early Childhood and the Preschool Period." In M. Cole and I. Maltzman, eds. *A Handbook of Contemporary Soviet Psychology.* New York: Basic Books, 1969.

NOTE: A list of further readings appears at the back of the book. Brackets indicate titles translated from the original Russian by the present authors.

24

Developmental Psychology: Childhood, Adolescence, and the Life Span

What house more stately hath there been or can be, than is man? to
   whose creation
All things are in decay.

GEORGE HERBERT

(So some folks told you, but they knew
No more of Jove's designs than you.)
JONATHAN SWIFT

It is convenient to distinguish between the "space arts," those in which a glimpse of the world is cast into permanent form in picture, statue, or building, and the "time arts," those in which the arrangement of words, tones, or bodily movements captures the flowing character of all temporally ordered experience. We may, in a similar fashion, distinguish between the sciences which capture and describe the structured and episodic arrangements of the world of things and events and those which concern themselves with change through time. The life sciences have been rapidly moving from structural-episodic inquiry to temporal-development inquiry. Ordinarily we distinguish nowadays, as did Lewin (1935), between the short-time changes and the long-time changes. But even here it is suggested by some physicists and astronomers that the physical laws which relate to relatively short time cycles may themselves undergo long-range shifts. Perhaps all reality is a kind of change, as Heraclitus said, and *all* science is an attempt to glimpse at change.

Such issues are worth a moment's reflection because our theme is the transition from the study of human nature as it *is* to the study of human nature as it *becomes* — the significance for man of the fact of development, including the facts that as a species he has lived a million years or so and that his evolution has left distinct changes in his individual ontogenetic development. Today we see further than Darwin did into the meaning of the geological and paleontological backgrounds of mammalian life. With every year comparative physiology and psychology and now, too, behavior genetics show the moving point, or the system of points, generating new lines into the future. As one studies the cognitive or affective life of rodents, monkeys, and man, one begins to ask multidimensional questions about the changing character of cognition and of affect as basic organic realities. One begins to see how and where the possibilities for symbolic life, and for cultural life as a whole, grew, through eons of time, out of the tissue changes which are part of organic evolution.

Thus, for example, the classical problem of "cortical localization" nowadays points to differential growth trends which depend upon developmental sequences among species and among human stocks. Even so profound a student of the brain as Lashley (1929) could be deeply absorbed for many years in the problems of "equipotentiality," showing at first rather limited concern for the intricacies of the phylogenetic developmental questions. Not only is there today more and more comparative research; there is also more comparative study of the progressive developmental differences between species. Specificity of localization may be largely a question of where one stands on a phylogenetic developmental ladder.

Problems of phylogeny continually reappear in problems of ontogeny. The large time span casts its shadow over the short time span. Indeed, it is to be doubted whether we are now in a position to see the full force of the large time span. Twentieth-century studies of the aggressive "aspects of human nature," by Freud (1920) on the one hand and Lorenz (1966) on the other, suggest only that we still do not have enough evidence to decide whether (1) aggression — or any other prime mover to action — begins at a biochemical level, antedating even the beginnings of a nervous system and therefore being part of the basic package of all life, or (2) really *new* motivating forces appear from time to time in the evolutionary sequence. If the former view is correct, then aggression is, so to speak, a dye in which tissue has been dipped. If the latter, we must work empirically toward discovery of the point at which each new developmental line of aggression begins.

Again, if we allow ourselves a large enough time span, we may find many new biological principles, ascertainable within the life of the individual, which have far-flung implications for the species. Population geneticists show us that when numbers reach a certain critical value, the individual dynamics of mutation may have a meaning which they could not have in a smaller population. With Waddington (1957), we see that habit patterns, developed in many individuals of the species, may set the stage for meaningful consequences from new mutations, but these same new mutations might not entail such meaningful consequences if the predisposing habit systems had not been so developed. We thus see how the appearance of new *habits* makes individuality and the selection process, at a genetic level, effective when it could not otherwise be so. With both we get results that *look* Lamarckian (see pp. 128–29), and though not truly Lamarckian, they affect the course of evolution. Shapiro (1939) and others in the field of physical anthropology show us how new functional patterns, however arising, can give survival value to new mutations in hand and brain from which new cultural innovations can follow. The problem is very complex indeed. It is, so to speak, a sheaf of time units within time units.

Our modern redefinition of reality in terms of the flow of time is a very recent matter. As the painters of a few centuries ago usually represented children with the bodily proportions of little adults, so the psychology with which the historian deals has been, until very recently, a psychology ignoring observations of childhood and arbitrarily assuming that in childhood we pass rapidly through a series of stages in order to become adults. The important part of life had been conceived to be the adult part; the important functions were the mature functions; the true or complete man or woman was the fulfilled man or woman. Almost never, until the eighteenth century, does one find any psychology of childhood at all. The eighteenth century began to put children on the map; the twentieth century has moved them toward the center of the map.

It is partly Darwinism that has taught us to use the time dimension. But to think in developmental terms is characteristic of our whole way of life. The term "man" no longer means simply the samples of today's *Homo sapiens* that are seen on the face of the globe. Today, in our newspapers and on our television screens, we note the diggings of skulls of men and their domesticated animals, the potsherds and flower pollens, as testimony to what human living was like at one or another remote period. We compare different contemporary preliterate societies in the way in which they rear their children, and we look for evidences of individual differences to determine whether these are qualitatively or quantitatively different from those we find among our own children. Psychoanalysis is perhaps the most abundant and systematic source of the conception that "the child is father to the man." The whole modern orientation to developmental or "longitudinal" sequence has come to be seen by many as the soundest approach to a study of the individuality of the adult. To paleontology, then, has been added prehistory; to prehistory, the conception of the biographical picture of the individual man. And add to them the various biologies which deal with short time spans. These short-time effects will have to be compared with the effects of longer and longer time spans, until ultimately the Lewinian distinction between short and long time spans will have to be dispensed with. We are on our way to a profoundly developmental conception of psychological reality.

Conceptions óf development have been growing more complex and sophisticated ever since Epicurus and, more specifically, Lucretius, who differentiated between the kinds of growth, their macrostructure and microstructure, their additive, compounding, synthesizing, and emerging forms. All that we have said above about the substitution of developmental and cross-sectional approaches may be regarded as trite as soon as one begins to ask about the *kinds* of development that can be observed.

Take first, for example, the distinction between continuous and discontinuous development. There is a prominent place in all modern science for the quantum and the "step function," the emergence of the indivisible new unit. To be sure, it may be argued that beneath the level of observation at which there are step functions, or observable and measurable jumps, there is really a sea of continuity. The practical job of observing and measuring must be based upon the observability of the *discontinuities;* but we strive nevertheless to conceptualize a continuity lying beyond the observed. The mutation in biology, discovered in the same year as the unit of action h (the quantum principle of Planck), has forced biology to question whether evolution is ultimately a smoothly developing movement or a series of step functions, the probability of which can indeed be assayed for a region or a period but the exact determination of which lies beyond our knowing. The mutation has become fundamental in evolutionary theory. For very *short*-time trends, such as tens of thousands of years in certain evolutionary records, mutations may be belittled on the ground that they are usually lethal; and even when nonlethal, they are responsible only for small—in fact, often hidden and unsuspected—gene changes. For all that, when time is long rather than short, a major place in shaping and inauguration of species must be assigned to mutations. The researches of Watson and Crick, and their followers, on the arrangement of nucleotides in a double helix form—from which the soma is guided by enzyme processes—lead into a beautiful analysis of structural and functional development. The questions, however, remain for the biologists as well as the psychologists: why and how, in the evolutionary process, the gradual or sudden rearrangements in structure brought about qualitative differences in morphological and behavioral functions, with all their attendant developmental consequences at a particular time and place.

These step functions are, of course, properties of the genetic material itself. Life can be represented by scintillations rather than by steadily flowing beams, such as Newton dealt with. One deals, in fact, with the ultimate light unit, or photon, and, as in the work of Hecht (1934), one studies the sensitivity of receptor cells, on an all-or-none basis, in which the smooth curves of rod and cone sensitivity are seen to be expressions of all-or-none jump-wise functions in individual receptor cells.

This principle is of direct importance in the embryological and postnatal growth process, as shown by Shirley (1931, 1938) in the systematic contrast which she established between continuous and discontinuous growth, between flowing and "saltatory" appearance of new behaviors. Maturation sequences may appear in steps only because the arrangement of smooth continuities is obscure; the eye picks out steps from flowing and continuous qualities. Or the picture may be reversed, and unless one uses special techniques one does not observe the saltatory components entering into the smooth appearances. The situation is comparable to the demonstration (Stevens, 1941) of the quantal nature of musical pitch. Though physical pitch is continuous, psychological functions move forward in step-wise or quantal terms; a slowly lowering tone may be heard to fall. As D'Arcy Thompson (1942) has shown, life is riddled with the quantum principle. We can thus have our discontinuity and, at the same time, live unaware of it except when employing special principles to make it visible.

How different the way of development turns out to be when regarded this way! We are confronted with scattered time-space points of one system moving forward to another by virtue of unknown underlying factors, which mobilize for us sudden rearrangements. The whole story of life becomes more a *staccato* than a *glissando* pattern; more a pattern of unexplained fresh creativity, moment by moment, than of the slow and steady unwinding of an infinite mainspring to which all else must respond.

These are the same philosophical conceptions of development to which we have been led also by fresh conceptualizations of the role of mathematics in the scientific task. Though dealing mainly with structured trends in what we have called the space arts, Lancelot Whyte (1951) has viewed general patterns in such a way as to bring them into articulate relation to the time-space orders of astronomy, geology, the biological sciences, the social sciences, and the arts. A psychology at home in all these fields would be much more of a time art than it is today. This is because it would see the relations between the various kinds of phylogenetic and ontogenetic time-tables, the articulation of which provides the moving system which we know as evolution. But as a time science, then, psychology begins with a *quantum* principle.

Can psychology establish a *universal* scheme of development, as offered in the "first principles" described by Herbert Spencer (see p. 143) over a century ago? According to him, evolution—defined in the broadest astronomical, biological, and social-science terms—consists of progress from an "indefinite incoherent homogeneity to a definite coherent heterogeneity." Whatever is "incoherent" undergoes differentiation into parts which, with their progressively clearer boundaries, display progressively clearer qualities differentiating the new areas that have come into being. Thus from the indefinite comes the definite by a process of differentiation. Sometimes differentiation follows from a change in temperature or momentum among colliding gases; sometimes it is a difference in the acid-base qualities of interacting fluids; sometimes, in life generally, it is a progressively acute contrast between regions on one side and regions on the other side of a natural boundary. Differentiation proceeds to a point at which the sharply separated components begin to interact with one another to produce an architecture, a higher unit. The movement is "dialectical" in the sense that a differentiated stage will never appear except as a forced requirement and when heterogeneous entities begin to interact and force differentiation upon the emerging substances or tissues: *integration can occur only when there are parts ready for integration.*

This comprehensive developmental schema, applied successfully by Herbert Spencer to the sciences as he knew them, became a specific working principle at the psychological level in the work of Werner (1926). He first applied it to the perceptual, conceptual, and affective life of small children. Werner proceeded to show the relation of developmental sequences in the child's mind to those which appear in psychopathology, in preliterate thinking, and in regressed or incomplete adult functioning. With Werner, development came to mean not just growth, but an orderly progression through three stages: the undifferentiated, the differentiated, and the integrated. His conceptions became highly experimentable and led to studies of everyday child perception and thought at the Hamburg Psychological Institute, and in the parks, streets, and docks of Hamburg.

At the undifferentiated level, the Werner principle was conceived to relate to the development of the child as a whole, especially to his central nervous system, and to the psychological functions expressing its development. There are, however, many phenomena of behavioral development in which the adult as much as the child, encountering a new situation, passes through an undifferentiated stage until freshly differentiated perceptual and cognitive events lead into conflict. Because the differentiated parts of an organism have to interact, the organism must proceed to some form of integration of the components. The unsophisticated listener to modern music may hear at first almost undifferentiated noise; then, as he observes the instruments and listens to the structure under the guidance of the conductor, he begins to disentangle various tones both at a given moment and in their sequences. He finally comes to a stage in which he can actually *hear* the music; that is, he has reached Werner's third level of integration.

Witkin's massive data (1954) on the emergence of "field-independent" ways of perceiving, a measurable degree of ability to separate the specific presentation from the context in which it is embedded, which some individuals reach sooner and some later with reference to each particular stimulus material, exemplify a similar principle. There is, in all probability, a constitutional factor setting certain limits upon the rate of differentiation and of integration. But there also appears to be a factor of early experience, an aspect of the process of perceptual learning (as shown also by Witkin's work with the blind), and evidence of preadolescent conflict as affecting the curve of development. The Spencer-Werner principle looks like a "general system" principle, a principle that holds broadly for both growth and learning. Helson's concept of "adaptation level" (1964) is another very general quantitative principle in which *time* is fundamental; so also is Piaget's principle of centration (see p. 412). Indeed, practically all "behavior models" of today bristle with time-dependent measures of developmental differentiation and integration.

Child Development

Child psychology can, if one likes, be dated from Comenius's picture book for children (1658), or from J. J. Rousseau's eager concern with the nature of the childhood beginnings of mind, his belief in spontaneity, and his demonstration of an open educational method (*Émile,* 1762). There soon followed Pestalozzi's articulate description in *Gertrude Teaching Her Children* (published in 1801) of children's spontaneous responses to flowers, animals, and the world of the senses; and Froebel's initiation of the "kindergarten." Stories for children—the traditional Grimm collections and the fabulous new stories of Hans Christian Andersen—reflected a wave of excitement about the nature of childhood which had found an articulate expression in Herbart's experimental education (see p. 52).

As early as 1787, Tiedemann had kept records of a small child's growth, and later Charles Darwin made sensitive observations on the development of his infant son. These notes laid the foundation for an experimental child study which began with Preyer (1882) and a widespread enthusiasm in Germany for the study of the child at home and at school: a study of children's drawings, play, and conversation. Two years after his founding of *The Pedagogical Seminary: A Journal of Child Study,* G. Stanley Hall continued to fan the flame. He arranged, at the World's Fair in Chicago in 1893, a meeting of child psychologists. Soon Sully (1895), in England, and Claparède (1905), in Switzerland, were devoting book-length studies to the mind of the child. It was in this era that Binet, reading the studies of thought processes which were coming from Würzburg, did thought experiments with his own two little girls. All through this era he was preoccupied with the measurement of intellectual powers in children (note especially his book on suggestibility, 1900) and soon broke the ground for "intelligence tests." The new preoccupation with child psychology is exemplified in William Stern's systematic *Psychology of Early Childhood* (1924).

The evolutionary viewpoint has thrown light on every aspect of child development. Before Darwin, even Rousseau could compare the unshaped mind of the child only to the unshaped mind of preliterate man. But with the new functionalism of evolutionary theory it was slowly realized that the period of early individual development may involve qualities of plasticity and of self-discovery that are unknown in the adult years. Putting aside the momentary extravagances of Hall (1904) and the literalism of his "recapitulation theory," it began to be realized that the period of "immaturity" was not a period of deficiency in being fully a human being, but a period of plasticity, with predispositions to grow in certain directions rather than in others. It began to be realized that the human organism, with its long infancy, had to utilize an enormous degree of plasticity, and that learning ability became the evolutionary criterion of its survival.

It is interesting at this point to view the earlier static conceptions that intelligence is simply "born in us"; that it is a fixed property of humanness; and that each individual level of intelligence is a fixed property, like a birthmark, which reflects what a particular combination of genes could produce. To the evolutionist, plants and animals have no such fixed functional limits; the principles of their adaptation include many important variables related to their plasticity. Consequently, the degree of modifiability of the characteristic pattern of the species has become an empirical question. It became evident that in many immature organisms, "intelligence" is one of the attributes quickly responsive to an enriched or challenging environment (see p. 456).

Evolutionary concepts, as we have seen, were concepts of measurable individuality. The measurement of perceptual-cognitive and motor skills carried forward that trend to quantification which Galton had stressed (see p. 138) and which Thorndike (1914) helped expand. It was assumed that children learned through association, especially with repetition, and through reward and punishment. These principles were systematized and experimentally documented in many university laboratories. Clinical concepts played as yet a rather small part. Witmer (1907) had founded at the University of Pennsylvania in 1896 a psychological clinic and for many years gave attention to individual case studies of children in trouble. This movement, however, was not closely articulated with the developing child psychology. It was with Healy (already a deviser of intelligence tests), in Chicago and later in Boston, that a new dynamic spirit, and in particular a psychoanalytic spirit, began to be effective. It is a curious coincidence that Healy's *Mental Conflicts and Misconduct* (1917), the first bold psychoanalytic glance at the dynamics of delinquency in this country, appeared about the same time as Terman's *The Measurement of Intelligence* (1916), which began a trend toward classifying children for school grouping. Later, Collins's finding (1928) that children of unskilled workers were twenty points lower in average IQ than children of professional workers was assumed to be evidence of innate differences in educability. Klineberg's pioneer data (1935) on the increase in IQs of rural children exposed for increasingly larger periods of time to the greater stimulation of urban schools were usually ignored, as were the challenging Iowa findings (see Skeels *et al.,* 1938) of changes in IQ of children from deprived settings after exposure to improved stimulation. More than a generation passed before adequate recognition was given to the role of experience in mental development.

At this point the mental hygiene movement began to develop. This can be said to have begun with the autobiographical *A Mind That Found Itself* (Beers, 1908). This book described the horrors of mental disease, especially under conditions of institutional treatment, and elicited new interest not only in the treatment of mental disease, but also in its possible origins in infancy and childhood.

A very small amount of money at the Phipps Clinic, in Baltimore, and a great deal of enthusiasm made possible Watson's studies of the behavior of the newborn, such as the grasping reflex and the startle and stiffening patterns subsumed under "fear" and "rage," respectively, together with a diffuse response of apparent outgoing character, called love. Shortly after these studies, Watson initiated some Pavlov-type studies of acquired fears in young children. Striking a metal bar with a hammer gave a dismal clang which elicited fear response in the infant; later the presentation of a furry animal at the time the bar was struck led to marked fear of the animal alone. The report was brief and vague, and the experiment was difficult to repeat. But the major idea that significant behavioral attributes arise through early Pavlovian conditioning was waiting for systematic elaboration, which was undertaken by Watson and Raynor (1920). Objective psychology had an idea and a program.

It soon had also a very lively intellectual and financial support: mental health, already in the public eye through the work of Beers and Healy, was a major preoccupation after the World War I "shell shock" experiences. The large number of men at borderline or definitely subnormal intellectual levels, as shown by Army testing in 1917 and 1918, had added to the concern with early development.

Shortly after World War I, large-scale objective studies of child development got under way in the United States, as a consequence of the awakening public interest in child welfare; the strong foundation support (especially by the Laura Spelman Rockefeller Fund under the initiative of Lawrence K. Frank); the behaviorist movement; and the availability of children in hospitals, nursery schools, and elementary schools. Elaborate studies of infant behavior were conducted at Ohio State University. A pioneer enterprise, early assuming large proportions, was the ambitious, long-range research program under Gesell (1928) at Yale. This resulted in a large number of publications on the norms of infant and child development, follow-up studies of individuals, and detailed analyses of specific behavior sequences. Other research centers (at the universities of California, Michigan, and Minnesota) also turned out voluminous data (for example, Shirley, 1931, 1933) describing physical and mental growth patterns, sensory and motor responses, emotions, social behavior, and language development in normal children in the favorable atmosphere of the rapidly growing number of nursery schools. Along with this comprehensive approach came a concern with behavioral responses to the environmental stimulation and challenge.

Through all of this work, however, there was no focus as yet on the level of integration and adaptive implications of the young child's behavior. There was even less focus on the fact that the testing procedures devised for adults (as in an intelligence test, for example) presented the infant and young child with very strange demands. However, Goodenough's early study of anger (1931) recognized the disintegrative effects of fatigue, hunger, and overstimulation. Later Dollard *et al.* (1939) formulated a relationship between frustration and aggression. By the late thirties Anderson (1937) had introduced the concept of integration in social behavior of young children. Lewin and his associates (1939) documented the disintegrative impact of autocratic leadership on the behavior of older boys and the negative effects of frustration on the play of preschool children.

The nature-nurture problem also interested many child psychologists. Gesell and Thompson (1929), for example, used identical twins as experimental and control subjects in a variety of developmental studies. In the same vein, McGraw (1939) taught one infant twin to roller-skate and to climb a steep slide, leaving his brother untrained; the latter quickly caught up when given the opportunity at a more advanced age and learned much faster than his precociously trained brother had learned. This study demonstrated the importance of maturational readiness to learn. Jersild (1932), among others, showed that equal training made dissimilar development in measurable skills, suggesting the importance of constitutional capacities. There were other studies comparing foster children with "own" children in their degree of intellectual resemblance to the parents in whose home they were reared. Experience in nursery school and institutions has been brought into relation to IQ changes. Gifted individuals have been studied in large numbers; thus Hollingworth (1942) studied a group made up entirely of children of exceptional intelligence, and Terman (1925) found that the mentally gifted children were superior also in most aspects of physical and social development.

The processes of conditioning and learning have also been analyzed in infancy and childhood. Skinner's reformulation of the earlier concepts of reward and punishment in terms of "reinforcement schedules" has been widely adapted in both education and therapy (see p. 427). The gradual infusion of psychoanalytic concepts was also steady and its effects on child psychology profound. It will be recalled that Freud's attention had been directed to neurosis in childhood quite early in his career and that he had formulated the theory of infantile sexuality even before his celebrated study of the phobia of a five-year-old child (1909). Until the 1920s psychoanalytic studies of children were, however, few and fragmentary. It was Freud's daughter, Anna Freud, who presented a major systematic view of child analysis (1936). Play techniques were initiated by her, and by Melanie Klein (1932), David Levy (1937, 1943), and others in the 1930s, for direct observation of personality dynamics in the course of therapeutic work with children. By allowing the child to manipulate toys representing father, mother, brother, sister, and self, and by allowing the expression of rivalry, fears, and sexual and other conflicts, it became possible to enrich the psychoanalytic theory of libidinal development and in some measure to test experimentally the adequacy of its formulations. After Freud's discussions of the Ego and the Id, in the late twenties and early thirties, came Isaacs's stimulating study (1933) of aggressiveness and love in small children. Meanwhile Anna Freud went on with her systematic formulation of ego development and the mechanisms of defense. The psychoanalysis of children became during the thirties a most fruitful field of investigation. It led in the mid-forties to the annual publication of the *Psychoanalytic Study of the Child.*

An important development in the history of child psychology was the gradual merging of psychoanalytic ways of thinking with other approaches to the study of child development. This was particularly apparent in the study of emotions (anger, anxiety, jealousy, phobic fears, and so on), dreams, and fantasies of children. Such studies were pursued as part of a clinical concern for the mental hygiene needs of children and as integral parts of research projects. Analysts such as Spitz (1965), Bowlby (1969), and Mahler (1968) reported on severe disturbances in development related to the interruption or distortion of the mother's relation with infant and young child—anaclitic depression, separation anxiety, autism, and symbiotic dependency. It is hard today to imagine a child psychology devoid of psychoanalytic concepts, for even the most objective of behavior analyses is heavily indebted to psychoanalytic thinking. Another equally influential line of thought came from Piaget and his followers.

Piaget

Jean Piaget began his career as a student of two themes: mollusks and intellectual history. He was trained in evolutionary biology, but some of his most penetrating ideas have related to the evolution of man's forms of thought. He began to see some broad developmental problems documented by history and also by the psychological development of children.

His own little children taught him a great deal, before he extended his studies to the children of Geneva's parks and streets. A key concept running through his early work (1923) is that of egocentrism. The child develops only very slowly an awareness of self and others; until he perceives himself as distinct from the environment he cannot recognize the subjectivity of his own outlook. Things *are* as they seem to be. To this acceptance of one's own viewpoint as conveying absolute reality the term "realism" was applied. The two concepts may be illustrated by reference to an experiment (1937) in which small children were placed, one at a time, near a table upon which stood a huge relief map of the Alps. Around the walls of the room were photographs showing how the Alps would look to observers stationed at different points on the mountain trails. Doll figures were placed here and there in the mountains, and the child was asked to indicate how the mountains would look to the doll as it was placed here or there. The child reported that the mountains would look as they did to him as he was standing beside the table. There was just one way in which the mountains could look.

From such egocentrism and realism followed a third concept: that of *participation,* in which the child failed so completely to distinguish himself from the external that he attributed life, mind, and purpose to all he encountered. As he rode his bicycle, the distinction between his thought of the tires and the actual tires themselves was so vague and blurred that he dared not think of them as punctured, lest the puncture automatically occur. This was analogous to Freud's conception and views of the omnipotence of thought; but it occurred for Piaget not by virtue of Freudian dynamic principles, but because at this stage of development he saw as yet no differentiation between self and not-self.

Practically the whole panorama of intellectual development in the small child was at first viewed by Piaget in terms of the gradual emancipation of the individual from the egocentric mode of thought. The dream, for instance, permitted the clear differentiation of a series of stages, beginning with one in which the dream, as a physical entity, came in through the window and lay down on the bed beside the child; through various stages of semiphysical existence in which the dream still occupied space; then on to a final stage in which the dream was a process carried out by the self.

Piaget's *The Child's Conception of the World* (1926) emphasized the tendency to find analogies between oneself and the forces of nature, analogies which lie in the impossibility of dissociating oneself from the world. By virtue of egocentrism, the child may declare that the cold wind which beats in his face is hostile, while the warm sun is generous. In the same way, the tree is sorry when the warm sun sets, and the rivers rejoice when the ice melts and sets them free in the spring. From this animistic tendency, similar to the animistic tendencies of primitive peoples, there is slow and arduous emancipation. To the small child, anything that moves has life. Later there must be movement that is self-initiated, and finally there must be activity that is purposive.

One of the great strokes of genius in Piaget's work had to do with his primary venture into social psychology in *The Moral Judgment of the Child* (1932). This investigation, influenced by the French sociological studies of ethics, was a systematic effort to define the stages through which judgments of right and wrong pass in a child from about two to fourteen. Piaget began by studying "the rules of the game." He became expert in the children's chosen games, learning how to make a good shot at marbles and a duffer shot. He wanted chiefly to find out what is regarded by the child as a *fair* or an *unfair* thing.

We may illustrate the stages he discovered in the evolution of moral judgment as follows. The little child of two or three tosses the marbles with great delight; his pleasure derives from sheer physical functioning. If asked at the end who has won, he says, "I won and John won and we all won." Competitive standards and man-made rules are not as yet clear. Later, the fact of rules begins to be understood. You must draw a square of given proportions, you must stand outside it, you must pitch one marble at a time, and you must use your own marble, instead of hitting and displacing your opponent's marble. Rules here are absolutely sacred. No one could possibly change them. (When the boys in Geneva were told that the boys over in Neufchâtel played differently, the only reply was, "Those guys over there never did understand marbles anyway!") We have then, as Lerner (1937) remarked, egocentrism at the social level, or *sociocentrism.*

Later still, the rigidity of these rules begins to give way. It is now permissible to alter the size of the square, or even to step on the line, provided all contenders follow the same rules. We have left the area of *moral realism,* in which the moral world is a rigid, external structure, and have entered the area of reciprocity, where social relationships are the basis of lawmaking. Finally, beyond such reciprocity comes a stage in the preadolescent period in which more subtle personality factors become matters of weight. The nearsighted boy may stand nearer than the others; just as in the sandlot ball game in the United States the crippled boy may bat, though someone else must run the bases for him. Reciprocity, says Piaget, is "colored by considerations of equity." One has achieved *autonomy.*

It was possible during the twenties and thirties to see a continuous change in Piaget's thinking: he remained charming and picturesque, but he was becoming a rigorous, systematic psychologist. There seemed almost to be three Piagets: the young Piaget of the first studies during the twenties and the middle-period Piaget of the studies of moral judgments (1932); but now came a third Piaget, tougher, more oriented to scientific abstractions, with a hardened demand to make psychology into a rigorous and self-consistent science. The third Piaget, the systematic psychologist (let us say 1935 and thereafter), began with observations of the infant's sensory-motor processes of *assimilation* and *accommodation*. Assimilation is the process by which input is received from the world which the mind uses for accommodation, that is, the modification of schemas for reciprocal relations of individual and environment. There is no longer a nature-nurture problem here; there is no longer the inevitable unfolding of an intrinsic developmental dynamic. On the contrary, there is a continuous reciprocity—the mind taking its shape from interaction with the outer world, with which it carries on perpetual commerce.

There are, moreover, *stages* in this assimilation-accommodation interaction which can be easily defined. During the end of the *sensorimotor period* the child develops a concept of objects as stable; inventiveness and imagery, including an "inner exploration of ways and means," become possible, and the child may reproduce an activity which he had previously observed and engage in concrete operations. Late in the second year of life symbolic functions appear, as in language, and *fictional invention* through symbolic play; perceptual-cognitive development moves on apace through a period of *centration*. From four to seven or eight comes a period of intuitive thought and *preoperational thinking,* in which the hallmark of maturity is the discovery of reversible relations, such as one has in the to and fro, back and forth, of the spatial order, and of the temporal, numerical, and other orders as well.

In all of these formulations, we find a primary reliance upon direct observation in natural settings, but substantially supplemented with experimental and comparative methods. With an aim to writing a systematic cognitive-perceptual psychology, there was a place for affect too, and a little for volition, but not very much. Nor was there a very large place for cross-cultural comparison. Rather, we have a biologist and historian's self-realization through half a century of creative research. The strong response to Piaget not only in the West but in the Soviet Union, in India, and in Japan, indicates his truly international role.

Some of the immediate impact of Piaget's later thinking is seen in the work of experimenters like Jerome Bruner (1969), Burton White (1969), and others who, stimulated by Piaget, have been studying details of the processes of differentiation and integration of steps in perception, sensory-motor development, development of object constancy, and logical thinking; it is seen also in the comprehensive review of contributions of experience to intelligence by J. McV. Hunt (1961).

The child's stages in cognitive development have, in fact, become the heart of a complete psychological system. Piaget, as *general* psychologist, can then be compared with other *general* psychologists, such as Pavlov or Freud. It is possible to articulate Piaget's system with the other systems as several psychologists have done, without dislodging or fraying its edges. It drops into place within the broad schema of psychology—this *despite* the fact that Piaget's system is still largely a cognitive system. We turn to Piaget for cognitive growth, as we turn to Freud for psychosexual, affective, and impulse-control systems and their development. Several preliminary efforts in reconciling these systems have been attempted, but the fragments that are fitted together so far do not represent a systematic whole.

In the late 1950s, the shock of the Soviet Sputnik with its implication of high scientific achievement, coupled later with the comparable shock of evidence of widespread failures in educational progress of American poor children, stimulated a new concern with processes and capacities for learning — their relation to nutrition, maternal care and neglect, and to disintegrative influences of racism, teacher's negative expectations, and the like. These paralleled the new wave of experiments stimulated by the translation of Piaget's work on the development of intelligence, with its focus on the integrative processes of assimilation and accommodation through early sensory-motor experiences. Piaget's concepts guided educational efforts and psychological experiments in the study of cognitive development and integration.

Nevertheless, many questions about the development of the child's capacity to organize words into structured sentences, about the relation of this capacity to basic identification with parents, and about the capacity to develop and maintain relationships which support communication are still unanswered. A method currently being applied to these issues is the longitudinal study of child development.

Longitudinal Methods

All three of the primary areas with which we have been concerned in this chapter — behavior study, the study of the child mind, and the study of unconscious childhood conflicts — have tended in recent years to require a larger place for longitudinal (as compared with "cross-sectional") methods. Whereas it was once considered adequate to slice through the behavior or the fantasy life of a few hundred children, with appropriate "samples" at each age level, it has more and more come to be recognized that individual variability in the maturation and interaction of many functions is so complex as to make this approach rather precarious. The many limited cross-sectional studies of relationships between socioeconomic level or ethnic origin and intelligence, for example, have led to misleading conclusions. It is recognized now that without a longitudinal approach to the process of development in different ecological settings and with their different quantities and qualities of nutriment for cognitive growth, the plastic nature of cognitive development is too easily ignored. During the sixties, public anxiety about widespread reading difficulties led to the advent of Head Start projects and to increased funds for studying factors in educational progress and failure. Parallel to this development and shortly thereafter, investigators like Hunt, Bruner, White, and others focused on those aspects of experience in infancy and early childhood which could affect the development of intelligence.

But quite a bit earlier, Bayley (1940) at Berkeley had demonstrated developmental variability in IQ, especially in the early years, through her longitudinal studies of mental growth. Other modern longitudinal approaches include Macfarlane's guidance study at the University of California at

Berkeley, the adolescent growth study at the same institution, the Cambridge-Somerville youth study in the Boston area, the Fels Foundation longitudinal study at Antioch College, and some more modest investigations in which the same individuals were followed for several years. In some studies — the Fels study, for example — the Rorschach test (see p. 434) was applied to the same group of children all the way from five or six to sixteen or eighteen. Other studies have taken a more complex overall pattern and were concerned with the personality as a whole; they pursued this pattern through successive phases of development, as have the studies by Murphy (1962) and her collaborators at the Menninger Foundation. It appears to us that such studies are less prone to reification of questionable generalizations than cross-sectional studies. Quite aside, however, from their specific methodological value in the increased understanding of development, the longitudinal studies have other advantages. They open a way toward the integration of conceptions from biology, social psychology, psychoanalysis, and the general psychology of personality. As we shall see in the discussion of ecological and cross-cultural problems later on, it is only when a full picture of the individual is provided (and then considered longitudinally in relation to its developmental setting and in terms of the life span), that one can really take hold of the problem of integrating all the relevant scientific disciplines.

To talk about "interdisciplinary research," or a wise integration of the best from many different scientific fields, has become trite indeed in recent years. The real question has proved to be *how* such an integration can be used to permit deeper insights and better understanding of development than could be achieved by the best methods of a single discipline. In the longitudinal studies, workers have the opportunity to check against one another the assumptions from different disciplines. They are forced to work through the tough problem of integrating a physical examination, a personal interview, a documentary analysis, a testing program, and a series of experimental procedures carried out against the backdrop of family, community, and culture as a whole. Child psychology, as the center in which all these forces gather and are observed, represents therefore the best proving ground for the integration of these disciplines and the contribution such integration might make to the understanding of problems in adaptation.

Child psychology has had to be much more than the psychology of the child. It has had to be in part a template for the construction of a more adequate general psychology. To think of the child as an "organism" or a "growing organism" prompts the mobilization of rich genetic, developmental, psychophysiological concepts. It may at times dovetail with the sociocultural approach, yet not with ideas of the child as an "individual." This is partly because individuality is largely defined in terms of the contexts and contrasts within which it appears. The frame of reference for an "individual" or a "person" and the kinds of questions that come to mind when one thinks in these terms are not likely to be the same ones as for an "organism." This is in part the issue raised by Gordon Allport (1937) in differentiating between the "nomothetic" (generalizing) and the "idiographic" (individualizing) approaches. However important the nomothetic aspects must be for certain purposes of science, there are realities viewed through the idiographic telescope which cannot be ignored if the science of development is to be complete.

Instead of comparing separate groups of three-year-olds and six-year-olds, the longitudinal approach of studying the same three-year-olds week by week, or at any rate month by month, until they are nine- (or ninety-) year-olds can lead to discovery of continuities in the idiosyncratic or unique responses that may be characteristic of a given individual, regardless of age. But even more importantly, there is a need to see *how* a particular kind of individuality grows. It is not just the study of child growth in general, but of the growth of particular individuality, that is required for sound education and work in mental health.

The methods have to include, of course, many of the cross-sectional approaches, but they have to do much more than this. They have to see how a going concern is changing and also continuous; they have to know what can be extrapolated and what cannot. They have to observe the changes in the ecology, parallel to the changes in individual responses, and they have to see the changing interaction patterns. The difficulties here are evident in the fact that there are so few longitudinal studies, and that of these few, several have already collapsed through lack of continued funding.

Yet a few longitudinal studies have persisted. We have mentioned the work of Bayley, and the monumental investigation, now in its third generation, launched and continued by Macfarlane at Berkeley. There is the Menninger Foundation study mentioned above, originally launched by Escalona and Leitch (1953) as an infancy project in the late forties but leading on into observations of some of the same children by L. B. Murphy, Alice Moriarty, and their collaborators, with observations from three to nineteen years of age. In addition to studies of continuity and change, studies of vulnerability, cognitive style, and coping patterns are considered as outcomes of the interaction of constitutional equipment, ecology and the vicissitudes of family life. From their studies it immediately becomes apparent that what cannot be gleaned by short-term observations (for example, the relation of certain events in infancy to the developments at three — or ten — years of age) can be precisely pinpointed in the individual record.[1] At the same time, intensive studies of these children have shown how success in coping with the challenges presented by early imbalances, sensitivities, or

[1] For example, it is among children with feeding and digestive difficulties in infancy that one finds at the preschool level, and also at the preadolescent level, the greatest interference with perceptual clarity — as in mistaking one animal for another in the Children's Apperception Test, and so on.

illness contributes to later resources for mastery. Of equal interest is the finding from longitudinal studies that a child's physical adequacy to the demands of the peer group may differ widely from one phase to another, and that along with this the child's social acceptance and status varies from phase to phase.

Adolescence and the Life Span

Adolescence, as a prominent phase of the developmental sequence, was early defined and given its own place by Hall (*Adolescence*, 1904), whose study of adolescent biological growth and turmoil had already been brought to the psychologist's attention in Starbuck's *Psychology of Religion* (1899) and William James's intensive use of Starbuck's records of adolescent experience. Its publication belongs to the same era in which Hall organized a conference at Clark University addressed by both Freud and Jung.

Psychoanalytic observations on adolescent psychosexual development and conflict came to be parts of a cross-cultural study of human maturing, to which cultural anthropologists (see p. 436), notably Benedict, Mead, and Kardiner, made their initial contributions in the second quarter of the century. Adolescence came to be conceived as an aspect of the life span (partly biologically, partly culturally defined) with its own unique attributes, such as the self-doubts and the negative phase, reported by Charlotte Bühler (1928), the temporary lapse into field dependence, reported by Witkin (1962), and the alternations between impulsiveness and idealistic asceticism discussed by Anna Freud (1936).

Adolescence, however, as an aspect of the life span as a whole, became also a gateway to a developmental conception of the whole life process. In Miles's experimental quantitative study of the life span (1933), from four years of age to the eighties, adolescence is only dimly separated from the preceding and succeeding stages of life; the period of rapidly waxing powers stands out for some individuals and is not distinctively marked for others. Indeed, the growth process begins to be conceived in terms of individual differences, with sophisticated measures of individuality in a variety of physical, intellectual, and social attributes; and also, of course, in terms of differences between the sexes, as in the studies of Shuttleworth (1939) and Stolz (1938), with attention here and there to racial and subracial differences, as observed by Franzblau (1935), and to cultural factors.

When, however, it began to be noted by cultural anthropologists that adolescence, middle age, and so on, are defined according to individual cultural traditions, each tradition entailing different understandings of life and different responsibilities and obligations, the whole conception of the life span was blown open to a fresh reconstitution of biological plasticity under ecological and cultural impacts. Studies of aging, influenced by anthropology, have looked for the social roles expected — or indeed, imposed — at various periods in life. The widely quoted study of Mead (1928) demonstrates that adolescent storm and stress, so widely observed in the Western world, is apparently lacking in Samoan culture, where psychosexual transitions are taken casually and are seldom sources of stress. The Comanche, as described by Kardiner *et al.* (1945), undergoes a very literal change of life; when failing strength means that he is no longer on the warpath he can settle for being a "good old man" or, if unwilling to accept this role, a troublesome "bad old man." As a good old man, however, he has enormous prestige and power in connection with the planning of tribal adventures in war and peace.

Biographical studies have been made of individuals able to achieve more in one period in life than another, or capable of displaying different responses to comparable challenges of the characteristic worlds to be dealt with at different phases in life. Studies of the human life span by Charlotte Bühler (1935) emphasized types of high creativity manifest in various periods in life in persons of the Western world. Recent studies edited by Bühler and Massarik (1968) which deal with aspects of human development at different periods in life articulate closely with the general creativity research interest of recent years (Guilford, 1968; Barron, 1969). This, and much other research, tends to show that in the West, at least, great intellectual powers in the fields of mathematics and the physical sciences may appear in adolescence or early adulthood; while in such fields as history, drama, and the novel, they appear late, as an expression perhaps of both biological growth and maturing and of types of experience possible at various stages.

The conception of periods in life, whether as defined in ordinary people or among the markedly creative, has been patterned to some degree upon Shakespeare's "seven ages." It has been patterned also, within recent years, upon Freud's conception of psychosexual stages. These were conceived to succeed one another rather abruptly and, at times, dialectically — one phase partially negating what has been asserted by the preceding phase and leading on into a higher reconciliation. Notable among these fresh formulations of psychosexual stages were those of Erikson (1950), which were based upon acceptance of the Freudian conception of the dominance of different organ systems and their contributions to such aspects of ego development as autonomy and initiative, intimacy and generativity at successive periods in life. Erikson gave a larger and larger place to the environmental challenges and responses to challenges whose mastery is required for the integration of a sense of identity and of commitment.

It is characteristic of most thinking about the life span that it entails a deep philosophical concern for completeness or for fulfillment. Just as with Cicero's celebrated essay on old age, the ragged edges, the general frustrations, however difficult for those experiencing them, have often been muted by the psychologist. Changing conceptions of the necessary shortness of man's life and the increasing number of aging persons may be expected to force some new changes in these perspectives.

REFERENCES

Allport, G. W. *Personality: A Psychological Interpretation*. New York: Holt, 1937.

Anderson, H. H. "Domination and Integration in the Social Behavior of Young Children in an Experimental Play Situation." *Genetic Psychology Monograph,* 19 (1937), 341–408.

Barron, F. *Creative Person and Creative Process*. New York: Holt, Rinehart and Winston, 1969.

Bayley, N. "Mental Growth in Young Children." *39th Yearbook of the National Society for the Study of Education,* Pt. II (1940), 11–47.

Beers, C. W. *A Mind That Found Itself*. London: Longmans, Green, 1908.

Binet, A. *La Suggestibilité*. Paris: Schleicher, 1900.

Bowlby, J. *Attachment and Loss*. Vol. 1. New York: Basic Books, 1969.

Bruner, J. S. "Eye, Hand, and Mind." In D. Elkind and J. H. Flavell, eds. *Studies in Cognitive Development*. New York: Oxford University Press, 1969.

Bühler, C. *Kindheit und Jugend* [*Childhood and Adolescence*]. Leipzig: Hirzel, 1928.

———. *From Birth to Maturity*. London: Kegan Paul, 1935.

Bühler, C., and Massarik, F., eds. *The Course of Human Life*. New York: Springer, 1968.

Claparède, E., *Psychologie de l'enfant et pédagogie expérimentale*. Geneva: Kundig, 1905. *Experimental Pedagogy and the Psychology of the Child*. Translated by M. Louch and H. Holman. New York: Longmans, 1911.

Collins, J. E. "The Intelligence of School Children and Paternal Occupation." *Journal of Educational Research,* 17 (1928), 157–69.

Comenius, J. A. . . . *Orbis Sensualium Pictus*. 1658. 12th ed. Translated by C. Hoole. London: Leacroft, 1777.

Darwin, C. "A Biographical Sketch of an Infant." *Mind,* 2 (1877), 285–94.

Dollard, J., Doob, L. W., Miller, N. E., Mowrer, O. H., Sears, R. R. (in collaboration with Ford, C. S., Hovland, C. I., and Sollenberger, R. T.). *Frustration and Aggression*. New Haven: Yale University Press, 1939.

Erikson, E. H. *Childhood and Society*. New York: Norton, 1950; rev. ed. 1963.

Escalona, S., and Leitch, M. *Early Phases of Personality Development: A Nonnormative Study of Infant Behavior*. Evanston, Ill.: Child Development Publications, 1953.

Franzblau, R. S. "Race Differences in Mental and Physical Traits Studied in Different Environments." *Archives of Psychology,* No. 177 (1935).

Freud, A. *Das Ich und die Abwehrmechanismen*. Vienna: Internationaler Psychoanalytischer Verlag, 1936. *Ego and the Mechanisms of Defense*. Rev. ed. New York: International Universities Press, 1967.

Freud, S. [*Analysis of a Phobia in a Five-Year-Old Boy*.] Leipzig: Deuticke, 1909. (SE, Vol. 10, 1955.)

Freud, S. [*Beyond the Pleasure Principle.*] Leipzig: Internationaler Psychoanalytischer Verlag, 1920. (*Standard Edition,* Vol. 18, 1955.)

Froebel, F. W. A. *Friedrich Froebel's Entwicklung-erziehende Menschenbildung
(Kindergarten-pädagogik) als system.* Herman Posche, eine umfassende,
Wortgetreue Zusammenstellung. Hamburg: Hoffman and Campe, 1862.

Gesell, A. *Infancy and Human Growth.* New York: Macmillan, 1928.

Gesell, A., and Thompson, H. "Twins T and C from Infancy to Adolescence: A
Biogenetic Study of Individual Differences by the Method of Co-Twin Control."
Genetic Psychology Monograph, 6 (1929), 1–124.

Goodenough, F. L. "The Expression of the Emotions in Infancy." *Child Development,* 2 (1931), 96–101.

Guilford, J. P. *Intelligence, Creativity and Their Educational Implications.* San
Diego, Calif.: Knapp, 1968.

Hall, G. S. *Adolescence: Its Psychology and Its Relations to Physiology, Anthropology, Sociology, Sex, Crime, Religion, and Education.* 2 vols. New York:
Appleton, 1904.

Healy, W. *Mental Conflicts and Misconduct.* Boston: Little, Brown, 1917.

Hecht, S. "The Nature of the Photoreception Process." In C. Murchison, ed. *Handbook of General Experimental Psychology.* Worcester, Mass.: Clark University
Press, 1934.

Helson, H. *Adaptation-Level Theory.* New York: Harper, 1964.

Hollingworth, L. S. *Children Above 180 I.Q.* New York: World Book, 1942.

Hunt, J. McV. *Intelligence and Experience.* New York: Ronald Press, 1961.

Isaacs, S. *Social Development in Young Children.* London: Routledge, 1933.

Jersild, A. T. "Training and Growth in the Development of Children: A Study of the
Relative Influence of Learning and Maturation." *Child Development Monograph,* No. 10 (1932).

Kagan, J., and Moss, H. A. *Birth to Maturity.* New York: Wiley, 1962.

Kardiner, A., Linton, R., DuBois, C., and West, J. *The Psychological Frontiers of
Society.* New York: Columbia University Press, 1945.

Klein, M. *The Psycho-analysis of Children.* Translated by A. Strachey. London:
Hogarth Press and The Institute of Psychoanalysis, 1932.

Klineberg, O. *Negro Intelligence and Selective Migration.* New York: Columbia
University Press, 1935.

Lashley, K. S. *Brain Mechanisms and Intelligence.* Chicago: University of Chicago
Press, 1929.

Lerner, E. *Constraint Areas and the Moral Judgment of Children.* Menasha, Wis.:
Banta, 1937.

Levy, D. M. "Studies in Sibling Rivalry." *Research Monograph of the American
Orthopsychiatric Association,* 2 (1937), 1–96.

———. *Maternal Overprotection.* New York: Columbia University Press, 1943.

Lewin, K. *A Dynamic Theory of Personality.* Translated by D. K. Adams and K. F.
Zener. New York: McGraw-Hill, 1935.

Lewin, K., Lippitt, R., and White, R. K. "Patterns of Aggressive Behavior in
Experimentally Created 'Social Climates.'" *Journal of Social Psychology,* 10
(1939), 271–99.

Lorenz, K. *On Aggression.* New York: Harcourt Brace Jovanovich, 1966.

Mahler, M. S. (with Furer, M.). *On Human Symbioses and the Vicissitudes of In-*

dividuation. Vol. 1. *Infantile Psychosis.* New York: International Universities Press, 1968.

McGraw, M. B: "Later Development of Children Specially Trained During Infancy: Johnny and Jimmy at School Age." *Child Development,* 10 (1939), 1–19.

Mead, M. *Coming of Age in Samoa.* New York: Morrow, 1928.

Miles, W. "Age and Human Ability." *Psychological Review,* 40 (1933), 99–123.

Murphy, L. B. *The Widening World of Childhood.* New York: Basic Books, 1962.

Pestalozzi, J. H. *Wie Gertrude Ihre Kinder Lehrt.* Vienna: Pichler, 1877. *How Gertrude Teaches Her Children.* Translated by L. E. Holland and F. C. Turner. Syracuse, N.Y.: Bardeen, 1894. (First published in 1801).

Piaget, J. *Le Langage et la pensée chez l'enfant.* Neuchâtel: Delachaux et Niestlé, 1923. *The Language and Thought of the Child.* New York: Harcourt Brace Jovanovich, 1926.

———. *Le Jugement et le raisonnement chez l'enfant.* Neuchâtel: Delachaux et Niestlé, 1924. *Judgment and Reasoning in the Child.* New York: Harcourt Brace Jovanovich, 1928.

———. *La Représéntation du monde chez l'enfant.* Paris: Alcan, 1926. *The Child's Conception of the World.* New York: Harcourt Brace Jovanovich, 1929.

———. *Le Jugement moral chez l'enfant.* Paris: Alcan, 1932. *The Moral Judgment of the Child.* London: Kegan Paul, 1932.

———. *La Naissance de l'intelligence chez l'enfant.* Neuchâtel: Delachaux et Niestlé, 1936. *The Origins of Intelligence in Children.* New York: International Universities Press, 1952.

Preyer, W. [Thierry Wilhelm]. *Die Seele des Kindes.* Leipzig: Grieben, 1882.

Rousseau, J. J. *Émile; ou, de l'education.* Amsterdam: Néaulme, 1762.

Shapiro, H. L. *Migration and Environment.* New York: Oxford University Press, 1939.

Shirley, M. M. *The First Two Years, A Study of Twenty-five Babies.* Vol. 1. *Postural and Locomotor Development.* Minneapolis: University of Minnesota Press, 1931. Vol. 2. *Intellectual Development.* Minneapolis: University of Minnesota Press, 1933. Vol. 3. *Personality Manifestations.* Minneapolis: University of Minnesota Press, 1933a.

———. "Development of Immature Babies During Their First Two Years." *Child Development,* 9 (1938), 347–60.

Shuttleworth, F. K. "Physical and Mental Growth of Boys and Girls Ages Six Through Nineteen in Relation to Age of Maximum Growth." *Monographs of the Society for Research in Child Development,* 4 (1939).

Skeels, H. M., Updegraff, R., Wellman, B. L., and Williams, H. M. "A Study of Environmental Stimulations: An Orphanage Preschool Project." *University of Iowa Studies in Child Welfare,* 15 (1938), 7–191.

Spitz, R. A. (in collaboration with Cobliner, W. G.). *The First Year of Life.* New York: International Universities Press, 1965.

Starbuck, E. D. *The Psychology of Religion.* New York: Scribner, 1899.

Stern, W. *Psychology of Early Childhood.* Translated by A. Barwell. New York: Holt, 1924.

Stevens, S. S. "Theory of the Neural Quantum in the Discrimination of Loudness and Pitch." *American Journal of Psychology,* 54 (1941), 315–35.

Stolz, H. R., *et al. The First Berkeley Growth Study.* Berkeley: Institute of Child Welfare, University of California, 1938.

Sully, J. *Studies of Childhood.* New York: Appleton, 1895.

Terman, L. M. *The Measurement of Intelligence.* Boston: Houghton Mifflin, 1916.

————, ed. *Genetic Studies of Genius.* Vol. 1. *Mental and Physical Traits of a Thousand Gifted Children.* Palo Alto, Calif.: Stanford University Press, 1925.

Thompson, D'A. W. *On Growth and Form.* Cambridge: Cambridge University Press, 1917. 2nd ed. New York: Macmillan, 1942.

Thorndike, E. L. *Educational Psychology.* New York: Lemcke and Buechner, 1903. Vol. 1. New York: Teachers College, Columbia University, 1913. Vol. 2. New York: Teachers College, Columbia University, 1913a. Vol. 3. New York: Teachers College, Columbia University, 1914.

Tiedemann, D. "Beobachtungen über die Enwickelung der Seelenfähigkeiten bei Kindern." *Hessische beiträge zur gelehrsamkeit und Kunst,* 2 (1787), 313–33; 3 (1787), 486–502.

Waddington, C. H. *The Strategy of Genes.* New York: Macmillan, 1957.

Watson, J. B., and Raynor, R. "Conditioned Emotional Reactions." *Journal of Experimental Psychology,* 3 (1920), 1–14.

Werner, H. *Einführung in die Entwicklungs-Psychologie.* Leipzig: Barth, 1926. *Comparative Psychology of Mental Development.* Translated by E. B. Garside. New York: Harper, 1940.

White, B. L. *The Initial Coordination of Sensorimotor Schemae in Human Infants— Piaget's Ideas and the Role of Experience.* In D. Elkind and J. H. Flavell, eds. *Studies in Cognitive Development.* New York: Oxford University Press, 1969.

Whyte, L. L., ed. *Aspects of Form.* New York: Pellegrini and Cudahy, 1951.

Witkin, H. A., Dyk, R. B., Faterson, H. F., Goodenough, D. R., and Karp, S. A. *Psychological Differentiation.* New York: Wiley, 1962.

Witkin, H. A., Lewis, H. B., Hertzman, M., Machover, K., Meissner, P. B., and Wapner, S. *Personality Through Perception.* New York: Harper, 1954.

Witmer, L. "The Hospital School." *Psychological Clinic,* 1 (1907), 138–46.

NOTE: A list of further readings appears at the back of the book.

25

Personality

If I could get within this changing I
JOHN MASEFIELD

Studies of personality began with the theater and with biographical sketches. In India, for example, they began with the traditional heroic figures of Ram and Sita, whose loyalty nothing could break. Among the Greeks, they began with Homer's "godlike Achilles" and "wily Odysseus" and with the figures portrayed by the men of tragedy—Aeschylus, Sophocles, and Euripides—and by the man of comedy—Aristophanes. They appear as literary "types," that is, figures which represent a group having something in common. The characters of the stage, their faces covered with masks, had to be austerely simplified; thus the defiant Prometheus, chained to the rock, had to be all benevolence toward man, all furious defiance toward the Lord of Heaven.

Plutarch, more than anyone else, stamped Western literature with the conception of noble, bold, and creative, or mean and despicable, types. Whether he drew greatly or only slightly upon the body types of Hippocrates—and probably he drew a good deal—he represented personality types in terms of dominant motives, often tied to dominant attributes of physique, as in the often-quoted remark of Caesar regarding Cassius: "Let me have men about me that are fat, / Sleek-headed men, and such as sleep o' nights." Shakespeare could assume that his audience, probably even the groundlings, could respond to this characterization. Such characterizations were greatly enhanced in the eighteenth century by the vivid theories of Lavater. He defined the attributes of skull and face, which reveal the charming or repulsive subtleties of the character of the owner to all who take time and trouble to study physiognomy. He also produced and distributed magnificent steel engravings to reinforce the point. The phrenologists who refined these theories were familiar with Lavater's physical and personal types. Darwin tells how he nearly lost his appointment on the *Beagle* because his nose, according to Lavater, disqualified him.

The next important step to be emphasized was the conception of measurable individuality, primarily in the work of Galton. He made himself a little paper cross, which he would carry in his vest pocket; one arm was for recording cases of average expression of a trait (the length of nose, for example), one arm for more than average, and one arm for less than average. As he walked through the Strand, he would prick the appropriate arm as he looked at noses, until he could get a suitable "distribution" of the length of noses. The laboratory was also soon pressed into service, and individual differences (which had hardly interested Fechner and Ebbinghaus) began to be noted in sensory, perceptual, motor, and affective functions.

The problem of individuality greatly interested Cattell (see p. 172) and Thorndike (see p. 366) at Columbia, who at the turn of the century were developing and applying many tests of simple sensory, associative, and motor functions. But individuality at the level of more complex functions first achieved prominence in the work of Binet. The Minister of Public Instruction in France asked him to develop tests which would differentiate dull children from those having difficulties in school work for other than intellectual reasons. The first systematic, orderly development of empirical intelligence tests followed. He even made very modern studies of some rare types, such as lightning calculators and chess players, and undertook quantitative studies of handwriting as related to personal-social characteristics.

In 1904, Charles Spearman offered a theory of "general intelligence" that marked, with Binet's work, the beginnings of a theoretical approach to intelligence and told how it could be measured. From this followed the study of the interrelations between kinds of abilities and the whole area of "mental organization," as it was called for some years. Soon the theoretical and practical work with "factor analysis" and later still the field of "mathematical models" emerged.

It was an era of preoccupation with individual differences and of metrical efforts to order these differences in systematic quantitative form. There was a good deal of medical measuring done in Italy, France, and Germany in relation to problems of proneness to one or another type of disorder. In England, the sphere of biometry was represented by Pearson (1904) and was applied to many psychological problems of personality. Even very complex personality functions were not beyond bold attack.

Binet's initial investigation of the properties of handwriting were carried further in Klages's (1917) work on a systematic theory of expression based upon the relation of the whole individual to the mode of his manual response in writing. All these efforts were under the influence of the new evolutionary approach which looked for individual diversity, preferably in quantitative terms, and tried to contain ultimately a biopsychological theory of individuality rich in concepts from genetics, embryology, histology, and biochemistry. They were also influenced by the industrial and general practical concerns with personality measures and, above all, with their utility in educational and vocational selection and guidance.

Wholeness, Structure, and Gestalt

Gestalt psychology pushed in the same direction. There were, to be sure, many who referred to personality measures as artificial, atomistic, or irrelevant to basic personality problems. Yet just as Freud found a place for the quantitative approach known as the *economic principle,* so Wertheimer and his colleagues found personality measures very useful indeed. The conception of structure or organization of personality emerged, in which each aspect of personality was viewed as identifiable and quantifiable within its proper context.

Outstanding among these approaches was the work initiated in Germany in the twenties, especially at Marburg and Hamburg. This was followed by the systematic elaboration of the concept of measurable individuality, in the Harvard Psychological Laboratories, by Allport (1937; and with Vernon, 1933). At Allport's invitation, a group of young men carried out a wide variety of tasks involving expressive movements—walking, writing, talking, and so on. These studies of individuality yielded a rich matrix of quantitative data, which allowed examination both of the "correspondence" of measures—measurement of one trait compared with measurement of another trait—and of the "congruence" of measures in which two or more measured attributes were seen as expressing the same characteristic in a personality disposition. More intuitive individual studies also fell naturally into place. In a separate study bound into the Allport and Vernon report, for example, there is an excellent quantitative analysis of handwriting by Powers, which shows that not only graphological experts but ordinary students can match handwriting against character sketches beyond chance level. Two of Wertheimer's own pupils, Arnheim (1928) and Wolff (1943), also conducted quantitative studies of the expression of personality and made a mark on the American personality psychology of the thirties. Wolff's work was an interesting combination of Gestalt and psychoanalytic concepts. Many of his subjects, while able to recognize the pattern of their own expressive movements, nevertheless showed at other times a strong tendency to be blind to them. They misidentified their own expressive movements as though rejecting them.

In the perceptual-cognitive field a popular method emerged for validating personality measures. It was reported by Rorschach (1921) that individual responses to inkblots can be matched rather successfully against personality sketches. (We shall return to his method on p. 434.) The Gestalt way of looking at personality, while not the only way which found favor, became a secondary aspect of almost every kind of personality investigation from that time forth, both in the laboratory and in the clinic. A personality was usually seen as a "whole," and its separate attributes were seen as having identifiable "membership character" in the particular personality and situational context. The body-type approach also implied the measurement of traits and the viewing of the individual as a whole. Here, too, the attempt to predict behavior in specific defined situations was integrated into a well-structured totality—into a *Gestalt*.

The Gestalt psychology of personality seems to have overcome most of the difficulties which the purely perceptual approaches of Gestalt theory did not achieve. As in the case of Wolff (1943), psychoanalytic and Gestalt concepts have frequently flowed together. The celebrated study, for example, of Barker *et al.* (1941) made use of the psychoanalytic concept of regression. Barker and his associates devised a simple rating scale of "degree of differentiation" and showed that frustrated children score lower on this scale than nonfrustrated children; repression could thus be identified by lowered differentiation. Blending, fusion, and integration of the different "schools" of psychology found their way rather easily into the study of personality.

This was especially clear in that branch of personality evaluation which has come to be called "assessment." This term is still used broadly and vaguely, but we refer here specifically to a branch of personality investigation which began with the work of the Office of Strategic Services (1948) in World War II. The task of this agency was to select men for "difficult and dangerous" assignments. Potential candidates from generals to privates, and civilians stripped of professional identification marks, passed through a grueling three-day screening process, being forced to carry out complex, difficult, or "impossible" tasks under glaring lights. "Naturalistic" laboratory-clinic measures had of course been used by psychiatrists and psychologists for a long time. But they achieved a new status in this situation, partly because of the powerful leadership offered by H. A. Murray. Assessment became a useful and respected method, demanding sophisticated personality theory to bear upon the assessment process. The work on assessment is being continued at many points, notably by the Institute of Personality Assessment and Research (at the University of California, Berkeley), by MacKinnon and Crutchfield and their associates. Assessment studies have often been concerned with the ability to cope with stress and have been guided largely by psychiatric—especially "psychosomatic"—thinking regarding both crisis breakdown and chronic anxiety (see Grinker and Spiegel, 1945).

In returning to "types" of personality, we should mention the typologies elaborated by Kretschmer (1921). According to his classifications, slender or spindle-shaped individuals are found mostly with a schizoid disposition, and globular, rounded types with cycloid or manic-depressive disposition. This way of thinking about temperamental types and their relation to physique was further developed by Sheldon (1942) in the late thirties and early forties. He used a standard photographic procedure for assessing body build according to three categories relating to the three embryonic tissue layers:

endoderm, mesoderm, and ectoderm. These reflected, respectively, at the psychological level: emotionally warm, affable tendencies; vigorous striped muscle action'tendencies; sensitivity and reflective tendencies. The investigation of these types has been one of the richest areas of personality research, with literally hundreds of publications; many supported Sheldon's theory, many opposed it, and many raised doubts regarding the general value of the system as a whole. There was a general tendency to agree that in extreme cases Sheldon's classification may be useful. These studies led to the recognition that the central nervous system, the autonomic and endocrine systems, and the system of organs and tissues as a whole are all relevant to the development of personality. At the other extreme, the negative data pointed to the need for considering the enormous impact of cultural factors in personality development, and of the specific family circumstances in which the individual is reared.

In the meantime, typologies had appeared in psychoanalysis, notably in Freud's conception of investment of the libido in oral, genital, and anal regions, and of the "fixation" of such investments. Other typologies stressed the "constitutional tendencies" predetermining the manner in which environmental pressures might exert their effects. Oral and anal types were described by Abraham (1924). Erikson (1950, 1956) extended the concept of developmental stages and delineated psychosocial aspects of ego development as outcomes of successive drive crises (see pp. 304–06). This was the era in which Jung (1921) was developing his widely popular extrovert-introvert typology, and Pavlov—and, a little later, Teplov (1964)—developed a typology appropriate to constitutional differences in normal functioning. But Freud's concepts of personality dynamics, and the response they elicited in those concerned with social determinants and psychological variables of personality, dominated the field. There can be little doubt that Freudian dynamics has played a very large part in the theory-building of the "personologist." Modified and enriched Freudian and Jungian conceptions, as in the work of Murray (1938) and his pupils, have continued to appear. At the same time the clinical psychologists of humanistic persuasion have made rich use of Jung, and occasionally of Adler. This trend has continued into more recent years, particularly in Maslow's work (1943). His conception of a hierarchy of needs and of "self-actualization" are useful in both defining the aim of the therapist and enabling him to see the otherwise obscure factors of internal conflict.

Personality and Learning Theory

There were also numerous attempts to combine learning theory and personality theory. Almost at the beginning of the procession we find Watson and his work on conditioned emotional responses, closely relating to the Pavlovian studies and conceptions of experimental neurosis. Later

Dollard and Miller (1950) applied learning theory to personality formation, which was conceived mostly in terms of the Hullian drive dynamics, with some admixtures from the early Freud. It became obvious that in personality theory one must find a place for "learnable drives"—for drives which owe their presence and force to definable past experiences and consolidate adaptive or maladaptive functions.

In general, the term "eclectic" was often used to describe systems which were built out of heterogeneous components, especially several conceptions of the learning process. The term was often used in a pejorative sense, in that the pieces were said to be torn from different systems of ideas and were awkwardly put together. Occasionally, however, it was used to show that observations achieved through different *methods* may prove to be related through a community of facts and ideas and may permit a deeper conception of unity. In the case of Lewin, for example, the disparity of his many sources of data did not prevent his achieving a high order of dynamic unity in relation to specific problems. It was a dynamic unity of personality that Stern (1935), and later Allport (1937), tried to achieve.

Such theories as these have been centered in the concept of the integrity of the living individual. They have not been much concerned with the enormous significance of the social milieu. The work of anthropologists and other social scientists during the twenties and thirties, however, began to make clear that the development of personality is profoundly influenced by the experience of growing up in the family and community; that persons with different cultural backgrounds are in a deep sense different persons. The issues of "culture and personality"—and the problem of growth membership in a society—became fused with earlier ideas that biological individuality is traceable to heredity and early individual growth. Here a great influence was exerted from the impressive anthropological studies of Mead (1928), Benedict (1934), and the Lynds (1929, 1937), as well as from numerous culturally oriented studies of early childhood such as those of Lois B. Murphy (1937). All these studies stressed the interdependence of cultural and individual factors in personality developments. Impressed by these studies, Gardner Murphy (1947) offered a biosocial view of personality which emphasized, against an evolutionary background, the development of the living system within a cultural milieu. He utilized the research materials which had become available through the work of psychiatrists, psychologists, and social scientists. In his approach, personality ceased to be simply what is within the skin: the biological individual. Personality was conceptualized, rather, as the product of endless, unremitting reciprocity between the environmental stimulus patterns and the responding organism. This approach looked for feedback relations in the symbolic life; it accepted the situationist's view that everything is determined (as Lewin had said) by the functional interactions between the surroundings and the person. It regarded the idiosyncrasies of personal behavior as depending in the same full measure upon the uniqueness of the situation, as upon the uniqueness of the biological individual. Similar conceptions have been developed by Campbell (1934) and Angyal (1941) and, within very different contexts, by Moreno (see p. 451). These conceptions offer alternative and complementary views.

But have the improved research methods and conceptual clarifications of recent years produced a unified theory of personality? When research shows that two or three expressions of the individual personality stem in large measure from the same root (as in the "congruence" of Allport and Vernon, 1933), or when longitudinal observations show that some early infant personality patterns are recognizable year by year and that there is a real interdependence or membership character of each attribute in the individual's growth pattern, it seems absurd to ask whether the evidence "favors" a holistic or an atomistic interpretation. Both terms, as a matter of fact, are somewhat pejorative and tend to bypass the issues. The investigators who take either of these extreme positions seem to be talking past one another, almost as much as they were two generations ago. The issues are the same as those we discussed regarding the application of Gestalt theory to problems of perception, memory, and thinking (see pp. 256–64). Maybe both are limiting cases; maybe once in a blue moon there is a real case of structure so *tight* that there is no observable "give" in any of the parts, or perhaps a character so *loose* that there are no solid sinews anywhere. However, neither of these extremes has been documented. Existing evidence suggests the interdependence of these two ways of looking at personality. This is less dramatic and less final than either of the extreme views and seems to require more complete formulations than are currently available. The facts about personality and the riches offered by such theoretical possibilities suggest that digestion of the mass of data (like a boa constrictor's meal) may take a very long time.

The modern "personologist" — as Murray calls one who studies persons — is preoccupied with the origins of personality in some clear and consistent understanding of heredity, growth, nutrition, pathology, vulnerability, coping capacity, and adaptive competence. He can no longer conveniently assign the attributes of personality to the bins of "heredity" and "environment." He can no longer be content with the sheer assertion of interdependence of biological and social factors. He must turn to sophisticated modern research approaches, to the broad resolution of the nature and nurture problem as it appears in contemporary laboratory studies. He must look for the special buffets of deprivation and enrichment, or of hostile environments, or of sheer accidents and disease. He must also look for enhancing, encouraging, and growth-stimulating factors, both personal and social, operating suddenly or gradually through a span of years — as was shown in the systematic studies of Witkin and his collaborators (*Personality Through Perception*, 1954; *Psychological Differentiation*, 1962). New observations emerging in the clinic, or the school, or the university, or any other professional life situation may irreversibly alter the perspective which earlier growth studies had given. Since the data-taking can never be complete, and since the perspectives constantly change with the advent of new methods, current personality theories cannot be regarded as anywhere near complete or exhaustive.

Clinical Psychology

Personality study in the clinic has come to be a rather sophisticated type of case analysis based upon a search for all material capable of throwing light on individual development. Until the mid thirties there was little readable material of this type except in manuscript form — that is, in the form of case studies in institutes of child welfare and in clinics serving maladjusted children and adults. The books on the psychology of personality that appeared in the twenties and early thirties were mostly popular books on psychoanalysis, or eclectic syntheses of theory, which sometimes made a gesture toward the rapidly accumulating case records. A marked advance from the point of view of simplicity and systematic clarity was Stagner's *Psychology of Personality* (1936), in which the emphasis was upon sociocultural dynamics in personality formation. This was followed immediately by a systematic integration: Gordon W. Allport's *Personality: A Psychological Interpretation* (1937). This volume, while inclined on the whole toward a Gestalt orientation, stressed the uniqueness and structural wholeness of the individual and made free use of conceptions from psychoanalysis and from behaviorism, and indeed from medical and sociological as well as literary sources. One of its most important conceptions was that of "functional autonomy." Human activities were regarded not just as continuations of instinctive tendencies, but as "contemporary systems," autonomous and developing in their own right.

In 1938 Murray's *Explorations in Personality* appeared. It presented a systematic conception of personality based in considerable measure upon psychoanalysis (Jungian as well as Freudian in spirit); but it was richly documented with experimental and clinical studies by Murray and his staff at the Harvard Psychological Clinic. An original list of human "needs" (need for achievement, for harm avoidance, and so on), theoretically clear and clinically observable, was considered in the context of each case history. Each need was to be understood in relation to the environmental impacts or "presses," which interacted with the dominant ("regnant") needs and were expressed by clinically recognizable "themas." In addition to life histories a variety of newly developed personality tests was applied. The "assessment" of personality was undertaken by clinically trained "teams" of psychologists; the modern conception of "assessment" was the later expression of this procedure. The *experimental* aspect of the work of the Murray group played a prominent part in initiating and shaping the modern movement toward investigation of perceptual and cognitive processes in personal-dynamics teams, as in R. N. Sanford's study of the relation of *hunger* and the eating cycle to the frequency of *food* response to pictures. The combined experimental and clinical uses of pictorial material had even before the publication of the *Explorations in Personality* been reported in the systematic work on the Thematic Apperception Test (see p. 435). Many of Murray's pupils and colleagues banded together in 1964 to show the huge range and rich sensitivity of his methods in a volume signalizing the focus of personality as being used not merely in a cross-sectional approach, but in the full life study, in a volume entitled *The Study of Lives: Essays on Personality Presented in Honor of Henry A. Murray* (Robert W. White, ed.).

The psychology of personality was thus becoming a recognized subdivision of general human psychology. It is not implied that Stagner's, Allport's, and Murray's books suddenly altered the academic situation as far as interest in personality problems was concerned. The journals were carrying annually hundreds of papers on the biological foundations of personality, on early habit formation, on the measurement of adult attitude and opinion, and on many other topics relevant to personality study. It was, however, common practice to refer to the biologically oriented studies as part of physiological psychology, and to the socially oriented ones as part of social psychology, or even of anthropology or sociology. Until the time of Stagner and Allport the world of psychology was hardly ready for a psychology of personality as such, allowing personality itself to become the central problem, separated for the moment from either primary concern with physiology or problems of the community. It was the decades of the thirties and forties which finally realized in full-fledged form the conception of personality study for its own sake.

Our present sketch relates mainly to American practices. In Britain, new approaches involving both laboratory and clinic have been represented in the studies by Eysenck (1953) in London, involving the construction and application of many personality tests, use of many normal and pathological subject samples, and a search for large and socially significant personal dimensions by combining tests which overlap so as to yield rich information about a few major attributes of clinical importance. Especially well known are extensive studies of extroversion and introversion, which in contrast to many earlier American studies have indicated that these Jungian concepts can be put to objective quantitative use in a broad research program.

It is difficult indeed to draw any meaningful line between personality research as pure science and personality research as an investigation of ways of diagnosing, assessing, predicting, guiding, protecting the individual, or giving him an opportunity to find himself and achieve self-actualization. Yet an attempt must be made to characterize in a few words the general spirit of the psychology of clinicians. The term is used, with no attempt to be invidious, mainly in reference to American psychology. European clinical studies of personality are still overwhelmingly the preoccupation of physicians, especially psychiatrists, while, since World War II, American psychologists have flocked in large numbers into training in a kind of psychology which proceeds from basic principles into more and more specialized studies of testing, interviewing, evaluating, guidance, and therapeutic efforts. Of all the practical or applied psychologies which have been recently thriving in this country, clinical psychology is easily the most widespread.

We should note the earlier establishment of the Psychological Clinic by Witmer at the University of Pennsylvania; the development of school testing by Binet and his followers; the development of personality tests of various sorts, especially the projective tests of Rorschach and Murray, and a spate of new projective tests which were developed in the 1930s. An almost boundless array of paper-and-pencil tests emerged in their wake in which the individual reports on himself in verbal terms or compares himself with others. These tests have gone through a process of "standardization" in which "norms" have been prepared and empirical standards given. The "batteries" of such tests are too much for the briefcase capacity of most clinicians, but very extensive experience with a few of them, notably the Rorschach test, the Thematic Apperception Test, and the MMPI (Minnesota Multiphasic Personality Inventory), together with an intelligence test, are presupposed and emphasized in most clinics. We will turn shortly to the discussion of those tests.

The usual route to the status of a "clinical psychologist" has included an exposure to: (1) the dynamics of development and adjustment; (2) the conception of syndromes of adaptive and maladaptive functions; (3) the theory and practice of psychological testing in a broad sense; and (4) a great deal of testing and diagnostic work, then psychotherapeutic experience, under close supervision. Closer and closer integration within private and public community services—hospitals, clinics, schools, industrial plants, and so on—has given clinical psychology a professional status, a local habitation, and a name. This has at times diverged considerably from the "science of the laboratory," but it has also at times led to genuine interchange of ideas and methods.

Professional applications of psychology have preoccupied more and more psychologists and have had a return effect upon the parent science. The first conspicuous public or community applications came in the educational field in the era of Herbart. Education and child study were invaded by psychology late in the nineteenth century. Industrial, vocational, and personnel needs made conspicuous demands upon psychology before, during, and after World War I. The use of intelligence tests with retarded and disturbed children began on a small scale in the first decade of the twentieth century. A clinical psychologist in that era was a person qualified to give psychometric tests, including performance scales as well as verbal scales. Then as child guidance clinics became established (see Healy, p. 406), the psychologist was expected to make personality assessments as well as intellectual evaluations. Rapid development of clinical skills with children coincided with the development of the Alpha and Beta tests in the Army, in 1917 and 1918. Clinical psychology emerged as a profession after World War I. The mental-hygiene movement (see p. 407) was moving rapidly ahead. David M. Levy brought the Rorschach test from Switzerland to New York in 1924, and Morgan and Murray (1935) were soon working on their Thematic Apperception Test at Harvard in the early thirties.

Many universities began to give the doctorate in clinical psychology during the thirties, but many others took the position that the degree was based on the scientific, not the applied, part of the work, and that clinical skills were like engineering skills, more or less ancillary to basic scientific training. There followed a movement for standardization and for professional dignity. Clinical psychology achieved status as a division of the American Psychological Association; and the American Board of Examiners in Professional Psychology established qualifying examinations and interviews and began to confer a diploma in clinical psychology (diplomas in other branches of applied psychology followed thereafter). Clinical psychologists, of course, have had to be heavily involved in community affairs and have had to take a firm professional position against the exploitation of the public by inadequately trained clinicians.

"The problem of lay analysis" dovetails here with the problem of basic standards to be met for diagnostic and therapeutic accreditation. Psychoanalysts have their own standards, distinctive training programs, and types of accreditation. The psychoanalytic movement continues to *influence* clinical psychology profoundly, but it has been far from being the controlling factor in the evolution of clinical psychology. Academic and university matters and the willingness of the public to accept clinical psychology continue to shape the evolution of professional training. They constitute the most distinctive criteria now available as to the directions in which clinical psychology will move and the type of impact it will exert on the science of psychology.

The movement of clinical psychology toward a mature professionalism has involved some regrets at the global, or even fuzzy, manner in which personality theory is often scratched out and applied. Projective tests have usually turned out to yield unsatisfactory reliabilities when independent clinical evaluations were made from the same materials. In most respects, most projective tests involve such a global attack that one cannot independently evaluate the various kinds of information which each part of a test purports to offer. These were among the reasons why straightforward verbal propositions about a person have tended more and more to acquire a major place in personality assessment techniques, along with ratings and check lists which had been used even in the first decade of the century. There have developed an extraordinary number of inventories and scales, such as Woodworth's 1919 Personal Data Sheet, used with Army recruits, and dozens of scales purporting to measure specific personal attributes such as extroversion, introversion, ascendance, submission, and of course attitudes and values of countless varieties.

The most widely known and the richest in clinical yield at the present time is the Minnesota Multiphasic Personality Inventory (MMPI), developed by Hathaway and his collaborators (1943) during World War II. It is a series of over five hundred propositions which can be considered as possibly applicable to a given individual. There are among these statements some which can be grouped together as relating to hysterical, neurotic, schizoid, and so on, attributes. A great deal of work on reliability and validity has been published and several volumes of clinical guides made available. The MMPI has long been widely useful, as, for example, at the Mayo Clinic, where this test is administered routinely to new patients, not with the idea that it is a guide to psychiatric practice, but as an instrument useful to the general diagnostician, no matter what the physical symptoms may be.

As we noted above, there may perhaps be a certain amount of double talk in the insistence—found in practically all modern personality theory— that personality must be viewed as a whole, while saying at the same time that it must be viewed in terms of specific tissue reactions and specific family and neighborhood interactions. The difference between the wholeness, or Gestalt, approach and the itemizing and measuring approach of the modern clinical psychologist cannot be altogether resolved by saying that they are a matter of emphasis. Some of the modern psychologies have almost nothing to say about the measurement of part functions and almost everything to say about the interrelations between observable aspects. At one extreme, some dismiss even the problem of interrelations among observable aspects and seek to find a primary, comprehensive, universal style of self-fulfillment, with some single cardinal attribute and uniqueness in the totality. At the other extreme, there is a great finesse in the isolation and measurement of personal attributes, as in the factor analysis of R. B. Cattell (1966) and of J. P. Guilford (1959); wide varieties of attributes are identified and teased out by meticulous concern with problems of true independence and partial interdependence. If this be "the psychology of *personality*," say the holists, where is the structure, the totality of the person? Can it lie in a unique, never-duplicable pattern? Is the analytical-metrical approach inappropriate for the central issues? The questions raised by Gordon W. Allport (1937) regarding *idiographic* and *nomothetic* conceptions of personality remain unresolved. There are many reconcilers to be found, but the nonreconcilers appear on the whole to be more numerous, and more vocal.

Issues in Personality Diagnosis

There are, in the meantime, many urgent research problems which appear to utilize both these warring conceptions. There are more and more verbal tests, depending upon ratings and self-ratings; adjective check lists; incomplete sentences; yes-no and multiple-choice questionnaires; structured, semistructured, and unstructured questions allowing both global and intuitively-arrived-at impressions. There are also arrays of data ready for the computer and perhaps for factor analysis or other modalities of analytic treatment. But the need for tests which attempt to catch the person as a whole, functioning as a totality, has been keenly and almost universally felt by the clinician. We must venture a few more words about methods developed to serve the purpose. As we have noted above, Klages (1917) and Binet demonstrated, and later Lewinson and Zubin (1942) and others systematically supported the assertion that handwriting reflects various personal attributes. The work of Powers (1933) and others indicated that a small bit of script can be matched (beyond chance levels) against a personality sketch of the person who produced it. A new projective procedure was introduced in the studies of verbal responses to inkblots, first undertaken by the Swiss psychiatrist Rorschach (1921), as expressions of the individual's basic way of perceiving, thinking, and feeling. Leonardo da Vinci had pointed out to his pupils that mud spattered on a wall stimulated the imaginative faculties. But it was Rorschach who recognized the value of such "stimulation of imaginative faculties" in personality assessment. He had reported on the basis of some hundreds of diagnostic studies that the perceptual-cognitive life is to some degree expressed in the way in which one sees wholes, large details, and small details in unstructured patterns. He had shown that the affective life is reflected in response to color; that the combined expression of cognitive and affective factors can be shown by responses in which both form and color exert an ascertainable effect; that response to the white spaces may indicate negativism toward the test or toward life; that human and animal movement may be perceived in different ways by different individuals and may be significant for the fantasy life. The method was soon introduced into the United States by David M. Levy and was successfully applied in 1930 by Beck (1937). Thereafter it spread quickly. After World War II the use of the Rorschach test became standard clinical practice all over the world. Questions of reliability and validity proved to be very complicated indeed, but the clinical usefulness of the test has been generally accepted. In 1960 W. H. Holtzman and his collaborators (1961) developed an inkblot test which appears to have many of the values of the classical Rorschach test and allows for a much higher level of objectivity.

Picture tests of various sorts have also been used with both children and adults in clinical practice, sometimes to test comprehension levels, sometimes to probe emotional responses. In 1935 Morgan and Murray, in the course of Murray's systematic work at the Harvard Psychological Clinic, offered a standard set of pictures presenting ambiguous human situations, allowing the respondent to make up a story, tell what has happened, and tell what will happen next. In this way the "need," the "press" acting upon the subject, and the resulting manifestation of a "thema" conveyed a miniature glimpse of the structure of personal meanings for each individual. This was the Thematic Apperception Test (TAT). It became widely accepted. Suitable variations in the ambiguous pictures, as in clothing and background of figures, permitted cross-cultural investigations. A Children's Apperception Test (CAT) was developed also. In its original form the TAT was not offered as a quantitative device, but the measurement of needs, presses, and themas was early conceived in quantitative terms, and their large-scale evaluation in various populations have been undertaken for years. A great quantity of work was produced by McClelland (1953) and his associates, in measuring the *need for achievement* and the widely varying achievement orientations of different peoples over the face of the globe.

Many other perceptual and motor tasks are being widely examined. Clinical practice almost everywhere uses the tests described and many make use of other projective tests such as finger painting, brush painting, figure drawing, house-tree-person drawing, etc. In most clinics and laboratories the projective tests are combined with personal inventories and other verbal and paper-and-pencil tests in the assessments of individual personalities.

The term "projective test" was introduced by Frank in 1939. The projective approach came to be regarded as a "view into the private world" of the individual. Standard tests of perceptual and motor skills, which had long been used for assessment of *abilities,* have come to be seen as a reflection of certain limited aspects of the total personality. No sharp line can be drawn between "projective tests" and other laboratory tests, such as those of Witkin *et al.* (1954) and Gardner *et al.* (1959) who look for broad personality attitudes as a guide to understanding adjustment and use those tests in a scientific approach to the understanding of the organization of functions within the person as a whole.

The Cross-Cultural Approach

A refreshingly new and promising approach to personality came from cultural anthropology. Some testing of the sensory, cognitive, and learning abilities of preliterate peoples had been undertaken at the turn of the century (see Rivers, 1901, 1903, for example). But the idea of cultural diversities in basic personality types was not ready for study, or even for a nod of recognition, until Boas (*The Mind of Primitive Man,* 1911) suggested in his studies of Eskimos and of the Kwakiutl Indians of Vancouver Island that there were rich culture-personality issues to be worked through. While Sapir (1934) was working on problems of "personality and culture," Malinowski (1927) undertook, in the western Pacific, a study of some psychodynamic assumptions of psychoanalysis. He had found that among the people of the Trobriand Islands it is the mother's brother, rather than the child's biological father, who takes on the primary role of socialization and thus becomes the focus of conflict for the child. This finding contradicted the psychoanalytic postulate that the parent-child conflict is primarily of the known Oedipal type. Such cross-cultural studies introduced the problem of social dynamics and cultural arrangements into the study of personality.

We have already mentioned the immediate impact of Margaret Mead's work in the thirties. Of great importance in the same era was the appearance of Ruth Benedict's *Patterns of Culture* (1934), with its demonstration that personality is shaped by dominating attitudes, values, and dynamic interpersonal situations of a given culture. In the meantime, working with a psychoanalytic frame of reference, Abram Kardiner developed a good working relationship with a cultural anthropologist, Ralph Linton. Together they applied psychoanalytic insights (1945) to observations on the Comanche Indians, the Betsileo of Madagascar, and the people of the Marquesas Islands. Later, many other analyses were carried out by Kardiner on further anthropological records. Taking for granted the constitutional predisposition of each individual, Kardiner emphasized the "basic character structure" which depends upon the cultural modes of mother-child interactions; thus Kardiner conceived of the early mother-child interaction as leading later into the individual's way of interpreting the world as a whole. According to him, the patterns of ideas which go with these relationships result in distinct philosophies and theologies and in basic ways of thinking — in a "projection" of infantile experience into the laws of the unseen world. Kardiner demonstrated that both the collective personality pattern of a *group* and the unique personality pattern of the *individual* within the group can be approached if there are sound ethnological observations to build upon.

The question naturally arose as to whether the methods and concepts of the anthropologist could be applied not only to preliterate men but to Western culture, to the study of our own social life. The Lynds (1929, 1937), as early as 1929 in their epoch-making study of the life of Middletown, had raised the question of whether a "naïve anthropological observer" could study the complexities and get outside of the presuppositions of our own Western culture. They had at least made a magnificent beginning. West (1945), within the approach marked out by Kardiner, studied another small midwestern town; and similar studies followed. A community does not have to be "preliterate" to come within the anthropological domain. Thus the studies of the "culture of poverty" (Oscar Lewis, 1959) deal with the individual personality as well as with his socioeconomic and cultural condition.

Such studies, when truly "multidisciplinary," tend to bring personality back from laboratory and clinic to community life. While anthropologists have been cautious in their response to these bold innovations, the methods of anthropology have been gradually extended to more and more problems of personality development. The conception that cultural and social diversities provide the best naturalistic setting for developing and testing personality theories continues to enjoy high popularity among psychologists. But their commitment to this approach may not fully measure up to the rapidly increasing urgency of the task. It is all too apparent that the relentless homogenizing pressure of Western civilization and technology has already numbered the days of the natural laboratory of diverse cultures. All the more apparent is the need for more and more sophisticated ways of viewing the complicated impact of the cultural milieu in all its richness upon the biologically developing individual.

REFERENCES

Abraham, K. *Versuch einer Entwicklungsgeschichte der Libido auf Grund der Psychoanalyse seelischen Störungen.* Leipzig: Internationaler Psychoanalytischer Verlag, 1924.

Allport, G. W. *Personality: A Psychological Interpretation.* New York: Holt, 1937.

Allport, G. W., and Vernon, P. E. *Studies in Expressive Movement.* New York: Macmillan, 1933.

Angyal, A. *Foundations for a Science of Personality.* New York: Commonwealth Fund, 1941.

Arnheim, R. "Experimentell-Psychologische Untersuchungen zum Ausdrucksproblem." *Psychologische Forschung,* 11 (1928), 1–132.

Barker, R. G., Dembo, T., and Lewin, K. "Frustration and Regression: An Experiment with Young Children." *University of Iowa Studies in Child Welfare,* 18, (1941).

Beck, S. J. "Introduction to the Rorschach Method." *American Orthopsychiatric Association Monographs,* No. 1 (1937).

Benedict, R. *Patterns of Culture.* Boston: Houghton Mifflin, 1934.

Binet, A. *L'Étude expérimentale de l'intelligence.* Paris: Schleicher, 1903.

Boas, F. *The Mind of Primitive Man.* New York: Macmillan, 1911.

Campbell, C. M. *Human Personality and the Environment.* New York: Macmillan, 1934.

Cattell, R. B. *The Scientific Analysis of Personality.* Chicago: Aldine, 1966.

Dollard, J., and Miller, N. E. *Personality and Psychotherapy: An Analysis in Terms of Learning, Thinking and Culture.* New York: McGraw-Hill, 1950.

Erikson, E. H. *Childhood and Society.* 1950. 2nd ed. New York: Norton, 1963.

———. "The Problem of Ego Identity." *Journal of the American Psychoanalytic Association,* 4 (1956), 56–121.

Eysenck, H. J. *The Structure of Human Personality.* New York: Wiley, 1953.

Frank, L. K. "Projective Methods for the Study of Personality." *Journal of Psychology,* 8 (1939), 389–413.

Gardner, R. W., Holzman, P. S., Klein, G. S., Linton, H. B., and Spencer, O. P. "Cognitive Control: A Study of Individual Consistencies in Cognitive Behavior." *Psychological Issues,* 1, No. 4 (1959).

Gray, J. A., ed. *Pavlov's Typology.* Translated by J. A. Gray. Oxford: Pergamon Press, 1964.

Grinker, R. R., and Spiegel, J. P. *Men Under Stress.* Philadelphia: Blakiston, 1945.

Guilford, J. P. *Personality.* New York: McGraw-Hill, 1959.

Hathaway, S. R., and McKinley, J. C. *The Minnesota Multiphasic Personality Inventory.* Minneapolis: University of Minnesota Press, 1943.

Holtzman, W. H., Thorpe, J. S., Swartz, J. D., and Herron, E. W. *Inkblot Perception and Personality: Holtzman Inkblot Technique.* Austin: University of Texas Press, 1961.

Jung, C. G. *Psychologische Typen.* Zürich: Rascher, 1921. *Psychological Types.* Translated by H. G. Baynes. New York: Harcourt Brace Jovanovich, 1923.

Kardiner, A., Linton, R., Du Bois, C., and West, J. *The Psychological Frontiers of Society.* New York: Columbia University Press, 1945.

Klages, L. *Handschrift und Charakter.* Leipzig: Barth, 1917.

Kretschmer, E. "Körperbau und Charakter." Berlin: Springer, 1921. *Physique and Character.* Translated by W. H. J. Sprott. New York: Harcourt Brace Jovanovich, 1925.

Lewinson, T. S., and Zubin, J. *Handwriting Analysis.* New York: King's Crown Press, 1942.

Lewis, O. *Five Families.* New York: Basic Books, 1959.

Lynd, R. S., and Lynd, H. M. *Middletown.* New York: Harcourt Brace Jovanovich, 1929.

———. *Middletown in Transition.* New York: Harcourt Brace Jovanovich, 1937.

MacKinnon, D. W. "Tests for the Measurements of Personal Effectiveness." *Invitational Conference on Testing Problems, 1951.* Princeton, N.J.: Educational Testing Service, 1952.

Malinowski, B. *Sex and Repression in Savage Society.* London: Kegan Paul, Trench, Trubner, 1927.

Maslow, A. H. "Dynamics of Personality Organization, I and II." *Psychological Review,* 50 (1943), 514–39, 541–58.

McClelland, D. C., Atkinson, J. W., Clark, R. A., and Lowell, E. L. *The Achievement Motive.* New York: Appleton-Century-Crofts, 1953.

Mead, M. *Coming of Age in Samoa.* New York: Morrow, 1928.

Morgan, C. D., and Murray, H. A. "A Method for Investigating Fantasies: The Thematic Apperception Test." *Archives of Neurology and Psychiatry,* 34 (1935), 289–306.

Murphy, G. *Personality.* 1947. Rev. ed. New York: Basic Books, 1966.

Murphy, L. B. *Social Behavior and Child Personality.* New York: Columbia University Press, 1937.

Murray, H. A., Barret, W. G., Homburger (Erikson), E., *et al. Explorations in Personality.* New York: Oxford University Press, 1938.

Office of Strategic Services Assessment Staff. *Assessment of Men.* New York: Rinehart, 1948.

Pearson, K. "On the Laws of Inheritance in Man: II. On the Inheritance of the

Mental and Moral Characters in Man, and Its Comparison with the Inheritance of Physical Characters." *Biometrica,* 3 (1904), 131–90.

Powers, E. "Matching Sketches of Personality with Script." In G. W. Allport and P. E. Vernon. *Studies in Expressive Movement.* New York: Macmillan, 1933.

Rivers, W. H. R. "The Colour Vision of the Eskimo." *Proceedings of the Cambridge Philosophical Society,* 11 (1901), 143–49.

———. "The Psychology and Sociology of the Todas and the Tribes of Southern India." *Reports of the British Association for the Advancement of Science,* 73 (1903), 415–16.

Rorschach, H. *Psychodiagnostik: Methodik und ergebnisse eines Wahrnehmungsdiagnostischen Experiments.* Bern: Bircher, 1921. *Psychodiagnostics.* Translated by P. Lemkau and B. Kronenberg. New York: Grune and Stratton, 1942.

Sapir, E. "The Emergence of the Concept of Personality in a Study of Cultures." *Journal of Social Psychology,* 5 (1934), 408–15.

Sheldon, W. H. (in collaboration with Stevens, S. S.). *The Varieties of Temperament: A Psychology of Constitutional Differences.* New York: Harper, 1942.

Spearman, C. "General Intelligence, Objectively Determined and Measured." *American Journal of Psychology,* 15 (1904), 201–93.

Stagner, R. *Psychology of Personality.* New York: McGraw-Hill, 1936.

Stern, W. *Allgemeine Psychologie auf Personalistischer Grundlage.* The Hague: Nijhoff, 1935.

Teplov, B. M. "Problems in the Study of General Types of Higher Nervous Activity in Man and Animals." In J. A. Gray, ed. *Pavlov's Typology.* Translated by J. A. Gray. Oxford: Pergamon Press, 1964.

West, J. *Plainville, U.S.A.* New York: Columbia University Press, 1945.

White, R. W., ed. (assisted by Bruner, K. F.) *The Study of Lives: Essays on Personality Presented in Honor of Henry A. Murray.* New York: Atherton Press, 1964.

Witkin, H. A., Dyk, R. B., Faterson, H. F., Goodenough, D. R., and Karp, S. A. *Psychological Differentiation.* New York: Wiley, 1963.

Witkin, H. A., Lewis, H. B., Hertzman, M., Machover, K., Meissner, P. B., and Wapner, S. *Personality Through Perception.* New York: Harper, 1954.

Wolff, W. *The Expression of Personality.* New York: Harper, 1943.

Woodworth, R. S. *Personal Data Sheet (Psychoneurotic Inventory).* Chicago: Stoelting, 1919.

NOTE: A list of further readings appears at the back of the book.

26

Social Psychology

A few strong instincts, and a few plain rules.
WORDSWORTH

It is not consciousness that determines life, but life that determines consciousness.

MARX

From the Greeks until late in the nineteenth century, psychology was essentially the study of individual minds. The problem of society – the problem of group interaction and of interpersonal relations – was a different matter. Frequently, it was the problem of the historian, the moralist, the jurist, or, to an increasing degree in the eighteenth century, the political economist. Adam Smith, whose *Inquiry into the Nature and Causes of the Wealth of Nations* (1776) could be regarded as the beginning of systematic formal political economy, was also an incisive theorist in the matter of the "moral sentiments" (1759) and the social role of fellow feeling and altruism. In the same era in which Jeremy Bentham and James Mill were applying association psychology to the factory and the marketplace, Malthus was uttering his dire analysis of the bitter choices that mankind must make; philosophical anarchists like Godwin (1793) were asking for a society without a government, and the massive impact of the French and American revolutions was forcing wave after wave of Utopian thinking upon western European and American scholars. Although there was not a social psychology under that name, everywhere there were the makings of a serious philosophy and a serious psychology of group life.

In the philosophical thought of early nineteenth-century Germany, rich in the romanticism of Goethe and the movement of *Sturm und Drang,* the meaning of universal social change lay in the development of Hegel's "Absolute idea." To those more oriented to the stress and suffering of economic transition, it lay in the revolutionary materialist reconstruction offered by Marx (1867). There was more gross and obvious economic and political material to work with than there was psychological material. The Darwinian period was also a period of rethinking the nature of society and of social change, the nature of societal struggle for existence and adaptation to the environment. It prepared for a psychological way of posing problems, which until then had been left largely in economic and political forms.

The beginnings of social psychology in the modern sense came through the growth of psychiatry, and in particular through the work of the Paris and Nancy schools. As the reader will recall, Charcot had defined the hysterical disposition, and Liébeault the nature of suggestibility, in such a way as to provide a scaffolding for a naturalistic conception of the relations of leaders and followers. It was exactly at this point that Tarde defined his *"laws of imitation,"* the first truly modern work in social psychology (1890). It was in these same terms that Sighele (1891) defined the "criminal crowd" and Le Bon (1895) wrote his monumental studies of crowd psychology. A glance through Tarde's work or Le Bon's will show how heavily these authors drew upon studies of pathological suggestibility. In other words, it was the work of the clinic that gave the new conceptions from which the theory of the crowd mind was derived. These theories were of importance chiefly in their contradiction of the classical rationalistic conceptions which underlay not only political economy, but also all of the major theories of social conduct. Even Descartes's "passions" had turned out to be the result of calculations of inherent pleasure and pain in the various possible courses of action. For this reason, we must emphasize the importance of Darwinism, also, in terms of its consistent underscoring of blind and impulsive factors in adaptation to the environment. It was in the soil prepared by Darwin that studies of pathological suggestibility developed into a nonrationalistic social psychology.

But it is necessary to note that as social psychology took shape, it tended to bifurcate into the social psychology of the *psychologist,* emphasizing the individual in social situations, and the social psychology of the *sociologist,* emphasizing group life. We cannot do justice here to the latter, with its intensive and systematic study of social *attitudes, values,* and *roles* — as these relate to society, social organization, and social institutions (G. H. Mead, 1934). The two psychologies share a great deal, yet each continues to have a distinctive focus. The social psychology of sociologist Ross (1908) and psychologist McDougall (1908) appeared at almost the same moment.

McDougall, trained in the Scottish and English schools, found himself, as a Darwinian, profoundly dissatisfied with all associationistic assumptions. In later years, he told with some emotion how he had been seated at dinner next to a personage who, in kindness to the younger man, had asked his area of interest. When the older man heard the word "psychology," he commented: "Oh yes! Association of ideas, and all that sort of thing. Very important!" To this McDougall inwardly replied, "Very *unimportant,* he means!" From that time forth he began to muse more actively upon the question of making psychology really important by getting to the mainsprings of conduct.

Such mainsprings he found in the instincts provided through natural selection. There had been, as a matter of fact, in the early days of Darwinism, a series of exquisitely clear inventories of animal instincts, several of which showed their relation to human instincts. McDougall took hold of an aspect of instinct theory which was as much in need of clarification as was the physiological core of emotion defined by James and Lange (see p. 199). The two problems—the problem of instinct and the problem of emotions—were to be solved simultaneously, along with the problem of conation (specific strivings toward specific ends). The thesis was stated in McDougall's *Introduction to Social Psychology* in 1908. By a single clear and brilliant stroke, he defined instinct in terms of successions of processes always occurring in a given order. (1) There was an innate tendency to perceive a situation in a given way. (There would be, for example, according to a McDougallian interpretation of current evidence on imprinting, an innate tendency of the gosling to follow a moving object.) (2) Such perception was said to be followed immediately by an appropriate affective or emotional response—appropriate in the sense that survival was said to be possible only for those in whom such affect follows. (We have, then, our gosling perceiving the moving object and experiencing contentment.) (3) The experience of emotion led physically into the impulse to act. (It is only among those of our goslings which strive to approach their mothers that survival is possible.)

Natural selection has provided all three of the essential innate tendencies. Each postulated instinct, then, involved a perceptual, an emotional, and a striving aspect, or, in slightly more rigorous language, a cognitive, an affective, and a conative disposition.[1] Every instinct contained, therefore, an emotional core, and every motion was the core of an instinct. Social life, according to McDougall, springs ultimately not from suggestibility nor from the association of ideas, but from the instincts which underlie behavior.

These instincts, however, were conceptualized as being at first rather nonspecific, not prototypes of adult social responses, but raw materials from which social responses are derived. The child may fear many things or be curious about many things. In time, however, the instinctive activities come to be called out more and more consistently in relation to those specific situations which have habitually elicited them. The child has become specifically curious about fire, or about the seats of authority in the community in which he lives, and potentially, therefore, may become a primitive engineer or a primitive politician.[2] For McDougall, however, there were typically two or more instincts focused in a given direction. The child both loves and fears his father, and in the authoritarian family the two are so

---

[1] Here we have the recurrence of Kant's threefold division of mind.

[2] The same conception of progressive narrowing of drives is considered by Janet under the term "canalization" and by Freud under the term "cathexis."

intimately fused that the separate components cannot easily be observed. The term "sentiment" was used by McDougall as the core of the habit system of the social individual; for in social development a person has developed fusions of specific "instinctive responses" in regard to most of the people and institutions around him; these are the "sentiments" that dominate his life.

Of special importance was the sentiment related to the perception of oneself. This system of attitudes toward oneself McDougall called the "self-regarding sentiment." Organized, continuous membership in the social group was chiefly derived from this sentiment. Self-regarding sentiments were the key to those sustained and persistent activities to which we may give the term "will," and they were likewise the basis for self-respect and moral order.

The self-regarding sentiment was built by McDougall into a general theory of voluntary action. The will had frequently been important in medieval and modern psychology; "conation" was one of the three functional descriptive terms for the classification of irreducible psychological realities. There was cognition, affection, and conation. Many psychologists after Kant and before McDougall were inclined to make some conception of impulse or of the will the central dynamic conception of all psychology. It was sometimes replaced by a vague dynamic, or striving, principle, which was difficult to define or describe in the concrete working details of psychological acts. McDougall, however, as one of the first evolutionary psychologists, thought of voluntary function as fundamental and central in his system of purposive psychology. When he had constructed his theory of sentiment, and in particular the self-regarding sentiment, he saw a way to make the will a direct derivative from it. Those with strong wills were those who have organized and enduring sentiments (many current psychologists would here write "values"). When the self was weak, as in the grossly defective child, there was not much "will" to observe, only impulse, or stubbornness, or an irrational thrust against life's difficulties. There was a very curious parallel here with the psychoanalytic system, which beyond the level of analysis of the ego stresses the superego (see p. 284).

In recent decades, the will as a basic conception in psychology appears to be phasing out. We regard each act as a function of an ongoing personality system and of a situation embedded in a cultural matrix. Often, indeed, we think of needs and presses as Murray and his collaborators (1938) did, and the themas which result when needs and presses come to terms with one another. While the concept of "the will" has been phasing out, the conceptions of voluntary controls and of the process of "decision" have continued to be very important indeed in the study of integrated activities at various levels of complexity. The voluntary control is often the highest, the apex, in the individual control system; and the experimental studies of the control of the inner physiology and the inner self are really, in all but name, studies of the will and its works seen in modern instrumental and laboratory terms. Most human operants (see p. 325) correspond roughly or indeed exactly to the "voluntary acts" of fifty years ago, in which language symbols—terms of reference related to values and decisions—are continued in new settings. The problem of spontaneity, or of "free will," a vital problem for Bergson and James over half a century ago, pushes one today to the question whether, if one watches a polygraph record of one's own inner activities, one encounters the will. As one makes a "decision," does one confront the will? The will seems to be a name for intricate systems of inner control, with their physiological aspects, their symbolic reference to social controls, and the confrontation of choice points in which these realities come to terms with one another. The problem of will has not completely disappeared; but any modern discussion of the issue must come to terms with the intricacy of the internal factors that operate when decisions are made, especially in times of high spontaneity and creativity, as described by both McDougall and Freud.

The appearance of McDougall's book marked the beginning of a new era in social psychology. About one new edition a year appeared during the following twenty years, and well over a hundred thousand copies were disposed of, largely in college classes. More important, psychologists and social scientists came rapidly to accept a dynamic, or a Darwinian, approach to problems of social behavior. Lists of instincts were made right and left—for example, by Thorndike in *The Original Nature of Man* (1913) and by Woodworth in *Dynamic Psychology* (1918). Economists such as Veblen (1914) found themselves carried forward by the new tide, and new volumes dealing with World War I and its aftermath were laden with interpretations of the world's predicament in terms of the clash of instincts. To this category belongs Trotter's *Instincts of the Herd in Peace and War* (1916). The instinct doctrine became the center of social psychology. As Bernard made clear in 1924, the term "instinct" was applied, more and more loosely, to almost any type of uniformity in human conduct to which some sort of hereditary basis might, with or without evidence, be assigned.

It was into this situation that Dunlap (1919) hurled the first of the "anti-instinct" bombshells. He indicated that behind all McDougall's views lay a *purposive* definition of instinctive activity. When truly impulsive acts occur at the animal or early childhood level, they can hardly be attributed to a clear purpose. If a strictly biological view of such impulses is taken as a basis for the dissection of human social life, the observable purposive, or goal-seeking, activities may be without proper justification, relegated to blind and unobservable forces in which there is an axiomatic assumption of purpose without proper causal justification. For a period of nearly ten years thereafter, anti-instinct writings of various types flooded the journals. There was an increasing emphasis upon the vagueness and the incompleteness of the evidence that this or that type of behavior is actually inborn.[3] The result was to leave social psychology, toward the end of the twenties, without any generally accepted theoretical basis and without any common agreement as to the kinds of entities or principles to which the complexities of social life should be reduced. At the same time, however, two new trends were serving to bring relief to the situation: new alternative conceptions of human nature emerged, and a series of new devices were developed for the gathering of authentic information. The latter, consisting of a revision in the *methods* of social psychology, are simpler and may be considered first.

The Rise of Experimental Method

Just before the outbreak of World War I, Moede had written an extraordinary little pamphlet on "experimental group psychology." In it he suggested that groups be constituted in various ways for laboratory investigation, with appropriate variables under control, so that the effects of group membership upon thinking, feeling, and action might be sharply defined. He began some investigations, which did not actually appear in published form until 1920. These investigations dealt with the influence of group membership upon various types of intellectual operations, as association and imagination, in a group of boys and young adults. The unwitting imitation of what was being done by others was systematically studied. He showed, for example, that an individual in a group gave words in a chain-association reaction more rapidly than he did when alone. Moede also compared the processes of competition between teams with the processes of competition between single individuals.

These investigations were known to Münsterberg (1914) at Harvard, who had himself carried out a few years earlier a pioneer study showing that individuals in the classroom influence one another in reporting upon an objective situation, as the number of dots appearing on a screen. Under the influence of Münsterberg and Moede, Floyd H. Allport began at Harvard, and continued elsewhere, an extraordinarily fruitful series of investigations on the influence of the group upon the individual. He showed, as had Moede, that one associates more rapidly in the group—*social facilitation*—but he was also able to show that when the quality of a more complex reasoning process is investigated, group membership seems in general to depress quality while adding to quantity. Allport also investigated the problem of whether membership in the group tends to force individuals into more central and less extreme judgments.

Systematic experimental work in social psychology was thus definitely launched. It is true that highly competent investigations of a strictly experi-

[3] A good historical survey of the reaction to McDougall's instinct theory is given by Krantz (1967).

mental type had already been carried out. Triplett had experimentally studied competition as early as 1898. Moore (1921) had measured the relative effect of expert opinion and majority opinion upon the moral and aesthetic judgments of students. The fact remains, however, that such investigations had been sporadic and without much influence until Allport brought together a group of interrelated experiments and demonstrated the revolutionary implications of the experimental method for the study of group behavior. His *Social Psychology* (1924), in which these experimental methods and their results were made generally available for the first time, is full of clear and practical implications for broader problems.

Allport's experimental methods introduced something decidedly new, exciting, and interesting, which was a definite improvement upon the rather formal, schematic outlines that had been laid down earlier. For Allport himself, however, there were two other notes to be sounded, each of them as important as that of experimental method. One was an objective behavioral approach essentially similar to that of Watson, but with emphasis upon observable reflex tendencies in the newborn, rather than upon theoretical constructs like the McDougall instincts. The other was an insistence that social psychology is not a study of group minds but of *individuals* in social situations.

The "prepotent reflexes" of the newborn were classified by Allport under six headings. It was the conditioning of these reflexes which was conceived to constitute the objective basis for social growth and for the interaction of group members. Complex types of social behavior were reduced to this type of formulation. Indeed, one of the most original chapters in Allport's book deals with the explanation of crowd behavior in terms of the reflex and "social facilitation." Individuals were not viewed as helpless pawns of crowd situations. There was no "crowd mind"; there was no subservience of the individual to the mass. The same thing which people wanted when they were considered as individuals they also wanted when they were in the group situation. But social facilitation *accentuated* their wants. Words were used which touched off the appropriate behaviors in situations in which alternative suggestions were found to be wanting.

The Allport formulation swiftly dominated American social psychology, partly through its experimental approach and partly through its behavioral emphasis. In later studies, Allport (1933) went on to demonstrate that "institutional behavior"—the response of individuals to institutional patterns—is quantitatively distinguishable from noninstitutional behavior. In the former case, most people conform; and those who do not conform to the institution may be ranged on a J-curve (Allport, 1934), in which fewer and fewer people appear on the chart as one moves further and further to the right from the point which indicates absolute conformity. Another theoretical contribution (Allport, 1940) was the definition of the interactions of individuals as "event systems," in which one can define and measure the degree to which each person actually contributes toward a social goal. These measurements can be compared with the degree to which the same person believes himself to be so contributing.

The Influence of Anthropology

In the meantime, the conception of ingrained-action tendencies was taking a beating. The instinct theory, already in serious trouble, was being belabored by another force as hostile to it as was the movement toward behaviorism. This was the growth of cultural anthropology, which had begun to emphasize the cultural molding of the individual. Social psychology had for the most part been a psychology of the nineteenth- and twentieth-century man of the Western world. Here and there, to be sure, there were gestures of recognition of the meaning of cultural diversity for the child's personality. But the general assumption seems to have been that the difference between societies would be found to lie only in specific content—for example, in the particular things that are said, or believed, or done—while in general the dynamics of human nature would remain everywhere the same. But in the decade of the twenties came a series of hammer blows directed at the conception that human nature, as we know it, is to be found in the same form everywhere. Studies of cultural diversity began to show that both content and form—both the specific thing done and the way of doing it, both the specific belief and the feeling tone associated with it—bear the marks of cultural arrangements.

The first of these investigations to capture the imagination of psychologists came from the pupils of Boas, who had himself suggested in *The Mind of Primitive Man* (1911) how profoundly the basic psychological processes reflect cultural adaptation to the environment. The whole approach became more concrete upon publication of Malinowski's study of the psychology of the Trobriand Islanders (1927) and Mead's *Coming of Age in Samoa* (1928). Mead's study contained straightforward tests of familiar hypotheses regarding the dynamics of psychological development, including the hypothesis that the "storm and stress" of adolescence is due to biological changes in puberty and that society must reconcile itself to the difficulties entailed by such changes. Mead's study of girls before, during, and after puberty in Samoa failed to reveal anything much by way of storm and stress, and the conclusion was therefore reached that in earlier formulations a biological explanation had mistakenly been given to a phenomenon which was essentially cultural (cf. p. 427).

Quite aside from the question of the acceptance or the rejection of the thesis of Mead's and Malinowski's work, American social psychology was struck as if by a blinding force. Could we, in fact, describe the laws of social psychology at all until we had an infinitely bigger cultural basis from which to work? Mead's volume was followed shortly by a companion study, *Growing Up in New Guinea* (1930), in which the emphasis was laid upon the hard, competitive, commercial model of living. This study was undertaken among the Manus people, who, in their regulation of many types of behavior in childhood, adolescence, and early adulthood, produce constraints and rigidities utterly different from the casual attitudes of the Samoans. Then followed, from Mead and many others, a series of further demonstrations of profound cultural molding of personality.

The instinct theory had already been weakened by Dunlap (1919) and the anti-instinct movement, and by F. H. Allport's conceptions of social behavior. From the anthropological studies came cultural relativism, which undertook to make environmental forces, especially cultural forces, nearly all-sufficient in the determination of personality and of its readiness for community living. Social psychology was called upon to make concessions to anthropology and sociology, just as in McDougall's day it had made concessions to biology. In the late twenties the psychologist began to throw in the phrase "in our culture" after every generalization about human conduct, just as he had begun, in the earlier twenties, to put quotation marks around the word "instinct." A void had been created by the rejection of McDougall's instinctivistic approach, and new conceptions gathered around the edges, waiting to be drawn in. It was clear that a new conceptual system had to take shape and that it was shaped under the influence of new anthropological and sociological discoveries.

In the meantime, the late twenties and the early thirties were periods of great activity in the gathering of empirical data by the methods of experimental social psychology. An enormous amount of careful work was undertaken on the formation of attitudes in children, on the effects of participation in various types of social groups, and in the formulation of more and more adequate methods for sampling and experimenting upon various types of response to education, to family membership, to propaganda, and to social pressure. It was, in fact, during these years that Lasker (1929) introduced us to the first careful studies of race attitudes in childhood, and that Horowitz (1936) measured accurately the development of one representative attitude (attitude toward the Negro) from the kindergarten through the school years, with appropriate samples and quantitative data at each age level. Thurstone (1931) and Likert (1932) developed scales for the measurement of the *intensity* of attitude – scales which became very serviceable in the more precise definition of individual variation in prejudice, in radicalism-conservatism, and so on, and in response to various types of opinion-making forces. To the same period belong large-scale experimental studies of propaganda, with more and more recognition of the fact that what is sociologically a rather simple problem becomes psychologically an intricate one. It was demonstrated that there are great individual differences in susceptibility to propaganda; that many individuals move in a direction opposite from the intended; and that all sorts of subtle personality factors appear which can only be fully understood by recourse to clinical and experimental methods.

The study of attitudes and propaganda remain among the major concerns of current social psychology.

Sherif and "Frames of Reference"

In this period of seething activity and conflicting theoretical formulations, many began to turn to the great systematic psychologies of the period for keys to the specific problems of social psychology. A psychoanalytic version of social psychology was already available. Gestalt formulations began to appear, and field theory successfully invaded the area through the efforts of Kurt Lewin and J. F. Brown.

But if these and other approaches were to be brought into a systematic form, a definition of the nature of social responses was required and so formulated as to bring laboratory studies into full alignment with observations made in the field. It was a Turkish student, working at Harvard and at Columbia, who achieved these definitions and formulated within their frame of reference a research program. Muzafer Sherif, while still in Ankara, had begun to note the influence of the group upon the individual at the level of social *perception:* the fact that the individual learns to *perceive* as a member of his cultural group perceives; he forms an individual "frame of reference." He used the autokinetic effect: the apparent movement of a point of light in the dark (1936, 1937). He showed that this effect is governed by factors of previous learning and of present attitude. Placing his experimental subjects in the company of others, he showed that the individual is progressively molded into the group's way of seeing the movement. In other experiments he studied the degree of excellence of literary passages, defined by group participation. Under group conditions of work, the norms and variabilities which had characterized the individual when alone were rapidly forced in a direction determined by others in the group. It was possible after each session to trace the degree to which each individual had given up his autonomy of judgment in favor of the tendency of the group as a whole. The curves indicated the convergence, or, as Sherif calls it, the "funnel-shaped relationship" which characterizes indoctrination into group norms. Sherif was closely associated in research with Hovland and his collaborators at Yale, dealing with the psychology of communication processes in terms of persuasion as affected by order of presentation, cognitive needs, and so on.

Sherif's data from laboratory experimentation were combined with anthropological materials to show that in general the individual's perceptual habits are adaptations to current cultural habits. It became apparent that the redefinition of social psychology in perceptual terms had the most profound implications for the study of language, family life, religion, politics, and indeed all social behavior. Behavioral interaction was to be studied not in conditioned-reflex terms as such, but at the level of the molding of the perceptual and cognitive processes. Koffka's conception of the process of perceiving (1922) was espoused and developed: namely, that the perceptual reactions are bipolar, with external structure and internal predispositions jointly determining the perceptual organization. The more rigidly defined the external structure, the smaller the play of internal factors, and vice versa. Other cognitive processes, such as recall, imagination, and thought, were also envisaged in cultural terms.

From this conceptual scheme and experimental exemplification, there soon followed scores of studies in social psychology devised to bring out the determination of the cognitive life by the existing norms. Many studies of value judgments and of recall and recognition of material followed in the wake of Sherif's investigation and Murray's contemporary studies of the influence of needs upon perception and cognition: Clark (1940), for example, reported differences between men and women in recalling material bearing on a struggle between a man and a woman, and Bruner and Goodman (1947) studied the influence of socioeconomic background and related motivational factors upon perception (the apparent size of coins, for example, was markedly overestimated by poor children).

Sherif's work, moreover, represents not only the experimental study of the influence of the group upon the individual, but also progress in the study of the group as a group. This latter concern, rapidly making headway in sociology, was very notably advanced by Lewin (see p. 266) as it appeared in industrial, military, and educational situations. Lewin, more than any other single individual, guided the theoretical and practical beginnings of "action research" (research in which the action itself gathers the "data") and of group dynamics (the study of interpersonal patterns of understanding and misunderstanding, and the related forces tending to conflict and adjustment).

The picture of man as gullible, almost formless in the face of a powerful leader, or of sheer mob depersonalization, seemed to be cut down to size by the moderate and orderly empirical data of Sherif. But his findings certainly did indicate a high degree of plasticity in response to pressure. This seemed to offer sinister implications for the robotlike character of men in society and aroused considerable uneasiness among those who were more concerned with the orderly and the rational in human living. Specifically, as an ardent companion and colleague of Max Wertheimer, Asch (1956) found this conception of group plasticity inaccurate and unpalatable. He undertook to set the record straight in a long and bold series of experiments with groups, in which he provided for group pressure to be directed upon a single member of the group. All members of the group but one were in collusion in reporting, for example, the lengths of lines, and the subject found himself caught between the self-evident reality which he wanted to report and the reports by all of his peers, in the light of which he himself was apparently grossly incorrect. Some gave verbal reports agreeing with their peers, but later denied that they had really been misled. In general, the data did indeed find some who moved in a pliable way under group pressure, and there were many who were caught in a painful predicament generating considerable confusion and self-blame. The demonstration of a wide range of responses in this situation, and the far from homogeneous nature of such "suggestibility" made a considerable mark, just as Hovland's data (1957) showed the rich and complex roots of "persuasibility."

Sociometry

After World War I, J. L. Moreno, a Viennese psychiatrist, had found himself drawn to the social theater about him through the seemingly irreconcilable difficulties between Austrians and Italians. An invention he made in the field of radio yielded income for him and helped to free him for involvement in his social research interests. His interest was drawn to American prison life and to penal theory and practice. This led to a vital relation with the New York State Training School for Girls at Hudson, New York. The school's superintendent, Fanny French Morse, was one of the great creative forces in the modernization and renewal of a generous spirit in the institutions for the troubled and delinquent. Moreno, with the help of Helen Jennings, came to the aid of Mrs. Morse and developed new methods for applied social psychology. He had the girls recreate their institutional world (twenty-five cottages with about thirty girls per cottage) by choosing their cottage mates, their work groups, and with whom they would spend various allotments of time. "Sociometry" was the name given to the mutual choices and rejections which were free to express themselves in these terms.

Sociometry, fused with spontaneity testing and spontaneity training, became the system of ideas presented in his 1934 volume, *Who Shall Survive?* The three ideas are developed in the following way. (1) *Sociometry* is a device for the measurement of social-choice processes. A sociometric procedure consists of each person choosing those persons with whom he would like to be placed, in relation to a series of activities. With whom would he like to eat, or to work, or to form a club, or to develop a community activity? Typically, individuals indicated their personal choices from first to third, or from first to fifth. In an investigation at the New York State Training School for Girls, mutual first choices were automatically put into effect; individuals were actually placed with those with whom they wanted to be placed. Where the reciprocation was not so clean-cut—as, for example, when B was A's first choice, but A was B's third choice—Moreno looked for the maximum adjustment which the entire mass of choices permitted. The reaching out of one person to another was considered to have a deep emotional core, to which the term "tele" was applied. (2) Persons may, however, "warm up" to each other; their choices may in time become more spontaneous. The second of Moreno's conceptions was therefore *spontaneity testing*. Here two individuals were placed together and told to begin a conversation. The study of their verbal and postural interactions gave some conception of the background for the "tele" and the choice which stems from it. (3) The third major conception was *spontaneity training*. Moreno regarded the adult as typically a hardened or encrusted form of what had been once the flexible, social creature of early childhood. The child had learned to do the things society demanded and had built up a shell which became more and more difficult to pierce.

Spontaneity training has been developed chiefly in the form of the drama — a drama, however, without detailed plot, written lines, or sharply defined roles. In the spontaneity theater one may call upon member after member of the audience to come on the stage and act out this or that role which may be educationally or therapeutically valuable. The drama is plastic and creative: it has made possible self-realization through the constant demand for a vital and meaningful response to a new situation. The neurotic might in this way relive upon the stage the harrowing struggle through which his own indecisiveness or conflict has dragged him. At times it may be necessary for the psychiatrist to appoint an alter ego (an assistant psychiatrist, perhaps) who takes over those functions of the individual patient's ego which the patient himself is unable at the time to realize.

Research in Natural Settings

Confidence in the feasibility of adapting significant social problems to the miniature theater or the experimental psychology laboratory gained rapidly during the twenties and thirties. But this was by no means the only way in which social psychology took on its "modern" form. Survey techniques of sampling opinions and attitudes, crudely expressing the casualness of a "straw poll," emerged into sophisticated sampling and question-framing, notably by George Gallup in 1932, to be followed by "cross-tabulation" methods by which it was possible to compare, with very small samples (for example, a few thousand to represent two hundred million), groups differentiated in terms of age, sex, religion, occupation, and so on, with surprisingly consistent results and with the possibility of useful prediction. These methods pushed on in the direction of becoming more intimately "psychological." Attempts were made to probe the factors of motivation or unconscious conflict which emerge in all expressions of opinion.

Verbal expression thus became more and more central in social psychology and was joined with new concerns regarding the role of language in society. One of the first problems was the relation of thought to language. Systematic and profound studies of thought and symbolism in general were undertaken in the German-speaking world by Karl Bühler (1932); formal analysis of phonetics, philology, and semantics have all been prominently interacting in recent years with learning theory and with conceptions of communication and information theory. There are indeed several distinct areas today of the "psychology of language," some of which require extensive study of both modern philosophy and information theory. The psychology of abstraction and concept formation, the psychology of expressive acts, the role of words in structuring and stylizing thought have all become research problems. Among those of particular significance was the "semantic differential" of Osgood *et al.* (1957), by which each socially significant person or process was made to elicit from the subject verbal expressions. These were rated according to *value, potency,* and *activity.* Subjects indicated, by rating a word in these terms, the fine structure of the individual meaning system so that attitude and value patterns could be evaluated and combined with other assessment techniques, relating to the symbolic and semantic roles.

Again, the public dimension of individual conduct has been brought into relation to the many private dimensions familiar to developmental and clinical psychology, as in the studies by M. B. Smith *et al.* (1956). Newcomb (1943) studied the relationships between Bennington College women's experience and their expressed attitudes on public issues. He followed up a quarter of a century later (1967) with a study of the same group of women (and a fresh group of undergraduate women), showing the manner in which the attitudes inculcated in college held fast against many eroding factors in marital and community life. Among a small group of college men, he investigated closely the processes by which acquaintanceships and friendships are formed (1961), successfully testing Heider's "balance hypothesis" (1958), as in instances in which "individuals achieve perceptual constancy with regard to persons by attributing stable orientations to them; such attributed orientations are not capricious, but are governed by the principles of balance. There is thus psychological stability amidst the inrush of new information."

A widely quoted clinically oriented study of socially significant attitudes is *The Authoritarian Personality* (Adorno *et al.,* 1950). It dealt with extreme ethnocentrism and fascistlike attitudes brought into relation to psychoanalytically conceived defense structures, displaced aggressions, and the like. Studies such as these had much in common with the life-history studies of Cantril (1938). The latter concentrated on the personal dynamics of participation in a political movement, and on the psychological dissection of social-political trends, as in the studies initiated earlier by Lasswell (1930).

The Influence of Kurt Lewin

Among social psychologists, the work of Kurt Lewin has continued to be prominent. This is attributable partly to his clean-cut manner of handling problems of life-space in terms of dynamics appropriate for the study of movement within bounded (and unbounded) areas and partly to the full utilization of a sort of quasi-geometrical manner of perceiving issues that can be represented in terms of lines, surfaces, barriers, and vectors; he made use of the branch of mathematics known as topology (the nonquantitative study of space). Even more, it was due to Lewin's ingenuity in experimenting with attention, motivation, interest, frustration, regression, leadership, and role-playing. His prolific mind and his enthusiasm inspired many able students. A large share, however, of his impact was surely due to sheer personality, charm, and charisma. His influence remains strong, because the men and women whom he inspired have been extraordinarily productive in research and in communication of his vivid message. His straightforward, appealing, and workable system of identifying, representing, and coding psychosocial realities remain applicable to the most challenging problems of community reintegration. One encounters the pupils of Lewin in many vigorous modern movements: in group dynamics, in race and community relations, in the development of ecological psychology, in conflict resolution, in dissonance theory, in studies of individual development and the life span, and so on. Many of his terms (aspiration level, life space, barrier, vector, and so on) have become part of the language of psychology.

As we noted earlier, social psychology arose in the late nineteenth century largely in clinical settings, and through all the decades of the present century it has continued to welcome and utilize clinical discoveries and clinical thinking. MacKinnon (1946) drew attention shortly after World War II to what was happening. The concept of "assessment of men" (Office of Strategic Services, 1948), so urgently needed in relation to the vast military undertakings of that crisis period, meant that personal social qualities, roughly evaluated in an intuitive manner by a recruiting officer or even a sergeant, might need to be studied by the most sophisticated of modern devices.

Along with clinical, personnel, and cultural problems we see studies of man's social setting in the large; from the more intimate settings of family, friendship, and neighborhood life to the studies of well-defined groups such as clubs, fraternal orders, dormitory groups, and especially industrial coworking groups. In the second quarter of this century the starkly individualistic study of men and women as they did their industrial tasks was in large measure replaced by the "social psychology of the industrial plant." One such study, the Western Electric Hawthorne plant study (Roethlisberger and Dickson, 1939) in Chicago, became celebrated for its investigation of industrial morale. In the Hawthorne plant the effects of illumination, rest periods, and so forth, on attitudes were studied. It turned out that people were responding positively to the fact that they were being studied; whatever was done to their life in the plant, insofar as it meant that someone noticed them, made them produce more. The "Hawthorne effect" became a paradigm for the results of taking seriously the personal meanings surrounding the worker, especially when such effects are new. Other industrial studies began in this spirit. They looked closely at the atmosphere in which work was done. Likert (1961), among others, has produced a series of studies suggesting that in place of the traditional, individualistic rewards and emoluments, the emphasis on cooperation, cohesion, and respect make a great difference in terms of productivity. Such methods of studying the role of attitudes in relation to productivity quickly found their way to the class-room—as, for example, in the dramatic and controversial study of Rosenthal and Jacobson (1968), which reported the influence of teachers' attitudes and preconceptions on the child's educational progress and self-esteem.

Social Ecology

We find the sophisticated psychology of human attitudes and field relationships leading into the study of the environment—indeed, to speak as biologists do, of a systematic study of human ecology. The concept of human ecology was occasionally mentioned during the second quarter of the present century, but systematic descriptive work, based on empirical studies of village and city life, made its appearance only in the middle of the century. The earlier description of "delinquency areas" by Shaw (1929), and of the regions of political radicalism and conservatism laid out on political maps by Rice (1928), were essentially unique museum pieces. Psychologists studied the "cultural background" or the "impact of industrialism" as supplying part of the context within which behavior appeared. But while the behavior itself and the events within the organism which were conceived to lead to the behavior were studied with a fine-toothed-comb, there was practically no concern with the *fine texture* of the urban, or rural, or maritime, or domestic, and so on, *contexts* within which behavior occurred.

It was Brunswik (1947) who first clearly saw and enunciated the fact that behavior science must sample and select from concrete situations, just as individual organisms sample and select. The processes of sampling may often lead to misrepresenting the total reality which is acting upon the organism and to assigning a total organized quality to the sampled reality which it does not in fact possess. The organism must pursue a "probabilistic" method of confronting the environment. The stimulus sampling theory developed by Estes (1950) moved toward finer analysis of the environment actually acting on the organism.

Ecology as used in botany could have partially solved the problem of fine texture analysis, and it is perhaps rather remarkable that R. A. Fisher, who was himself dealing with plots of ground, fertilizers, water, sunshine, and similar variables in his studies of plant growth, was used by psychologists almost solely for his mathematics, not for his conception of ecology. Indeed, even Fisher himself did not make much use of the conception of patterning or order among the components of natural forces acting on the growing plant. He dealt with probability theory and with independent events as far as he could. His concept of "interaction" applied to certain classes of patterned events, which were not studied further in terms of the dynamics of their own structural relations.

During this period, however, Roger Barker and Herbert Wright (1955), in a small Kansas town, and Roger and Louise Barker (1961), in a small town in the British Midlands, introduced systematic sampling studies in the whole public life of the town—street corner, school, church, supermarket, filling station, and so on—isolating and describing the "behavior settings" in which meaningful units of social interaction go on. They showed the relations between the stimulus complexes and the patterned responses and studied the individual through all the moments of his day. Those included the analysis of "social weather," the ups and downs in stimulus configurations which lead to ups and downs in individual responses.

One might, of course, conceive the term "ecology" so broadly as to include the study of cultures at one extreme and the study of specific responses to subdetails of the individual environment at the other—such as street-corner behavior or cockpit behavior. There are plenty of such studies. Among the most interesting ones today are those that have to do with man-machine systems. These include studies of spaceship astronauts and their response to environments representing what may soon become floating palaces of interplanetary and interstellar journeys. As we think back to Bernard (1859) and the "constancy of the internal environment," we may think likewise of the extraordinary demand for constancy of the immediate *external environment* of a small group of men shut up for a prolonged journey through space. The experience of whaling ships, of submarine crews, and of men in Arctic radar stations have done a little to prepare for an essentially new kind of psychology in which the great problem is not the ability to meet new situations but to tolerate stimulus deprivation and boredom. It will force upon us a new kind of "adaptive" psychology, an adaptive psychology which is drastically different from the one applicable to sudden change and crisis, as appears vividly in the current "disaster" studies (Taylor *et al.,* 1970).

New Perspectives on Social Deprivation and Enrichment

All psychologies, and especially social psychology, have been undergoing revision as a result of new ways of viewing the ancient problem of "nature and nurture." In fact, the formless mind, the mind as "white paper," has again come into prominence as a theoretical construct. Moving rapidly beyond the sheer documentation of effects of the "environment" upon the infant's and the child's mind, it has occurred to many to take quite seriously the notion that the mind, regarded in cognitive terms, is at birth essentially blank. Donald Hebb, a physiological psychologist and learning theorist, showed the inevitable corollaries of this conclusion. In his conception the mind was essentially blank before it became capable of newly organized response. The central nervous system manifested a capacity for forming "cell-assemblies," out of which as a functioning unit the habits of attending and perceiving may develop.

But the concept of cell-assembly was relevant not only to the newborn. The organism is in constant reciprocity with its environment at every age, and to shut it off from its milieu makes it qualitatively as well as quantitatively different from what it has been. From this conception followed the idea of "sensory deprivation." It had long been known that men in solitary confinement, men drifting alone on rafts through endless ocean wastes, men in outlying Arctic posts without human companionship might function in ways not quite human. It occurred then to Hebb and his associates to simplify the human environment by an extreme isolation technique (cf. pp. 232–33). From these studies of "sensory deprivation" developed devices for pocketing men off away from their ordinary environment. Sometimes there was no interference in seeing; sometimes communication with the outside world was available through a speaking tube; sometimes there was extreme limitation of movement, as in placing subjects in a respirator allowing almost no trunk and limb activities.

The anomalies of psychological response to these conditions of limited sensory input suggested a number of problems, belonging both to physiology and to social psychology. With the rapid development of information theory, it became possible to think of these states of deprivation in terms of a simplification of the channel system, including at times a possibility that the exclusion of some sources of information may allow other sources to play a predominant part.

Let us turn to "sensory deprivation" in animals or human beings reared under conditions of extreme environmental-cultural simplification. We should mention here the experiments by Krech and his collaborators (1966), in which young rats were randomly assigned to three types of early environment. The first group received a stimulating array of problems with which to keep busy and make increasingly complex responses. The second group received the usual cage treatment with others of similar age; and the third received full isolation treatment. When sacrificed at eighty days of age, these groups of animals showed considerable differences in brain weight. The shelled-off cortex of the brain was heavier in the first group than in the second, and heavier in the second group than in the third. Independent biochemical assessments were made (by technicians unacquainted with the anatomical findings) which indicated significant differences between the groups in terms of the cholinesterase activity in the brain, a result to be expected if there was a biochemical difference in the brains dependent upon sheer use of the nerve cells. Much replication and many studies of indirect effects suggest that we are indeed dealing here with physiological effects of gross sensory deprivation in the case of one group, and with enrichment in the case of another.

Such results are rich with reference to the whole "nature-nurture" issue and raise difficult questions about all groups which function in different cultural and socioeconomic settings. We may compare different groups of institutional children, especially children in monotonous orphanage environments, where quite commonly IQs go down, year after year. Instead of remaining (as they do in normal environments) an expression of a more or less stable relation between mental age and chronological age, IQs can go up or down, and do go up or down, in enriched and deprived environments. Indeed, a twenty-year follow-through of the Skeels studies, by Skodak (1966), showed that almost all of those who received early attention had been maintaining themselves effectively in a life on their own, whereas most of those who had not received such stimulation became public charges.

It is unfortunately still hard to tell what *aspects* of the enriched environment produce the most difference. Indeed, there is very little analytical work among the contemporary studies of sensory deprivation and sensory enrichment to show what really counts over the years. We do have the cogent evidence of J. McV. Hunt (1961) attesting that verbal and/or conceptual training can make an enduring difference. But it is still difficult to say what individual factors and interpersonal factors need to be underscored for maximal long-range results. There may even be much of the "Hawthorne effect" (see p. 454) in the favorable outcomes of early sensory stimulation. Indeed, the Hawthorne effect may itself be regarded as either a special case of stimulus input or of an affective stimulation. As just noted, there often appears an "experimenter effect," as different investigators manage somehow to record different social realities.

The applications of these new kinds of information have, of course, profoundly altered the form of the controversy regarding socioeconomic class differences. The work of Davis (1948), Eells *et al.* (1951), Haggard (1954), and other investigators has strongly suggested that the form of questions put to boys of different economic classes may result in very different types of indicators, or indeed in some cases can lead to the conclusion that when questions are part of the everyday world of social contact for all groups of boys, the group differences tend to disappear.

There is no single source, however, of information on an issue as complex as this. A general trend toward vigorous environmentalism has been apparent for many years among all who work directly with environmental variables. Information regarding human behavior genetics is still very scant, and it is not surprising that the balance, as new information has come to hand, has been strongly in the environmentalist direction. It is, however, more than a *general trend* that impresses the modern analyst of the data; it is its tendency to become specific, analytical, functional, realistic. Instead, for example, of asking whether the southern rural Negro home with its lack of stimulating qualities results in broadly reduced intelligence-test capabilities, we have been settling into the habit of asking what kinds of messages from the larger American cultural world can get through to such a home and what kinds of messages cannot. We no longer look for general intelligence as a primary expression of a gross and general handicap, but for specific functions which can be enriched or deprived.

There remain, of course, those who continue to emphasize the likelihood of basic genetic differences between members of different socioeconomic classes and of different races. Striking, for example, is the evaluation of the data by Shuey (1958), in terms of quantities of data on inferior Negro test-intelligence performance, which she apparently regards as an answer to the environmentalist viewpoint. The parties to this debate are, however, "talking past one another," for one is dealing in the classical terms within which the studies of group differences have been conducted, in which deep-seated or intrinsic attributes are sought, while the other is dealing with contemporary analytical conceptions of functions which arise in specific settings and which will vary with the texture of these specific settings.

This may serve to introduce the whole reconceptualization of the problem of human environments. Home environment used to be measurable on a one-dimensional scale, as, for example, on the Chapman-Sims scale of socioeconomic backgrounds. One might compare this with the Taussig fivefold differentiation of economic status from "Professional and Higher Business" down to unskilled. The quest for fine structure and texture has led to discoveries in which socioeconomic status ceases to be a one-dimensional continuum. Some studies of American class organization suggest that a multifaceted classification of the American public, calling for ethnic, religious, and other factors and including specific roles to be played by the members of different categories, may make it impossible to speak in the grosser terms of yesterday regarding such differentials.

Attitudes

The subject matter of social psychology has been utterly transformed at several different points in modern history. Social psychology consisted largely, in the 1890s, of crowd and mob behavior. When the full impact of the evolutionary approach was assimilated, instincts became key concepts and, as we saw in the work of McDougall, made the instincts the ultimate keys to social behavior. Behavioristic emphasis upon the methods of Pavlov and Watson replaced the instincts by "conditioned reflexes." In the meantime, those who had approached social behavior from the vantage point of sociology had been emphasizing "attitudes." And, as the observation, analysis, and measurement of attitudes became a major concern of social psychology, the instinct period waned. Quantitative methods made refined scaling of attitudes a professionally challenging undertaking. The sophisticated use of scaling techniques in the hands of Thurstone (1924, 1931) and Likert (1932) made attitude measurement and attitude change just as amenable to a systematic quantitative approach as were the "primary mental abilities." In fact, Thurstone's scales with "equal appearing intervals" offered opportunities for rapid resolution of complicated issues about factors which increase or decrease prejudice, or make propaganda more effective or less effective, or determine the form and extent of persuasibility (Hovland, 1957). In certain identifiable situations, social attitudes, along with other social attributes (like ascendance and submission, extroversion and introversion, proneness to one or another type of instability or abnormality), made up a large part of the socially meaningful behavior measurements that were so widely hailed and gratefully pursued during the decades of the thirties and forties.

These studies of attitudes have led also into the study of attitude patterns found in industrial society, to be related to everyday ways of handling challenging issues. Rokeach (1960) has extensively studied "the open and closed mind," systematic and generalized orientations to kinds of information not foreordained solely by one's own personal "apperception mass" (see p. 52). Harvey et al. (1961) have pursued a similar way of thinking and have identified four basic ways of confronting new ideas. All of this kind of research into the cognitive life can be brought into relation to social attitudes of friendliness and prejudice; and at the other edge of a study of these "cognitive maps" one may find oneself in the midst of cognitive psychology generally, or of cognitive and perceptual psychology.

The Rokeach-Harvey type of approach to cognitive function does not deal with the simple objects often used in the cognitive laboratory. A sort of multidimensional map of the human cognitive life emerged from this approach. It became uncertain whether the affective dimension can really be stripped away from the cognitive dimension. Theories of cognition as they appear in social judgment have become prominent in recent social psychology. In addition to the Sherif conception, and the various conceptions expressing Murray's approach, much research has resulted from Festinger's (1957) *Theory of Cognitive Dissonance,* relating to the need to close the gap between two discordant cognitions. Heider's conception (1958) that imbalance must be adjusted between perceived units and experienced sentiments was also relevant in these approaches.

It has long been evident that personality psychology and social psychology are hard to separate from one another or to distill from a larger field which might be called simply a study of personal and interpersonal behavior dimensions. In general, however, when the attributes of individuals are considered in their own right, a wide variety of measurable attributes appears, some of which look as if they were primarily conative or impulsive. What will remain for social psychology, on this basis, will be attributes which appear most clearly in social situations, such as the attitude patterns just described or attributes which reflect the momentary and enduring relations of persons to one another.

The complex and changing pressures of society on personality development appeared in the work of Cantril, a student of Gordon W. Allport and Murray. He conducted pioneer research in the area of communication and mass media (Cantril and Allport, 1935) and later vigorously applied Ames's approach to perception in studies of social psychology (*The "Why" of Man's Experience,* 1950). Still later, Cantril undertook a series of public-opinion analyses and creative studies of individuality under political pressures (*The Politics of Despair,* 1958). Such studies as these represent the fusion of social psychology with the study of perception, political science, economics, and a broad sociocultural view of our own society. This literature is now becoming abundant. If social psychology tends to lose its identity somewhat in this process of merging with all knowledge and wisdom realting to man and society, it will gain much new realism and perspective.

We noted that ever since the early studies of Moede, Floyd H. Allport, and Sherif, the alert social psychologist has tried not only to domicile broad social problems in a form capable of laboratory analysis, but to deal with the broadest social issues in their *natural setting,* in the general manner of the social scientist. As already noted, fascism, communism, social prejudice, and war have prompted many systematic studies. But more, *much* more, is expected of social scientists in this era, and even the boldest attempts to meet new demands are judged wanting. Why, ask many citizens, must we put up with the bullheaded clinging to ancient stupidities, like imperialist war, sex and race prejudice, poverty in the midst of fabulous plenty, a straightjacketing type of public education offered to children in the years of their richest flexibility? Why do not social psychologists go forth to meet all these and countless other demands? The Society for the Psychological Study of Social Issues, the brain child of Krech, was formed in 1936 to confront such issues. Several other movements, notably Lewin's "action research," vigorously accepted the same response to social challenge. The steady pressures to make psychology a "hardnosed" science were difficult indeed to integrate with the urge to create this kind of immediately applicable social psychology, a social psychology which would be committed to these most pressing emotion-laden issues. Clinical and child psychology have had similar professional and moral issues to face. It would be pleasant to believe that *all* science is partly evaluative and normative—a quest for the good as well as the true—and that social psychology is in the same boat with all other kinds of psychology. But at the realistic level, at which research is done, it is a long way from the study of "social facilitation" in a laboratory to the understanding of campus turmoil or international hatred. The two issues—rigor of method and the moral or emotional content of research work—tend to be confused. Either one by itself is enough to complicate or even jeopardize the scientific issue: the issue of understanding man and society.

In the present era, social psychology has one foot in experimental science and the other in the welter of social change. Its task of describing and meeting the vast and intricate forces at work even in a remote society is difficult enough; it may become terrifying when the scientist's microscope is focused on the fine structure of his own rapidly changing society.

Perhaps the social psychology of the full educational process – the process of growing up in the community, whether pursued in home or neighborhood or school or college – offers the most accessible target for imaginative research endeavors. These are now being carried on to bridge the study of laboratory behavior with the study of society. The psychology of personality, the psychology of the learning process, and the psychology of group functioning and leadership are especially characteristic of contemporary thinking about the task of an integrative social psychology.

The problem of what is worth studying and how to develop a way to study it is of course one of those broad problems in the "sociology of knowledge" in which one attempts to view the behavior of the investigator in terms of the whole system of social driving forces that work upon him. For example, studies of aggression, conflict, and hostility were very prominent in the research literature on both adults and children in the 1920s and 1930s (see Jersild and Markey, 1935), during a period of "rugged individualism" and emphasis upon "each for himself." The study of sympathy and cooperation (as, for example, L. B. Murphy's *Social Behavior and Child Personality,* 1937) was a rather lonely adventure in such a period. Though all psychology reflects an era and its ethos, social psychology is particularly sensitive to such influences.

REFERENCES

Adorno, T. W., Frenkel-Brunswik, E., Levinson, D. J., Sanford, R. N. (with Aron, B., Levinson, H. H., and Marrow, A. W.). *The Authoritarian Personality.* New York: Harper, 1950.

Allport, F. H. *Social Psychology.* Boston: Houghton Mifflin, 1924.

———. *Institutional Behavior.* Chapel Hill: University of North Carolina Press, 1933.

———. "The J-Curve Hypothesis of Conforming Behavior." *Publications of the American Sociological Society,* 28 (1934), 124–25.

———. "An Event-System Theory of Collective Action, with Illustrations from Economic and Political Phenomena and the Production of War." *Journal of Social Psychology,* 11 (1940), 417–45.

Asch, S. E. "Studies of Independence and Conformity: I. A Minority of One Against a Unanimous Majority." *Psychological Monographs,* 70 (1956).

Barker, R. G. *Ecological Psychology.* Palo Alto, Calif.: Stanford University Press, 1968.

Barker, R. G., and Barker, L. S. "Behavior Units for Comparative Study of Cultures." In B. Kaplan, ed. *Studying Personality Cross-Culturally*. Evanston, Ill.: Row, Peterson, 1961.

Barker, R. G., and Wright, H. F. *Midwest and Its Children*. Evanston, Ill.: Row, Peterson, 1955.

Bernard, C. *Leçons sur les propiéties physiologiques et les alterations pathologiques des liquides de l'organisme*. 2 vols. Paris: Ballière, 1859.

Bernard, L. L. *Instinct: A Study in Social Psychology*. New York: Holt, 1924.

Boas, F. *The Mind of Primitive Man*. New York: Macmillan, 1911.

Bruner, J. S., and Goodman, C. C. "Value and Need as Organizing Factors in Perception." *Journal of Abnormal and Social Psychology*, 42 (1947), 33–44.

Brunswik, E. *Systematic and Representative Design of Psychological Experiments*. Berkeley: University of California Press, 1947.

Bühler, K. "Das Ganze der Sprachtheorie, Ihr Aufbau und Ihre Teile." *Berichte über den Kongress der Deutschen Gesellschaft für Psychologie*, 12 (1932), 95–122.

Cantril, H. "The Predicting of Social Events." *Journal of Abnormal and Social Psychology*, 33 (1938), 364–89.

———. *The "Why" of Man's Experience*. New York: Macmillan, 1950.

———. *The Politics of Despair*. New York: Basic Books, 1958.

Cantril, H., and Allport, G. W. *The Psychology of Radio*. New York: Harper, 1935.

Clark, K. B. "Some Factors Influencing the Remembering of Prose Materials." *Archives of Psychology*, No. 253 (1940).

Davis, A. *Social Class Influences Upon Learning*. Cambridge, Mass.: Harvard University Press, 1948.

Dunlap, K. "Are There Any Instincts?" *Journal of Abnormal Psychology*, 14 (1919), 35–50.

Eells, K., Davis, A., Havighurst, R., Herrick, V., and Tyler, R. *Intelligence and Cultural Differences*. Chicago: University of Chicago Press, 1951.

Estes, W. K. "Toward a Statistical Theory of Learning." *Psychological Review*, 57 (1950), 94–107.

Festinger, L. *The Theory of Cognitive Dissonance*. Palo Alto, Calif.: Stanford University Press, 1957.

Godwin, W. *An Inquiry Concerning Political Justice, and Its Influence on General Virtue and Happiness*. 2 vols. London: Robinson, 1793.

Haggard, E. A. "Social-Status and Intelligence: An Experimental Study of Certain Cultural Determinants of Measured Intelligence." *Genetic Psychology Monographs*, 49 (1954), 141–86.

Harvey, O. J., Hunt, D. E., and Schroder, H. M. *Conceptual Systems and Personality Organization*. New York: Wiley, 1961.

Heider, F. *The Psychology of Interpersonal Relations*. New York: Wiley, 1958.

Horowitz, E. L. "The Development of Attitudes Toward the Negro." *Archives of Psychology*, No. 194 (1936).

Hovland, C. I., ed. *The Order of Presentation in Persuasion*. New Haven: Yale University Press, 1957.

Hunt, J. McV. *Intelligence and Experience*. New York: Ronald Press, 1961.

Jersild, A. T., and Markey, F. V. "Conflicts Between Preschool Children." *Child Development Monographs*, No. 21 (1935).

Koffka, K. "Perception: An Introduction to *Gestalttheorie.*" *Psychological Bulletin,* 19 (1922), 531–85.

Krantz, D. L., and Allen, D. "The Rise and Fall of McDougall's Instinct Doctrine." *Journal of the History of Behavioral Sciences,* 3 (1967), 326–38.

Krech, D., Rosenzweig, M. R., and Bennett, E. "Environmental Impoverishment, Social Isolation, and Changes in Brain Chemistry and Anatomy." *Physiology and Behavior,* 1 (1966), 99–104.

Lasker, B. *Race Attitudes in Children.* New York: Holt, 1929.

Lasswell, H. D. *Psychopathology and Politics.* Chicago: University of Chicago Press, 1930.

Le Bon, G. *Psychologie des foules.* Paris: Alcan, 1895.

Likert, R. "A Technique for the Measurement of Attitudes." *Archives of Psychology,* No. 140 (1932).

———. *New Patterns of Management.* New York: McGraw-Hill, 1961.

MacKinnon, D. W. "The Use of Clinical Methods in Social Psychology." *Journal of Social Issues,* 2 (1946), 47–54.

Malinowski, B. K. *Sex and Repression in Savage Society.* London: Kegan Paul, Trench, Trubner, 1927.

McDougall, W. *An Introduction to Social Psychology.* London: Methuen, 1908.

Marx, K. *Das Kapital.* 3 vols. Hamburg: Meissner, 1867.

Mead, G. H. *Mind, Self and Society.* Chicago: University of Chicago Press, 1934.

Mead, M. *Coming of Age in Samoa.* New York: Morrow, 1928.

———. *Growing Up in New Guinea.* New York: Morrow, 1930.

Moede, W. *Experimentelle Massenpsychologie.* Leipzig: Hirzel, 1920.

Moore, H. T. "The Comparative Influence of Majority and Expert Opinion on Individual Judgments." *American Journal of Psychology,* 32 (1921), 16–20.

Moreno, J. L. *Who Shall Survive?* Washington, D.C.: Nervous and Mental Disease Publishing, 1934.

Müller, F. M. *Lectures on the Science of Language, Delivered at the Royal Institute of Great Britain . . . in 1861 and 1863.* London: Longman, Green; Longman, Roberts, 1861–64.

Münsterberg, H. *Grundzüge der Psychotechnik.* Leipzig: Barth, 1914.

Murphy, L. B. *Social Behavior and Child Personality.* New York: Columbia University Press, 1937.

Murray, H. A., Barret, W. G., Homburger (Erikson), E., *et al. Explorations in Personality.* New York: Oxford University Press, 1938.

Newcomb, T. M. *Personality and Social Change.* New York: Dryden, 1943.

———. *The Acquaintance Process.* New York: Holt, Rinehart and Winston, 1961.

Newcomb, T. M., Koenig, K. E., Flacks, R., and Warwick, D. P. *Persistence and Change: Bennington College and Its Students After Twenty-Five Years.* New York: Wiley, 1967.

Office of Strategic Services Assessment Staff. *Assessment of Men.* New York: Rinehart, 1948.

Osgood, C. E., Suci, G. J., and Tannenbaum, P. H. *The Measurement of Meaning.* Urbana: University of Illinois Press, 1957.

Rice, S. A. *Quantitative Methods in Politics.* New York: Knopf, 1928.

Roethlisberger, F. J., and Dickson, W. J. *Management and the Worker—An Account of a Research Program Conducted by Western Electric Company,*

Hawthorne Works, Chicago. Cambridge, Mass.: Harvard University Press, 1939.

Rokeach, M. *Open and Closed Mind.* New York: Basic Books, 1960.

Rosenthal, R., and Jacobson, L. *Pygmalion in the Classroom: Teacher Expectation and Pupil's Intellectual Ability.* New York: Holt, Rinehart and Winston, 1968.

Ross, E. A. *Social Psychology.* New York: Macmillan, 1908.

Shaw, C. R., Zorbaugh, F., McKay, H. D., and Cottrell, L. S. *Delinquency Areas.* Chicago: University of Chicago Press, 1929.

Sherif, M. *The Psychology of Social Norms.* New York: Harper, 1936.

———. "An Experimental Approach to the Study of Attitudes." *Sociometry,* 1 (1937), 90–98.

Shuey, A. M. *The Testing of Negro Intelligence.* Lynchburg, Va.: Bell, 1958.

Sighele, S. *La coppia criminale.* Turin: Bocca, 1891.

———. *La Foule criminelle.* Translated by P. Vigny. Paris: Alcan, 1892.

Skeels, H. M. "Adult Status of Children with Contrasting Early Life Experiences." *Monographs of the Society for Research in Child Development,* 31 (1966).

Smith, A. *Theory of Moral Sentiments.* London: Millar, 1759.

———. *An Inquiry into the Nature and Causes of the Wealth of Nations.* 2 vols. London: Strahan and Cadell, 1776.

Smith, M. B., White, J. S., and White, R. W. *Opinions and Personality.* New York: Wiley, 1956.

Tarde, G. *Les Lois de l'imitation.* Paris: Alcan, 1890. *The Laws of Imitation.* Translated by E. C. Parsons. New York: Holt, 1903.

Taylor, J. B., Zurcher, L. A., and Key, W. H. *Tornado: A Community Responds to Disaster.* Seattle: University of Washington Press, 1970.

Thorndike, E. L. *Educational Psychology.* Vol. 1. *The Original Nature of Man.* New York: Teachers College, Columbia University, 1913.

Thurstone, L. L. *The Nature of Intelligence.* New York: Harcourt Brace Jovanovich, 1924.

———. "The Measurement of Change in Social Attitudes." *Journal of Social Psychology,* 2 (1931), 230–35.

Triplett, N. "The Dynamogenic Factors in Pacemaking and Competition." *American Journal of Psychology,* 9 (1898), 507–33.

Trotter, W. *Instincts of the Herd in Peace and War.* London: Unwin, 1916.

Veblen, T. *The Instinct of Workmanship.* New York: Macmillan, 1914.

Woodworth, R. S. *Dynamic Psychology.* New York: Columbia University Press, 1918.

NOTE: A list of further readings appears at the back of the book.

27

History
in the Making:
Marginalia and the
Open Frontier

> *The great tragedy of science — the slaying of a beautiful hypothesis by an ugly fact.*
>
> T. H. HUXLEY

Of all the fast-moving current trends, surely the most general is the continued movement of psychology in the direction of becoming a science — in the sense in which chemistry became a science in the nineteenth century and physiology and embryology became sciences in the late nineteenth and early twentieth centuries. Psychology breathes their spirit, exchanges ideas and methods with them, looks for physical or chemical foundations in its general theoretical formulations, seeks to emulate their authority and criteria for scientific acceptability, and shares the ups and downs of the newly emerging epistemological issues which unite or separate them all. A quarter of a century ago, there was a clearly organized hard core of general systematic psychology; but there were still large fringes of undigested data from the humanities and social sciences. Even more importantly, there was a prevailing authoritative certainty that logical positivism had indeed blunted the edge of age-old philosophical questions regarding the nature of knowledge, that psychology had come into the possession of all the needed tools of rationality for the remaining single and uniform task — the task of collecting and explaining data.

Since that time many things have happened in psychology and in science at large. Psychology did indeed become more scientific. It has also lost some of its former breadth in the process. This was seen as a justifiable, or perhaps even an indispensable, sacrifice on the altar of logical positivism and operationalism. But true to the tradition of all jealous gods, logical positivism and operationalism [1] did not live up to their promises. We may personally take comfort in believing that psychology, too, has contributed to their demise; but we are here not to praise or blame, not to reject or regret, but to attempt a résumé of the situation, which we believe is clear indeed. Psychology has ceased to be a cloudlike area of scattered groups of observations. Most of the current sources we can turn to, in an attempt to get a picture of modern psychology, bristle with facts which are part of that "general science" which has been coming into existence in the books and journals of the last few decades. Yet questions of epistemology and of the unity of science, and of psychology's place within science, are still very much on the agenda.

Psychology and the Unity of Science

We will devote the remainder of this book to examining the current status of psychology as a scientific discipline. Our first task is to locate psychology's position in the web of relationships commonly referred to by the term "the unity of science." Unity, of course, means for some simply the desire or possibility of reducing all complex phenomena to progressively simpler levels: those of behavior to biology and physiology; those of biology and physiology to biochemistry; those of biochemistry to physical chemistry; and perhaps ultimately all to physics. For others, the issue is whether there are uniform principles and methods of experimentation and logical analysis that can be applied equally well in all areas of science. With all its progressive concretization and legitimate claims to full scientific status, psychology has not yet dealt satisfactorily with these problems; nor has science solved these issues vis à vis psychology.

The unity of the reductionist hinges upon the success or failure of the reduction, isolation, and idealization of observed empirical phenomena for abstract mathematical manipulation. This, is, of course, the approach of basic physical and exact sciences, in which (the categorically differentiating label "exact sciences" notwithstanding) the aim and method is isolation and idealization in a process of formulating predictive theories and laws. Biologists and psychologists, by contrast, still deal primarily with the description of concrete, or one might say exact, rather than idealized happenings. The great complexity of the matrix of variables which determine biological and behavioral events often militate against the possibility of full and complete isolation and idealization of particulars; and thus the door is closed to reduction in many areas. When the descriptive concreteness is given up in

---

[1] Operationalism, of course, survives in the current "methodological behaviorism" within which there remains a vigorous emphasis on clearly stated "operational definitions," but such definitions are not taken as final substitutes for content. It is only the Skinnerians who continue to cling to the original tenets of behaviorism and who appear to have espoused operationalism both as method and as the final procedure for the definition of content.

favor of predictive generalization, the problem of complexity may step in and redirect attention either to isolated but marginal causal connections, or to artificial idealization and abstract manipulation of large irreducible entities, which themselves encompass highly complex and sometimes undefinable causal connections.

Two examples come to mind. First, the almost-canonized name of William James can be brought into this examination: here, if we speak as modern scientists, the issue immediately narrows down to the present scientific value of James's conceptions of attention, emotion, and the will. Second, the overarching genius of Sigmund Freud can be invoked with reference to the unconscious. Here, the emerging experimental problem would seem to be the kind of reductionistic investigation of the subliminal dynamics of perception and thought processes that would vindicate, or repudiate, the position to which Freud felt himself driven by his clinical observations. Such studies are in fact currently in progress (Shevrin and Fritzler, 1968, for example). But the majority of current investigators, applying their most recent and most sophisticated instruments to isolated problems of perception, motivation, and thought processes, can very well dispense with the concepts of both James and Freud. The clinician concerned with the *totality* of human behavior cannot do the same; James's and Freud's approaches to personality continue to survive quite well in their works without any overwhelming reductionist support.

This lack of unity, as viewed through the eyes of the reductionist, has not prevented the rapid growth and cross articulation between the various disciplines of psychology—between child psychology, social psychology, personality, comparative and physiological psychology, and so on. Their respective journals are similar in spirit and editorial aims. The criterion of acceptability of articles for publication is the same general scientific methodology and compatibility of findings which holds for psychology as a whole. Psychology has been tending to become monolithic; but at the same time it has proceeded along clear lines of increasingly detailed specialization. There is a general frame of reference that is astonishingly clear and uniform, especially when one considers how recently the basic sciences of physics, chemistry, biology, physiology, and their subdisciplines have taken their own shape. But reductionism has not worked very well for psychology. Psychology remains in search of new facts, new principles, and new logical procedures of abstraction—perhaps in search of a Kuhnian paradigm (see p. 471) of sorts—in its striving to draw the clear lines of unity within itself and with the totality of science. Thus, while psychology is nesting within a proud brood, and almost ready to fly with the rest, it is not quite flying yet. Hopefully, it will grow strong enough to take a legitimate position of leadership when the flight does come to pass.

Psychology and the Development of Science

The unity of science is one of the great central ideas of our time. Much has been said about our scientific age, but these statements could merely mean that there is a universal respect for the methods of science. There could still be a dozen or a hundred sciences, each with its own discipline, its own modalities and methodologies and conceptualizations, its own established methods of observations and treatment and interpretation of data. Such a view on science may be quite different from our present notion of the unity of science. Actually, it is the modern concept of the unity of science that dramatically invites the attention of the historian who looks at spans of time separated from one another by large epochs. We look for the growth of all human thought in the great periods of Periclean Athens, of Caesar's and Cicero's Rome, of Dante and the medieval development of the Italian city-state, or of rapid geographical expansion which followed upon the bold adventure of Columbus. Each of these epochs is characterized by a readiness to look and to feel in particular ways, by social creativity of men sharing in a collective thinking enterprise. From this viewpoint the Alexandrian period could be called a scientific era; and the ideas of Galileo, Descartes, and Newton certainly all shared in a new scientific era. But science in each of these periods was one among a group of exciting new adventures. It might squabble, incidentally, with artistic, theological or humanitarian organization of values, but it was not yet mature enough to show a united front and close ranks in support of a world-view against the views alien to it. An Alexandrian observation of nerves did not join forces with Ptolemaic astronomical ideas; Gilbert's work on the magnet did not predetermine the course of Harvey's thoughts about the circulation of the blood. Science today, however, appears to be in the process of becoming a structured whole: an architectonic so finely contrived that one may, when the edifice finally grows to its full stature, move from any one point to any other point and encounter no chilling problems of adaptation. Psychology is certainly called upon to form a significant part in this structure.

Until a few decades ago, the ambition to make psychology a science was considered to be possible only in those aspects of psychology which, by their content, were closest to physics. This was notable in studies of thresholds in psychophysics, in psychophysiology, and in those aspects of learning theory which were most clearly mathematical. But this is no longer the case. The severity of criteria for research design, the elaborateness of controls, the care given to the null hypotheses, the attempt to define how far a conclusion may be generalized and where the generalization must cease on the basis of a specific piece of research work — all these apply to all psychology. These apply as much to abnormal as to social psychology, as much to developmental psychology as to neurophysiology, and to the learning process.

From this viewpoint, it is not a portion of psychology that is conceived to belong fully to science; *all* of psychology is moving in the direction of standardization of concepts and methods to make itself a part of today's general science.

What of the manifest protests and countermovements of the last few years? What about the fierce light of phenomenology and existentialism? What have they made clear within the citadel of scientific structure? What about the leadership of humanistic psychology in the rejection of logical positivism and operational methods so prized only a short time ago by the general field? What of Maslow's *Psychology of Science* (1966) and his clear warning that science is throwing out babies with the bath and is missing the central reality of human nature, or indeed of life itself? What about the ever more nagging current questions of "relevance"?

One of the possible answers, of course, is that these are countermovements – perhaps to be understood dialectically, perhaps to be understood in terms of the unrest which comes when values are very rapidly changing in an individual's lifetime. Rearguard actions against Darwin took several decades, and the rearguard action against Einstein's work took nearly as long. It would seem reasonable to expect these protests, being very vital, very human, and very intelligible, to continue. They have been going on and gaining momentum for a number of years, and they may lead to forming a more orderly action against the psychological "establishment." A renewed interest in spontaneity, subjectivism, and eagerness to vindicate the role of direct experience rather than the role of systematic conceptualization, instrumentation, and measurement may come in their wake. It may be the hope of the dominant "center" of modern psychology that once a variety of safeguards has been established (as directed by guidelines that will have evolved in a postlogical positivistic, postoperationalistic, but still primarily quantification-oriented science) the currently rejected movements will once again be accepted within the total system – accepted insofar as their aims, concepts, and methods are those of general science. So explicit may this wish become, as time goes on, that if one were to write a book for a doctoral dissertation on the development of Freud's ideas, one might find himself forced to do this in a department of English or German literature, but not in a department of psychology. Or, if one wished to consider a quantitative approach to beauty of line, shadow, or shape, one might find himself encouraged in such an effort by a department of philosophy or a department of fine arts, but not by a department of psychology.

But suppose such an isolation of psychology does in fact take place (some signs of it are already apparent). What will be its necessary effects on the emerging new science? It may result in the rejection of much of that which we had considered in this book as the intellectual heritage of psychology. The unity of science, as we understand it now – whether through reduction of complex to elementary phenomena, or through a uniformly objective rationality — may necessarily imply exclusion of the many central human concerns and behaviors which do not readily lend themselves to isolation, idealization, or fully objective assessment. By excluding them as proper subject matter for "scientific scrutiny" we may very well do more harm than good, by the criteria of long-range scientific history. It is not only their "scientific" understanding that is at stake, but, more importantly, the evolution of science itself. In the final analysis, it is not that psychology must be restricted and limited to the central approaches and methodologies of a science as we know it today; rather, science must be formed in such a way that it can take full account of, and deal in full competence with, all the central and essential human issues and behaviors. If science has no place for James's ideas on the stream of thought, it is the poorer, not the richer, for it. It is with such understanding that psychology must seek the paths of its future growth and strive for a kind of leadership among the sciences.

Science, as Conant (1947) and many others have shown, has regularly had the habit of rejecting observations because the system cannot incorporate them. More recently, Kuhn (1962) has brilliantly shown the long series of arduous processes by which the practitioners of a "normal science" (physics, chemistry, and closely related disciplines) hold together a systematic view of nature and develop related central paradigms. The reason given is that such paradigms permit unity in perception and action, while the new discordant observations fail precisely in that respect. Discordant observations, when persistent, produce dislocation (breakdown in paradigms) rather than unity. It is only when fully digested, and in the aftermath of revolutionary changes in the original paradigm, that such new information is accepted and made the cornerstone in the revised new systematic view of nature.

It is apparent that in terms of Kuhn's analysis much of modern psychology is still in a preparadigm phase. Even the generally accepted central theories, such as the theory of evolution and the unity of mind and body, have not yet led to a single systematic view of the psychological nature of men on which all available information can be reflected in a clearly affirmative or clearly discordant fashion. It is rather likely, though, that the Kuhnian analysis does not fully fit the life sciences and psychology. The reason, one might argue, is that "normal sciences" have evolved around those central paradigms which were fully pertinent to them and fully testable by their methods. Psychology, on the other hand, evolved and revolved around paradigms and examples which were borrowed from, and emulated, the normal sciences and biology. The issue thus became not only the degree of harmony and dissonance of one or another central idea and available empirical information, but also a question of harmony or dissonance between a new psychological idea and the current conceptualizations in other better established scientific disciplines. This in turn brought into the forefront institutional issues of prestige, acceptance, communication, and so on. Most of those issues were outside the immediate problem of empirical verification and reform of ideas. This is not to deny the importance of empirical verification in the development of psychology, but to point out some difficulties in applying uniform models to the history of different scientific disciplines. This issue, however, belongs to another more directly focused discussion. Here we should state only that the development of psychological ideas may not fully fit the evolutionary process outlined by Kuhn; although many of the specifics in the history of psychology could be written in Kuhn's terms.

The most notable nineteenth-century support of Kuhn's interpretation would be the manner in which the static conceptions of human psychology as basically different from animal psychology were maintained until Darwinism broke into the field. After Darwin, the most radical evolutionary conceptions could rapidly coordinate vast areas of animal and human behavior. Another illustration of smaller magnitude and different nature indicates the difficulties in the full application of a straightforward Kuhnian view to the history of psychology. The rather simple sleeplike phenomenon demonstrated by Puységur was rejected for over fifty years, apparently because it was called "animal magnetism." Braid changed the term to "nervous sleep" and almost instantly got the medical men of the era to accept what had been rejected as ludicrous imposture. There was no marked change in any world view or paradigm here, nor any precisely affirmative or negative understanding of the observed phenomenon vis à vis such; rather, the issue revolved, at least in part, around the general scientific respectability of verbal tags.

A volume edited by Farberow (1963) spelled out a dozen areas of modern research and clinical practice which are still in the no man's land of scientific reputability. A number of aspects of human sexual function, both normal and pathological, had belonged for a long time in this category. Before Freud there were strong medical taboos on many branches of such investigation; and even after thirty years of ventilation of such issues by psychoanalysis, the Kinsey reports (1948, 1953) produced a great deal of heat and a great deal of normative thinking in areas which, by general agreement, needed scientific exploration.

In terms of the sociology of knowledge we may think of all these skirmishes on the fringe of science as related to the incompatibility of ideas. The problem of *incompatibility* of two explanations would seem to be a logical problem: a statement cannot be both true and false. Today, however, the assumption of incompatibility needs a frank assessment as a possible case of psychological "resistance," that is, the rejection of an idea *not* because it is logically *incompatible* with other ideas, but because it is *threatening* to one's world-view and self-esteem — often in ways which are outside of purely logical or scientific considerations. Experiments in the thought processes, whether with syllogisms or with political slogans, strongly suggest that psychological propositions may become threatening either to man's collective image of himself or to the particular self-image of the individual who is confronting the evidence. Thomas Reid said that he would entertain no idea which impugned "the dignity of man." Bishop Wilberforce said, in 1860, that he could not credit the conception of man's descent from a monkey; and Disraeli assured the Parliament that, in a choice between the monkeys and the angels, he was "on the side of the angels."

No science is a finished structure. The attempt to make it tight, with no open window, is a normal process in a familiar context. The attempt will continue as long as the atmosphere favors it. It will be even stronger in psychology than in other rapidly expanding sciences because of the unfulfilled need for unity-coherence and self-containedness. To admit that we have many open windows would imply that we do not yet have a really solid backing of uniform principles, methods and facts.

We will now turn, as a first example, to an area which has received a great deal of attention by many outstanding psychologists of the past and present, but not even a modicum of scientific accreditation: to parapsychology. Following this we will discuss two sources of creative and disruptive tension in current psychology: the humanistic protest and the continuing dissonance in national psychologies.

Psychology and Parapsychology

If we retrace our steps, we find that almost all the important forward steps in psychology were taken through the importation of an idea from another science, or even from a domain of experience which is not a science at all. Fisher's conception of the measurement of coworking and interacting components in plant growth (1935) fitted so perfectly into the then developing experimental psychology that it literally transformed experimental thinking. Köhler's idea about physical forms, derived mostly from physics, had an explosive effect upon development of form theory in psychology. Pavlov, the physiologist, gave the newly constituted field of psychology of learning both major methods and major concepts. Indeed, these imported methods and concepts tended to force out existing methods and concepts. Freud's observations and ideas ran through many formulations. Many of them found a place in the ongoing psychological systems, but some were kept out. Almost all of the modern world of genetics fitted; almost nothing from parapsychology fitted.

All the problems in establishing the validity of reports and fitting new materials to an existing system are apparent in the response of scientific psychology to the field of parapsychology, which, in the late nineteenth century, was known as psychical research. This field is concerned with alleged communication and perceptual and cognitive responses to persons, objects, or events, without any apparent use of the known sense organs. The term "telepathy," for example, refers to alleged direct perceptual and cognitive contact of one person with another through means other than the known senses. The term "clairvoyance" refers to direct perception of an event without known direct sensory contact with it.

In 1882, a group of Cambridge University scholars and the Dublin physicist William Barrett organized the Society for Psychical Research in London. This group immediately started very ambitious studies of long-range telepathy (Gurney *et al.*, 1886) and of a variety of hypnotic and other phenomena. The aim was to break open a sealed off region which, as Henry Sidgwick put it, represented a mass of human experience, the neglect of which was a "scandal" in an "enlightened age." William James was intensely interested, partly because the empirical spirit of all his work meant looking for odd or unpalatable events which could not easily be classified. He was also interested because his attention was drawn to a young medium, Mrs. L. E. Piper, whose utterances contained factual statements which, in his judgment, were utterly beyond any possibility of being normally acquired (James, 1909).

Later experimental studies of telepathy and related phenomena appeared here and there like sparks in a half-extinguished fire. These studies were given a little new life by the long-distance telepathic experiments of the French chemical engineer Warcollier (1921) and by three members of the psychology department at the University of Gröningen, in the Netherlands (Brugmans, 1922). These three reported on their ability to control the responses of a subject in another room. The subject, in each trial, selected one out of forty-eight checkerboard squares as the target for the specific trial and quickly rolled up highly significant scores under the telepathic suggestion of the experimenters. Estabrooks (1929) at Harvard reported a successful series in similar experiments, while Coover's study of this same phenomenon, at Stanford University, offered nothing which he regarded as positive.

The issue did not become one of major concern to psychologists until the late nineteen twenties, when McDougall came from Oxford to Harvard and then to Duke University and encouraged the work of two young botanists and foresters, J. B. Rhine and his wife, L. E. Rhine. In the span of four years they collected through a wide variety of tests abundant material on telepathy and the related process of clairvoyance (Rhine, 1934). For several years an emotionally intense battle raged between pro-Rhine and anti-Rhine groups. But the issue settled itself as might be expected, in a general rejection and dismissal of these findings by the major body of psychology. This, however, did not prevent other scientists from conducting Rhine-type and other experiments and publishing them in the *Journal of Parapsychology* and the *Journal of the American Society for Psychical Research*. The work continues actively; parapsychological research has been carried on in more than fifty university laboratories and medical sleep-dream laboratories, frequently with positive results and with increasing use of automated methods (Ullman *et al.*, 1966).

Most psychologists continue to be negative toward parapsychology for two main reasons. There has never been a clearly "repeatable" experiment, which anyone could carry out in his own laboratory, with positive and confirmatory results. Also, there is no systematic theory which would bind the new research materials into the organized and generally accepted scientific framework. These, of course, are weighty reasons for hesitation and certainly justify skepticism. But the current practitioners of parapsychological research take seriously the rules of clean-cut experimentation and relentless replication of each positive observation; and they continue to come up with further supportive evidence. Daring efforts are being made to develop a theory which would bridge the concepts of scientific psychology and parapsychology. Parapsychology may possibly soon become a part of organized psychology; but at this time it is a separate field.

The Protest of Humanistic Psychology

Psychology has embarked upon a great new adventure of making itself a full-fledged science, but it continues to remain in need of new models and new ground rules for drawing the lines of unity within itself and within the totality of sciences. The assessment of the gains and losses will be the responsibility and privilege of the historian of the twenty-first century. All we can do at present is to point to some possible frontiers and indicate some current marginalia which may in time move to the forefront of scientific respectability and may play an important role in the continued search for coherence. Phenomenology and existentialism are currently important. Their message is being sifted until it becomes clear; their postulates are currently formulated as to fit or not to fit. The fit, of course, will never be perfect; and the creative instability and unpredictability of a few great seminal figures will continue to leaven the loaf. But the main trend is clear, at least for our era, this closing fourth of the twentieth century.

As we said earlier, the influence of these two philosophical trends, existentialism and phenomenology, constitutes a massive "humanistic protest" against the psychological establishment. The major concern of this protest relates to the nature of man and of man's contact with reality. It is beyond our capacity here to give the reader a full account of the philosophical postulates of existentialism and phenomenology, or to show the totality of effort in relating these to psychology. At their present state of development these trends and efforts may be regarded neither as systematized philosophies nor as well-articulated psychological systems; but rather primarily as a variety of discontinuous, and sometimes even self-contradictory, revolts against the current philosophical and scientific establishments, against the remoteness from life of both academic philosophy and scientific psychology. The major quarrel of existentialism and phenomenology is with the marked suppression in all sciences of the role of subjective experience and individuality. They argue against the prevailing positivistic emphasis on the objectively defined and clearly communicated particulars in experience and behavior. They argue that this emphasis pays a heavy toll in failing to grasp the totality of human experience, in failing to see the alleged ultimate essence of reality to be found in individual consciousness.

It had become clear by the mid 1950s that the infusion of phenomenology and existentialism into psychology was heightened by many rich cultural trends—trends that were evident in literature and the arts, in various protests against formalism and the firmly structured social patterns that go with industrialization and technology. The sources of these trends were the anti-Victorianism, anticlassicism, and antiformalism of the period just prior to World War I. One could argue that the period of World War I, the Depression, the brutality and horrors of fascism during the thirties, World War II, the dismal failures of Russian communism with respect to individual freedom, and the moral burden of the conflict in Southeast Asia all added up to a profound distrust of industrial societies, and indeed of science, of technology and all its works. Existentialism and phenomenology invaded academic and clinical psychologies just as behaviorism, Gestalt psychology, and psychoanalysis had invaded psychology before them. They entered the vacuum of psychology's apparent inability to say anything about human nature which would have adequately explained, foreseen, and warded off these enormous social failures and betrayals of hope.

Humanistic psychology thought of itself as a "third force," a countertrend both to psychoanalysis and to behavioristic psychology. It is a psychology which, in the declaration of aims by the *Journal of Humanistic Psychology,* "is concerned with the publication of theoretical and applied research, original contributions, papers, articles, and studies in values, autonomy, being, self, love, creativity, identity, growth, psychological health, organism, self-actualization, basic need-gratification and related concepts" (Sutich *et al.,* 1961, p. ii). These broad concerns, especially the concern with spontaneity and creativity, were frequently expressed in vigorous protests against behavioristic and Freudian approaches. Similar protest movements were under way in Britain and continental western Europe. In the German-speaking world there had been, for a century, a continuing protest of many against the reduction of all psychology to a natural-science basis. But the movement we are describing here is primarily American.

Humanistic psychology was soon incarnated in a national body with annual meetings (the Association for Humanistic Psychology) and with a journal. It has plainly moved toward stability and a new center of gravity. However, there was always a place in humanistic psychology for the abrogation of competitive individualistic self-assertion. And there was a place for the positive cultivation of goals that go *beyond* "self-actualization" toward an egoless, or depersonalized, or transcendent kind of existence—the kind of existence that is very close to, or indeed at times identical with, the *samadhi* of Yoga or the *satori* of Zen Buddhism. While remaining nontheo-logical, the new humanistic trend was plainly rooted in the craving for some-thing beyond *personal* fulfillment: a need for something that could be called truly "transpersonal." By the late sixties the trend in this direction could no longer be subsumed within humanistic psychology as such, and "transper-sonal psychology" announced itself as a "fourth force."

But it is time to pick up some threads from the clinical and personality psychology of the era, which, though existing as individual components in psychology, take on an added meaning because of their "membership character" in the humanistic and transpersonal trends. These threads from clinical and personality psychology have to do with (1) the very marked extension, range, and depth of research into hypnosis, passing from what we might call the Janet period, through the Freud period, through the Hull period, through the experimental-clinical period until it appears now in a context related to "altered states of consciousness"; (2) the reactivation of an intense interest in pharmacopsychology, taking up where Kraepelin and James had stood in their experiments with drugs at the turn of the century, and later expressed in the widespread use of tranquilizing and antidepressant drugs and more recently in the appearance of the psychedelic, or mind-transforming, drugs; (3) the cosmopolitan pressures, as shown through a vastly augmented amount of travel all over the world and the need to read and talk with cultural emissaries of other parts of the world; (4) the disil-lusionment or despair with organized religion as a force neither satisfying the deeper individual needs nor serving as a creative guide toward a kind of fulfillment of human living; and (5) the consequent craving for self-actualiza-tion through sharing of common human experiences across national-cultural boundaries.

In the context of all this, and in combination with the protest against mech-anization and the technical revolution, a massive movement toward re-making the image of man took place. One aspect of this movement which it seems appropriate to deal with here is the research into "altered states of consciousness" or "altered ego states."

Altered States of Consciousness

The possibility of inducing a wide variety of relaxed, drowsy, suggesti-bility-prone, highly focused or highly diffused states of awareness appears to have been known both in the East and in the West. Aldous Huxley's *The Devils of Loudun* is a representative study of a seventeenth-century episode containing some of these features.

We have already noted the Janet era (see p. 157). The psychoanalytic era may be said to have begun partly in consequence of Freud's observations of the Charcot and Bernheim methods of induction of suggestible states. His own experiments, jointly with Breuer (Breuer and Freud, 1893–95), dealt with the observation of passive, yet conflictful, states. These were states in which the hypnotic trance was used at first both to recover the origins of conflict and to redirect the stream of associations into less conflictful or more ego-controlled channels. The failure of the cures to last, and the conclusion that they often dealt with relatively superficial regions of conflict, led to the development of the "talking out method" to replace the hypnotic trance and its attendant utilization of suggestibility. During this time, it became more evident to Freud that the theoretical clue to the hypnotic state was the phenomenon of transference (see p. 275); and so it remained even in his much later reconstruction of the facts in *Group Psychology and the Analysis of Ego* (1921). Suggestibility was the clue not only to psychopathology, but to normal group life — whether of the stressful type associated with the concept of mobs and crowds or taking the everyday form of group cohesion, as in church and army. A well-developed conception of hypnotic transference phenomena in the work of Gill and Brenman (1959) may be said to put the capstone on the classical psychoanalytic view of hypnosis.

In the meantime, dissatisfaction with the basic psychoanalytic definition of hypnotic phenomena and a fresh and vigorous experimental approach to hypnotic induction and hypnotic phenomena had taken shape as early as World War I. This kind of work became articulate in the studies of Wells (1940, 1941), with his emphasis especially upon the experimental use of "waking hypnosis"; of Erickson (1939, 1941, 1941a), Hilgard (1965), and Weitzenhoffer (1957), with objective definitions of hypnotic phenomena and the development of scales to measure its depth and other attributes. From this effort toward objectivity there developed, in time, a skepticism over whether or not there is, in fact, a hypnotic state and the question of what more there is to study than the various forms and style of suggestion, set, and expectancy. Some would draw these phenomena into close relation to drowsiness, sleepiness, and a set toward inactivity (and irresponsibility); while others would point out the presence of all these phenomena while maximal alertness remains which can frequently result in a battle between the will of the hypnotist and some portion of the personality of the hypnotized subject which cannot go along with the suggestions given. In this connection the old question of whether a person may be "hypnotized against his will" and whether he may be "induced to commit a crime under hypnosis which he would not otherwise be capable of performing" suggests that not one but many phenomena are being experimented upon. There is no doubt, however, that a variety of fundamentally "altered states of consciousness" are being probed which had earlier been lumped together either under the term "hypnosis" or under the term "suggestibility."

The general association of hypnotic practice with the relaxed free-association condition became evident during World War I, when traumatized or shattered personalities could be led under "hypnoanalysis" to recall, and then face, the horrors of the battlefield. These problems recurred during

World War II, and at that time new pharmacological devices were developed to make possible the more rapid recall and assimilation of traumatic episodes. Pentothal, notably, was often successfully used to bring back traumatic episodes — episodes which, according to Freudian formulation, had involved a massive overload breaking through the "stimulus barrier" and producing neurological and not simply "psychogenic" problems. This points, incidentally, to the reentry of neurological concepts, which had in general been put aside as irrelevant, or even misleading, in the daily activities of the psychoanalyst.

The availability of many new compounds as an expression of rapidly developing biochemistry and pharmacology paved the way for the development in the early fifties of a wide variety of new "ataractic" drugs, including tranquilizers, antidepressants, and similar psychiatrically useful drugs. These, all over the civilized world, shortened and simplified many management problems in institutions and complicated the assessment of psychotherapeutic methods. On the heels of the ataractic drugs followed the psychedelic drugs.

The history of the modern use of psychedelic drugs offers a fascinating opportunity to point out the oldness of the new — the recapitulation of discoveries which have utterly different meanings in different scientific and cultural contexts. Preliterate man has, in several times and places, discovered psychedelic, or "mind-revealing," drugs: the yage of the Indians of the Colombia River Valley in Venezuela and Colombia, the Mexican mushroom derivatives known today as psilocybin, and the more familiar mescaline. These drugs were often under suspicion because of the religious revelations which they purported to offer; thus, for example, the Spanish confessional to American Indian converts sometimes went into the question of whether or not the convert was making use of mind-revealing drugs. The opiates, of course, had been known from time immemorial in the Far East, as had Indian hemp, or *cannabis indica*. Opium and hashish were "discovered" by Western travelers and empire builders early in the nineteenth century, and opium breaks into Western literature in the spectacular dreams of De Quincey and Coleridge. William James (1882) drew attention to the extraordinary effects of nitrous oxide in yielding experiences of "affirmation"; while systematic pharmacological research in the interests of psychiatry began vigorously in the work of Kraepelin (1892). From the scientific point of view, these were simply drugs; they belonged with bodily produced toxins, poisons from infected foods, and a host of other disorganizing agents, comparable to fatigue, sleeplessness, prolonged hunger, or the semiacute conditions of exposure to extremes of heat and cold.

However, a radically different point of view was in the making. Some of the pharmacologically oriented psychiatrists began to think of some of these drugs as capable of powerfully transforming or reworking the personality. The drugs could induce mystical or trance states; they could be bracketed together with creative as well as with destructive biochemical agencies. It is in this atmosphere that we may note the extraordinary discovery during World War II of lysergic acid diethylamide by the Swiss pharmacologist Hofman (1959), in a series of far-flung experiments with new compounds. He swallowed some of the new preparation and became so affected that he could hardly make his way home. Soon he and others were announcing the discovery of a "psychotomimetic" group of drugs. These were drugs which produced psychosislike conditions. For several years those who took the drug with this anticipation behaved like very seriously disturbed psychotics, and the condition was compared with schizophrenia and various psychotic states. Gradually two facts emerged, as they did with regard to countless other drugs: (1) the atmosphere in which the drug is taken, the basic setting, and anticipation make an enormous difference in the type of phenomena engendered; (2) even when the psychological factors are given great weight, there still remains very striking individual differences connected with individual thresholds — the amounts to be taken in order to induce certain effects — and qualitative variations of great complexity. In some of the more systematic studies (Masters and Huston, 1966), there appeared to be stages or levels of drug impact through which many subjects passed: from relatively simple sensory effects, like increasing visual vividness, through states of altered meanings and basic ego transformations, to the more advanced level of depersonalization, and even religious ecstasy. It is apparently because of these various types of higher ecstatic experiences that use of these drugs became widespread expressions of the eagerness of youth to plumb the range and depth of new experience. Unsupervised confrontation with very powerful mind-altering agencies, however, like all serious attempts to alter the mind, involved grave risks along with a possible profound promise of new meanings; almost everything depends on the handling of the situation by responsible or irresponsible persons.

Early it had begun to be noted that the higher levels of such drug-induced experience were often described in language very similar to the language used to describe ecstatic and mystical states: for example, in James's *Varieties of Religious Experiences* (1902) and especially in Bucke's *Cosmic Consciousness* (1901). One direct statement of this question — the question of whether psychedelic drugs produce experiences indistinguishable from profound spontaneous mystical experiences — appears in the works of Pahnke (1966, 1969), indicating that LSD states and nondrug states of the higher mystical level are not clinically distinguishable from one another. But since there are many LSD phenomena and many mystical phenomena, the statement leads into complex unresolved problems.

National Psychologies

As we have seen, the psychology of a given time and place is profoundly biased by the dominant ideas of that time and place. It might be worthwhile therefore to look once more at the more dramatic deviations in our modern time from the general themes projected in this book.

Most modern Western psychology is Greek in origin and in spirit. It is derived from the renaissance of Greco-Roman ideas in medieval and early modern times. It took shape specifically under the influence of experimental and evolutionary biology, the two still remaining distinguishable within the structure of today's science. As we have tried to show in the chapter on learning, some psychologists have felt free to leap beyond the bounds of experimental and evolutionary biology and to attach themselves as closely as possible to the physical science model. It is this post-Greek, post-Renaissance modern psychology that we have been describing. But what of the other great traditions?

Of the basic civilizations which have taken shape in the last few thousand years, very few produced a recognizable psychology. The men of the Middle East and the Iranian plateau built an animistic system in which the deities were conceived to be like men and women. For them, the observable principles of human perception, thought, and passion were believed to be cut from the same cloth as the necessary or universal psychology represented by the gods themselves; that is, men "projected" the psychological world that they knew into the cosmic spaces. In general this is where they stopped in their attempt to systematize and order the basic principles of psychology. But the religious genius of the Hebrews went on to monotheism and to an ethical concern with all humanity.

If we take as our standard the inventiveness, the search for psychological whys and wherefores that characterized the Greeks, we shall find these developing to a high level in India and in the lands to which Indian ideas traveled, notably Burma, Ceylon, Tibet, Thailand, China, and Japan; and we shall find the basic Indian insights, modulated but not utterly transformed, in all these cultures. It appears that the early animistic psychology, prevalent in the *Rig Veda* (1500 B.C. and thereafter), continued in interaction with native South Indian Dravidian ideas of a mystical sort and of a sort inclined to challenge the confident aggressive individualism of the earlier period of the *Rig Veda*. Whatever the factors involved, it is plain that by 800 B.C., with the earliest *Upanishads,* Indian thinkers, both warriors and priests, had discovered the phenomenon of depersonalization, the disappearance of competitive individuality, the serene sense of identification with the one central cosmic spirit or *atman.* It is also clear that within the next few centuries rather rapid progress was made through psychophysical exercises (relaxation, breath control, and so on) and speculative analysis to develop a rich psychological system. This system was concerned both with the basic nature of perception, memory, thought, emotion, and the will, and with the application of such general principles to self-discipline, to moral purity, to intellectual power, and even to statecraft and law. Indian psychology contained a central core of profound thought relating to the discovery of a real reality, transcending the deceitfulness of the senses; and at the same time a very broad system of treatises in applied psychology, more reminiscent of Machiavelli and Sir Thomas More than of Aristotle and Descartes.

The word "discipline" is appropriate to apply here, for it pervaded both the intellectual quest and the bodily control. But the poverty, sickness, and misery of the masses continued. At about 500 B.C. Gautama Buddha, a prince who taught the middle way (avoiding both license and asceticism) and the "noble eightfold path," addressed himself to the common people as well as to the élite and offered the possibility of escape from the endless "cycle of rebirths." Buddhism was carried all over eastern and southeastern Asia, and Buddhist psychology became almost as sophisticated as that of Hinduism. Buddhist psychology contains its own account of the process of discipline and deals very specifically with the need for poise and moderation in all things, especially as devices for preventing those excesses of emotional intensity which lead to suffering both in this world and in all later lives (which derive some of their properties from the earlier extravagances of their predecessors). Though Chinese Buddhism became as powerful as the ethical system of Confucius, and in many ways interacted with it, it did not achieve distinctiveness as a psychology wholly separate from the Buddhism of India. It did, however, cultivate those mystical states which had been known in India as *samadhi,* a trancelike unification of the soul with the divine principle; and from the thirteenth century onward these doctrines of skilled detachment and quiet ecstasy were practiced under the name of Zen. Zen Buddhism has maintained a prominent place in popular Japanese religion and philosophy over the centuries.

The Europeanization of Asian philosophy and psychology began with the British, Dutch, and French vessels of war and trade which established the powerful economic links with Asia. These links may be summarized in the word "colonialism." By 1800, British scholars were sending Indian ideas, along with Indian jewels and precious metals, to Britain. And, under the influence of such scholars as Macaulay, British ideas regarding education were imported into India. Missionary efforts in India, China, Japan, and elsewhere began to influence the thinking of the high-caste Hindus and other Asian élites.

After 1868 Westernization became rapid in Japan, and Western university education began to undermine the classical beliefs — religious and philosophical — in favor of science as understood by Western physicists, chemists, evolutionary biologists, and, in time, social scientists, too. In fact, the cold and impersonal science of the West achieved high prestige everywhere in

Asian thought. With this came the evolutionary conception of adaptation to the environment, and hence the relativity of the superiorities and inferiorities of the various groups encountering one another in contests of military and economic strength. There was, then, a two-way osmotic pressure, conveying Indian thought and feeling to the West and vice versa; while, to some degree, the same occurred in China and in Japan, Western science became dominant.

This Westernization may very well bring about negative as well as positive consequences regarding the development of psychology. It may lead to the loss of some vigorous and original components in the psychology of the Far East. The positive side, of course, consists in the rapid orientation of all of southern and eastern Asia to the common human values found in experimental science and in its applications in medicine, engineering, and agriculture. Perhaps the door here is still open for a synthesis of the new and old, of the East and West, and a healthier science may be the product.

European psychology has also changed a great deal in the last few decades. First must be emphasized the literally enormous development of Soviet psychology (see Chapter 23) since the late forties. This has been in the great tradition of the physiologists Sechenov and Pavlov and their remarkably modern conceptions of psychophysiology. As we have seen, a great deal of good research on conditioning, sensory functions, homeostatic and feedback functions, and so on, is now under way and ready to engage the interest of all psychologists. Here, too, one might hope for new syntheses for the benefit of all science.

British psychology is still recognizably British. There has been a notable development of laboratory psychology since World War II. This is true not only within the classical atmosphere represented by Cambridge, Oxford, and the University of London, but by a score of newly established British laboratories concerned with a very wide range of problems. These range from perception, memory, psychometrics, ethology, to individual differences accessible to factorial methods on a large scale. Canadian and Australian psychology still clings rather closely to British standards.

Beyond this, it would be tedious to go into the national diversities which lead both to different conceptions of what psychology must be and to different types of university allocations of space and status with the resulting different levels of research achievement. Psychology in West Germany has not yet fully recovered from World War II; although its Lorenzian ethology (see p. 359) has already made strong new marks. Italy and France continue to emphasize medical psychology rather than general experimental psychology. The Low Countries and all the Scandinavian countries have been productive out of proportion to their population size, responsive both to American and to the German-language traditions. Switzerland has had the express advantage of a high internationalism and a high quota of brilliant leadership: Jung, Rorschach, Piaget.

The present status of world psychology inevitably prompts some remarks about the extraordinary degree to which American laboratories, American child-guidance clinics, American doctoral degrees in every kind of psychological endeavor, have become dominant. By several rough counts, based upon listings of members, listings of those holding Ph.D. degrees, samplings of book and periodical publications, and so on, it is safe to say that at least 90 per cent of the world's professional psychology is today American. To pursue this theme may seem invidious, but there are some consequences that need to be faced. An obvious one is that the American psychologist, with so many rich facilities at his command, seldom thinks it necessary to read much of the newer psychology from other lands. Almost everything which he regards as important is available in English—in fact, in several translations. Open and vigorous protests against modern-language requirements continue. However, it should be noted that most of the major psychological ideas of today, as taught in American universities, are ideas which arose in Europe between the time of Darwin and World War II. This fact may be a telling argument against allowing young psychologists to become too provincial. If the current European psychology becomes for Americans so remote that it is not even worthwhile to get acquainted with it, we shall have succeeded in creating an insular psychology, the applications of which even within our own provincial boundaries will have had an insufficient human "working through," an insufficient systematic testing before the general bar of science, and of civilization. And we shall be fortunate indeed if we can still hear the international and intercultural voices as the din of our own chorus continues in its confident intensity.

But, there are some powerful counterquestions to the above argument that must also be raised here: Can we seriously entertain the possibility of growing isolation in the light of the truly international character of our general scientific endeavor? Does not man's quest for understanding his world and himself stem from a common origin of shared needs and curiosities? Are not the objective methods and theories of science truly supranational, perhaps even supracultural? Do they not present true possibilities for filling the void of diverse values and claims of a national and cultural supremacy in this painfully small and convulsed world of ours? A case for existing and growing scientific internationalism must be made in the light of the undeniably positive, even though qualified, answers to these questions. Ours is indeed a small globe; but ours are also the infinite horizons of shared needs, imagination, and creativity. Will the efforts of psychology be directed to these horizons? Is it reasonable to entertain the hope that the science of psychology—the study of man's behavioral and imaginative continuities from his past, within his present, and into his future—will go forth in expanding, in enriching, and in fulfilling its promise?

REFERENCES

Boring, E. G. "The Psychology of Controversy." *Psychological Review,* 36 (1929), 97–121.

Breuer, J., and Freud, S. [*Studies on Hysteria.*] Leipzig: Deuticke, 1893–95. (SE, Vol. 2, 1955.)

Brugmans, H. I. F. W. *Le Compte rendu officiel du premier congrès international des recherches psychiques.* Copenhagen, 1922.

Bucke, R. M. *Cosmic Consciousness.* Philadelphia: Innes, 1901.

Conant, J. B. *On Understanding Science.* New Haven: Yale University Press, 1947.

Erickson, M. H. "An Experimental Investigation of the Possible Antisocial Uses of Hypnosis." *Psychiatry,* 2 (1939), 391–414.

———. "Hypnosis: A General Review." *Diseases of the Nervous System,* 2 (1941), 13–18.

Erickson, M. H., and Erikson, E. H. "Concerning the Nature and Character of Post-Hypnotic Behavior." *Journal of General Psychology,* 24 (1941a), 95–133.

Estabrooks, G. H. "The Enigma of Telepathy." *North American Review,* 227 (1929), 201–11.

Farberow, N. L. *Taboo Topics.* New York: Atherton Press, 1963.

Fisher, R. A. *The Design of Experiments.* Edinburgh: Oliver and Boyd, 1935.

Freud, S. [*Group Psychology and the Analysis of the Ego.*] Leipzig: Internationaler Psychoanalytischer Verlag, 1921. (SE, Vol. 18, 1955.)

Gill, M. M., and Brenman, M. *Hypnosis and Related States: Psychoanalytic Studies in Regression.* New York: International Universities Press, 1959.

Gurney, E., Myers, F. W. H., and Podmore, F. *Phantasms of the Living.* 2 vols. London: Trubner, 1886.

Hilgard, E. R. *Hypnotic Susceptibility.* New York: Harcourt Brace Jovanovich, 1965.

Hodgson, R. "A Record of Observations of Certain Phenomena of Trance." *Proceedings of the Society for Psychical Research,* 8 (1892), 1–168.

Hofman, A. "Psychotomimetic Drugs." *Acta Physiologica et Pharmacologica Neerlandica,* 8 (1959), 240–58.

James, W. "On Some Hegelisms." *Mind,* 7 (1882), 186–208.

———. *The Varieties of Religious Experience.* New York: Longmans, Green, 1902.

———. "Report on Mrs. Piper's Hodgson-Control." *Proceedings of the Society for Psychical Research,* 28 (1909), 1–121.

Kinsey, A. C., Pomeroy, W. B., and Martin, C. E. *Sexual Behavior in the Human Male.* Philadelphia: Saunders, 1948.

Kinsey, A. C., Pomeroy, W. B., Martin, C. E., and Gibbard, P. H. *Sexual Behavior in the Human Female.* Philadelphia: Saunders, 1953.

Kraepelin, E. *Ueber die Beeinflussung einfacher psychischer Vorgänge.* Jena: Fischer, 1892.

Kuhn, T. S. *The Structure of Scientific Revolutions.* Chicago: University of Chicago Press, 1962.

Maslow, A. H. *The Psychology of Science.* New York: Harper & Row, 1966.

Masters, R. E. L., and Huston, J. *Varieties of Psychedelic Experience.* New York: Holt, Rinehart and Winston, 1966.

Myers, F. W. H. *Human Personality and Its Survival of Bodily Death.* 2 vols. London: Longmans, Green, 1903.

Pahnke, W. "Drugs and Mysticism." *International Journal of Parapsychology,* 8 (1966), 295–320.

Pahnke, W., and Richards, W. A. "Implications of LSD and Experimental Mysticism." In C. T. Tart, ed. *Altered States of Consciousness.* New York: Wiley, 1969.

Rhine, J. B. *Extra-Sensory Perception.* Boston: Boston Society for Psychical Research, 1934. Boston: Humphries, 1935.

Shevrin, H., and Fritzler, D. E. "Visually Evoked Response Correlates of Unconscious Mental Processes." *Science,* 161 (1968), 295–98.

Sutich, A. J., O'Neill, H., Winthrop, H., *et al. Journal of Humanistic Psychology,* 1 (1961).

Ullman, M., Krippner, S., and Feldstein, S. "Experimentally Induced Telepathic Dreams: Two Studies Using EEG-REM Techniques." *International Journal of Neuropsychiatry,* 2 (1966), 420–37.

Warcollier, R. *La Télépathie. Recherches experimentales.* Paris: Alcan, 1921.

Weitzenhoffer, A. M. *General Techniques of Hypnotism.* New York: Grune and Stratton, 1957.

Wells, W. R. "Ability to Resist Artificially Induced Dissociation." *Journal of Abnormal and Social Psychology,* 35 (1940), 261–72.

———. "Experiments in the Hypnotic Production of Crime." *Journal of Psychology,* 11 (1941), 63–102.

Notes
on Further Reading

Chapter 1. The student who has time for parallel or independent reading in connection with the history of psychology will find it worthwhile to get his own (paperback if possible) copy of a general history of science (such as G. Sarton, *Introduction to the History of Science,* 1927) and a general history of philosophy (such as B. A. G. Fuller, 1945; W. Windelband, 1958; or B. Russell, 1945). A good encyclopedia like the *Encyclopaedia Britannica* will be helpful in looking up particular movements or life sketches of individual philosophers or scientists. One very valuable book is B. Russell's *Wisdom of the West* (1959). B. G. Rosenthal, *The Images of Man* (1971), shows the basic character of Greek, medieval, and Renaissance life as it influenced the structure of psychology. For a comparison of West and East, see L. Yutang, *The Wisdom of China and India* (1942). The student whose orientation is chiefly in terms of psychology as an experimental science will surely begin with E. G. Boring's *A History of Experimental Psychology* (1950).

If the student wishes to relate the history of psychology to the history of philosophy or the history of science, he can be helped by reading J. H. Robinson, *The Mind in the Making* (1921).

Chapter 2. For further work, the student will need at least one broad, sound, inspiring discussion of the Renaissance as it relates to the origins of modern science. Any of the recent paperback reprints of the seventeenth-century classics —Descartes, Hobbes, Locke, Spinoza—could be read side by side with some first-hand contact with the work of the intellectual giants of the physical sciences, especially Galileo and Newton. J. B. Conant, *On Understanding Science* (1950), and T. S. Kuhn, *The Structure of Scientific Revolutions* (1970), are especially useful representations of the scientific mood which took shape as the medieval period faded or passed into the Renaissance and modern era.

Chapter 3. Reading the great philosophers and scientists of the eighteenth century can well be accompanied by studies of the rise of the experimental method, for which G. S. Brett, *A History of Psychology* (1912–21; 1965), and E. G. Boring, *A History of Experimental Psychology* (1950), are especially valuable. The general literature of the eighteenth century, especially the writings of Pope, Swift, Voltaire, Franklin, Jefferson, help the student get some understanding of the Age of

Enlightenment. The Mentor paperbacks are useful here: *Age of Reason: The Seventeenth Century Philosophers* (S. Hampshire, ed., 1956), *Age of Enlightenment: The Eighteenth Century* (I. Berlin, ed., 1956). We are leaving behind the rationalists (Descartes, Leibnitz, and Spinoza) and moving toward philosophical romanticism. Dipping into the romantic movement, as represented by Rousseau, Wordsworth, and Goethe, should give a useful exposure to this trend. These giants of course are not to be understood by one evening's quick browsing; but the student is much better off with even a glimpse of a giant than he is with only a textbook-writer's second-hand evaluation. For a history of specific scientific contributions—who made them, when, why, and where—a general history of science will be valuable.

Chapter 4. The story of the struggle between classicism and romanticism is helpful for an understanding of the development of the life sciences, which were profoundly influenced by both. To go with one jump from the rationalists to the romanticists—as from Hume to Goethe—will help the student to understand both the romanticism of the "philosophy of nature" and the growth of a feeling of poetic intensity in figures like Goethe and Fechner. The student should by all means read what Boring has to say in *A History of Experimental Psychology* (1950). Then, for social context, he should take a look at the Industrial Revolution, as background for a more impersonal or even mechanical view of life. It is advisable to read both those authors who saw the new industrialism as benign and those who thought of it as a malignant force—to compare, for example, H. Spencer, *Evolution of Society* (1967), with T. Carlyle, *Carlyle Reader: Selections from the Writings of Thomas Carlyle* (1968). The "atomism" of the nineteenth-century psychology may fruitfully be compared with the atomism developing in the physical sciences. Again, a good look at a general history of science is useful. The student will probably get a great deal from J. T. Merz, *A History of European Thought in the Nineteenth Century* (1965).

Chapter 5. The student who has time for extra reading will use it well by getting both a broad picture of the history of science from the seventeenth to the nineteenth centuries, as suggested in the reference notes following each of the first four chapters, and some concrete images of specific individual psychologists who use the experimental approach. He will also gain some understanding of the increasing prestige of mathematics and the urge to translate all observations into quantitative form. The history of science and the history of medicine are useful, and encyclopedia references for the work of men like Lavoisier (the chemist who discovered respiration) and Helmholtz (a physicist as well as a physiologist) will be useful especially as background for Herbart, Weber, and Fechner. The books by J. T. Merz, *A History of European Thought in the Nineteenth Century* (1965), and T. S. Kuhn, *The Structure of Scientific Revolutions* (1970), will again be useful. The student should note the successes of atomism in chemistry and physics and of quantitative science (conservation of energy and so on) and its applications in physiology and psychology. Any one of these paths will suggest something about the unity of the scientific endeavor.

Chapter 6. A distinction between natural sciences and cultural sciences briefly noted above can be of very great value and offer much insight to the student who has time to pursue such lines of thought, especially as they relate to the world of the German universities in the nineteenth century. W. Dampier, *A History of Science* (1966), and H. W. Tyler, *A Short History of Science* (1939), may be useful here, and the two great volumes by Helmholtz, *Treatise on Physiological Optics* (1963) and *On the Sensations of Tone* (1954), will make their impact in personal terms. Again, we have found very useful J. T. Merz's *A History of European Thought in the Nineteenth Century* (1965).

Chapter 7. The student interested in the flavor of nineteenth-century

British thought will get a great deal out of the study of the impressions which British thought made upon such Americans as Henry Adams, Henry James, William James, and Ralph Waldo Emerson. Mill was well known among American intellectuals. Spencer (*Principles of Psychology,* 1969) and Bain (*Mind and Body: The Theories of Their Relation,* 1971) were not only culminations of British systematic associationist psychology with a mixture of the Scottish school, but also a pioneering influence on American thought as far as it dealt in a formal way with psychology as such. A primary reason, however, for reading British psychology of the mid-nineteenth century is to get ready to understand our own William James, who was deeply steeped in the British tradition and yet personally needed to rebel against it. It is, for example, a useful exercise to compare Bain's treatment of habit formation with James's chapter on habit.

Chapter 8. As noted already, there is no substitute for first-hand contact with the experimental genius of Helmholtz, as shown in his *Treatise on Physiological Optics* (1963) and *On the Sensations of Tone* (1954). Use must be made here of E. G. Boring's *A History of Experimental Psychology* (1950) and *Sensation and Perception in the History of Experimental Psychology* (1942). The story of the founding of the first psychological laboratory can best be understood by looking first at W. Wundt's *Principles of Physiological Psychology* (1904) and then at the life and work of any of his outstanding pupils, such as E. B. Titchener (*Experimental Psychology,* 1901–05). W. Dennis, ed., *Readings in the History of Psychology* (1948), highlights excerpts from the writings of a great many giants of early psychology. The student will find material in this book from Weber, Müller, Helmholtz, Fechner, Pavlov, and others dealt with in this chapter. He may want to supplement these with reading parts of J. C. Eccles, *The Physiology of Nerve Cells* (1957), G. T. Ladd and R. S. Woodworth, *Elements of Physiological Psychology* (1911), and G. S. Holt, *Founders of Modern Psychology* (1912).

Chapter 9. The student eager to understand the full impact of evolutionary thinking can start by comparing old-time standard preevolutionary treatises — such as the medical textbooks of 1850 — with the intellectual ferment and systematic reorientation which followed the work of Darwin. Marvelously personal are Darwin's own accounts of his work in *The Autobiography of Charles Darwin and Selected Letters* (1958), and several new studies are available of Darwin's journey on the *Beagle* (*Voyage of the Beagle,* 1962). The student must read for himself some chapters from *The Origin of Species* (1962), *The Descent of Man* (1965), and *The Expression of Emotions in Man and Animals* (1965). Some of the early experimental psychologists caught fire from Darwin. First of course is Galton, whose *Inquiries into Human Faculty and Its Development* (1883) is fascinating reading. The student should look forward also to the chapter on William James and be prepared to see in what way evolutionary theory formed the foundation of William James's psychology. For a broader view of modern evolutionary thinking, J. C. Greene's *The Death of Adam: Evolution and Its Impact on Western Thought* (1961) is a must. The works of T. Dobzhansky (such as *Mankind Evolving,* 1970) are also valuable.

Chapter 10. Encyclopedia references to celebrated names, such as Burton, Sydenham, Mesmer, Seguin, and Kraepelin, are worth the time. The appealing history of the unconscious by L. L. Whyte, *Unconscious Before Freud* (1960), and H. Ellenberger's *A History of Dynamic Psychiatry* (1970) will help to prepare for the later study of Freud and his contemporaries. G. Zilboorg and G. W. Henry, *A History of Medical Psychology* (1941), should also be helpful.

Chapter 11. To grasp the conception of an experimental psychology and the reasons why it led to the founding of Wundt's laboratory, read E. G. Boring, *A History of Experimental Psychology* (1950), especially what he says about Weber,

Fechner, Helmholtz, and Wundt, and R. J. Herrnstein and E. G. Boring, *A Sourcebook in the History of Psychology* (1965), especially Chapters 5-6. H. E. Barnes, *An Intellectual and Cultural History of the Western World* (1965), provides a skeleton of the history of modern experimental psychology.

Chapter 12. A good picture of the early development of laboratory work on learning and memory is obtainable by looking at Ladd and Woodworth's *Elements of Physiological Psychology* (1911) and E. L. Thorndike's *Psychology of Learning* (1913). A wide range of dogmatic positions were entertained from the mechanistic view of the learning process represented by J. Loeb to the mind-body dualism of H. Bergson. Bergson's *Matter and Memory* (1959) should not be overlooked. The student should also look in Chapter 22 for the physiological and biochemical approaches to memory, so characteristic of the present era.

Chapter 13. There is no substitute for extensive reading in William James. The student with any time at all for the sheer luxury of enjoying psychological reading must at least read the following chapters from James's *Principles of Psychology* (1950): "Habit," "The Stream of Thought," "Consciousness of Self," "Emotion," "Will." (It is not necessary to read the very extensive quoting by James of other authors.) The student should also read at least the first half-dozen chapters of *The Varieties of Religious Experience* (1958) and at least one of the collections of essays of a philosophical cast, such as *The Will to Believe*, and other essays cited at the end of this chapter. There is a very useful biography of James by G. W. Allen (*William James: A Biography*, 1967). The monumental picture of James as a very broad and great man appears in R. B. Perry, *The Thought and Character of William James* (1935), now available in paperback. There are many collections and evaluations of James's work by his many pupils and admirers.

Chapter 14. One can judge a main trend or thrust in psychology by choosing its most creative figure, and for this reason it is fair to emphasize here the charm, appeal, and masterful position of E. B. Titchener. One could begin by looking at his *Textbook of Psychology* (1909-10) or *A Beginner's Psychology* (1923). Any sample will serve to show Titchener's attempt to break up the mind into introspectively observed experiences, organized in various ways and following various sequences —an approach that had great prestige for twenty or thirty years. It faded slowly, being replaced by Gestalt emphasis, by psychodynamics, by psychiatry, by behaviorism, and by objective methods generally. It is nevertheless worthwhile to look at these works by Titchener and to ask oneself very general questions, such as those raised by T. S. Kuhn, *The Structure of Scientific Revolutions* (1970). How was Titchener out of line with the *Zeitgeist?* What is permanent in the specific content of his work? And most important, what is permanently left by way of *method?* Is psychology today beginning to study again the "immediate consciousness," to which Titchener dedicated his prolonged and brilliant labors? One can get most of the meaning of American functionalism by reading the quoted article by John Dewey or by noting what E. Heidbreder has to say in *Seven Psychologies* (1961) or R. S. Woodworth and M. R. Sheehan in *Contemporary Schools of Psychology* (1964). These schools have become in a way whipping boys for more "modern" psychology. But they were led by intelligent men, and the great deal they had to offer can be made real to the student if he reads at least a little of Titchener and Dewey.

Chapter 15. One of the great issues that comes into focus around the beginning of the twentieth century is the question of whether the new experimental psychology should stick to its elementary task of examining the simplest or most rudimentary processes, or whether it should also encompass the complexities of thought, value, intuition, creativity. Controversies that we think of today in terms of "reductionism" appear in connection with all our present sequences of chapters

(Chapters 12–16); consequently, we would urge the thoughtful student to look at the history of mechanism from the time of La Mettrie and from the time of Kant and see how this ancient battle was transformed through new evolutionary theory and new experimental method. We would also suggest reading as much history of modern philosophy as possible, especially the works of philosophers like William James, A. N. Whitehead, Bertrand Russell. The student should read the simpler studies of thought processes, such as those by F. C. Bartlett (*Remembering: A Study in Experimental and Social Psychology*, 1932) and by J. S. Bruner, J. J. Goodnow, and G. A. Austin (*A Study of Thinking*, 1956); but he should also look at the complexities revealed, for example, in D. Rapaport, *The Organization and Pathology of Thought* (1959), and look at the newer attempts to get at the nature of thought through studies of language (see C. E. Osgood, G. J. Suci, and P. H. Tannenbaum, *The Measurement of Meaning*, 1959). This may not explain the technical problems of the Würzburg school, but it will aid understanding of the modern controversies about these great issues: Does psychology start with the simple build *up*, watching for the simple even at the highest level? Or does it first face complexities and try to view the details by going *down* with structure as a whole?

    Chapter 16. Anyone who wants to understand the complexities of the behaviorist movement will do well to look at the controversial literature mentioned at the end of the preceding chapter and then plunge into the studies by three great personalities: Sechenov (*Selected Works*, 1935), Pavlov (*Lectures on Conditioned Reflexes*, 1928, 1941), and J. B. Watson (*Behavior: An Introduction to Comparative Psychology*, 1914). He might include V. M. Bekhterev, *General Principles of Human Reflexology* (1933), and if he is charmed by the philosophical issues, he should read E. B. Holt (*The Freudian Wish and Its Place in Ethics*, 1915). The student who wishes to grasp the struggle of an expanding science of biology to comprise all of psychology within its domain should first read Sechenov and his great pupil, Pavlov, and should then understand the somewhat parallel movement by which the comparative psychologist J. B. Watson (*Psychological Review*, 20, 1913, 158–77) at the University of Chicago decided to blow up the "introspective psychology" of this era and succeeded. K. S. Lashley (*Psychological Review*, 30, 1923, 237–72) regards behaviorism in various other senses of the term, as, for example, simply behavior analysis (as an emphasis upon behavior study). For modern behaviorism read B. F. Skinner, *The Behavior of Organisms: An Experimental Analysis* (1938).

    Chapter 17. Assuming a good background in William James and a familiarity with the controversy (in Germany) between atomistic and more holistic ways of thinking, it will be well worthwhile for the student to sample the scattered works of Max Wertheimer, including those brought together in the volume edited by D. C. Beardslee and Michael Wertheimer, *Readings in Perception* (1958). The student should also read Max Wertheimer, *Productive Thinking* (1959), K. Koffka, *The Principles of Gestalt Psychology* (1935), any of W. Köhler, from the charming *Mentality of Apes* (1924) to the abstruse studies dealing with cortical physiology, *Dynamics in Psychology* (1940). Very refreshing is R. Arnheim, *Art and Visual Perception* (1954). An introduction to Gestalt ways of thinking in general appears in W. D. Ellis, *Source Book of Gestalt Psychology* (1959). For the influence of Gestalt psychology upon the study of personality the student should read G. W. Allport and P. E. Vernon, *Studies in Expressive Movement* (1937).

    Chapter 18. There is unlimited literature on Freud; books, articles, monographs, evaluations, and critiques come out faster than they can be read. The student should by all means read a few basic works by Freud himself, such as *The Origin and Development of Psychoanalysis* (Vol. 11 in *The Standard Edition of the Complete Works of Sigmund Freud*, 1953), "The Clark University Lectures," or any equivalent paperback edition. For a systematic presentation of the early psychoanalytic ideas, the student may read *The Interpretation of Dreams* (Vol. 4, *Standard Edition*). For developmental theory related to the libido, he may read especially *Three Contributions to the Theory of Sex* (Vol. 7, *Standard Edition*), and for the later construction of relations of id, ego, and superego, he may read *The Ego and the Id* (Vol. 14, *Standard Edition*), and *Inhibitions, Symptoms, and Anxiety* (Vol. 20, *Standard Edition*). The Hartmann and Erikson volumes cited at the end of this chapter present contemporary psychoanalytic thinking that remains essentially within the Freudian fold. E. Jones's biography gives a fine background (*The Life and Work of Sigmund Freud*, 1953).

 Chapter 19. To get the general spirit of Jung's early work, *The Psychology of the Unconscious* (1912) is a good starting point. And to get his extroversion-introversion theory, it is worthwhile to dip into his *Psychological Types* (1923). For the middle period, in which he is beginning to show more and more his "prophetic" leanings, the student may read *Modern Man in Search of a Soul* (1932). *Memories, Dreams, Reflections* (1961) covers Jung's whole life span and shows how very far he is from Freudian psychoanalysis and how rich he is in reflecting upon and expressing a tremendous range of human cultural achievements and aspirations. This will also provide a background for the better understanding of the humanistic psychology of today. For the earlier contributions of Adler, *The Practice and Theory in Individual Psychology* (1924) will serve, and for Adlerian thinking in recent years, the *Journal of Individual Psychology* should be consulted. To get the feeling of Fromm, the student should read *Escape from Freedom* (1965) or any of the many recent semipopular books. Horney's *The Neurotic Personality of Our Time* (1937) or Sullivan's "Conceptions of Modern Psychiatry" (*Psychiatry,* 1940) should be helpful. R. Munroe, *Schools of Psychoanalytic Thought* (1955), gives a good panoramic view of post-Freudian psychoanalysis. After reading E. Erikson, *Childhood and Society* (1963), the student may want to go on to the other studies mentioned in this text. He should include if possible Erikson's *Gandhi's Truth* (1970).

 Chapter 20. To get a view of the general direction being taken in recent years in the psychology of learning, the first edition of E. R. Hilgard, *The Psychology of Learning* (1948), with the latest edition of this book by Hilgard and Bower (1966) should be helpful. To cover the work of all the major theorists is hardly possible for anyone but the very mature specialist; but the student must read something substantial by Hull, by Pavlov, and by Skinner and then go back and compare this reading with the material offered by Hilgard and Bower. For the student wishing to round out the discussions of this chapter, Volume 2 of *Psychology: A Study of a Science* (S. Koch, ed., 1959) offers chapters by W. K. Estes ("The Statistical Approach to Learning Theory"), F. C. Frick ("Information Theory"), E. R. Guthrie ("Association by Contiguity"), H. F. Harlow ("Learning Set and Error Factor Theory"), F. A. Logan ("The Hull-Spence Approach"), N. E. Miller ("Liberalization of Basic S-R Concepts: Extensions of Conflict Behavior, Motivation and Social Learning"), B. F. Skinner ("A Case History in Scientific Method"), and E. C. Tolman ("Principles of Purposive Behavior"). The physiological aspects of learning theory are discussed later in the present book.

 Chapter 21. For basic material in this area, the student should consult S. S. Stevens, ed., *Handbook of Experimental Psychology* (1951), and R. S. Woodworth and H. Schlosberg, *Experimental Psychology* (1954). For a workout in perception theory, he may compare F. H. Allport, *Theories of Perception and the Concept of Structure* (1955), with J. J. Gibson, *The Senses Considered as Perceptual Systems* (1966). And for the thought processes, he may compare D. Rapaport, *The Organization and Pathology of Thought* (1959), with Max Wertheimer, *Produc-*

tive Thinking (1959), and D. Berlyne, *Structure and Direction in Thinking* (1965). The philosophically minded student will be interested in A. N. Whitehead's *Science and the Modern World* (1967) and S. Langer's *Philosophy in a New Key: A Study in the Symbolism of Reason, Rite and Art* (1957). For cognitive style, the student should see the work of R. W. Gardner and A. E. Moriarty, *Personality Development at Preadolescence: Exploration of Structure Formation* (1968), and the recent volumes of the *Journal of Cognitive Psychology*.

Chapter 22. The thoughtful student might begin with a physiologist's philosophy, such as C. Sherrington's *Man on His Nature* (1941), and then dip into a standard text in physiological psychology (S. P. Grossman, *A Textbook of Physiological Psychology,* 1967, is particularly recommended) and look through a few current issues of the *Journal of Comparative and Physiological Psychology*. He must include some of the work of K. S. Lashley and must deal attentively with the problem of localization as seen in the work of Olds and Delgado mentioned in this chapter; he must also review Hilgard and Bower, *The Psychology of Learning* (1966), once again to see how far he can go on a tentative integration of physiological theory and learning theory. P. H Klopfer and J. P. Hailman, *An Introduction to Animal Behavior: Ethology's First Century* (1967) will be helpful for understanding ethology. It may be followed by reading on the current state of specific topics that have captured the student's interest. For this the books of R. A. Hinde, *Animal Behaviour: A Synthesis of Ethology and Comparative Psychology* (1970), J. L. Fuller and W. R. Thompson, *Behavior Genetics* (1960), or J. Hirsch, ed., *Behavior-Genetic Analysis* (1967) should be helpful. The student may want to round out his inquiry by reading K. H. Pribram's chapter ("Interrelations of Psychology and the Neurological Disciplines") in S. Koch, ed., *Psychology: A Study of a Science* (1962).

Chapter 23. The writings of G. Razran and J. Brozek should be helpful to the student needing orientation beyond the material presented in this chapter: for example, G. Razran, "Russian Physiologist's Psychology and American Experimental Psychology: A Historical and Systematic Collation and Look into the Future" (*Psychological Bulletin,* 1963), or J. Brozek, "Fifty Years of Soviet Psychology: An Historical Perspective" (*Soviet Psychology,* 1968). Access to current issues in Soviet psychology is to be found in M. Cole and I. Maltzman, eds., *A Handbook of Contemporary Soviet Psychology* (1969), which includes an excellent historical sketch (by the editors) and a great number of specific chapters dealing with the various areas and topics of Soviet psychology (written by Soviet specialists). The Russian-speaking student may want to compare this English-language handbook with the earlier Russian-language handbook (*Psikhologicheskaia Nauka v SSSR,* 1959–60). Major Soviet psychological journals are now available in the English language, and translations of influential works continue to appear. For the latter, the student should examine publications of Akademiia Nauk and of the Soviet Foreign Language Publishing House.

Chapter 24. A good way to evaluate the changing content of a field is to compare subsequent revised editions of a single book dealing with its particular topics. The student of developmental psychology is fortunate in having this method available to him in the 1946, 1954, and 1970 editions of *The Manual of Child Psychology* (L. Carmichael, ed., for the 1946 and 1954 editions and P. Mussen, ed., for the 1970 edition). Issues of development, perhaps more than anything else, cut across boundaries of different fields and disciplines in psychology. This makes it rather difficult to pinpoint those publications that may fit the student's interest. Two books that should orient him to particular problems and research approaches within developmental psychology are L. K. Frank, *The Importance of Infancy* (1966), and L. W. Hoffman and M. Hoffman, eds., *Child Development Research* (1966). For the breadth and variety of research issues, the new journals *Developmental Psychology* (American Psychological Association) and *Developmental Psychobiology* (Interscience Publishers) should be helpful. For the increasing influence of the concept of development upon the theory of knowledge, and philosophy in general, the student should read Piaget's latest book, *Psychology and Epistemology* (1971).

Chapter 25. It is not easy to get a broad view of modern approaches to personality at this time, but it will be helpful to read some of the volumes that compare different personality theories with one another, for example, C. S. Hall and G. Lindzey, *Theories of Personality* (1970), or L. Bischof, *Interpreting Personality Theories* (1970). Then the student should pick out one or two major conceptions, perhaps those of C. Rogers or G. W. Allport, pursue them through the various writings of each man, and then come back and compare the notes on these authors with what is offered above, in Chapters 18 and 19, regarding the Freudian and other early dynamic theories. It will no doubt be difficult to integrate the results of this comparison, for the problem is an extremely intricate one, and the wealth of material is likely to overwhelm the student. The student who looks forward to work in clinical psychology may do very well at this point to make himself familiar with the brilliantly original work of Rorschach, *Psychodiagnostics* (1942), to compare it with the views of Freud, Jung, and the Gestalt thinkers, and try to incorporate it in this preliminary conception of what the term *personality* might mean.

Chapter 26. A perspective on the social sciences after World War I is obtainable in R. S. Lynd and H. M. Lynd, *Middletown* (1929). This work may be compared with the then new *Social Psychology* (1924) of F. H. Allport. G. Murphy and L. B. Murphy, *Experimental Social Psychology* (1931), and the revision by Murphy, Murphy, and T. M. Newcomb (1937) will show the development of research method and of the new enthusiasm and achievement. The systematic social psychologies developed by M. Sherif and C. W. Sherif, *Outlines of Social Psychology* (1956), and by D. Krech and R. S. Crutchfield, *Theories and Problems in Social Psychology* (1948), will show the rapid modernization and systematization of the field. A good integration of social psychology and sociology with a conception of education and the learning process is available in T. M. Newcomb, R. H. Turner, and P. E. Converse, *Social Psychology* (1965); and the Bennington Studies mentioned in the reference notes at the end of Chapter 26 will give a rich introduction to stability in social attitudes over the years. A good example of a naturalistic experimental study of life situations is presented by Sherif *et al., Intergroup Conflict and Cooperation: The Robers Cave Experiment* (1961). The student of social psychology will do well to get a broad social-science perspective, and he should make himself familiar with the resources of modern research in psycholinguistics (for example, C. E. Osgood, *Psycholinguistics,* 1965). G. Lindzey and E. Aronson, *Handbook of Social Psychology* (1968), bring the history more nearly up to the present.

Chapter 27. There are many attempts to define the direction in which psychology is now moving. There is probably no better course than to visit the psychology reading room for a few days and notice what is happening in the psychological journals (say from World War II to the present time). Hot points of controversy regarding learning theory and personality structure are worth reviewing at this time. A few very important figures may be evaluated from time to time in the literature. Consider, for example, the evaluations of the work of Clark Hull, Edward Tolman, Kurt Lewin. Books and journals can give a refreshing and integrative picture of what it takes to make a *lasting* impression in psychology. This, however, is also a good time to reread T. S. Kuhn, *The Structure of Scientific Revolutions* (1970), and to compare one's picture of the history of psychology with what one gets regarding the history of medicine and the history of philosophy. The *Annual Review of Psychology* (Stanford University Press) should help with the contemporary picture and the look ahead.

In reviewing this book as a whole, the student might indicate trends beginning and ending at various points and then pull everything together as of the present moment and try to predict *what* will happen *and why*. How far will world events and general scientific progress influence his extrapolations? What are the essential, realistic possibilities, and what are the great roadblocks and booby traps the student must get around when making his predictions? What does he hope will happen? How well are his sober judgments able to restrain his hopes, wishes, or fears? Can psychology actually influence history? Why or why not?

Adler, A. *The Practice and Theory in Individual Psychology.** Translated by P. Radin. New York: Harcourt Brace Jovanovich, 1924.

Allen, G. W. *William James: A Biography.* New York: Viking, 1967.

Allport, F. H. *Social Psychology.* Boston: Houghton Mifflin, 1924.

————. *Theories of Perception and the Concept of Structure.* New York: Wiley, 1955.

Allport, G. W., and Vernon, P. E. *Studies in Expressive Movement.* New York: Macmillan, 1937.

Arnheim, R. *Art and Visual Perception.** Berkeley: University of California Press, 1954.

Bain, A. *Mind and Body: The Theories of Their Relation.* Lexington, Mass.: Gregg International, 1971.

Barnes, H. E. *An Intellectual and Cultural History of the Western World.** 3 vols. New York: Dover, 1965.

Bartlett, F. C. *Remembering: A Study in Experimental and Social Psychology.** Cambridge: Cambridge University Press, 1932.

Beardslee, D. C., and Wertheimer, Michael, eds. *Readings in Perception.* Princeton: Van Nostrand, 1958.

Bekhterev, V. M. *General Principles of Human Reflexology.* Translated by E. Murphy and W. Murphy. New York: International Publishing, 1933.

Bergson, H. *Matter and Memory.** Translated by N. M. Paul and W. S. Palmer. New York: Doubleday Anchor, 1959.

Berlin, I., ed. *Age of Enlightenment: The Eighteenth Century.** New York: Mentor, 1956.

Berlyne, D. *Structure and Direction in Thinking.* New York: Wiley, 1965.

Bischof, L. *Interpreting Personality Theories.* 2nd ed. New York: Harper & Row, 1970.

Boring, E. G. *Sensation and Perception in the History of Experimental Psychology.* New York: Appleton-Century, 1942.

————. *A History of Experimental Psychology.* 2nd ed. New York: Appleton-Century-Crofts, 1950.

Brett, G. S. *A History of Psychology.** 3 vols. London: Allen & Unwin, 1912–21. Rev. ed., R. S. Peters, ed. Cambridge, Mass.: M.I.T. Press, 1965.

Brozek, J., ed. "Fifty Years of Soviet Psychology: An Historical Perspective." *Soviet Psychology,* special issue, 6, No. 3–4, (1968), 1–127.

Bruner, J. S., Goodnow, J. J., and Austin, G. A. *A Study of Thinking.** New York: Wiley, 1956.

* Available in paperback.

Carlyle, T. *Carlyle Reader: Selections from the Writings of Thomas Carlyle.**
G. B. Tennyson, ed. New York: Modern Library, 1968.

Carmichael, L., ed. *The Manual of Child Psychology.* New York: Wiley, 1946, 1954.

Cole, M., and Maltzman, I., eds. *A Handbook of Contemporary Soviet Psychology.* New York: Basic Books, 1969.

Conant, J. B. *On Understanding Science.* New Haven: Yale University Press, 1950.

Dampier, W. *A History of Science.** 4th ed. Cambridge: Cambridge University Press, 1966.

Darwin, C. *The Autobiography of Charles Darwin and Selected Letters.** F. Darwin, ed. New York: Dover, 1958.

———. *Voyage of the Beagle.** Garden City, N.Y.: Doubleday Natural History, 1962.

———. *The Origin of Species.** New York: Collier, 1962.

———. *The Descent of Man.** Chicago: University of Chicago Press, 1965.

———. *The Expression of Emotions in Man and Animals.** Chicago: University of Chicago Press, 1965.

Dennis, W., ed. *Readings in the History of Psychology.* New York: Appleton-Century, 1948.

Dobzhansky, T. *Mankind Evolving.** New York: Bantam, 1970.

Eccles, J. C. *The Physiology of Nerve Cells.** Baltimore: Johns Hopkins Press, 1957.

Ellenberger, H. *A History of Dynamic Psychiatry.* New York: Basic Books, 1970.

Ellis, W. D. *Source Book of Gestalt Psychology.* New York: Harcourt Brace Jovanovich, 1959.

Erikson, E. H. *Childhood and Society.** Rev. ed. New York: Norton, 1963.

———. *Gandhi's Truth.** New York: Norton, 1970.

Estes, W. K. "The Statistical Approach to Learning Theory." In S. Koch, ed. *Psychology: A Study of a Science.* Vol. 2. New York: McGraw-Hill, 1959.

Frank, L. K. *On the Importance of Infancy.** New York: Random House, 1966.

Freud, S. "The Clark University Lectures." *American Journal of Psychology,* 21, No. 2. (1910), 181–218.

———. *The Standard Edition of the Complete Works of Sigmund Freud.* J. Strachey, ed. London: Hogarth Press & The Institute of Psychoanalysis, 1953.

Frick, F. C. "Information Theory." In S. Koch, ed. *Psychology: A Study of a Science.* Vol. 2. New York: McGraw-Hill, 1959.

Fromm, E. *Escape from Freedom.** New York: Avon, 1965.

Fuller, B. A. G. *A History of Philosophy.* 2 vols. in 1. Rev. ed. New York: Holt, 1945.

Fuller, J. L., and Thompson, W. R. *Behavior Genetics.* New York: Wiley, 1960.

Galton, F. *Inquiries into Human Faculty and Its Development.* London: Macmillan, 1883.

Gardner, R. W., and Moriarty, A. E. *Personality Development at Preadolescence: Exploration of Structure Formation.* Seattle: University of Washington Press, 1968.

Gibson, J. J. *The Senses Considered as Perceptual Systems.* Boston: Houghton Mifflin, 1966.

Greene, J. C. *The Death of Adam: Evolution and Its Impact on Western Thought.** Ames: Iowa State University Press, 1959. New York: Mentor, 1961.

Grossman, S. P. *A Textbook of Physiological Psychology.* New York: Wiley, 1967.

Guthrie, E. R. "Association by Contiguity." In S. Koch, ed. *Psychology: A Study of a Science.* Vol. 2. New York: McGraw-Hill, 1959.

Hall, C. S., and Lindzey, G. *Theories of Personality.* 2nd ed. New York: Wiley, 1970.

Hampshire, S., ed. *Age of Reason: The Seventeenth Century Philosophers.** New York: Mentor, 1956.

Harlow, H. F. "Learning Set and Error Factor Theory." In S. Koch, ed. *Psychology: A Study of a Science.* Vol. 2. New York: McGraw-Hill, 1959.

Heidbreder, E. *Seven Psychologies.** New York: Century, 1933; New York: Appleton-Century-Crofts, 1961.

Helmholtz, H. L. *Treatise on Physiological Optics.** 3 vols. in 2. Translated by J. P. Southall. New York: Dover, 1963.

――――. *On the Sensation of Tone.** Translated by A. F. Ellis. New York: Dover, 1954.

Herrnstein, R. J., and Boring, E. G., eds. *A Sourcebook in the History of Psychology.* Cambridge, Mass.: Harvard University Press, 1965.

Hilgard, E. R. *The Psychology of Learning.* New York: Appleton-Century, 1948.

Hilgard, E. R., and Bower, G. H., eds. *The Psychology of Learning.* 3rd ed. New York: Appleton-Century-Crofts, 1966.

Hinde, R. A. *Animal Behaviour: A Synthesis of Ethology and Comparative Psychology.* 2nd ed. New York: McGraw-Hill, 1970.

Hirsch, J., ed. *Behavior-Genetic Analysis.* New York: McGraw-Hill, 1967.

Hoffman, L. W., and Hoffman, M., eds. *Child Development Research.* 2 vols. New York: Russell Sage Foundation, 1966.

Holt, E. B. *The Freudian Wish and Its Place in Ethics.* New York: Holt, 1915.

Holt, G. S. *Founders of Modern Psychology.* New York: Appleton, 1912.

Horney, K. *The Neurotic Personality of Our Time.** New York: Norton, 1937.

James, W. *Principles of Psychology.** New York: Dover, 1950.

――――. *Varieties of Religious Experience.** New York: Mentor, 1958.

Jones, E. *The Life and Work of Sigmund Freud.** 3 vols. New York: Basic Books, 1953.

Jung, C. *The Psychology of the Unconscious.** Translated by B. M. Kinkle. New York: Moffat, Yard, 1912.

――――. *Psychological Types.** Translated by H. G. Baynes. New York: Harcourt Brace Jovanovich, 1923.

――――. *Modern Man in Search of a Soul.** Translated by D. Baynes and C. Baynes. London: Routledge, 1932.

――――. *Memories, Dreams, Reflections.** Translated by R. Winston and C. Winston. New York: Pantheon Books, 1961.

Klopfer, P. H., and Hailman, J. P. *An Introduction to Animal Behavior: Ethology's First Century.* Englewood Cliffs, N.J.: Prentice Hall, 1967.

Koch, S., ed. *Psychology: A Study of a Science.* 6 vols. New York: McGraw-Hill, 1959–62.

Koffka, K. *The Principles of Gestalt Psychology.** New York: Harcourt Brace Jovanovich, 1935.

Köhler, W. *Mentality of Apes.* London: Kegan, 1924.

――――. *Dynamics in Psychology.** New York: Liveright, 1940.

Krech, D., and Crutchfield, R. S. *Theories and Problems in Social Psychology.* New York: McGraw-Hill, 1948.

Kuhn, T. S. *The Structure of Scientific Revolutions.** 2nd ed. Chicago: University of Chicago Press, 1970.

Ladd, G. T., and Woodworth, R. S. *Elements of Physiological Psychology.* New York: Scribner, 1911.

Langer, S. *Philosophy in a New Key: A Study in the Symbolism of Reason, Rite and Art.** 3rd ed. Cambridge, Mass.: Harvard University Press, 1957.

Lashley, K. S. "The Behavioristic Interpretation of Consciousness I." *Psychological Review,* 30 (1923), 237–72.

Lindzey, G., and Aronson, E., eds. *Handbook of Social Psychology.* 6 vols. 2nd ed. Reading, Mass.: Addison-Wesley, 1968.

Logan, F. A. "The Hull-Spence Approach." In S. Koch, ed. *Psychology: A Study of a Science.* Vol. 2. New York: McGraw-Hill, 1959.

Lynd, R. S., and Lynd, H. M. *Middletown.** New York: Harcourt Brace Jovanovich, 1929.

Merz, J. T. *A History of European Thought in the Nineteenth Century.** 4 vols. Edinburgh: Blackwood, 1896–1914. New York: Dover, 1965.

Miller, N. E. "Liberalization of Basic S-R Concepts: Extensions to Conflict Behavior, Motivation and Social Learning." In S. Koch, ed. *Psychology: A Study of a Science.* Vol. 2. New York: McGraw-Hill, 1959.

Munroe, R. *Schools of Psychoanalytic Thought.* Boston: Dryden Press, 1955.

Murphy, G., and Murphy, L. B. *Experimental Social Psychology.* New York: Harper, 1931. Rev. ed. by Murphy, Murphy, and T. M. Newcomb. New York: Harper, 1937.

Mussen, P., ed. *The Manual of Child Psychology.* New York: Wiley, 1970.

Newcomb, T. M., Turner, R. H., and Converse, P. E. *Social Psychology.* New York: Holt, Rinehart & Winston, 1965.

Osgood, C. E. *Psycholinguistics.* Bloomington: Indiana University Press, 1965.

Osgood, C. E., Suci, G. J., and Tannenbaum, P. H. *The Measurement of Meaning.** Urbana: University of Illinois Press, 1959.

Pavlov, I. P. *Lectures on Conditioned Reflexes.** Vol. 1. Translated by W. H. Gantt. New York: International Publishers, 1928.

———. *Lectures on Conditioned Reflexes.** Vol. 2. Translated by W. H. Gantt. New York: International Publishers, 1941.

Perry, R. B. *The Thought and Character of William James.** 2 vols. New York: Little, Brown, 1935.

Piaget, J. *Psychology and Epistemology.* Translated by A. Rosin. New York: Grossman, 1971.

Pribram, K. H. "Interrelations of Psychology and the Neurological Disciplines." In S. Koch, ed. *Psychology: A Study of a Science.* Vol. 4. New York: McGraw-Hill, 1962.

Psikhologischeskaia Nauka v SSSR. 2 vols. Moscow: APN-RSFSR, 1959–60.

Rapaport, D. *The Organization and Pathology of Thought.* New York: Columbia University Press, 1959.

Razran, G. "Russian Physiologist's Psychology and American Experimental Psychology: A Historical and Systematic Collation and Look into the Future." *Psychological Bulletin,* 63 (1965), 42–64.

Robinson, J. H. *The Mind in the Making.* New York: Harper, 1921.

Rorschach, H. *Psychodiagnostics.* Translated by P. Lemkau and B. Kronenberg. W. Margenthaler, ed. New York: Grune & Stratton, 1942.

Rosenthal, B. G. *The Images of Man.* New York: Basic Books, 1971.

Russell, B. *History of Western Philosophy.** New York: Simon & Schuster, 1945.

———. *Wisdom of the West.** New York: Doubleday, 1959.

Sarton, G. *Introduction to the History of Science.* Baltimore: Wilkins & Wilkins, 1927.

Sechenov, I. M. *Selected Works.* Moscow and Leningrad: Gozmedizdat, 1935.

Sherif, M., Harvey, O. J., White, B. J., Hood, W. R., and Sherif, C. W. *Intergroup Conflict and Cooperation: The Robers Cave Experiment*. Norman: University of Oklahoma Book Exchange, 1961.

Sherif, M., and Sherif, C. W. *Outlines of Social Psychology*. Rev. ed. New York: Harper, 1956.

Sherrington, C. *Man on His Nature*.* New York: Macmillan, 1941.

Skinner, B. F. *The Behavior of Organisms: An Experimental Analysis*.* New York: Appleton-Century, 1938.

———. "A Case History in Scientific Method." In S. Koch, ed. *Psychology: A Study of a Science*. Vol. 2. New York: McGraw-Hill, 1959.

Spencer, H. *Evolution of Society*. R. Carneiro, ed. Chicago: University of Chicago Press, 1967.

———. *Principles of Psychology*. London: Longman, Green, 1885. Reprinted by Gregg International, 1969.

Stevens, S. S., ed. *Handbook of Experimental Psychology*. New York: Wiley, 1951.

Sullivan, H. S. "Conceptions of Modern Psychiatry." *Psychiatry*, 3 (1940), 1–117.

Thorndike, E. L. *Psychology of Learning*. New York: Teachers College Press, 1913.

Titchener, E. B. *Experimental Psychology*. 4 vols. New York: Macmillan, 1901–05.

———. *Textbook of Psychology*. New York: Macmillan, 1909–10.

———. *A Beginner's Psychology*. New York: Macmillan, 1923.

Tolman, E. C. "Principles of Purposive Behavior." In S. Koch, ed. *Psychology: A Study of a Science*. Vol. 2. New York: McGraw-Hill, 1959.

Tyler, H. W. *A Short History of Science*. Rev. ed. New York: Macmillan, 1939.

Watson, J. B. "Psychology as the Behaviorist Views It." *Psychological Review*, 20 (1913), 158–77.

———. *Behavior: An Introduction to Comparative Psychology*. New York: Holt, 1914.

Wertheimer, Max. *Productive Thinking*. New York: Harper, 1959.

Whitehead, A. N. *Science and the Modern World*.* (Lowell Lectures, 1925). New York: Free Press, 1967.

Whyte, L. L. *Unconscious Before Freud*. New York: Basic Books, 1960.

Windelband, W. *History of Philosophy*.* 2 vols. New York: Torch, 1958.

Woodworth, R. S., and Schlosberg, H. *Experimental Psychology*. Rev. ed. New York: Holt, Rinehart and Winston, 1954.

Woodworth, R. S., and Sheehan, M. R. *Contemporary Schools of Psychology*. 3rd ed. New York: Ronald Press, 1964.

Wundt, W. *Principles of Physiological Psychology,* Vol. 1. Translated by E. B. Titchener. New York: Macmillan, 1904.

Yutang, Lin. *The Wisdom of China and India*. New York: Random House, 1942.

Zilboorg, G., and Henry, G. W. *A History of Medical Psychology*.* New York: Norton, 1941.

Index
of Names

The following abbreviations have been used: *m* to indicate a name briefly mentioned, *n* to indicate a footnote, and *r* to indicate a reference. An asterisk indicates material contained in the Notes on Further Reading.

Index
of Subjects

A
B
C
D
E
F
G
H
I
J